D[illegible]
E[illegible]

70

One Day Adventures From the Great Cities by Rail, Bus or Car

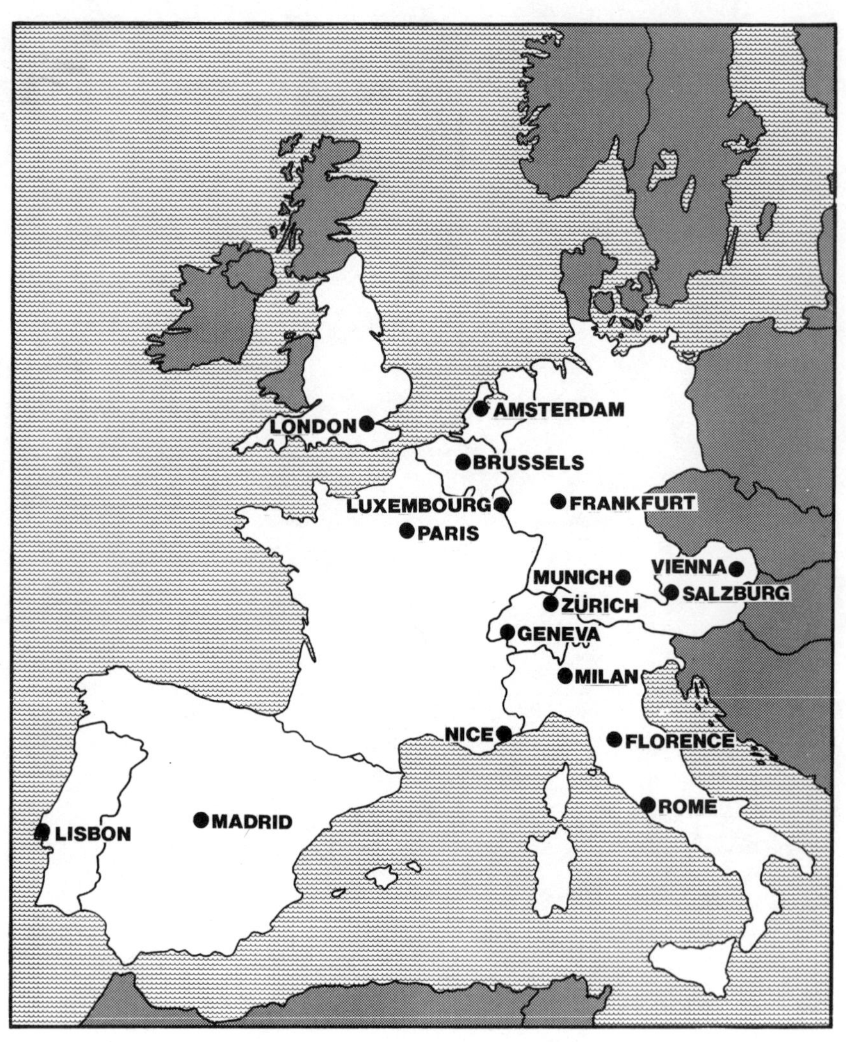
AMSTERDAM
LONDON
BRUSSELS
LUXEMBOURG
FRANKFURT
PARIS
VIENNA
MUNICH
SALZBURG
ZÜRICH
GENEVA
MILAN
NICE
FLORENCE
ROME
MADRID
LISBON

DAYTRIPS IN EUROPE

70 One Day Adventures From the Great Cities by Rail, Bus or Car

by
Earl Steinbicker

HASTINGS HOUSE
MAMARONECK, NEW YORK

We are always grateful for comments from readers, which are extremely useful in preparing future editions of this or other books in the series. Please write directly to the author, Earl Steinbicker, ℅ Hastings House, 141 Halstead Avenue, Mamaroneck, NY 10543; or FAX (914) 835-1037. Thank you.

All photos and maps are by the author.
Distributed to the trade by Publishers Group West, Emeryville, CA.

ISBN: 0-8038-9330-2

Printed in the United States of America
10 9 8 7 6 5 4 3 2 1

Contents

Introduction

However exciting the major cities of Europe are, the real adventures begin in the countryside just outside them. That's where you'll find the castles surrounded by natural splendor; the mountains, lakes, and seaside resorts; the charming villages, unspoiled historic towns, and even a few other cities that have miraculously escaped the tourist hordes. Out of the hundreds of enticing daytrip destinations scattered throughout Europe, this book takes a fresh—*and very thorough*—look at 70 of the most intriguing spots, and describes in step-by-step detail a pleasurable way of exploring them on self-guided walking tours.

Walking is by far the best way to probe most places. Not only is it undeniably healthy, but it also allows you to see the sights from a natural, human perspective; and to spend just as much or as little time on each as you please. The carefully tested walking tours were designed to take you past all of the attractions worth seeing without wasting time, effort, or money. Which of these you actually stop at is up to you, but you won't have any trouble finding them with the large, clear maps provided. There is never a need to rush as you'll have plenty of time for each walk, taking pleasant rest stops along the way.

The destinations were chosen to appeal to a wide variety of interests. In addition to the usual cathedrals, castles, palaces, and art galleries there are such attractions as country walks, wine villages, great seaports, folk museums, Roman ruins, boat cruises, steam train rides, pilgrimage centers, salt mines, towns where time stands still, homes of famous writers and artists, places where history was made, and even a few snowcapped mountain peaks. Not only do most of these reflect a delightful sense of the past, but some also expose you to the dramatic changes that are sweeping through Europe today.

Dining (and drinking) well is a vital element in any travel experience. For this reason, a selection of particularly enjoyable restaurants and cafés along the walking routes has been included for each of the daytrips. These are price-keyed, with an emphasis on the medium-to-low range, and have concise location descriptions that make them easy to find.

All of the daytrips can be made by rail, although in a very few cases you'll find buses to be more practical. Specific transportation information is given in the "Getting There" section of each trip, and general information in the "Daytrip Strategies" chapter and in the introduction pages for each country. Road directions are also given in case you'd rather drive.

Time and weather considerations are important, and they've been included in the "Practicalities" section of each trip. These let you know, among other things, on which days the sights are closed, when the colorful outdoor farmers' markets are held, and which places should be avoided in bad weather. The location and telephone number of the local Tourist Information Office is also given in case you have questions.

Many of the attractions have a nominal entrance fee—those that are free will come as a pleasant surprise. Cathedrals and churches depend on small donations in the collection box to help pay their maintenance costs, so it is only fair to leave some change when making a visit.

Please remember that places have a way of changing without warning, and that errors do creep into print. If your heart is absolutely set on a particular sight, you should check first to make sure that it isn't closed for renovations, or that the opening times are still valid. The local tourist offices are always the best source of such up-to-the-minute information.

One last thought—it isn't really necessary to see everything at any given destination. Be selective. Your one-day adventures throughout Europe should be fun, not an endurance test. If they start becoming that, just saunter on over to the nearest outdoor café, take a seat, and enjoy yourself while watching the world stroll past. There will always be another day.

Happy Daytripping!

Section I

The pleasures of the Chiemsee are only an hour from Munich

DAYTRIP STRATEGIES

The word "Daytrip" may not have made it into dictionaries yet, but for many experienced independent travelers it represents the easiest, most natural, and often the most economical approach to exploring a European country. This strategy, in which you base yourself in a central city (or its suburbs) and probe the surrounding regions on a series of one-day excursions, is an effective way to experience most of what Europe has to offer.

ADVANTAGES:

While not the answer to every travel situation, daytrips have significant advantages over point-to-point touring following a set itinerary. Here are a dozen good reasons for considering the daytrip approach:

1. Freedom from the constraints of a fixed itinerary. You can go wherever you feel like going whenever the mood strikes you.
2. Freedom from the burden of luggage. You bags remain in your hotel while you run around with only a guidebook and camera.
3. Freedom from the anxiety of reservation foul-ups. You don't have to worry each day about whether that night's lodging will actually materialize.
4. The flexibility of making last-minute changes to allow for unexpected weather, serendipitous discoveries, changing interests, new-found passions, and so on.
5. The flexibility to take breaks from sightseeing whenever you feel tired or bored, without upsetting a planned itinerary. Why not sleep late in your base city for a change?
6. The opportunity to sample different travel experiences without committing more than a day to them.
7. The opportunity to become a "temporary resident" of your base city. By staying there for a while you can get to know it in depth, becoming familiar with the local restaurants, shops, theaters, night life, and so on—enjoying them as a native would.
8. The convenience of not having to hunt for a hotel each day, along with the security of knowing that a familiar room is waiting back in your base city.
9. The convenience of not having to pack and unpack your bags each day. Your clothes can hang in a closet where they belong, or even be sent out for cleaning.
10. The convenience (and security!) of having a fixed address in your base city, where friends, relatives, and business associates can reach you in an emergency. It is exceedingly difficult to contact anyone who changes hotels daily.
11. The economy of staying at one hotel on a discounted longer-term basis, especially in conjunction with airline package plans. You can make advance reservations for your base city without sacrificing any flexibility at all.
12. The economy of getting the most value out of a railpass. Daytripping is ideally suited to rail travel as the best train service operates out of base-city hubs.

Above all, daytrips ease the transition from tourist to accomplished traveler. Even if this is your first trip abroad, you should be able to handle uncomplicated one-day excursions such as those to Canterbury or Delft on your own. The confidence gained will help immensely when you tackle more complex destinations, freeing you from the limitations of guided tours and putting you in complete control of your own trip.

DISADVANTAGES:

For all of its attractions, the daytrip concept does have certain restrictions. There are always a few areas where geography and the available transportation have conspired to make one-day excursions impractical, or at least awkward. To see these, you'll have to temporarily resort to more conventional travel.

Another disadvantage is that you may have to forego the pleasures of staying at country inns, manor houses, or converted castles. To some extent, you can overcome this by basing yourself in a nearby suburb with good commuter transportation instead of checking into a downtown hotel. You could also use daytrips most of the time, and the "touring" approach when traveling from one base city to the next.

Perhaps the greatest drawback to daytripping is that all of the to-ing and fro-ing involved can significantly increase your total travel mileage. This will surely result in higher costs if you're using a rental car. Rail travelers, however, often have the option of purchasing economical one-day round-trip excursion tickets for little more than a one-way fare; and those wisely using railpasses (see page 17) get unlimited transportation in any case. The extra time spent on trains is not wasted as you continue meeting people, seeing, and learning even as you travel.

ESCORTED DAY TOURS:

Commercially operated one-day bus tours to nearby towns and other attractions are available in nearly every European city of any size. Described in colorful brochures, these are heavily promoted by hotels (who get a commission) and by local tourist offices. On the surface, they may seem like an effortless way to take in the countryside. While certainly better than no tour at all, they are no substitute for exploring on your own. Among their many shortcomings is the fact that the tours go where their operators want to go, not where you want to. All too often, this is where it's easiest to park the bus. Some of the "attractions" visited are downright tourist traps from which they get extra income, while others reflect someone's idea of the "average" person's interests. The spoken commentary is usually tediously given in a succession of tongues that you must suffer through before finally getting to English. Worse, people who take these tours are treated as part of a mob to be efficiently catered to for profit rather than as real guests. You'll get no genuine adventure on these tours, and feel no sense of accomplishment on completing them. On top of that, they tend to be rather expensive.

WALKING TOURS:

Each daytrip in this book includes a highly-detailed do-it-yourself walking tour. No one has yet invented a better way to experience the towns of Europe than to stroll through them on foot. Not only do you get to see the sights from a human, eye-level perspective (the way they were meant to be seen), but all along the way you'll be mixing with local residents, meeting with and absorbing their culture as if by osmosis.

Walking is good for you as well. Besides being an excellent aerobic exercise, it also stimulates the brain while it burns off all of those nasty calories from last night's feast.

The suggested walking routes described in the text and shown on the maps are designed so as not to waste time or effort. They include more sights than you'll care to see in a day, but this allows you to pick and choose.

BASE CITIES

The 17 cities used as bases for the daytrips in this book represent the most popular urban destinations in Europe, both with tourists and business travelers alike. There are, of course, many others that are equally suitable, some of which—such as Edinburgh, Marseille, Berlin, and Naples—are covered in our series of "Daytrip" guidebooks for individual countries and regions (see page 431).

For several of the base cities there are **alternatives** that might be more appealing, cheaper, or just good to know about in case the main city is "all booked up" for some event. A few examples of this are: Cannes or Monte Carlo instead of Nice, Augsburg or Starnberg instead of Munich, and Lausanne instead of Geneva. The one thing they all have in common is great commuter transportation to the main city.

In choosing a base, you should consider whether it is interesting enough to be worth exploring when you don't feel like making daytrips, and whether it's livable enough to be worth coming back to each night.

FINDING ACCOMMODATIONS:

For the best choice of hotels, you should make advance reservations through your travel agent, possibly choosing one of the **airline package plans** that combine transatlantic air fares, a hotel room, and other features into one discounted price. Failing that, you can always

This street scene in Canterbury is typical of the sights you'll find close to London

find a room of some sort upon arrival by going straight to a hotel booking agency at the airport, or the nearest local **Tourist Information Office**, usually at the airport and/or main train station. The latter will be more helpful about finding less expensive rooms, such as Bed-and-Breakfast (B&B) accommodations, *pensions, gastzimmers,* college dorms during the summer, or even at youth hostels. There is always *something* available, even if it's out in the suburbs.

Look for a room that is convenient from a standpoint of making daytrips. If you're traveling by train, this means either near the station or close to a subway, bus, or commuter train stop from which you can easily get to the main station.

GETTING AROUND

All of the daytrips in this book can be taken by either rail or bus, or by private car. Special considerations for each country are outlined in its introduction pages. In general, these are your transportation options:

BY RAIL:

Trains are usually the fastest way to cover the medium distances involved on most of the daytrips. Passenger railroads throughout western Europe range from the absolutely superb to the merely good. Their very best efforts are represented by the dozens of TGV trains that zip around France at 186 mph, by Germany's brand-new and quite luxurious ICE expresses, by the swift British InterCity 225 electrics, by the amazing Italian Pendolinos, and by the completely articulated Spanish Talgos.

But the really outstanding aspect of rail travel in Europe is the manner in which thousands of ordinary trains go about their business so frequently and so reliably, taking millions of people to their destinations every day. The best of these are the **EuroCity (EC)** expresses, which must meet strict international standards of comfort and speed; and the **InterCity (IC)** expresses, which are nearly as good. Even the workhorse commuter locals are more than adequate for the shorter runs on some of the trips. The "Getting There" section of each daytrip chapter tells you how frequently the trains run, how long they take, what station they leave from, and how late in the evening the return services operate.

Seasoned travelers know that riding trains is one of the best ways to meet the local people and make new friends. It is not unusual to strike up an engaging conversation with your seatmate, making your trip all the more memorable. You also get a good view of the passing countryside from the large windows, and have time to catch up on your reading. Then, too, you are spared the worries of driving, especially after a little indulgence in the local beer or wine.

Schedules for train services are available at all stations. The personnel at the information window may not always speak English, but you will have no trouble if you write out the name of your destination and the time you would like to leave. Doing this avoids the confusion caused by towns with similar-sounding names. It also prevents misunderstandings of day-to-day variations when, for example, a particular train only runs on Saturdays in summer. At the same time, always check the return schedule so you don't get stranded. Tables of **departures** (usually printed on yellow paper) and **arrivals** (most often on white paper) are posted throughout the stations, and are stated in terms of the 24-hour clock. Thus, a departure at 3:32 p.m. would be marked as 15.32. Some stations have free printed schedules for popular destinations; others feature multi-lingual computer terminals that dispense schedule information and plan your routes. Complete schedule books may be purchased, but they're too big to carry around. The compact **Thomas Cook European Timetable**, sold in some travel book stores in America, by mail from the **Forsyth Travel Library** (P.O. Box 2975, Shawnee Mission, Kansas 66201-1375, phone toll-free 1-800-FORSYTH), or at Thomas Cook offices in Britain, is extremely useful even though it does not list *every* local service.

Reservations are required for all TGV trains and for a few other high-speed expresses, especially in Spain, Portugal, and Italy. They are also desirable for travel on EC or IC trains during peak periods. Railpass holders are charged a small fee for this. The reservation will assign you to a specific car and seat, with your choice of smoking or non-smoking and a window or aisle seat. Those traveling without reservations should be careful not to sit in someone else's reserved seat, which is marked by a card at the compartment entrance or above the seat. Careful observation of these may gain you a seat even when the entire train is full, as most passengers seem to believe that a reservation card always means that the seat is taken. Not so. It only indicates that the seat is reserved from a certain station to another certain station, and these are marked on the card. Outside of that specific trip segment the seat is free.

It is always best to arrive at the station a few minutes before departure time and go directly to the track platform shown for your train on the departure board. There you will often find a sign that shows the exact makeup of every express leaving from that platform, including the location of each car. This serves two major purposes. First, you won't have to make a last-minute dash when you discover that the first-class cars stop at the opposite end of a long platform. Secondly, and more important, it shows which—if any—cars are dropped off en route to your destination.

The **routing** and final destination of each car is usually shown just outside its door as well as in its vestibule. First-class cars are marked with the numeral "1" near the door, and often with a yellow stripe above the windows.

Most express trains offer a **food and beverage service** of some sort, as shown on the schedules. Riding in a regular dining or self-service café car can be a delightful experience, but beware the push-carts in other cars that sell well-shaken cans of warm beer. You are much better off stocking up on snacks and refreshments at the station and bringing them with you, as most Europeans do.

Railpasses can be a terrific bargain if you intend to do any real amount of train travel. Ask your travel agent about them before going to Europe as most passes are difficult or impossible to purchase once there. Passes for individual countries and regions are described in the introduction pages of each section of this book. All of the countries ***except Great Britain*** accept the popular **Eurailpass** for unlimited travel on their national railways, and for other travel bonuses. This is the best pass to get **if** you are traveling in several different countries, especially those north of the Alps where regular train fares are high. The pass is available in the following versions:

EURAILPASS—Allows unlimited first-class rail travel throughout Austria, Belgium, Denmark, Finland, France, Germany, Greece, Holland, Hungary, Ireland, Italy, Luxembourg, Norway, Portugal, Spain, Sweden, and Switzerland. It is available for periods of 15 or 21 consecutive days, or 1, 2, or 3 consecutive months. The Eurailpass includes a wide variety of fringe benefits such as free rides on Rhine or Danube river steamers, on Swiss lakes, some free buses, discounts on some popular mountain railways and cable cars, and several free international ferry steamers.

EURAIL FLEXIPASS—The latest innovation in railpasses allows unlimited first-class travel on any 5 days within a 15-day period, on any 9 days within a 21-day period, or on any 14 days in a month. It is valid in the same 17 countries as the regular Eurailpass and has the same fringe benefits, but naturally costs more per travel day. This is a particularly attractive deal **if** you intend to spend much time exploring your base cities between making daytrips from them.

EURAIL SAVERPASS—An economical version of the Eurailpass that offers the same first-class benefits as above, but for groups of 3 or more people traveling together. Between October 1st and March 31st the group size can be as small as 2 persons. This pass is available for a period of 15 consecutive days only, and the travel must always be done as a group.

EURAIL YOUTHPASS—This low-cost version is available to anyone under the age of 25 on the first day of use and allows unlimited *second-class* travel in the same 17 countries for one or two consecutive months. It also comes as a **YOUTH FLEXIPASS**, good for travel on any 15 or 30 days within a 3-month period.

All railpasses must be **validated** before their initial use. The first and last days of validity will be entered on the pass at that time. Be certain that you agree with the dates *before* allowing the validating station agent to write them in. Read the specific instructions that come with each railpass to get all of the benefits you're entitled to.

If you intend to take several of the daytrips in this book, and especially if at least one of them is to a distant location such as Lyon and you travel by train from one base city to another, a railpass will probably wind up saving you a considerable amount of money. Even if the savings are less than that, a pass should still be considered for the convenience it offers in not having to line up for tickets (only to find that you're in the wrong line!), and the freedom of just hopping aboard almost any train at whim. Possession of a railpass encourages you to become more adventurous, to seek out distant and offbeat destinations (yes, first-class passes are valid on even the most obscure second-class trains). You can also use them to save money by "going native" and staying at inexpensive inns in the suburbs instead of costlier city hotels, commuting each day by train. And, should you ever manage to get on the wrong train by mistake (or change your plans en route), your only cost will be your time—not an extra fare back!

Eurail and other passes are sold by most travel agents, who also have current information and prices, and by mail from the Forsyth Travel Library mentioned on page 17. If you're visiting only one country you should consider its **national railpass**, which is often a better deal. These are described in the appropriate pages of this book. Visitors going to both Britain and France can check out the **BritFrance Railpass** mentioned on pages 24 and 80; while those staying in Holland, Belgium, and Luxembourg may be interested in the **Benelux Tourrail Pass** (see pages 146 and 175).

BY BUS:

A few of the daytrips in this book are easier to take by bus than by train. Details are given in the "Getting There" section for those particular excursions. None of these bus services are covered by railpasses.

BY CAR:

Many tourists prefer to explore Europe by car, especially when several people are traveling together. Although generally slower, cars offer a complete freedom from schedules. Europe's network of superhighways is superb, but be prepared to pay some rather stiff tolls in France, Italy, Spain, and Portugal. Cars using Switzerland's highways must have a road-tax sticker affixed. An **International Driving Permit**, available in America from the AAA, is required in Spain and may be useful in other non-English-speaking countries as well.

The "Getting There" section of each trip description tells you the direction, the driving distance in miles, and the most efficient route to follow. You'll still need a good **road map** for the country you're in—those published by Michelin are excellent and updated annually. Be sure to get a current edition as new roads are constantly being opened. Rand McNally's maps and its annual *Road Atlas of Europe* are also very good, and generally easier to find.

Most transatlantic airlines offer **fly/drive plans** that combine air fares with car rentals at discounted rates. These can be extended to include hotel package plans and other features. Ask your travel agent about current offerings, which change frequently.

BY BICYCLE:

Not for traveling from a base city, of course, but once you've gotten to your destination by train or car you might want to **rent a bicycle** to use on the suggested tour instead of walking or taking local buses. Bikes can be rented in nearly all towns; just ask at the local tourist office for details. The railroads of France, Belgium, Holland, Germany, Austria, and Switzerland rent bicycles at many of their stations, and often offer discounts if you come by train. Whenever applicable, these services are mentioned in the "Practicalities" section of each daytrip.

FOOD AND DRINK:

Several choice restaurants that make sense for daytrippers are listed for each destination in this book. Most of these are long-time favorites of experienced travelers, are open for lunch, are on or near the walking route, provide some atmosphere, and serve local cuisine unless otherwise mentioned. Their approximate price range, based on the least expensive complete meal offered, is shown as:

$ — Inexpensive, but may have fancier dishes available.
$$ — Reasonable. These establishments may also feature daily specials.
$$$ — Luxurious and expensive.
$$$+ — Very expensive
X: — Days or periods closed.

If you're really serious about dining you should consult an up-to-date restaurant and hotel guide such as the classic red-cover *Michelin* guides to *Great Britain & Ireland, France, Benelux, Deutschland, Italia,* and *España & Portugal.* These are issued annually in the spring and generally available at good bookstores.

Restaurants, of course, are forever changing. What is good one year may not be the next. Far more important than any list of suggestions is to develop the ability to spot good establishments. It is always wise to check the prices posted outside the restaurant, and to take a peek at who's dining there. A large proportion of locals, especially businessmen, almost guarantees an excellent meal—while a place full of foreign tourists may not. Those prominently displaying menus in English festooned with little British or American flags are at least suspect. You won't need the security blanket of the English menu if you use a discreet pocket-size translator book such as the *Berlitz European Menu Reader,* which helps you cope with nearly all European cuisines in 14 languages.

If you're in a hurry to get on with sightseeing, you can save both time and money by eating lunch at a British pub, an outdoor farmers' market, from a sidewalk vendor, or in a museum or department store cafeteria. The food in these places is often delicious, usually indigenous, and always cheap. American-style fast-food chains have invaded most of Europe, along with the ubiquitous pizzerias.

SUGGESTED TOURS

The do-it-yourself walking tours in this book are relatively short and easy to follow. They always begin at the local train station or bus stop since most readers will be using public transportation. Those going by car can make a simple adjustment. Suggested routes are shown by heavy broken lines on the maps, while the circled numbers refer to major attractions or points of reference along the way, with corresponding numbers in the text.

Trying to see everything in any given town could easily become an exhausting marathon, and possibly lead to the dreaded Stendhal's

Hallstatt makes an enticing daytrip from Salzburg

Syndrome, a temporarily disabling condition that afflicts those who grossly overindulge in culture. The only known cure for this is to go to a quiet, isolated village where there are no museums. In any case, you will certainly enjoy yourself more by being selective and passing up anything that doesn't catch your fancy in favor of a friendly pub, café, or *Bierstube*. Forgiveness will be granted if you fail to visit *every* church.

Practical information, such as the opening times of various attractions, is as accurate as was possible at the time of publication. Everything is, of course, subject to change. You should always check with the local tourist office if seeing a particular sight is crucially important to you.

You can estimate the amount of time that any segment of a walking tour will take by looking at the scaled map and figuring that the average person covers about 100 yards a minute. The walks will be easier if you wear real walking shoes, especially those sneakers that are specifically designed for walking rather than jogging or sports. Layered clothes are a good idea to cope with changing weather conditions, mountain peaks, ice caves, and so on. Carrying a folding umbrella is always good insurance against rain, particularly in England.

*OUTSTANDING ATTRACTIONS:

An * asterisk before any attraction, be it an entire daytrip or just one painting in a museum, denotes a special treat that in the author's opinion should not be missed.

TOURIST INFORMATION

Virtually every town, or even village, of any tourist interest in Europe has its own information office that can help you with specific questions or book local accommodations. Usually identified by the letter "**i**," they almost invariably have English-speaking personnel on staff. The smaller ones are frequently closed on Saturday afternoons and all day on Sundays. Their locations are shown on the town maps in this book by the word "**info.**," and repeated along with the phone number in the "Practicalities" section for each trip.

ADVANCE PLANNING INFORMATION:

All of the countries in this book have **National Tourist Offices** with branches in North America and elsewhere in the world. They will gladly provide help in planning your trip if you contact them at the address or phone number shown in the introductory pages for each section.

Section II

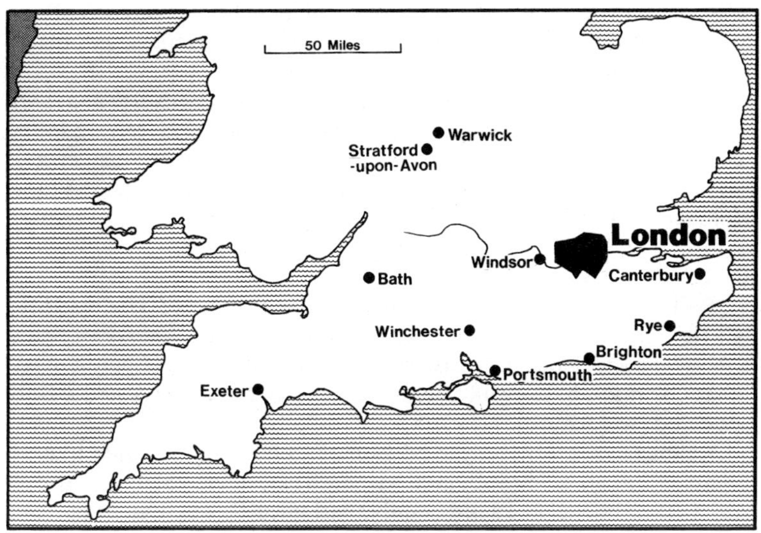

DAYTRIPS IN
ENGLAND

• from London

By any reckoning, southern England just has to be the world's most fertile ground for daytripping. Not only are the distances short, but many of the attractions are among the very best that Europe has to offer. Language is no problem and getting around on your own is as simple as it is back home. Whether by rail or car, it's only an hour or so from central London to such destinations as Canterbury, Brighton, Windsor, or Bath. Extend the time just a bit and you can soon be deep in the West Country at the ancient port of Exeter, or reliving the life of Shakespeare in Stratford-upon-Avon. When you've seen enough, you can just as easily return to your London base for dinner and a night's entertainment.

The ten daytrips described in this section offer a little something for everyone. There are two of the world's greatest medieval castles, some of its most memorable cathedrals, Roman ruins, pubs galore, a leading seaside resort, a fishing village whose salty charm has hardly changed since the 16th century, a naval base with warships from the 1500s to the present, and a floating maritime museum where you can climb aboard everything from a Chinese junk to a Danish steam tug. There are also short country walks through England's green and pleasant land, boat trips on its rivers, quirky regional museums, and many places of historical and literary association.

Even more possibilities for one-day adventures are explored in two of our companion guidebooks. ***Daytrips London*** covers walking tours within the capital city and its suburbs plus 23 nearby one-day excursions, while ***Daytrips in Britain*** goes farther afield with 60 daytrips from London and in Scotland.

GETTING AROUND:

Rail is the most practical way to make daytrips out of London. **British Rail** operates an extremely dense network of train services, with such frequent departures that reference to schedules is hardly necessary. London has several major stations, so be sure to use the one specified for each trip.

Railpasses can be terrific bargains, but must be obtained before going to Britain as they cannot be purchased there. See your travel agent. The **BritRail Pass** offers unlimited travel throughout Britain for periods of 8, 15, or 22 consecutive days, or for one month; and is available in both first- and standard (2nd)-class versions, with price breaks for seniors, youths, and children. The more expensive **BritRail Flexipass** provides the same benefits but does not have to be used on consecutive days. It is available for use on any 4 days in an 8-day period, any 8 in 15, or any 15 in one month. The **BritFrance Railpass** allows unlimited travel in both Britain and France including round-trip Channel crossings. It is offered for any 5 days in a 15-day period, or any 10 days in a month, in both first- and standard (2nd)-class versions, with a reduced standard-class rate for youths.

If you're primarily visiting London and plan to make daytrips in southeastern England only, your best bet is the **London Extra**, which combines a pass for London's Underground and buses with a special pass for rail travel within the Network SouthEast. The two passes do not have to be used at the same time, and are sold in 3+3, 4+4, and 7+7-consecutive-day versions, in both classes, for adults or children. It covers all of the destinations in this section *except* Bath, Warwick, and Stratford-upon-Avon. The trip to Exeter must be made from Waterloo Station via Salisbury.

ADVANCE PLANNING INFORMATION:

The **British Tourist Authority** has branches throughout the world, including New York, Chicago, Dallas, Los Angeles, Toronto, London, Sydney, Auckland, and Tokyo. There New York office is at 40 West 57th St., New York NY 10019-4001, phone (212) 581-4700.

A Daytrip from London

*Canterbury

Over two thousand years of history have left their mark on Canterbury, a magnet for countless pilgrimages since the 12th century. St. Augustine established the Christian Church in England here as far back as A.D. 597, and in 1170 the martyr Thomas à Becket was murdered in its cathedral. As a convenient place to ford the River Stour, Canterbury was a strategic settlement ever since the Iron Age. Under the name *Durovernum,* the Romans made it an important center of trade in the 1st century A.D. This status increased during Anglo-Saxon times, when the name was changed to *Cantwarabyrig,* and it became the capital of the Kingdom of Kent. Much of Canterbury's colorful past remains intact today, despite the ravages of Cromwell's troops and the bombs of World War II.

GETTING THERE:

Trains to Canterbury East Station depart from Victoria Station in London twice an hour. The journey takes about 80 minutes. Be sure to get on the correct car, as the train splits at Faversham. Return service operates until late evening.

By car, Canterbury is 58 miles southeast of London via the A-2 and M-2 highways.

PRACTICALITIES:

Any day is a good day to visit Canterbury, bearing in mind that some minor sights are closed on Sundays. The local **Tourist Information Centre**, phone (0227) 76-65-67, is at 34 St. Margaret's Street, three blocks southwest of the cathedral. You might ask there about renting a **bicycle** in town as this is good cycling country. Canterbury is in the county of **Kent**, and has a **population** of about 35,000.

FOOD AND DRINK:

Having attracted pilgrims and their modern counterparts since the Middle Ages, Canterbury has no shortage of restaurants and pubs in all price ranges. Some particularly good choices are:

Tuo e Mio (16 The Borough, opposite the King's School) Noted for its fine Italian cuisine. X: Tues. lunch, Mon. $$$

George's Brasserie (71 Castle St., 2 blocks northeast of the Norman Castle) Mostly traditional French bistro food. X: Sun. $$

Sweeney Todd's (8 Butchery Lane, near the Roman Pavement) A popular basement restaurant featuring pizza, burgers, salads, and the like. $

Caesar's (46 St. Peter's St., between the Weavers' House and Westgate) A favorite with the young crowd for its salads and burgers. $

SUGGESTED TOUR:

Leaving **Canterbury East Station** (1), cross the footbridge over the A-2 highway and turn right on the ancient city walls. Dating from the 13th and 14th centuries, these were built on Roman foundations. To your left is **Dane John Gardens** (2), a pleasant 18th-century park with a strange mound of unexplained but probably prehistoric origin. Continue atop the walls and turn left by the bus station onto St. George's Street. The tower on the right is all that remains of St. George's Church, where Christopher Marlowe was baptized in 1564.

St. George's Street soon becomes High Street. Stroll down this and make a right into narrow **Mercery Lane**, the traditional pilgrim's approach to the cathedral. During medieval days this was lined with stalls selling healing water from Becket's Well, medallions of St. Thomas, and other mementos of the pilgrimage. At its far end is the Butter Market, an ancient center of trade. The magnificent **Christchurch Gate** (3), opposite, dates from the early 16th century and is the main entrance to the cathedral grounds.

Pass through the gate and enter the grounds of ***Canterbury Cathedral** (4), the mother church of the Anglican faith throughout the world. For centuries it has been a center of pilgrimage and in a sense still is, although today's visitors are more likely to be tourists. Neither the largest, the tallest, nor the most beautiful of English cathedrals, it nevertheless has an attraction that is second to none.

A cathedral was built on this site by St. Augustine, the first Archbishop of Canterbury, in 602. This lasted until 1067, when it burned down. The present structure was begun in 1070 and completed in 1503, although little of the earlier work remains.

Enter the cathedral by way of the southwest porch. The lofty nave was built in the Perpendicular style during the 14th century, replacing an inadequate Norman original. Above the crossing you can see up the entire height of the magnificent **Bell Harry Tower**, whose bell is rung every evening for curfew and tolled on the death of a sovereign or an archbishop. A flight of steps to the right of the screen leads to the elevated **Choir**, one of the longest in England.

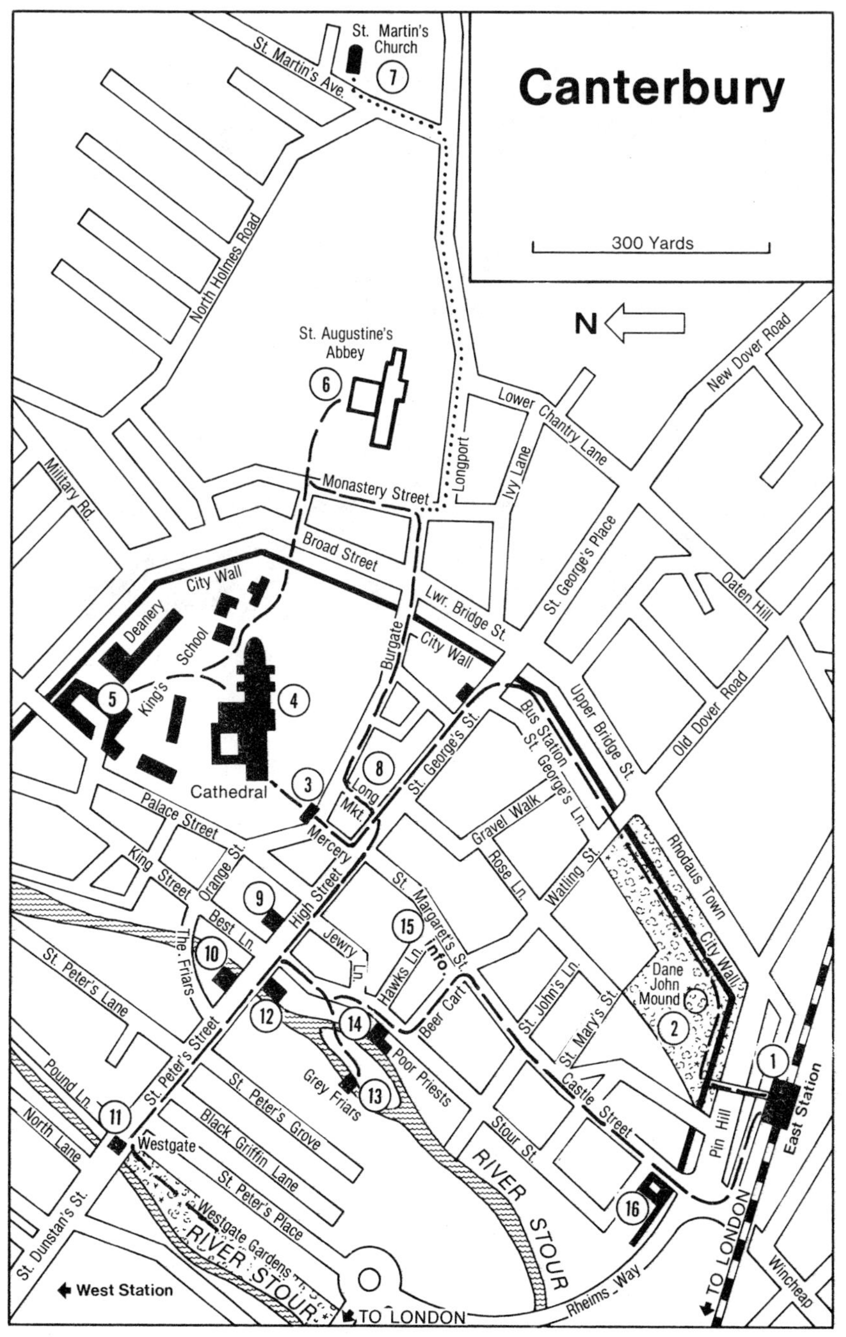
Canterbury
300 Yards
N
St. Martin's Church
St. Martin's Ave.
North Holmes Road
St. Augustine's Abbey
Monastery Street
Longport
Lower Chantry Lane
Ivy Lane
New Dover Road
Military Rd.
Broad Street
City Wall
Deanery
King's School
Cathedral
Burgate
Lwr. Bridge St.
St. George's Place
Oaten Hill
City Wall
Upper Bridge St.
Old Dover Road
Bus Station
St. George's Ln.
St. George's St.
Long Mkt.
Palace Street
Mercery
Gravel Walk
Rose Ln.
Watling St.
Rhodaus Town
King Street
Orange St.
High Street
St. Margaret's St.
Best Ln.
The. Friars
Jewry Ln.
Hawks Ln.
Info.
Beer Cart
St. John's Ln.
St. Mary's St.
Dane John Mound
City Wall
St. Peter's Lane
St. Peter's Street
Poor Priests
Grey Friars
Castle Street
Pin Hill
East Station
Pound Ln.
North Lane
Westgate
St. Peter's Grove
Black Griffin Lane
St. Peter's Place
Stour St.
RIVER STOUR
Westgate Gardens
RIVER STOUR
St. Dunstan's St.
West Station
TO LONDON
Rheims Way
TO LONDON
Wincheap
1
2
3
4
5
6
7
8
9
10
11
12
13
14
15
16

In the Choir of Canterbury Cathedral

Behind the High Altar is the **Trinity Chapel**, which held Becket's tomb until Henry VIII had it demolished and the bones scattered in 1538. The tomb of the only king to be buried at Canterbury, Henry IV, and that of Edward, the Black Prince, are also in this chapel. At the extreme east end is a circular chapel known as the **Corona**, or Becket's Crown. The marble chair in its center is used for the enthronement of every archbishop.

The north aisle leads past the choir to the northwest transept, the scene of the martyrdom. It was here that Archbishop Thomas à Becket was murdered on December 29, 1170. The four knights who committed the deed thought they were carrying out the desire of their king, Henry II, although his part in it is disputed by historians. Henry certainly had reason to get rid of "this turbulent priest," his former friend and ally who had challenged the power of the State. Whatever the rationale behind the killing, it led to the canonization of Becket, the chastisement of Henry II, the role of Canterbury as a place of pilgrimage, and helped further the cause of individual freedom.

The spacious **Crypt** is the oldest part of the cathedral, dating from Norman times. Along its south aisle there is a Huguenot chapel where services in French are still held. Becket was first buried at the east end, which was also the scene of Henry II's penance.

Stroll into the early-15th-century **Cloisters** by way of the northwest transept. Adjoining it is the Chapter House and Library. Follow the passageway and turn left into the grounds of the **King's School** (5). Although it was refounded by Henry VIII, the school claims an ancestry going back to the time of St. Augustine, which would make it the oldest in England. The 12th-century Norman staircase near the northwest corner of the Green Court is truly magnificent, as are the views of the cathedral from this point.

Returning, bear left and walk around the rear of the cathedral to the Kent War Memorial Gardens. Go through the gate in the far corner and follow the map to the ruins of **St. Augustine's Abbey** (6). Originally founded in 598 and rebuilt several times since, it was destroyed by Henry VIII following the Reformation. Excavations have revealed the layout of several buildings including the church, monk's dormitory, kitchen, refectory, and cloisters. The abbey is open on Mondays through Saturdays, from 9:30 a.m. to 6:30 p.m.; and on Sundays from 2–6:30 p.m. It closes at 4 p.m. in winter.

From here you might want to make a little side trip to an interesting old church. To do this, walk back around St. Augustine's and turn left on Monastery Street, then left again on Longport. Just past the jail make another left to **St. Martin's Church** (7), said to be the oldest church in England that is still in use. Parts of it date from before the time of St. Augustine and were used by Queen Bertha, Christian wife of King Ethelbert. Explore the interior, noting in particular the Saxon font, then stroll through the tranquil graveyard.

Returning to town via Longport and Church Street, walk down Burgate and turn left into Butchery Lane. In a basement below a modern shopping center is an excavated **Roman Pavement** (8), once part of a large villa erected around A.D. 100. It is presently closed for reconstruction and will re-open in late 1992.

Continuing along High Street, you will pass Queen Elizabeth's Guest Chamber, a Tudor house on the left in which the queen entertained her French suitor, the Duke of Alençon. It is now a restaurant. Farther along on the right is the **Royal Museum and Art Gallery** (9), otherwise known as the Beaney Institute. It has a fine collection of Roman and other antiquities as well as local art, and may be visited on Mondays through Saturdays, from 10 a.m. to 5 p.m. The famous **Weavers' House** (10) on the edge of the River Stour was occupied by Huguenot weavers who settled in Canterbury after fleeing France in the 17th century. Boat rides on the river are offered here.

Walk along St. Peter's Street to the **Westgate** (11). Built in the late 14th century, this imposing fortification once guarded the western approach to Canterbury. Its upper floor served as the city jail until 1829. Now a museum of arms and torture instruments, it is open daily except on Sundays, from 10 a.m. to 1 p.m. and 2–5 p.m.; with winter hours being 2–4 p.m. There is a superb ***view** from the top.

A stroll through Westgate Gardens is very inviting. Return to St. Peter's and turn right. Opposite the Weavers' is the **Eastbridge Hospital** (12), a well-preserved 12th-century hostel for poor pilgrims. Its crypt, chapel, and hall are open to visitors on Mondays through Saturdays, from 10 a.m. to 1 p.m. and 2–5 p.m.

Turn right on Stour Street and then right again into a tiny lane marked "to Greyfriars." Follow the path onto a small island. The extremely picturesque 13th-century **Greyfriars** (13) is all that remains of the first Franciscan friary in England. From inside you can get a feeling of what monastic life in medieval Canterbury was like.

Just beyond this, also on Stour Street, is the **Poor Priests' Hospital** (14). This 14th-century hostel is now the **Canterbury Heritage Museum**, where the latest techniques are used to re-create the city's past, from Roman times to the near present. It is open on Mondays through Saturdays, from 10:30 a.m. to 4 p..m., and on summer Sundays from 1:30–4 p.m.

Turn left on Beer Cart and left again on St. Margaret's Street to the latest attraction, the ***Canterbury Tales** (15), a magnificent exhibition based on Chaucer's masterpiece. Actors are used along with sets and the latest in audio-visual techniques to bring the classic story to life. Located in a former church, it is open daily from 9:30 a.m. to 5:30 p.m., closing at 4:30 p.m. in winter.

You can head back to the station via Castle Street. At its end, opposite the city wall, are the ruins of an 11th-century **Norman Castle** (16). Never very effective as a defensive bastion, it was later used as a jail, a coal dump, and a water tank.

A Daytrip from London

*Rye

A relic from the Middle Ages, the once-great seaport of Rye has been stranded ever since its harbor silted up in the 16th century. Today, only small craft can sail the two miles up the River Rother to the town's docks. In a way this is fortunate, as it left England with a well-preserved medieval port that still clings to its salty past. Rye is alive with the smell of the sea, and working fishermen still walk its ancient streets, side by side with their many visitors. It easily ranks among the prettiest towns in Britain, and is one of the most enjoyable for tourists.

GETTING THERE:

Trains depart London's Charing Cross or Victoria stations frequently for Ashford, where you change to a local for Rye. The total journey takes less than two hours. Return trains run until mid-evening. Service is reduced on Sundays and holidays.

By car, the shortest route is to take the A-21 from London to Flimwell and change to the A-268. Rye is 63 miles southeast of London.

PRACTICALITIES:

Rye may be savored on a fine day in any season. The local **Tourist Information Centre**, phone (0797) 22-66-96, is at The Quay, by the Town Model. Outdoor **markets** are held on Thursdays near the train station. Rye is in the county of **East Sussex** and has a **population** of about 4,000.

FOOD AND DRINK:

Rye has plenty of quaint old inns, tea shops, and pubs. Some choices are:

Flushing Inn (Market St., near the Town Hall) A 15th-century inn noted for its seafood. X: Mon. eve., Tues., Jan. $$ and $$$

Mermaid Inn (Mermaid St.) An old smugglers' haunt from the 15th century. $$

Fletcher's House (Lion St., just north of St. Mary's Church) Light meals in an historic medieval house. $$

Standard Inn (The Mint, near Needles Passage) A delightful pub with meals. $

SUGGESTED TOUR:

Leaving the **train station** (1), walk straight ahead and turn left on Cinque Ports Street. In a few yards you will pass remnants of the original 14th-century towns walls, just behind a parking lot. The **Land Gate** (2) is the only remaining town gate of the three that once protected Rye. It was probably constructed about 1340 and originally contained machinery for a drawbridge over the town ditch.

Walk uphill along Hilder's Cliff, with its marvelous views across the Romney Marsh. Much of this lowland was once an open ocean, but that was before the sea receded as the River Rother silted up and the tides washed countless pebbles onto the shore.

Make a right down Conduit hill to the **Augustine Friary** (3), commonly known as The Monastery. Originally built in 1379, it was used in the 16th century as a refuge for persecuted French Huguenots. Today it houses a pottery that you can visit. Now return to High Street and follow it to the old Grammar School, erected in 1636 and immortalized by Thackeray. Opposite this is the 400-year-old George Hotel.

A left onto Lion Street leads past Fletcher's House, once a vicarage and now a tea shop. The dramatist John Fletcher was born here in 1579. At the corner of Market Street stands the **Town Hall** (4), which contains some interesting artifacts, including the gruesome gibbet cage with the remains of a notorious 18th-century murderer who was executed in the town. Ask to be shown these.

In a few more steps you will come to ***St. Mary's Church** (5), first erected between 1150 and 1300. Facing the top of Lion Street is the ***church clock**, the oldest in England still functioning with its original works. Two figures above the clockface strike the quarter hours but not the hours. Between them is a plaque that proclaims, "For our time is a very shadow that passeth away." A climb to the top of the ***tower** is well worth the effort. The extremely narrow stairway leads to the bell-ringing room where various combinations of changes are posted. In the same room is the venerable clock mechanism, from which hangs an 18-foot-long pendulum. A ladder goes to the bell room itself, and another to the roof. From here there is an unsurpassed **view** of the entire area. A visit to the church interior is also worthwhile.

Across from the churchyard there is a curious oval-shaped brick **water reservoir**, built in 1735 but no longer used. Bear right and stroll down to **Ypres Tower** (6). Pronounced *Wipers,* this is the oldest existing structure in town. Largely unchanged since it was first constructed as a defensive fortification around 1249, it ceased to have any military value in later years and was sold to one John de Ypres as a private habitation. The town bought it back in 1513 for use as a jail, a function it served until 1865, when it became a mortuary. The tower is now the **Rye Museum**, housing artifacts of the town's history. A visit to its var-

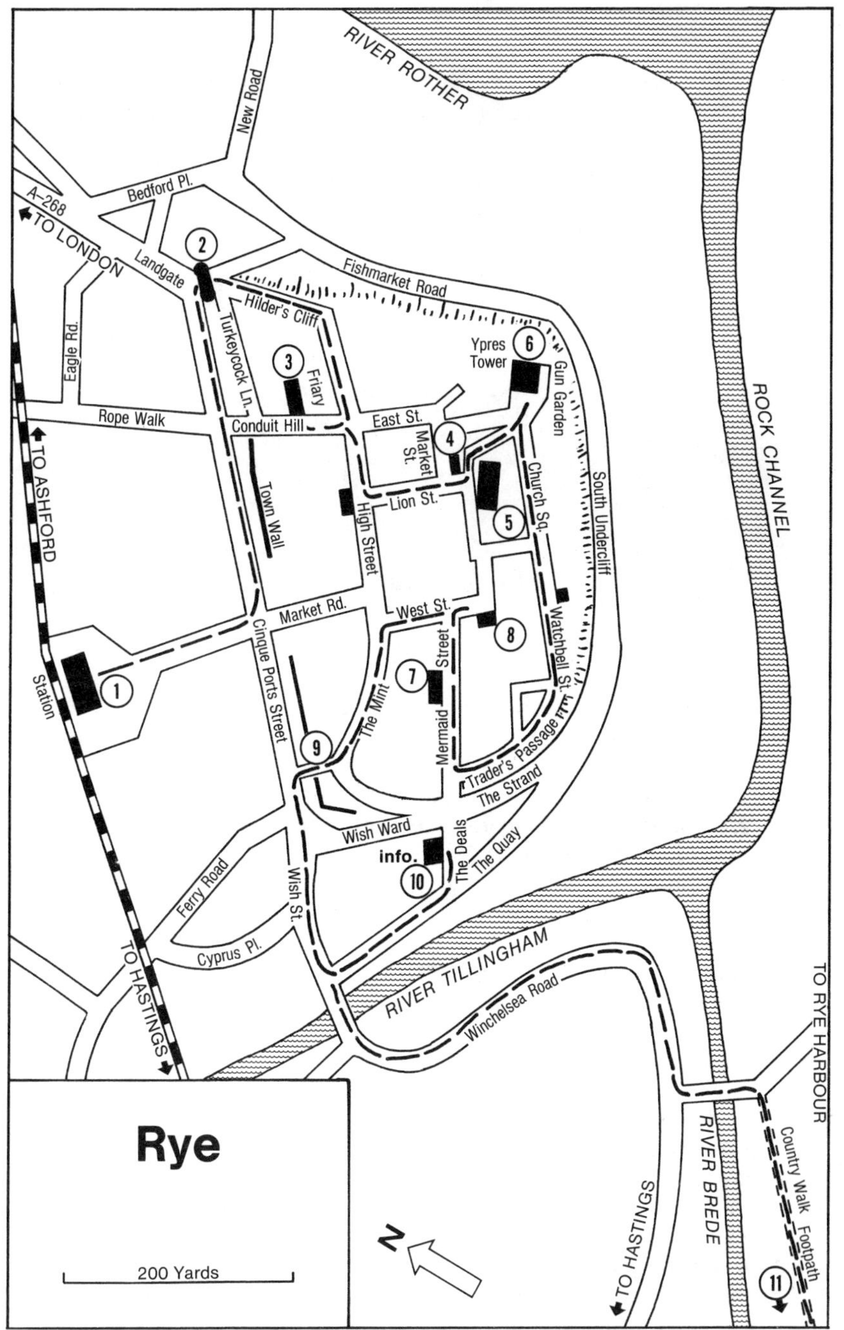

RIVER ROTHER
New Road
Bedford Pl.
A-268
TO LONDON
Landgate
Fishmarket Road
Hilder's Cliff
Turkeycock Ln.
Eagle Rd.
Friary
Ypres Tower
Gun Garden
ROCK CHANNEL
Rope Walk
Conduit Hill
East St.
Market St.
TO ASHFORD
Town Wall
Lion St.
High Street
Church Sq.
South Undercliff
Market Rd.
West St.
Watchbell St.
Cinque Ports Street
Station
The Mint
Mermaid Street
Trader's Passage
The Strand
Wish Ward
info.
The Deals
The Quay
Ferry Road
Wish St.
Cypress Pl.
TO HASTINGS
RIVER TILLINGHAM
Winchelsea Road
TO RYE HARBOUR
Country Walk Footpath
RIVER BREDE
TO HASTINGS
Rye
N
200 Yards
1
2
3
4
5
6
7
8
9
10
11

Along Church Square

ious rooms and cells is very interesting and may be made between Easter and mid-October, daily from 10:30 a.m. to 1 p.m. and 2:15–5:30 p.m. Just below this is the **Gun Garden**, an emplacement for artillery pieces that once helped defend England's shores.

Walk down Church Square, an exceptionally lovely cobbled street. This becomes Watchbell Street, whose name derives from the warning bell once housed there. Along the way you will pass a Spanish-style Catholic church. At the end is the **lookout**, overseeing the harbor.

Traders Passage leads to ***Mermaid Street**, quite possibly the most picturesque thoroughfare in all England. Go uphill to the **Mermaid Inn** (7), a famous hiding place for smugglers and highwaymen, first built in the late 15th century and much altered over the years. It is now a hotel and restaurant, the perfect spot for a refreshment break. Walk through a passage into the courtyard for a look.

Continue up Mermaid Street and turn right on West Street. Here, where the street bends, you will find the **Lamb House** (8), formerly the residence of the Lamb family, which for a long time provided many of the mayors of Rye. Henry James lived in this house from 1897 until 1916, writing many of his best-known novels there. It is now owned by the National Trust and receives visitors on Wednesdays and Saturdays, April through October, from 2–5:30 p.m.

Mermaid Street

Stroll back down West Street to High Street and turn left to The Mint, then make a right into **Needles Passage** (9). This narrow path takes you through a gap in the old town wall and down a few steps to Cinque Ports Street. Turn left and follow Wish Street.

Another left, just before the bridge, leads onto The Strand, where you will find an interesting group of 19th-century **warehouses** (10) that bear testament to the town's past as a trading port. The **Rye Town Model**, a highly entertaining sound-and-light show, is held in one of these every half-hour, daily from 9:30 a.m. to 5:30 p.m. The Heritage Centre and tourist office are in the same building.

Before leaving Rye, you might want to take a delightful walk in the countryside. From the bridge at the foot of Wish Street it is only about 1½ miles to **Camber Castle** (11), built by Henry VIII in the 16th century. To get there just follow the map to the public footpath along the River Brede. This trail leads through some pleasant sheep-grazing land and is well marked.

A Daytrip from London

Brighton

Londoners have been tripping down to Brighton in search of amusement since the mid-18th century, when a local doctor first promoted his famous sea cure. What made the town fashionable, though, was the frequent presence of naughty George IV, then the pleasure-loving, womanizing Prince of Wales, who began construction on his Royal Pavilion in 1787. Brighton remained an aristocratic resort until the coming of the railway turned it into the immensely popular "London-by-the-Sea" that it is today.

The town itself is actually very old, dating from at least Roman times. It was mentioned in the famous *Domesday Book* of 1086 as *Brighthelmstone,* then a tiny fishing village. Traces of what Brighton looked like before becoming a resort can still be found in the area of The Lanes, a colorful district between the Pavilion and the sea.

Brighton has no equal as an easy and fun-filled daytrip from London. Here you will mix with every sort of Englishman, from aristocrats to cockneys, and visit elegant places as well as popular amusements.

GETTING THERE:

Trains leave London's Victoria Station at least hourly for Brighton, a ride of about one hour. There are also direct hourly trains from London's King's Cross ThamesLink and Blackfriars stations, a 90-minute ride. Return service operates until late evening.

By car, Brighton is 54 miles south of London via the A-23, bypassing Gatwick on the M-23.

PRACTICALITIES:

Most of the major sights are open daily, but the art museum is closed on Mondays and some major holidays. A bright, warm day will add to your enjoyment. The local **Tourist Information Centre**, phone (0273) 237-55, is in the Marlborough House at 54 Old Steine. You might ask them about local **bicycle** rentals or buses to nearby attractions. Brighton has a **population** of about 200,000 and is in the county of **East Sussex**.

The Royal Pavilion

FOOD AND DRINK:

Brighton offers the widest range of restaurants this side of London. Some good choices are:

English's Oyster Bar (29 East St., in The Lanes) Considered to have the best seafood in town. X: Sun. eve. $$$

Stubbs (14 Ship St., in The Lanes) Seafood and classic French cuisine in the middle of an historic district. X: Sat. lunch. $$$

Le Grandgousier (15 Western St., north of King's Rd., between Montpelier and Waterloo streets) French cuisine in a casual setting. X: Sat. lunch, Sun. $$

Brown's Café (3–4 Duke St., in The Lanes) Steaks, grills, chili, and the like. $

Food for Friends (17 Prince Albert St., in The Lanes) Innovative vegetarian food in an informal setting. $

Cricketers (15 Black Lion St., in The Lanes) A cozy 16th-century pub with good food. $

SUGGESTED TOUR:

Leaving the marvelously Victorian **train station** (1), follow the map to **Old Steine** (2), an easy stroll of about ten minutes. Along the way you will pass the Royal Pavilion, a treat best saved for the end of the tour. The Old Steine (pronounced *Steen*) is the center of activity in Brighton and is probably named after a stone on which fishermen dried their nets in those quiet centuries before the town became London's playground.

Continue straight ahead to the **Palace Pier** (3), a gaudy Victorian structure dating from 1899 that juts some 1,717 feet, nearly a third of a mile, into the English Channel. On it you will find a fantastic variety of fun houses, rides, shows, shops, and people from all over Britain, with accents ranging from pure North Country to London Cockney.

The best way to explore the beach is to take a ride on **Volk's Railway** (4). This quaint, open train has been operating since 1883, the first in Britain to run on electricity. It follows right along the edge of the beach from near Palace Pier to the marina at Black Rock, a distance of about a mile. Volk's Railway operates from April through September.

Brighton Marina (5, off the map) is the largest in Europe and can accommodate over 2,000 yachts. Just west of this is the "naturist" beach, where—as the tourist office so tactfully puts it—clothes need not be worn.

Return by walking along Marine Parade with its attractive 19th-century terraces, squares, and crescents. The distance is only a bit over a mile, but you could, of course, take a bus or Volk's Railway. At the end, near the Palace Pier, is the new **Sea Life Centre** (6), a modern aquarium where you can observe strange marine life in re-created natural surroundings. It is open daily all year round.

Just beyond Old Steine lies the original Brighton, now known as **The Lanes** (7). No longer inhabited by fishermen, this warren of narrow traffic-free alleyways has become a fashionable center of boutiques, antique shops, pubs, and restaurants. The Lanes are a good spot for aimless strolling, although you should not miss Brighton Square and Duke's Lane, the most attractive of the tiny byways. This is also a great place to stop for a refreshment break.

Walk out onto **King's Road** and turn right along the beach. This is the main promenade of Brighton, a stretch of seaside lined with the traditional entertainments. Fish-and-chips shops, ice cream stands, the famous Brighton rock candy—it's all here. As you approach the adjoining town of Hove the atmosphere changes to one of sedate elegance.

Make a right at **Adelaide Crescent** (8), a beautiful open area of green surrounded by Regency town houses from the early 19th century. From here you can either return along King's Road or take Western Road back to Brighton. Your next stop should be the **Church of St. Nicholas** (9) on Dyke Road. Originally built in 1380 and reconstructed in 1853, it has a remarkable 12th-century Norman font. The churchyard is a perfect spot to rest before pressing on.

A short stroll down Church Street leads to the **Art Gallery and**

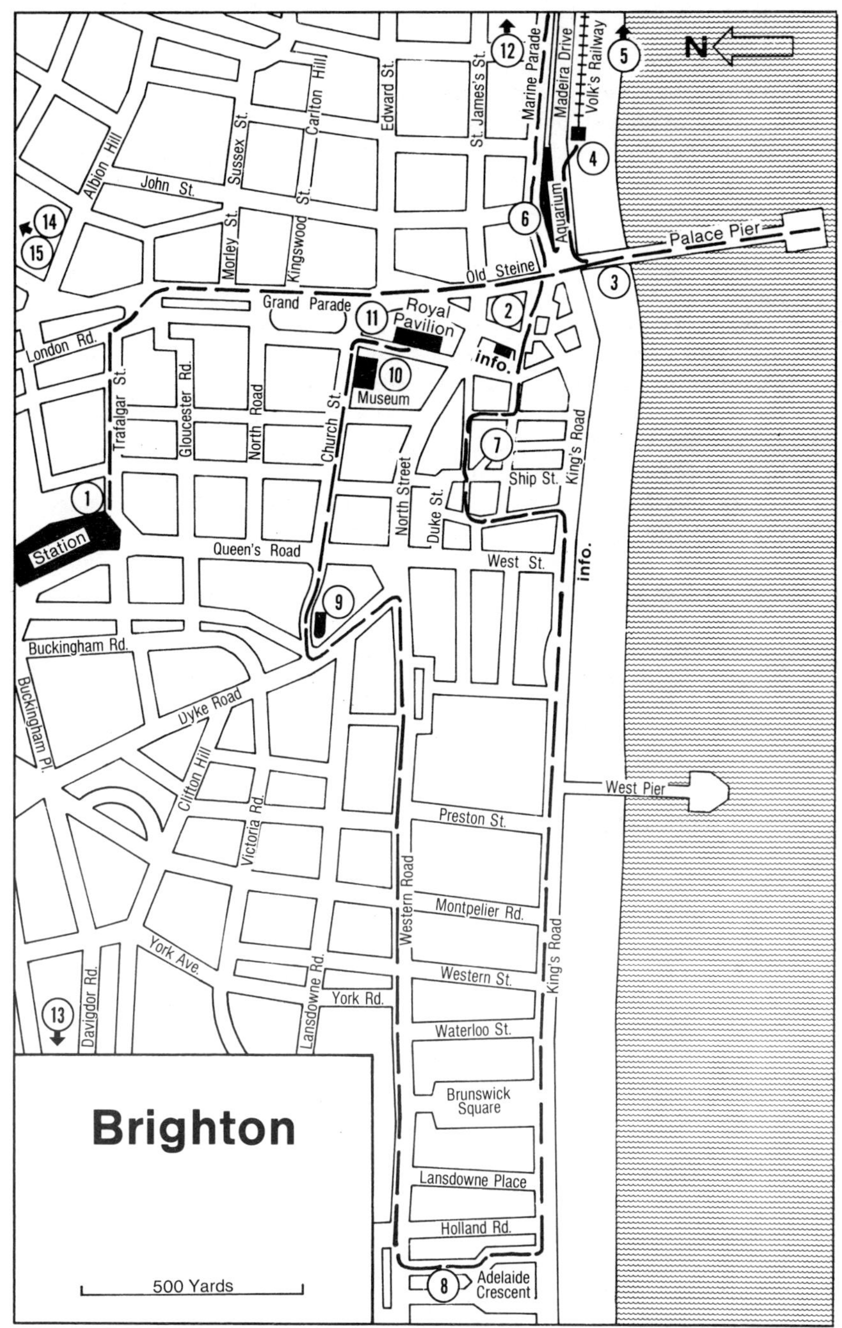

N
Brighton
500 Yards
Station
Queen's Road
Buckingham Rd.
Buckingham Pl.
Dyke Road
Clifton Hill
Victoria Rd.
York Ave.
Davigdor Rd.
Lansdowne Rd.
York Rd.
Western Road
Preston St.
Montpelier Rd.
Western St.
Waterloo St.
Brunswick Square
Lansdowne Place
Holland Rd.
Adelaide Crescent
King's Road
West Pier
West St.
info.
Ship St.
Duke St.
North Street
Church St.
North Road
Gloucester Rd.
Trafalgar St.
London Rd.
Museum
Royal Pavilion
Grand Parade
Old Steine
Palace Pier
Aquarium
Madeira Drive
Volk's Railway
Marine Parade
St. James's St.
Edward St.
Carlton Hill
Kingswood St.
Morley St.
Sussex St.
John St.
Albion Hill
1
2
3
4
5
6
7
8
9
10
11
12
13
14
15

Museum (10), a very worthwhile stop. Its collection of Art Nouveau and Art Deco pieces is probably the best in Britain. In addition, there are several Old Masters, superb porcelains, silver, furniture, and a fascinating display of local history—along with a gallery of fashion history. The museum is open on Tuesdays through Saturdays, from 10 a.m. to 5:45 p.m.; and on Sundays from 2–5 p.m.; but not on Mondays or some major holidays.

Brighton's stellar attraction, the ***Royal Pavilion** (11), is just around the corner. King George IV, known as "Prinny," began this hedonistic pleasure palace when he was still Prince of Wales, and over the years from 1787 to 1822 it evolved from a classical structure into the bizarre pseudo-Oriental fantasy that it is today. The final design, from 1815 on, was the work of John Nash, the greatest architect of the Regency period. Before entering the pavilion you should stroll around it as the best views face Pavilion Parade.

The **interior** of the palace, every bit as extravagant as the outside, may be visited on any day except Christmas and Boxing Day, from 10 a.m. to 6 p.m. (until 4:30 p.m. from October through May). The king used the pavilion until 1827, and it was also used by his brother, King William IV and, in turn, by Queen Victoria. Its end as a royal residence came in 1850 when Victoria, not amused by the theatricality of it all, sold the pavilion to the town for a fraction of its value. Another century passed before the palace was fully restored to its former splendor as a result of a permanent loan, made by Queen Elizabeth II, of original furnishings.

NEARBY SIGHTS:

Brighton has several other interesting attractions that may be reached by local bus, car, or rented bicycle. Ask for directions at the tourist office on Old Steine. The best of these are:

Rottingdean Village (12), a picturesque spot four miles east of Brighton on a cliff overlooking the sea. Rudyard Kipling lived here and mementos of his life can be seen at **The Grange**, a former vicarage that is now a museum.

British Engineerium (13), located in a former pumping station on the edge of Hove Park on Nevill Road, has a magnificent collection of stationary steam engines and mechanical inventions from the Victorian era.

Preston Manor (14), two miles from Old Steine on London Road, is an 18th-century Georgian mansion in a lovely setting. The manor is open on Tuesdays through Sundays, from 10 a.m. to 5 p.m., except on some major holidays.

Stanmer Village (15) preserves a turn-of-the-century atmosphere of rural England and is located four miles north of Brighton along Lewes Road.

A Daytrip from London

Portsmouth

There is one very compelling reason to visit Portsmouth, and that is to go aboard H.M.S. *Victory,* Nelson's flagship at Trafalgar. Here you can relive one of the proudest moments in British history. Located on a naval base, the ship has been perfectly restored to the condition she was in on October 21, 1805, when she won the most decisive battle ever fought at sea.

Portsmouth, long known to sailors as "Pompey," has many other attractions as well, including the *Mary Rose,* a Tudor warship sunk in 1545, and H.M.S. *Warrior,* the sole survivor from the Royal Navy's ironclad era. There are also forts and fortifications, splendid harbor views, several museums, a cathedral, and best of all, Old Portsmouth, which retains much of its nautical atmosphere despite heavy bombing during World War II.

The town was originally founded in 1194 by Richard the Lionheart but did not achieve real importance until 1495, when the first dry dock in the world was established there by Henry VII. Since then, Portsmouth has grown to become one of the major naval bases in the world, a position it still holds.

GETTING THERE:

Trains to Portsmouth Harbour Station, the end of the line, leave frequently from London's Waterloo Station. The journey takes about 90 minutes, with returns operating until mid-evening.

By car, Portsmouth is 71 miles southwest of London via the A-3 road. You may want to drive around the town instead of walking or taking buses.

PRACTICALITIES:

Portsmouth may be visited at any time except during the Christmas holidays. Most of the sights are open daily. The local **Tourist Information Centre**, phone (0705) 82-67-22, is on The Hard, near the entrance to the naval base. Portsmouth is in the county of **Hampshire**, and has a **population** of about 175,000.

FOOD AND DRINK:

Some good choices of pubs and restaurants are:

Le Talisman (123 High St., Old Portsmouth, near the cathedral) Excellent seafood and Breton French cuisine in the Old Town. X: Sat. lunch, Sun., Mon. $$$

Bistro Montparnasse (103 Palmerston Rd., 2 blocks north of Southsea Castle) A popular French-style restaurant. X: Sun. $$$

Pendragon (Clarence Parade, 2 blocks northeast of Southsea Castle) English and Continental dining in a small hotel. $$

George (84 Queen St., near the naval base) A colorful old pub serving lunches. $

Pembroke (Pembroke Rd., Old Portsmouth, near the cathedral) A pub with meals in a nautical ambiance. $

The Lone Yachtsman (at The Point in Old Portsmouth) A pub restaurant with traditional fare. $

SUGGESTED TOUR:

Leaving **Portsmouth Harbour Station** (1), turn left on The Hard and enter the main gate of the naval base. Continue straight ahead to ***H.M.S. *Victory*** (2), where you join the queue for tours aboard the ship. Each group is escorted through the entire vessel by a guide who is well versed in its history. Built in 1759, H.M.S. *Victory* has been in continuous commission since 1778. Visits may be made on any day except Christmas, from 10:30 a.m. to 5 p.m., but not before 1 p.m. on Sundays.

The **Royal Naval Museum**, occupying three old storehouses just a few steps away, is an interesting place to visit after the tour. In addition to the expected material relating to Lord Nelson and the Battle of Trafalgar, there are exhibits of more contemporary naval matters, including a mock-up of a modern frigate's operations room. The museum is open daily, except Christmas, from 10:30 a.m. to 5 p.m.; closing at 4:30 p.m. in winter.

The **Mary Rose** was the flower of Henry VIII's fleet, a revolutionary warship lost while defending Portsmouth in 1545. Long forgotten, its oaken hull lay preserved in the seabed mud for four centuries. In 1979, a team led by Prince Charles began recovery work and in 1982

H.M.S. Victory

the remains of the ship were raised. These are now on display in a covered dry dock next to H.M.S. *Victory*. There is also a fascinating exhibition of *Mary Rose* artifacts in a boathouse close to the naval base entrance. Both may be seen daily except on Christmas, from 10:30 a.m. to 5 p.m.

A new addition to the naval base, just west of the entrance gate, is **H.M.S. *Warrior***. This iron-hulled warship was built in 1860 as the world's fastest and best protected. She is the only remaining 19th-century capital ship in existence, the sole survivor of the Royal Navy's ironclad era. Visits may be made daily, from 10:30 a.m. to 5 p.m. An inexpensive **cafeteria** next to the museum offers lunches, snacks, and refreshments.

Follow the map to High Street in Old Portsmouth. The **Cathedral of St. Thomas** (3) is a rather odd structure. It was begun in 1188 as a chapel, became a parish church in 1320, and a cathedral only in 1927. The old church now forms the choir and sanctuary, with a new, still unfinished nave having been started in 1935. Although not a great cathedral by any standard, it is certainly interesting and deserves a visit.

At the end of High Street, next to the sea, is the 15th-century **Square Tower** (4), one of the first forts specially designed for cannon warfare. On its side is a gilded bust of Charles I that mysteriously survived the Civil War.

Turn right on Broad Street and pass the **Sally Port**, the traditional point of embarkation for Britain's naval heroes. Just beyond this is the **Round Tower** (5). Begun in 1415, it was the first permanent defensive work to be built in Portsmouth. You can climb up on it for a good view. An iron chain ran across the harbor from here to prevent unfriendly ships from entering.

The Point (6) still retains some of the flavor of Old Portsmouth. Once known as Spice Island, this small peninsula fairly teemed with bawdy pubs and brothels. To this day it remains a colorful place for eating and drinking, and the perfect spot for a **refreshment break**.

Return on Broad Street and continue to the **Garrison Church** (7). Now in ruinous condition, it was founded in 1212 as a hospice but was disbanded in 1540. It then became an armory and later a residence for the military governors. Charles II was married here in 1622. The building was restored as a church in the 19th century and badly damaged during World War II. It may be visited.

Stroll down to **Clarence Pier** (8), a popular amusement area with the usual seaside amenities. From here you can walk or take a bus past the beautiful gardens of Southsea Common to **Southsea Castle** (9), built in 1545 by Henry VIII. Inside the fort is a museum of local military history and archaeology, which may be visited daily from 10:30 a.m. to 5:30 p.m. Nearby is the **D-Day Museum**, featuring the 272-foot-long Overlord Embroidery, audio-visual shows, vehicles, weapons, and the like. The only museum in Britain devoted solely to the Normandy Invasions, it is open daily from 10:30 a.m. to 5:30 p.m.

Return to Pier Road and follow it to Museum Road. You can also take a bus from the front of Southsea Castle if you're tired. The **City Museum** (10) displays decorative and fine arts from the 16th century to the present, and is open daily from 10:30 a.m. to 5:30 p.m. At this point you could return directly to Portsmouth Harbour Station (1), or follow Cambridge Road to the **Civic Centre** (11). The Guildhall there is an outstanding Victorian structure flanked by modern glass buildings. To the north is the main shopping area along Commercial Road. This street leads, off the map, to the **Charles Dickens Birthplace Museum** at 393 Old Commercial Road. It is open from March through October, daily from 10:30 a.m. to 5:30 p.m. The **Portsmouth and Southsea Station** (12) is a convenient place to get a train back to London.

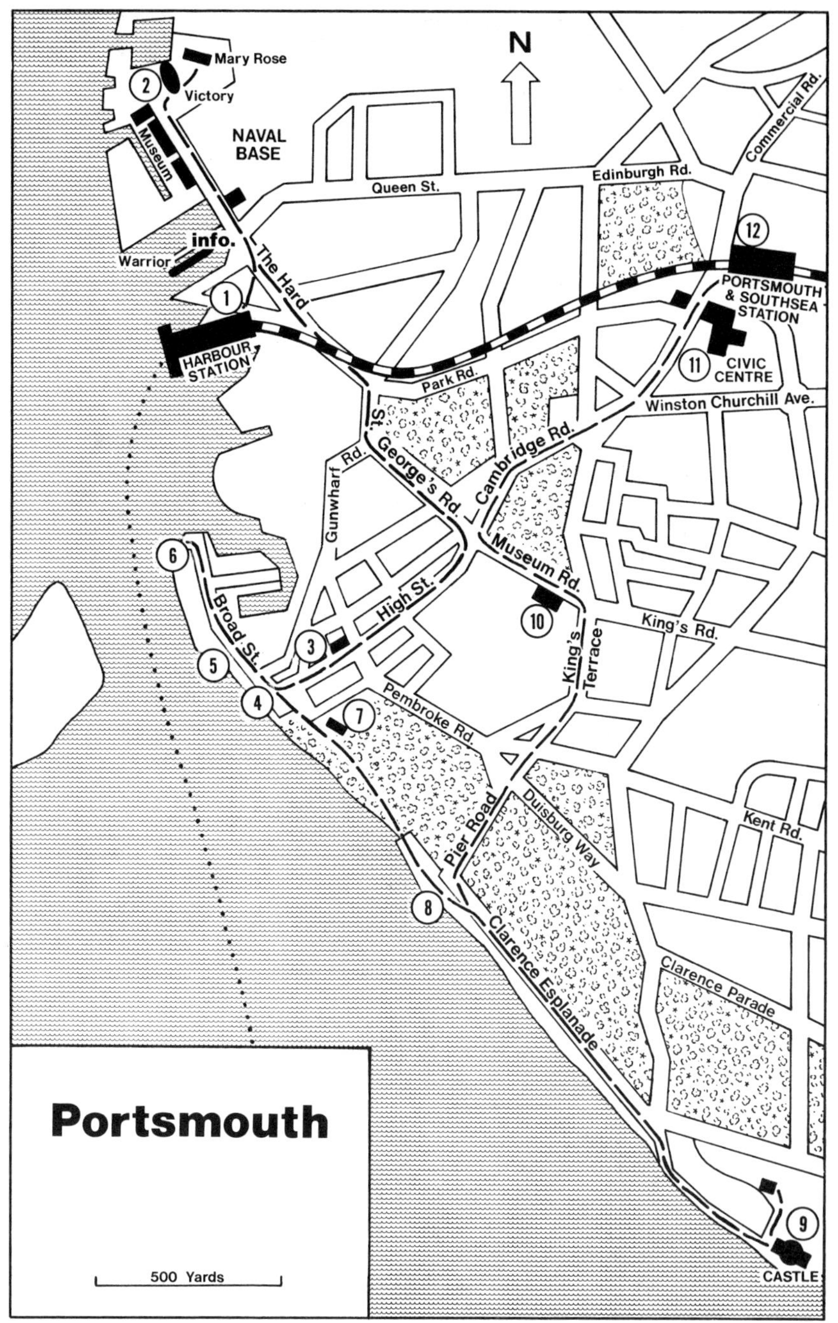
N
Mary Rose
Victory
NAVAL BASE
Museum
Queen St.
Edinburgh Rd.
Commercial Rd.
info.
Warrior
The Hard
HARBOUR STATION
PORTSMOUTH & SOUTHSEA STATION
CIVIC CENTRE
Park Rd.
Winston Churchill Ave.
St. George's Rd.
Cambridge Rd.
Gunwharf Rd.
Museum Rd.
High St.
Broad St.
King's Rd.
King's Terrace
Pembroke Rd.
Pier Road
Duisburg Way
Kent Rd.
Clarence Esplanade
Clarence Parade
CASTLE
Portsmouth
500 Yards
1
2
3
4
5
6
7
8
9
10
11
12

A Daytrip from London

Winchester

Winchester wears its history gracefully. The first "capital" of England, it was an important town from Roman times until the 12th century, when it lost out to rival London. Despite this decline, it remained a major religious and educational center, a role it still plays today. There are few places in England where the past has survived to delight the present quite so well.

The history of Winchester goes back to the Iron Age, when the Belgae, a Celtic tribe, settled in the valley of the River Itchen. This became the Roman town of *Venta Belgarum,* the fifth-largest in Britain. Following the collapse of the Roman Empire, the Anglo-Saxons took over and, changing the name to *Wintanceaster,* made it the capital of their kingdom of Wessex. Threats from marauding Danes caused the rival kingdoms of England to unite behind Egbert, the king of Wessex, in the mid-9th century; an act that made Winchester the effective capital of all England. A few decades later, under Alfred the Great, the town reached its peak of importance, and afterwards became the seat of such kings as Canute, Edward the Confessor, and William the Conqueror. Winchester's time had passed, however, and during the Norman era the center of power was gradually transferred to London.

GETTING THERE:

Trains leave London's Waterloo Station hourly for the one-hour ride to Winchester, with returns until late evening.

By car, Winchester is 72 miles southwest of London via the M-3 highway.

PRACTICALITIES:

This trip can be made at any time, although some sights are closed on Sundays, and sometimes on Mondays. Open-air **markets** are held in the town center on Wednesdays, Fridays, and Saturdays. The local **Tourist Information Centre**, phone (0962) 84-05-00, is in the Guildhall on The Broadway. Winchester is the county seat of **Hampshire**, and has a **population** of about 34,000.

Winchester Cathedral

FOOD AND DRINK:

Winchester has a wide selection of restaurants and pubs in all price ranges. A few good choices are:

- **The Elizabethan** (18 Jewry St., near High St.) A 16th-century Tudor house with Anglo-French cuisine. $$
- **Brann's** (9 Great Minster St., near the City Museum) A wine bar for snacks and a restaurant for full meals. X: Sun. $ and $$
- **Minstrels** (18 Little Minster St., a block west of the City Museum) Inexpensive lunches and vegetarian dishes, with an upstairs bar and restaurant. $ and $$
- **Wykeham Arms** (75 Kingsgate St., near Winchester College) An 18th-century inn, now a pub with excellent meals. X for food: Sun., Mon. eve. $
- **Royal Oak** (Royal Oak Passage, just off High St.) Lunch in an ancient pub with plenty of atmosphere. X for food: Sun. $

SUGGESTED TOUR:

From the **train station** (1), follow Sussex Street to the **Westgate** (2), one of Winchester's two remaining medieval gatehouses. Built in the 12th century, its upper floor was added in 1380 and later served as a debtors' prison. It is now a small museum with an interesting collection of ancient armor and related objects. The view from its roof is excellent. Visits may be made on Mondays through Saturdays, from 10 a.m. to 5 p.m.; and on Sundays from 2–5 p.m. From October through March it is closed on Mondays, and closes on Sundays at 4 p.m.

Strolling down High Street, you will pass the **Old Guildhall** on the right. Its projecting clock and figure of Queen Anne were given to the town to commemorate the Treaty of Utrecht in 1713. On the roof is a wooden tower that houses the curfew bell, still rung each evening at eight. The 16th-century **God Begot House**, opposite, occupies the site of a manor given by Ethelred the Unready to his Queen Emma in 1012.

A few more steps brings you to the **City Cross** (3). Also known as the Butter Cross, it was erected in the 15th century. Make a right through the small passageway leading to The Square. William the Conqueror's palace once stood here. The **City Museum** (4) has fascinating displays of local archaeological finds, including Celtic pottery, a Roman mosaic floor, and painted walls. It is open during the same times as the Westgate, above.

***Winchester Cathedral** (5) is among the largest in Europe. It was begun in 1079 on the site of earlier Saxon churches. During the 14th century the cathedral was altered with a new Gothic nave, resulting in a mixture of styles ranging from robust Norman to graceful Perpendicular. Several of England's earliest kings are buried here, including Ethelwulf, Egbert, Canute, and William II Rufus, son of the Norman conqueror.

Enter the nave through the west doorway. The windows retain some of the original 14th-century stained glass, most of which was destroyed by Puritan zealots during the Civil War. About halfway down the nave, on the right, is the magnificent **Wykeham's Chantry**, dedicated to Bishop William of Wykeham, who was also the founder of Winchester College and New College at Oxford, as well as a noted statesman. Almost opposite this, on the north aisle, is an outstanding 12th-century **font**, carved with the story of St. Nicholas. The tomb of the authoress Jane Austen is nearby in the north aisle.

The massive transepts are almost unchanged since Norman times. Near the southeast corner is a chapel containing the tomb of Izaak Walton, author of *The Compleat Angler,* who died here in 1683. A doorway in the south wall leads to the **Library**, which has a 10th-century copy of the Venerable Bede's *Ecclesiastical History* as well as a rare 12th-century illuminated Bible. During the summer it is open every day except on Sundays; and in winter on Saturdays and Wednesdays.

Continue up the south aisle and enter the **Presbytery**. Above the screens are six mortuary chests containing the bones of early English kings. Behind the **High Altar** is a magnificently carved 15th-century ornamental screen. Adjoining this is the **choir** with some outstanding early-14th-century stalls and misericords. The tomb of William II Rufus

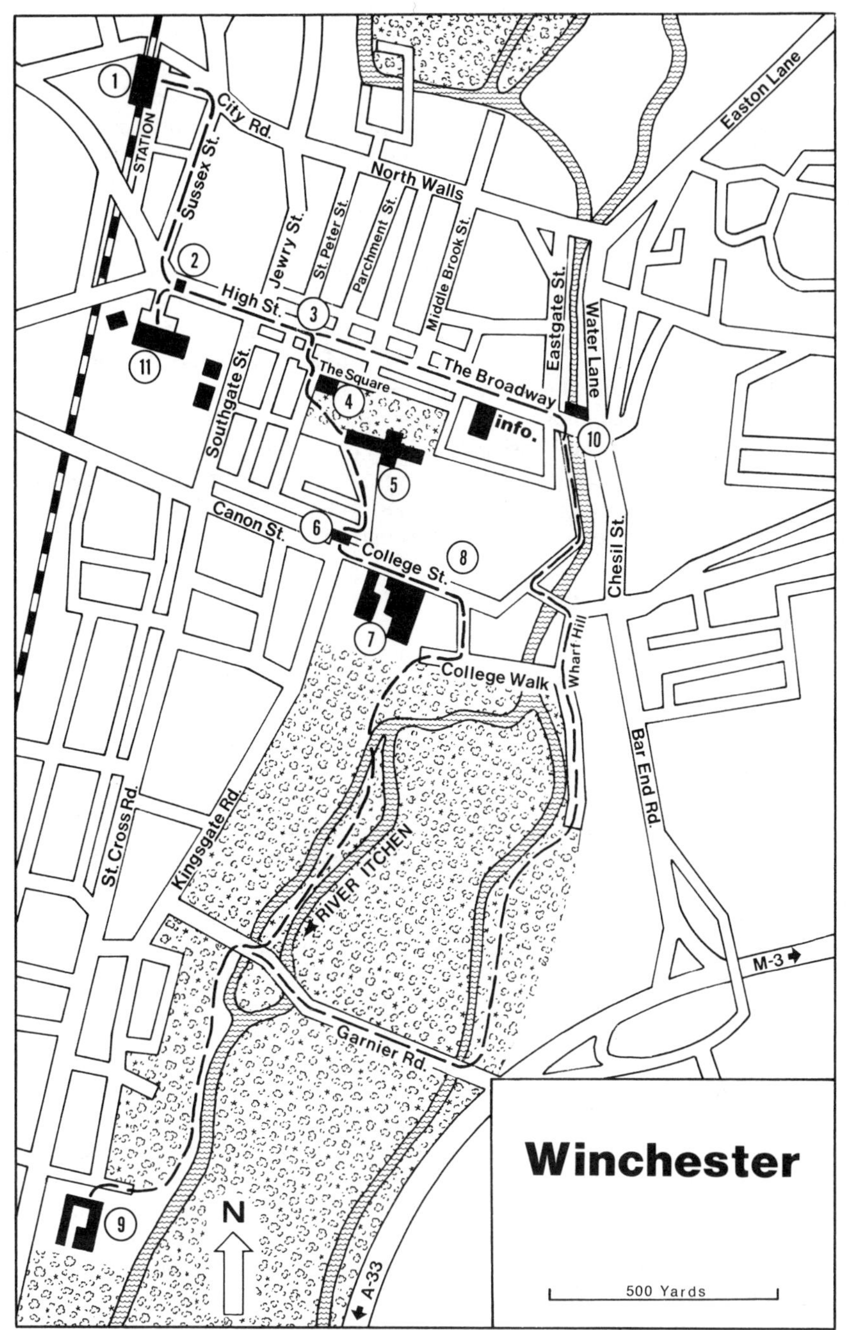
Winchester
STATION
City Rd.
Sussex St.
North Walls
Jewry St.
St. Peter St.
Parchment St.
Middle Brook St.
Eastgate St.
Water Lane
Easton Lane
High St.
The Square
The Broadway
info.
Southgate St.
Canon St.
College St.
Chesil St.
Wharf Hill
College Walk
Bar End Rd.
Kingsgate Rd.
St. Cross Rd.
RIVER ITCHEN
Garnier Rd.
M-3
A-33
N
500 Yards
1
2
3
4
5
6
7
8
9
10
11

is under the tower. At the east end of the cathedral is the 12th-century **Chapel of the Guardian Angels**, and the modern **Shrine of St. Swithun,** the patron saint of British weather. If it rains on his day, July 15th, you're in for another 39 soggy days. Other sights include the crypt and the treasury.

Leave the cathedral and stroll through the Close, partially surrounded by the ancient monastery's walls. An arcade of the former Chapter House links the south transept with the Deanery. Dome Alley has some particularly fine 17th-century houses. Pass through the **Kingsgate** (6), the second of the two surviving medieval town gates. Above it is the tiny 13th-century **Church of St. Swithun-upon-Kingsgate**, which should definitely be visited.

Winchester College (7), the oldest "public" school in England, was founded in 1382 and is associated with New College at Oxford. You may visit the chapel or wander around the courtyards on your own whenever the college is open. Guided tours are available from April through September, on Mondays through Saturdays, at 11 a.m., 2 p.m., and 3:15 p.m.

Continue down College Street to the ruins of **Wolvesey Castle** (8), begun in 1129 and destroyed in 1646 by Cromwell's forces during the Civil War. They are enclosed by part of the old city wall, but you can enter and take a look from April through September, daily from 10 a.m. to 1 p.m. and 2–6 p.m. The adjacent Wolvesey Palace, thought to have been designed by Sir Christopher Wren, is now the bishop's residence.

From here there is a wonderfully picturesque **riverside walk** to the venerable Hospital of St. Cross, the oldest functioning almshouse in England. It is about one mile away and can be reached by bus along St. Cross Road, but the delightful stroll along the stream is too lovely to miss. You can always ride back. To get there, just follow the map.

The ***Hospital of St. Cross** (9) has always had a tradition of providing a dole of bread and ale to weary wayfarers, which includes you. Ask and ye shall receive. Founded in 1136 by Bishop Henry de Blois, grandson of William the Conqueror, the institution cares for 25 brethren who live in 15th-century quarters and wear medieval gowns. There is a 12th-century Norman chapel and a 15th-century hall and kitchen that can be visited. It is open all year, except on Sundays and Christmas Day, from 9:30 a.m. to 12:30 p.m. and 2–5 p.m.; with shorter hours in winter. Don't miss this.

Those returning on foot can take the alternative route via Garnier Road. St. Catherine's Hill, across the river, has an Iron Age fort and the foundations of an early chapel at its summit, as well as an excellent view.

Back in Winchester, the footpath leads across the River Itchen

The Hospital of St. Cross

alongside the medieval walls to the **City Mill** (10), now a youth hostel. There has been a mill at this location since Anglo-Saxon days. The present one, built in 1744, may be visited from April through September, daily except Mondays and Fridays, from 1:45–4:45 p.m.

Turn left and follow **The Broadway** past the statue of King Alfred, who made Winchester a center of learning over a thousand years ago. The huge Victorian **Guildhall** of 1873 houses the tourist office. From here, High Street leads to The Castle, an administrative complex that includes the **Great Hall** (11), the sole remaining part of Winchester Castle. Dating from the early 13th century, the hall was the scene of many important events in English history. Go inside and take a look at the famous Roundtable, once associated with King Arthur but now known to be of 14th-century origin. It is open daily from 10 a.m. to 5 p.m., closing at 4 p.m. on winter weekends. There are five military museums in the immediate vicinity that might interest you: the **Royal Green Jackets**, the **Light Infantry**, the **Gurkha**, the **Royal Hussars**, and the **Royal Hampshire Regiment**. From here it is only a short stroll back to the train station.

A Daytrip from London

Windsor and Eton

Windsor, like Stratford, Oxford, and the Tower of London, is one of England's greatest tourist attractions. It has just the right combination of elements to make an ideal daytrip destination for first-time visitors and seasoned travelers alike. To begin with, it is very close to the capital and easy to reach. Second, it contains within a small area much of what is considered to be typically English. There is the Royal Castle, still in use after 850 years, a picturesque riverside location on the Thames, a colorful Victorian town, and in Eton one of the great public schools that have molded British character since the Middle Ages. Add these together and you have a carefree and thoroughly delightful day ahead of you.

GETTING THERE:

Trains depart London's Paddington Station frequently for Slough, where you change to a shuttle train for Windsor and Eton Central. The total journey takes about 40 minutes, with returns until late evening. Service is reduced on weekends. There is also direct service from London's Waterloo Station to Windsor and Eton Riverside, taking about 50 minutes and running about twice an hour, less frequently on Sundays. Most travelers will find the route via Paddington to be more convenient.

By car, Windsor is 28 miles west of London via the M-4 motorway. Get off at Junction 6.

PRACTICALITIES:

The castle grounds are open daily except for special events. The State Apartments are also open daily, with the exception of Sundays in winter, but closed when the Queen is in residence. If in doubt, check with the local **Tourist Information Centre**, phone (0753) 85-20-10, in the Windsor and Eton Central Station. Windsor is in the county of **Berkshire**, and has a **population** of about 30,000.

A statue of Queen Victoria guards the Castle

FOOD AND DRINK:

Some good pubs and restaurants are:

In Windsor:

The Orangerie (Thames St., near the bridge) English and French cuisine at an inn, once the home of Sir Christopher Wren. $$$

La Taverna (2 River St., near the bridge) Good Italian food in a nice location. X: Sun. $$

Carpenters Arms (Market St., behind the Guildhall) A comfortable pub with lunches. X for meals: Sun. $

Windsor Chocolate House (8 Church St., behind the Guildhall) Light lunches and afternoon teas. $

In Eton:

Eton Buttery (High St., by the bridge) Excellent food with a French touch, in view of the castle. $$

Eton Wine Bar (82 High St., near the bridge) Healthy, imaginative cooking with a changing menu. $$

SUGGESTED TOUR:

Start your walk at **Windsor and Eton Central Station** (1). Directly adjacent to this is the wonderful **Royalty and Empire** exhibition that re-creates moments of the Victorian era with replicas of old railway equipment, animated figures of Queen Victoria and other notables, and a 15-minute audio-visual extravaganza. This perfect introduction to Windsor is open every day except Christmas and the second and third weeks of January, from 9:30 a.m. to 5:30 p.m., closing at 4:30 p.m. in winter.

Cross the main street, passing the statue of Queen Victoria, and enter the castle grounds. Begun by William the Conqueror in the 11th century, ***Windsor Castle** has been altered by nearly every succeeding monarch. it is the largest inhabited castle in the world and remains a chief residence for the sovereigns of England.

Enter through Henry VIII's Gateway and visit ***St. George's Chapel** (2), one of the most beautiful churches in England. Many of the country's kings and queens are buried here. Continue on past the massive **Round Tower** and go out on the North Terrace, which has magnificent views up and down the River Thames. The entrance to the **State Apartments** (3) is nearby. A stroll through them is worthwhile, but don't fret if they are closed because the Queen is here. Much more interesting is ***Queen Mary's Dolls' House,** a miniature 20th-century palace in exquisite detail, also entered from the North Terrace. Both are usually open on Mondays through Saturdays, from 10:30 a.m. to 5 p.m.; and on Sundays from 12:30–5 p.m.; closing at 3 or 4 p.m. in winter. They are also closed on winter Sundays and on some holidays. The rest of your tour of the castle can be spent just poking about any area that is not off limits, and visiting the **Curfew Tower** (4).

Leave the castle and stroll down Church Street, perhaps stopping at the Parish Church and Brass Rubbing Centre. Walk through the graveyard to St. Alban's Street, near the foot of which is the **Royal Mews Exhibition** (5), a display of ceremonial carriages and various gifts received by the Queen. From here you might go down Park Street for a walk in the **Home Park**.

The elegant **Guildhall** (6) on High Street was completed in 1707 by Sir Christopher Wren. Step on to its porch and note that the center columns do not quite reach the ceiling they allegedly support, a trick played by the architect to prove the soundness of his design. Continue down High Street and Thames Street, making a left at the footpath to the river. Along the way you will pass a bowling green, tennis courts, and a lovely waterside park. **Boat trips**, some as short as 35 minutes, are available here.

The old **cast-iron bridge** (7) to Eton is reserved for pedestrians. Once across it follow High Street past numerous shops and pubs to

Windsor and Eton

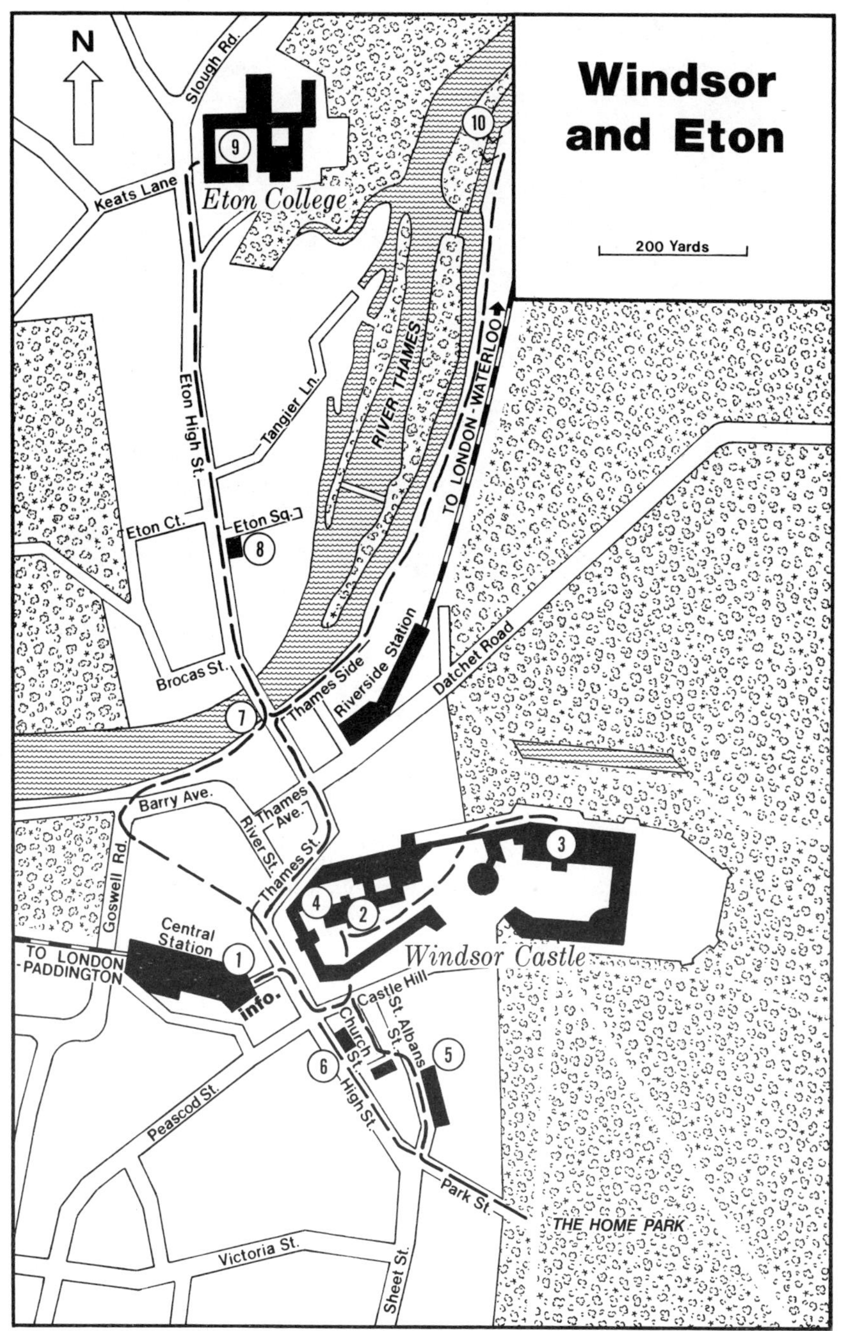

Boat trips on the Thames

the **Cock Pit** (8), a 15th-century timbered inn where cockfighting was once patronized by Charles II, the Merry Monarch. Outside it are the **town stocks** and an unusual Victorian mailbox.

Eton College (9) was founded in 1440 by Henry VI, himself a teenager at the time. It is the most famous of England's public (meaning very private) schools and has educated many of the nation's greatest leaders. As you walk around you will notice the peculiar traditional garb of the students, which makes them look a little like penguins. Parts of the school are open to visitors, including the schoolyard, cloisters, and the chapel. The Upper and Lower schools may also be seen at times. Guided tours, led by senior boys, are available. Be sure to visit the **Museum of Eton Life**, which re-creates life among the students in bygone times. Located in the cellars of the original 15th-century buildings, it is usually open from 2–5 p.m., depending on school activities.

Return to the bridge. If you have any strength or time left you may want to take a pleasant walk along the Thames to the **Romney Lock** (10), or visit a pub before returning to London.

A Daytrip from London

*Bath

Legend has it that the hot mineral springs of Bath were discovered about 500 B.C. by Prince Bladud who, suffering from leprosy, was cured and became king. Whatever truth lies behind this story, we do know that the Romans built a settlement there named *Aquae Sulis,* which served as their spa for nearly 400 years.

During the Middle Ages the waters of Bath were well known for their curative properties, but the splendor of the Romans had vanished. The town was renovated for Queen Anne's visit in 1702 and a master of ceremonies appointed to oversee the spa. This post remained after the queen's departure and was filled in 1705 by a bizarre young gambler named Richard "Beau" Nash, who in the next 40 years virtually invented the resort business.

Nash began by persuading the local leaders to invest vast sums into building a town of unmatched elegance. Much of the design fell to one John Wood, an architect with visionary ideas. Under his plan, individual houses were only components of a larger structure behind a common façade. This thinking reached its height in that triumph of the Palladian style, the Royal Crescent, designed by his son in 1767.

Today, Bath remains much the same as it was when the Georgian aristocracy made it their playground. The remains of the Roman era have since been unearthed, adding to its many attractions. Despite its stylish refinement, Bath makes a great daytrip destination largely because it is such a fun place to visit. Many travelers, in fact, consider it to be nothing less than the most enjoyable town in England.

GETTING THERE:

Trains leave London's Paddington Station at least hourly for Bath Spa Station, a ride of about 80 minutes. Return service operates until late evening.

By car, take the M-4 highway to Junction 18, then south on the A-46. Bath is 119 miles west of London.

PRACTICALITIES:

Nearly all of the attractions are open daily. The local **Tourist Information Centre**, phone (0225) 46-28-31, is in The Colonnades on Bath Street, just west of the Roman Baths. Bath is in the county of **Avon**, and has a **population** of about 84,000.

FOOD AND DRINK:

Bath has an enormous range of restaurants and pubs, a few of the better choices being:

Popjoys (Beau Nash House, Sawclose, adjacent to the Theatre Royal) An elegant Regency restaurant with inventive English cuisine. Reservations recommended, phone (0225) 46-04-94. X: Sat. lunch, Sun., Mon. $$$

Royal Crescent Hotel (16 Royal Crescent) Very fine food with an outstanding wine selection. For reservations phone (0225) 31-90-90. $$$

Flowers (27 Monmouth St., west of the Theatre Royal) A delightfully pleasant restaurant with a reasonably priced lunch menu. X: Sun. $$ and $$$

Moon and Sixpence (6a Broad St., east of the Octagon) Simple lunches and full dinners, with outdoor tables available. $$ and $$$

Woods (9 Alfred St., near the Assembly Rooms) Famous for its good food and Georgian elegance. X: Sun. $$

Sweeney Todd's (15 Milsom St., near the Octagon) Pizza, burgers, chili, and the like, in a nice setting. $

The Grapes (Westgate St., 2 blocks northwest of the Roman Baths) An old-fashioned pub with good food and a lively crowd. X: Sun. $

Huckleberry's (34 Broad St., east of the Octagon) A fine place for vegetarian meals. X: Sun. $

SUGGESTED TOUR:

Leaving **Bath Spa Station** (1), walk straight ahead on Manvers Street past the bus station and turn left on North Parade. In one block this becomes a colorful lane called **Old Lilliput Alley**, lined with some of the oldest houses in Bath. One of these is **Sally Lunn's House** (2), built in 1482 on Roman foundations, which as a coffee shop has been famous for its hot Bath buns since the late 17th century. They are still just as delicious, making this a favorite place for a break. You can also just pop in to see the original **kitchen** in the cellar, and the Roman walls. At the end of the passage is **Abbey Green**, an especially attractive spot.

The Abbey

Turn right on Church Street and follow it for two blocks to the **Abbey** (3). This splendid example of the Perpendicular style was begun in 1499, although it did not gain a roof until the 17th century. Earlier churches existed on the same spot for several hundred years before a cathedral was built in 1088, a Norman structure that was destroyed by fire in 1137. The present abbey is noted for its enormous clerestory windows that flood the interior with light, and for its vaulted ceiling, planned from the start but not added until 1864.

Walk across the Abbey Churchyard to the entrance of the ***Roman Baths and Pump Room** (4). The tour through this ancient complex includes a fascinating **museum** of Roman and prehistoric relics, featuring the renowned gilt-bronze head of the goddess Minerva. An overflowing part of the original Roman reservoir is in the area, as is the **Great Bath**, a marvelously preserved pool that is today open to the sky. The original Roman lead plumbing is still in use, while the columns and statues above are Victorian additions. Another group of small baths and hypocaust rooms lie beyond, along with the King's Bath and the Circular Bath. A few of the ruins were discovered in the 18th century, but it was not until the 19th that the major finds were excavated. Above all of this is the famous **Pump Room**, an elegant Georgian assembly hall reflecting a gentility long vanished elsewhere.

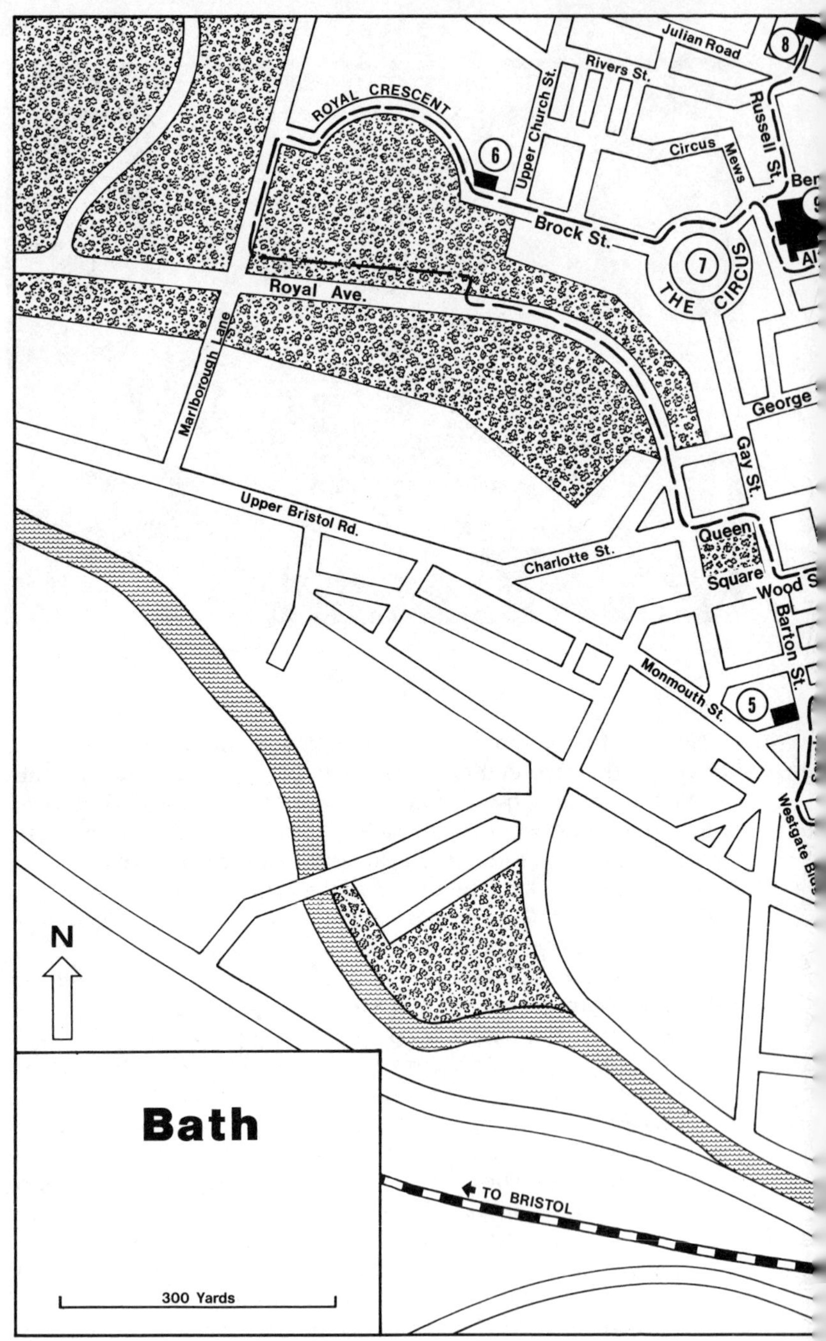
Julian Road
Rivers St.
Upper Church St.
ROYAL CRESCENT
Russell St.
Circus
Mews
Brock St.
THE CIRCUS
Royal Ave.
Marlborough Lane
George
Gay St.
Upper Bristol Rd.
Charlotte St.
Queen
Square
Wood S
Barton St.
Monmouth St.
Westgate
N
Bath
TO BRISTOL
300 Yards
6
7
8
5

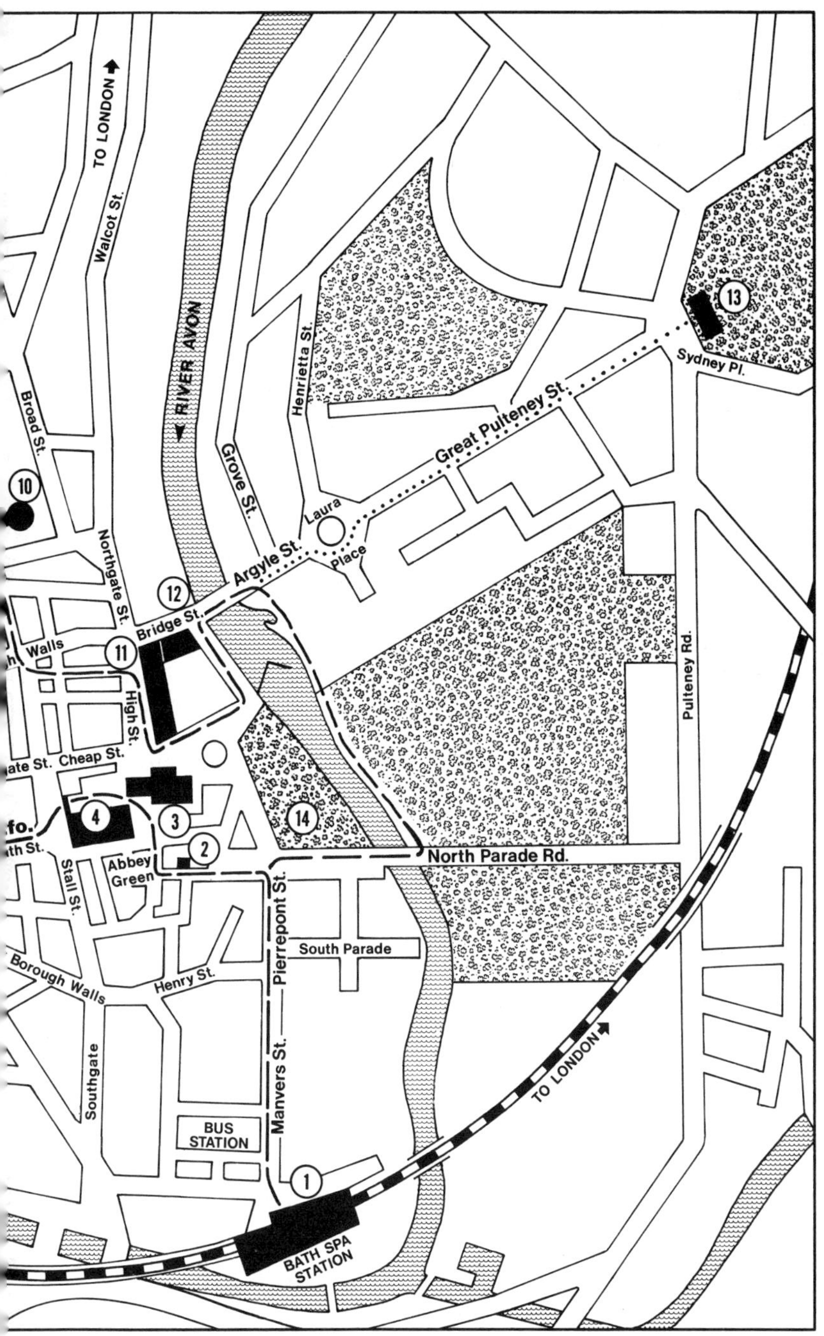
TO LONDON
Walcot St.
RIVER AVON
Broad St.
10
Northgate St.
Grove St.
Henrietta St.
13
Sydney Pl.
Great Pulteney St.
Laura
Place
Argyle St.
12
Bridge St.
Walls
11
High St.
Cheap St.
4
3
2
14
North Parade Rd.
Stall St.
Abbey
Green
Pierrepont St.
South Parade
Borough Walls
Henry St.
Pulteney Rd.
Southgate
Manvers St.
BUS
STATION
TO LONDON
1
BATH SPA
STATION

Be sure to see the wonderful equation clock of 1709, as well as the charming prints and 18th-century furniture. Needless to say, this is the perfect spot for a **tea break**, served along with live music by the Pump Room Trio from 10 a.m. to noon and 2:45–5 p.m., daily in summer and on Sundays in winter. The entire complex is open daily from 9 a.m. to 6 p.m., closing at 5 p.m. in winter.

Continue down Bath Street past the tourist office and turn right into St. Michael's Place, then left through a narrow passage called Chandos Buildings to Westgate Buildings. Another right brings you to the **Theatre Royal** (5), first erected in 1720 but later rebuilt. It is adjacent to Beau Nash's last home, now a restaurant named after his mistress, Juliana Popjoy. Follow the map by way of the narrow, cobbled **Queen Street** and continue through Queen Square, heading uphill through Royal Victoria Park.

From the gravel walk you have an excellent view of the ***Royal Crescent** (6), a magnificent sweep of 30 houses joined together in one continuous façade of 114 Ionic columns. Designed in 1767 by John Wood the Younger, this is regarded as the epitome of the Palladian style in England. Follow it around to **Number 1**, whose interior has been restored to its 18th-century splendor. This exquisite house is open to the public from March through October, on Tuesdays through Saturdays, from 11 a.m. to 5 p.m.; and on Sundays from 2–5 p.m. During the rest of the year it is open on weekends only, from 11 a.m. to 3 p.m.

Stroll down Brock Street to **The Circus** (7), a circular group of Georgian houses considered to be John Wood's finest work. It is arranged so that no street goes straight through, resulting in a view from every angle. Continue along Bennet Street, from which you can take an interesting little side trip by turning up Russell Street and making a right on Rivers Street to the **Bath Industrial Heritage Centre** (8). This Victorian engineering shop, brass foundry, and mineral-water plant is complete with all of its original machinery and related items. An unusually fascinating place to visit, it is open daily from 2–5 p.m., March through November, and on weekends only during the rest of the year.

Now head for the **Assembly Rooms** (9). Also built by John Wood the Younger, this structure was the center of social activity in Bath, having witnessed many grand balls, banquets, receptions, and the like. The ***Museum of Costume** on its lower floor is the largest of its kind in the world. Clothes dating from as far back as the 16th century up to the present are very well displayed, many of them in period room settings. It is open daily from 10 a.m. to 5 p.m.

The route now takes you down to Milsom Street, the main shopping thoroughfare. The 18th-century **Octagon** (10) now houses the **National Centre of Photography**. This intriguing museum has displays of both contemporary and early camera work as well as an outstanding collection of antique and modern photo equipment, including a vast number of Leicas. It also serves as the headquarters of the Royal Photographic Society, and is open daily from 9:30 a.m. to 5:30 p.m.

Continue straight ahead past Upper Borough Walls and turn left through the very charming **Northumberland Place** to High Street. The building on the other side is the **Guildhall** (11), whose banqueting room is one of the finest interiors in Bath. This may be seen on Mondays through Fridays, from 8:30 a.m. to 4:30 p.m. Next to it is the **Covered Market**, which was founded in medieval times and remains very much alive in its 19th-century building.

Turning left around the Orange Grove brings you to Grand Parade. To the left, on Bridge Street, is the **Victoria Art Gallery**, which displays changing exhibitions of interest. It is open on Mondays through Fridays, from 10 a.m. to 6 p.m.; and on Saturdays from 10 a.m. to 5 p.m. The **Pulteney Bridge** (12) spanning the Avon is one of the few left in Europe to be lined with shops. Built in 1770 with obvious inspiration from the Ponte Vecchio in Florence, it makes a spectacular sight rising above the weir.

Once across it, you might want to make a **side trip** down Argyle Street and Great Pulteney Street to the **Holburne of Menstrie Museum** (13), which specializes in the arts of the Age of Elegance. Silver, porcelains, miniatures, and paintings by Gainsborough and others are among its attractions. Visits may be made on Mondays through Saturdays, from 11 a.m. to 5 p.m.; and on Sundays from 2:30–6 p.m. It is closed between mid-December and mid-February, and on Mondays between November and Easter.

Return almost to the bridge, then go down a flight of steps marked Riverside Walk to the River Avon and stroll past the weir. From the embankment on this side you can take a **boat ride** lasting about one hour. Check the tourist office for current schedules. When you get to the next bridge, climb the stairs and cross it. You are now on North Parade. The **Parade Gardens** (14) on the right are a good place to relax before returning to the station.

A Daytrip from London

Exeter

There are two excellent reasons that make the rather long journey to Exeter practical as a daytrip from London. The first is its fabulous Maritime Museum and the second is the opportunity it affords to experience at least some of the West Country's many charms without having to stay for a few days.

Exeter began as a Celtic settlement, being taken over in A.D. 55 by the Romans, who called it *Isca Dumnoniorum* and used it as a frontier outpost. Portions of their stone walls, erected in the early 3rd century, can still be seen. Continuously occupied ever since, it became the *Exanceaster* of the Saxons and was frequently plundered, right down to modern times, when much of it was wiped out by the bombs of World War II. Now a thriving modern city, Exeter still retains many of its medieval treasures as well as reminders that this was once an important seaport.

GETTING THERE:

Trains depart London's Paddington Station several times in the morning for the less-than-2½-hour ride to Exeter's St. David's Station. Those going on a Saturday in summer should make reservations. Return trains run until mid-evening. If you're using the London Extra Pass, you'll have to travel via the slower route from London's Waterloo Station to Exeter Central Station.

By car, Exeter is 172 miles southwest of London via the M-3 followed by the A-30 through Salisbury.

PRACTICALITIES:

A trip to Exeter requires good weather and an early start. Some of the sights are closed on Sundays and Mondays, but the exciting Maritime Museum is open every day except Christmas and December 26. The local **Tourist Information Centre**, phone (0392) 26-52-97, is in the Civic Centre on Paris Street. Exeter is the county town of **Devon**, and has a **population** of about 97,000.

In the Maritime Museum

FOOD AND DRINK:

Exeter has a number of historic inns and pubs, as well as several good restaurants. Some choices are:

Ship Inn (Martin's Lane, just north of the cathedral) An historic inn favored by Sir Francis Drake and other sailors, with a pub and an upstairs restaurant. X: Sun. $ and $$

White Hart (66 South St., between the cathedral and the Maritime Museum) An old inn, partly 14th century. Bar lunches and full meals. $ and $$

Turk's Head (High St., near the Guildhall) A pub with traditional English fare. $ and $$

Coolings Wine Bar (11 Gandy St., just southeast of the Royal Albert Museum) A casual and very popular place for traditional dishes and salads. X: Sun. $

Port Royal Inn (The Quay, near the Maritime Museum) A riverside pub with good food. $

SUGGESTED TOUR:

Leaving **St. David's Station** (1), you have a choice of walking or taking a bus or taxi to the cathedral, nearly a mile away. Those on foot should follow the route on the map.

***Exeter Cathedral** (2) is famous for its gorgeous interior and the unusual placement of its two Norman towers. Begun in the 12th century on the site of an earlier Saxon church, the cathedral was transformed during the 14th century into the lovely Gothic structure it is today. Its west front is heavily decorated with an amazing array of sculpted figures. "Great Peter," a six-ton bell in the north tower, still tolls the curfew each evening, as it has for nearly 500 years.

Enter the nave and look up at the richly colored roof **bosses**. The charming **Minstrels' Gallery**, midway down on the left, is used for Christmas carol recitals. In the north transept there is a superb 15th-century wall painting of the Resurrection and an **astronomical clock** from the same era that shows the Sun revolving around the Earth. The choir has a fabulous 14th-century **Bishop's Throne** and interesting old misericords.

Complete your exploration of the cathedral and stroll out into the **close**. At the end of St. Martin's Lane is the small St. Martin's Church. Next to that is **Mol's Coffee Shop** (3), a 16th-century inn now used as a shop. You can enter it and ask to see the room where famous seamen such as Raleigh, Drake, and Hawkins once sipped their brew.

Now follow the map to the ***Maritime Museum** (4), across the river from The Quay. Occupying several old warehouses on a canal basin and reached by taking a hand-operated ferry, this is a fun place where visitors are encouraged not only to touch but to climb aboard many of the exhibits. Crawl into the engine room of a coal-burning tug, picnic on an exotic Chinese junk, or wear yourself out turning capstans. Well over a hundred boats from all over the world are on display, several of them floating in the basin. Portuguese rowboats may be rented by the hour for a short trip down the River Exe. If you love boats at all, you will rejoice in this wonderful place. It is open daily, from 10 a.m. to 5 p.m., closing at 6 p.m. in July and August.

While still in a maritime mood, you can take a short walk along the ancient **canal**, first opened in 1566 and now used for pleasure craft. The route is easy to follow and returns you to The Quay and the **Quay House Interpretation Centre** (5), a 16th-century structure now used for historic exhibitions and an audio-visual introduction to the city. From here walk past the 17th-century **Customs House**, built on the site of the Roman quay. Continue on to West Street and the parish church of **St. Mary Steps** (6), which has a curious 17th-century clock in its bell tower as well as a Norman font. Opposite it, at number 24, is the **House that Moved**, a timber-framed structure dating from about 1500 that was moved on rollers in 1961 to make way for road construction. Take a look up Stepcote Hill, a steep medieval street that is little changed.

A right on Fore Street will take you past **Tucker's Hall**, a 15th-cen-

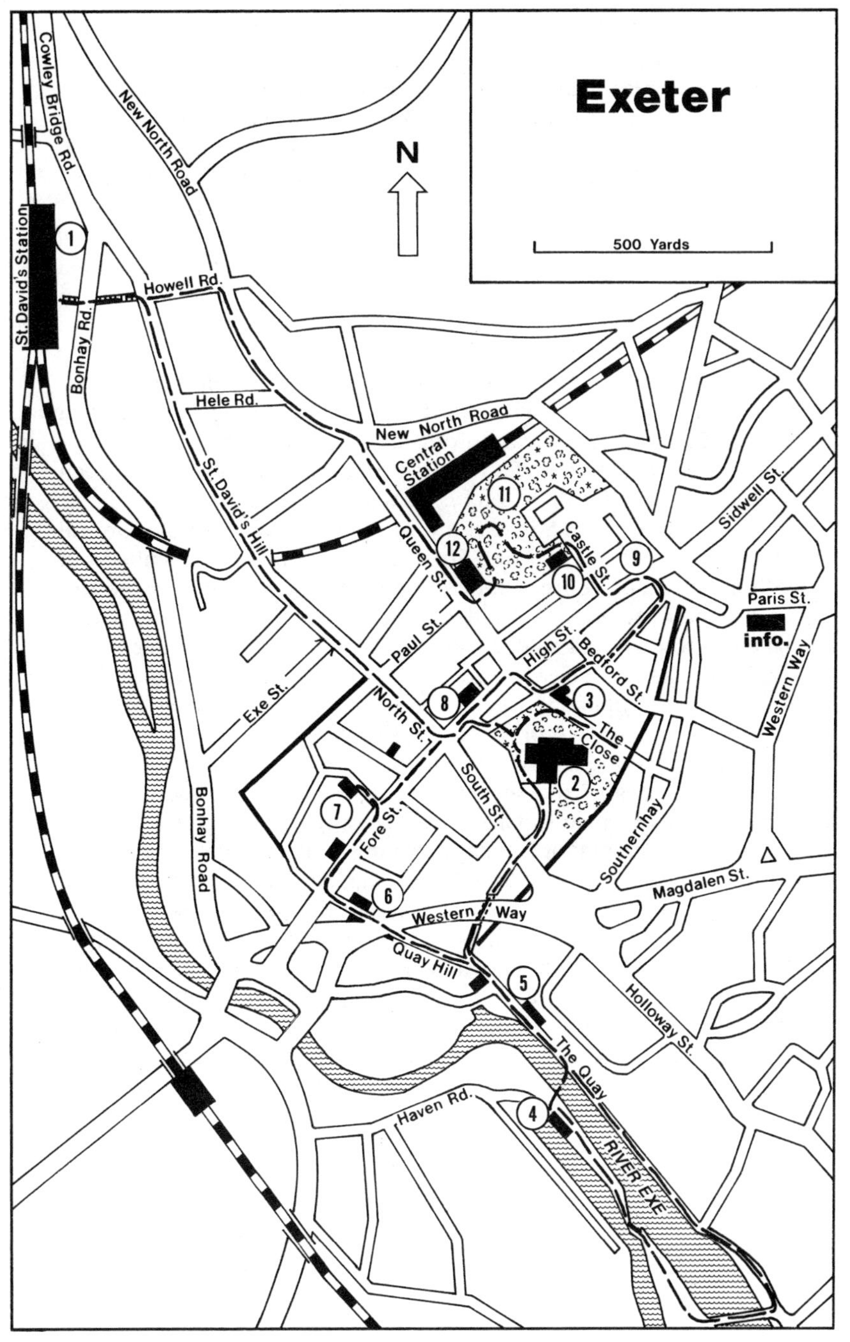
Exeter
N
500 Yards
Cowley Bridge Rd.
New North Road
St. David's Station
Bonhay Rd.
Howell Rd.
Hele Rd.
New North Road
Central Station
St. David's Hill
Queen St.
Castle St.
Sidwell St.
Paris St.
info.
Paul St.
High St.
Bedford St.
Exe St.
North St.
The Close
Western Way
South St.
Fore St.
Southernhay
Bonhay Road
Magdalen St.
Western Way
Quay Hill
Holloway St.
The Quay
Haven Rd.
RIVER EXE
1
2
3
4
5
6
7
8
9
10
11
12

tury guildhouse that is sometimes open. Turn left on The Mint and visit **St. Nicholas Priory** (7), once a Benedictine monastery founded in 1080 by William the Conqueror. Disbanded in 1536, it is now a **museum** featuring a fine Norman **undercroft**, a 15th-century **guest hall**, an ancient **kitchen**, and other rooms fitted with period furniture. Visits may be made on Tuesdays through Saturdays, from 10 a.m. to 1 p.m. and from 2–5 p.m.

Two other interesting churches in the area are **St. Olave's**, a strange building of the 14th century on Fore Street, and **St. Mary Arches** on Mary Arches Street, a 12th-century parish church with a Norman nave and Jacobean memorials.

Fore Street soon becomes High Street. On your left is the **Guildhall** (8), believed to be the oldest municipal building still in use in Britain. Built in 1330, it has an outstanding 16th-century façade projecting out over the sidewalk. Visitors are welcome on Mondays through Saturdays, from 10 a.m. to 5 p.m., subject to civic functions.

Continue up High Street and turn right on Martin's Lane for one block, then left on Catherine Street past the ruins of a bombed-out 15th-century almshouse. Follow the map to the entrance of the **Underground Passages** (9). Guided tours are run through these medieval water tunnels that date from the 13th century and remained in use until about a hundred years ago. *This trip is somewhat spooky and not for the claustrophobic.* They can be explored on Tuesdays through Saturdays, from 2–5 p.m. Near the exit are remains of the ancient town walls, and the tourist office in the Civic Centre.

Return to High Street and make a right up Castle Street. To your left are scanty remnants of a Norman gateway and, beyond, a Norman tower. The **Rougemont House Museum** (10) has exhibits of costume and lace, and is open on Mondays through Saturdays, from 10 a.m. to 5:30 p.m. Stroll through the very pleasant **Rougemont Gardens** (11) and exit onto Queen Street. A right brings you to the **Royal Albert Memorial Museum and Art Gallery** (12), which has something for everyone. There are displays of art, ethnography, exploration, natural history, and many other subjects. it is open on Tuesdays through Saturdays, from 10 a.m. to 5:30 p.m. This is a good place to spend your remaining time before returning to the train station.

A Daytrip from London

Warwick

Many visitors go to see the magnificent castle at Warwick but completely overlook the town itself. That's a pity, because this is surely one of the least spoiled places in England. Small and compact, it has a wonderful blend of Tudor and Georgian architecture, a splendid church, and several fine museums.

Warwick grew up around its castle, whose origins date back to a fortification built here in 914 by Ethelfleda, daughter of Alfred the Great, to protect her kingdom of Mercia. Nothing of this remains, but there are still traces of the motte built by William the Conqueror in 1068. The castle you see today is largely of 14th-century construction with great modifications made down through the years to convert the interior into a luxurious home. Sold to Madame Tussaud's in 1978, it is now a showcase combining medieval elements with those of a more recent stately home, and outfitted with the inevitable wax figures.

GETTING THERE:

Trains depart London's Paddington Station several times in the morning for Leamington Spa, where you change for a local to Warwick. The total time is about 2 hours, with return service until mid-evening.

Buses operated by National Express connect London's Victoria Coach Station with Warwick several times a day.

By car, Warwick is 96 miles northwest of London via the M-40 to Junction 15.

PRACTICALITIES:

The castle is open every day except Christmas, but some of the other sights are closed on Sundays or Mondays. Those coming by train should avoid Sundays or holidays, when service is virtually nil. The local **Tourist Information Centre**, phone (0926) 49-22-12, is in the Court House on Jury Street. Warwick is the county town of **Warwickshire**, and has a **population** of about 22,000.

FOOD AND DRINK:

Some choice places for lunch include:

Lord Leycester (17 Jury St., east of the tourist office). Dining in a small country hotel. $$

Porridge Pot (Jury St., east of the tourist office) Traditional British country fare in a medieval house. X: Sun. eve., Mon. $$

Zetland Arms (Church St., near St. Mary's) A popular pub with lunches. $

There is also a popular-price restaurant in the castle.

SUGGESTED TOUR:

Leave the **train station** (1) and follow the map to ***Warwick Castle** (2). Considered by many to be the finest medieval castle in England, it will easily take two or three hours to explore. Everything is very well marked and explained. The main attractions include the **Barbican and Gatehouse**, a 14th-century complex of some 30 rooms; the **Armoury** with its superb collection of weapons; and the **Dungeon and Torture Chamber**, which has fascinating if grisly displays of medieval torture instruments. Beyond this, **Guy's Tower** may be climbed and the ramparts walked. The **Ghost Tower** is allegedly haunted by a 17th-century apparition. More Victorian in character, the ***State Apartments** make a gorgeous show of baronial splendor. Next to them is the **Royal Weekend**, a re-creation of a turn-of-the-century house party enlivened with wax figures of famous nobility.

Beyond the castle are lovely **gardens** designed by "Capability" Brown in the 18th century. Peacocks roam about the trees, some of which were planted by such luminaries as Queen Victoria and Prince Albert. Cross the bridge over the River Avon to an **island** (3) that has wonderful views of the south face. The **Conservatory** (4) is a fantasy recalling the spirit of Georgian times. Warwick Castle is open every day except Christmas, from 10 a.m. to 5:30 p.m., closing at 4:30 p.m. from November through February.

Leave the castle and return to Castle Hill. A short walk down Mill Street will reward you with splendid views. Now follow the map to **Oken's House** (5), an Elizabethan dwelling that survived the devastating fire of 1694. It now houses an utterly delightful collection of antique and period dolls and toys, which may be seen from Easter through September; on Mondays through Saturdays from 10 a.m. to 5 p.m., and on Sundays from 2–5 p.m.

Continue up Castle Street and make a left on High Street to the **Lord Leycester Hospital** (6), a group of picturesque 14th-century almshouses that have been used since the 16th century as a retirement home for old soldiers. One of these gentlemen will be happy to show you around on Mondays through Saturdays, from 10 a.m. to 5:30 p.m.,

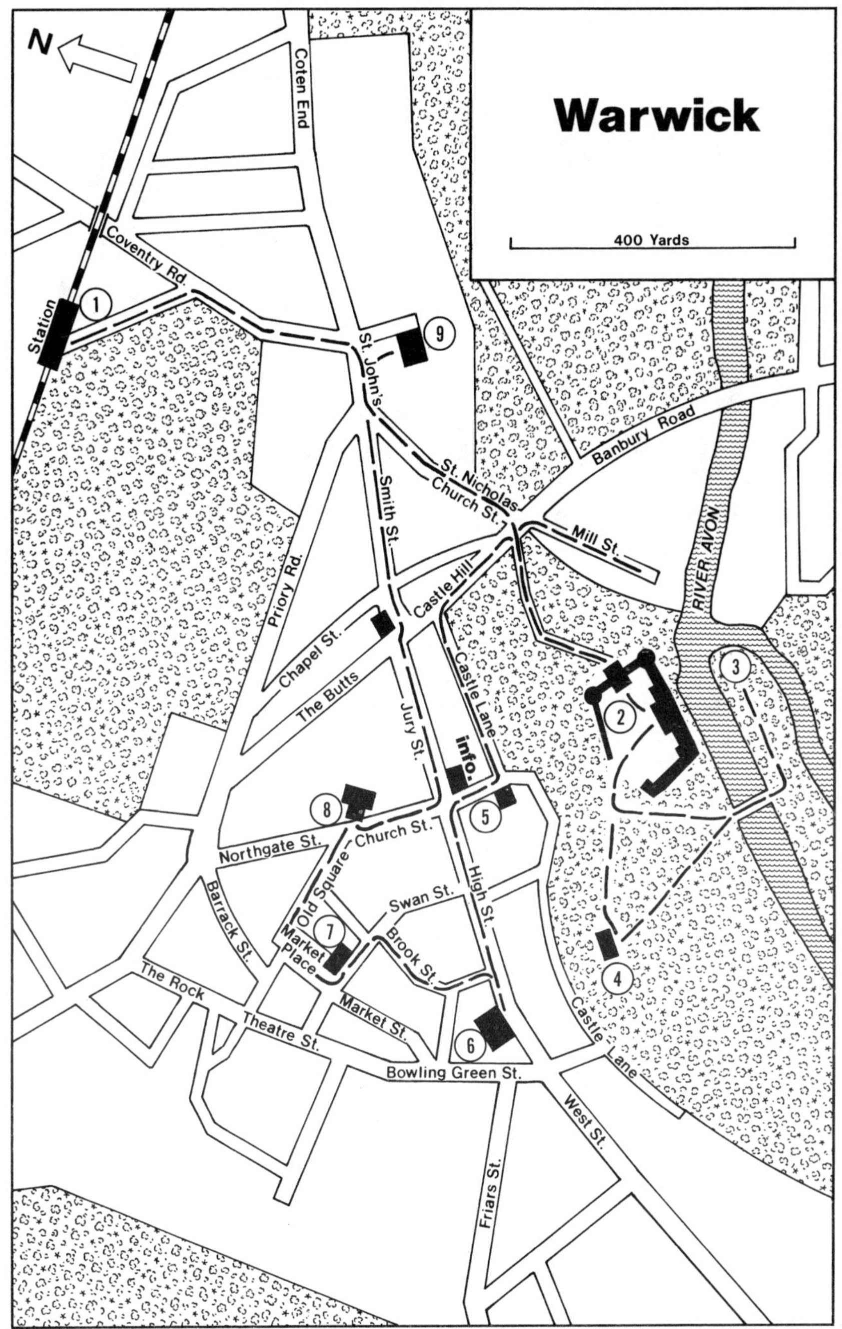

N
Warwick
400 Yards
Coten End
Station
Coventry Rd.
St. John's
St. Nicholas
Church St.
Banbury Road
Mill St.
RIVER AVON
Smith St.
Priory Rd.
Castle Hill
Chapel St.
The Butts
Jury St.
Castle Lane
info.
Northgate St.
Church St.
Old Square
Swan St.
High St.
Barrack St.
Market Place
Brook St.
The Rock
Theatre St.
Market St.
Bowling Green St.
Castle Lane
West St.
Friars St.
1
2
3
4
5
6
7
8
9

Warwick Castle and the River Avon

but not after 4:30 p.m. from October through March.

Walk down Brook Street to the **County Museum** (7) in the Market Place. Displays here cover archaeology, natural history, and local bygones in addition to changing exhibitions. The museum is open on Mondays through Saturdays, from 10 a.m. to 5:30 p.m.; and on Sundays from May through September, from 2:30–5:30 p.m.

St. Mary's Church (8), nearby, has parts dating from the 12th century, although it was largely rebuilt after the 1694 fire. Its 15th-century **Beauchamp Chapel** is incomparable.

Jury Street leads past the **East Gate**, a relic of the old town wall, and as Smith Street to **St. John's House** (9). This beautiful 17th-century mansion is now a **museum** of local crafts, costumes, and furniture. There is a regimental military exhibition on the floor above. It is open on Tuesdays through Saturdays, from 10 a.m. to 12:30 p.m. and 1:30–5:30 p.m.; and on Sundays from May through September, from 2:30–5 p.m. A short walk in the garden completes your tour before returning to the nearby station.

A Daytrip from London

*Stratford-upon-Avon

As someone once remarked, there's no business like show business. That, put simply, is what Stratford-upon-Avon is all about. The whole town is one vast theater, entertaining thousands of visitors a day. Despite this, it has miraculously managed to avoid the worst of tourism's trappings and still retains a quite genuine charm. Just about everyone who goes there enjoys the experience.

William Shakespeare was born in Stratford in 1564. This is also where he lived a great deal of his life and where he died in 1616. Many of the buildings associated with the Bard have been lovingly preserved and may be visited. The Royal Shakespeare Theatre, one of the greatest anywhere, is beautifully situated on the banks of the quiet Avon. There are several other attractions, some relating to Shakespeare and others not, but perhaps in the long run it is simply the atmosphere of this delightful old market town that is so memorable.

The best way to savor Stratford is to stay overnight and perhaps take in a performance at the theater. Those with cars will find that it makes an ideal base for exploring the midlands and the Cotswolds. If you can't do this, however, a daytrip from London is still very enjoyable.

GETTING THERE:

Trains depart London's Paddington Station around 9 and 10:30 a.m. for Leamington Spa, perhaps requiring a change en route. At Leamington change to a local for Stratford-upon-Avon. The total journey takes about 2½ hours, with return trains running until mid-evening. Service is poor or non-existent on Sundays and holidays.

"The Shakespeare Connection," a **train/coach** combination, leaves London's Euston Station every morning for Coventry, where you change to a special bus. The total ride takes about 2 hours. It is usually possible to make a late-night return on this *on performance days only* if you want to see a performance at the theater and first make a reservation with the coach operator. BritRail Passes cover the train portion only. Check the schedule in advance or with the coach operator, Guide Friday Ltd., at Stratford, phone (0789) 29-44-66.

Special Packages including rail and/or coach transportation, overnight accommodations, theater tickets, and dinner are available through travel agents in London and elsewhere.

By car, take the A-40 and M-40 to Junction 15, then the A-46 to Stratford-upon-Avon, which is 96 miles northwest of London.

PRACTICALITIES:

The major sights in Stratford are open daily except on December 24, 25, and 26, with generally longer hours from March through October. A colorful **outdoor market** is held on Fridays at the square joining Greenhill and Wood streets. The local **Tourist Information Centre**, phone (0789) 29-31-27, is at Bridgefoot, between the canal and the bridge. You might ask them about renting a **bicycle** for a ride in the country. Stratford is in the county of **Warwickshire**, and has a **population** of about 21,000.

FOOD AND DRINK:

Some outstanding restaurants and pubs are:

Box Tree (Waterside, in the theater) Classic food with a wonderful view of the Avon. Proper dress and reservations required, phone (0789) 29-32-26. X: when theater is closed. $$$

Da Giovanni (8 Ely St., near Harvard House) Classic Italian cuisine. X: Sun. $$$

Shakespeare Hotel (Chapel St., near New Place) An atmospheric 16th-century inn. $$

Hussain's (6a Chapel St., near New Place) Indian food, with tandoori specialties. $$

Black Swan (Waterside St., near the theater) Also known as the Dirty Duck, very famous with actors. Pub and restaurant. $ and $$

River Terrace (Waterside, in the theater) Self-service cafeteria. X: when theater is closed. $

Garrick Inn (High St., near Harvard House) A charming historic pub with lunches. $

SUGGESTED TOUR:

Leave the **train station** (1) and follow the map to that most logical of beginnings, ***Shakespeare's Birthplace** (2). This is actually two houses joined together, the eastern part having been his father's shop and the western half the family residence. To the left of it is the modern **Shakespeare Centre**, which houses exhibitions, a library, and a study center. Enter this and wander through the delightful **garden**, complete with flowers, shrubs, and trees mentioned in his plays. The well-marked trail then takes you into the old house itself, where you

Shakespeare's Birthplace

will visit the bedroom in which Shakespeare was presumably born on or about April 23, 1564. The entire house is furnished as it might have been in his youth, including an interesting period kitchen and an oak-beamed living room. Visits may be made on any day except December 24, 25, or 26. On Mondays through Saturdays it is open from 9 a.m. to 5:30 p.m., closing at 4 p.m. from November through February. On Sundays from March through October it is open from 10 a.m. to 5:30 p.m., closing at 4 p.m. in winter. A reduced-price joint ticket covering all of the "Shakespeare Properties" is available.

Return on Henley Street, walk down Bridge Street, and turn right at Waterside. The **World of Shakespeare** at the **Heritage Theatre** (3) provides a good, if somewhat commercialized and pricey, introduction to Elizabethan England. This multimedia extravaganza surrounds the audience with 25 stage sets depicting such events as the London plague and Queen Elizabeth I's epic journey to Kenilworth, all brought to life through the clever use of sound, light, and special effects. The show runs continuously every half-hour. It is open daily from 9:30 a.m. to 5:30 p.m.

Stroll through **Bancroft Gardens**, going past the canal basin and locks. Overlooking this pleasant scene is the **Gower Memorial**, a life-size bronze statue of the Bard with figures of Hamlet, Lady Macbeth, Falstaff, and Prince Hal. The tourist office is nearby. Continue on and cross the footbridge over the Avon, a span formerly used by the horse-drawn tramway that once connected Stratford with Moreton-in-Marsh. From here you will have a beautiful view of the river and the modern Royal Shakespeare Theatre. Just beyond the bridge is the **Butterfly and Jungle Safari** (4), where exotic flora and fauna exist in an indoor "natural" setting, the largest of its kind in Europe. The 15th-century **Clopton Bridge** with its 14 arches, to the left, still carries heavy traffic.

Return and walk over to the **Royal Shakespeare Theatre** (5). Built in 1932 to replace a smaller 19th-century theater that burned down, its performances of Shakespearian plays are world famous. Although tickets should be booked well in advance, they are frequently available on the day of performance. The attached **RSC Collection** has interesting mementos of theatrical personalities and other Shakespeariana. You can ask here about **backstage tours** of the theater. Near this is the new **Swan Theatre**, specially designed to present plays by Shakespeare's contemporaries and playwrights influenced by him.

Thirsty travelers can refresh themselves at the famous **Black Swan Pub**, a.k.a. the *Dirty Duck,* closeby on Waterside. From here, a path leads along the river's edge, passing the **Brass Rubbing Centre** where you can make your own inexpensive souvenir of Stratford.

Continue on to ***Holy Trinity Church** (6), the scene of Shakespeare's baptism in 1564 and burial in 1616. Copies of the church registers showing both events are on display. His **tomb** is inscribed with the famous lines ending in *"and curst be he that moves my bones."* There are a few other interesting items in this 14th-century church, particularly the humorous **misericords** under the choir seats.

Hall's Croft (7) on Old Town is the next stop. This splendid Tudor house was the home of Shakespeare's eldest daughter, Susanna, and her husband, Dr. John Hall. Its interior is well worth visiting for a glimpse of how a prosperous doctor's family lived in those days. Be sure to see the dispensary with its surgical instruments, herbs, and potions. A stroll through the **garden** in the rear is a delight. Hall's Croft is open on Mondays through Saturdays from 9:30 a.m. to 5 p.m., closing at 4 p.m. in winter; and on Sundays from 10:30 a.m. to 5 p.m., except in winter when the hours are 1:30–4 p.m.

Turn right on Church Street and pass, on the right, the **King Edward VI Grammar School**, where the young Shakespeare learned his "small Latin and less Greek." Adjoining this is the 15th-century **Guild Chapel** with its noted fresco of the *Last Judgement* above the chancel arch. Just beyond, on Chapel Street, is the site of Shakespeare's own home, **New Place** (8), which he purchased in 1597 and in which he died in 1616. Its last owner demolished it in 1759, and today only the foundations and the **garden** remain. These can be reached by going through the **New Place Museum** in the former home of Thomas Nash, who was married to Shakespeare's granddaughter, Elizabeth Hall. It is

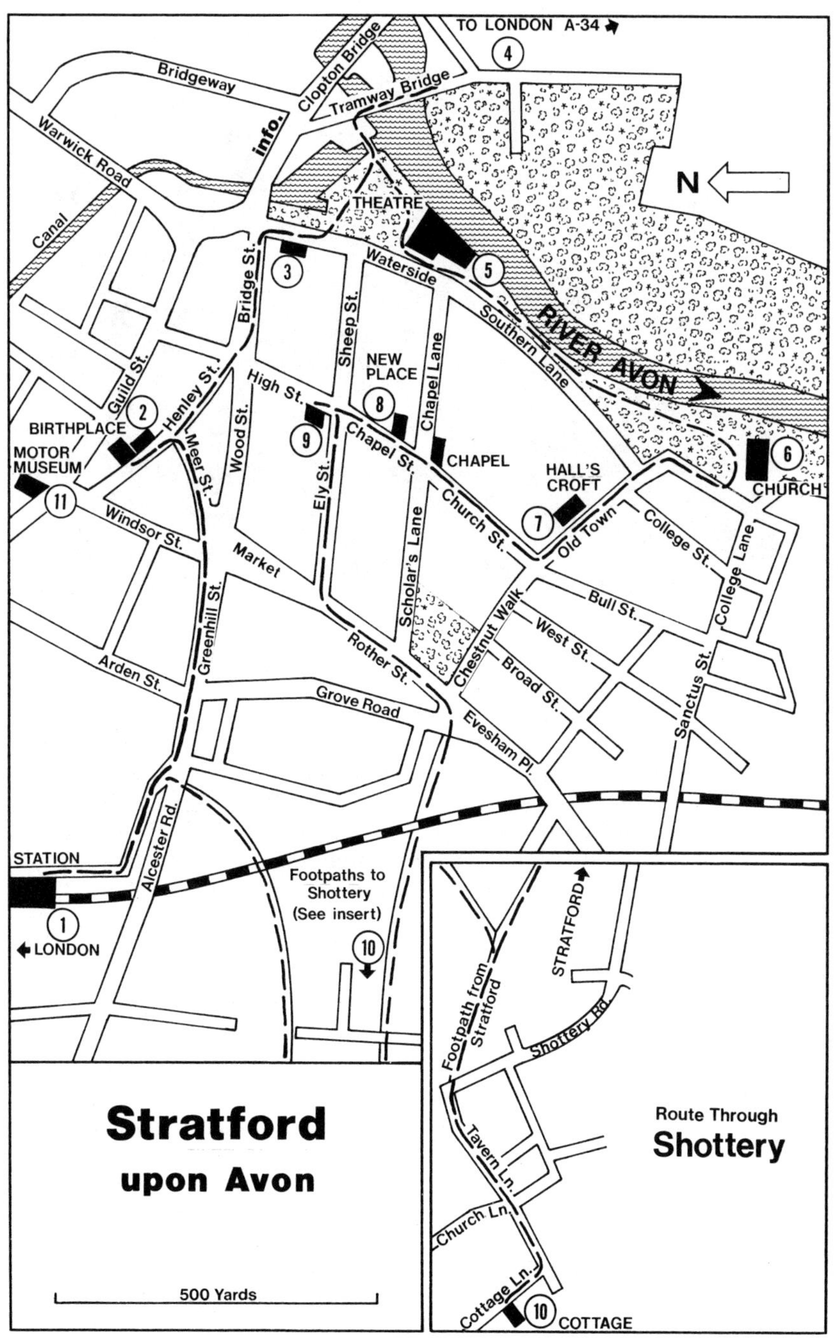

Stratford upon Avon

Route Through **Shottery**

Anne Hathaway's Cottage

open during the same times as Hall's Croft, above.

Harvard House (9) has nothing to do with the Bard, but a lot to do with Harvard University. This outstanding example of a half-timbered Elizabethan structure was the home of the mother of John Harvard, whose donations helped found the famous institution in the U.S.A. Its richly decorated interior may be visited. Adjacent to this are two other buildings of similar style and age, one of them being the well-known **Garrick Inn**, named for the actor David Garrick who organized the first Shakespeare Festival here in 1769. This is a great place to stop for a break.

While in Stratford you will probably want to see ***Anne Hathaway's Cottage** (10), certainly one of the prettiest (and most visited) sights in England. The home of Shakespeare's wife before their marriage, this 16th-century thatched-roof farmhouse is set in gorgeous surroundings. The furnishings are fairly authentic as the cottage remained in her family until late Victorian times. Located in the nearby hamlet of Shottery, about one mile from Stratford, it is easily reached by bus from Bridge Street or, better still, by rented bicycle, or on foot via a country path that begins at Evesham Place. The route is well marked and is shown on the map and its insert. The cottage is open during the same times as the Birthplace (2). Return by way of the other path to Alcester Road and the train station.

Section III

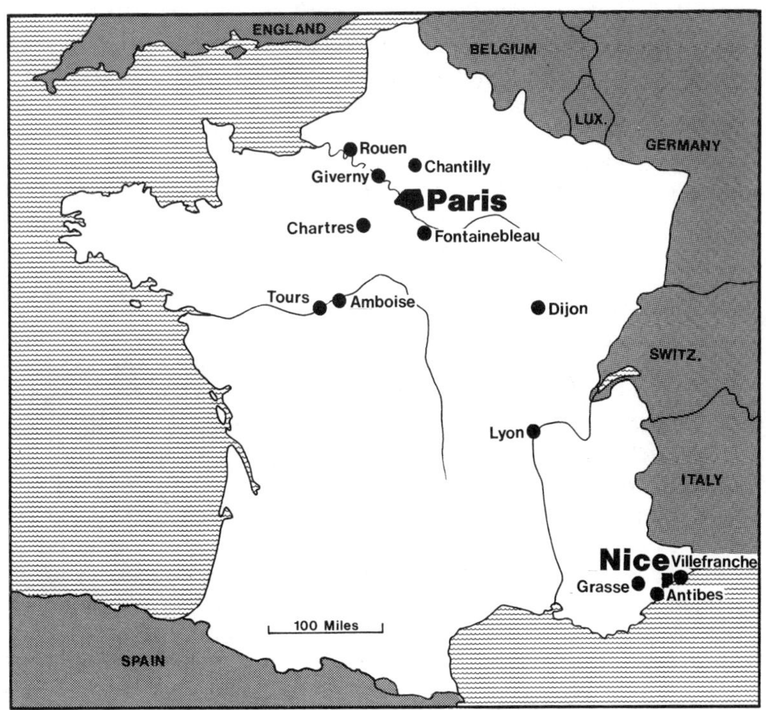

DAYTRIPS IN FRANCE

- from Paris
- from Nice

Even a nation as large and varied as France can be pretty thoroughly explored on a daytrip basis. Its two favorite cities, Paris and Nice, are well situated for this and make excellent bases for one-day probes into their respective regions. The introduction of high-speed TGV trains, especially, has brought destinations as distant as Lyon within easy daytrip range of Paris, while the entire Riviera lies just minutes from Nice by train, bus, or car. This simple fact also makes it possible to stay in any of the Riviera towns and make the same daytrips that can be taken from Nice.

The 12 one-day adventures described in this section cover a very broad spectrum of interests, ranging from medieval cathedrals and Renaissance châteaux to quiet, half-forgotten villages where time seems to stand still; from the homes of great people in historic cities to renowned meccas of gastronomy; and from the last unspoiled reaches of the Riviera to hill towns clinging to mountainsides.

An even greater range of possibilities is explored in our companion guidebook, ***Daytrips in France***, whose recently revised edition now includes five one-day walking tours of Paris, much more practical information, and a section on Daytrips in Provence.

GETTING AROUND:

Trains are generally the most practical way of daytripping through France, especially if only one or two persons are making the trip. The French rail system is for the most part excellent and features the world's fastest trains, the TGVs that travel as fast as 186 mph. Reservations are necessary for these, but can be made up to five minutes before departure if seats are still available.

Eurailpasses (see page 18) are accepted for travel by train throughout France. If you are visiting both France and Britain, you should consider the **BritFrance Railpass** instead, which gives you unlimited rail travel in both countries on any five days within a 15-day period, or on any ten days within a month, and includes round-trip travel across the English Channel via Hovercraft. It is sold in both first- and second-class versions, for either adults or children, or in second-class only for youths between 12 and 25, by most travel agents in North America. For those visiting only France, the cheapest rail deal is the **France Railpass**, offering unlimited train travel on any four days within a 15-day period, or any nine days within a month, and including substantial extra benefits such as a Paris *Métro* pass. Again, it comes in both first- and second-class versions, for adults or for children, from your friendly travel agent.

Those traveling by **car** will find the roads to be quite good, especially the **Autoroutes**, a network of limited-access highways with rather steep tolls. Driving may be less expensive than trains when three or more people share the cost, and certainly allows greater flexibility.

ADVANCE PLANNING INFORMATION:

The **French Government Tourist Office** has branches throughout the world, including New York, Chicago, Beverly Hills, Dallas, Montreal, Toronto, London, Sydney, and Tokyo. Their New York office is at 610 Fifth Avenue, New York NY 10020, phone (900) 990-0040 (Toll call).

A Daytrip from Paris

*Chartres

Rising majestically above the Beauce Plain, the Cathedral of Chartres is one of the great legacies of the Middle Ages and the quintessential Gothic cathedral. Pilgrims and tourists from all over the world are drawn to it by the thousands, yet most overlook the charms of the town itself. And that's a pity—for Chartres is one of those rare French *villes* that kept its essentially medieval character intact.

It may seem surprising that a town as small as Chartres should possess one of the largest cathedrals on Earth. The place, however, appears to have a long history of religious significance. Ancient Druids probably worshipped at the well under the cathedral crypt. Later the capital of the Gallic Carnutes, it was called *Autricum* by the Romans, who built a temple on the same site. Early Christians replaced this with a basilica, saving the statue of the Roman goddess whom they took to be the Virgin. Five subsequent churches were built on the spot, culminating in the present 13th-century masterpiece. A precious relic believed to be a garment worn by the Virgin Mary, which has been in the cathedral since 876, is responsible for Chartres being a place of pilgrimage for over a thousand years.

GETTING THERE:

Trains leave Montparnasse Station in Paris fairly frequently for the 50-minute trip to Chartres. Return service operates until late evening.

By car, Chartres is 55 miles southwest of Paris via the A-10 and A-11 Autoroutes. A slower but more interesting route is to take the N-10 through Versailles and Rambouillet.

PRACTICALITIES:

Try to visit Chartres in good weather, when sunshine illuminates the incredible stained-glass windows to best effect. The art museum is closed on Tuesdays and major holidays. The local **Tourist Information Office**, phone 37-21-50-00, is at the far end of the cathedral square. Chartres is in the **Ile-de-France** region, and has a **population** of about 40,000.

FOOD AND DRINK:

Chartres has many restaurants that cater primarily to tourists. Among the better choices are:

La Vieille Maison (5 Rue au Lait, near the cathedral) Modern regional cuisine in an attractive 14th-century house. Proper dress expected, for reservations phone 37-34-10-67. X: Sun. eve., Mon., Jan. $$$

Café Serpente (2 Cloître Notre-Dame, facing the cathedral) An old-fashioned bistro. X: Tues. eve., Wed. $$

Le Minou (4 Rue Mar.-de-Lattre-de-Tassigny, 3 blocks south of the cathedral) An exceptional value. X: Sun. eve., Mon., July. $

Le Biniou (7 Rue Serpente, one block south of the cathedral) Crêpes in a Breton atmosphere. X: Tues., Wed. $

SUGGESTED TOUR:

From the **train station** (1) you will have a clear view of the cathedral. Follow the map to its fascinating ***West Front** (2), much of which survives from an earlier 12th-century structure largely destroyed by fire in 1194. The two asymmetrical towers make a dramatic study in architectural evolution. On the right is the **Old Tower**, representing the fullest development of the Romanesque style. The **New Tower**, to the left, is capped with a 16th-century spire, a masterpiece of the Flamboyant Gothic. Between them stands the **Royal Portal**, three arched doorways from the 12th century. Look carefully at the stunning *Christ in Majesty* carving above the center door. The figures over the right portal depict the Nativity, while those on the left are of the Ascension.

Step inside to witness the true glory of ***Chartres Cathedral**—its miraculous ***stained-glass windows**. Almost all of these are original, mostly 13th-century with some dating from the 12th. Replacements account for less than six percent of the total 26,000 square feet, making this the largest collection of medieval glass in the world.

Guided tours of the interior are available—those in English being particularly good—or you can pick up a printed guide and explore on your own. Binoculars can be a great help for studying the biblical stories depicted in the windows. Be sure to visit the **Treasury**, behind the choir, which displays the venerated garment thought to have been worn by the Virgin Mary.

A climb to the top of the ***North Tower** will reward you with spectacular views. The entrance to this is by the door in the **North Transept** (3). Another sight not to be missed is the ancient **Crypt** of the original church, which can be visited on special guided tours only. These depart, oddly enough, from a souvenir shop called *La Crypte* in front of the **South Porch** (4).

The West Front of Chartres Cathedral

Leave the cathedral and follow the map to the Rue des Écuyers. On the right, at number 35, you will find a curious old house with a 16th-century turret staircase of carved oak known as the **Escalier de la Reine Berthe** (5). Continue on to the **Église St.-Pierre** (6). If its great cathedral did not exist, Chartres would still be noted for this magnificent medieval church, whose flying buttresses and original stained glass are truly impressive.

Stroll over to the Eure River and cross it. There is a nice view of the cathedral from here. Turn left on Rue de la Foulerie and follow along to **Porte Guillaume** (7) to see what little remains of the old town walls. Return to the stream and walk along Rue de la Tannerie, passing several delightful old waterside buildings. Across the Eure stands the 12th-century **Église St.-André** (8), a Romanesque church whose choir once spanned the water on a daring arch, long since destroyed.

Continue by following the map to the **Musée des Beaux-Arts** (9), reached via the steep Tertre Saint-Nicolas steps that open into lovely gardens. The museum, housed in the former Bishop's Palace, contains a superb collection of paintings (particularly those by Vlaminck), enamels, tapestries, furniture, and artifacts of regional history. It is open from 10 a.m. to noon and 2–6 p.m. (5 p.m. in winter), every day except Tuesdays and holidays.

Another attraction you may want to visit is the **Cellier de Loëns** (10) at number 5 Rue du Cardinal Pie. This 13th-century cellar once stored tithes and is now the **International Stained-Glass Center**, offering rotating exhibits of the art that made Chartres famous. It is open daily from 10 a.m. to 12:30 p.m. and 1:30–6 p.m.

Some visitors might also be interested in the new **Conservatoire du Machinisme et des Pratiques Agricoles** *(Le Compa)* (11, off the map), an exhibition of farm machinery from early times to the present. It is housed in a 19th-century steam locomotive depot just west of the train station, and is open daily except on Mondays.

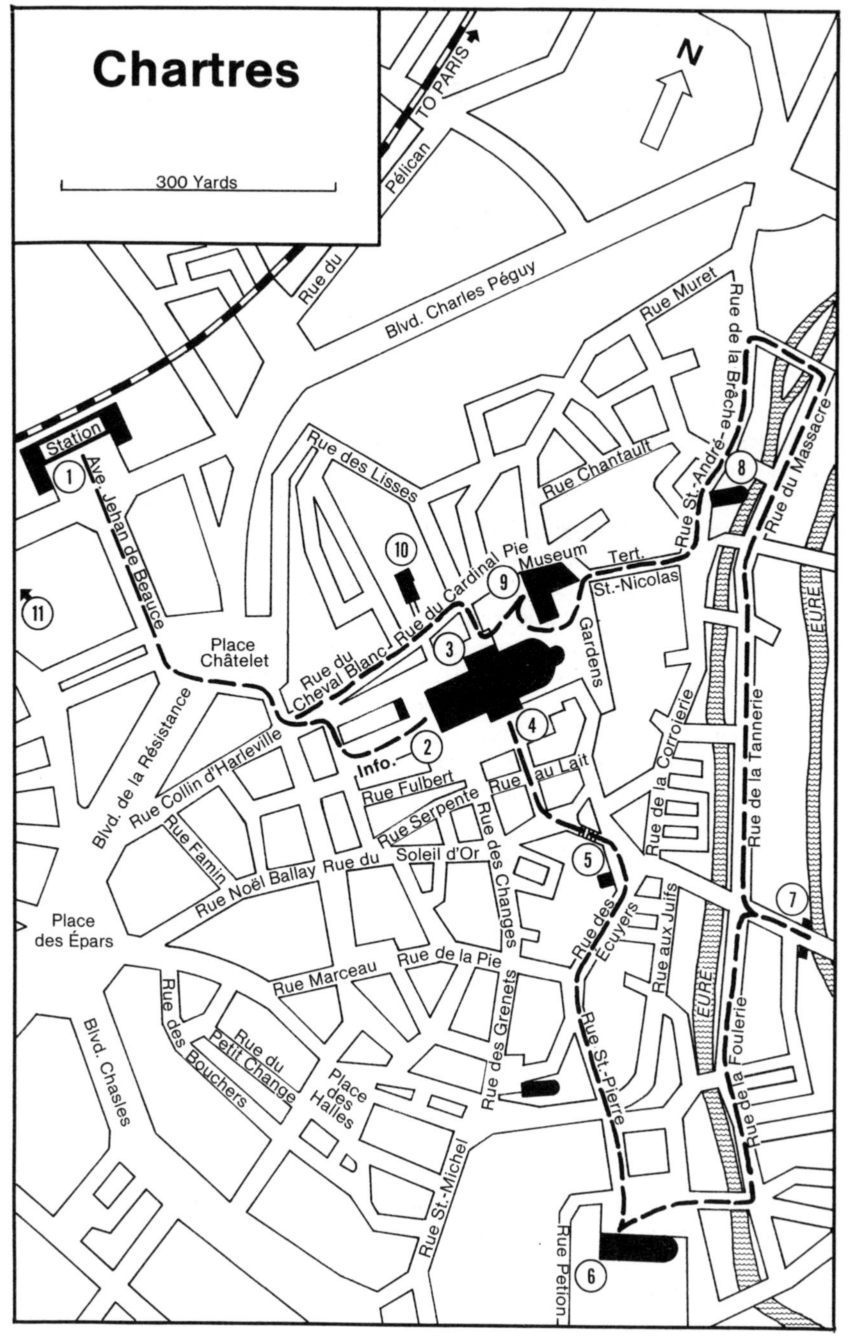
Chartres
300 Yards
N
TO PARIS
Pélican
Rue du
Blvd. Charles Péguy
Rue Muret
Rue de la Brêche
Rue du Massacre
Station
Ave. Jehan de Beauce
Rue des Lisses
Rue Chantault
Rue St.-André
Rue du Cardinal Pie
Museum
Tert. St.-Nicolas
Gardens
Place Châtelet
Rue du Cheval Blanc
EURE
Info.
Blvd. de la Résistance
Rue Collin d'Harleville
Rue Fulbert
Rue au Lait
Rue de la Corroierie
Rue de la Tannerie
Rue Serpente
Rue des Changes
Rue Famin
Rue Noël Ballay
Rue du Soleil d'Or
Rue des Écuyers
Rue aux Juifs
Place des Épars
Rue Marceau
Rue de la Pie
Rue des Grenets
Rue St.-Pierre
Rue de la Foulerie
Blvd. Chasles
Rue des Bouchers
Rue du Petit Change
Place des Halles
Rue St.-Michel
Rue Petion
1
2
3
4
5
6
7
8
9
10
11

A Daytrip from Paris

Fontainebleau

Haunted by memories of François I and Napoleon Bonaparte, the Château of Fontainebleau beguiles with its marvelously haphazard layout and intimate atmosphere. Many prefer it to Versailles. This was a real home for the rulers of France, from the 12th century right down to Napoleon III in the 19th.

The palace as it stands today is mostly the result of an extensive reconstruction carried out in the 16th century by François I, the king most credited with bringing the Renaissance to France. Only the keep *(donjon)* in the Oval Court survives from the Middle Ages. Later kings, including Louis XIV, made frequent use of the château, drawn primarily by the sporting opportunities of the surrounding forest. Fontainebleau became the favorite residence of Napoleon I, who had it thoroughly redecorated. It was also the scene, in 1814, of his abdication and departure for Elba.

The Forest of Fontainebleau is exceptionally lovely with its wide variety of wild, natural beauty. Those with cars or bikes may want to pick up a map at the tourist office and go exploring, particularly to the charming village of Barbizon.

GETTING THERE:

Trains depart Gare de Lyon station in Paris frequently for Fontainebleau-Avon, less than 45 minutes away. These are met by a bus marked "Château," which goes to the palace. Return trains run until mid-evening.

By car, the fastest way is via the A-6 Autoroute, followed by the N-37 and N-7 roads. Fontainebleau is 40 miles southeast of Paris.

PRACTICALITIES:

Avoid coming on a Tuesday, when the château is closed. Pleasant weather will make a walk in the gardens more enjoyable. The local **Tourist Information Office**, phone 64–22–25–68, is at 31 Place Napoléon-Bonaparte, near the château. **Bicycles** may be rented at the train station. Fontainebleau is in the **Ile-de-France** region, and has a **population** of about 19,000.

The Château of Fontainebleau

FOOD AND DRINK:

The town of Fontainebleau has a great many restaurants and cafés in all price ranges, particularly on and near Rue Grande and Place Général-de-Gaulle. Among the better choices are:

Aigle Noir (27 Place Napoléon-Bonaparte, near the tourist office) Excellent modern cuisine in the renowned hotel's Le Beauharnais restaurant. Proper dress expected, reservations advised, phone 64–22–32–65. Garden dining in season. $$$

Le Filet de Sole (5 Rue du Coq-Gris, near the tourist office) Good food in an ancient house. X: Tues., Wed., July. $$

Chez Arrighi (53 Rue de France, 2 blocks northwest of the château) Corsican dishes near Napoleon's palace. X: Mon. $$

Le Dauphin (24 Rue Grande, near the tourist office) An exceptional value. X: Tues. eve., Wed., Feb. $

Le Grillardin (12 Rue des Pins, 4 blocks northeast of the tourist office) Good-value dining in a rustic atmosphere. X: Sun. eve., Mon.

SUGGESTED TOUR:

The **Fontainebleau-Avon Train Station** (1) is nearly two miles from the palace. Get there by one of the frequent buses marked "Château," on foot through the park, or by rented bike.

Enter the ***Château** (2) via the White Horse Courtyard, also known

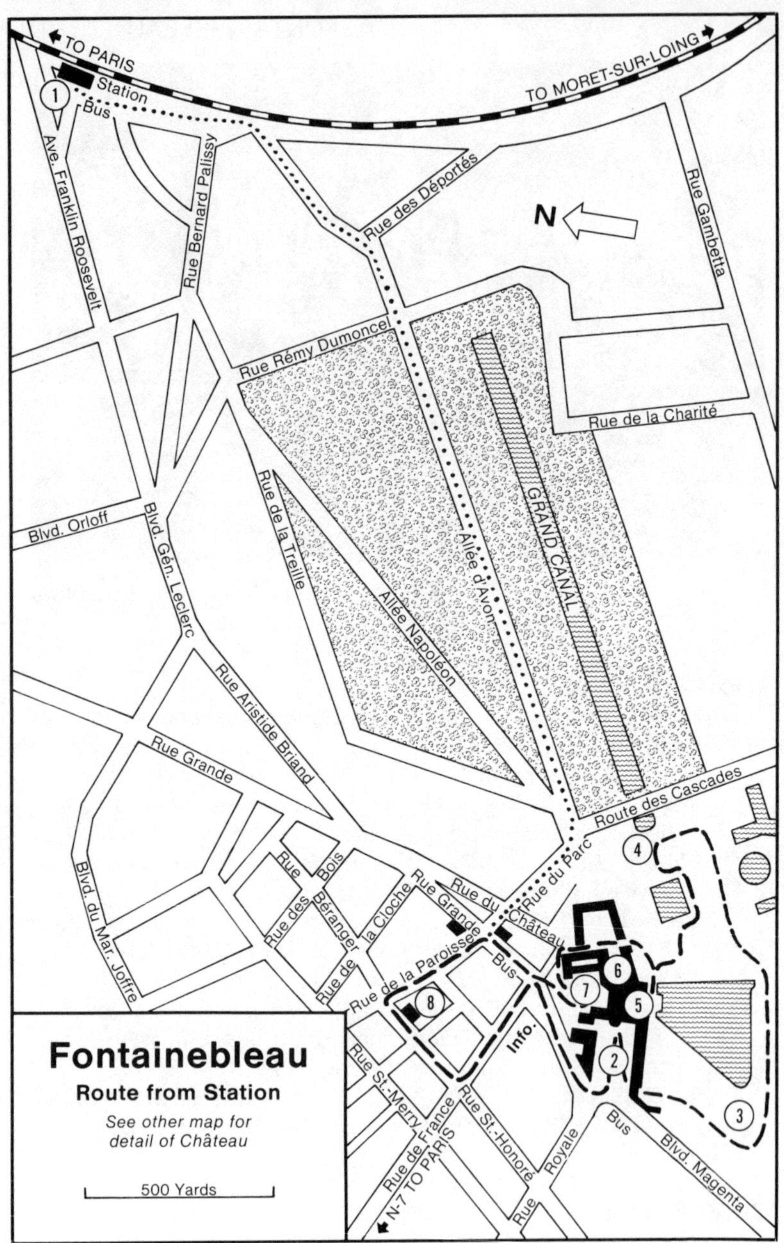

Fontainebleau

Route from Station

See other map for detail of Château

500 Yards

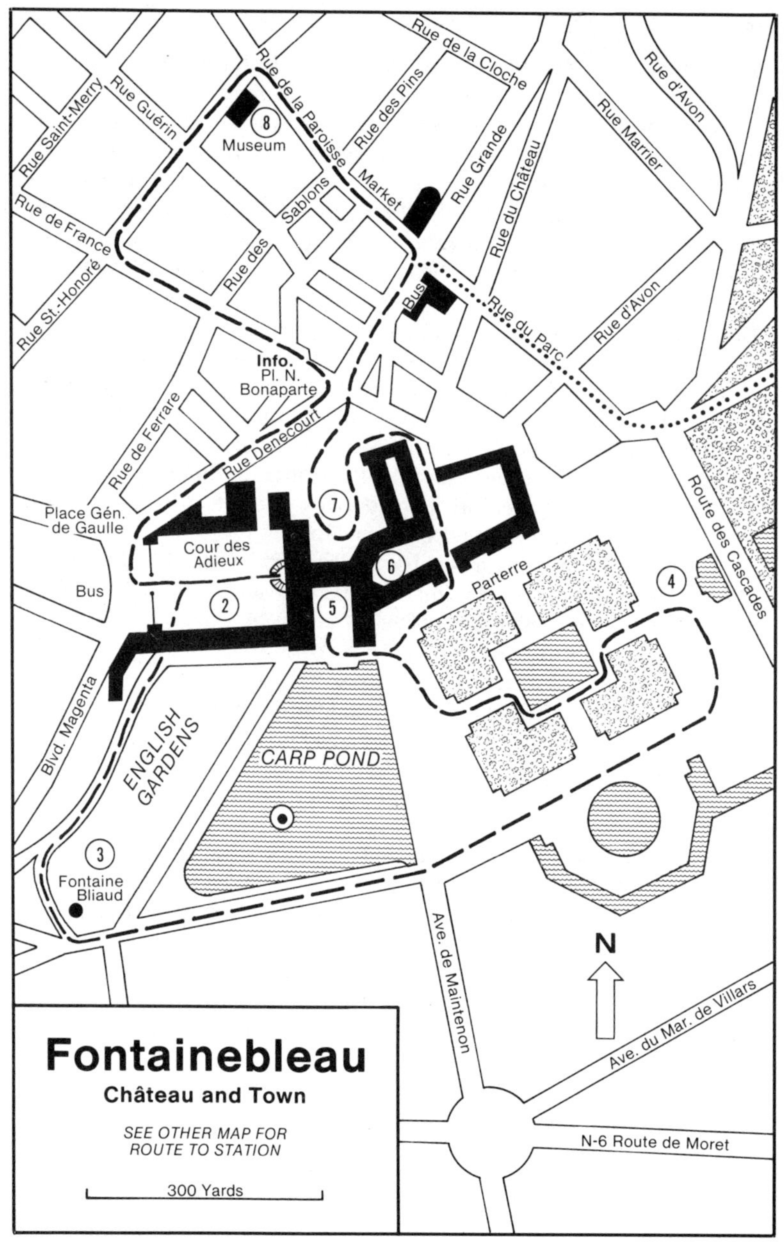
Rue de la Cloche
Rue d'Avon
Rue Marrier
Rue de la Paroisse
Rue des Pins
Rue Grande
Rue du Château
Rue Saint-Merry
Rue Guérin
8
Museum
Rue des Sablons
Market
Rue de France
Rue St.-Honoré
Bus
Rue du Parc
Rue d'Avon
Info.
Pl. N.
Bonaparte
Rue Denecourt
Rue de Ferrare
Place Gén.
de Gaulle
Cour des
Adieux
7
6
Parterre
4
Route des Cascades
Bus
2
5
Blvd. Magenta
ENGLISH
GARDENS
CARP POND
3
Fontaine
Bliaud
N
Ave. de Maintenon
Ave. du Mar. de Villars
N-6 Route de Moret
Fontainebleau
Château and Town
SEE OTHER MAP FOR
ROUTE TO STATION
300 Yards

as the **Cour des Adieux**, where Napoleon I bid a tearful farewell to his troops in 1814 as he went into exile. You may stroll through the **Grand Apartments** at your own leisure, following a well-marked route. In order to understand what you're seeing, however, it will help to purchase an illustrated guide in English, available at the entrance. The most outstanding sights are the 16th-century **Galerie François I,** the **King's Staircase**, the **Ballroom**, the **Royal Apartments**, and **Napoleon's Apartments**. To see the more intimate **Petit Apartments** requires taking a guided tour. The château is open every day except Tuesdays, from 9:30 a.m. to 12:30 p.m. and again from 2–5 p.m. In either case, the last admission is 45 minutes before the closing time.

Leave the château and follow the map through a passage in the south wing to an intriguing 16th-century grotto. This opens into the informal **Jardin Anglais** (English Gardens) (3) laid out by Napoleon. Continue on past the original spring, the **Fontaine Bliaud**, from which the name of the palace and town derives. Next to this is the **Carp Pond** with its delightful little island pavilion.

You are now in the formal gardens, the Parterre designed for Louis XIV by the architect Le Vau, which offers marvelous views of the château. Stroll down to the **Cascades** (4) and look out over the Grand Canal, a center of pageantry in the time of the Sun King, then return to the palace. Horse carriage rides are usually available along here.

The **Cour de la Fontaine** (5) is a beautiful courtyard overlooking the carp pond. Take an admiring glance, then follow around past the ancient **Oval Court** (6) with its 12th-century keep—used by François I as his bedroom. This is usually locked, but you can peek in through the grill. Continue on past the 17th-century Cour des Offices and visit the **Jardin de Diane** (7), a wonderfully romantic garden noted for its elegant fountain dating from 1603.

Those who would like to see some of the town should exit onto Rue Grande and turn right. A left on Rue Paroisse leads past a market place to the interesting **Musée Napoléonien d'Art et d'Histoire Militaire** (8) on Rue St.-Honoré. Noted for its fine collection of swords, the Napoleonic Museum is open on Tuesdays through Saturdays, from 2–5:30 p.m.

Return to Place Général-de-Gaulle, facing the entrance of the château. From here you can get a bus back to the train station.

A Daytrip from Paris

*Chantilly

The Ile-de-France region is justly renowned for its many splendid châteaux. Some of these, especially Versailles, are monumental in scope while others, such as Fontainebleau, leave the visitor endowed with an immensely satisfying sense of history. For sheer beauty, however, the dream-like Château of Chantilly is by far the most outstanding. Many even consider it to be the loveliest in all France. This is surely reason enough to make the easy daytrip, but Chantilly gilds the lily with yet more sumptuous attractions. There are enchanted gardens, a magnificent forest, one of the nation's best art museums, stables that resemble a palace, a world-famous racetrack, a great horse training center and—of course—the delicious whipped cream and black lace for which the town is noted.

Chantilly has an illustrious history going back to a Roman named Cantilius. The present château—actually two separate châteaux joined by a common entrance—is the fifth on the same site. Its larger part, the impossibly romantic Grand Château, is a late-19th-century pastiche while the older Petit Château dates from the 16th century. It was here that a well-known event (or story?) occurred in 1671, when Louis XIV came calling for a three-day visit—along with five thousand of his retainers. The greatest chef in France at the time, François Vatel, was employed at the château and had to feed all those hungry mouths on virtually no notice. Things went wrong and finally, when the promised fish failed to arrive in time, the overwrought Vatel ended it all with a sword thrust through his body.

GETTING THERE:

Trains leave Nord Station in Paris almost hourly for the 30-minute ride to Chantilly-Gouvieux Station. Return service operates until mid-evening.

By car, leave Paris on the A-1 Autoroute, switching to the N-1 near St.-Denis and then to the N-16. Chantilly is about 25 miles north of Paris.

PRACTICALITIES:

Good weather is essential for a visit to Chantilly. Avoid coming on a Tuesday, when nearly everything is closed. The local **Tourist Information Office**, phone 44–57–08–58, is on Avenue Maréchal-Joffre, one block from the train station. You might want to call them first to avoid coming on a crowded race day, usually held on certain Sundays in June. **Bicycles** may be rented at the station. Chantilly is in the **Ile-de-France** region, and has a **population** of about 10,000.

FOOD AND DRINK:

There are a few good restaurants between the train station and the château. Some choices are:

Le Relais Condé (42 Av. du Mar.-Joffre, near the station) Classic cuisine with good wines in an elegant restaurant with a terrace. Proper dress expected, reservations advised, phone 44–57–05–75. X: Sun. eve., Mon. $$ and $$$

Les Quatres Saisons (9 Ave. du Général-Leclerc, south of the station) Both French and Scandinavian specialties, terrace. X: Mon., Feb. $$

Tipperary (6. Ave. du Mar.-Joffre, on the way to town) A pleasant place for regional specialties. $$

Château (22 Rue du Connétable, near the Grandes Ecuries) Good dining on the garden terrace or indoors. X: Mon. eve., Tues., late Aug. $$

Capitainerie (in the château) A self-serve cafeteria for light lunches. X: Tues. $

SUGGESTED TOUR:

Leave the **train station** (1) and follow the map past the tourist office to the **Hippodrome** (racetrack) (2), where the prestigious *Prix de Diane* and *Prix du Jockey Club* races are run each June. This beautifully situated course has been attracting Paris society since 1836.

Continue on to the ***Château** (3), rising from the middle of a tiny lake like a fantastic scene from a fairy tale. One single admission covers both the castle and its grounds. Cross the bridge and enter the ***Musée Condé**, a museum that occupies the entire château. The sumptuous collection of art, along with the estate, was bequeathed to the *Institut de France* in 1897 by its last owner, the Duke of Aumale, fifth son of Louis-Philippe, the last king of France. A small guide brochure in English is available at the entrance.

The rooms to your right, in the **Grand Château**, contain the picture galleries and may be seen at your own leisure. Laid out in a charming 19th-century style, the walls are covered from top to bottom with an amazingly good collection of canvases. To see the rest of the château

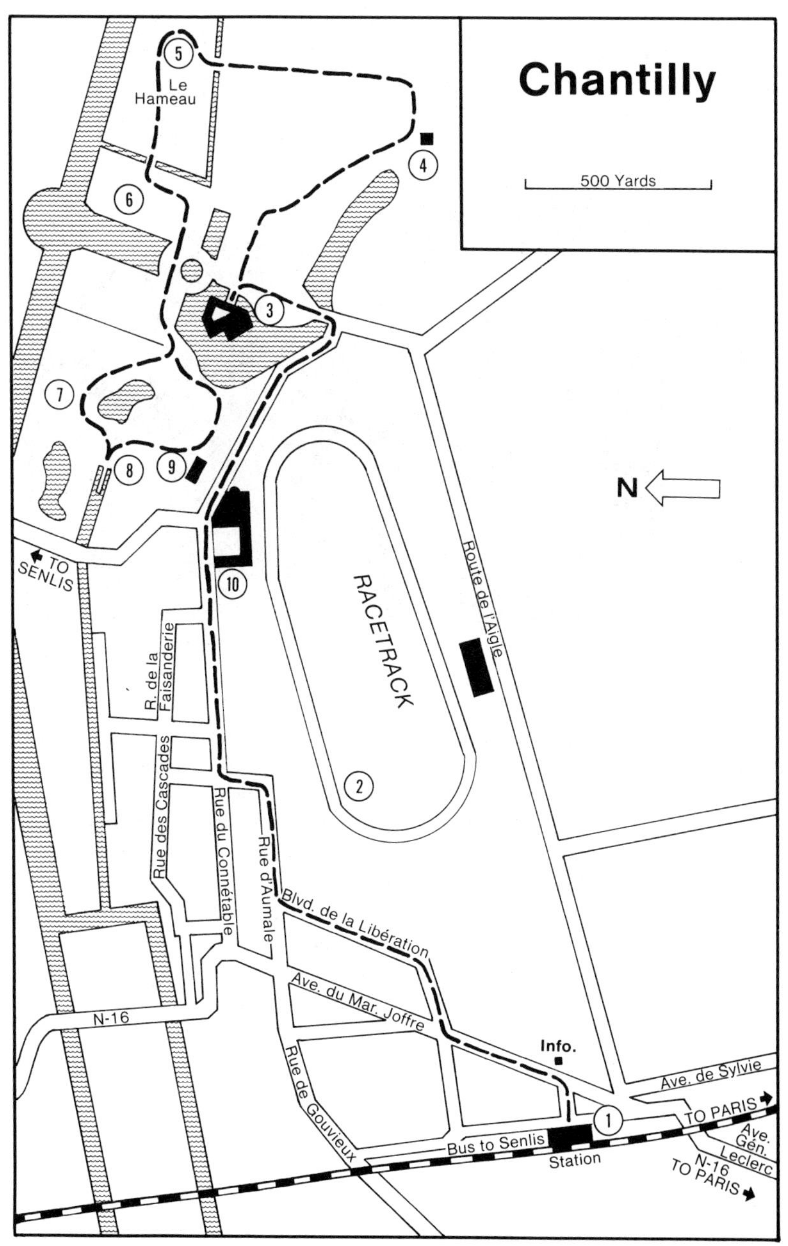
Chantilly
500 Yards
N
Le Hameau
TO SENLIS
R. de la Faisanderie
Rue des Cascades
Rue du Connétable
Rue d'Aumale
RACETRACK
Route de l'Aigle
Blvd. de la Libération
Ave. du Mar. Joffre
N-16
Rue de Gouvieux
Info.
Ave. de Sylvie
TO PARIS
Ave. Gén. Leclerc
N-16 TO PARIS
Bus to Senlis
Station
1
2
3
4
5
6
7
8
9
10

The Château of Chantilly

you will have to take a guided tour, included in the admission price. Don't miss the private apartments in the **Petit Château,** especially the Chapel and the Library, whose greatest treasure is the **Très Riches Heures du Duc de Berry,* one of the great masterpieces of the Middle Ages. Because of its fragile condition this is rarely exhibited, but copies are on display. The château is open every day except Tuesdays, from 10:00 a.m. to 6 p.m., closing at 5 p.m. in winter.

Leave the castle and walk straight ahead into the park. Once in the woods, turn right and follow the map past the tiny Chapel of St.-Paul to the **Maison de Sylvie** (4), a house with a long history of romantic affairs. The paths now lead through an enchanted forest, complete with statuary in little clearings, to **Le Hameau** (5), a rustic hamlet where the nobility played at being peasants. This was the prototype for Marie-Antoinette's famous *hameau* at Versailles. Continue around to the formal **gardens** and **waterways** (6) designed by that great landscape artist, André Le Nôtre, who was also largely responsible for the gardens at Versailles.

The picturesque ***Jardin Anglais** (English Gardens) (7) come as a great contrast. Stroll through them to the **Ile d'Amour** (8), an idyllic

In the Forest

little island, then continue on to the **Jeu de Paume** (9), which is sometimes open.

One last sight remains at Chantilly, just outside the palace precincts. This is the ***Grandes Écuries** (10), a stable built like a fabulous palace. The story is told about the Duke of Bourbon, owner of the Château during the early 18th century, having this luxurious barn erected because he expected to be reincarnated as a horse and wanted to assure his future comfort. Whether this event actually occurred is not known, but the posh interiors are open to visitors as the **Musée Vivant du Cheval** (Living Museum of the Horse). Demonstrations of dressage, a great treat, are given several times daily. The stables are open from April through November, daily except Tuesdays and Sundays, from 10:30 a.m. to 6:30 p.m.; and on Sundays as well from May through October, from 10:30 a.m. to 7 p.m. In July and August they are also open on Tuesdays.

A Daytrip from Paris

Giverny and Vernon

The Monet Gardens

Born in 1840, the celebrated French painter Claude Monet was one of the founding fathers of Impressionism and a vital force in the modern art movement it led to. After a long period of ridicule and poverty, his talent finally received broad public recognition. By then fairly prosperous, Monet in 1883 created for himself and his family a lovely home surrounded by lush gardens near the Seine, in the tiny hamlet of Giverny. It was in this serene environment that his greatest works were achieved.

Following Monet's death in 1926, the property deteriorated badly until 1966, when it was willed to the *Institut de France* by his son Michel. Generous donations, primarily from the United States, have made possible a stunning restoration of this extraordinary place. Ever since its public opening in 1980 as the Claude Monet Foundation, the gardens—along with his remarkably charming house and cavernous studio—have become an extremely popular daytrip destination, indeed a pilgrimage, for art lovers and tourists alike.

Organized bus tours to Giverny are offered by several firms in Paris, which are certainly a convenient way to reach this secluded spot. They have the disadvantage, however, of limiting the amount of time you can spend savoring its enchanting atmosphere. They also overlook nearby Vernon, an ancient town of considerable charm, worthy of a trip in itself.

GETTING THERE:

Trains depart St.-Lazare Station in Paris several times daily for Vernon, less than an hour away. From here you can take a taxi the three-mile distance to Giverny. It is also possible to walk or rent a **bicycle** at the Vernon station. Return trains run until early evening.

By car, take the A-13 Autoroute to the Bonnières-Vernon exit, then the N-15 into Vernon, cross the Seine and follow signs to the Monet Museum. It is about 50 miles northwest of Paris.

PRACTICALITIES:

The Monet gardens and house are open from April through October, daily except Mondays, from 10 a.m. to 6 p.m. Avoid coming on a rainy day. The **Tourist Information Office** in Vernon, phone 32–51–39–60, in on Rue Carnot near the church. You can call the Monet Museum at 32–51–28–21. **Bicycles** may be rented at the station. Giverny and Vernon are in the **Normandie** region.

FOOD AND DRINK:

There are several simple eating places in Giverny—ask at the museum about this. The town of Vernon offers a much wider selection of restaurants, including:

Au Beau Rivage (13 Av. Mar.-Leclerc, near the river) An attractive place for good food. X: Sun. eve., Mon. $$

Les Fleurs (71 Rue Carnot, near the Archives Tower) A local favorite. X: Sun. eve., Mon. $$

Le Strasbourg (6 Place d'Évreux, 2 blocks northeast of the station) Dining in a small hotel. X: Sun. eve., Mon. $

SUGGESTED TOUR:

From the **Vernon Train Station** (1) you can take a taxi to the *Musée Monet* in Giverny, a trip of nearly three miles. Walking is also possible by following the map, or you can rent a bicycle at the station.

Visits at the ***Claude Monet Foundation** (2) in Giverny begin in the huge **Water Lily Studio**, built in 1916 to accommodate large canvases. The paintings on the wall are, of course, copies; the originals being in leading museums.

Stroll over to the painstakingly restored ***house**, surfaced in pink crushed brick with green doors and shutters. Its exquisite interior, looking like the pages from a fashionable architectural magazine, is perhaps a bit too tidy for the home of an artist, but very beautiful nonetheless. It was here that Monet entertained his closest friends, including the French premier Georges Clemenceau and fellow artists Renoir, Degas, Rodin, and Cézanne, among others.

The **Clos Normand Garden**, facing the house, is totally French in concept. Monet loved gardens, and as his fortunes improved he employed several gardeners to maintain them. From here, a tunnel leads under the public road to the famous ***Water Garden** (3), which he created by diverting a nearby stream. This part of the property exudes a distinctly Oriental aura. Much of it seems familiar, especially the wisteria-entwined **Japanese Bridge**, a subject for many of his best-known paintings, around which clusters of water lilies float on the pond.

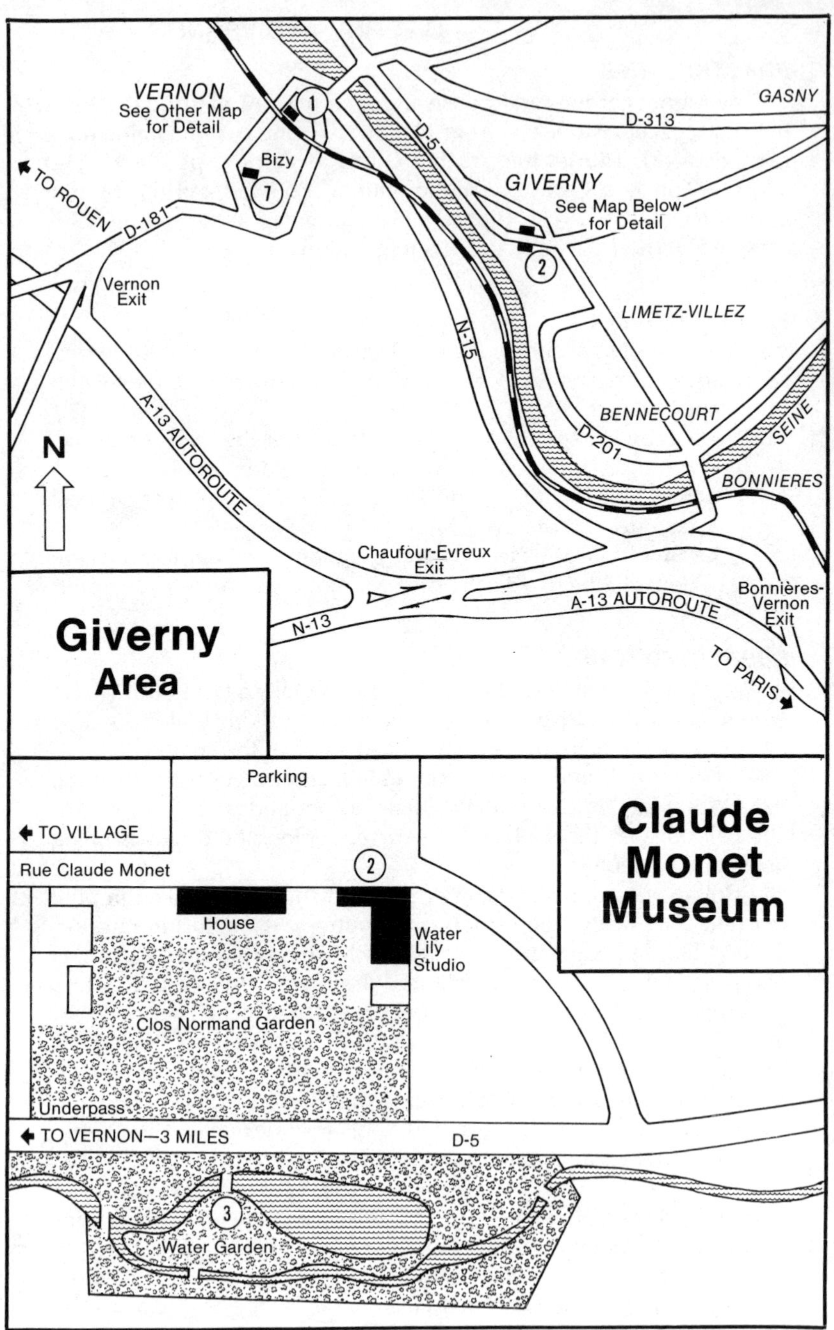
VERNON
See Other Map
for Detail
1
Bizy
7
TO ROUEN
D-181
Vernon
Exit
GASNY
D-313
D-5
GIVERNY
See Map Below
for Detail
2
LIMETZ-VILLEZ
N-15
A-13 AUTOROUTE
N
BENNECOURT
D-201
SEINE
BONNIERES
Chaufour-Evreux
Exit
N-13
A-13 AUTOROUTE
Bonnières-
Vernon
Exit
TO PARIS
Giverny
Area
Parking
TO VILLAGE
Rue Claude Monet
2
Claude
Monet
Museum
House
Water
Lily
Studio
Clos Normand Garden
Underpass
TO VERNON—3 MILES
D-5
3
Water Garden

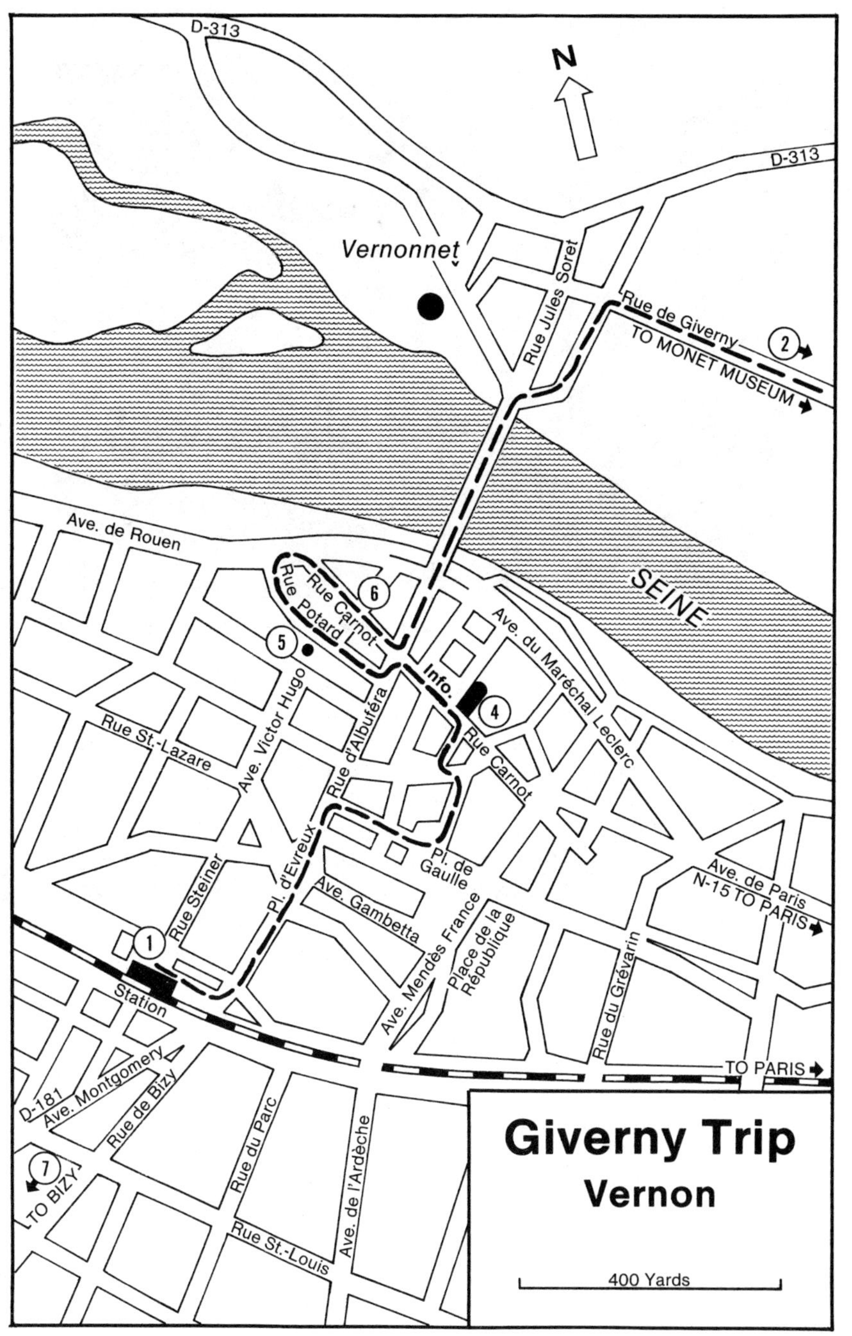

D-313
N
D-313
Vernonnet
Rue Jules Soret
Rue de Giverny
2
TO MONET MUSEUM
SEINE
Ave. de Rouen
Rue Carnot
Rue Potard
6
5
Info.
4
Ave. du Maréchal Leclerc
Rue Carnot
Rue St.-Lazare
Ave. Victor Hugo
Rue d'Albuféra
Pl. d'Evreux
Pl. de Gaulle
Ave. Gambetta
Rue Steiner
1
Station
Ave. Mendès France
Place de la République
Rue du Grévarin
Ave. de Paris
N-15 TO PARIS
TO PARIS
D-181
Ave. Montgomery
Rue de Bizy
7
TO BIZY
Rue du Parc
Ave. de l'Ardèche
Rue St.-Louis
Giverny Trip
Vernon
400 Yards

The Japanese Bridge in the Water Garden

Returning to **Vernon**, you will have a beautiful view from its bridge of the town, the Seine and the woods beyond. Visit the 12th-century **Church of Notre-Dame** (4), noted for its splendid west-front rose window and lavish interior. In the immediate vicinity stand a number of medieval half-timbered houses, lending atmosphere to this ancient settlement founded by Rollo, the first duke of Normandy, in the 9th century. Stroll along Rue Carnot and Rue Potard. The **Archives Tower** (5) is all that remains of a massive castle built in 1123 by King Henry I of England. Closeby, in another venerable building, is the **Poulain Municipal Museum** (6), which proudly displays two paintings by Monet along with items of local interest. It is open daily except on Mondays and holidays, from 2–5:30 p.m.

NEARBY SIGHT:

The **Château of Bizy** (7), an 18th-century mansion set in a charming park, may also be visited. Its interior contains many superb pieces in the Empire style along with Napoleonic souvenirs. The château is open from 10 a.m. to noon and 2–6 p.m., daily except Fridays, from April through October. To get there, follow the D-181 for one mile southwest of Vernon.

A Daytrip from Paris

*Rouen

One of the best-preserved medieval cities in all of Europe, Rouen is also a thriving modern commercial center. This unusual combination of past and present results from a deliberate decision on the part of local government to strip away decades of "modernization" in the old part of town and restore its ancient features. At the same time, cars were banned from many of the streets, creating an unusually pleasant—and very beguiling—pedestrian shopping zone. If ever there was a city designed to be explored on foot, Rouen is it.

Over two thousand years ago, Rouen was already in existence as a Celtic encampment on the banks of the Seine. This evolved into a market town known as *Ratuma* to the Gauls and later as *Rotomagus* to the Romans. Its real history, however, begins with an invasion by the Vikings from Scandinavia, who made it the capital of their Norman duchy in 912. The brilliant Norse leader Rollo established an able administration that did much to develop the local economy. His linear descendant, William the Bastard, known to history as the Conqueror, defeated the English near Hastings in 1066 and became king of England, bringing Norman civilization to that island country.

Centuries later it was the English who invaded Normandy. During the Hundred Years War a strange leader arose among the French, Joan of Arc, who persuaded the king to allow her to lead troops in battle. Eventually she was captured by the Burgundians and sold to the English, who brought her to Rouen in 1431 for a mockery of a trial—after which she was burned at the stake in the town's market place.

In the years that followed the re-establishment of French rule, Rouen blossomed into a beautiful and prosperous city with many fine Renaissance buildings. Although it suffered badly during the 16th-century Wars of Religion and again during World War II, it has today regained its place as one of the great cities of France.

GETTING THERE:

Trains leave St.-Lazare Station in Paris frequently for Rouen's Rive Droite Station, a trip of about 70 minutes. Return service operates until mid-evening.

By car, Rouen is 86 miles northwest of Paris via the A-13 Autoroute.

PRACTICALITIES:

Rouen may be enjoyed in any season, but avoid coming on a Tuesday or holiday if you plan on visiting any of the major museums. The local **Tourist Information Office**, phone 35–71–41–77, is in front of the cathedral. Rouen is the **Normandie** region, and has a **population** of about 105,000.

FOOD AND DRINK:

The city offers an extraordinarily wide range of excellent restaurants, many of which specialize in the rich, highly caloric Norman cuisine. Some good choices are:

Bertrand Warin (9 Rue de la Pie, just west of Place du Vieux-Marché) A highly refined restaurant with inventive cuisine, rather dressy. Reservations needed, call 35–89–26–69. X: Sun. eve., Mon., Aug. $$$

Le Beffroy (15 Rue du Beffroy, 2 blocks east of the Fine Arts Museum) Norman and modern cuisine in a fashionable restaurant. For reservations call 35–71–55–27. X: Sun., Mon. $$$

La Couronne (31 Place du Vieux-Marché) Norman specialties, especially duck, in a 14th-century house. Proper dress expected, for reservations phone 35–71–40–90. $$$

La Réverbère (5 Place de la République, 3 blocks southeast of the cathedral) A broad selection of well-prepared cuisine in a simple setting. X: Sun. $$

Les P'tits Parapluies (46 Rue Bourg-l'Abbé, 2 blocks north of St.-Ouen) A stylish restaurant with innovative cooking. X: Sun., Mon. lunch, Aug. $$

La Vieille Auberge (37 Rue St.-Etienne-des-Tonneliers, 3 blocks south of the Great Clock) An exceptional value. X: Mon. $

Les Flandres (5 Rue des Bons-Enfants, 3 blocks southwest of the Fine Arts Museum) Simple and very popular, with good steaks. X: Sat. eve., Sun., Aug. $

La Tarte Tatin (99 Rue de la Vicomté, 1 block southeast of Place du Vieux-Marché) An outstanding crêperie. $

SUGGESTED TOUR:

Follow the map from Rouen's **Rive Droite Train Station** (1) to Place de la Cathédrale, where the tourist office is housed in an elegant 16th-century Renaissance building. Along the way you will pass many examples of old half-timbered houses that have been put to modern use while still retaining the town's medieval atmosphere.

The ***Cathedral of Notre-Dame** (2), one of the finest Gothic structures in existence, is familiar to art lovers as the subject for a series of Impressionist paintings by Monet that captured its spirit under changing atmospheric conditions. Its **west front** displays at a glance the entire history of Gothic cathedral construction. The base of the left tower dates from the early 12th century and, along with two doors, is the only portion of the church that survived the devastating fire of 1200. On the right is the so-called **Butter Tower**, supposedly financed by the sale of indulgences allowing the faithful to eat butter during Lent. This Flamboyant structure was erected in the 15th century. The next hundred years saw the addition of the central portal and the rose window. Construction continued through the 19th century, when the delicate open-ironwork spire, the tallest in France, was completed.

A stroll through the cathedral's majestic interior is impressive. Note in particular the **Booksellers' Staircase**, in the north transept and the **tombs** of several historical figures, including those of Rollo, the first duke of Normandy, and Richard the Lionheart, king of England. Guided tours are conducted through the fascinating 11th-century **crypt** and the ambulatory, several times daily during the summer season, and on weekends and some holidays the rest of the year.

Walk down Rue du Gros-Horloge, a pedestrians-only shopping street of well-preserved houses, many of them half-timbered. The ***Gros-Horloge** (Great Clock) (3), a famous symbol of Rouen, was relocated here in 1527. Its adjoining 14th-century **Belfry** may be climbed between Palm Sunday and September 30th, from 10 a.m. to noon and 2–6 p.m., but not on Tuesdays, Wednesday mornings, or holidays. Splendid views of the old city make the climb very worthwhile.

Stroll over to the magnificent **Palais de Justice** (4), one of the great civic structures of Europe. Originally built in the 16th century and later modified, its Gothic façade becomes increasingly Flamboyant as it rises above the ground floor. You can visit its Prosecutors' Room, reached via the staircase in the left wing, on weekdays. Recent excavations in the courtyard have unearthed an underground 12th-century **synagogue** or yeshiva, which can be seen by arrangement with the tourist office.

On May 30th, 1431, Joan of Arc was burned at the stake in Rouen's **Place du Vieux-Marché** (Market Place) (5), the next stop on the walking tour. A huge cross now marks the spot where she met her fiery end. The strikingly contemporary **Église Sainte-Jeanne-d'Arc**, adjacent to this, was consecrated in 1979 and contains a large area of marvelous 16th-century stained-glass windows from a previous church on the site. Also in the square is a modern covered marketplace, several inviting outdoor cafés, and the tiny but fascinating **Musée Jeanne-d'Arc** (6), a somewhat kitschy waxworks crammed with re-created scenes from the life of the Maid of Orléans. Another nearby sight that might be of interest is the **Maison Natale de Corneille** (7) at number 4 Rue de la Pie, where the famous French playwright Pierre Corneille

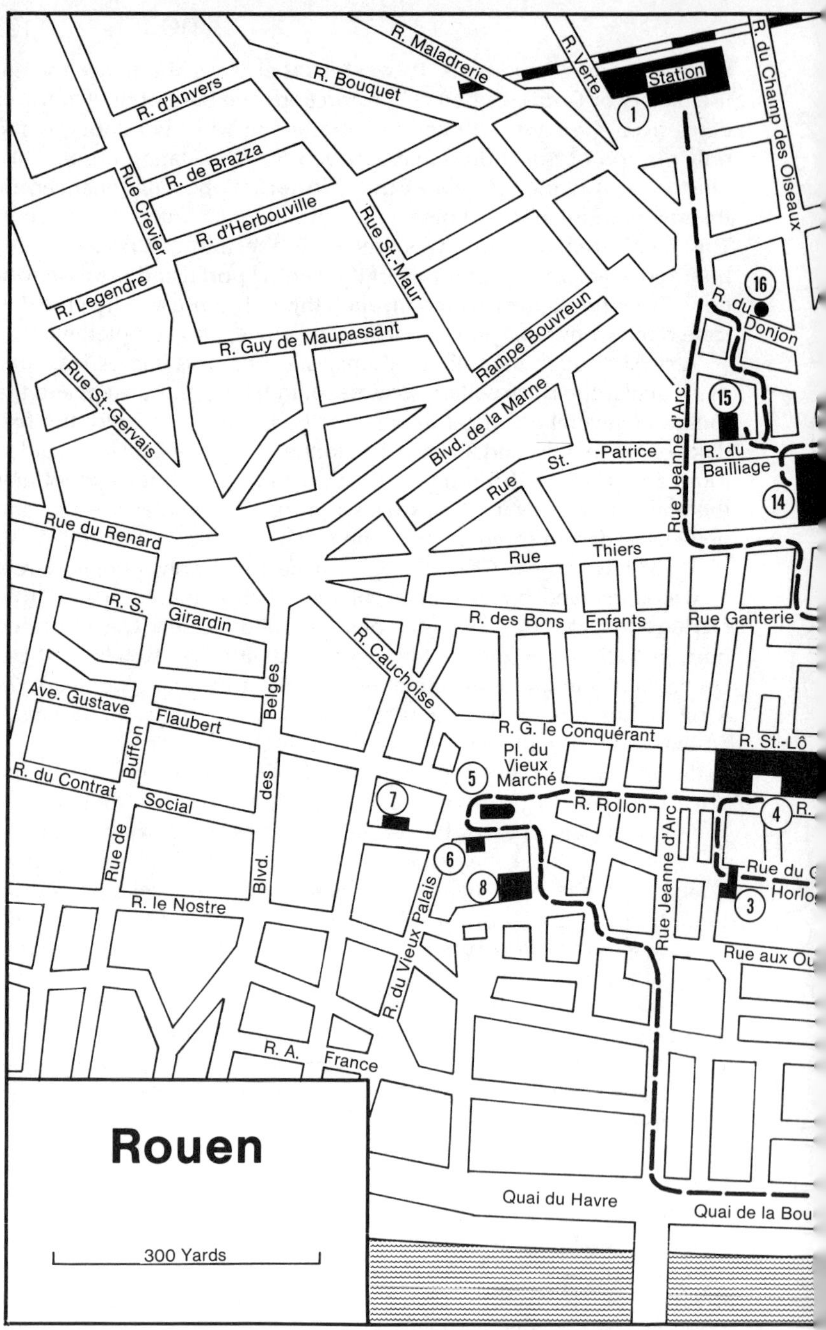
R. Maladrerie
R. Verte
Station
R. du Champ des Oiseaux
R. d'Anvers
R. Bouquet
R. de Brazza
Rue Crevier
R. d'Herbouville
Rue St.-Maur
R. Legendre
R. Guy de Maupassant
Rampe Bouvreun
R. du Donjon
Rue St.-Gervais
Blvd. de la Marne
Rue St.-Patrice
R. du Bailliage
Rue Jeanne d'Arc
Rue du Renard
Rue Thiers
R. S. Girardin
R. des Bons Enfants
Rue Ganterie
R. Cauchoise
Belges
Ave. Gustave Flaubert
R. G. le Conquérant
R. St.-Lô
Buffon
Pl. du Vieux Marché
R. du Contrat Social
des
R. Rollon
Rue de
Blvd.
R. du Vieux Palais
Rue du Gros Horloge
R. le Nostre
Rue aux Ou
R. A. France
Quai du Havre
Quai de la Bou
Rouen
300 Yards
1
3
4
5
6
7
8
14
15
16

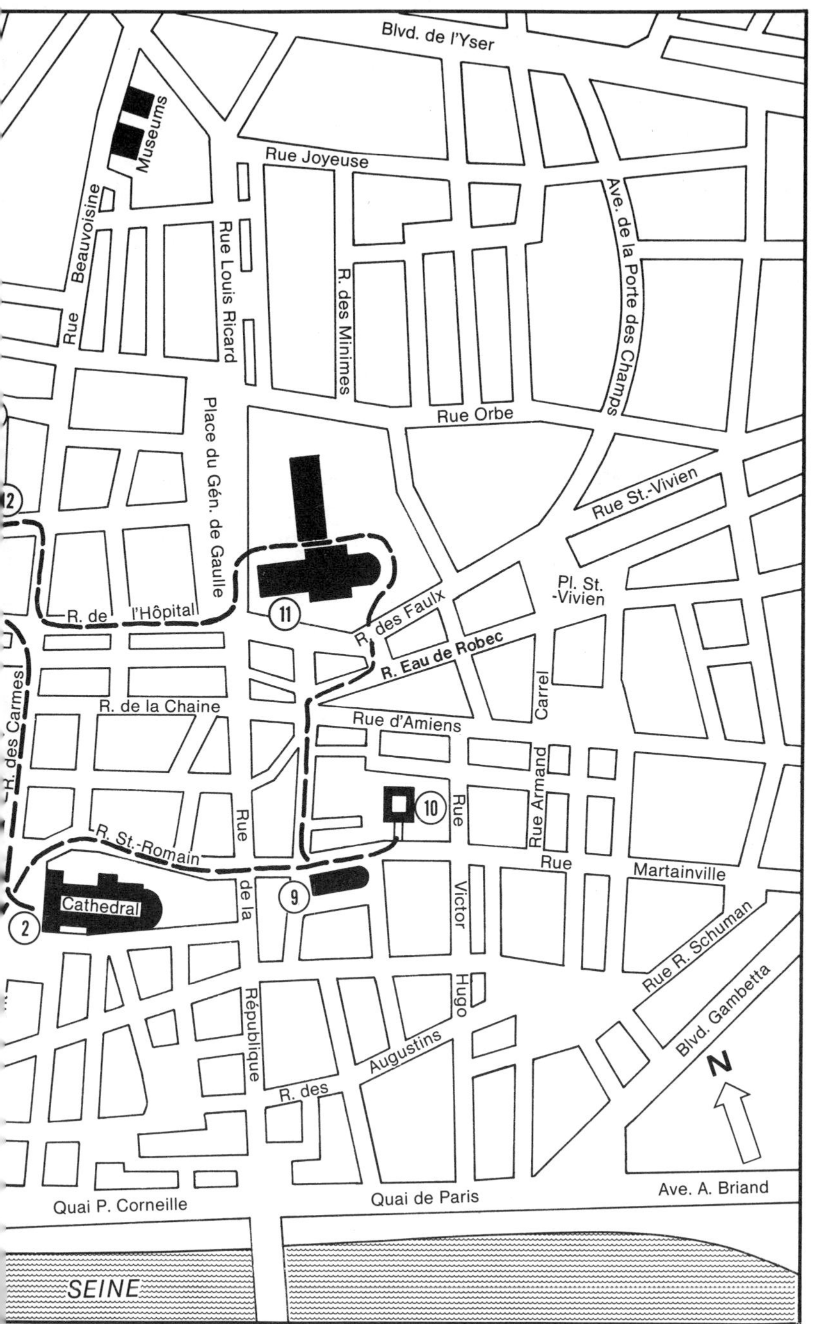

Blvd. de l'Yser
Museums
Rue Joyeuse
Rue Beauvoisine
Rue Louis Ricard
R. des Minimes
Ave. de la Porte des Champs
Rue Orbe
Place du Gén. de Gaulle
Rue St.-Vivien
Pl. St. -Vivien
R. de l'Hôpital
11
R. des Faulx
R. Eau de Robec
R. des Carmes
R. de la Chaine
Rue d'Amiens
Carrel
Rue Armand
10
Rue Victor Hugo
R. St.-Romain
Rue de la République
Rue Martainville
9
Cathedral
2
Rue R. Schuman
Blvd. Gambetta
N
R. des Augustins
Quai P. Corneille
Quai de Paris
Ave. A. Briand
SEINE

was born in 1606 and where he lived most of his life. It is open daily except on Tuesdays, on Wednesday mornings, and on holidays.

It is only a few steps to the Place de la Pucelle, site of the elegant **Hôtel de Bourgtheroulde** (8). This sumptuous 16th-century mansion, now a bank, combines Gothic with early Renaissance elements. Step into the courtyard to admire the decorations, some of which depict the meeting of François I and England's Henry VIII at the Field of the Cloth of Gold in 1520.

Return to the cathedral via the route shown on the map, which takes you along the right bank of the Seine. Colorful Rue St.-Romain, lined with picturesque half-timbered medieval and Renaissance houses, leads past the **Archbishop's Palace.** It was here that Joan of Arc was sentenced to death and, 25 years after the execution, at last found innocent.

The ***Église St.-Maclou** (9) is perhaps the most striking example of Flamboyant Gothic church architecture in France. Badly damaged in World War II, it is now completely restored. Don't miss seeing its lovely interior, particularly the remarkable organ loft.

Another absolute "must" sight in Rouen is the ***Aître St.-Maclou** (10), a 16th-century cloister that once served as a plague cemetery. Its ossuary galleries, now occupied by an art school, are carved with exceptionally macabre figures of death. Go in for a peek.

Return to the church and follow the gorgeous Rue Damiette to the **Abbatiale Saint-Ouen** (11). This enormous abbey church, dating mostly from the 14th century, replaces earlier churches on the same site going back as far as the 7th century. Stroll through the gardens behind it and return through the **Hôtel de Ville** (City Hall).

Now follow the map to the **Musée Le Secq des Tournelles** (12), an unusual museum located in a desanctified former church. Its vast collection of wrought-iron objects dating from the 3rd through the 19th centuries is totally fascinating, and can be seen during the same times that the Fine Arts Museum, below, is open. Continue on to the nearby **Église St.-Godard** (13), a late-15th-century church noted for its unusual wooden roof and outstanding stained-glass windows, especially the one depicting the Tree of Jesse at the choir end of the south aisle.

The **Musée des Beaux-Arts** (Fine Arts Museum) (14) has one of the best provincial collections in France. There are paintings by Gérard David, Rubens, Ingres, Delacroix, Velázquez, Corot and many others, along with those by native-son Géricault. Impressionism is well represented by Sisley and Monet *(Rouen Cathedral)*. There are also several rooms of contemporary art including one devoted to the local Duchamp family. The museum is open daily except on Tuesdays and holidays; from 10 a.m. to noon and 2–6 p.m., but closed on Wednesday mornings.

The Great Clock on Rue du Gros-Horloge

Now amble over to the splendid **Musée de Céramique** (15), an exhibition of lovely ceramics located in a former mansion just one block away. The opening times are the same as for the Fine Arts Museum.

Before leaving Rouen, it would be fitting to visit the **Tour Jeanne-d'Arc** (16) on Rue du Donjon near the train station. This former keep is all that remains of a 13th-century castle, and is the place where the Maid of Orléans was confronted with the instruments of torture. You can climb to its top for a nice view. The tower is open daily except on Tuesdays and holidays, from 10 a.m. to noon and 2–5:30 p.m.

A Daytrip from Paris

*Dijon

There is a lot to see in Dijon—if you can just tear yourself away from the pleasures of the table long enough to feast the eyes as well as the palate. Long renowned as the region's gastronomic center, this ancient city is also the traditional capital of Burgundy. Its rulers left behind a rich heritage that today makes it a veritable treasury of the arts. Dijon is an exceedingly likeable place, and an eminently walkable one as well.

Originally a Roman encampment on the military road linking Lyon with Mainz, *Divio,* as Dijon was then known, became the capital of the Burgundian kingdom during the Dark Ages, only to be destroyed by fire in 1137. The late 12th century saw its reconstruction as a fortified city, while the Cathedral of St.-Bénigne was begun a hundred years later.

Philip the Bold, son of King John II of France, inherited Burgundy in 1364, thus starting the powerful line of Valois dukes whose loyalty to the Kingdom of France wavered with each succeeding generation. During this time Burgundy was greatly expanded, making Dijon in effect the capital of much of what is now the Netherlands, Belgium, Alsace and Lorraine as well as the present region of *Bourgogne*. This enormous growth coincided with the beginning of the Renaissance, attracting many leading artists to Dijon, where there was both work and money. The golden days came to an end in 1477 when Duke Charles the Bold was killed fighting Louis XI, thus reunifying Burgundy with France.

GETTING THERE:

Trains for Dijon leave Gare de Lyon station in Paris fairly frequently. The speedy TGVs *(reservations required)* make the run in about 100 minutes; others take about 2½ hours. Return service operates until mid-evening.

By car, Dijon is 195 miles southeast of Paris via the A-6 Autoroute. This may be too far for a daytrip, although Dijon makes an excellent stopover en route between Paris and the Riviera.

PRACTICALITIES:

Most of the major sights are closed on Tuesdays and some holidays. The local **Tourist Information Office**, phone 80–43–42–12, is at Place Darcy. Dijon is in the **Bourgogne** region, and has a **population** of about 145,000.

FOOD AND DRINK:

The overall quality of dining in Dijon is exceptionally high, with such local specialties as *boeuf bourguignon* and *coq au vin* being international favorites. The city is also famous for its mustard, a jar of which makes a nice souvenir. Some outstanding restaurants located on or near the suggested walking route are:

Jean-Pierre Billoux (Hôtel la Cloche, 14 Place Darcy) Regarded as the best restaurant in Dijon, and among the best in France. Proper dress expected, garden tables available. For reservations call 80–30–11–00. X: Sun. eve., Mon., Feb. $$$+

Le Chapeau Rouge (5 Rue Michelet, 1 block east of the cathedral) Serious classic dining in a tranquil setting. For reservations call 80–72–31–13. $$$

Le Toison d'Or (Les Oenophiles) (18 Rue Ste.-Anne, 5 blocks southwest of the Palace of the Dukes) In an old mansion, with ancient wine *caves* and a museum. A unique experience. X: Sat. lunch, Sun., holidays, Aug. $$

La Porte Guillaume (in the Hôtel du Nord on Place Darcy) An old traditional establishment. $$

Brasserie du Théâtre (place du Théâtre, a block southeast of the Palace of the Dukes) A lively place with outdoor tables in summer. X: Wed. $$

Le Dôme (16 bis Rue Quentin, 2 blocks northwest of Notre-Dame Church) A popular little restaurant facing the Central Market. X: Sun., holidays $

Au Bec Fin (47 Rue Jeannin, a block north of the Church of St.-Michel) An excellent value. X: Sat. lunch, Sun. $

SUGGESTED TOUR:

Leave the **train station** (1) and follow the map to **Place Darcy** (2), an attractive square with a tourist office, a small park and an 18th-century triumphal arch. Continue on Rue de la Liberté past the venerable **Grey Poupon** mustard store—which has an exhibit of antique jars on display—to **Place François Rude** (3). In the center of this lively square there is a fountain that once ran with new wine at harvest time, topped by a statue of a naked youth treading the grapes. The Central Market *(Les Halles),* two blocks north of this, bustles with activity on Tuesday, Friday and Saturday mornings.

Follow the narrow Rue des Forges past several exquisite old houses, the most notable being the 15th-century **Hôtel Morel-Sauvegrain** at number 56; the 13th-century exchange—much restored—at number 40; and the **Maison Milsand** dating from 1561, at number 38. A left at Place Notre-Dame leads to the ***Église de Notre-Dame** (4), a unique jewel of 13th-century Gothic architecture. Its façade is literally cov-

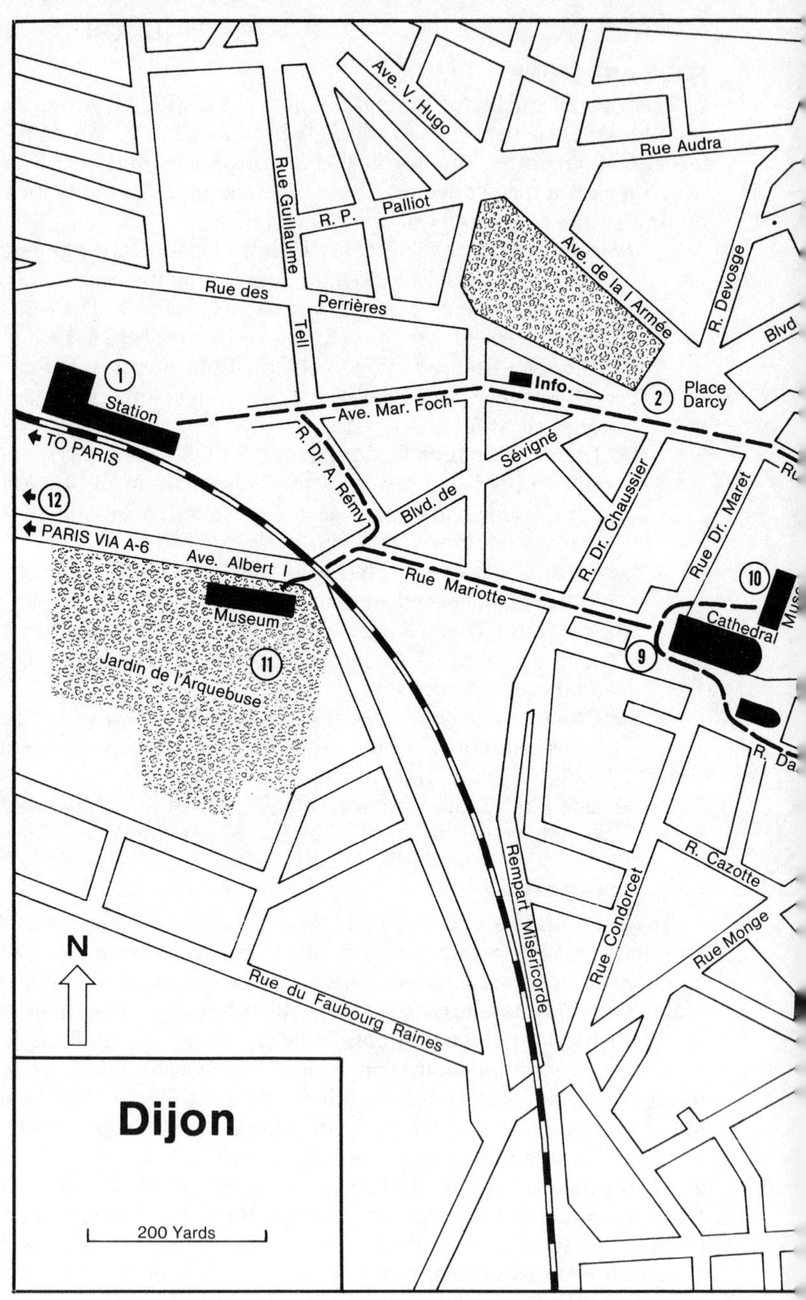
Ave. V. Hugo
Rue Audra
Rue Guillaume
R. P. Palliot
Ave. de la I Armée
R. Devosge
Blvd
Rue des Perrières
Tell
1
Station
Info.
2
Place Darcy
Ave. Mar. Foch
TO PARIS
R. Dr. A. Rémy
Blvd. de Sévigné
R. Dr. Chaussier
Rue Dr. Maret
12
PARIS VIA A-6
Ave. Albert I
Rue Mariotte
10
Museum
Cathedral
9
11
Jardin de l'Arquebuse
Rempart Miséricorde
R. Cazotte
Rue Condorcet
Rue Monge
N
Rue du Faubourg Raines
Dijon
200 Yards

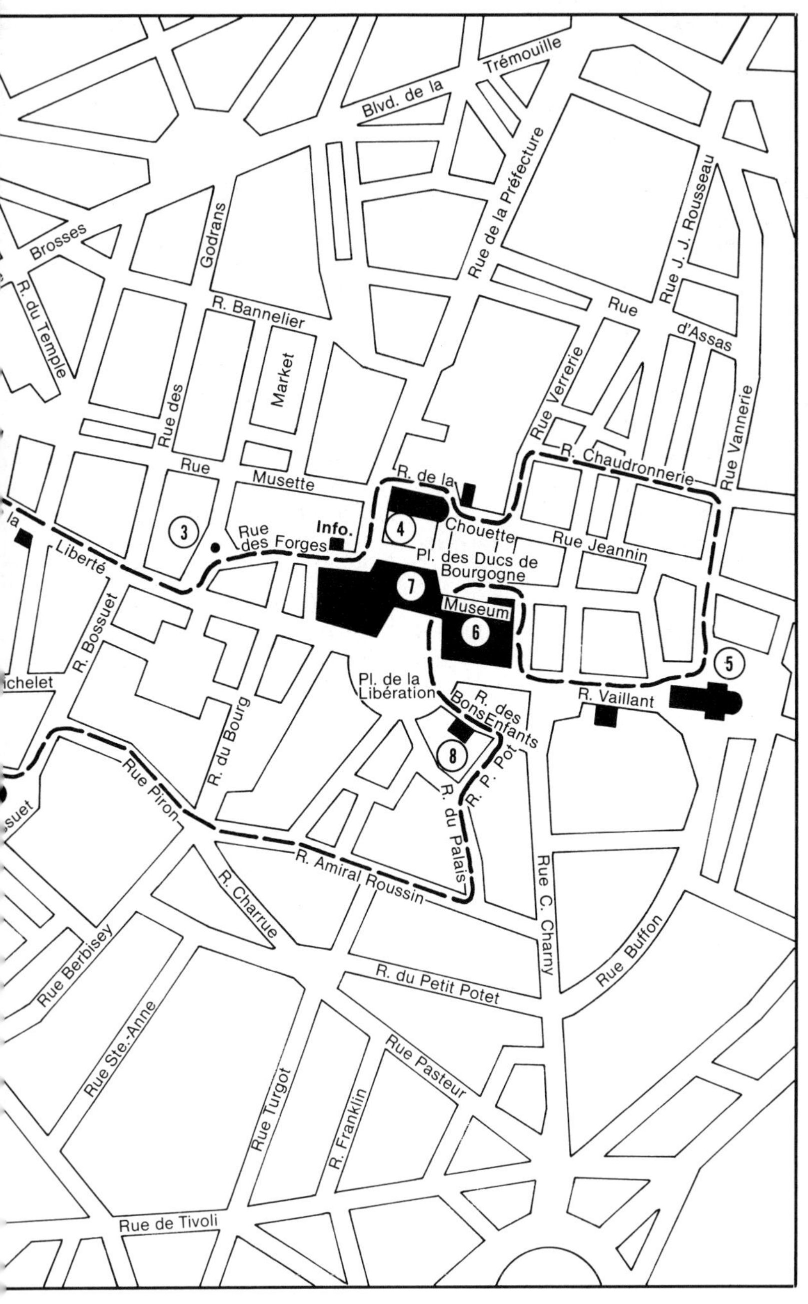

Blvd. de la
Trémouille
Rue de la Préfecture
Rue J. J. Rousseau
Brosses
Godrans
R. du Temple
R. Bannelier
Rue d'Assas
Market
Rue des
Rue Verrerie
Rue Vannerie
R. Chaudronnerie
Rue
Musette
R. de la
Chouette
Info.
Rue des Forges
Rue Jeannin
Pl. des Ducs de Bourgogne
Liberté
Museum
R. Bossuet
ichelet
Pl. de la Libération
R. des Bons Enfants
R. Vaillant
R. du Bourg
R. P. Pot
R. du Palais
Rue Piron
ssuet
R. Amiral Roussin
R. Charrue
Rue C. Charny
Rue Buffon
Rue Berbisey
R. du Petit Potet
Rue Ste.-Anne
Rue Pasteur
Rue Turgot
R. Franklin
Rue de Tivoli
3
4
5
6
7
8

ered with hideous gargoyles, while from the roof rises the Jacquemart, a mechanical chiming clock that Philip the Bold brought back as war booty from the Flemish town of Courtrai in 1389. Be sure to visit the remarkably harmonious interior, noted for its ancient stained-glass windows and an 11th-century Black Virgin carved in wood.

Stroll around to the rear of the church on Rue de la Chouette. At number 8 you will pass the **Hôtel de Vogüé**, a lovely residence in the Renaissance style dating from 1614. Make a left into Rue Verrerie, and the next right on Rue Chaudronnerie, followed by another right on Rue Vannerie—a short walk taking you down three very picturesque streets lined with medieval buildings. At the end you will come to the **Église St.-Michel** (5), a curious mixture of Gothic and Renaissance styles built during the 15th, 16th and 17th centuries.

The major attraction in Dijon, besides its food and wine, is the ***Palais des Ducs de Bourgogne** (6). Begun in the 14th century, the Palace of the Dukes of Burgundy was continually enlarged and modified until the 19th, with much of its classical façade designed by Louis XIV's architect, Jules Hardouin-Mansart of Versailles fame. This enormous complex of structures now houses both the *Hôtel de Ville* (City Hall), which may be strolled through, and the world-famous ***Musée des Beaux-Arts** (Fine Arts Museum), one of the very best in all France.

The entrance to the museum is on Place de la Ste.-Chapelle. Allow plenty of time for a visit—an hour at the very least—and carefully study the posted layout maps as it is quite easy to get disoriented and risk missing some of its best treasures. These include the ducal kitchens, the **tombs** of Philip the Bold and John the Fearless; Italian, Swiss, Flemish and German as well as French paintings and sculptures; and, of course, the outstanding galleries of modern and regional art. The museum is open daily except on Tuesdays and major holidays, from 10 a.m. to 6 p.m.

Now stroll into Place des Ducs-de-Bourgogne, a charming square facing the original parts of the palace. A portal at the corner leads back into the palace complex, from which you can climb up the **Tour Philippe-le-Bon** (7) for an excellent view of the city, the mountains beyond and the beginnings of the Burgundy wine district. It is a steep 150 feet to the top of this 15th-century tower, but well worth the effort.

Follow the map through the elegant Place de la Libération to the **Musée Magnin** (8), housed in a fine 17th-century mansion, the Hôtel Lantin on Rue des Bons-Enfants. Step inside to view a sumptuous collection of paintings displayed in the gorgeous environment of original room settings reflecting period bourgeois life. It is open from 9 a.m. to noon and 2–6 p.m., daily except on Tuesdays and major holidays.

Continue on past the Palais de Justice and turn right on Rue Amiral

Place François Rude

Roussin. The route now leads through a colorful old part of town to the **Cathedral of St.-Bénigne** (9), a 13th-century example of the Burgundian Gothic style. You can make an interesting visit to its unusual circular crypt, dating from 1002 with some 9th-century segments, which survives from an earlier basilica on the same site.

Next to this is the **Musée Archéologique** (10), housed in the dormitory of a former Benedictine abbey. Displays here include some fascinating Gallo-Roman and medieval artifacts. The museum is open daily except on Tuesdays, from 10 a.m. to 6 p.m. during the summer season and from 9 a.m. to noon and 2–6 p.m. the rest of the year.

On the way back to the train station you may want to stop at the **Jardin de l'Arquebuse** (11), a large and very lovely garden which also houses the **Natural History Museum.** Those with a bit more time can make a short excursion of less than a mile to the famous **Chartreuse de Champmol** (12, off the map). Originally the burial place of the dukes of Burgundy, this 14th-century monastery was destroyed in the Revolution and the site is now occupied by a mental hospital. Some of its fabulous sculptures by the noted medieval master Claus Sluter are still there, a deserve to be seen by anyone interested in the art of the Middle Ages.

A Daytrip from Paris

Lyon

In the past, a daytrip to Lyon would have been nearly unthinkable as the second city of France lies some 288 miles southeast of Paris. All that changed with the introduction of high-speed TGV trains, which cover the distance in an astonishing two hours flat. This is a good excursion for railpass holders—you really get your money's worth—and an excellent reason to purchase one of these bargains.

Strangely, Lyon has never been much of a tourist attraction. Visitors yes—about five million a year, mostly on business—but travelers in search of pleasure have largely avoided it. Lyon deserves better than that. Its older sections are surprisingly beautiful, and endowed with enough first-rate attractions to make just about any other city in France besides Paris pale by comparison.

And then there is the food. Lyon is usually regarded as the gastronomic capital of all France, which in practical terms means that it probably has the best cooking in the world. You could make a trip there just to eat, especially if your object was to indulge in one of the legendary temples of *haute cuisine* the area is famous for.

Over two thousand years old, Lyon was founded in 43 B.C. as the Roman colony of *Lugdunum*. Even before then, the site at the confluence of two rivers had long been occupied by Celts and other people. Under the emperor Augustus it became the capital of Gaul and later, in A.D. 478, the capital of the Burgundians. The city's strategic situation at the crossroads of trade routes favored its development as a mercantile center, a position it still holds. Textile manufacturing took root in the early 16th century, establishing a strong economic base along with banking and printing. Although Lyon—sometimes spelled *Lyons* in English—is now a very modern city, the walking tour suggested below is limited to the handsome and well-preserved older parts of town.

GETTING THERE:

TGV trains *(reservations required)* depart Gare de Lyon station in Paris frequently for the two-hour run to Lyon. Most of these stop at both of Lyon's two main stations, Part-Dieu and Perrache. If your train does this, *do not get off at Part-Dieu but stay on to Perrache*. If your train does not, you will have to get off at Part-Dieu and take another train to Perrache Station, where the walking tour begins. Return service operates until mid-evening.

By car, the distance from Paris is too great for a daytrip. You may, however, want to make a stopover en route to or from the Riviera. Lyon is 288 miles southeast of Paris via the A-6 Autoroute.

PRACTICALITIES:

Some of the major attractions are closed on Mondays, some on Tuesdays, and others on both days. The **Tourist Information Office**, phone 78–42–25–75, is located in Place Bellecour (2), with a branch in the Perrache Station and another atop the Fourvière hill. Lyon has a city **population** of about 413,000, with over a million in its greater urban area, and is in the **Rhône-Alpes** region.

FOOD AND DRINK:

Lyon abounds in superb restaurants and friendly cafés, with the selections listed below limited to a few along or near the suggested walking route. For choices in other parts of town you should consult an up-to-date restaurant guide.

Léon de Lyon (1 Rue Pleney, 1 block south of the Fine Arts Museum) Inspired Lyonnais cuisine in the grand tradition. Proper dress expected. For reservations call 78–28–11–33. X: Sun., Mon. lunch. $$$

La Tour Rose (16 Rue du Boeuf, in Old Lyon, 3 blocks north of the cathedral) Inventive modern cuisine in a 17th-century house. Dressy, reservations needed, phone 78–37–25–90. X: Sun., Aug. $$$

La Voûte—Chez Lea (11 Place Antonin-Gourju, 1 block northwest of Place Bellecour, near the river) Traditional Lyonnais cooking in an old establishment. X: Sun., July. $$

Café des Fédérations (8 Rue Major-Martin, 1 block west of the Fine Arts Museum) An old-fashioned place with simple local cuisine. X: Sat., Sun., Aug. $$

La Mére Vittet—Brasserie Lyonnaise (26 Cours de Verdun, between the rail and bus stations at Perrache) Serving good meals 24 hours a day. X: May 1. $$

Le Comptoir du Boeuf (3 Place Neuve-St.-Jean in Old Lyon, 3 blocks north of the cathedral) An attractive café-restaurant with hearty food and many wines by the glass. X: Sun. $$

Chez Sylvain (4 Rue Tupin, 6 blocks south of the Fine Arts Museum) A favorite of the neighbors for its local dishes. X: Sun., Mon., Aug. $

La Mère Jean (5 Rue Marronniers, 1 block east of Place Bellecour) Local home-style cooking at low prices. Always crowded. X: Sat. eve., Sun., Aug. $

SUGGESTED TOUR:

Leave the **Perrache Train Station** (1), a huge modern complex that includes a bus terminal, and descend the escalators to Place Carnot. From here the pedestrians-only Rue Victor Hugo leads through a lively shopping district to **Place Bellecour** (2), a vast open space with a flower market, the main tourist office, and an equestrian statue of Louis XIV. Turn left and cross the Pont Bonaparte, a bridge spanning the Saône. Continue straight ahead to the funicular station, buy a ticket from the vending machine, and board the car on the right-hand side marked for Fourvière. This will take you to the top of a very steep hill, from which there is a wonderful panoramic view of Lyon.

The outlandish **Basilique Notre-Dame-de-Fourvière** (3), at the top of the funicular and overlooking the city, has to be seen to be believed. This marvelously extravagant basilica, a curious *mélange* of architectural styles, was begun in 1870 as thanks to the Virgin for saving Lyon from the Germans during the Franco-Prussian War. Step inside for a look at the elaborate stained-glass windows, mosaics, and the crypt. A tower on the left affords an even better view of the city. The basilica is closed between noon and 2 p.m.

The Fourvière hill was the site of the original Roman settlement and is rich in archaeological finds. Follow the map to the ***Musée Gallo-Romain** (4), a superb modern structure, mostly underground, which spirals its way down part of the hillside. As you descend its ramps you will pass many fascinating artifacts from Lyon's ancient past. A descriptive booklet in English is available at the entrance. Visits may be made from 9:30 a.m. to noon and 2–6 p.m., daily except on Mondays and Tuesdays.

Leave the museum from its lowest level and stroll over to the two **Théâtres Romains** (5), unearthed in the 1930s. The larger of these Roman theaters is the oldest in France and was built by the emperor Augustus in 15 B.C. It is now used for occasional festival performances, but you can usually climb all over it.

Continue down the hill via Montée du Chemin Neuf to the **Cathedral of St.-Jean** (6). Begun in the 12th century, it displays a mixture of styles ranging from Romanesque to Flamboyant Gothic. The interior is noted for its 13th-century stained-glass in the choir, apse, and rose windows of the transepts. In the north transept there is an interesting 14th-century **astronomical clock** that puts on a show at noon, 1, 2, and 3 p.m. Don't miss the **Chapel of the Bourbons** on the north side of the nave. The **Treasury**, to the right of the entrance, exhibits rare

The Basilica of Notre-Dame-de-Fourvière

pieces of religious art. The cathedral is closed between noon and 2 p.m.

Adjacent to the cathedral, on its north side, is an outdoor archaeological garden with excavations of earlier churches. Stroll down Rue St.-Jean turn left to the **Hôtel de Gadagne** (7), a magnificent 16th-century Renaissance mansion now housing both the **Musée Historique de Lyon** and the intriguing ***Musée de la Marionnette**. Puppets have been a tradition of the city since the late 18th century when one Laurent Mourguet, an unemployed silk worker who lost his job after the Revolution made silk undemocratic, created a satirical marionette character named Guignol. The plays, larded with broad humor in the local dialect, are still very popular. Ask at the tourist office for details of performances given in various theaters. Besides the classic Guignol characters, the museum also has puppets from all over the world, notably those from Cambodia. It is open from 10:45 a.m. to 6 p.m., daily except on Tuesdays, and remains open until 8:30 p.m. on Fridays.

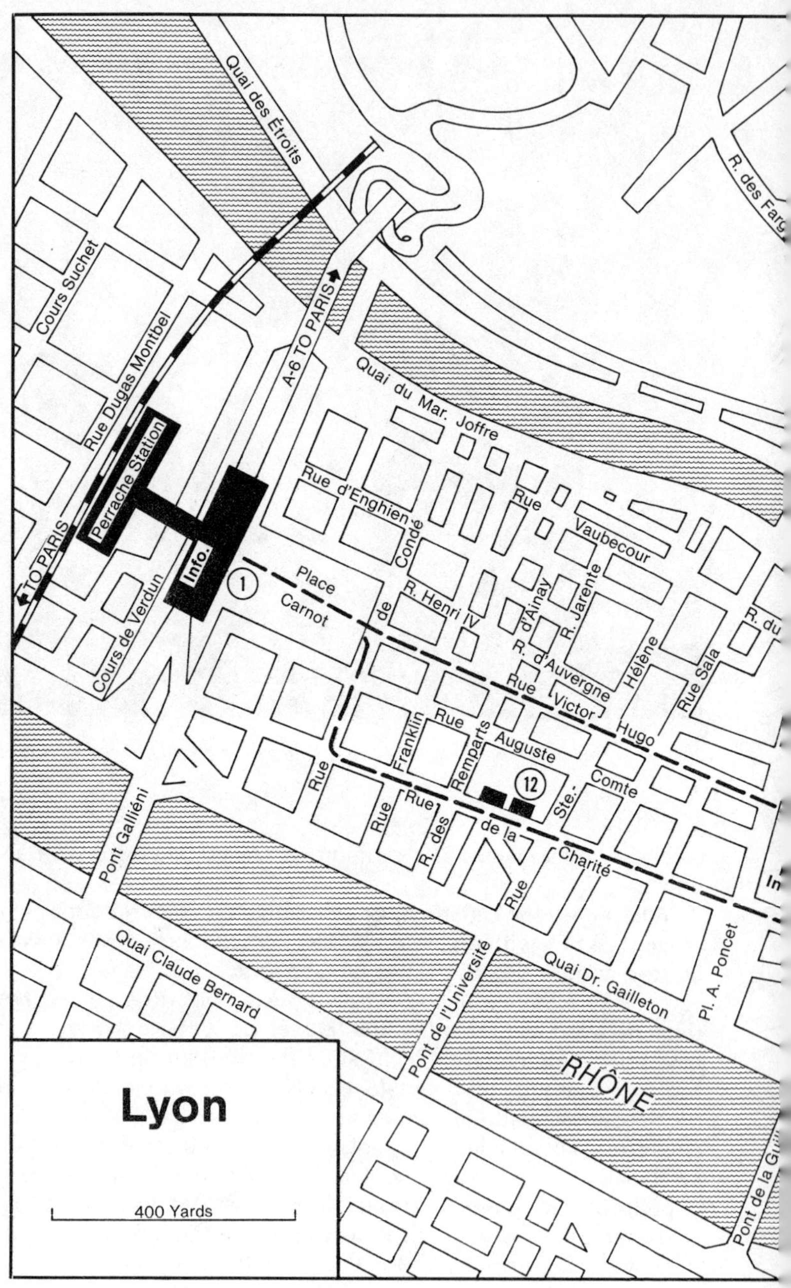
Quai des Étroits
R. des Farg
Cours Suchet
Rue Dugas Montbel
A-6 TO PARIS
Quai du Mar. Joffre
Perrache Station
TO PARIS
Info.
Rue d'Enghien
Condé
Rue
Vaubecour
Place
Carnot
1
de
R. Henri IV
d'Ainay
R. Jarente
R. d'Auvergne
Hélène
Rue Sala
R. du
Cours de Verdun
Rue
Victor
Hugo
Franklin
Rue
Remparts
Auguste
12
Comte
Ste.-
Rue
Rue
Rue
R. des
de la
Charité
Rue
Pont Galliéni
Quai Claude Bernard
Pont de l'Université
Quai Dr. Gailleton
Pl. A. Poncet
RHÔNE
Pont de la Gui
Lyon
400 Yards

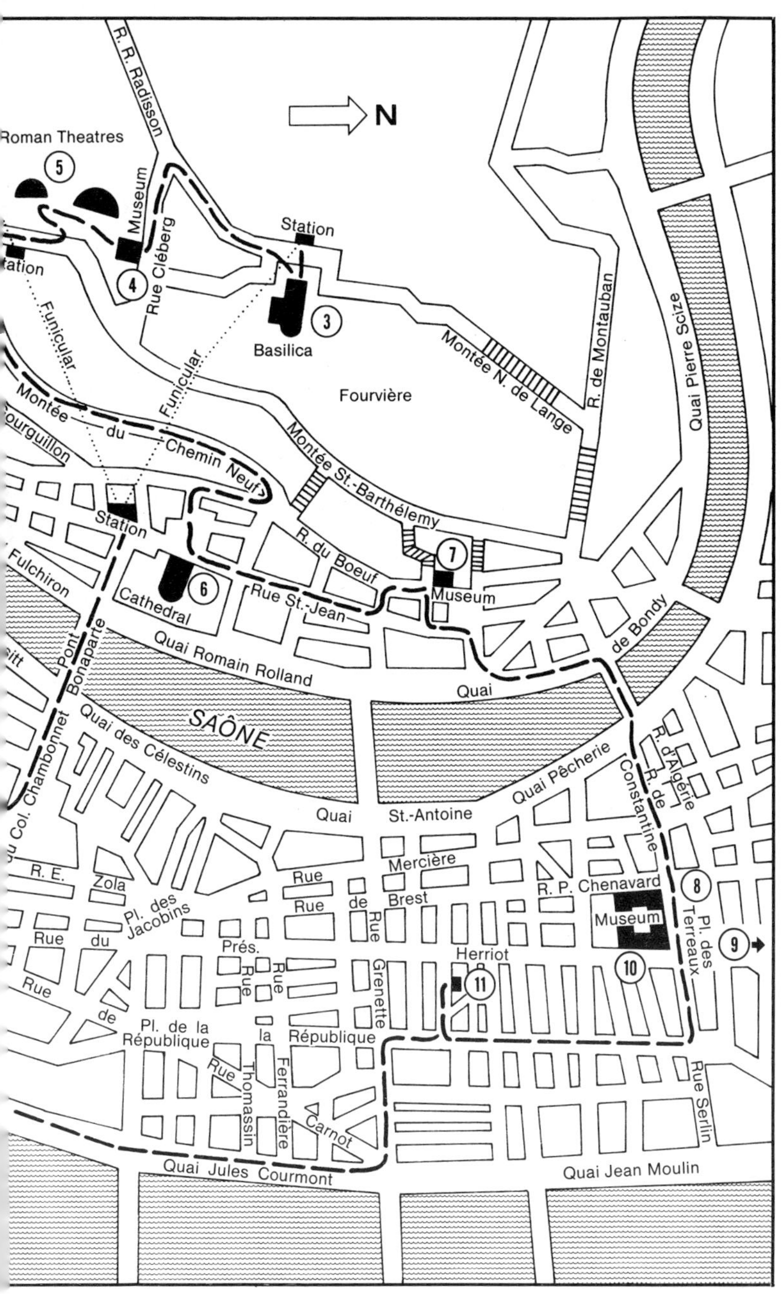

N
Roman Theatres
5
R. R. Radisson
Museum
Rue Cléberg
4
Station
Station
3
Basilica
Fourvière
Funicular
Funicular
Montée N. de Lange
R. de Montauban
Quai Pierre Scize
Montée du Chemin Neuf
Gourguillon
Montée St.-Barthélemy
Station
R. du Boeuf
7
Museum
6
Cathedral
Rue St.-Jean
Fulchiron
Quai Romain Rolland
Quai de Bondy
Pont Bonaparte
SAÔNE
Quai des Célestins
Col. Chambonnet
Quai St.-Antoine
Quai Pêcherie
R. d'Algérie
R. de Constantine
R. E. Zola
Pl. des Jacobins
Rue Mercière
Rue de Brest
R. P. Chenavard
8
Museum
Pl. des Terreaux
9
10
Rue du Prés.
Rue Herriot
Rue Grenette
11
Rue de la République
Pl. de la République
Rue Thomassin
Rue Ferrandière
Carnot
Rue Serlin
Quai Jules Courmont
Quai Jean Moulin

While still in this colorful old area, known as **Vieux Lyon**, you should take the opportunity to explore its numerous tiny streets and alleyways. For many years this was a notorious slum, but recent restoration has made it fashionable once again. Some of its narrowest passages, known as *traboules,* makes interior connections between the ancient buildings and adjacent streets, and were used by members of the Resistance during World War II to hides from the Nazis. Maps guiding you through these mazes are available at the tourist office and elsewhere.

Now follow the map across the river to **Place des Terreaux** (8) with its grandiose fountain by the 19th-century sculptor Frédéric Bartholdi, who also created the Statue of Liberty in New York. Those with boundless energy may want to head north up the Croix-Rousse hill and into the evocative quarter of **Les Traboules** (9, off the map), which offers endless possibilities to *trabouler,* as the sport of exploring the tiny passageways is known. As in Old Lyon, these architectural eccentricities are best seen with a specialized and highly detailed map. Don't get lost.

The ***Musée des Beaux-Arts** (Fine Arts Museum) (10), facing Place des Terreaux, has one of the best collections in France. Originally a Benedictine nunnery, the building is slightly seedy, although not without charm. Its many rooms contain major works covering just about the entire scope of Western art. It is open from 10:30 a.m. to 6 p.m., daily except on Mondays and Tuesdays.

Continue on, following the map down the pedestrianized Rue de la République, to the **Musée de l'Imprimerie et de la Banque** (Printing and Banking Museum) (11), installed in a 15th-century mansion on Rue de la Poulaillerie. This is a splendid place to visit if the subject holds any interest to you. It is open daily except on Mondays and Tuesdays.

The walking route now swings over to the banks of the Rhône, then leads past Place Bellecour (2) to two more attractions. The **Musée des Arts-Décoratifs** (12) and its next-door neighbor, the **Musée Historique des Tissus** (Historical Museum of Textiles), share the same admission ticket. As its name implies, the Decorative Arts Museum features exquisite room settings, primarily of the 18th century. If you like fabrics you will love the Textile Museum, which has the largest collection in the world. Both are open from 10 a.m. to noon and 2–5:30 p.m., daily except on Mondays and holidays. From here it is only a short walk back to Perrache Station.

A Daytrip from Paris

Tours

Tours, the major city of the Loire region, appears at first glance to be nothing but an endless sprawl of modern industries; certainly prosperous but hardly attractive to tourists. In its ancient heart, however, lurk enough medieval and Renaissance treasures to make this a highly worthwhile daytrip from Paris. A visit here is further enhanced by the presence of a large student population, breathing life into the picturesque alleyways of the Old Town district. All of this activity makes Tours one of the better spots in France to just relax at outdoor cafés and enjoy the passing parade.

GETTING THERE:

TGV trains *(reservations required)* depart Montparnasse Station in Paris frequently for the 70-minute ride to Tours. **Regular trains** take about 2¼ hours for the trip, and leave from Austerlitz Station in Paris. In either case it may be necessary to change trains at St.-Pierre-des-Corps on the outskirts of Tours. Return service runs until late evening.

By car, Tours is 145 miles southwest of Paris via the A-10 Autoroute, going by way of Orléans.

PRACTICALITIES:

Avoid coming to Tours on a Tuesday or major holiday, when many of its attractions are closed. The local **Tourist Information Office**, phone 47–05–58–08, is in front of the train station. **Bicycles** may be rented at the station. Tours has a **population** of about 136,000 and is in the **Loire** region.

FOOD AND DRINK:

Tours is once again a great gastronomic center, with excellent restaurants spread all over the sprawling city. Some good choices in the area covered by the walking tour are:

Barrier (101 Av. de la Tranchée, just across the Pont Wilson bridge) Classic French and Touraine cuisine from a renowned chef. Proper dress expected, for reservations call 47–54–20–39. X: Sun. $$$

Les Tuffeaux (19 Rue Lavoisier, across from the Château) A restful place for contemporary cuisine. X: Sun., Mon. lunch. $$

La Rôtisserie Tourangelle (23 Rue du Commerce, by the Hôtel Gouin) An old-time favorite for traditional dining infused with new ideas. X: Sun. eve., Mon. off-season, early Mar. $$

Le Lys (63 Rue Blaise-Pascal, 2 blocks southwest of the station) Sophisticated modern cuisine. X: Sun. eve. $ and $$

Les Trois Canards (16 Rue de la Rôtisserie, 1 block south of Place Plumereau) A good value in romantic dining. X: Sat. eve., Sun. $

Be sure to try the local Loire wines, especially the Vouvray!

SUGGESTED TOUR:

Leave the **train station** *(Gare)* (1) and follow the map past the tourist office and the Préfecture, housed in an 18th-century convent, to the ***Musée des Beaux-Arts** (Fine Arts Museum) (2). This occupies the former Archbishop's Palace, which dates from the 17th and 18th centuries and incorporates vestiges of the Gallo-Roman town wall. The collections displayed in its elegant rooms were begun around 1800 with pieces seized during the French Revolution. Today they range all the way from the Italian Primitives to the most contemporary Moderns, including such masterpieces as Mantegna's *Christ in the Garden of Olives* and *The Resurrection,* Ruben's *Madonna and Child,* and Rembrandt's *Flight into Egypt*. The museum's courtyard and **gardens** are quite nice, shaded by a gigantic cedar tree planted in 1804. Visits may be made on any day except Tuesdays and major holidays, from 9 a.m. to 12:45 p.m. and 2–6 p.m.

Next to the museum stands the **Cathedral of St.-Gatien** (3), built between 1220 and 1547 in a variety of styles tracing the entire evolution of the French Gothic form. Its **flying buttresses** are particularly dramatic, especially when seen from the rear. Inside, the cathedral is most noted for its glorious 13th-century **stained-glass windows** in the chancel; and for the **tomb** of Charles VIII's infant children, guarded by small angels, just off the south transept. Try to see the adjoining **cloisters**, known as the **Psalette**, which has an elegant Renaissance staircase and offers close-up views of the buttresses. The cathedral is closed between noon and 2 p.m.

One block to the north, facing the Loire River, are the scanty remains of the great **Château** (4) built in 1160 by Henry II of England. Part of the original structure, the **Tour de Guise**, has been restored and now houses an interesting wax museum called the **Historial de Touraine**, in which some 165 figures in 31 settings act out the history of the region from the 4th century until modern times. Operated by the Grévin Museum of Paris, it is open daily but closes between noon and 2 p.m. during the off-season. There is also a **tropical aquarium** with a separate admission.

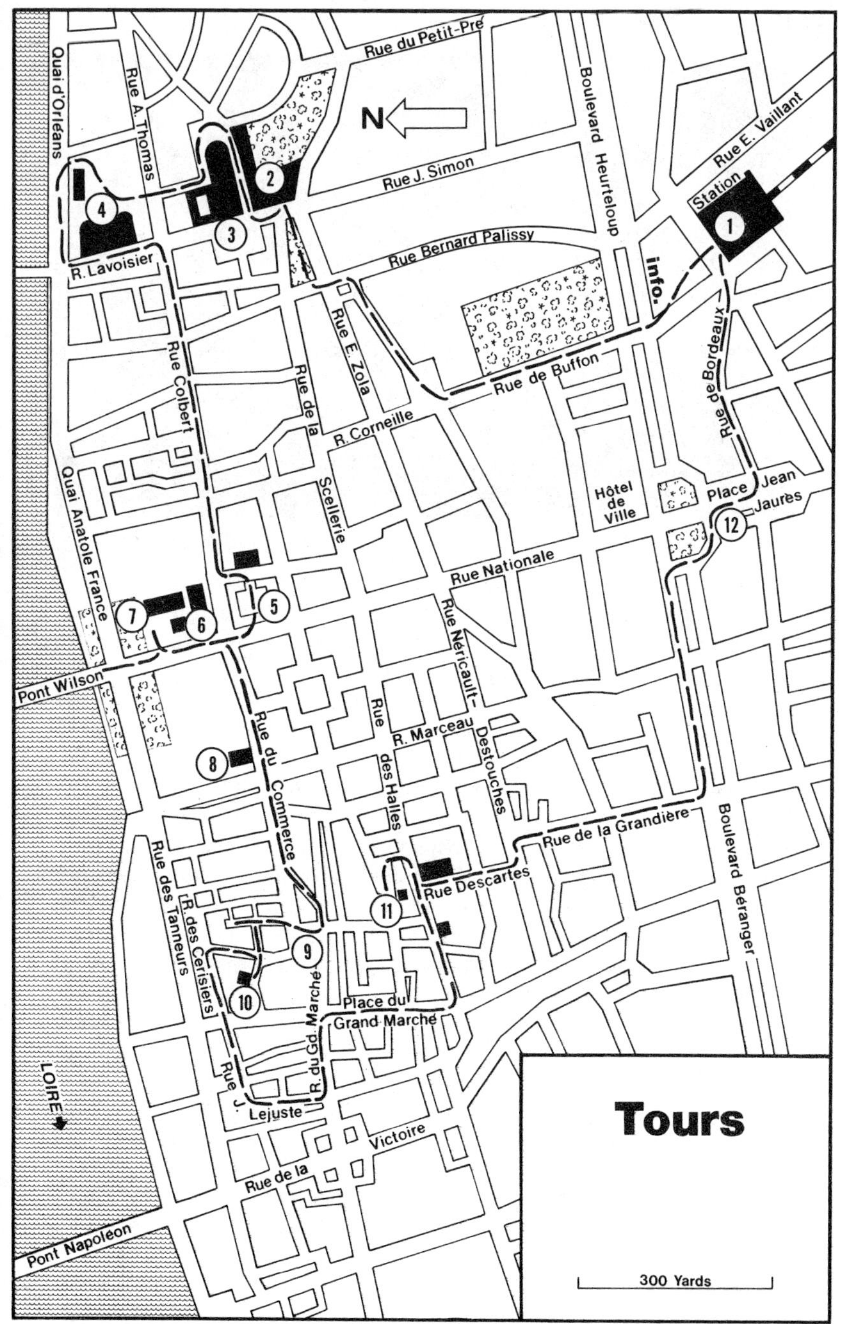

Tours
N
Rue du Petit-Pré
Quai d'Orléans
Rue A. Thomas
Boulevard Heurteloup
Rue E. Vaillant
Station
Rue J. Simon
Rue Bernard Palissy
R. Lavoisier
info.
Rue de Bordeaux
Rue E. Zola
Rue de Buffon
Rue Colbert
Rue de la Scellerie
R. Corneille
Quai Anatole France
Hôtel de Ville
Place Jean Jaurès
Rue Nationale
Rue Néricault-Destouches
Pont Wilson
Rue du Commerce
Rue des Halles
R. Marceau
Rue de la Grandière
Boulevard Béranger
Rue Descartes
Rue des Tanneurs
R. des Cerisiers
Place du Grand Marché
R. du Gd. Marché
Rue J. Lejuste
LOIRE
Rue de la Victoire
Pont Napoléon
300 Yards
1
2
3
4
5
6
7
8
9
10
11
12

In the Wax Museum

Follow the map down Rue Colbert, ambling through the **Beaune-Semblançay Garden** (5) with its nicely sculpted 16th-century fountain and the remains of a Renaissance mansion.

The nearby **Église St.-Julien** dates from the 13th century and has a belfry porch from the 11th, part of an abbey founded in the early 6th century by Clovis, king of the Franks. The ancient cellars of the complex now house the **Musée des Vins de Touraine** (6), a museum devoted to the local wines and their enjoyment. It is open during the same times as the Beaux-Arts Museum. Almost adjacent to it is the **Musée du Compagnonnage** (Craft Guilds Museum) (7), located upstairs in a former monks' dormitory above a chapter house. This fascinating museum displays the masterpieces submitted by candidates for membership in craft guilds, many of which are bizarre in concept but of extraordinary quality. Again, it is open during the same times as the Beaux-Arts Museum. From here you might want to stroll out on the **Pont Wilson** bridge for a good view of the Loire River, then return.

Continue down Rue du Commerce to the 16th-century **Hôtel Gouin** (8), a Renaissance mansion of exceptional beauty. Today it is home to an archaeological museum with collections of artifacts from the Gallo-Roman, medieval, and Renaissance periods. It is closed on Fridays in the off-season and during December and January.

You are now entering ***Vieux Tours** (Old Tours), a highly restored and very picturesque neighborhood of gabled façades and half-timbered houses connected by narrow pedestrian alleyways. Its most delightful square is **Place Plumereau** (9), lined with 15th-century houses

Place Plumereau

and a multitude of **outdoor cafés;** the perfect spot for a break in your walk. When you feel like moving on, head north through a vaulted passageway to **Place St.-Pierre-le-Puellier** with its open **Gallo-Roman excavations**.

Wander over to the **Musée du Gemmail** (10) on Rue Des Moûrier. Installed in a 19th-century mansion, this museum is devoted to the highly unusual (and very French) art of making three-dimensional back-lit creations from broken fragments of colored glass. It is open from April through mid-October, on Tuesdays through Sundays, from 10 a.m. to noon and 2:30–6 p.m.

Continue on the very attractive Rue Briçonnet and follow the map around, passing many old houses, artists' studios, and craft workshops, until you wind up at **Place de Châteauneuf** (11). This was the site of the once-great **Basilique St.-Martin**, built in the 11th century over the tomb of the 4th-century saint. For centuries this was a stop on the pilgrims' route to Spain, but it was sacked by the Huguenots in 1562 and fell to ruin during the Revolution. All that remains today is the **Tour de l'Horloge** on the Rues des Halles and the **Tour Charlemagne** on Rue de Châteauneuf.

Head south on Rue Descartes and Rue de la Grandière, then turn left on Boulevard Béranger to **Place Jean-Juarès** (12). Facing the splendid **Hôtel de Ville** (Town Hall) of 1905, this shady square is lined with inviting **sidewalk cafés**, where you can once again just sit down and enjoy the fine old town. The best way to return to the train station is via Rue de Bordeaux.

A Daytrip from Paris

Amboise

Rising majestically above the banks of the Loire, the magnificent château of Amboise totally dominates its attractive little town. A castle has stood on this rocky spur, guarding the strategic bridgehead since Gallo-Roman times, when it was known as *Ambacia*. The present structure, however, is a product of the 15th century and incorporates some of the earliest examples of Renaissance architecture in France. Charles VIII, who was born and raised at Amboise, had invaded Italy in 1494. While there, he became captivated by the new Italian style and brought some of its craftsmen back with him to finish off his favorite château.

The real effect of the Renaissance came with the succession to the throne of François I in 1515. This outstanding king also spent his childhood at Amboise and continued residence there during the first years of his reign. It was he who invited Leonardo da Vinci to France, installing him in a luxurious home just blocks from the château, where the great artist and inventor spent the last years of his life.

GETTING THERE:

Trains leave Austerlitz Station in Paris in the morning for Amboise, a trip of under 2½ hours. Be careful to get on the correct car as some trains split en route. Return service operates until early evening. A change at Orléans or Blois might be necessary.

By car, take the A-10 Autoroute to Blois, then the D-751 or N-152 into Amboise, which is 137 miles southwest of Paris.

PRACTICALITIES:

Amboise may be visited at any time. The Clos Lucé is closed in January, and the Postal Museum on Mondays and some holidays. The local **Tourist Information Office**, phone 47–57–01–37, is on the Quai du Général-de-Gaulle, near the bridge. **Bicycles** may be rented at the station. Amboise has a **population** of about 11,000 and is in the **Loire** region.

FOOD AND DRINK

Being a popular tourist center, the town has quite a few restaurants and cafés. Some of the better choices are:

Le Manoir Saint-Thomas (Place Richelieu, 3 blocks south of the château) Superb local specialties in a Renaissance building

The Château and the Loire from the Gardens

with a garden. Proper dress expected. For reservations phone 47–57–22–52. X: Mon., mid-Jan. to Mid-March. $$$

L'Auberge du Mail (32 Quai du Général-de-Gaulle, 4 blocks west of St.-Denis Church) A delightful little country inn. X: Fri. in low season, early Dec. $$

La Brèche (26 Rue Jules Ferry, 2 blocks south of the train station) A small inn with good meals. X: Sun. eve, Mon. in low season, Dec. $

SUGGESTED TOUR:

Leave the **train station** (1) and follow the map across the Loire to the ***Château** (2), perched dramatically above the river and town. You may prefer to have lunch before visiting any of the sights as they are closed between noon and 2 p.m. except in July and August. A long ramp leads up to the castle grounds. Climb this and join one of the frequent guided tours, which are given in French with a printed English translation provided. During its time of glory the château was considerably larger than it is today, much of it having been demolished in the early 19th century for lack of maintenance funds. Some of the best parts, however, remained intact and have been beautifully restored to the delight of today's visitors.

The tour begins with the exquisite **Chapel of St.-Hubert**, dedicated to the patron saint of huntsmen. Begun in 1491, shortly before Charles

VIII acquired his passion for the Renaissance, it is a triumph of the Flamboyant Gothic style. What are thought to be the bones of Leonardo da Vinci are buried here, under a slab in the north transept.

Following this you will enter the **Logis du Roi** (King's Apartments), consisting of two wings, one Gothic and the other Renaissance. These are the only major buildings of any size left at the castle. Their interiors are splendidly decorated in a variety of period styles, ranging from the 15th through the 19th centuries. From the fascinating **Minimes Tower** with its spiral equestrian ramp there is a stunning view up and down the Loire Valley. Don't miss taking a stroll through the **gardens** behind the château after the guided tour has ended. The château is open every day, from 9 a.m. to noon and 2–6:30 p.m., closing an hour earlier in winter. In July and August it remains open over lunch.

A ten-minute walk along Rue Victor-Hugo leads to ***Clos Lucé** (3). This was the home of Leonardo da Vinci, that visionary genius of the Renaissance, from 1516 until his death three years later. Prior to that it was the residence of Anne of Brittany, the wife of King Charles VIII. The manor house has marvelous period furnishings, worth a visit in themselves, but the main interest lies in the many ***models of Leonardo's inventions**, built by IBM from his original plans. Frequent guided tours, with a printed English translation, are conducted daily between 9 a.m. and 6 p.m. During the summer the hours are from 9 a.m. to 7 p.m. The house is closed during January.

Return along Rue Victor-Hugo and follow the map to the **Postal Museum** (4). Located in an elegant 16th-century mansion, the museum features an intriguing exhibition of the history of transportation from horse-drawn coaches to modern airlines. There are also, of course, many rare stamps to be seen, along with old manuscripts and engravings. The museum is open from 9:30 a.m. to noon and 2–6:30 p.m., closing at 5 p.m. during the winter season. It is closed on Mondays and some holidays.

Continue on to the 15th-century **Beffroi** (Clock Tower) (5), a picturesque structure built by Charles VIII on earlier foundations. Now follow the pedestrians-only Rue Nationale to the **Église St.-Denis** (6). This 12th-century example of the Romanesque style was built on the site of a Roman temple. Step inside for a look at some exceptional works of art including a fine *Pietà* and an astonishingly realistic sculpture of a drowned woman.

Returning via Quai du Général-de-Gaulle you will pass an outstanding modern fountain designed by Max Ernst, the tourist office, the 15th-century Église St.-Florentin, and the 16th-century Hôtel de Ville (Town Hall).

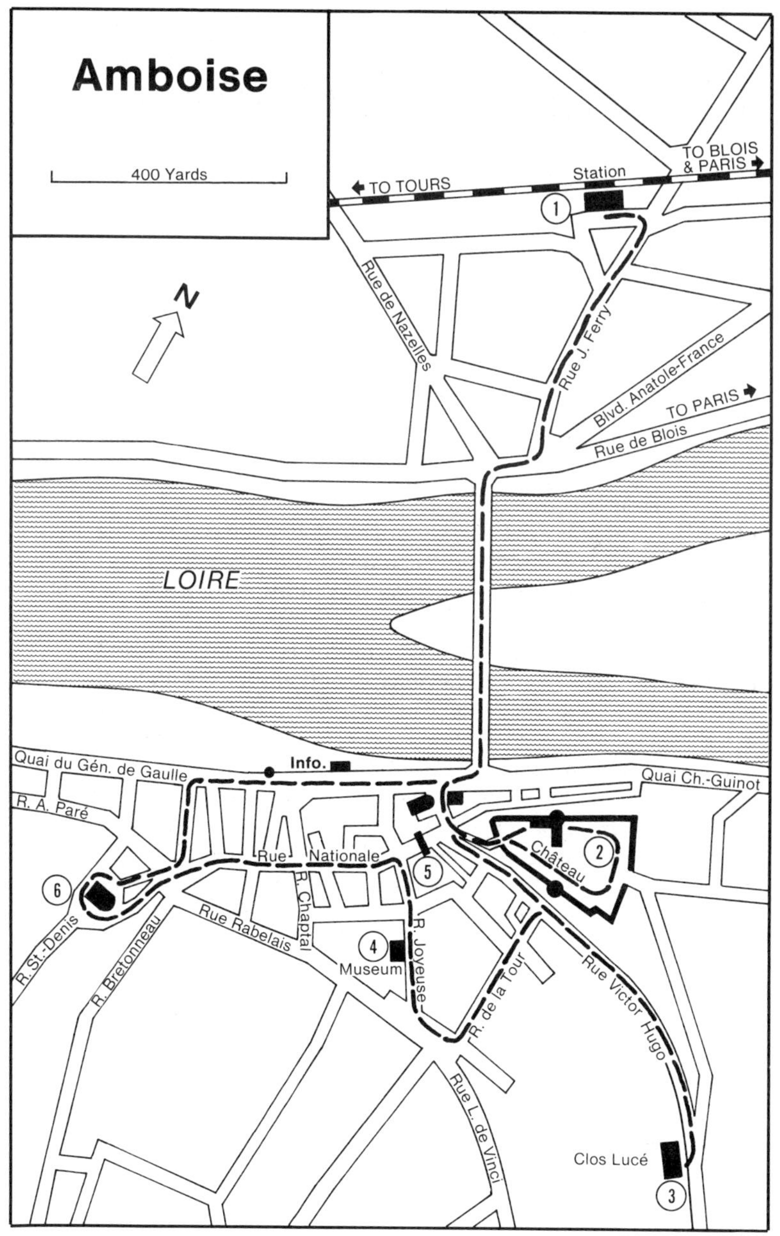
Amboise
400 Yards
N
TO TOURS
Station
TO BLOIS & PARIS
1
Rue de Nazelles
Rue J. Ferry
Blvd. Anatole-France
TO PARIS
Rue de Blois
LOIRE
Info.
Quai du Gén. de Gaulle
Quai Ch.-Guinot
R. A. Paré
Rue Nationale
Château
2
5
6
R. Chaptal
R. Joyeuse
Rue Rabelais
R. St.-Denis
R. Bretonneau
4
Museum
R. de la Tour
Rue Victor Hugo
Rue L. de Vinci
Clos Lucé
3

A Daytrip from Nice

Villefranche, Cap-Ferrat, and Beaulieu

Despite rampant commercialization, isolated pockets of the romantic old Riviera do still exist, largely unchanged since the Roaring Twenties. This classic daytrip from Nice takes you just a few miles in distance, but decades in time, to some very unusual sights in a setting of spectacular natural beauty.

The picturesque old port of Villefranche is a largely unspoiled 18th-century town whose ancient streets sometimes tunnel under the jumble of colorful houses. Among its attractions is a bizarre art museum in the dungeons of a 16th-century fortress, and a highly unusual chapel decorated by Jean Coacteau. From there you can walk (or take a bus) along the coast and out onto the Cap Ferrat peninsula, whose lush Mediterranean vegetation shelters homes of the rich and famous. One of the most magnificent of these, a villa built for the Baroness Ephrussi de Rothschild, is open to the public, as are the lovely gardens.

Passing through the port village of St.-Jean-Cap-Ferrat, the route follows a coastal promenade to the old resort of Beaulieu-sur-Mer, snuggled between mountains and the sea, which is noted for its exceptionally mild climate. Its sole tourist attraction, the strange Villa Kérylos, is alone worth a trip.

GETTING THERE:

Trains depart Nice frequently for the 7-minute ride to Villefranche-sur-Mer. Be sure to take a local. Return service from Beaulieu-sur-Mer operates until late evening. The same line serves practically all spots on the Riviera coast.

By car, take the N-98 *Basse Corniche* road, which begins in Nice as Boulevard Carnot. Exit to the center of Villefranche-sur-Mer, less than 4 miles to the east. By modifying the route, you can drive the entire suggested tour route and not have to walk.

PRACTICALITIES:

The Rothschild estate is closed on Mondays and all of November, while the Villa Kérylos closes on Mondays from September through June. The Cocteau chapel is closed on Fridays, and the Citadel on Tuesdays. The local **Tourist Information Offices** are: **Villefranche**, 1 Square Binon, 3 blocks west of the Citadel, phone 93-80-73-68; **St.-Jean-Cap-Ferrat**, 59 Avenue Denis-Semeria, 3 blocks south of the Rothschild estate, phone 93-01-36-86; and **Beaulieu**, by the train station, phone 93-01-02-21. This daytrip is in the **Côte d'Azur** region.

FOOD AND DRINK:

Some restaurant suggestions are:

In Villefranche-sur-Mer:

Le Saint-Pierre (1 Quai Courbet, near the Cocteau chapel) Classical cuisine overlooking the sea, with a glassed-in terrace. $$ and $$$

Provençal (4 Av. Maréchal-Joffre, 2 blocks northwest of the Citadel) A small hotel with good-value meals. X: Nov., Dec. $

In St.-Jean-Cap-Ferrat:

Le Provençal (2 Av. Denis-Semeria, 1 block west of the port) Specializes in fish, especially bouillabaisse. X: Tues. $$

Le Sloop (at the north end of the port) Inventive cuisine on a terrace facing the yachts. $$

In Beaulieu-sur-Mer:

African Queen (Port de Plaisance, near Villa Kérylos) A huge brasserie with an open terrace, renowned for its seafood. $$

La Pignatelle (10 Rue Quincenet, in the town center) A very popular local bistro, always crowded. Excellent value. X: Wed. $

SUGGESTED TOUR:

Leave the **Villefranche Station** (1) and follow the map to **Rue du Poilu**, a main street of the Old Town *(Vieille Ville)*. Parallel to this, towards the sea, is the mysterious **Rue Obscure**, a dark passageway tunneling beneath the brightly-colored houses. One block to the west stands the **Église St.-Michel** (2), a 17th-century church in the Italian Baroque style, noted for its striking figure of Christ carved from a single piece of wood by a forgotten 17th-century convict.

Continue on Rue de l'Église and the vaulted Rue Obscure to the **Old Port**, founded in the 14th century as a duty-free area. It faces a sheltered bay of exceptional depth, a roadstead that easily accommodates large liners and warships. Next to the harbor is the **Chapelle**

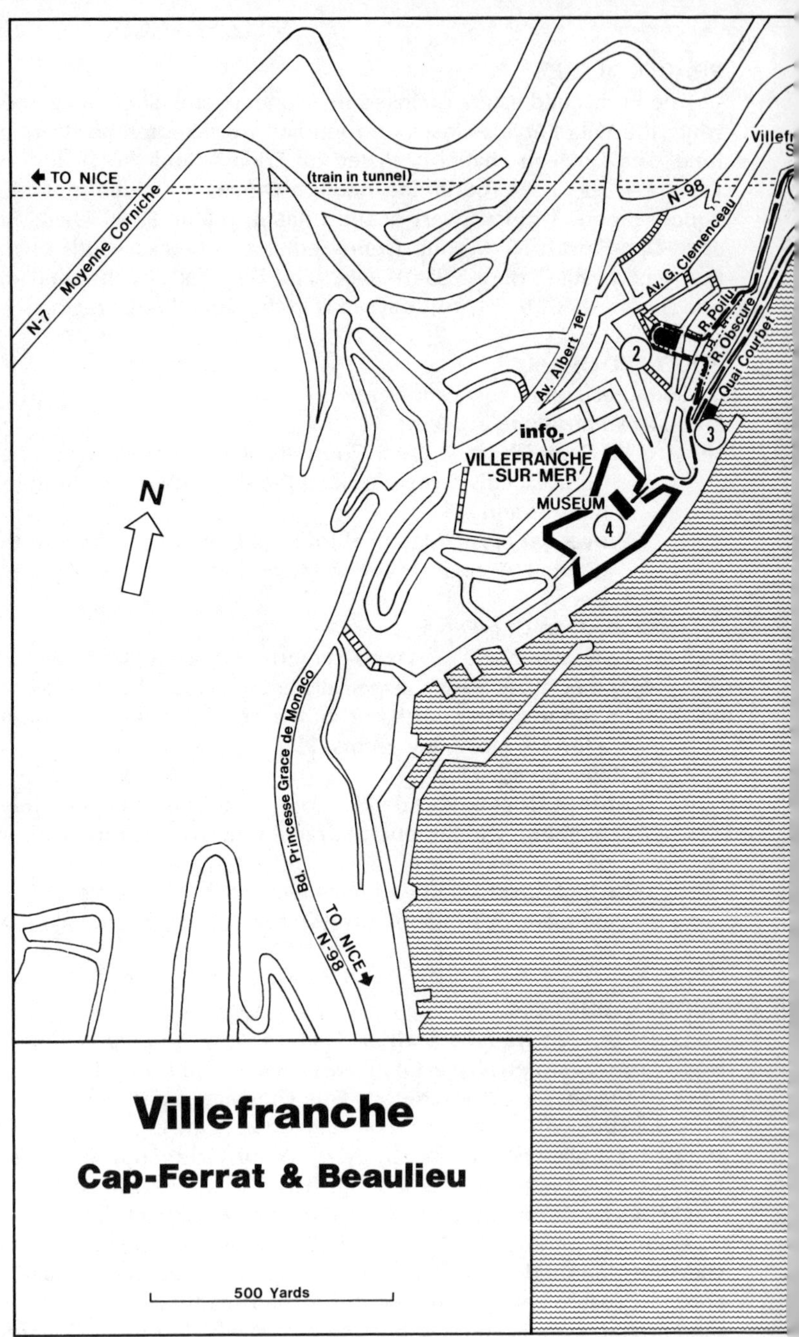

Villefranche

Cap-Ferrat & Beaulieu

500 Yards

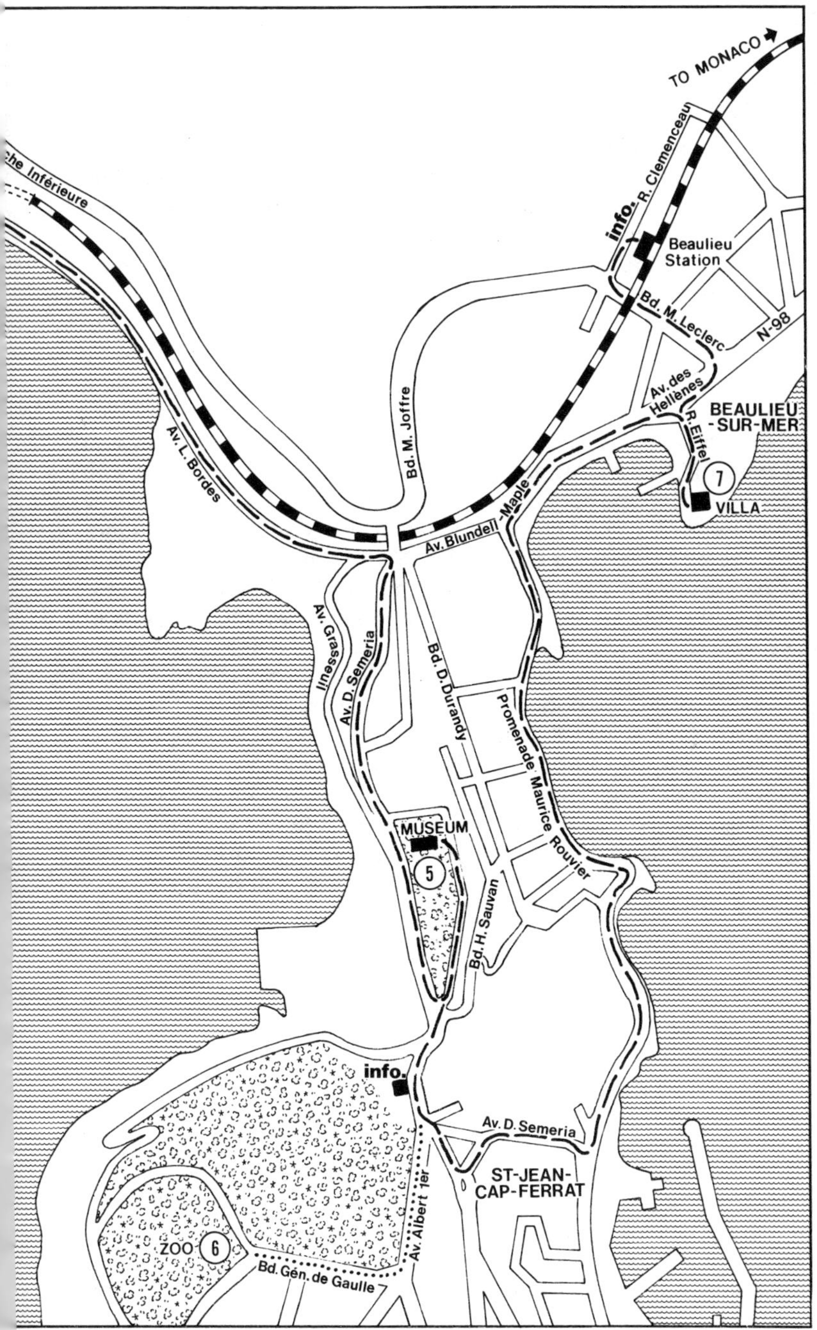
TO MONACO
info.
R. Clemenceau
Beaulieu Station
Bd. M. Leclerc
N-98
Av. des Hellènes
R. Eiffel
BEAULIEU-SUR-MER
7
VILLA
Av. Blundell-Maple
Bd. M. Joffre
Av. L. Bordes
Inférieure
Av. Grasseuil
Av. D. Semeria
Bd. D. Durandy
Promenade Maurice Rouvier
MUSEUM
5
Bd. H. Sauvan
info.
Av. D. Semeria
ST-JEAN-CAP-FERRAT
Av. Albert 1er
ZOO
6
Bd. Gén. de Gaulle

St.-Pierre (3), a 14th-century fishermen's chapel that was decorated in 1957 by the avant-garde writer and film maker Jean Cocteau. His staring-eye ceramics represent the flames of the Apocalypse, while the pastel **frescoes** depict the life of Saint Peter, gypsies, and the women of Villefranche. It is open daily except on Fridays, from 9 a.m. to noon and 2:30–7 p.m., with shorter hours in the off-season, but closed from mid-November through mid-December.

The huge **Citadel** (4) overlooking the port was built in the 16th-century by the dukes of Savoy, who then ruled this region. Today it houses the **Volti Museum**, where strange modern sculptures by a local artist are displayed in the courtyard and deep in the surrounding casemates. The museum is usually open daily except on Tuesdays and on Sunday mornings, from 11 a.m. to noon and 2–5 p.m.

Now follow the map on foot (or take a bus) around the bay and out onto the **Cap Ferrat peninsula**, a hilly spit of land covered with exotic vegetation and dotted with the mansions of the super rich. Nearly all of these are exceedingly private, but you can visit one of the grandest of them all, the ***Villa Ephrussi de Rothschild** (5). Built in 1912, it was bequeathed in 1934 to the Académie des Beaux-Arts and is now the **Ile-de-France Museum**, where the rather eclectic collections of the Baroness de Rothschild are displayed in a jewel of a setting. Among the many treasures are Renaissance furniture, Aubusson tapestries, Sèvres porcelains, period costumes, and paintings by Boucher and Fragonard. One gallery is devoted to the 19th-century Impressionists, with important works by Renoir, Sisley, and Monet. Surrounding the villa are some 17 acres of fabulous ***gardens** in various styles, some with dramatic views over the Mediterranean. The estate is open during July and August, on Tuesdays through Sundays, from 3–7 p.m.; during September, October, and December through June, on Tuesdays through Sundays, from 2–6 p.m. The gardens alone are also open on the same days, from 9 a.m. to noon. Admission to the villa includes a guided tour.

While in the neighborhood, you might want to visit the nearby **Jardin Animé** (6), a private **zoo** on an estate that once belonged to King Léopold II of Belgium. Exotic animals, birds, and butterflies can be viewed in the setting of a tropical garden. Trained chimpanzees give performances six times a day. The zoo is open daily from 9:30 a.m. to 6:30 p.m., closing at 5:30 from October through April.

The route leads across the peninsula to the former fishing village of **St.-Jean-Cap-Ferrat**, now a small resort. From its harbor follow the **Promenade Maurice Rouvier**, a coastal pedestrian path with fabulous views, to the old resort of **Beaulieu-sur-Mer** . The sole tourist attraction in this lovely town is the curious ***Villa Kérylos** (7). Built in 1900 by the archaeologist Théodore Reinach as an exact replica of a Greek

View of the mainland from the Cap Ferrat Peninsula

villa from antiquity, it is perched on a promontory overlooking the town and bay. Its **library** displays genuine art from that era, while the furniture is mostly reproductions copied from those depicted on ancient vases. Classified as a historic monument, the villa has belonged to the Institut de France since the owner's death in 1928. Entering it is like stepping back three millennia in time, at least visually, yet it retains a strangely decadent ambiance from the early 1900s. Don't miss this very unusual sight, which is open daily during July and August, from 3–7 p.m.; and on Tuesdays through Sundays the rest of the year, from 2–6 p.m. From here it is a short walk to the **Beaulieu Train Station** (8).

A Daytrip from Nice

Antibes

Dating from the 4th century B.C., the ancient Greek trading post of *Antipolis* grew up to become the delightfully unpretentious Antibes of today. The narrow streets of its picturesque Old Town are an open invitation for pleasant wanderings, particularly to the seaside promenade and its castle, which today houses the fabulous Picasso Museum. Ambitious walkers, or those with cars or rented bicycles, can also explore the lovely Cap d'Antibes, a place of great natural beauty.

GETTING THERE:

Trains depart Nice frequently for the 15-minute ride to Antibes, with returns until late evening. The same line serves practically all coastal towns on the Riviera.

By car, use the N-7 or N-98 road. Antibes is 15 miles southwest of Nice.

PRACTICALITIES:

The Picasso Museum is closed on Tuesdays, some major holidays, and during November. Good weather is essential for a pleasant side trip to Cap d'Antibes. The local **Tourist Information Office**, phone 93-33-95-64, is at 11 Place du Général-de-Gaulle, 5 blocks south of the train station. **Bicycles** may be rented at the station. The town's full name is Antibes-Juan-les-Pins. It has a **population** of about 75,000, and is in the **Côte d'Azur** region.

FOOD AND DRINK:

Antibes has a broad range of restaurants in all price brackets. Some excellent choices are:

Bacon (Blvd. de Bacon, near Pointe Bacon) Renowned for its fresh seafood. Proper dress expected. For reservations phone 93-61-50-02. X: Sun. eve., Mon., mid-Nov. through Jan. $$$

L'Auberge Provençale (61 Place Nationale, 3 blocks west of the Picasso Museum) A charming country inn with modern variations on traditional cuisine. X: Mon., Tues. lunch. $$

Restaurant du Bastion (1 Ave. du Général-Maizière, next to the Archaeological Museum) Regional specialties in a picturesque garden restaurant. X: Sun. eve., Mon., Feb. $$

A game of Boules *at the Bastion St.-André*

L'Oursin (16 Rue de la République, 6 blocks west of the Picasso Museum) A popular place for seafood. X: Sun. eve., Mon., Aug. $$

L'Armoise (2 Rue de la Touraque, 2 blocks southwest of the Picasso Museum) A very small place with loads of atmosphere; nouvelle and Provençale cuisine. X: Wed. Nov. $$

SUGGESTED TOUR:

Leave the **train station** (1) and follow the town map, passing the tourist office on Place du Général-de-Gaulle. Rue de la République leads to Place Nationale. You are now entering the **Old Town** with its picturesque maze of narrow streets.

Thread your way through past the colorful market place on Cours Masséna to the **Château Grimaldi** (2), home of the marvelous ***Musée Picasso.** Built between the 13th and 16th centuries, this medieval stronghold overlooking the sea was for centuries home to a branch of the ruling Grimaldi family of Monaco. After seeing service as a governor's residence and later as an army barracks, the castle was bought by the town after World War I for use as a museum.

In 1946, Pablo Picasso was invited to use part of it as a studio. During the months that followed he produced some of his greatest works, many of which the artist later donated to the museum in memory of

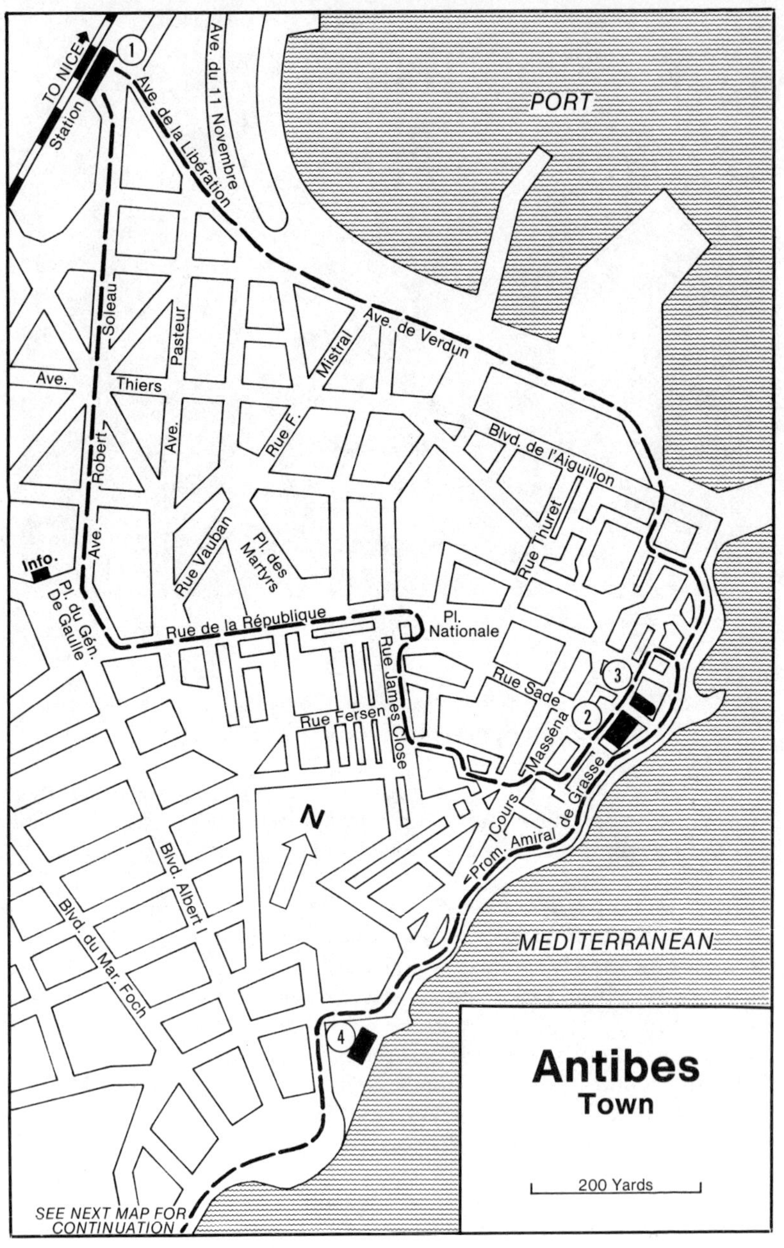
TO NICE
Station
Ave. du 11 Novembre
Ave. de la Libération
PORT
Soleau
Pasteur
Mistral
Ave. de Verdun
Ave.
Thiers
Robert
Ave.
Rue F.
Blvd. de l'Aiguillon
Rue Thuret
Ave.
Info.
Rue Vauban
Pl. des Martyrs
Pl. du Gén. De Gaulle
Rue de la République
Pl. Nationale
Rue James Close
Rue Sade
Rue Fersen
Masséna
Cours
de Grasse
Prom. Amiral
N
Blvd. Albert I
Blvd. du Mar. Foch
MEDITERRANEAN
Antibes
Town
200 Yards
SEE NEXT MAP FOR CONTINUATION

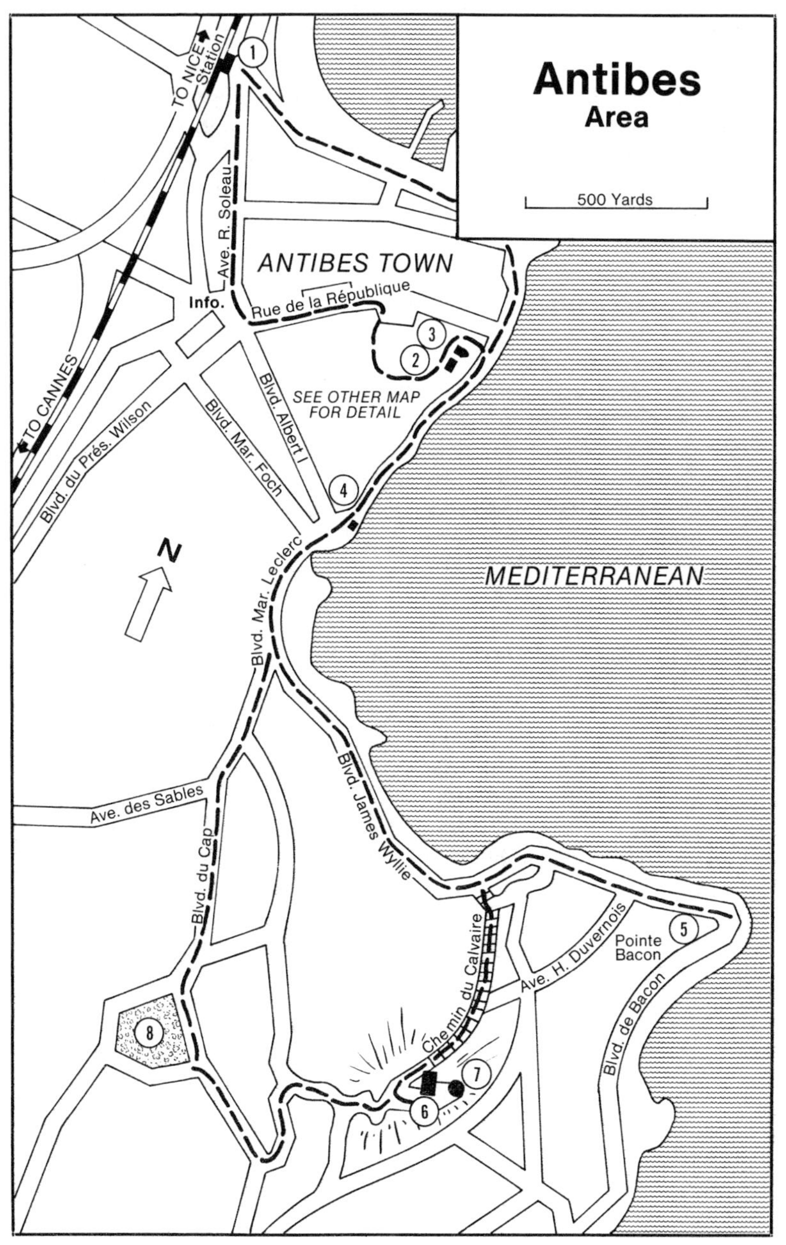

Antibes
Area
500 Yards
TO NICE
Station
ANTIBES TOWN
Ave. R. Soleau
Info.
Rue de la République
TO CANNES
SEE OTHER MAP
FOR DETAIL
Blvd. du Prés. Wilson
Blvd. Mar. Foch
Blvd. Albert I
N
MEDITERRANEAN
Blvd. Mar. Leclerc
Blvd. James Wyllie
Ave. des Sables
Blvd. du Cap
Chemin du Calvaire
Ave. H. Duvernois
Pointe
Bacon
Blvd. de Bacon
1
2
3
4
5
6
7
8

the happy times he had there. Although primarily devoted to Picasso, the museum also displays works by other contemporary artists along with some archaeological pieces. To wander through its well-arranged rooms and passageways is a sheer joy. Don't miss the sculpture-filled **terrace** overlooking the sea. The museum is open daily from 10 a.m. to noon and 2–6 p.m., but closed on Tuesdays, some holidays, and during November.

The **Church of the Immaculate Conception** (3), next door, is still referred to as a cathedral although it lost that status as far back as 1244. Much of the present structure is from the 17th century, but the 12th-century belfry is original. Step inside to see the noted altarpiece in the south transept, attributed to Louis Bréa.

Now meander through the oldest parts of Antibes and follow the 16th-century ramparts to the **Musée d'Archeologie** (4) in the 17th-century Bastion of St.-André. The archaeological collections in this museum, covering some 4,000 years of local history, include jewelry, coins, and pottery. They may be seen from 9 a.m. to noon and 2–6 p.m. (7 p.m. in summer), daily except on Tuesdays, some holidays, and during November.

Ambitious walkers have a real treat ahead of them. Turn to the area map and follow the coastal road past the public beach to **Pointe Bacon** on Cap d'Antibes (5), a distance of slightly over one mile. The views from here are spectacular, encompassing the Bay of Angels as far as Nice. Those with cars or rental bicycles can, of course, drive or pedal there and continue completely around the wooded peninsula, long a haunt of the very rich.

Retrace your steps and turn into a stepped path called Chemin du Calvaire. This leads uphill past some Stations of the Cross to the ***La Garoupe Plateau**, which offers a sweeping panorama of the seacoast, extending from Cannes to Nice, with part of the Alps in the background. The delightful **Chapel of Notre-Dame-de-la-Garoupe** (6), dating in part from the Middle Ages, has a strange and wonderful interior. Its walls are covered with touchingly naïve ex-votos offered by sailors and others in thanks for deliverance from some awful fate. You could literally spend hours examining the tales they so graphically depict. The chapel is open from 10:30 a.m. to 12:30 p.m. and 2–5 p.m., with shorter hours in the winter. Nearby is a **lighthouse** *(phare)* (7), which may also be visited.

The route shown on the map takes you past the interesting **Jardin Thuret** (8), a research garden for exotic trees and plants. These may be seen from 8 a.m. to 12:30 p.m. and 2–5:30 p.m., daily except on Saturdays, Sundays, and some holidays. Return to Antibes via Boulevard du Cap.

A Daytrip from Nice

Grasse

The medieval hill town of Grasse is widely known as the undisputed world center of perfume essences. A visit to one of its scent factories is a must, of course, but don't miss exploring the town itself. A veritable maze of ancient alleyways and half-hidden passages wind their way along the hillside, opening here and there for magnificent views. With its interesting cathedral and four small but intriguing museums, Grasse offers enough attractions to entertain you for an entire day.

GETTING THERE:

Buses to Grasse depart fairly often from the east side of the train station in **Cannes**, easily reached from Nice in 30 minutes by frequent trains. The bus ride takes about 45 minutes, with return service until early evening. There is also some direct service between the bus terminal in Nice and Grasse.

By car, take the N-85 north from Cannes, a distance of 10 miles. Grasse is 26 miles west of Nice. Park by the bus station.

PRACTICALITIES:

Grasse may be visited at any time, but at least one museum is closed on Sundays, another on Mondays and Tuesdays, and some in November. The local **Tourist Information Office**, phone 93-36-03-56, is on Place de la Foux, near the bus station. Grasse has a **population** of about 38,000, and is in the **Côte d'Azur** region.

FOOD AND DRINK:

Grasse has an adequate number of restaurants, some good choices being:

Amphitryon (16 Blvd. Victor-Hugo, 2 blocks west of the Fragonard Villa Museum) Light classical cuisine from the Southwest of France in a small traditional restaurant. X: Sun., holidays, Aug. $$

Maître Boscq (13 Rue de Fontette, 2 blocks east of Place aux Aires) A tiny and very romantic restaurant with traditional local cooking. X: Sun., Mon. off season, Nov. $

La Voute (Rue du Thouron, 2 blocks west of Place aux Aires) Provençal cooking, grills, and pizzas. $

SUGGESTED TOUR:

Leave the **bus station** *(Gare Routière)* (1) and follow the map past the tourist office to **Place aux Aires** (2). This thoroughly delightful open area has some find arcaded 18th-century houses and several sidewalk cafés arranged around a bubbling fountain. A lively outdoor market is held there in the mornings.

Follow the map down Rue des 4 Coins and descend the steep Rue de Fontette to Place Jean-Jaurès. Continue on, trying not to get lost in the tiny alleyways, to the 12th-century **Cathedral of Notre-Dame-du Puy** (3), heavily restored in the 17th century. Step inside to view the two paintings by Rubens in the south aisle, an altarpiece attributed to Louis Bréa and, above the sacristy door, one of Fragonard's rare religious works, the *Washing of the Feet.*

The square in front of the cathedral has an impressive square tower from the 12th century. Stroll around to **Place du 24 Août** (4), which offers a sweeping panorama of the countryside.

A series of steps leads to Rue Mirabeau and the **Musée d'Art et d'Histoire de Provence** (5). Housed in an 18th-century mansion, the museum's splendid collections are mostly concerned with the folk arts and traditions of the region, although there are also some fine paintings and archaeological displays. These may be seen daily except on holidays, from 10 a.m. to 1 p.m. and 2–7 p.m. From October through May it is closed on Mondays and Tuesdays, and has shorter hours.

Grasse produces most of the world's supply of the essences used in perfume manufacturing. This industry had its origins in the 16th-century fashion for scented gloves, which were made locally. It grew with the nearby cultivation of roses, jasmin and other plants; with more exotic ingredients now being imported from all over the world. Several of the larger factories offer free guided tours explaining their operations. One of the most interesting of these is the **Parfumerie Fragonard** (6), conveniently located a few steps away, whose tours in English are given daily at frequent intervals.

Now wander past a lovely park to the **Villa-Musée Fragonard** (7). If that name seems common around here, it is because the famous painter Jean-Honoré Fragonard was born in Grasse in 1732. Although he lived most of his life in Paris, he returned to his hometown during the Revolution and spent a year in this villa. Most of the paintings on display are copies, albeit very good ones; the originals being in the

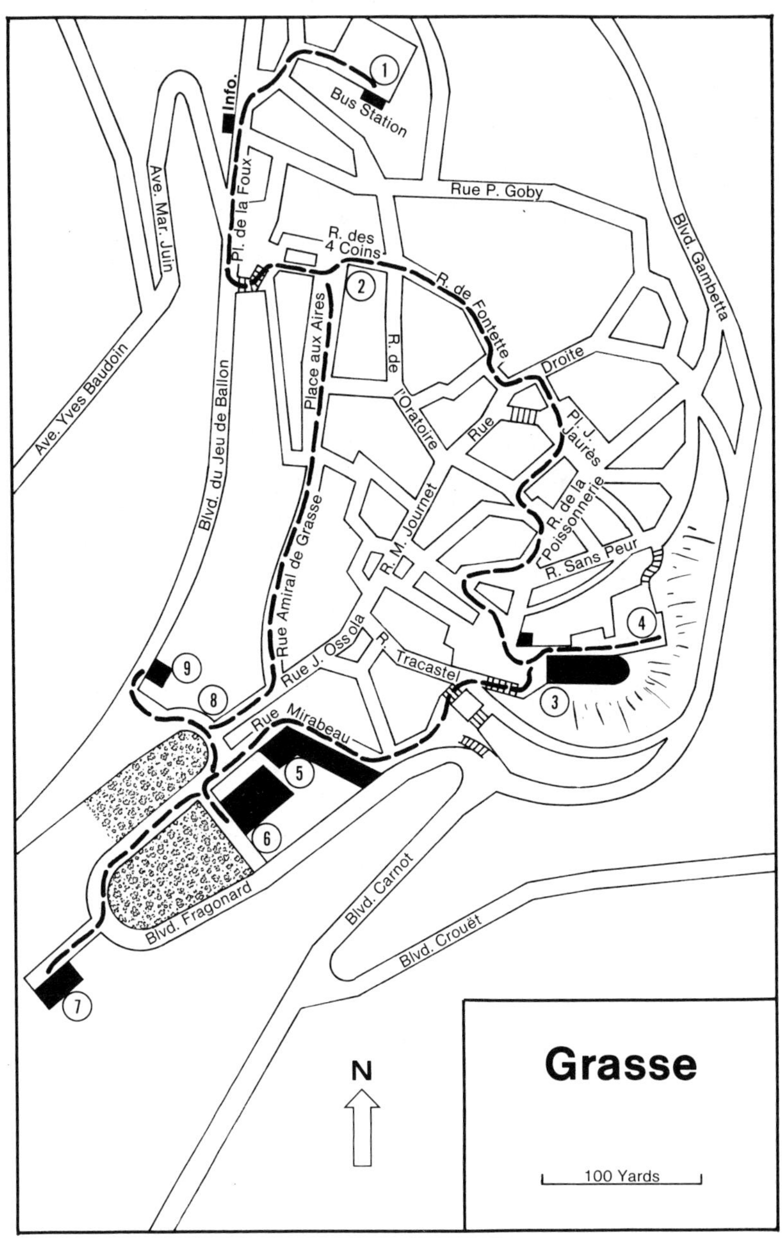
Info.
Bus Station
Rue P. Goby
Ave. Mar. Juin
Pl. de la Foux
R. des 4 Coins
R. de Fontette
Blvd. Gambetta
Place aux Aires
R. de l'Oratoire
Droite
Rue
Pl. J. Jaurès
R. de la Poissonnerie
R. Sans Peur
R. M. Journet
Rue Amiral de Grasse
Blvd. du Jeu de Ballon
Ave. Yves Baudoin
Rue J. Ossola
R. Tracastel
Rue Mirabeau
Blvd. Fragonard
Blvd. Carnot
Blvd. Crouët
1
2
3
4
5
6
7
8
9
N
Grasse
100 Yards

Place aux Aires

Frick Museum in New York. Still, a visit to this charming small museum is very worthwhile and can be made during the same times that the Art and History Museum (above) is open.

The new **International Perfume Museum** (8) at 8 Place du Cours is now open, with displays on the history of perfume making and marketing. It is open on Wednesdays through Sundays, from 10 a.m. to 6 p.m., but closed on holidays and the month of November.

American tourists will be particularly interested in the **Musée de la Marine** (9), devoted primarily to the life of Amiral de Grasse. Born in nearby Bar-sur-Loup, this 18th-century French naval hero is remembered for his role in the American War of Independence, when he blockaded the British at Yorktown, Virginia. Souvenirs of the battle are on display along with ship models and related items. The museum is open on Mondays through Saturdays, from 10 a.m. to noon and 2–6 p.m. It is closed in November. From here follow the map back to Place aux Aires and the bus station.

Section IV

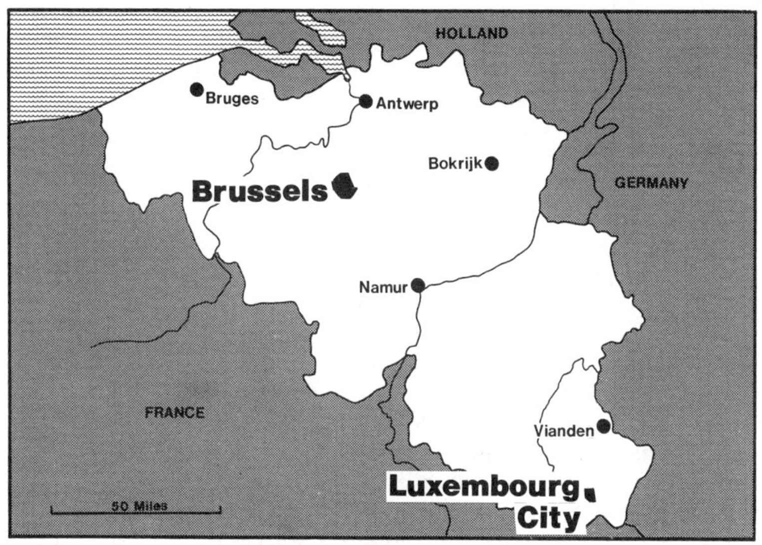

DAYTRIPS IN

BELGIUM and LUXEMBOURG

- from Brussels
- from Luxembourg City

Belgium is so compact a nation that nearly all of its attractions lie within comfortable daytrip range of Brussels. This multifaceted, multilingual city; practically the *de facto* capital of Europe, is centrally located near the line that divides Belgium into a Flemish-speaking north, with its strong Dutch and Germanic influences, and the southern Latin-based world of the French-speaking Walloons. Both sides are represented in the four daytrips that follow, which include the near-magical medieval town of Bruges; the bustling, cosmopolitan port city of Antwerp; the preserved rural past of Bokrijk; and the magnificent fortress town of Namur.

Tiny Luxembourg offers only a few first-rate daytrip possibilities, the very best being to the fairy-tale castle village of Vianden, described at the end of this chapter.

More one-day adventures in both countries are featured in our companion guidebook, ***Daytrips in Holland, Belgium and Luxembourg***, which follows the same format and includes do-it-yourself explorations on foot of the three base cities: Amsterdam, Brussels, and Luxembourg City.

GETTING AROUND:

Belgium has the densest **rail** network in Europe, with most of its busy passenger lines radiating outwards from Brussels. Note that the capital has three major **stations**, and that virtually all trains stop at all three. They are, bilingually, *Nord/Noord, Central/Centraal,* and *Midi/Zuid.* Express trains of the **IC** and **IR** categories are your best bet for travel within Belgium. **EC** luxury trains may also be used, but you'll pay a supplementary fare unless you have a Eurailpass. Most **destinations** in Belgium have both a French and a Flemish name. This book uses the name most familiar to English-speaking people, followed by the alternative name(s) in parenthesis. Please note that the train station for Bruges is marked *Brugge.*

Luxembourg has good rail service to neighboring countries, but most public transportation within the country is by bus. Fortunately, railpasses are accepted on all of these except for urban services within Luxembourg City and to its airport.

Eurailpasses (see page 18) are honored throughout both countries, but if you're only visiting Belgium, Luxembourg, or Holland you might consider these less expensive regional passes: The **Benelux Tourrail Pass** is valid for unlimited train travel in Belgium, Luxembourg, and Holland on any 5 days within a 17-day period. It is sold in both a first- and second-class version, for either adults or juniors up to age 25. Buy it at any major station in the Benelux countries, or overseas offices of the *Netherlands Board of Tourism* (see next chapter). Cheaper yet is the **B-Tourrail Pass**, basically the same but limited to Belgium only, and sold only at stations there.

Driving is easy in both countries, but be aware that in Belgium the road signs are usually only in the language of the region you happen to be in at the moment. Thus, in heading for Antwerp, the signs may begin as *Anvers* and later direct you to *Antwerpen.* Be sure you know the alternative names.

ADVANCE PLANNING INFORMATION:

The **Belgian Tourist Office** has branches in Western Europe and a few other parts of the world, including New York, Montreal, and London. Their New York address is: 745 Fifth Avenue, New York NY 10151, phone (212) 758-8130. The **Luxembourg National Tourist Office** has a branch in New York at 801 Second Avenue, New York NY 10017, phone (212) 370-9850; and one in London as well.

A Daytrip from Brussels

*Bruges

(Brugge)

Time has long stood still in medieval Bruges, a romantic city that went to sleep in the Middle Ages and didn't wake up until this century. Virtually all of the events of modern history have passed it by, leaving behind a perfectly preserved gem that is today among the loveliest places in Europe. No visitor to Belgium should miss seeing it.

In its heyday Bruges was a very wealthy town, attracting great artists and erecting splendid houses. Built around a 9th-century castle, its position near the Zwin estuary made it an ideal inland port, well protected from the storms of the North Sea. By the 12th century it was one of the most important trading centers in Europe. Shiploads of wool from England arrived daily to be woven into cloth at Bruges.

Gradually, however, the Zwin began to silt up and, at first, expensive efforts were made at dredging it. Around the same time, the English started to make their own cloth for export. The weavers at Bruges—defending their own privileges—prohibited this from entering their harbor, and so the trade naturally shifted to rival Antwerp. This was the beginning of the end. Investment in a canal, new harbor facilities, and a change in the guild rules might have saved the day, but the merchants of Bruges balked at the price, with the result that the town slowly declined and became known as "Bruges-la-Morte," or the "dead city."

Ironically, the necessary canal finally got built, and it opened in 1907 along with the modern harbor of Zeebrugge. By then, however, the citizens of Bruges had discovered a gold mine in their own past and took steps to insure that the town's medieval appearance would forever remain intact to delight the tourists.

And Bruges does get more than its share of visitors. Everything is so well organized, though, that even in the peak travel season it remains an extraordinarily pleasant place and never seems overcrowded. The suggested walking tour, besides covering the basics, also takes you into parts of town that relatively few tourists ever get to see.

GETTING THERE:

Trains depart Brussels' three major stations at half-hour intervals for the 1-hour ride to Bruges (Brugge). Return service operates until late evening.

By car, Bruges is 60 miles northwest of Brussels via the A-10 highway to exit 9. Park as close to the train station as possible and avoid driving in the Old Town.

PRACTICALITIES:

Any time is a good time to visit Bruges, but note that some of the major attractions are closed on either Tuesdays or Wednesdays between October and the end of March. The local **Tourist Information Office**, phone (050) 44-86-85, is at Burg 11, by the Town Hall. **Bicycles** may be rented at the train station, and reserved by calling (050) 385-871. There is a discount if you come by train. Bruges has a **population** of about 118,000, and is the provincial capital of **West Vlaanderen**. Known locally as **Brugge**, the town is in the **Flemish** speaking part of Belgium.

FOOD AND DRINK:

Being a major tourist area, Bruges offers a wide range of restaurants and cafés in every possible price range. Some choices are:

Duc de Bourgogne (Huidenvettersplaats 12, 1 block southeast of the Basilica of the Holy Blood) A world-famous inn with classic cuisine. Reservations are essential, phone (050) 33-20-38. X: Mon., July. $$$

De Witte Poorte (Jan van Eyckplein 6) Excellent seafood and other dishes. X: Sun., Mon. $$$

't Kluizeke (Sint Jacobstraat 58, 3 blocks northwest of the Markt) In a quiet part of town. X: Wed. $$

De Postiljon (Katelijnestraat 3, opposite the Memling Museum) Conveniently near the major attractions. X: Sun. eve., Tues. $

Malpertus (Eiermarkt 9, 1 block northwest of the Markt) Exceptional value. X: Thurs., July. $

SUGGESTED TOUR:

Leave the **Brugge Train Station** (1) and follow the map through a park to the **Minnewater** (2), popularly known as the "Lake of Love." During the Middle Ages this was the commercial harbor of the town, defended in part by the powder tower of 1398 at its south end.

Stroll through this peaceful scene and turn left into the ***Begijnhof** (Beguinage) (3), a sheltered world of meditation that has hardly changed since its foundation in the 13th century. In those days its tiny houses

View of the Belfry from the canal

were occupied by single lay women, or widows who wished to live a religious life without taking formal vows. Today it is inhabited by Benedictine nuns wearing 15th-century costumes. Amble quietly through its courtyard and visit the small church, first erected in 1245 and rebuilt in 1605. The **house** at the northeast corner has been restored to its 17th-century condition and is open to visitors at the times posted. Don't miss this unusual treat. If the south gate to the Beguinage is closed, you can usually get in via the main north gate.

Follow the map to the bridge on Katelijnestraat. This is one of the four places where you can take a delightful half-hour ***boat cruise** through the town's picturesque canals. These depart whenever there are enough customers, between March and November, and are a "must" for all visitors to Bruges.

Just across the bridge stands the **Onze Lieve Vrouwekerk** (Church of Our Lady) (4). Built in a variety of styles between the 13th and 15th centuries, it has the tallest spire in the Low Countries. Step inside to see the famous ***Virgin and Child*** statue by Michelangelo, one of the few pieces by that renowned artist to have left Italy during his lifetime. Among the many other works of art are the 16th-century **monumental tombs** of Mary of Burgundy and Charles the Bold. High above the north ambulatory there is an enclosed **balcony** that opens into the

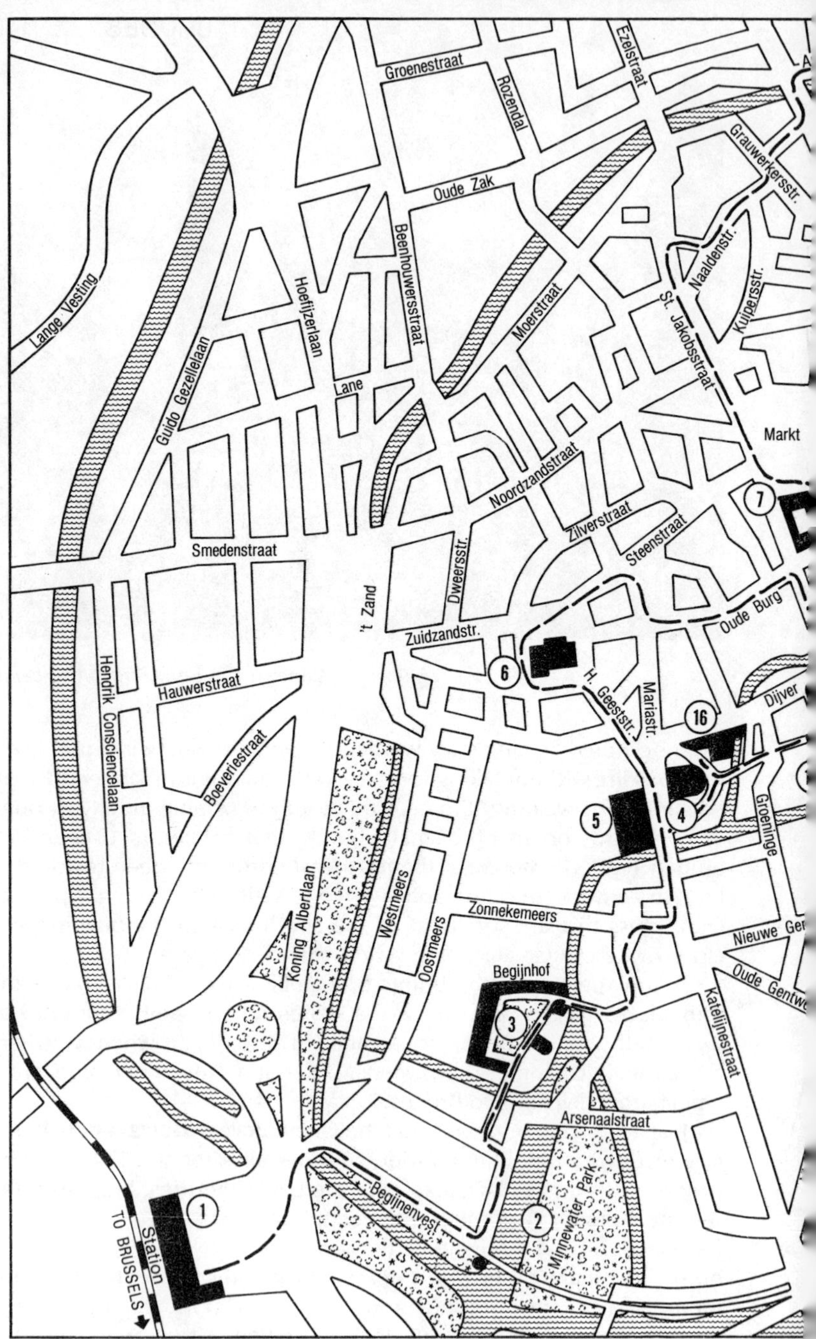
Groenestraat
Rozendal
Ezelstraat
Grauwerkersstr.
Oude Zak
Beenhouwersstraat
Hoefijzerlaan
Lange Vesting
Guido Gezellelaan
Moerstraat
Naaldenstr.
Kuipersstr.
St. Jakobsstraat
Lane
Markt
Noordzandstraat
Zilverstraat
Steenstraat
Smedenstraat
Dweersstr.
't Zand
Oude Burg
Zuidzandstr.
Hendrik Consciencelaan
Hauwerstraat
H. Geeststr.
Mariastr.
Dijver
Boeveriestraat
Groeninge
Westmeers
Zonnekemeers
Koning Albertlaan
Oostmeers
Begijnhof
Katelijnestraat
Arsenaalstraat
Begijnenvest
Minnewater Park
Station
TO BRUSSELS
1
2
3
4
5
6
7
16

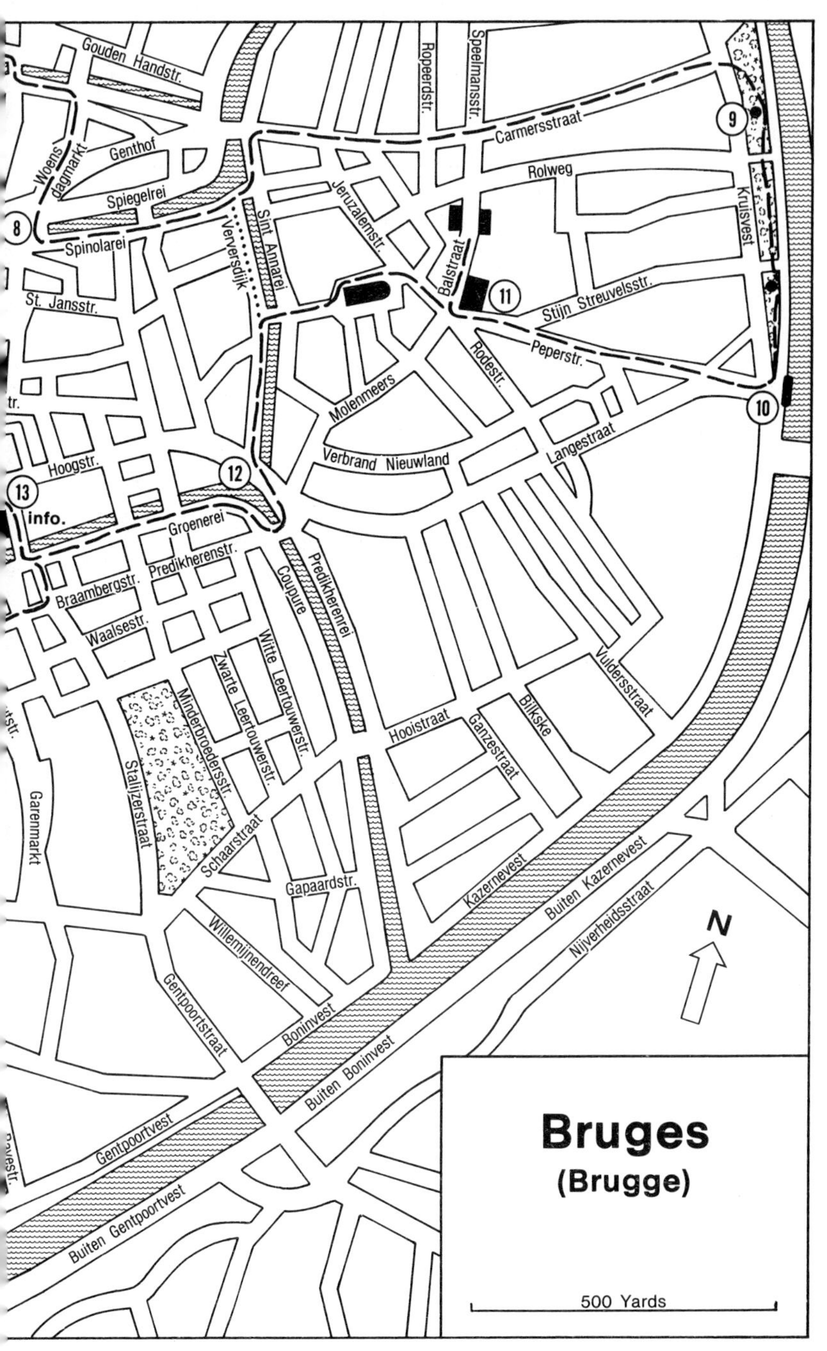
Bruges
(Brugge)
500 Yards
N
Gouden Handstr.
Woensdagmarkt
Genthof
Spiegelrei
Spinolarei
St. Jansstr.
Hoogstr.
info.
Groenerei
Predikherenstr.
Braambergstr.
Waalsestr.
Verversdijk
Sint Annarei
Jeruzalemstr.
Balstraat
Ropeerdstr.
Speelmansstr.
Carmersstraat
Rolweg
Kruisvest
Stijn Streuvelsstr.
Peperstr.
Rodestr.
Molenmeers
Verbrand Nieuwland
Langestraat
Coupure
Predikherenrei
Witte Leertouwerstr.
Zwarte Leertouwerstr.
Minderbroedersstr.
Stalijzerstraat
Garenmarkt
Schaarstraat
Gapaardstr.
Hooistraat
Ganzestraat
Bilkske
Vuldersstraat
Kazernevest
Buiten Kazernevest
Nijverheidsstraat
Willemijnendreef
Gentpoortstraat
Boninvest
Buiten Boninvest
Gentpoortvest
Buiten Gentpoortvest
8
9
10
11
12
13

adjacent Gruuthuse Museum. The balcony was put there in the 15th century so that the wealthy merchant who lived in the mansion could attend services without leaving home. The church is usually open on Mondays through Saturdays from 10–11:30 a.m. and 2:30–5 p.m.; and on Sundays in the afternoons only.

Directly across the street is the **St. Janshospitaal** (Hospital of St. John) (5), which houses the magnificent ***Memling Museum**. Founded in the 12th century to care for Bruges' sick and indigent, this former hospice contains a stunning collection of works by Hans Memling, a 15th-century German-born painter who became the leading artist of Medieval Bruges. The most outstanding pieces are the ***Reliquary of St. Ursala***, in which the legend of the saint and her 11,000 virgins being massacred in Cologne is depicted on the sides of an oak reliquary; and the ***Mystical Marriage of St. Catherine***, a sublimely beautiful altarpiece dedicated to St. John the Baptist and St. John the Evangelist, the patron saints of the hospital. While there, be sure to visit the restored 17th-century **Dispensary**, which remained in use until 1971. The museum is open daily from 9:30 a.m. to noon and 2–6 p.m., but is closed on Wednesdays from October through March.

Continue along Mariastraat and Heilige Geeststraat to **St. Salvator's Cathedral** (6), an essentially Gothic structure grafted onto an earlier Romanesque base. Architecturally undistinguished, it has suffered much during the centuries and was only elevated to cathedral status in 1834. Nevertheless, its interior does have some exquisitely carved choir stalls and misericords, splendid tapestries, and a lovely Baroque rood screen. The adjoining **Cathedral Museum** features some works by the old Flemish masters Dirk Bouts and Hugo van der Goes.

The route now follows a complicated but colorful path to the **Markt** and its rather extravagant (and slightly askew) 13th-century **Belfry** (7), the very symbol of Bruges. Soaring some 270 feet above the old marketplace, it may be climbed for a spectacular ***view** on any day from 9:30 a.m. to 12:30 p.m. and 1:30–6 p.m., with slightly shorter hours in winter. On the way up you can glimpse the famous 47-bell **carillon** that plays tunes every quarter-hour.

Stroll through the lively Markt, an unusually attractive square lined with restaurants and outdoor cafés. The route now leaves the tourists behind and explores a quiet part of town where a medieval atmosphere still lingers. Follow the map through a series of narrow streets and alleyways to **Jan van Eyckplein** (8), named after the great 15th-century Flemish painter.

Continue along the canalside Spinolarei until you come to a bridge. From here you could cut the tour short by turning right and following the map to the Basilica of the Holy Blood (14). If you prefer to see more sights, however, you should cross the bridge and turn down

The Bonifacius Bridge

Carmersstraat to the outer ring canal, where you will find several restored **windmills**. One of these may be visited. Known as **St. Janshuismolen** (9), it is of the stilt type and was rebuilt in 1770. You can climb up into its working mechanism for a good look on any day between May and the end of September, from 9:30 a.m. to noon and 2–6 p.m.

Amble through the park to the early-15th-century **Kruispoort Gate** (10), once a part of the ramparts that were largely demolished during the 18th century. Head back into town on Langestraat and Peperstraat, which take you to the 15th-century **Jerusalem Church** (11), supposedly built to the same plans as the Holy Sepulchre in Jerusalem. It is noted for its 15th-century stained-glass windows and its interesting crypt.

Just north of this, in the medieval almshouses, is the popular **Kantcentrum** (Lace Center). Sponsored by the state, this is where the ancient skills of lace making are passed on to younger generations. You can pay a visit on Mondays through Saturdays, from 10 a.m. to noon and 2–6 p.m., closing at 5 p.m. on Saturdays. Across the street is the **Folklore Museum**, which you might also want to see.

Continue on past St. Anne's Church and cross a small canal. Turn left and follow around to one of the prettiest sights in Bruges, the

Groenerei (12). From here you get a lovely ***view** into the old part of town. Stroll along the water and turn right on Blinde Ezelstraat to the flamboyant **Stadhuis** (Town Hall) (13). Begun in the 14th century, its magnificent façade is a veritable forest of statuary. Step inside to see its splendid Gothic Hall, decorated with murals depicting the history of Bruges, and to admire its vaulted ceiling. Visits can usually be made daily, from 9:30 a.m. to noon and 2–6 p.m.

The large open square known as **Burg**, in front of the Town Hall, occupies the site of the original 9th-century castle around which Bruges developed. Facing this is the **Heilig Bloedbaziliek** (Basilica of the Holy Blood) (14), where what is said to be blood washed from the body of Christ is venerated. The 12th-century basilica consists of a lower and an upper chapel, the lower being a dark Romanesque structure that remains virtually unchanged. The sacred relic is in the upper chapel, which was rebuilt in the Gothic style during the 16th century. On Ascension Day, it is carried through the streets in a colorful procession. The basilica is open nearly every day, from 9:30 a.m. to noon and 2–6 p.m., closing at 4 p.m. in winter.

Return across the canal and follow the map to the world-famous ***Groeninge Museum** (15). Covering the entire scope of Flemish art from the 15th through the 20th centuries, this superb museum displays works by Jan van Eyck, Hans Memling, Rogier van der Weyden, Hugo van der Goes, Breugel, Bosch, and such moderns as Magritte and Delvaux. It is open daily from April through September, 9:30 a.m. to 6 p.m.; and on Wednesdays through Mondays the rest of the year, from 9:30 a.m. to noon and 2–5 p.m. Don't miss it.

Leave the museum by a side passage and stroll around to the tiny ***Bonifacius Bridge**, beyond which lies one of the most enchanting and evocative corners of old Bruges. From here it is only steps to the **Gruuthuse Museum** (16), housed in a fabulous 15th-century merchant's mansion. In it are displayed several thousand antiques of all sorts, covering the entire sweep of Bruges' history. As you wander through the complex of rooms, you may be startled to look out directly into the interior of the Church of Our Lady, reminding you that this tour has come full circle. The museum is open daily from 9:30 a.m. to noon and 2–6 p.m. From October through March it has shorter hours and is closed on Tuesdays.

A Daytrip from Brussels

*Antwerp

(Antwerpen, Anvers)

If you haven't already discovered it, a visit to Antwerp should come as a wonderful surprise. Belgium's second-largest city and major seaport is not only a great cultural center, it is also a highly entertaining, beautiful, vital, and immensely likeable place. Don't miss this urban Flemish treat!

Legend has it that Antwerp began during the Roman era with the riverside castle of a giant named Druon Antigonus, who exacted tolls from passing ships and cut off the hands of sailors who refused to pay, which he then threw into the Schelde—thus the name *Handwerpen,* meaning "to throw a hand." Historians, however, offer a less picturesque theory, insisting that the name derives from *Aan de Werpen,* literally "at the wharf." Whatever the truth of the matter, Antwerp's reason for existence has always been its strategic location on a deep river that runs through Dutch territory to the North Sea.

The port city's most famous citizen was Peter Paul Rubens (1577–1640), the German-born painter who spent most of his life in Antwerp and left behind an astonishing legacy of art. You'll be seeing much of this along the walking route, although the city possesses far more masterpieces than can possibly be seen in a day.

GETTING THERE:

Trains depart Brussel's three major stations frequently for the 35-minute ride to Antwerp's Centraal Station. Return service runs until mid-evening.

By car, Antwerp is 32 miles north of Brussels via the A-1 highway.

PRACTICALITIES:

Antwerp is a pleasure to visit at any time, but note that some of the main museums are closed on Mondays and/or major holidays. **Harbor cruises** operate from Easter through September. The local **Tourist Information Office**, phone (03) 232-01-03, is located at Grote Markt 15. Antwerp has a **population** of about 475,000 and is the capital of **Antwerpen** province. The principal local language is **Flemish**.

FOOD AND DRINK:

Some good restaurant choices are:

Sir Anthony Van Dijck (Oude Koornmarkt 16, 1 block southwest of the cathedral) World famous for its ancient atmosphere and superb seafood. For reservations call (03) 231-61-70. X: Sat., Sun. $$$

In de Schaduw van de Kathedraal (Handschoenmarkt 17, opposite the cathedral) Delicious Belgian specialties. X: Tues. $$

Roden Hoed (Oude Koornmarkt 25, just south of the cathedral) The oldest restaurant in town, specializing in seafood but with other dishes. X: Wed., Thurs. $$

De Peerdestal (Wijngaardstraat 8, 3 blocks northeast of the cathedral) A large country-style restaurant with a broad menu. X: Sun. $$

't Hofke (Oude Koornmarkt Vlaeikensgang 16, 1 block southwest of the cathedral) A bargain. $

SUGGESTED TOUR:

Centraal Station (1) is about one mile east of the Old Town's center, where the sights begin. The entire distance is along a series of attractive shopping streets, but if you prefer to ride you can take the underground tram *(Pre Métro)* to Groenplaats.

The ***Cathedral of Our Lady** (2) is just north of the Groenplaats, once the town graveyard and now a pedestrian area with a statue of Rubens. Although it is the largest Gothic church in Belgium, it is so hemmed in by houses that its immense size does not become immediately apparent. The present cathedral was begun in 1352 and was essentially finished during the 16th century. Its fantastically ornate north tower soars some 404 feet above the street, while the south tower was never completed.

The cathedral's spacious interior is undergoing a long-term restoration, so its many art treasures are moved around from time to time. Three masterpieces by Rubens to be on the lookout for are his *Elevation of the Cross,* the *Descent from the Cross,* and the *Assumption.* Visits may be made on Mondays through Fridays from 10 a.m. to 5 p.m.; on Saturdays from 10 a.m. to 3 p.m.; and on Sundays and holidays from 1–4 p.m., but not during services.

Continue on to the nearby **Grote Markt** (3), the impressive main square of Antwerp. In its center stands the Brabo Fountain, atop which the legendary hero Silvius Brabo tosses the hand of Antigonus into the Schelde, thus saving the town from the evil giant's tyranny. The entire west side of the square is occupied by the magnificent 16th-century **Stadhuis** (Town Hall) whose essentially 19th-century interior

The Stadhuis in the Grote Markt

may usually be visited on any day except Sundays. Ornate **guild houses**, mostly from the 16th century, line the other sides of the square. Many of these now contain **restaurants** or **cafés**, contributing to the generally festive atmosphere.

A short stroll down Suikerrui brings you to the Schelde River. ***Harbor cruises** offered by the Flandria Company depart frequently from the landing stage at **Steenplein** (4). These are a lot of fun, although only the longer trips get into the modern port, quite a distance downstream. Still, the views are interesting and refreshments are available on board. The cruises, lasting 50 or 80 minutes, or even longer, operate from Easter through September.

At the north end of Steenplein stands a forbidding medieval fortress called the **Steen** (5), whose foundations date from the 9th century. The remaining parts of the castle were built around 1250 and have been altered several times since. Originally the residence of the ruling counts, it was later used as a notorious prison and now houses the **Scheepvaartmuseum** (National Maritime Museum). The modern statue at its entrance is of the "Lange Wapper," a giant who was the scourge of drunkards. Inside, the museum has a fascinating collection of nautical artifacts, ship models, and displays concerning Antwerp's maritime development. There is a colorful café in the basement, and an outdoor collection of real boats and barges. The museum is open daily, except on major holidays, from 10 a.m. to 5 p.m.

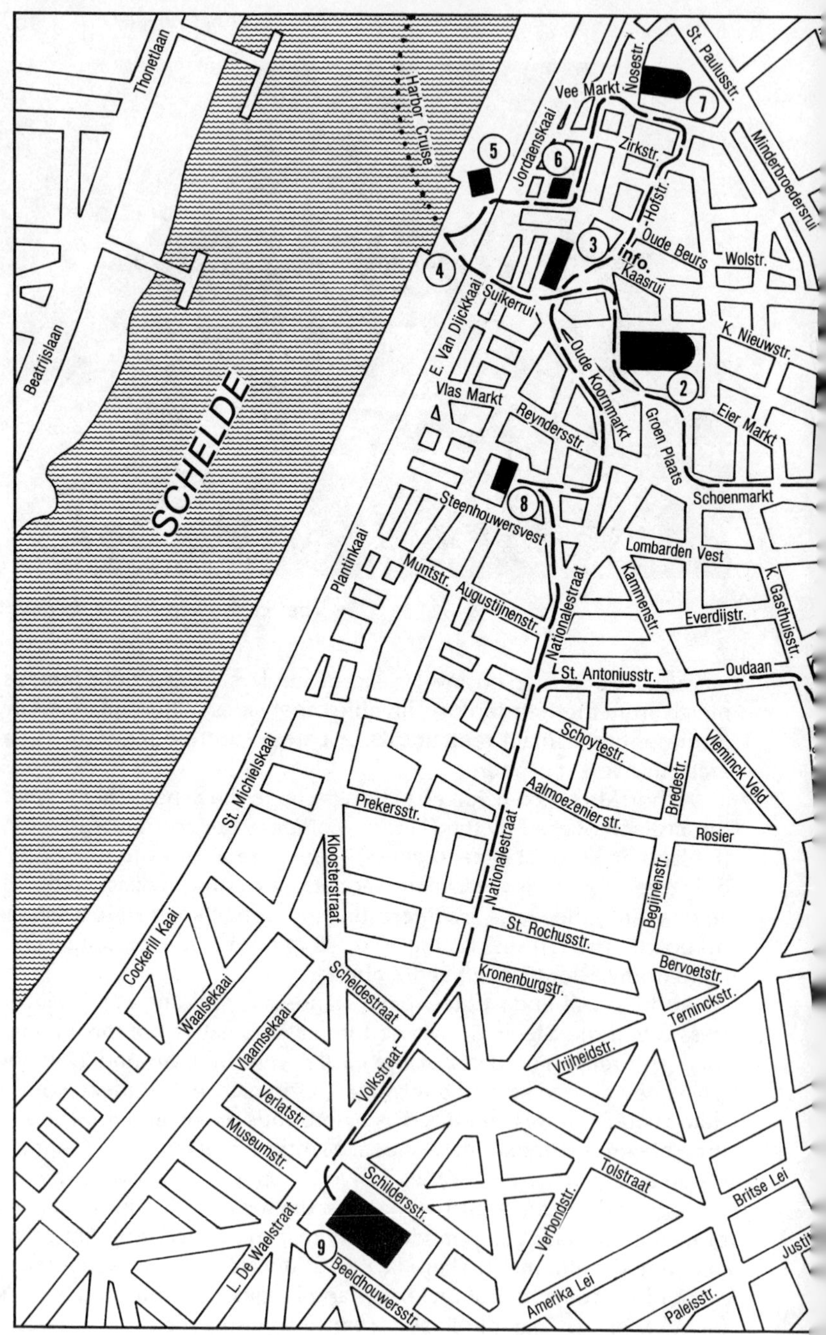

Thonetlaan
Harbor Cruise
Vee Markt
Nosestr.
St. Paulusstr.
Jordaenskaai
Zirkstr.
Minderbroedersrui
Hofstr.
Oude Beurs
Wolstr.
info.
Kaasrui
Suikerrui
E. Van Dijckkaai
K. Nieuwstr.
Oude Koornmarkt
Groen Plaats
Eier Markt
Vlas Markt
Reyndersstr.
Beatrijslaan
SCHELDE
Schoenmarkt
Steenhouwersvest
Lombarden Vest
Plantinkaai
Muntstr.
Augustijnenstr.
Nationalestraat
Kammenstr.
K. Gasthuisstr.
Everdijstr.
St. Antoniusstr.
Oudaan
Schoytestr.
Vleminck Veld
St. Michielskaai
Prekersstr.
Aalmoezenierstr.
Bredestr.
Rosier
Kloosterstraat
Begijnenstr.
St. Rochusstr.
Cockerill Kaai
Bervoetstr.
Kronenburgstr.
Scheldestraat
Terninckstr.
Waalsekaai
Vlaamsekaai
Volkstraat
Vrijheidstr.
Verlatstr.
Museumstr.
Schildersstr.
Tolstraat
Britse Lei
L. De Waelstraat
Verbondstr.
Beeldhouwersstr.
Amerika Lei
Paleisstr.

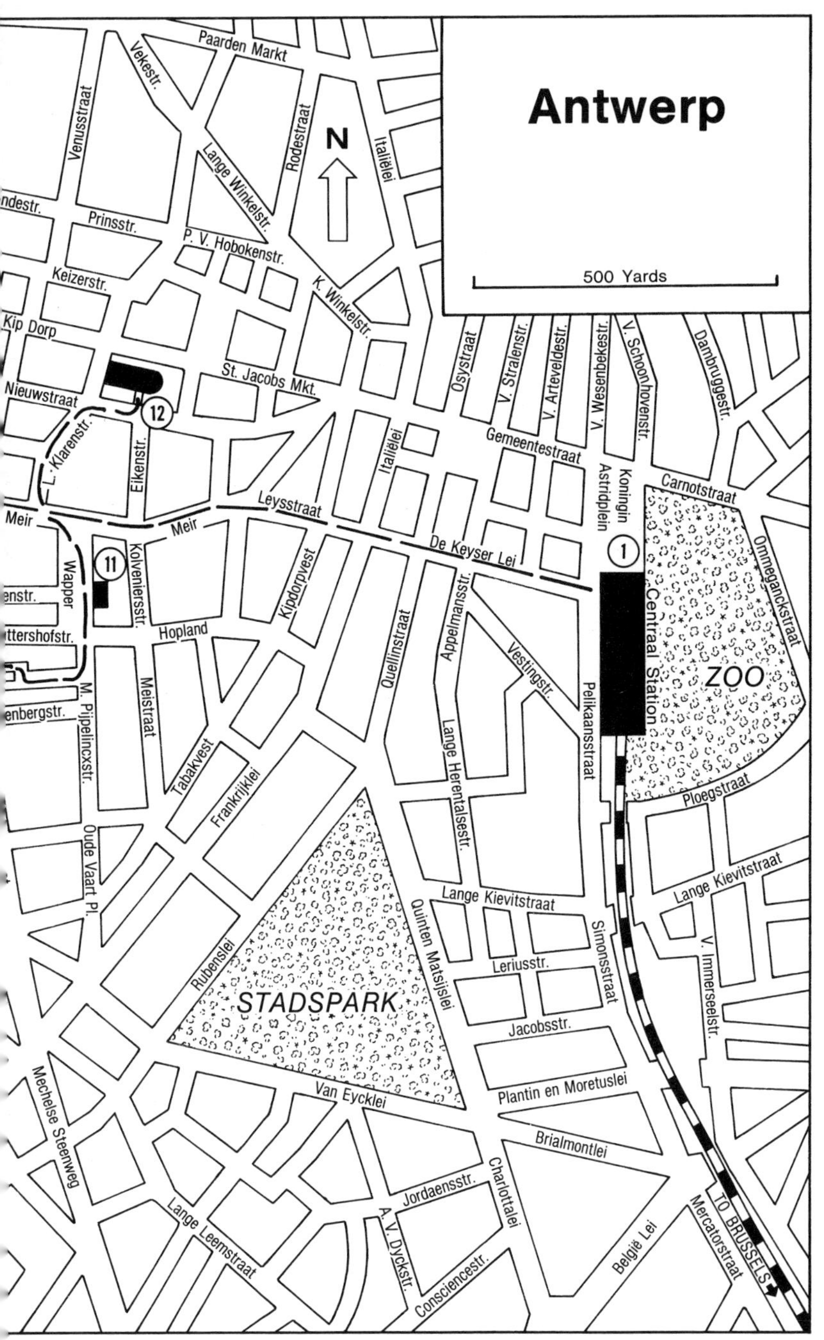
Antwerp
500 Yards
N
Paarden Markt
Vekestr.
Venusstraat
Lange Winkelstr.
Rodestraat
Italiëlei
Prinsstr.
P. V. Hobokenstr.
Keizerstr.
K. Winkelstr.
Kip Dorp
St. Jacobs Mkt.
Nieuwstraat
L. Klarenstr.
Eikenstr.
Osystraat
V. Stralenstr.
V. Arteveldestr.
V. Wesenbekestr.
V. Schoonhovenstr.
Dambruggestr.
Gemeentestraat
Italiëlei
Koningin Astridplein
Carnotstraat
Leysstraat
Meir
Meir
De Keyser Lei
Wapper
Kolveniersstr.
Kipdorpvest
Appelmansstr.
Quellinstraat
Vestingstr.
Centraal Station
Ommeganckstraat
ZOO
Hopland
Meistraat
M. Pipelincxstr.
Tabakvest
Frankrijklei
Lange Herentalsestr.
Pelikaansstraat
Ploegstraat
Oude Vaart Pl.
Lange Kievitstraat
Lange Kievitstraat
Quinten Matsijslei
Simonsstraat
V. Immerseelstr.
Rubenslei
Leriusstr.
STADSPARK
Jacobsstr.
Plantin en Moretuslei
Van Eycklei
Brialmontlei
Mechelse Steenweg
Jordaensstr.
Charlottalei
Lange Leemstraat
A. V. Dyckstr.
Conscienceestr.
België Lei
Mercatorstraat
TO BRUSSELS

Now follow the map to the **Vleeshuis** (6), a masterful gabled and turreted mansion built for the Butchers' Guild in 1503. Its elegant interior today houses an excellent museum for the applied arts that is especially noted for its collection of old **musical instruments**. Visits may be made on any day except Mondays and some major holidays, from 10 a.m. to 5 p.m.

Continue on to Veemarkt, the former cattle market, and **St. Pauluskerk** (7), a late-Gothic church of the 16th century ornamented with a 17th-century Baroque tower. Its lovely interior contains some fine wood carvings, choir stalls, and confessionals. There are also several paintings by Rubens and other local artists.

The route now leads through a charming old part of town and returns to the Grote Markt. Head south on Oude Koornmarkt and follow around to Vrijdagmarkt, where an **antiques market** is held on Wednesday and Friday mornings. Facing this is the ***Plantin-Moretus Museum** (8), an absolutely essential stop for anyone who loves books. The publishing firm founded in 1555 by Christopher Plantin grew to become the most important in Europe, was taken over by his son-in-law Jan Moretus, and remained in business until 1867. The complex of buildings in which the museum is housed served as both the family mansion and printing shops. In it are displayed a vast collection of publishing artifacts; including a type foundry, printing presses, many rare volumes, and a Gutenberg Bible. There are also several paintings by Rubens, who was a family friend. Don't miss this special treat, which is open daily, except for a few major holidays, from 10 a.m. to 5 p.m.

From here, you can make a **side trip** on foot or by bus or tram to the Royal Art Museum; or you could skip that and head straight for the Mayer van den Bergh Museum.

The ***Koninklijk Museum voor Schone Kunsten** (Royal Museum of Find Arts) (9) is easily among the most impressive in the Low Countries. Its monumental collections include works by such masters as Van Eyck, Van der Weyden, Memling, Dirk Bouts, and Quentin Massys, among others. Rubens gets two entire galleries to himself, and his contemporaries such as Van Dyck and Jordaens are well represented. You will also find paintings by Bruegel, Cranach, Frans Hals, and Rembrandt. Modern art is well covered with works by such Belgian luminaries as Ensor, Margritte, and Delvaux. The museum is open daily, except on Mondays and some major holidays, from 10 a.m. to 5 p.m.

Return via the route on the map and turn east to the **Mayer van den Bergh Museum** (10), where a small but exquisite collection of medieval and Renaissance art is displayed in a reconstructed 16th-century town house. The most important piece here is Bruegel's *Dulle Griet* (Mad Meg), an astonishing painting that touches on the super-

The Steen and the Lange Wapper *statue*

natural. Visits may be made on any day except Mondays and major holidays, from 10 a.m. to 5 p.m.

Continue on to what is probably Antwerp's most popular attraction, the ***Rubens House** (11). The great painter Peter Paul Rubens began construction on this large town house and studio around 1610 and lived there until his death in 1640. After that it deteriorated badly, and by the time it was acquired by the city in 1937 there was not much left beyond the framework. A meticulous reconstruction was finished and it opened to the public in 1946. None of its present furnishings actually belonged to Rubens, but they are all authentic antiques from his time and show just how well this prosperous artist, diplomat, and scholar really lived. Be sure to go into the garden, laid out as it appeared in his paintings. The house is open daily, except for a few major holidays, from 10 a.m. to 5 p.m.

While on the subject of Rubens, you may want to visit the nearby **St. Jacobskerk** (12), a patrician church where the artist and his family are buried. Above the altar in the Rubens Chapel is one of the master's last works, *Our Lady Surrounded by Saints,* in which he depicted himself as St. George, his two wives as Martha and Mary, his father as St. Jerome, and his son as Christ. From here you can walk or take a tram back to the station.

A Daytrip from Brussels

Bokrijk

Europe has an ever-increasing number of outdoor folk museums where the rural past is brought back to life, but perhaps none of them surpass Bokrijk in sheer entertainment value. Although it may have certain "cultural" overtones, for the foreign tourist a visit here is just plain fun.

Farm structures, village houses, churches, schools, country inns, wind and water mills, and even urban buildings have been brought here from all over the Flemish provinces of Belgium and reassembled into typical villages as well as a small corner of a great city. Dating from the 12th through the late-19th centuries, many of the preserved buildings are furnished with authentic antiques to appear as they would have in times past. The old crafts and farming methods continue to be practiced as a way of keeping ancient traditions alive.

Located in the large Provincial Domain of Bokrijk, the Flemish Open-Air Museum opened in 1958 and is now the largest outdoor folk museum in Europe. A guide booklet in English is available at the entrance so you can explore the entire area on your own, traveling on foot or riding one of the horse-drawn wagons. Authentic rural inns with outdoor tables, serving real country beer and home-cooked meals make for pleasant stops along the way. The suggested route described here takes you past all of the interesting highlights, which are described in greater detail in the guide booklet.

GETTING THERE:

Trains bound for Genk depart Brussel's three major stations hourly for the 1½-hour ride to Bokrijk. Be sure to get on a car marked for Genk, as the trains split en route. Bokrijk has no station, but the trains stop along the tracks close to the museum entrance between April and late October. Return service runs until mid-evening.

By car, leave Brussels on the A-3 highway and go east, almost to Leuven, then take the A-2 northwest to exit 30 and follow signs south to Domein Bokrijk Openluchtmuseum. The total distance is 52 miles.

A horse wagon passes the Dolphin Inn

PRACTICALITIES:

The open-air museum at Bokrijk operates from April through October, daily from 10 a.m. to 6 p.m., closing at 5 in October. Good weather is essential for this trip. The provincial **Tourist Information Office**, phone (011) 222-958, is at the museum entrance. Bokrijk is in the **Flemish** speaking province of **Limburg**.

FOOD AND DRINK:

There are several places to eat and drink within the open-air museum, as well as a good restaurant just outside. They are:

St. Gummarus Inn (#5 on the map) A huge inn with a turn-of-the-century ambiance. Indoor and outdoor tables. Very popular. $

Dolphin Inn (#6 on the map) A 17th-century inn with a good food selection, outdoor tables available.$

In't Paenhuys (#4 on the map) An old country brewery with a small choice of snacks and beers. Outdoor tables. $

Bierkelder (#8 on map) A typical beer cellar from Antwerp. A huge variety of beers are available, but only snack food. $

't Koetshuis (Bokrijklaan, outside the northeast entrance) In a mock castle near the open-air museum. Regional cuisine in a rustic setting. X: Tues. off-season. $$

SUGGESTED TOUR:

Leave the **train halt** (1) and walk a short distance to the **Openlucht-museum** (Flemish Open-Air Museum) entrance (2). Follow the map to a **Limburg Village** (3), complete with a 17th-century farmstead, a 16th-century granary, a laborer's cottage, a 19th-century school, a 15th-century chapel, and other similar buildings.

Continue on to a 17th-century brewery that now houses a café called the **In't Paenhuys** (4). Grouped around this is a 17th-century half-timbered house, an especially nice pigsty, a bakehouse with a latrine, and a small chapel. Head towards the octagonal **windmill** of the 18th century, the 12th-century Romanesque church, the archers' mast, and the cave hut.

Turn left at the next windmill and left again at another farmstead. You are now in a village typical of Antwerp Province. Opposite the pillory is the **St. Gummarus Inn** (5), an 18th-century structure restored to its condition of 1900. This is a great place for simple meals and especially for the local Hoevebier—a full-bodied and tasty brew. A souvenir shop is nearby, as is the 18th-century vicarage. Also nearby are more pigstys and outhouses, and a 17th-century farmhouse.

The route now leads past an ancient abbey farmstead, a water mill, and more farms to the **Dolphin Inn** (6), a 17th-century meeting place from West Flanders. Restored to its early-20th-century condition, it offers a good selection of regional dishes and brews, including the very strong, black Abbey Beer.

Continue on through a rural area typical of **West Flanders** (7) and an undeveloped part of the museum to the **Urban Section** (8). City buildings from Antwerp are being moved here brick by brick to save them from the wrecker's ball. Dating from as far back as the 15th century, the ones that are now finished house exhibitions as well as a delightful and very popular **beer cellar** that features a fabulous choice of brews. This is the perfect place to relax before heading back to the train halt.

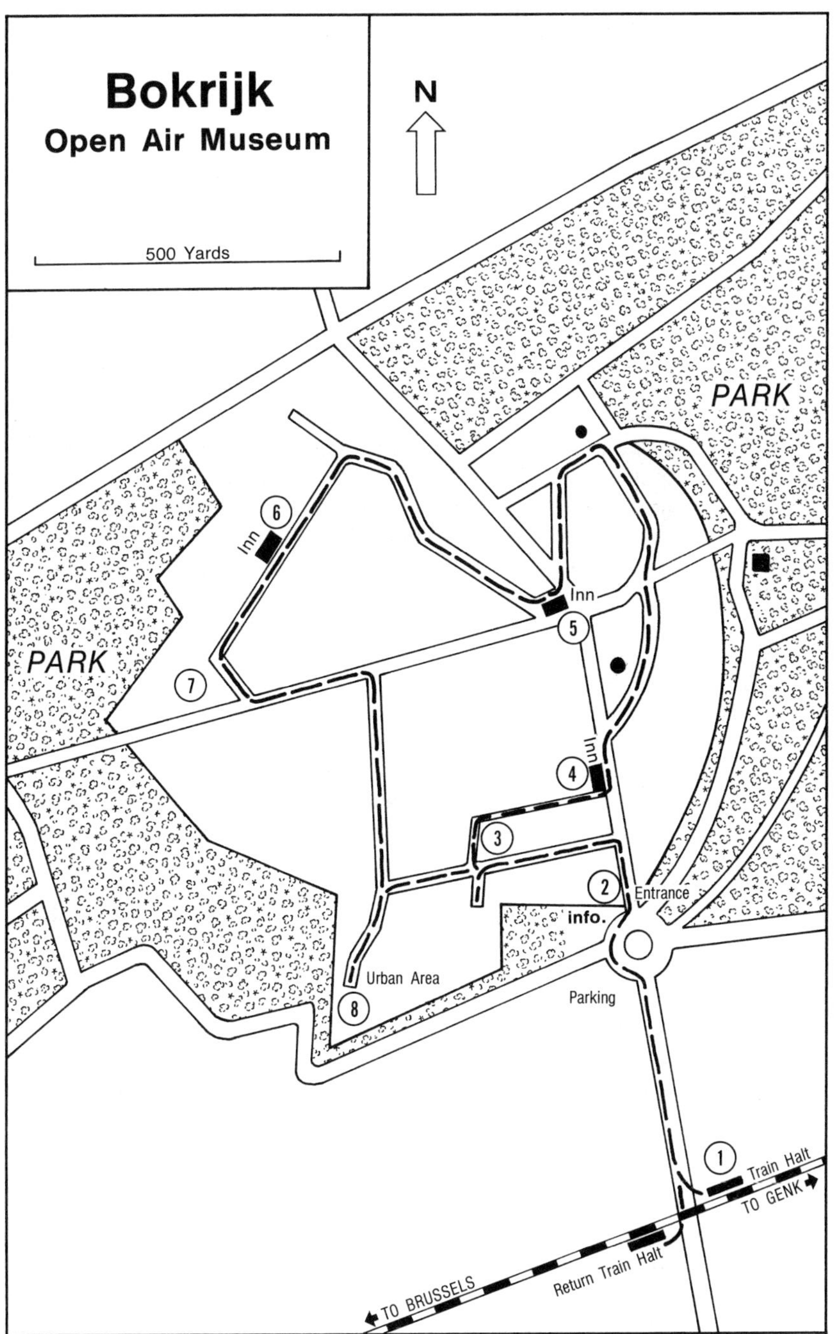
Bokrijk
Open Air Museum
N
500 Yards
PARK
PARK
Inn
6
Inn
5
7
Inn
4
3
2
Entrance
info.
Urban Area
8
Parking
1
Train Halt
TO GENK
Return Train Halt
TO BRUSSELS

A Daytrip from Brussels

Namur

(Namen)

Guarding the confluence of the Meuse and Sambre rivers and acting as the gateway to the Ardennes, French-speaking Namur has always been a strategic military bastion. Its enormous citadel originally dates from Roman times and has been frequently rebuilt throughout nearly 2,000 years of an often-violent history. Today it is a major tourist attraction, reached by cable car or by a long, winding road. The town itself is unusually pleasant, with several good museums and a wealth of 17th- and 18th-century buildings.

GETTING THERE:

Trains depart Brussel's three major stations at half-hour intervals on weekdays and hourly on weekends for the 54-minute ride to Namur. Return service operates until mid-evening.

By car, Namur is 40 miles southeast of Brussels via the A-4 highway.

PRACTICALITIES:

The most important attraction of Namur, its Citadel, is open daily from April through late October. Some of the museums are closed on Tuesdays, while others have various closing days. Good weather is essential for this trip. The local **Tourist Information Office** *(Syndicat d'Initiative)*, phone (081) 22-28-59, is at Square Léopold, just east of the train station. **Bicycles** may be rented at the station. Outdoor **markets** are held on Saturdays. The town has a **population** of about 102,000, and is the capital of French-speaking **Namur** province.

FOOD AND DRINK:

Some good restaurant choices in Namur are:

Château de Namur (Av. Ermitage 1, at the top of the cable car) Good food with a wonderful view. $$$

La Bruxelloise (Av. de la Gare 2, near the station) A good value, with mussels in season. $$

The Citadel from the river

La Soupière (Rue Saint-Loup 8, 2 blocks southwest of Museum of Old Namur) In the center of town. X: Sun. $$

Le Parisien (Rue Emile Cuvelier 16, a block southeast of the Museum of Old Namur) An exceptional value in French cuisine. $

SUGGESTED TOUR:

Leave the **train station** *(Gare)* (1) and follow Avenue de la Gare to the tourist office, then turn down Rue de Fer to the **Musée des Arts Anciens du Namurois** (Museum of Old Namur Arts) (2). Housed in an 18th-century mansion, the collections here are predominantly sculptures, paintings, and metalwork of the region, from both the Middle Ages and the Renaissance. The museum is open on Wednesdays through Mondays, from 10 a.m. to 12:30 p.m. and 1:30–5 p.m.

Now follow the map to the **École des Soeurs de Notre-Dame** (School of the Sisters of Our Lady) (3), which houses Namur's greatest art treasures. The collection of early-13th-century gold plate by the master Brother Hugo of Oignies is a superb example of the stylistic lengths to which reliquaries, chalices, crosses, and other items of religious art could be carried. They may be seen on Wednesdays through Mondays, from 10 a.m. to noon and 2–5 p.m.; but not on Tuesdays, holidays, or Sunday mornings.

The route leads across a bridge to the lower station of the **Téléférique** (cable car) (4) that carries you slowly and gently to the heights of the Citadel. The cars operate daily from Easter until October, and then on weekends until mid-November; from 10 a.m. to 7 p.m. You can also drive or walk up.

Once at the **top** (5), stroll down Avenue d'Artois and into the woods to the **Musée de la Forêt** (Museum of the Forest) (6), a charming rustic structure from 1910 in which subjects such as forestry, hunting, and fishing are explored along with samples of the flora and fauna of the Ardennes region. The museum is open from April through October, daily from 9 a.m. to noon and 2–5 p.m.

Continue on past a sports stadium to the entrance of the ***Citadel** (7), a massive complex of fortifications spread over an area of 20 acres. It is believed that a stronghold has stood on this site since at least Roman times, but most of what exists today is from the 17th through the 19th centuries. Parts of it remained in use by the Belgian Army until 1975, and the whole fortress was opened to the public in 1978. You can visit it on foot or by riding the little "tourist train;" or you can take a guided tour lasting about 90 minutes. Either way, be sure to visit the small museum in the former barracks *(Caserne)*. The Citadel is open daily from April through late October, from 11 a.m. to 7 p.m.

Return to town via the cable car or on foot. Just across the bridge is the **Musée Archéologique** (8), housed in a 16th-century meat hall. The archaeological collections here are particularly rich in prehistoric, Gallo-Roman, Merovingian, and Early Christian artifacts from the region. It is open on Wednesdays through Fridays and Mondays, from 10 a.m. to noon and 1–5 p.m., and on weekends from 11 a.m. to 5 p.m.

Stroll ahead to Place d'Armes and turn left near the 14th-century **Belfry**, once a part of the medieval town walls. The route leads through a delightful part of town to the new **Musée Félicien Rops** (9) at Rue Fumal 12, where some 600 works by the popular 19th-century artist can be seen daily except on Tuesdays, from 10 a.m. to 5 p.m. Continue on to the **Musée de Groesbeeck de Croix** (10), an 18th-century mansion with a splendid interior. It contains some marvelous local paintings and other artworks from the 17th and 18th centuries, and is open on Wednesdays through Mondays, from 10 a.m. to noon and 2–5 p.m.

Close to this is the **Cathedral of St. Aubain** (11), a neo-classical structure of the 18th century, built on the site of churches dating back to the 3rd century. Just behind it is the **Diocesan Museum** (12) with a notable collection of medieval religious art and artifacts, generally open daily except on Mondays, from 10 a.m. to noon and 2:30–6 p.m., but closed in the mornings between November and Easter. From here walk back through the town to the train station.

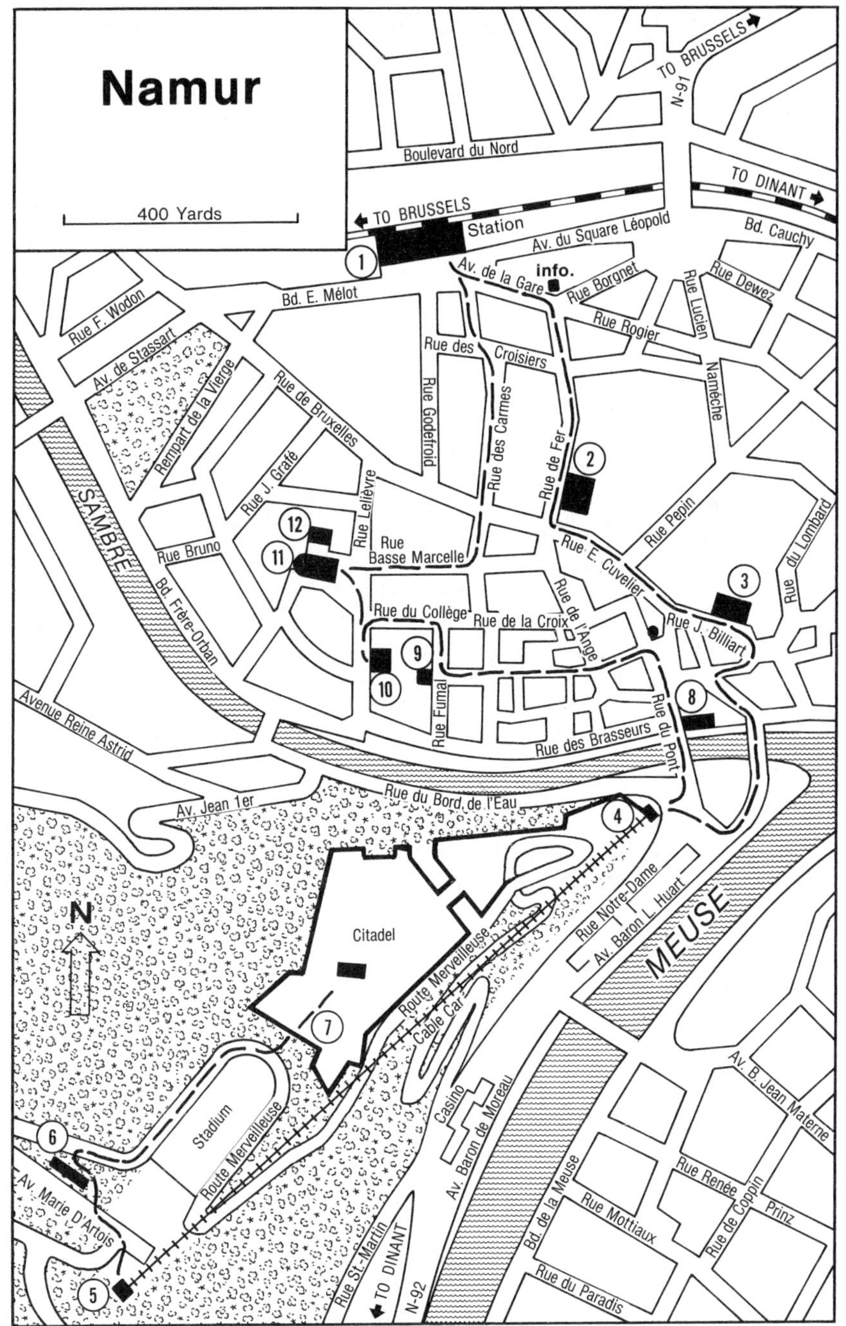
Namur
400 Yards
TO BRUSSELS
N-91
Boulevard du Nord
TO DINANT
TO BRUSSELS
Station
Av. du Square Léopold
Bd. Cauchy
Av. de la Gare
info.
Rue Borgnet
Rue Dewez
Rue Lucien Namêche
Bd. E. Mélot
Rue Rogier
Rue F. Wodon
Av. de Stassart
Rue des Croisiers
Rempart de la Vierge
Rue de Bruxelles
Rue Godefroid
Rue des Carmes
Rue de Fer
Rue J. Grafé
Rue Lelièvre
Rue Pepin
Rue du Lombard
SAMBRE
Rue Bruno
Rue Basse Marcelle
Rue E. Cuvelier
Bd. Frère-Orban
Rue du Collège
Rue de la Croix
Rue de l'Ange
Rue J. Billiart
Rue Fumal
Rue du Pont
Avenue Reine Astrid
Rue des Brasseurs
Av. Jean 1er
Rue du Bord de l'Eau
Rue Notre-Dame
Av. Baron L. Huart
MEUSE
N
Citadel
Route Merveilleuse
Cable Car
Casino
Av. Baron de Moreau
Av. B. Jean Materne
Stadium
Route Merveilleuse
Av. Marie D'Artois
Bd. de la Meuse
Rue Renée Prinz
Rue Mottiaux
Rue de Coppin
Rue du Paradis
Rue St.-Martin
TO DINANT
N-92
1
2
3
4
5
6
7
8
9
10
11
12

A Daytrip from Luxembourg City

Vianden

Towering high above a romantic village, the fairy-tale castle of Vianden casts its spell on the narrow, cobbled streets below. This is, quite simply, the most picturesque little town in the Grand Duchy, and the most enticing destination for a daytrip from Luxembourg City. In addition to its restored medieval castle, Vianden offers a visit to the exile home of Victor Hugo, an excellent folklore museum, magnificent scenery, and a delightful atmosphere that attracts visitors from all over Europe.

The story of Vianden is the story of its castle. A small fort had existed on this hill since Roman times, over which a castle was built in the 9th century. This was greatly enlarged during the 11th, 12th, and 15th centuries, and became an ancestral home of the House of Orange-Nassau, the dynasty that supplies both the kings and queens of the Netherlands as well as the grand dukes of Luxembourg.

GETTING THERE:

Trains depart the Luxembourg City Station several times in the morning for the half-hour ride to Ettelbruck, where you change to a connecting bus for Vianden. The bus ride takes about 30 minutes, and railpasses are accepted. Return service operates until early evening.

By car, head north from Luxembourg City on the N-7 to Diekirch, then take local roads into Vianden. The total distance is 27 miles.

PRACTICALITIES:

Vianden may be visited on any fine day from April through October. During the rest of the year the castle is open on weekends and holidays only. The local **Tourist Information Office**, phone 842-57, is in the Victor Hugo House. Despite its **population** of only 1,500, Vianden has legally held city status since 1308!

The Castle of Vianden

FOOD AND DRINK:

A few good restaurant choices are:

Veiner Stuff (Rue de la Gare 26, 1 block southeast of the tourist office) A romantically elegant place noted for fine cuisine. X: Tues. except July–Aug., Mon. eve., Nov. $$$

Le Châtelain (Grand-Rue 126, just below the castle) A popular restaurant with an outdoor terrace. X: Mon., Thurs. eve., except in July–Aug. $$

Heintz (Grand-Rue 55, near the Trinitarian Church) A small inn with good food, in an ancient building with a terrace and garden. X: Wed. from Oct.–July. $

SUGGESTED TOUR:

Leave the **bus station** *(Gare Routière)* (1) and stroll down Rue de la Gare to the **Maison Victor-Hugo** (2). The great French writer loved Vianden and stayed here several times, including a period of political exile in 1871. Reconstructed after World War II damage, the house is now a small museum containing some of the author's belongings and documents relating to his visits. It also houses the local tourist office and is open daily from April through October, from 9:30 a.m. to noon and 2–6 p.m., but closed on Wednesdays during April, May, September, and October.

Just before the bridge there is a bust of Victor Hugo. In the middle of the span you'll see a statue of St. Nepomuk, the patron saint of bridges. Continue across the Our River and head up Grand Rue to the **Église des Trinitaires** (3), a Gothic parish church with a double nave dating from 1248. It is one of the oldest religious buildings in Luxembourg and is noted for its fine rococo altar. A short visit here is definitely worthwhile, as is a few moments spent in the 14th-century **cloisters** behind it.

The route now leads uphill and climbs steeply around to the ***Château de Vianden** (Castle) (4), one of the great architectural treasures of the region. Until fairly recently it had been in a state of semi-ruin, but a major restoration project has now revived its medieval splendor. The roof is back on, and many of the rooms are now furnished with period pieces. A printed diagram in English leading you through its four levels will be given to you at the entrance. The castle is open daily from April through October, and on weekends and holidays the rest of the year. The hours are: April, 10 a.m. to 5 p.m.; May through August, 9 a.m. to 7 p.m.; September, 9 a.m. to 6 p.m.; October, 10 a.m. to 5 p.m.; other months, 10 a.m. to 4:30 p.m.

Return to the village and follow the charming Vieille Rue until it joins Grand Rue. Across the street is the **Musée d'Art Rustique** (Folklore Museum) (5), where local crafts, antiques, and household items of the past are displayed in an attractive old house. It is open from April through mid-October, daily from 10 a.m. to noon and 2–6 p.m.

You could easily return to the river by strolling down Grand Rue, but a more interesting, if slightly rugged, way to get there is by following the remnants of the ancient **Town Walls** (6). Now recross the bridge and turn left on Rue Victor-Hugo, which brings you to the **Télésiège** (chair lift) (7). From here you can take an enjoyable ride across the river and up to the top of a hill overlooking the valley, town, and castle. The lift operates daily from early April until late September.

Ambitious walkers may want to continue on to the **Barrage** (dam) (8). This forms the lower reservoir of a vast pumped-storage hydroelectric complex, whose inner workings several miles up the road may be visited. Ask the tourist office for details.

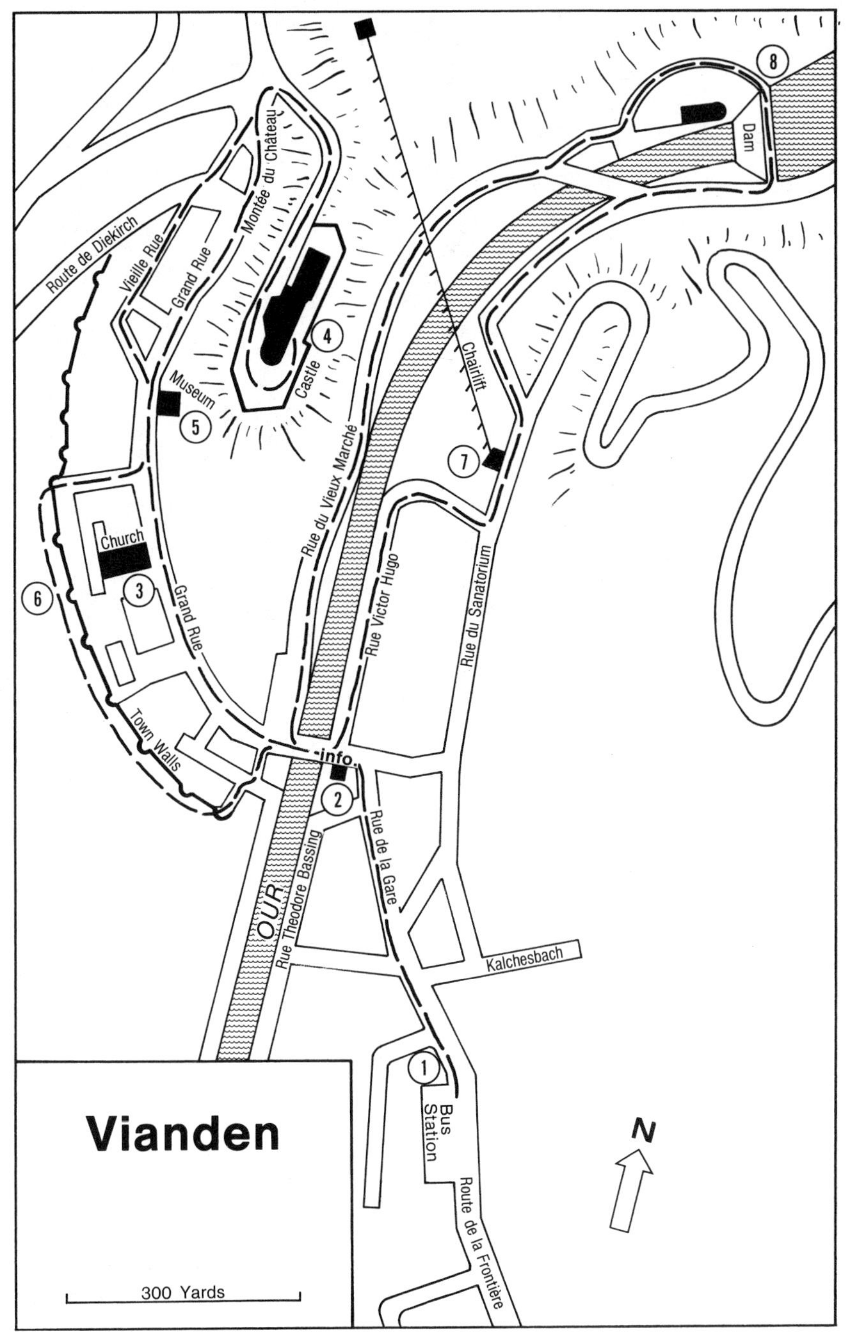
Vianden
300 Yards
N
Route de Diekirch
Vieille Rue
Grand Rue
Montée du Château
Castle
Museum
Church
Grand Rue
Town Walls
Rue du Vieux Marché
OUR
Rue Theodore Bassing
info.
Rue de la Gare
Rue Victor Hugo
Rue du Sanatorium
Chairlift
Dam
Kalchesbach
Bus Station
Route de la Frontière
1
2
3
4
5
6
7
8

Section V

DAYTRIPS IN
HOLLAND

• from Amsterdam

If ever a country was made for daytripping, Holland is surely it. The entire Kingdom of the Netherlands, as it is correctly called by almost no one, lies within such easy reach of Amsterdam that virtually all of its varied attractions may be enjoyed on one-day excursions. The six destinations described in this section cover two of the country's favorite outings, one to Delft and the other to Alkmaar; a steam-train-and-boat trip through the "Historic Triangle" to the old port of Hoorn; the great university and museum town of Leiden; the sophisticated city of Utrecht; and to what may be your only opportunity to see rural life as it was in days gone by—now preserved in an open-air museum near Arnhem.

Additional one-day adventures are described in our companion guidebook, ***Daytrips in Holland, Belgium and Luxembourg***, which follows the same format and also features walking tours of the three bases: Amsterdam, Brussels, and Luxembourg City.

GETTING AROUND:

Rail is usually the fastest and easiest way to get around Holland, with train departures so frequent that reference to schedules is unnecessary. International express trains, marked **EC** or **D**, often charge a supplementary fare unless you are using a Eurailpass. **IC** express trains are usually your best bet, otherwise use the slower *Sneltreins* or local *Stoptreins*.

Eurailpasses (see page 18) are accepted for travel on the Netherlands Railways, but if you're only visiting Holland or the Benelux countries you should consider these more economical passes: The **Benelux Tourrail Pass** is valid for unlimited train travel throughout Holland, Belgium, and Luxembourg on any 5 days within a 17-day period. It is sold in both first- and second-class versions, for either adults or for juniors up to age 25. Buy it at any major train station in the Benelux countries, or from overseas offices of the Netherlands Board of Tourism. Cheaper yet is the **Netherlands Rail Ranger**, available for 7 consecutive days of unlimited travel in Holland only, in either first- or second-class versions. To this may be added the **Public Transport Link Ranger**, which extends the pass to include virtually all buses, trams, and subways in the nation. It is sold at major train stations in Holland, as well as by overseas offices of the Netherlands Board of Tourism (see below). Ask the tourist office for a current copy of "Touring Holland by Rail," a free booklet that explains everything in English.

By car, Holland has what is arguably the most intensive road network in Europe. Driving is exceptionally easy outside the big cities, but you may have trouble parking in Amsterdam and coping with the notorious congestion.

Bicycles may be rented at many train stations, with a discount if you got there by train.

Local Tourist Offices, known by the letters **VVV**, will provide current information as well as reserve accommodations for you. Ask them about the **Museum Card**, which for one low price admits you to some 375 of the best museums in Holland. They can also tell you about the **Tourist Menu** and **Neerlands Dis** menu programs that offer excellent meals at quite reasonable prices in hundreds of participating restaurants.

ADVANCE PLANNING INFORMATION:

The **Netherlands Board of Tourism (NBT)** has branches throughout the world, including New York, Chicago, San Francisco, Toronto, London, and Sydney. Their New York address is: 355 Lexington Avenue, New York NY 10017, phone (212) 370-7367.

A Daytrip from Amsterdam

Hoorn and the Historic Triangle

Here is an easy and thoroughly enjoyable daytrip that is just filled with sun and fun. You can travel by train or car to the historic port of Hoorn, then ride an ancient steam train through the lovely North Holland landscape to Medemblik, where you board an excursion boat to Enkhuizen. From there it's a short train ride back to Hoorn, a most delightful place to explore on foot.

Known as the "Historic Triangle," *(Historische Driehoek)*, this rich agricultural area is loaded with memories of the former Zuider Zee, the arm of the North Sea that became the land-locked IJsselmeer. Many of its traditions may be probed at the Westfries Museum in Hoorn, while the magnificant and fascinating outdoor museum at Enkhuizen brings the rural past to life.

First settled in the early 14th century, Hoorn was a major port for international trade until the late 17th century. It gave its name to Cape Horn, the southernmost tip of South America, which was discovered in 1616 by the locally-born navigator, Willem Schouten. This was an important center of the Dutch East Indies Company, which brought about the prosperity so clearly seen in the town's many beautiful old buildings. Alas, as trade increased, so did the draught of the ships needed to carry it. The local waters are relatively shallow and subject to silting, and so the maritime trade gradually moved to deeper ports. One of the most attractive towns in Holland, Hoorn thrives today as a regional shopping and yachting center.

GETTING THERE:

Trains, marked for Enkhuizen, depart Amsterdam's Centraal Station at half-hour intervals for the 36-minute run to Hoorn. Return service operates until late evening.

By car, the most attractive route to follow from central Amsterdam is through the IJ Tunnel, then the N-10 and N-247 roads north by way of Edam to Hoorn. It may be slightly faster to take the A-7 motorway instead. In either case, the distance is about 25 miles.

In the Steam Train Station at Hoorn

PRACTICALITIES:

This trip may be taken on any day from mid-July through late August; and on Tuesdays through Saturdays during May, June, and early September. The "Historic Triangle" steam train and boat combination does not operate at other times. To avoid disappointment you should check first with the information office in Amsterdam's Centraal Station, or with the tourist office in Hoorn. Good weather is essential, as is an early start—around 9 a.m. at the latest. The local **Tourist Information Office** (VVV) in Hoorn, phone (02290) 183-42, is in the former Town Hall at Nieuwstraat 23. Current schedules for the "Historic Triangle" combination can be had by phoning (02290) 148-62. **Bicycles** may be rented at the Hoorn Station; for reservations call (02290) 170-96. Hoorn is in the province of **Noord-Holland**, and has a **population** of about 56,000.

FOOD AND DRINK:

Snacks and drinks are available on both the steam train and the boat. Some good restaurants in Hoorn are:

De Waag (Rode Steen 8, near the Westfries Museum) Meat and fish specialties. X: Tues. $$

Bontekoe Taverne (Nieuwendam 1, near the Binnenhaven) Upstairs, in a 17th-century warehouse. X: Mon., Tues., between Oct. and April. $$

Stationsrestauratie (in the train station) Inexpensive and convenient. $

SUGGESTED TOUR:

Begin your tour at the **Hoorn Train Station** (1), where you cross a pedestrian bridge over the tracks to the **Steam Train Station** (2). There is a great deal of intriguing activity here as locomotives and open-ended cars, some nearly a century old, are shunted about. Buy a combination ticket for the steam train and boat *(combi stoomtram + boot)* and study the printed schedule carefully. These rides are privately operated and are not covered by any railpass.

You will probably have time before departure to enjoy visiting the yards and special steam exhibitions. No one seems to mind your walking around on the tracks or even in the train sheds and machine shops.

Now board the ancient train and take delight in the passing countryside. The ride to Medemblik takes about one hour, and there is a primitive bar car to help you pass the time. Upon arrival at **Medemblik Station** (3), walk straight ahead past **De Oude Bakkerij**, a unique little bakery museum, and down the main street to the **harbor** (4), where you will find the large excursion boat (probably the *Stad Enkhuizen*) that will take you to Enkhuizen. This delightful cruise on the IJsselmeer takes about 75 minutes. Again, snacks and drinks are available.

From the **Enkhuizen Pier** (5) it is only a few steps to the train station, where there are frequent trains back to Hoorn. While here, however, you might want to visit the famous ***Zuider Zee Outdoor Museum** *(Buitenmuseum),* where some 130 old houses, churches, shops, and other rural structures from the region have been relocated to preserve them for posterity. Grouped into villages, some are staffed with people performing the old crafts and trades. Various events are staged throughout the day, and all is well explained. The museum is easily reached by boat from the Enkhuizen Pier, and is open daily from mid-April through late October, from 10 a.m. to 5 p.m.

Return to Hoorn by train and begin your walking tour of the old port town by following the map to the former **Stadhuis** (Town Hall) (6), a lovely twin-gabled building from 1613 that now houses the tourist office *(VVV).* Continue down Nieuwstraat past the enormous **Grote Kerk**, a 19th-century church that has been strangely converted into shops. Kerkstraat leads to Rode Steen, the town's main square. Named after the red stone that was once a place of public execution, this large open area is surrounded by exquisite old buildings.

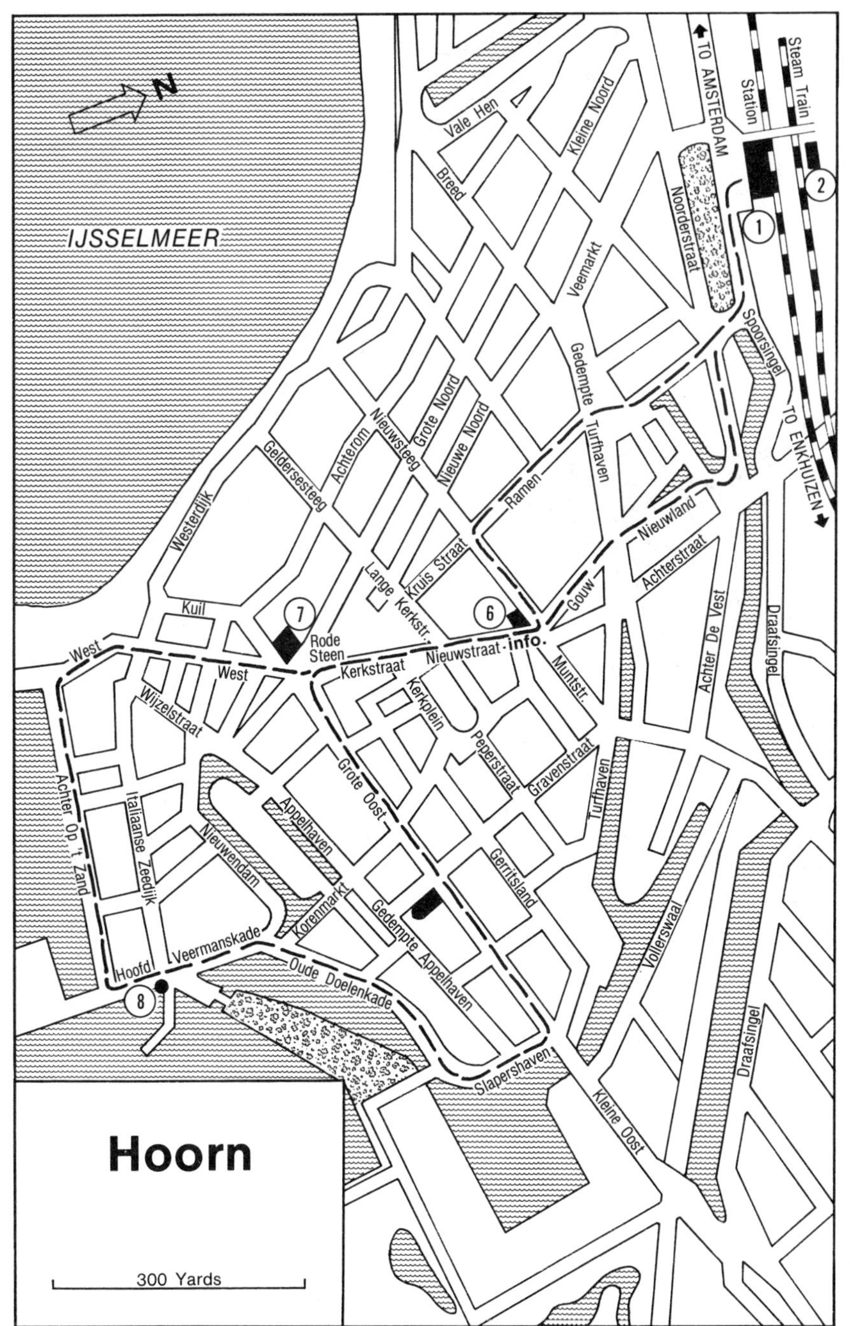
N
IJSSELMEER
TO AMSTERDAM
Station
Steam Train
TO ENKHUIZEN
Vale Hen
Kleine Noord
Breed
Noorderstraat
Veemarkt
Spoorsingel
Gedempte
Turfhaven
Grote Noord
Nieuwe Noord
Nieuwsteeg
Achterom
Geldersesteeg
Westerdijk
Ramen
Nieuwland
Achterstraat
Gouw
Kruis Straat
Lange Kerkstr.
Kuil
Rode
Steen
West
Kerkstraat
Nieuwstraat
info.
Muntstr.
Achter De Vest
Draafsingel
Kerkplein
Wijzelstraat
Peperstraat
Gravenstraat
Turfhaven
Grote Oost
Appelhaven
Achter Op 't Zand
Italiaanse Zeedijk
Nieuwendam
Gerritsland
Vollerswaal
Korenmarkt
Gedempte Appelhaven
Veermanskade
Hoofd
Oude Doelenkade
Slapershaven
Kleine Oost
Draafsingel
1
2
6
7
8
Hoorn
300 Yards

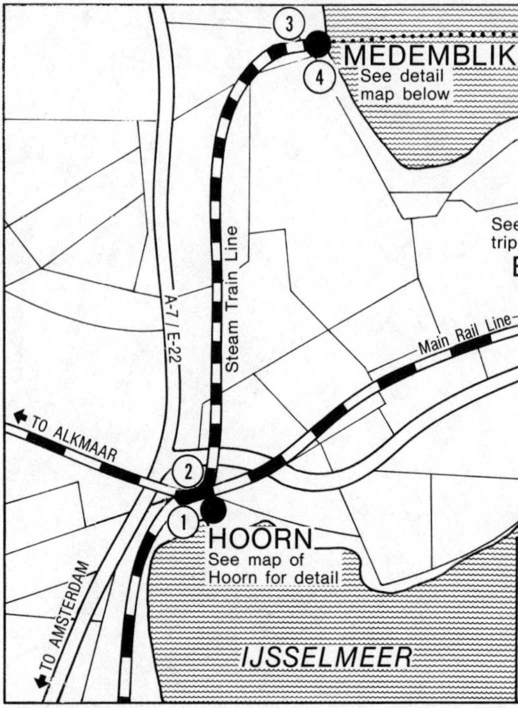

MEDEMBLIK
See detail map below
Boat
N
See map of Enkhuizen trip for detail
ENKHUIZEN
A-7 / E-22
Steam Train Line
Main Rail Line
TO ALKMAAR
HOORN
See map of Hoorn for detail
TO AMSTERDAM
IJSSELMEER

Historic Triangle
Area

5 Miles

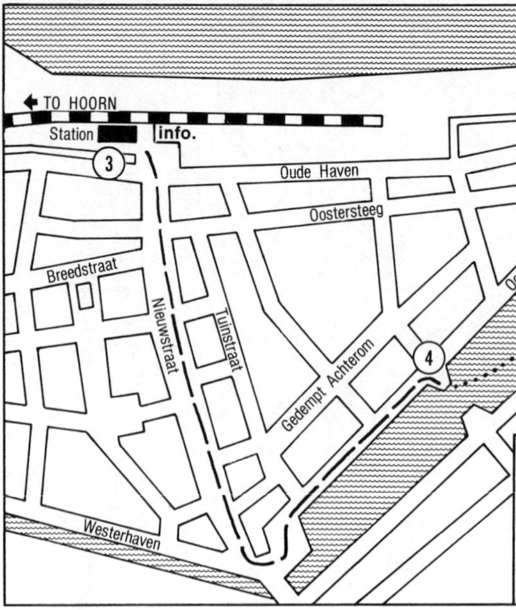

TO HOORN
Station
info.
Oude Haven
Oostersteeg
Breedstraat
Nieuwstraat
Tuinstraat
Gedempt Achterom
Oosterhaven
Boat
Westerhaven

Route Through Medemblik

The Rode Steen and the Westfries Museum in Hoorn

One of these structures, the highly-ornate 17th-century Staten College (State Council) is now the home of the **Westfries Museum** (7). Step inside to witness the wealth this town once possessed. Sumptuous furniture, paintings, weapons, ship models, and anything else associated with the history of the region—they're all there, all displayed in elegant surroundings. The museum is open Mondays through Fridays, from 11 a.m. to 5 p.m.; and on Saturdays and Sundays from 2–5 p.m.

On the opposite side of the square is the **Waag**, an especially nice weigh house from 1609. Stroll down Grote Oost past the **Oosterkerk**, a Gothic church founded in 1450. Its stained-glass window from 1620 depicts a famous naval battle. Turn right at Slapershaven and amble along the picturesque harbor, busy with pleasure boats. The early-16th-century **Hoofdtoren** (8) was a part of the old fortifications, and sports a delicate belfry from 1651. From here you may want to just wander around and soak up the delicious atmosphere before returning to the train station and Amsterdam.

A Daytrip from Amsterdam

Alkmaar

The world-famous Cheese Market at Alkmaar is a tradition going back to the early 17th century. Although more efficient distribution methods have been developed over the years, this colorful weekly wholesale auction is still held, partly as a tourist attraction and partly to preserve a worthwhile link with the past.

But there is much more to this lovely old town than cheese. The historic center, surrounded by moats and canals, still maintains its Old World character, with many fine buildings from the 15th through the 18th centuries remaining in use today.

Alkmaar was first mentioned in the 10th century and received its charter in 1254. It played a pivotal role in the Dutch struggle for independence when the town defeated the Spaniards in 1573 by opening the sluices, thus flooding the surrounding area. This marked the beginning of the end of Spanish domination in the Low Countries, and led eventually to self rule.

GETTING THERE:

Trains leave Amsterdam's Centraal Station frequently for the 30-to-45 minute ride to Alkmaar, with return service until late evning.

By car, the fastest route is the N-5/A-5 highway west in the direction of Haarlem, then the A-9 north to Alkmaar. The total distance from central Amsterdam is 25 miles.

PRACTICALITIES:

Tourists by the thousands flock to Alkmaar on Friday mornings between mid-April and mid-September to see the famous **Cheese Market** in action. The Municipal Museum is closed on Mondays and Saturdays, the Cheese Museum on Sundays, and the Beer Museum on Mondays. The local **Tourist Information Office** (VVV), phone (072) 11-42-84, is in the historic weighhouse at Waagplein 2. **Bicycles** may be rented at the station, phone (072) 11-79-07. Alkmaar is in the province of **Noord-Holland**, and has a **population** of about 87,000.

Cheese porters in the Waagplein

FOOD AND DRINK:

Being a favorite tourist attraction, Alkmaar has a wide variety of restaurants and cafés in all price ranges. Some good choices for lunch are:

Hof van Sonoy (Hof van Sonoy 1, 2 blocks northwest of the Waag) Luxury dining in an old almshouse just off Nieuwesloot. $$$

Koekenbier (Kennemerstraatweg 16, 3 blocks south of the windmill) Scandinavian food. X: Mon. $$

't Pannekoekschip De Kajuit (at the Fries Bridge 3 blocks east of the Beer Museum) All kinds of pancakes served on a boat in the canal. X: Mon. $

Stationsrestauratie (in the train station) Good food at low prices. $

SUGGESTED TOUR:

Leave the **train station** (1) and follow the map into the historic center. On your left is the **Noord Hollands Kanaal**, opened in 1825 to link Amsterdam directly with the North Sea. Much too shallow for large ships, it was later superseded by the larger North Sea Canal. A right turn on Doelenstraat leads to the **Stedelijk Museum** (Municipal Museum) (2), located in an impressive building from 1520. Its exhibits, including a great deal of good art, artifacts, and historic objects, relate mainly to the town and surrounding areas; with a particular emphasis on the famous siege of 1573. If you come on a Friday morning in season you might want to return here after seeing the Cheese Market, which is all over by noon. The museum is open on Tuesdays through Fridays, from 10 a.m. to 3 p.m.; and on Sundays and holidays from 1–5 p.m.

Turn left on Nieuwesloot and follow it to Waagplein, where the famous ***Cheese Market** is held on Fridays from 10 a.m. to noon, between mid-April and mid-September. A delightful anachronism in an age of efficient distribution, this staged event carries on traditions begun in the early 17th century, primarily for the benefit of the thousands of tourists who come to witness the spectacle. The cheeses, sold by auction to wholesale dealers, are mostly of the Edam variety, although usually without the red export covering you are probably familiar with. Brought to the large open square by truck, they are tested by prospective buyers, who accompany their bids with a brisk clapping of hands. Deals are consummated by handshakes, after which the real ceremony begins.

Cheese porters, wearing immaculate white uniforms and belonging to an ancient guild, carry heavy loads of the cheeses on traditional litters to the weighhouse *(Waag)*, where the totals are tallied, then to the purchasers' trucks. Working in pairs, they jog along with a peculiar gait to prevent spills. There are four companies of porters, each with its own hat color, and each consisting of six porters, a weigher, and a foreman.

A good place to watch all of this activity is from the windows of the **Kaas Museum** (Cheese Museum), located upstairs in the weighhouse, or **Waag** (3). Originally built as a church in 1341, this magnificent structure was converted to its present use as early as 1582. The lovely Renaissance façade and ornate tower were added soon after that. A carillon plays between 11 a.m. and noon on market days, and jousting figures on horseback appear as a trumpeter blows a clarion call. Exhibits in the museum are concerned with both past and present methods of cheese production, with delicious samples on sale. The museum may be visited on Mondays through Saturdays, from 10 a.m. to 4 p.m., April through October. It opens at 9 a.m. on Fridays.

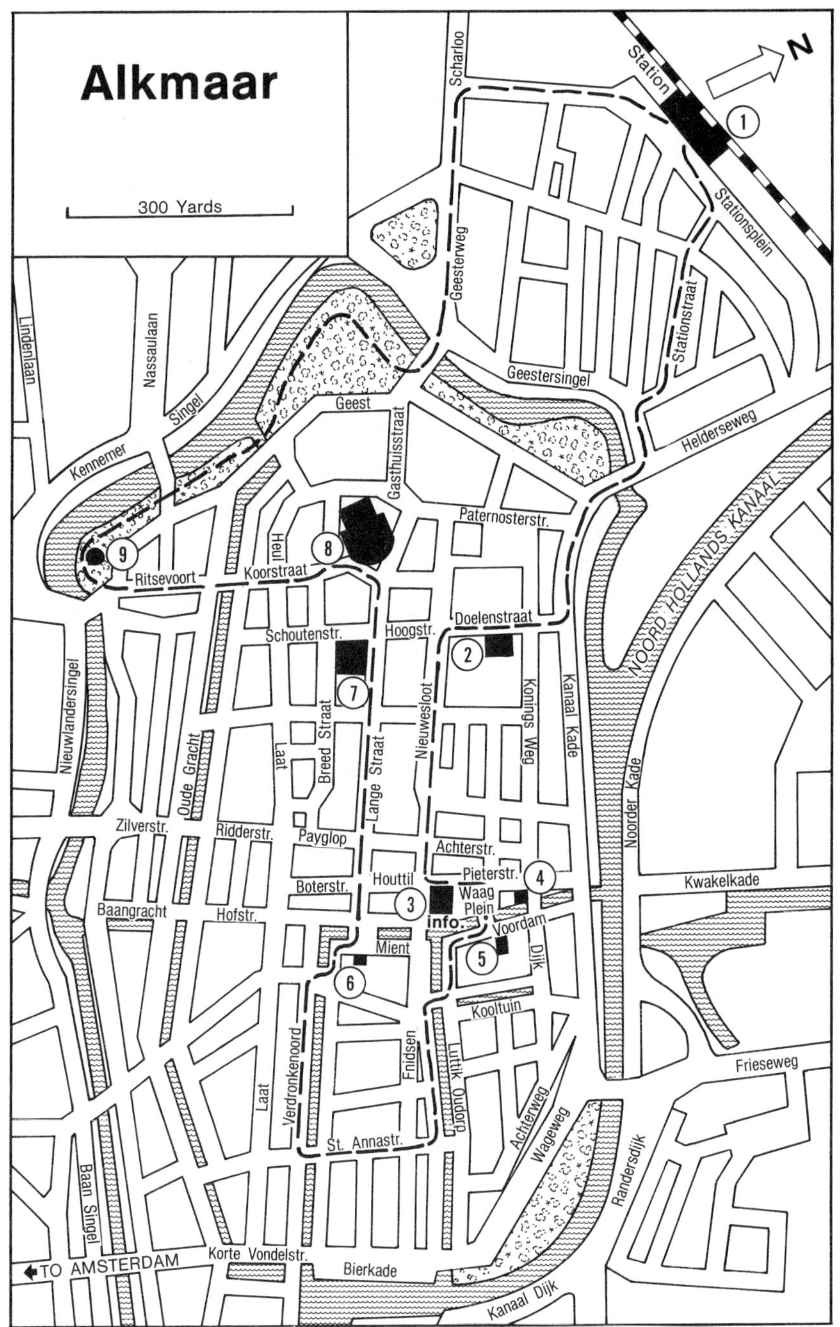
Alkmaar
300 Yards
N
Station
Stationsplein
Stationstraat
Scharloo
Geesterweg
Geestersingel
Helderseweg
NOORD HOLLANDS KANAAL
Lindenlaan
Nassaulaan
Kennemer
Singel
Geest
Gasthuisstraat
Paternosterstr.
Heul
Ritsevoort
Koorstraat
Doelenstraat
Schoutenstr.
Hoogstr.
Nieuwlandersingel
Oude Gracht
Laat
Breed Straat
Lange Straat
Nieuwesloot
Konings Weg
Kanaal Kade
Noorder Kade
Zilverstr.
Ridderstr.
Payglop
Achterstr.
Pieterstr.
Houttil
Boterstr.
Waag Plein
info.
Voordam
Dijk
Kwakelkade
Baangracht
Hofstr.
Mient
Kooltuin
Verdronkenoord
Fnidsen
Luttik Oudorp
Achterweg
Wageweg
Frieseweg
Randersdijk
St. Annastr.
Baan Singel
TO AMSTERDAM
Korte Vondelstr.
Bierkade
Kanaal Dijk
1
2
3
4
5
6
7
8
9

Having tasted the cheese, you may be ready for the **National Beer Museum** (4), just a few steps beyond the Waagplein. Housed in the former *"De Boom"* brewery, it traces the history of beer making throughout the ages. You can enjoy some of the liquid refreshment in the bar or at the adjoining canal-side café. The Beer Museum is open on Tuesdays through Saturdays, from 10 a.m. to 4 p.m.; and on Sundays from 1–5 p.m.

Cross a bridge to Voordam and the new **Hans Brinker Museum** (5), housed in five warehouses from 1635. The famous story of the silver skates is retold with period room sets, costumes, and artifacts. It is open from April until October, on Tuesdays through Fridays and on Sundays, from 1–5 p.m.

Now follow the map through some of the most colorful streets in town. Along the way you will pass the 16th-century **Vismarkt** (Fish Market) (6), which also operates on Friday mornings, and which is noted for its sculpted roof figures and old pump from 1785. Around the corner from this, at number 23 Mient, is a house whose gable displays Alkmaar's coat of arms—with the lions facing the wrong way as an insult to the town fathers.

Continue down Lange Straat, the main shopping street, to the **Stadhuis** *(Town Hall)* (7), a late Gothic structure begun in 1509. Some of its beautifully decorated rooms may usually be seen by asking at the reception desk, but only on Mondays through Fridays, from 9 a.m. to noon and 2–4 p.m.

Just a few more steps and you are at the **Grote Kerk** (8), a splendid Dutch Reform church dedicated to St. Laurens. Built between 1470 and 1516 in the Gothic style, it has a very impressive interior. The large organ in the nave dates from 1643, while the small one in the north ambulatory—from 1511—is the oldest still in use in Holland. Recitals are frequently held on Cheese Market days.

The route now wanders down to the old waterside ramparts, along which is the 18th-century **Molen van Piet** (9). Still grinding flour as it has for centuries, this ancient windmill may usually be visited. A stroll through the park and a left turn over the bridge onto Geesterweg will return you to the station.

A Daytrip from Amsterdam

Leiden

Holland's first university was established at Leiden in 1575 and is still going strong. Especially renowned for its faculties of medicine and law, it remains the nation's most prestigious center of higher learning. With such a scholarly background, it is perhaps not surprising that the city possesses an exceptionally broad range of museums. These are, in fact, its major attraction to tourists. If you enjoy visiting museums, you will love Leiden.

The town is also noted as the birthplace of Rembrandt, Jan Steen, and several other famous painters. The Pilgrim Fathers, having fled England for Amsterdam, moved here in 1609, and remained until departing for the New World in 1620.

GETTING THERE:

Trains leave Amsterdam's Centraal Station very frequently for the 35-minute ride to Leiden. Return service operates until late evening, after which hourly trains run all night long.

By car, take the A-4 highway past Schiphol Airport. Leiden is 25 miles southwest of central Amsterdam.

PRACTICALITIES:

Avoid coming to Leiden on a Monday, when practically everything is closed. Most museums are open on Sundays and holidays after 1 p.m., although the Pilgrim Fathers Documents Center is closed on weekends. October 3rd is the local **festival** day—expect all attractions to be closed. Leiden makes a fine rainy day destination. The local **Tourist Information Office** (VVV), phone (071) 14-68-46, is just across from the train station at Stationsplein 210. **Bicycles** may be rented at the station, phone (071) 13-13-04. Leiden is in the province of **Zuid-Holland**, and has a **population** of about 107,000.

FOOD AND DRINK:

Some good restaurant choices in the old part of town are:

Rôtisserie Oudt Leyden (Steenstraat 51, 4 blocks south of the station) Fine dining in an Old Dutch atmosphere, possibly the best in town. X: Sun. $$$

De Doelen (Rapenburg 2, just north of the Oudheden Museum) On a canal, with a nice ambiance. X: Sat., Sun. $$

't Pannekoekenhuis (Steenstraat 51, 4 blocks south of the station) Pancakes and the like, with a *Tourist Menu.* Not to be confused with the expensive adjoining Oudt Leyden restaurant. $

Bernsen (Breestraat 157, near the town hall) Features the *Tourist Menu.* $

Surakarta (Noordeinde 51, 3 blocks northwest of the Oudheden Museum) Indonesian cuisine, with a *Tourist Menu.* $

SUGGESTED TOUR:

From the **train station** (1) walk straight ahead on Stationsweg until you get to the first canal. On the right are two of the many museums for which Leiden is famous. At this point you will have to decide which of these interest you most since you can't possibly see all of them in one day without suffering a terminal case of museum burnout. The **Boerhaave Museum** (2) specializes in the history of science from a Dutch point of view, displaying a formidable collection of antique instruments and medical devices. These may be seen on Tuesdays through Saturdays, from 10 a.m. and 5 p.m.; and on Sundays from 1–5 p.m. Just beyond it is the **Rijksmuseum voor Volkenkunde** (Ethnology Museum), a sweeping survey of civilizations from outside the European world. Of particular interest here are the marvelous Buddhas from Japan; religious artifacts from Indonesia, Tibet, China and elsewhere; houses and boats from the South Pacific; and displays on American Indian, Eskimo, Mexican, and South American cultures. The main focus is, naturally, on the former Dutch colonies. Visits can be made on Tuesdays through Saturdays, from 10 a.m. to 5 p.m.; and on Sundays and holidays from 1–5 p.m.

Continue down Steenstraat and follow the map across the canalized waters of the Rijn *(Rhine)* river, whose main flow is now to the south through Rotterdam. The lovely Rapenburg canal leads to what is perhaps Leiden's most outstanding museum, the ***Oudheden** *(Rijksmuseum van Oudheden)* (3). Housing one of the major archaeological collections in Europe, it gets off to an impressive start right in the entry hall with the entire *Temple of Taffeh,* donated by Egypt in 1969 in recognition of Holland's role in the rescue of Nubian treasures threatened by the construction of the Aswan dam. Originally built in

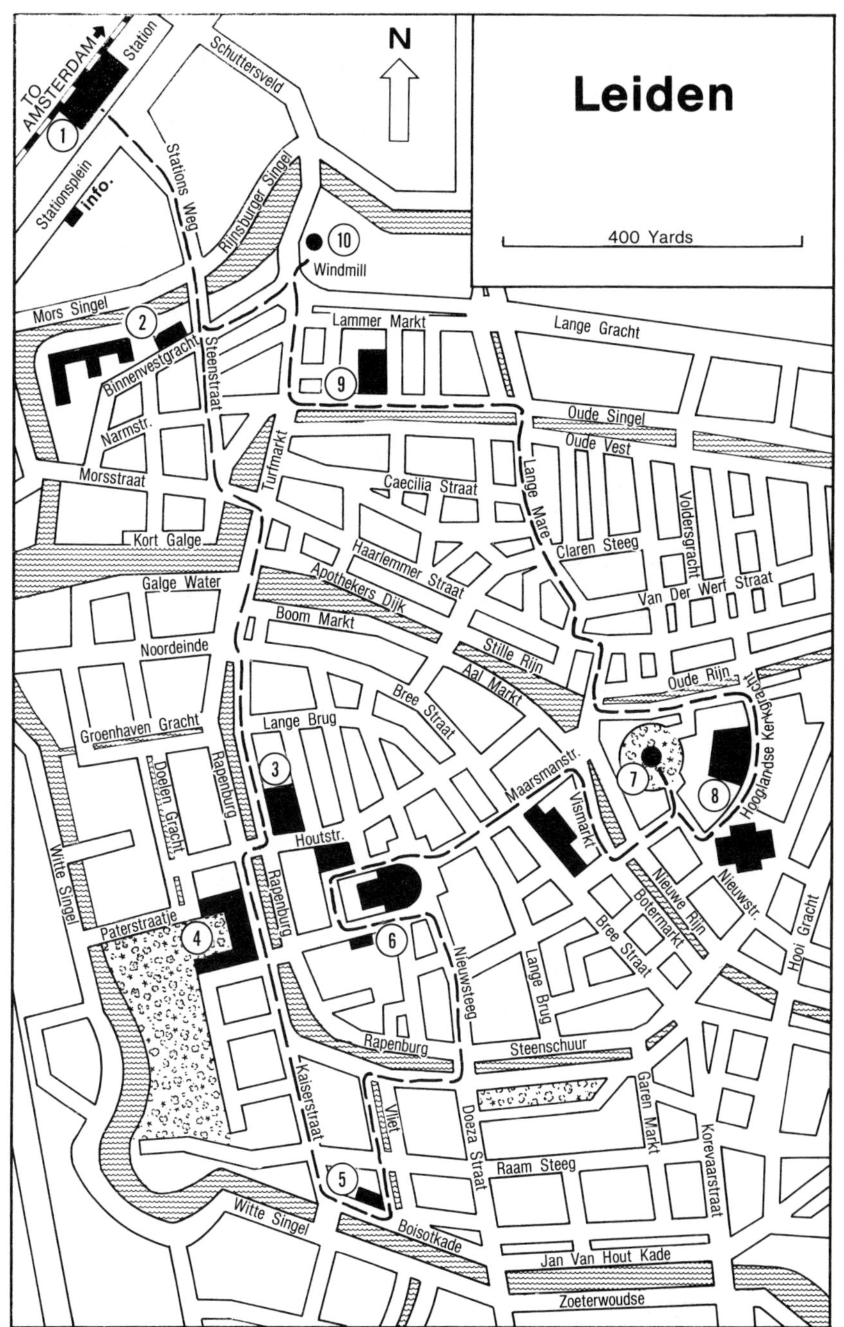

Leiden
N
400 Yards
TO AMSTERDAM
Station
Stationsplein
info.
Schuttersveld
Stations Weg
Rijnsburger Singel
Windmill
Mors Singel
Binnenvestgracht
Steenstraat
Lammer Markt
Lange Gracht
Oude Singel
Oude Vest
Narmstr.
Morsstraat
Turfmarkt
Caecilia Straat
Lange Mare
Voldersgracht
Kort Galge
Haarlemmer Straat
Claren Steeg
Apothekers Dijk
Van Der Werf Straat
Galge Water
Boom Markt
Noordeinde
Stille Rijn
Aal Markt
Oude Rijn
Bree Straat
Hooglandse Kerkgracht
Groenhaven Gracht
Lange Brug
Doelen Gracht
Rapenburg
Maarsmanstr.
Vismarkt
Witte Singel
Houtstr.
Nieuwe Rijn
Botermarkt
Nieuwstr.
Paterstraatje
Hooi Gracht
Nieuwsteeg
Bree Straat
Lange Brug
Rapenburg
Steenschuur
Kaiserstraat
Vliet
Doeza Straat
Garen Markt
Korevaarstraat
Raam Steeg
Witte Singel
Boisotkade
Jan Van Hout Kade
Zoeterwoudse
1
2
3
4
5
6
7
8
9
10

the 1st century A.D., it was converted during the 4th century for the worship of Isis and later used as a Christian church. Other displays here are of equal caliber, covering Egyptian, Greek, Roman, and other eras of classical antiquity. The top floor is devoted to archaeology in the Netherlands, from prehistoric times through the Middle Ages. All of this may be seen on Tuesdays through Saturdays, from 10 a.m. to 5 p.m.; and on Sundays and holidays from 1–5 p.m.

Now cross the canal and wander down to the **Academie** (4), the main building of the university since 1581. Originally built as a church, it has a fine bell turret and now houses, among other things, the small **Academisch Historisch Museum**. Displays here all relate to the long history of the university and may be seen on Wednesdays through Fridays, from 1–5 p.m. Close to this, at Rapenburg 65, is the **Prentenkabinet** (Print Room) of the university. You can step inside for a look at the collection of prints and drawings, and especially at the interesting material on the history of photography, including old cameras. It is open on Tuesdays through Fridays, from 2–5 p.m. Admission to both university museums is free.

Behind the Academie building is one of the oldest botanical gardens in Europe, the **Hortus Botanicus.** A perfect place to relax, it was laid out in 1590 and belongs to the university. You can enter the gates at Rapenburg 73.

A short stroll down Kaiserstraat and a left at the next canal brings you to the **Pilgrim Fathers Documents Center** (5), whose displays concern the life of the Pilgrims in Leiden before they left for America in 1620. It is open on Mondays through Fridays, from 9:30 a.m. to 4:30 p.m., and admission is free.

Now follow the map to the **Pieterskerk** (6), a large 15th-century church with a fine interior. Next to it is the **Jan Pesijnshofje**, a 17th-century almshouse built on the site of the home of John Robinson, the leader of the Pilgrims. A plaque in English explains all.

The route continues past the **Stadhuis**, or Town Hall, with an impressive restored façade of 1600 in the Dutch Renaissance style. Behind this, along the Nieuwe Rijn canal, is held a lively outdoor market. Cross the unusual bridge and wander through some narrow streets to the **Burcht** (7), a 12th-century fortress atop a mound of Saxon or possibly Roman origin. It once guarded the confluence of the Old and New Rhine *(Rijn)* rivers, both of which have long since been turned into canals with most of the water diverted to the south. You can climb to the top of the citadel for a superb view of Leiden.

Return to Nieuwstraat and take a look at the **Hooglandse Kerk**, an imposing church from the 15th century. Hooglandsekerkgracht leads to a former orphanage from the 17th century that now houses the **National Museum of Geology and Mineralogy** (8), where you can see

The market along the Nieuwe Rijn Canal

all sorts of stones and bones, including minerals and a treasury of precious gems. It is open on Mondays through Fridays, from 10 a.m. to 5 p.m.; and on Sundays from 2–5 p.m.

Continue on through the old town, following the map to Leiden's superb art gallery, the **Stedelijk Museum "De Lakenhal"** (9). Erected in 1640, this former cloth weavers' guildhall now exhibits 16th- and 17th-century paintings by such local artists as Jan Steen and Lucas van Leyden. Native-son Rembrandt is represented by an early work. There are also period room settings, sculptures, decorative art works, armor, tiles, and historical artifacts on display. The museum is open on Tuesdays through Saturdays, from 10 a.m. to 5 p.m.; and on Sundays and holidays from 1–5 p.m.

On the way back to the station you will pass a windmill used as the **Molenmuseum "De Valk"** (10). Built in the mid-18th century, it has been restored to its condition of about 1900, and may be visited on Tuesdays through Saturdays, from 10 a.m. to 5 p.m.; and on Sundays and holidays from 1–5 p.m.

A Daytrip from Amsterdam

*Delft

Long famous for its distinctive blue porcelain, historic Delft is among the best preserved and most picturesque places in Holland. Its lovely old buildings and tree-shaded canals make it everything a Dutch town should be, a scene right out of a painting by Vermeer. That renowned 17th-century artist was in fact born in Delft, and lived and died here. Another celebrated resident was William the Silent, in some ways the father of modern Holland, who was murdered here in 1584.

Settled since at least the 11th century, Delft received its charter in 1246. Trade grew with the development of a harbor on the Maas river, a short distance away in what is now Rotterdam. A great fire in 1536 almost totally destroyed the town, but it was soon rebuilt. The manufacture of porcelain brought about a great prosperity that lasted until the late 18th century. Later revived, this industry today plays only a minor role in the town's economy.

As you will quickly discover, Delft is very popular with tourists. Fortunately, most of them never get beyond the pottery shops in the market place, leaving the tranquil streets and narrow canals there for you to enjoy in peace.

GETTING THERE:

Trains depart Amsterdam's Centraal Station frequently for the 55-minute ride to Delft. A local *(stoptrein)* runs at half-hour intervals and goes directly there, while the express *(IC)* trains require a change at Den Haag HS Station. Return service operates until late evening, followed by hourly departures all night long.

By car, take the A-4 highway southwest to Den Haag, followed by the A-13 into Delft. The total distance from Amsterdam is 36 miles.

PRACTICALITIES:

Most of the museums are closed on Mondays, except that the two major ones are open daily during June, July, and August. The main churches are not open to tourists on Sundays. A colorful **outdoor market** is held on the Markt every Thursday from 9 a.m. until 5 p.m.,

The bridge behind the Nieuwe Kerk

and there is a fascinating **flea market** along the canals on Saturdays from May through September. The local **Tourist Information Office** (VVV), phone (015) 12-61-00, is in the market square at Markt 85. **Bicycles** may be rented at the train station, phone (015) 14-30-33 for reservations. Delft is in the province of **Zuid-Holland** and has a **population** of about 88,000.

FOOD AND DRINK:

Delft has an unusually broad range of restaurants and cafés, mostly geared to the tourist trade. Among the better choices are:

Prinsenkelder (Schoolstraat 11, in the Prinsenhof Museum) Elegant French-inspired dining. Reservations preferred, phone (015) 12-18-60. X: Sat. lunch, Sun. $$$

Spijshuis De Dis (Beestenmarkt 36, 2 blocks south of the Nieuwe Kerk) Good Dutch food. X: Wed. $$

Le Vieux Jean (Heilige Geest Kerkhof 3, by the Oude Kerk) Classic French cuisine. X: Sun., Mon. $$

Monopole (Markt 48, on the market square) Light meals and drinks, *Tourist Menu*. $

Stationsrestauratie (in the station) Convenient and inexpensive dining. $

SUGGESTED TOUR:

It is an easy and rather pretty walk from the **train station** (1) to the **Markt**, a busy market square lined with outdoor cafés and shops. Just follow the map. At its west end stands the imposing **Stadhuis** (Town Hall) (2), a Renaissance structure built in 1618. The tower dates from the 14th century and was part of the original building that was destroyed in the great fire of 1536. It may be possible to step inside to view the richly decorated council chamber and wedding hall. Horse carriage rides depart from the outside of the building during the tourist season, every day except Thursdays—when the traditional outdoor market fills up the square.

The east end of the square is dominated by the ***Nieuwe Kerk** (3), a Gothic church which, despite its name, is not all that new, having been built between 1384 and 1496. Its tower—all 365 feet of it—may be climbed for a fine view, and contains a noted 17th-century carillon that serenades the square below. Step inside to see the magnificent **mausoleum** of Holland's greatest hero, William the Silent, who was assassinated in Delft in 1584. In the vaults below (not open to the public) lie the remains of more than 40 other members of the royal House of Orange, including Queen Wilhelmina, who died in 1962. Other features of the church include some fine **stained-glass** windows and an exhibition on royal funerals. Visits may be made on Mondays through Saturdays, from 9 a.m. to 5 p.m.; with shorter hours off season. There is an admission charge.

The walk now leads around the rear of the church, passing a small canal, a remarkably picturesque little bridge, and some gorgeous houses. Turn left on Voldersgracht, a narrow lane alongside an equally narrow canal. On Saturdays in summer a **flea market** is held here, where you can have fun bargaining for all kinds of junk and perhaps a few treasures. Some of the 17th-century façades along the street are interesting, notably that at number 6 as well as the former meat market *(Vleeshal)*, decorated with animal heads, at the west end. The **Waag** (4), a former weighhouse built in 1770, was once the guildhall of the gold and silversmiths, and today serves as a small theater.

Continue on, following the map, to the ***Oude Kerk** (5). The tower of this 13th-century Gothic church leans precariously, but since it hasn't toppled over yet it is presumably safe to enter for a look at the tombs of several national heroes. Among these are **memorials** to the great artist Johannes (Jan) Vermeer (1632–1675) and the scientist Antony van Leeuwenhoek, who is reputed to have invented the microscope. While inside, be sure to take a look at the strangely carved 16th-century **pulpit** and the modern stained-glass windows depicting recent Dutch history. The church doors are open for tourists from the beginning of April until the end of October, on Mondays through Saturdays, from

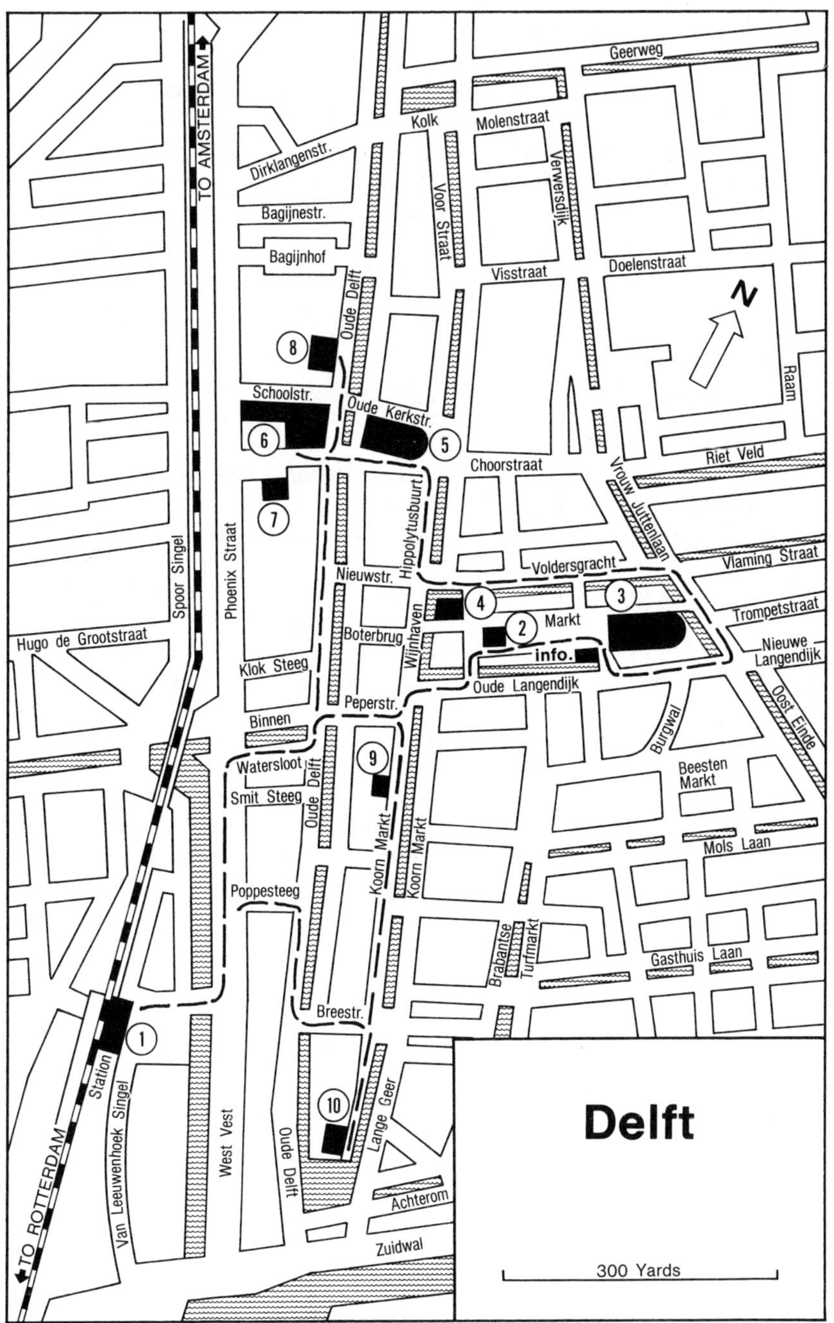
TO AMSTERDAM
TO ROTTERDAM
Geerweg
Kolk
Molenstraat
Dirklangenstr.
Verwersdijk
Voor Straat
Bagijnestr.
Bagijnhof
Visstraat
Doelenstraat
Oude Delft
N
Raam
Schoolstr.
Oude Kerkstr.
Riet Veld
Choorstraat
Vrouw Juttenlaan
Hippolytusbuurt
Phoenix Straat
Spoor Singel
Voldersgracht
Vlaming Straat
Nieuwstr.
Trompetstraat
Markt
Boterbrug
Wijnhaven
info.
Nieuwe Langendijk
Hugo de Grootstraat
Klok Steeg
Oude Langendijk
Peperstr.
Oost Einde
Binnen
Burgwal
Watersloot
Beesten Markt
Smit Steeg
Oude Delft
Koorn Markt
Koorn Markt
Mols Laan
Poppesteeg
Brabantse
Turfmarkt
Gasthuis Laan
Breestr.
Station
Van Leeuwenhoek Singel
West Vest
Oude Delft
Lange Geer
Achterom
Zuidwal
Delft
300 Yards
1
2
3
4
5
6
7
8
9
10

10 a.m. until 4 p.m. There is an admission charge.

Now stroll over to the ***Prinsenhof Museum** (6), housed in a 15th-century convent that was once the residence of William the Silent. It was also the scene of his assassination, and the bullet marks are still there on the wall at the foot of the stairs. The museum that now occupies the premises is mostly devoted to the struggle for Dutch independence from Spain and also has exhibits relating to the royal House of Orange-Nassau, which has supplied Holland with its monarchs down to the present. It is well worth a visit for its elegantly decorated interior, as well as for its splendid paintings, tapestries, silverware, and porcelain. The museum is open on Tuesdays through Saturdays, from 10 a.m. to 5 p.m.; and on Sundays and holidays from 1–5 p.m. During the months of June, July, and August it is also open on Mondays from 1–5 p.m.

Just across the square from this is the **Nusantara Museum** (7), which specializes in ethnology with an emphasis on Indonesian artifacts. It is open during the same times as the Prinsenhof Museum (above) and shares a common entrance ticket.

Another nearby museum is the **Huis Lambert van Meerten** (8). This is of great interest for its collection of antique Delft tiles, beautiful room settings, and lovely old furniture. Again, it is open at the time as the Prinsenhof Museum (above), and the same ticket will get you in.

Before heading back to the train station, you might want to visit the small **Museum Tétar van Elven** (9). Named after a very obscure 19th-century painter who lived here, it is noted more for its stylish atmosphere than for the art it contains. The museum is open from May through mid-October, on Tuesdays through Saturdays, from 1–5 p.m.

Continuing down the same street will bring you to the **Armamentarium** (10), a 17th-century warehouse that now houses the Dutch Army Museum. Military buffs will enjoy the weapons on display here, ranging from ancient times to the present. They may all be seen on Tuesdays through Saturdays, from 10 a.m. to 5 p.m.; and on Sundays from 1–5 p.m.; but not on major holidays. From here it is only a short stroll back to the station.

A Daytrip from Amsterdam

*Utrecht

One of the easiest and most satisfying daytrips you can take from Amsterdam is to Utrecht, a fair-sized city noted for its engaging combination of the past and the present. The area near its train station is as contemporary as any place on Earth, yet step beyond this and you enter a world of preserved charm. Its picturesque sunken canals are unique, while some of its museums are among the most enjoyable in the nation. Home to Holland's largest university, Utrecht is alive with a youthful spirit.

The Romans built a fortification here around A.D. 47 to guard their crossing point on what was then the Rhine river. A town developed around this and a church was built as early as A.D. 500, from which Christianity spread throughout the Netherlands. During the Middle Ages, Utrecht was frequently the residence of the Holy Roman emperors. In 1589 it was the setting for the *Union of Utrecht,* a pact that united the northern provinces against Spain. The troubled times that followed were finally resolved by the signing of the *Treaty of Utrecht* in 1713, ending the War of the Spanish Succession.

GETTING THERE:

Trains depart Amsterdam's Centraal Station at very frequent intervals for the 30-minute run to Utrecht's Centraal Station (CS). Return service operates until late evening, with reduced service all night long.

By car, Utrecht is 22 miles southeast of Amsterdam via the A-2 highway to the Utrecht-West exit. Convenient parking is available around the Hoog Catharijne-station complex.

PRACTICALITIES:

Avoid going to Utrecht on a Monday, when nearly all of its attraction are closed. The local **Tourist Information Office** (VVV), phone (0) 6-34-03-40-85 (toll call), is at the northern end of the Hoog Catharijne shopping center, adjoining the station. **Bicycles** may be rented at the station, phone (030) 31-11-59. Utrecht has a **population** of about 230,000, and is the capital of **Utrecht** province.

FOOD AND DRINK:

The city offers a wide choice of restaurants and cafés, especially around the Hoog Catharijne and the Oude Gracht canal. Some choices are:

Café de Paris (Drieharingstraat 16, 1 block northeast of the Hoog Catharijne) Traditional French cuisine in a turn-of-the-century environment. $$$

Eethuis Het Draeckje (Oude Gracht 114, on the canal, near the Town Hall) Dutch food, *Neerlands Dis* menu. X: Sun. $$

Graaf Floris (Vismarkt 13, near the Domtoren) Dutch food, *Neerlands Dis* menu. X: Sat., Sun. $$

La Pizzeria (Voorstraat 23, 3 blocks north of the Town Hall) Long popular for pizzas and other Italian dishes. X: Mon., holidays. $ and $$

De Werfkring (Oude Gracht 123, on the canal, near the Town Hall) Noted for its vegetarian food and young crowd. X: Sun. $

SUGGESTED TOUR:

Utrecht's **Centraal Station** (1), one of the busiest in Europe, is connected to the immense **Hoog Catharijne** complex. This climate-controlled indoor city-within-a-city, embracing some 180 shops plus theaters, restaurants, cafés, offices, a hotel, and even apartment houses, was built in the late 1970s. Spanning the streets below, it can be somewhat confusing to negotiate although there are floor plans everywhere. Just follow the signs through it to Clarenburg, descend the escalators, and exit onto Lange Elisabeth Straat.

Make a right on Mariastraat and follow the map to the fascinating ***Rijksmuseum van Speelklok tot Pierement** (Musical Clock to Street Organ Museum) (2). Located in the Buurkerk, a former church dating in part from the 13th century, this is one of the most utterly joyful museums anywhere—and a favorite with children. Its displays of mechanical musical instruments from the 18th to the 20th centuries, some of which are quite huge, don't just sit there to be admired. They make music, lots of very loud barrel-organ music, to the delight of everyone present. You can join the fun on Tuesdays through Saturdays, from 10 a.m. to 5 p.m.; and on Sundays from 1–5 p.m., but not on some major holidays. Guided tours with demonstrations begin every hour on the hour, or you can just walk through.

Now continue around to the **Vismarkt** (3), a market place on the Oude Gracht canal, where fishermen have been selling their catch since the 12th century. Note how the canals of Utrecht are sunk well below the level of the streets, with old warehouse entrances opening directly onto them. Many of these have been turned into restaurants, with outdoor café tables facing the water.

In the Rijksmuseum van Speelklok tot Pierement

A left on Servetstraat brings you to the **Domtoren** (4), at 367 feet the tallest church tower in Holland. It was completed in 1382 and stands apart from the cathedral of which it was a part. The nave of the cathedral collapsed during a storm in 1674 and was never replaced, although the rest of the church is still there. The tower, luckily, can be climbed for a wonderful ***view**.

As you stroll across Domplein you can see the outline of the former nave, indicated by colored paving stones. The present **Domkerk** occupies the choir and transepts of the one-time cathedral, built between 1254 and 1517 on the site of the Roman settlement.

Adjoining the church is the 15th-century **Kloostergang** (Cloister) (5), a spot of unusual beauty and tranquillity. Amble through it to a picturesque old lane behind the church, named Achter de Dom. The route on the map now takes you down some interesting streets, along the Oude Gracht canal, and through a park to Utrecht's famous ***Centraal Museum** (6). Housed in a former convent, its displays cover a wide scope of interests, ranging from 20th-century Dutch art to period room settings to an unearthed 9th-century Viking ship. Upstairs, there is an excellent collection of Utrecht Old Master paintings, applied arts, and historical artifacts. The museum is open on Tuesdays through Saturdays, from 10 a.m. to 5 p.m.; and on Sundays and holidays from 1–5 p.m.

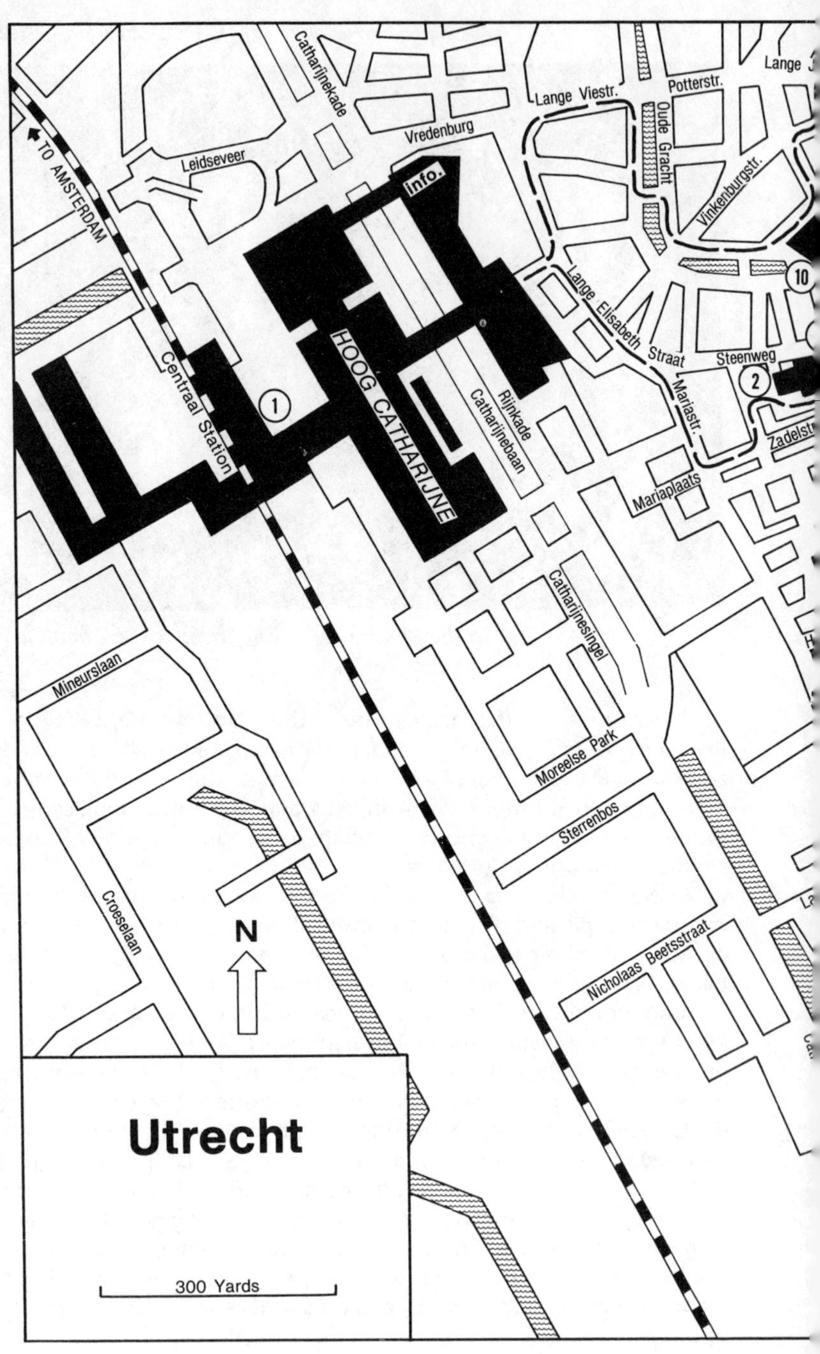
Utrecht
300 Yards
N
TO AMSTERDAM
Catharijnekade
Vredenburg
Leidseveer
Lange Viestr.
Potterstr.
Oude Gracht
Vinkenburgstr.
info.
HOOG CATHARIJNE
Centraal Station
Rijnkade
Catharijnebaan
Lange Elisabeth Straat
Steenweg
Mariastr.
Mariaplaats
Zadelstr.
Catharijnesingel
Mineurslaan
Moreelse Park
Sterrenbos
Croeselaan
Nicholaas Beetsstraat
1
2
10

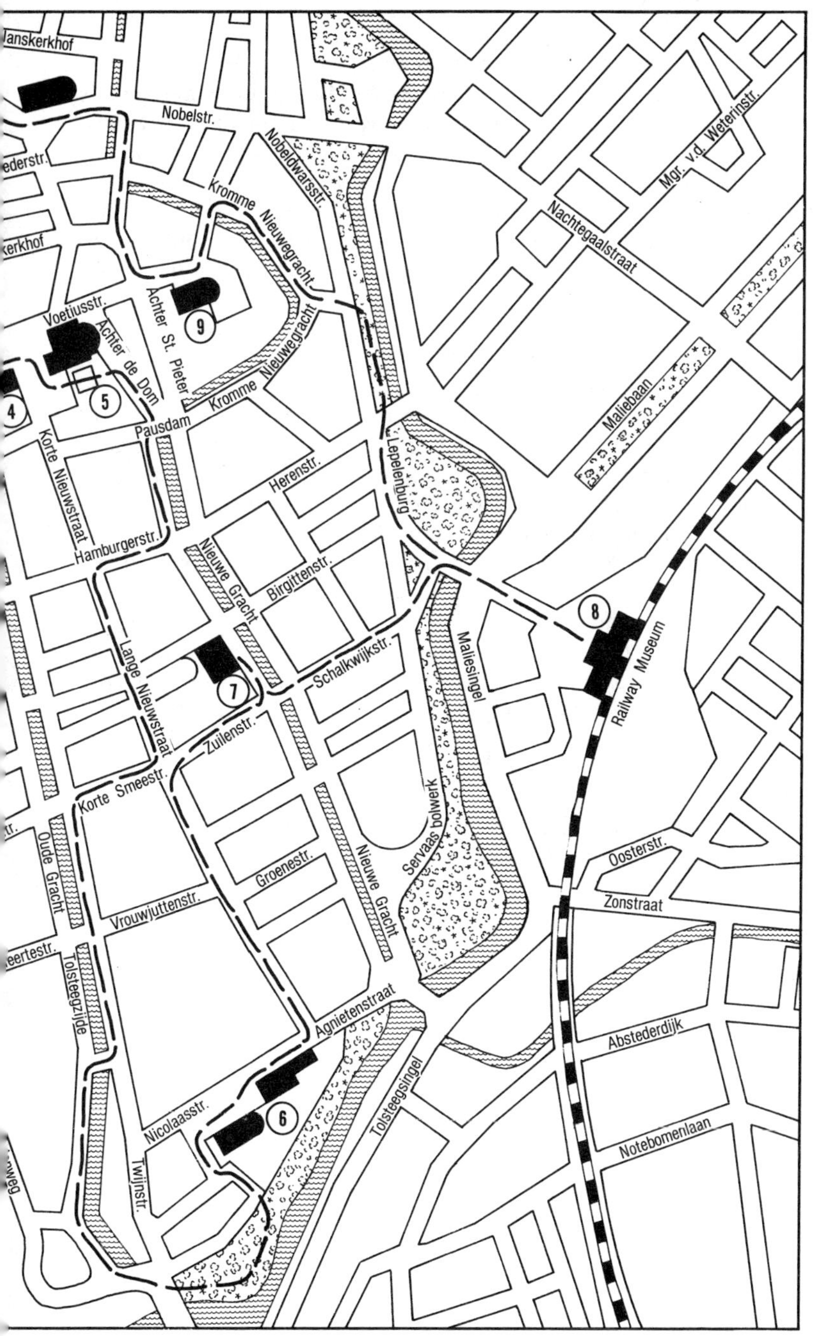

Janskerkhof
Nobelstr.
Nobeldwarsstr.
Kromme Nieuwegracht
Mgr. v.d. Weterinstr.
Nachtegaalstraat
Voetiusstr.
Achter St. Pieter
Achter de Dom
9
5
4
Pausdam
Maliebaan
Korte Nieuwstraat
Herenstr.
Lepelenburg
Hamburgerstr.
Nieuwe Gracht
Birgittenstr.
8
Railway Museum
Maliesingel
Lange Nieuwstraat
7
Schalkwijkstr.
Zuilenstr.
Korte Smeestr.
Servaas bolwerk
Oude Gracht
Groenestr.
Nieuwe Gracht
Oosterstr.
Zonstraat
Vrouwjuttenstr.
Tolsteegzijde
Agnietenstraat
Abstederdijk
Tolsteegsingel
Nicolaasstr.
6
Notebomenlaan
Twijnstr.

Return toward the center of town on Lange Nieuwstraat and turn right on Zuilenstraat. The **Rijksmuseum het Catharijneconvent** (7) is located in a former 16th-century convent, whose entrance is at Nieuwe Gracht 63. Its modern interior contains nothing less than the largest collection of medieval art in Holland, along with a vast amount of religious artifacts and a sweeping survey of Christianity in the Netherlands. This renowned museum is open on Tuesdays through Fridays, from 10 a.m. to 5 p.m.; and on Saturdays, Sundays, and holidays from 11 a.m. to 5 p.m.

Continue on across the town moat to the thoroughly enjoyable and very popular **Nederlands Spoorwegmuseum** (Railway Museum) (8), appropriately located in a former train station from the 19th century. Along its platforms and in its yards is a magnificent collection of locomotives, cars, and trams. Model trains speed along miniature tracks in the station itself, to the delight of railfans young and old. Indoors, there is also a collection of railroading artifacts, and you can get refreshments in the old dining car outside. The museum is open on Tuesdays through Saturdays, from 10 a.m. to 5 p.m.; and on Sundays from 1–5 p.m.

A rather interesting route back to the center is to follow along the canal and turn left into Kromme Nieuwe Gracht, a narrow street with a tiny canal. Another left brings you to **St. Pieterskerk** (9), an 11th-century Romanesque church that hasn't changed very much over the ages. Continue on Achter St. Pieter and Keistraat to Janskerkhof, then follow the map to the **Town Hall** *(Stadhuis)* (10) on the Oude Gracht canal. This area is particularly rich in outdoor cafés, mostly on the water's edge. ***Boat trips** through the canals are offered near here, and make a fine way to finish off your trip to Utrecht before returning to the station.

A Daytrip from Amsterdam

Netherlands Open-Air Museum at Arnhem

Outdoor folk museums have become increasingly popular in Europe as more of the countryside succumbs to modern development and the traditional ways of life disappear. In many cases they are the only realistic way of saving a nation's domestic heritage. Typically, threatened structures ranging from thatched farm cottages to early industrial buildings are moved into a protected park setting and reassembled in village groupings. Trained personnel, often in folk costumes, carry on the old crafts and farm the fields in the traditional way, while reconstructed country inns continue to serve age-old recipes. A visit to one of these places can be a lot of fun, and may be the only chance you'll ever get to experience some aspects of the Old World.

There are several open-air museums in Holland, but this one at Arnhem is by far the largest and most complete. Spread over an area of about 75 acres, it was begun in 1912 and now contains roughly 100 structures. All of these have been restored to their original appearance, and many are filled with period furnishings.

GETTING THERE:

Trains leave Amsterdam's Centraal Station frequently for the 68-minute ride to Arnhem, with returns until late evening.

By car, Arnhem is 62 miles southeast of Amsterdam via the A-2 and A-12 highways to the Arnhem-Apeldoorn exit. Follow local signs to the Openlucht Museum.

PRACTICALITIES:

The museum is open daily from April through October. The **Tourist Information Office** (VVV) in Arnhem, phone (085) 42-03-30, is across from the train station. You can call the open-air museum directly at (085) 57-61-11. **Bicycles** may be rented at the station, phone (085) 42-17-82. Arnhem is the capital of **Gelderland** province.

FOOD AND DRINK:

There are several places to eat and drink at the outdoor museum, including:

De Oude Bijenkorf (near the entrance) Full Dutch meals along with refreshments. $$

De Hanekamp (near the far end) Pancakes and snacks. $

SUGGESTED TOUR:

The easiest way to get from the **Arnhem Train Station** to the open-air museum is to take trolleybus number 3 in the direction of Alteveer. This departs frequently from the square in front of the station, and the ride takes 10 minutes. Otherwise, it is a 2½-mile taxi ride, walk, or bike ride.

The **Nederlands Openlucht Museum** (Netherlands Open-Air Museum) (1) is open from the beginning of April until the end of October, Mondays through Fridays from 9 a.m. to 5 p.m.; and on Saturdays and Sundays from 10 a.m. to 5 p.m.

Turn left just past the information booth and stroll down to the **Horse-Drawn Oil Mill** (2) from the province of Gelderland. Close to this is a small thatched-roof **Veluwe Farmhouse** (3) from around 1850, whose furnished interior may be visited.

The route now passes a small exhibition of bee keeping on the way to the **Betuwe Farmhouse** (4), a rather large structure originally built in 1646. Also from Gelderland province, it has an attached barn and a nicely-furnished interior.

Return past the bees and turn left to the romantically sited **Farmhouse from Giethoorn** (5), which is partially surrounded by water. Down the road from it stands the large **Staphorst Farmhouse** (6), a type still found in that conservative part of Holland. The small living quarters are beautifully decorated with tiles and painted furniture. Behind it is the **Farmhouse with a Pyramid Roof**, erected in 1745 in North Holland province, and associated with the making of Edam cheeses.

The route now enters a small village over a typical wooden drawbridge from around 1800. The **Merchant's House** (7) from Koog on the Zaan partially dates from 1686 and has the sort of comfortable interior favored by the 19th-century bourgeoisie. Turn left and stroll through the village to the **Fisherman's Cottage from Marken** (8), similar to those found today on the island in the IJsselmeer just north of Amsterdam. Its tiny interior has excellent examples of the traditional cupboard beds.

Continue on past an early-19th-century **Laundry** (9) that was brought here from an area near Haarlem. Close to it is a refreshment stand, where you can take a break before admiring the unusual **Post Windmill** (10). This was once used to grind grain in North Holland, and parts of it are over 300 years old. The **Paper Mill from the Veluwe** (11) is in a beautifully wooded location between two ponds. Powered by

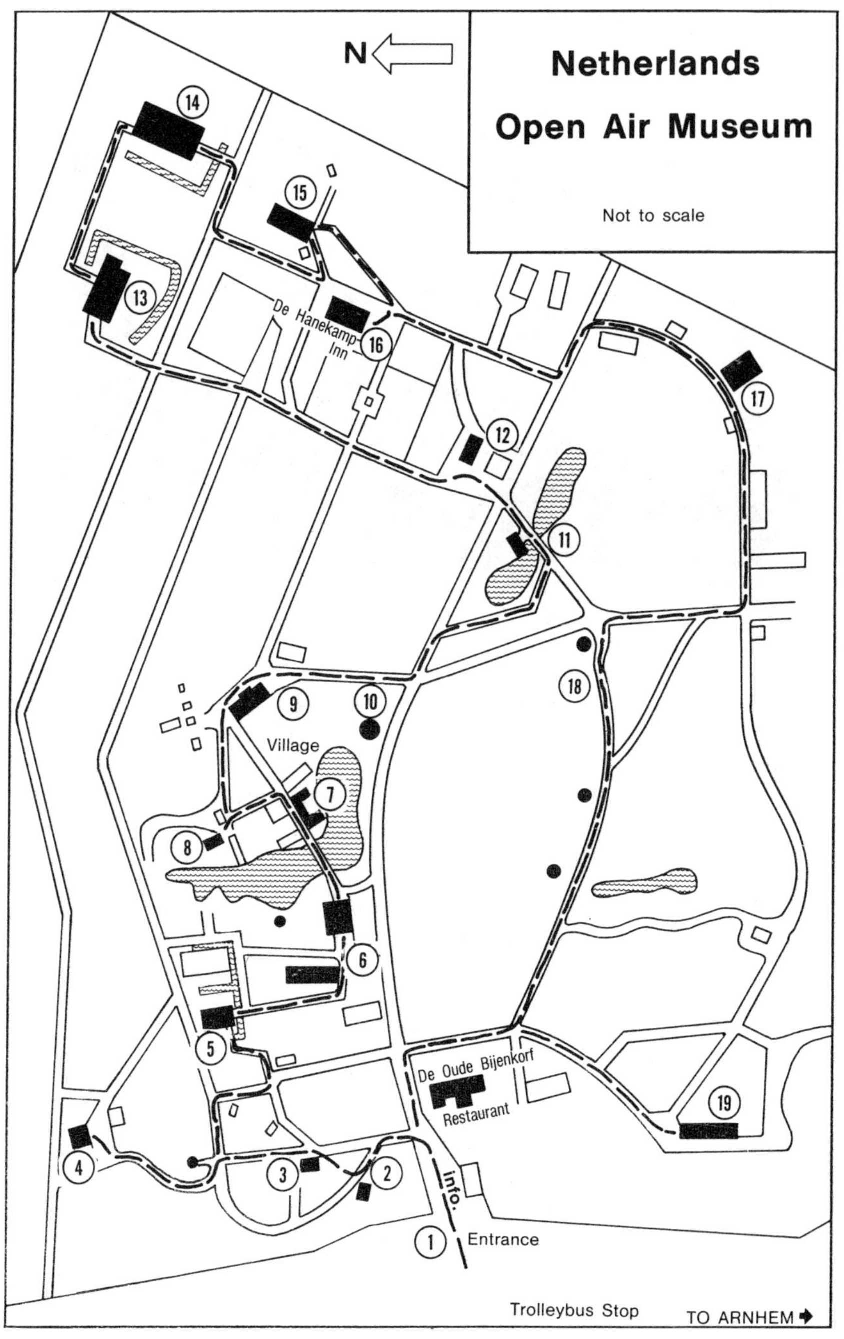
Netherlands
Open Air Museum
Not to scale
N
14
15
13
De Hanekamp Inn
16
12
17
11
18
9
10
Village
7
8
6
5
De Oude Bijenkorf
Restaurant
19
4
3
2
Info.
1
Entrance
Trolleybus Stop
TO ARNHEM

The drawbridge to the village

an overshot water wheel, its mechanisms still work and are used to give demonstrations of hand paper-making. Although it is a re-creation and not an original, the **Parlor from Hindeloopen** (12) is quite interesting for the stylized painted furniture associated with that former Zuider Zee town.

Now follow the map past the lovely **Herb Garden** to the **Frisian Farmstead** (13), whose rather elegant living quarters reflect the prosperity of that dairy region. Near this is the **Farmhouse from Beerta** (14), an area in Groningen province. Its living section has been restored to the state it was in around 1935, after electrification provided such luxuries as lighting, kitchen appliances, and a radio. In contrast, the **Drenthe Farmhouse** (15) is a large but rather primitive affair dating from around 1700.

Continue on to the **De Hanekamp Inn** (16), an 18th-century country inn from Zwolle. It now functions as a delightful café for museum visitors, with both indoor and outdoor tables.

Limburg province, in the south and much hillier than the rest of Holland, is represented by the **Krawinkel Farmstead** (17) and other nearby structures. From here the route passes a grouping of various **Windmills** (18) on the way back to the entrance. Before leaving, you might want to make a little side trip to the **Exhibition of Costumes** (19) to see what they wore in times past.

Section VI

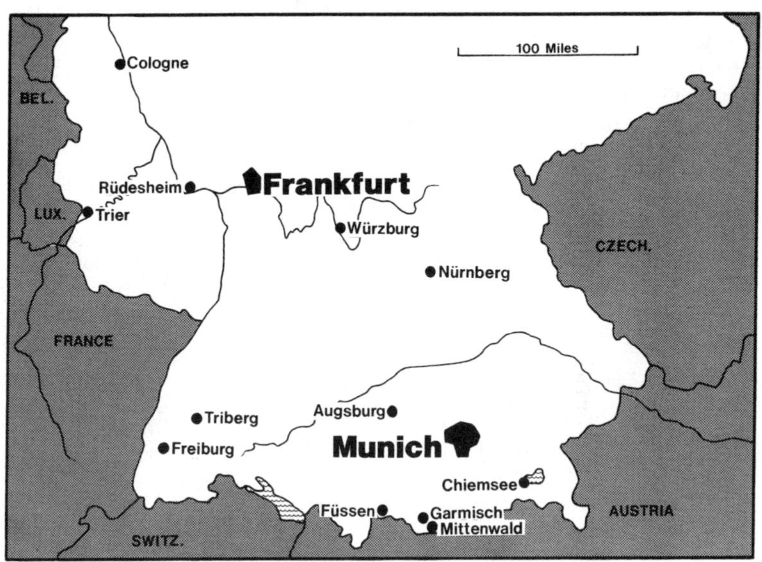

DAYTRIPS IN

GERMANY

- from Munich
- from Frankfurt

Munich and Frankfurt are the two German cities that are most likely to be visited by overseas tourists and business travelers. Both are major transportation hubs and make ideal bases for daytrips into their surrounding regions. Lying between the Alps and Franconia, Munich is blessed with fascinating destinations in all directions; while Frankfurt is close enough to the Rhineland for easy one-day excursions.

It is not necessary to actually stay in either city to take advantage of its central location, as both have alternative bases nearby, a good thing to know about if you arrive without reservations during the middle of a *fest*. In the case of Munich, you may prefer to stay in Augsburg, which is just as convenient, or in a suburb such as Starnberg. If Frankfurt is "all full up," as it frequently is, you'll find excellent accommodations in Mainz or Wiesbaden—both of which are near the Frankfurt Airport.

Of the 12 daytrips described in this chapter, five can be taken from the Munich area, five from around Frankfurt, and two from either base. They cover a broad range of interests, from such popular attractions as two of "mad" King Ludwig II's fantasy castles and the Rhineland wine village of Rüdesheim to country walks in the Black Forest and the Roman ruins of Trier. All are easy to make, whether you travel by train or by car.

These 12 daytrips are, of course, only a small sample of what so rich and diverse a nation as Germany offers. More possibilities are covered in our companion book, ***Daytrips in Germany***, which describes 55 one-day adventures in the same format, using Munich, Frankfurt, Hamburg, and Berlin as bases. Walking tours of these cities are included as well.

GETTING AROUND:

Trains are generally the easiest and often the fastest way to get to the daytrip destinations in this section. In both Munich and Frankfurt they always depart from a main station in the center of town, called the **Hauptbahnhof**. Modern luxury expresses are identified with the prefix **EC** or **IC**, and require payment of a supplementary charge called a *Zuschlag* unless you are using a railpass. Other expresses, marked **IR**, **FD**, or **D** carry an extra charge for journeys of less than 50 kilometers (31 miles), but not for railpass users. All express trains have both first- and second-class cars; none require reservations.

Eurailpasses (see page 18) are accepted throughout the country, but if you're only visiting Germany you'll save money by using the **GermanRail Flexipass**, good for unlimited rail travel on any 5, 10, or 15 days within a 30-day period. It is sold in both first- and second-class versions; for adults, children, or juniors (age 12 through 25, second-class only); and includes bonus benefits such as free cruises on the Rhine and rides on the Romantic Road buses. These passes can be ordered through travel agents.

Germany is famous for its **Autobahns** with their virtually unlimited speeds. **Driving** may be less expensive than trains when three or more people share the cost, and certainly allows greater flexibility.

ADVANCE PLANNING INFORMATION:

The **German National Tourist Office** has branches throughout the world, including New York, Los Angeles, Toronto, London, and Sydney. The address of their New York office is: 747 Third Avenue, New York NY 10017, phone (212) 308–3300.

A Daytrip from Munich

Garmisch-Partenkirchen

It was the Winter Olympics of 1936 that made Garmisch-Partenkirchen famous. Formerly two separate resort towns, they were merged for that event and have shared the unwieldy name ever since. Neatly split down the middle by the Partnach stream, with Garmisch to the west and Partenkirchen—once the Roman settlement of *Parthanum*—to the east, the combined entity has become Germany's leading center for winter sports. Today, most people just call it "Garmisch."

Mountains are what Garmisch is all about. The town lies in a broad, flat valley at the foot of the highest peak in Germany, the Zugspitze, and is surrounded on all sides by towering Alps, whose bases literally run right into the village streets. Despite immense popularity, Garmisch remains remarkably unspoiled in its easygoing Bavarian manner.

Most daytrippers come to Garmisch to ride to the top of the Zugspitze, a wonderful excursion that takes the better part of a day, and that can easily be done without special reference to a guidebook. This daytrip, however, is different. It explores the parts of Garmisch that most tourists miss, giving you a good idea of why this is one of Germany's favorite playgrounds. Besides the town itself, it includes a country walk through a spectacular white-water gorge and a lift to a mountain summit for the best possible panoramic views. If you also want to do the Zugspitze tour, you should plan on staying overnight or on coming back another day.

GETTING THERE:

Trains depart Munich's main station hourly for the 90-minute trip to Garmisch-Partenkirchen, with return service until mid-evening. Reduced-price excursion tickets *(Ausflugskarte)* valid for 2 days are available.

By car, Garmisch-Partenkirchen is 55 miles south of Munich via the A-95 Autobahn.

PRACTICALITIES:

The resort is open all year round, but the Partnachklamm may be closed after a heavy snow or spring melt. Those making this walk should be prepared to get a trifle wet, and need suitable shoes. The mountains can be chilly, even in summer. The local **Tourist Information Office**, phone (08821) 1806, is on Dr. Richard Strauss Platz, next to the

Kurpark. **Bicycles** may be rented at the station from April through October. Garmisch is in the Land of **Bayern**, and has a **population** of about 29,000.

FOOD AND DRINK:

Some good restaurants are:

Reindl Grill of the Partenkirchener Hof (Bahnhofstr. 15, 2 blocks east of the station) Well known for its International European cuisines. Reservations advised, phone (08821) 580-25 X: mid-Nov., mid-Dec. $$$

Mühlenstube (Mühlstr. 22, 4 blocks west of the casino) This hotel dining room is famous for its seafood. Reservations advised, phone (08821) 70-40. $$ and $$$

Forsthaus Graseck (Top of the cable car at the Partnachklamm) German food with excellent mountain views and an outdoor terrace. X: Nov. $$

Gasthof Fraundorfer (Ludwigstr. 15, near the Folk Museum) A rustic Bavarian inn, somewhat touristy but fun. X: Tues. $$

Clausings Post Hotel (Marienplatz 12, near the casino) Dining in a small, romantic hotel with 3 restaurants. $$

Stahl's Badstubn (Klammstr. 47, in the swimming complex by the ice rink) Very popular, with an extensive menu. $

There are also several inexpensive, rustic places along the way to the Partnachklamm, and a pleasant café atop the Wank.

SUGGESTED TOUR:

Leave the **train station** (1) and follow the map along the Partnach stream to the **Olympic Ski Stadium** (2). Accommodating about 80,000 spectators, this gigantic outdoor structure was built by the Nazi regime as a showcase. Removing the swastikas did little to improve the architecture, but functionally it is still excellent and remains in use every winter. Entry is free.

Follow the road leading away from town for an easy and pleasurable walk in the woods to the dramatic Partnachklamm, one of the most memorable sights in the Bavarian Alps. In about one mile, level all the way, you will come to the tiny **Graseckbahn cable car** (3). Ride this to its upper station at the Forsthaus Graseck, a delightful Alpine inn and a great place for lunch or just refreshments.

Cross the hotel terrace and continue along a trail with spectacular views, then descend a steep path to the upper end of the ***Partnachklamm** (4). This wildly romantic gorge, only a few feet wide but up to 263 feet deep, is filled with torrents of rushing white water. A narrow footpath with guardrails has been carved from the sheer rock sides, at times tunneling through impossible passages. You'll get a little wet,

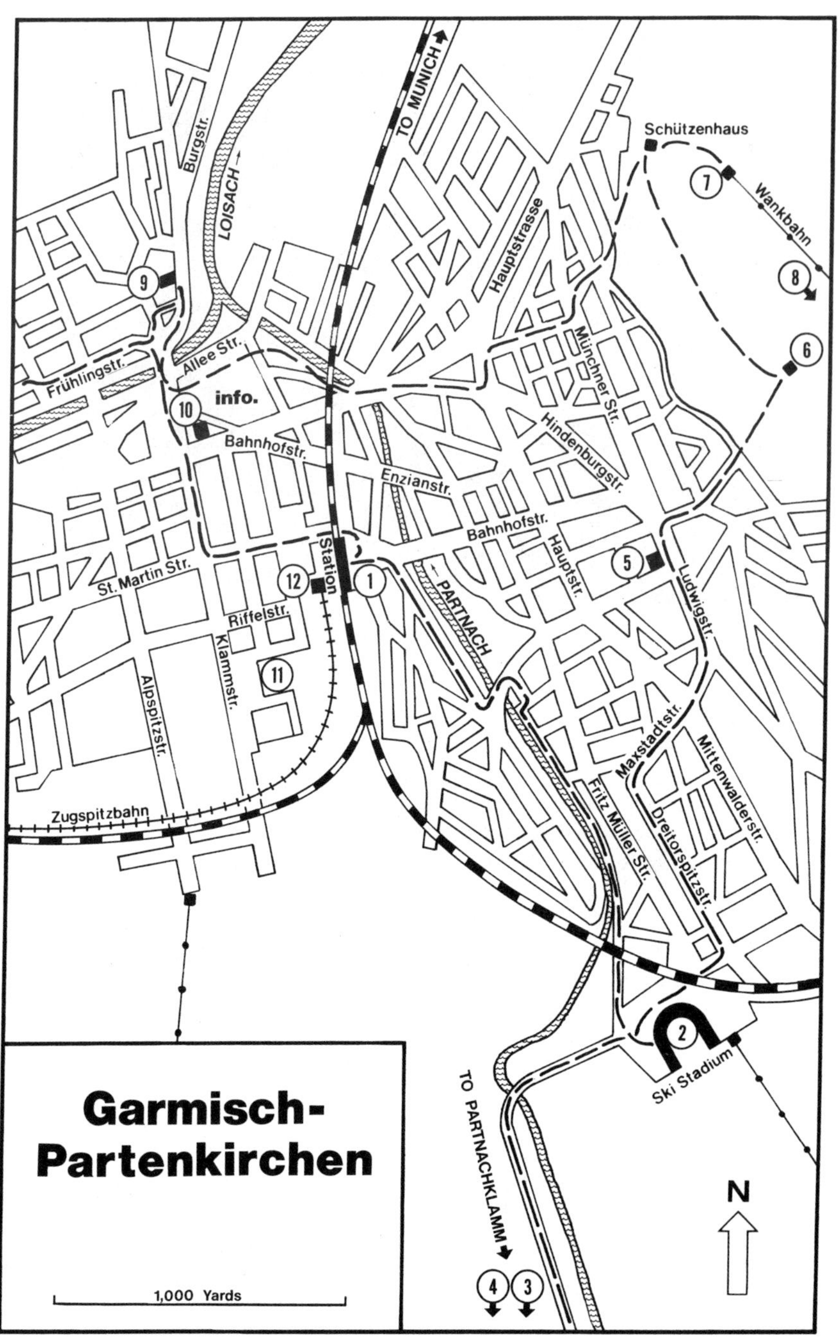

Garmisch-Partenkirchen

In the Partnachklamm

but that's a small price to pay for such a breathtaking experience. There is a modest admission charge, payable at the exit.

Leaving the gorge will put you back on the forest road to the Olympic Ski Stadium. Return there and either walk or take a bus to the **Werdenfels Heimat Museum** (5) on Ludwigstrasse. This folk museum of mountain life in olden times is open on Tuesdays through Fridays, 10 a.m. to 1 p.m. and 3–6 p.m.; and on weekends from 10 a.m. to 1 p.m.

Now follow the map to the early 18th-century **Pilgrimage Church of St. Anton** (6), going past some remarkable Stations of the Cross along the hilly path. The interior of this chapel, with its frescoed oval dome and elaborate plaster work, is quite attractive and well worth the climb. On the way in you will pass a touching display of plaques, some with photographs, in memory of local sons who never returned from the last two wars.

The **Philosophenweg**, a trail with stunning views of the Alps, leads to the Schützenhaus. From there take a steep but short footpath to the lower station of the **Wankbahn cable car** (7). Board one of the small cabins for a lift up the mountain, but don't get off at the first stop. Stay on all the way to the **Wank summit** (8) for the most glorious panorama possible of the Zugspitze and the Wetterstein range towering over a toylike Garmisch, safely nestled in its valley below. There

View from the Wank summit

is a sunny **outdoor café** to help you enjoy the scene even more.

At 5,850 feet, the summit is a center for the thrilling sport of hang gliding. This is a fast way down for some brave souls, but you will probably prefer to return on the cable car.

Leave the lower station and follow the map through Partenkirchen and into Garmisch. A path along the Partnach stream brings you to the **Kurpark**, from which it is a short stroll to the **Alte Kirche** (Old Church) (9). Located in a picturesque district, its origins may predate the spread of Christianity into this area. Or at least according to local tradition. Some of the mural paintings date as far back as the 13th century. The church itself was originally Romanesque, but later rebuilt in the Gothic style.

Take a look down **Frühlingstrasse**, a colorful street of quaint chalets. Straight ahead, at Zoeppritzstrasse 42, is the villa of the composer Richard Strauss, who died in Garmisch in 1949.

Along the way back to the station, you might want to stop at the **Spielbank** (Casino) (10) for a fling with Lady Luck, or visit the **Olympic Ice Stadium** (11) of 1936, which seats 12,000 spectators under one roof and is the largest in Europe. Close to this and adjacent to the train station is the **Zugspitz Bahnhof** (12), from which private cog-wheel trains depart for an excursion up the Zugspitze mountain by train and cable car. You can get current information there, and perhaps make the trip on another day.

A Daytrip from Munich

Mittenwald

If you were asked to design a stage set for an Alpine romance, you could hardly do better than to copy Mittenwald. This dreamy resort on the Austrian border has everything—a rugged mountain peak rising vertically from its own back yard, colorfully painted houses lining the peaceful streets, and a rich musical heritage as the "Village of a Thousand Violins."

The latter is Mittenwald's chief industry, next to tourism. Once a prosperous trading post on the Venice-to-Augsburg road, its economy fell to ruin as traffic moved to other passes. Then, in the 17th century, an unlikely miracle happened. A local lad named Matthias Klotz had moved to Cremona, where he learned the art of violin making from the legendary Nicolo Amati. On his return in 1684 he founded the trade that today exports Mittenwald sting instruments to the entire world.

Although not as high as Garmisch's Zugspitze, a ride up the Karwendel mountain at Mittenwald is a more satisfying experience as its summit is wide open, allowing good opportunities for hiking, climbing, or just playing in the snow.

GETTING THERE:

Trains depart Munich's main station hourly for Mittenwald, a trip of less than 2 hours. Be sure to board the correct car as some are dropped off en route. Return service operates until early evening.

By car, Mittenwald is 68 miles south of Munich. Take the A-95 Autobahn to Garmisch-Partenkirchen, then continue on the B-2 road.

PRACTICALITIES:

Mittenwald is a year-round resort, but good weather is really necessary to enjoy it. You might want to bring along hiking shoes and a sweater for a romp in the snow atop the Karwendel. The local **Tourist Information Office**, phone (08823) 339-81, is in the town hall at Dammkarstrasse 3. **Bicycles** may be rented from several local firms; ask the tourist office for details. Mittenwald is in the Land of **Bayern** and has a **population** of about 8,300.

Obermarkt and the Pfarrkirche

FOOD AND DRINK:

Among the many good restaurants are:

Arnspitze (Innsbrucker Str. 68, 2 blocks south of the bridge) Elegant dining in Mittenwald's best restaurant. For reservations call (08823) 24-25. X: Tues., Wed. lunch. $$$

Alpenrose (Obermarkt 1, near the church) Noted for its traditional Bavarian food, especially game dishes. Reservations suggested, phone (08823) 50-55. $$

Hotel Post (Obermarkt 9, just south of the church) A 17th-century Bavarian inn serving local dishes in a rustic setting. $$

Hotel Rieger (Dekan-Karl-Platz 28, 3 blocks south of the church) A Bavarian-style inn whose restaurant has a good view of the mountains. X: Mon. $$

SUGGESTED TOUR:

Leave the **train station** (1) and follow Bahnhofstrasse to the **Rathaus** (Town Hall) (2), which houses the tourist office. From here it is a short stroll to the stunning Baroque **Pfarrkirche** (Parish Church) (3). Built in the 18th century by the famous architect Josef Schmuzer, its beautifully frescoed tower and richly decorated interior are symbols of the town's prosperity. In front of it stands a **statue** of Matthias Klotz making a violin.

A few steps down Ballenhausgasse brings you to the **Geigenbau und Heimatmuseum** (Violin-Making and Folk-Life Museum) (4). Step inside to view the process of making stringed instruments in a traditional workshop. The museum is open on Mondays through Fridays from 10–11:45 a.m. and 2–4:45 p.m.; and on weekends and holidays from 10–11:45 a.m. only. It may be closed in early spring and late fall.

Follow the map along a street called **Im Gries** to see the oldest houses in Mittenwald, among which are some outstanding examples of *Lüftlmalerei,* the characteristic art of outdoor frescoes that originated during the Counter-Reformation to help proclaim the Catholic faith. Return to the church and turn right onto **Obermarkt**, the main street. This is also lined with some wonderfully frescoed structures. Walk along it to the edge of town, where it becomes Innsbrucker Strasse. Just before the first bridge a path leads off to the right.

Follow the country trail a short distance to the **Leutaschklamm** (5), a very narrow gorge filled with rushing white water. Actually in Austrian territory, the mountain ravine has a wooden gangway suspended above the torrent, which takes you to a spectacular 82-foot waterfall. The gorge may be entered during the summer season, or in winter if it is very cold. There is a tiny outdoor café at the entrance.

Return to Innsbrucker Strasse and stroll down Mühlen Weg. Cross a bridge and walk along the Isar, a river on which goods were once floated downstream to Munich. You will soon come to the lower station of the **Karwendelbahn** (6), a large cable car that transports you in 10 minutes to the heights of the Karwendel mountain.

At an altitude of 7,362 feet, the **upper station** (7) of the cable car looks nearly straight down on Mittenwald and offers fabulous ***views** across the Bavarian, Austrian, and Italian Alps. Follow the trail leading uphill through the snow and pass the *Freistaat Bayern* sign. You are now in Austria for the second time in one day, although there is no customs post. A circular route takes you all the way to the very pinnacle *(Gipfel)* at 7,825 feet. Be careful, however. The highest section of the trail is steep and can be difficult without proper boots when the snow has become icy. This treacherous section is bypassed by a lower, easier trail. When you tire of all the sunshine, clean air, and marvelous scenery you can visit the **café** and **restaurant** adjacent to the upper cable car station for a drink or snack before returning to the valley and the train station.

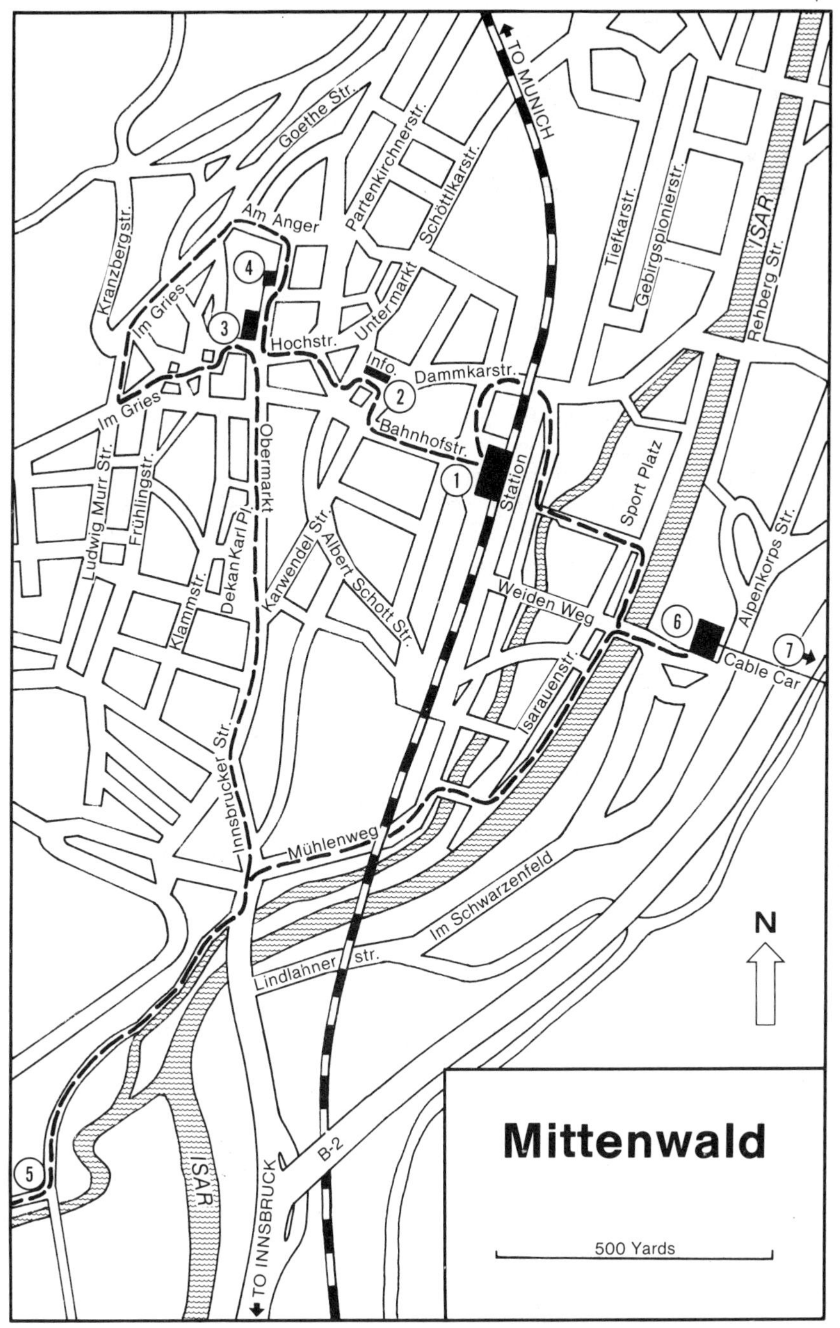
Mittenwald
TO MUNICH
Goethe Str.
Partenkirchnerstr.
Schöttlkarstr.
Tiefkarstr.
Gebirgspionierstr.
ISAR
Rehberg Str.
Kranzbergstr.
Am Anger
Im Gries
Untermarkt
Hochstr.
Info.
Dammkarstr.
Im Gries
Bahnhofstr.
Station
Sport Platz
Ludwig Murr Str.
Frühlingstr.
Obermarkt
Karwendel Str.
Albert Schott Str.
Dekan Karl Pl.
Klammstr.
Weiden Weg
Alpenkorps Str.
Cable Car
Isarauenstr.
Innsbrucker Str.
Mühlenweg
Im Schwarzenfeld
Lindlahner str.
N
B-2
TO INNSBRUCK
ISAR
500 Yards
1
2
3
4
5
6
7

A Daytrip from Munich

*Füssen and Neuschwanstein

The most instantly recognized symbol of Germany is undoubtedly Neuschwanstein, a sight that graces the covers of numerous guidebooks, brochures, and travel posters. Everything a fairytale castle should be, "mad" King Ludwig II's most spectacular creation has even served as a model for Disneyland.

While countless tourists trek through it every year, relatively few visit the neighboring castle of Hohenschwangau—in which Ludwig was actually raised—and only a small minority venture down the road to the delightful frontier town of Füssen. This trip combines all three for an exciting day filled with memorable sights, far more than you would get on a guided bus tour.

GETTING THERE:

Trains leave Munich's main station hourly for either Buchloe or Kaufbeuren, where you change to a local for Füssen. Check the schedule to determine where the change is made. Return service operates until early evening. The journey takes about 2 hours each way.

By car, leave Munich on the B-12 road, going west to Landsberg, then turn south on the B-17 to Hohenschwangau and Füssen for a total distance of 75 miles.

PRACTICALITIES:

The Royal Castles are open all year round, but are more crowded on weekends during the tourist season. There is a **Tourist Information Office** in Füssen at Augsburger Torplatz, 3 blocks east of the station. You can phone them at (08362) 70-77. **Bicycles** can be rented at the train station from April through October. Füssen has a **population** of about 15,000 and is in the Land of **Bayern**.

FOOD AND DRINK:

Restaurants near the Royal Castles tend to be touristy, with better values in Füssen. Some good choices are:

In Füssen:

Hirsch (Augsburger Torplatz, 4 blocks east of the station) A rustic inn with a friendly restaurant. X: Dec.-mid-Feb. $$

Reichenstrasse in Füssen

Gasthaus zum Schwanen (Brotmarkt 4, near Kloster St. Mang) Bavarian and Swabian dishes in a cozy setting. X: Sun. eve., Mon., Nov. $

In Hohenschwangau:

Müller (Alpseestr. 14, near the bus stop) Country-style dining. X: mid-Nov.-mid-Dec. $$

Lisl und Jägerhaus (Neuschwanstein Str. 1, just south of the bus stop) Local and Continental cuisine. X: mid-Jan.-Mar. $$

SUGGESTED TOUR:

Leave the **Füssen train station** (1) and walk over to the bus stop across the street. Check the posted schedule of service to Hohenschwangau, also called *Königsschlösser* or Royal Castles. From this you can determine the amount of time available for exploring Füssen, allowing at least three hours for Neuschwanstein and Hohenschwangau castles.

Stroll down Bahnhofstrasse to Augsburger Torplatz, where the tourist office is located. From here turn right on Reichenstrasse, a charming pedestrians-only street lined with outdoor cafés, which leads to **Kloster St. Mang** (2). This former Benedictine abbey was founded in the 8th century and rebuilt during the 18th. It now serves as the town hall and contains a small museum. In the courtyard is the Chapel of St. Anne, noted for its unusual *Totentanz* (Dance of Death) painting from 1602, and the parish church with its ancient 9th-century crypt. Both are worth a visit.

Climb uphill to the **Hohes Schloss** (Castle) (3), once a residence of the bishops of Augsburg, who claimed it after Emperor Heinrich VII forfeited on a loan they had made to him. The present structure, curiously painted, dates from the 13th and 16th centuries. Long before that, in the 3rd century A.D., the Romans had a castle on the same site to protect their Via Claudia road that ran from Verona to Augsburg. The splendid Knights' Hall and other rooms may be visited daily, from 2–4 p.m.

Now follow the map to the **Lech Waterfall** (4), a very beautiful spot just yards from the Austrian border. Cross the Maxsteg footbridge over the cascade and return via Tiroler Strasse. Once across the main bridge bear right onto Brotmarkt and Brunnengasse, then return to the bus stop.

Board the bus to Hohenschwangau *(Königsschlösser),* a distance of about two miles. You could, of course, walk or drive there instead, or even rent a bike at the station. Check the posted return bus schedule upon arrival.

From the **Hohenschwangau bus stop** (5) it is a fairly steep climb via a woodland trail to Neuschwanstein Castle, with park benches provided en route. This can be avoided by taking one of the rather touristy horse-drawn carriages, or by a special bus (still requiring a little uphill trek), both of which start from a point opposite the bus stop, next to the parking lot. At the top of the climb, just below the castle, there is a restaurant and **outdoor café** where you can rest before tackling the main attraction.

***Neuschwanstein Castle** (6) is pure fantasy. By comparison, King Ludwig II's other creations of Linderhof and Herrenchiemsee, although wildly extravagant, have at least some basis in reality—other kings have built lavish palaces for themselves before. For this one, however, there is no model except possibly the Wartburg in Thuringia. Ludwig was obsessed with strange notions of a transfigured past whose gods, knights, and swans form the hazy bedrock of Wagnerian opera. Completely withdrawn from the industrial world of the 19th century, this lonely monarch wrapped himself in a cloud of long-forgotten dreams, of which Neuschwanstein is simply the most spectacular manifestation.

The castle, rising from a rocky crag high above the Pöllat gorge, was designed by a theatrical scene-painter employed by the court. This was Ludwig's first creation, begun in 1869, but it remained unfinished at the time of his death 17 years later. He lived there for a total of 102 days, and it was from there that he was taken into custody after

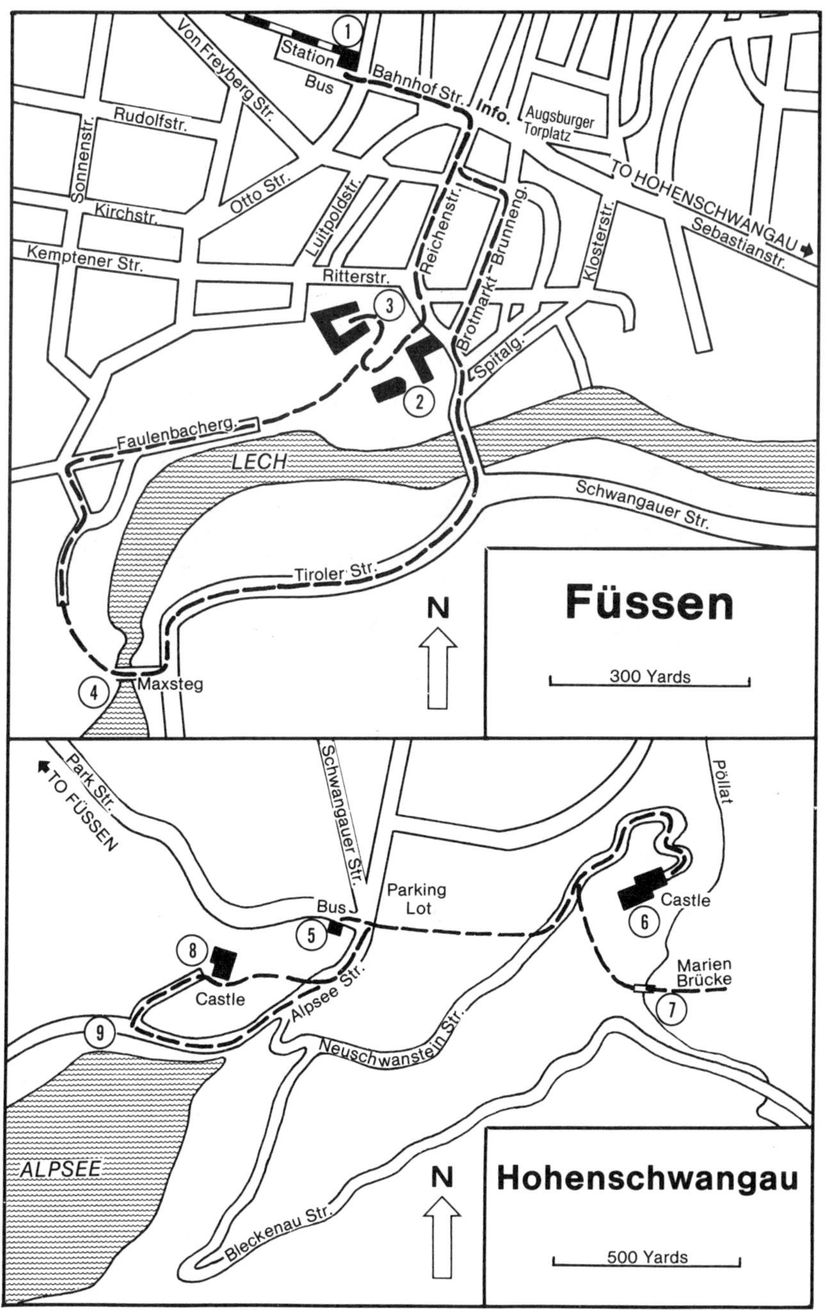

Füssen
300 Yards
N
Station
Bus
Bahnhof Str.
Info.
Augsburger Torplatz
Von Freyberg Str.
Rudolfstr.
Sonnenstr.
Otto Str.
Kirchstr.
Luitpoldstr.
Reichenstr.
Brunneng.
Brotmarkt
Klosterstr.
TO HOHENSCHWANGAU
Sebastianstr.
Kemptener Str.
Ritterstr.
Spitalg.
Faulenbacherg.
LECH
Schwangauer Str.
Tiroler Str.
Maxsteg
1
2
3
4
Hohenschwangau
500 Yards
N
TO FÜSSEN
Park Str.
Schwangauer Str.
Pöllat
Parking Lot
Bus
Castle
Marien Brücke
Castle
Alpsee Str.
Neuschwanstein Str.
ALPSEE
Bleckenau Str.
5
6
7
8
9

Neuschwanstein Castle from the Marienbrücke

being declared insane. The young king's life ended tragically in the waters of Lake Starnberg the very next day.

Enter the castle and join one of the very frequent guided tours, many of which are in English. Unlike the rococo fantasies of his later structures, Neuschwanstein is heavily Teutonic, with wall murals depicting those heroic sagas so dear to the hearts of Wagnerians. Tours are held from April through September, daily from 9 a.m. to 5:30 p.m.; and from October through March, daily from 10 a.m. to 4 p.m.

After the tour you may want to take a short but invigorating walk to the ***Marienbrücke** (7) for some truly splendid views.

Return to the bottom of the hill and visit **Hohenschwangau Castle** (8). Despite its excessive decoration, this *Schloss* has a homely, lived-in feel about it. Dating from the 12th century, it was heavily reconstructed by Ludwig's father, Maximilian II. The future king spent much of his youth here and was undoubtedly influenced by its dreamy, romantic atmosphere. It was here, too, that he entertained the composer Richard Wagner, who milked him for all he was worth. Tours of the castle are conducted during the same time periods as Neuschwanstein Castle, above.

From here, stroll down to the **Pindarplatz** (9) for another gorgeous view across the Alpsee, then return to the bus stop (5) and Füssen.

A Daytrip from Munich

The Chiemsee

The enchanting Chiemsee, Bavaria's largest lake, lies just north of the Alps within easy reach of Munich. It was on an island in these idyllic waters that Ludwig II, the unbalanced "Dream King," built a Teutonic version of Versailles as his final castle. He was not the first to appreciate the lonely beauty of this spot, however. As far back as 782 a Benedictine convent was founded on a neighboring island; its 15th-century replacement remains there to this day, as does an old fishing community that is fast becoming a modest resort. Between the nearby town of Prien and the ferry dock a 19th-century narrow-gauge steam train shuttles enthusiastic visitors out for a day of fun, sun, and exploration.

GETTING THERE:

Trains depart Munich's main station several times in the morning for the one-hour ride to Prien, the starting point of this trip. Return service operates until mid-evening.

By car, the Chiemsee is 60 miles southeast of Munich via the A-8 Autobahn. Use the Bernau exit and follow signs for Prien, parking at the ferry dock.

PRACTICALITIES:

The best time to visit the Chiemsee is between late May and late September, when boats are frequent and the steam train operates. The castle is open daily all year round, except for a few major holidays. Some boats operate during the off-season. The local **Tourist Information Office**, phone (08051) 690-50, is near the train station in Prien. **Bicycles** may be rented at the Prien station from April through October. The Chiemsee is in the Land of **Bayern**.

FOOD AND DRINK:

Some choice restaurants and cafés are:

At Stock-Hafen:

Reinhart (Seestr. 117, near the pier) Rustic country charm. X: Thurs. $$

Seehotel Feldhütter (Seestr. 101, near the pier) Has an outdoor beer garden. X: Nov.-Mar. $

On Herreninsel:

Schlosshotel Herrenchiemsee (by the Altes Schloss) Noted for its fish dishes, also has outdoor tables and a café. $$

SUGGESTED TOUR:

From the **Prien Train Station** (1) you can get to the ferry pier *(Stock-Hafen)* by either the 19th-century **Chiemsee Bahn** steam train departing from the adjacent station, or by bus, depending on which is running at the moment. Just follow the crowds—they're going to the same place. A combination round-trip ticket for the steam train or bus plus the ferry rides is available.

Ferries for the two islands depart from the **Stock-Hafen Pier** (2), and are timed to meet the arrival of trains and buses. Boat tickets are also sold there.

The **Chiemsee** (pronounced *keem-zay*) covers an area of over 31 square miles and has three islands; one of which, Krautinsel, is uninhabited. Of the other two, Herreninsel (Men's Island) has had a monastery since the Middle Ages, and Faueninsel (Ladies' Island) a nunnery since 782. According to legend, Krautinsel (Vegetable Island) was the spot where the monks and nuns got together, at least to grow veggies.

The boat ride to **Herreninsel** takes only 15 minutes. Upon arrival at its **landing stage** (3), walk uphill to the 17th-century **Altes Schloss** (4), once the home of Augustinian canons. There is an attractive **outdoor café** and restaurant in its precincts. From here a path leads through the woods, opening suddenly to reveal the palace in all its splendor.

King Ludwig II of Bavaria was just about the strangest monarch ever to rule a European country. Born centuries too late, he lived in a sheltered dreamworld of his own making. In the end, events swept him aside and he died tragically at the age of 40. The legacy he left behind, from the operas of Richard Wagner to the fantastic castles dotting the Bavarian landscape, has, however, enriched all of Western civilization.

Rising before you, the ***Palace of Herrenchiemsee** (5) was Ludwig's final paean to an age that vanished long before he was born. Ludwig purchased the island, a religious center until 1803, as the site for his Teutonic Versailles. Construction began in 1878 and continued until 1885, when funds gave out. Ludwig occupied the unfinished *Schloss* on only one occasion, during the fall of 1885, and then only for 10 days. Less than a year later he was deposed, and afterwards found drowned.

The interior of the palace is simply incredible. To see it you will have to join one of the frequent guided tours, some of which are in English. An illustrated booklet describing the entire palace is available

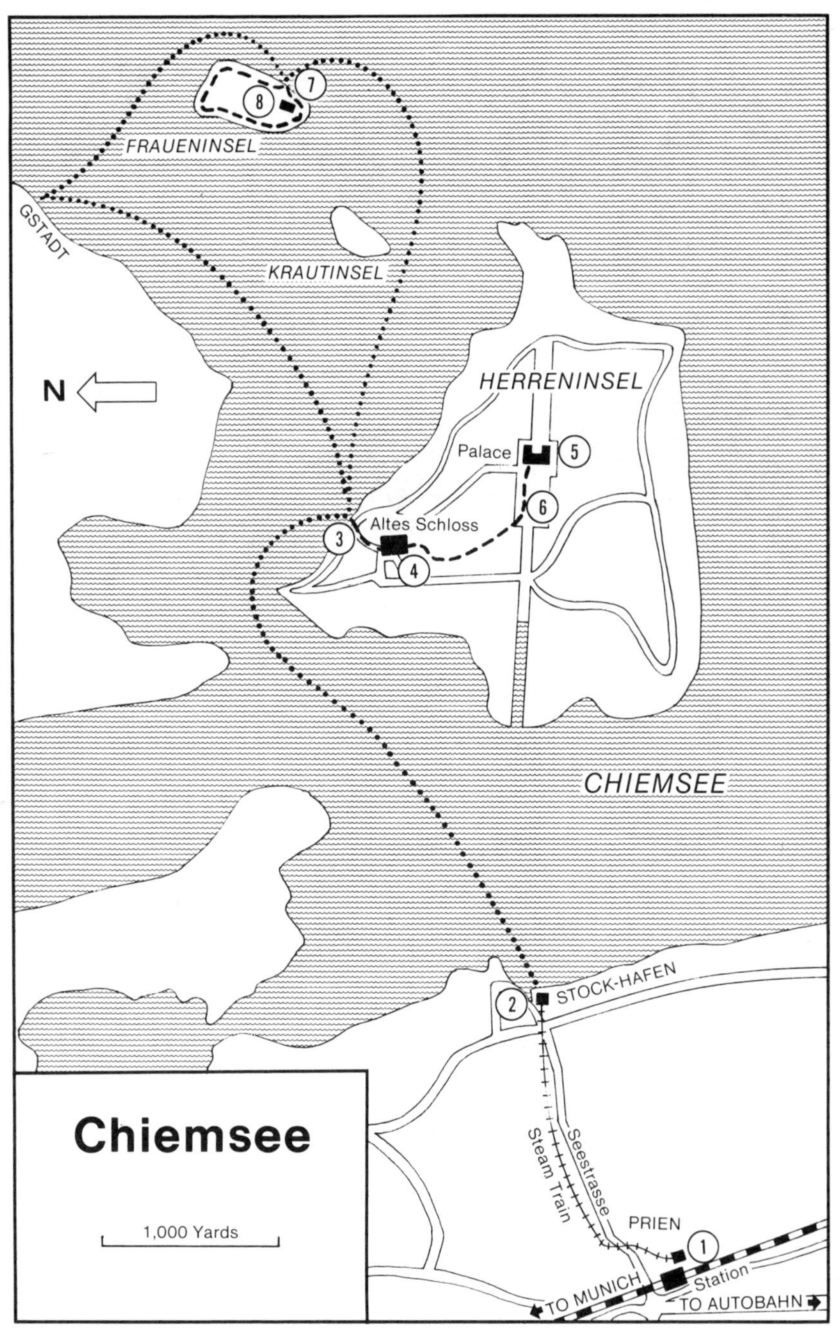
FRAUENINSEL
7
8
GSTADT
KRAUTINSEL
N
HERRENINSEL
Palace
5
6
Altes Schloss
3
4
CHIEMSEE
STOCK-HAFEN
2
Chiemsee
1,000 Yards
Seestrasse
Steam Train
PRIEN
1
Station
TO MUNICH
TO AUTOBAHN

Herrenchiemsee Palace

at the entrance, where there is also a small **museum** devoted to Ludwig's life. Visits may be made daily from April through September, 9 a.m. to 5 p.m.; and from October through March, 10 a.m. to 4 p.m.

Leaving the palace, walk straight ahead to the **Latona Fountain** (6), which erupts into jets of water at frequent intervals. From here stroll back to the landing stage and board the next boat bound for Fraueninsel.

Arriving at the **Fraueninsel landing stage** (7), recheck the posted schedule to determine just how much time can be spent there. Turn left and walk around the Benedictine nunnery, founded in 782 and rebuilt several times. Its **Abbey Church** (8), dating from the 13th and 15th centuries and combining Romanesque, Gothic, and Baroque elements, is well worth a visit.

Besides the convent, Fraueninsel is essentially a fishing village, albeit one that is being taken over by vacationers. A circular stroll around its perimeter reveals an oasis of quiet beauty with a panorama of mountains to the south, a perfect spot to relax at one of the **outdoor cafés** before returning to Stock-Hafen, Prien, and Munich.

A Daytrip from Munich

Augsburg

Although it was founded by the Romans as far back as 15 B.C., Augsburg is really a city of the Renaissance. At that time its merchant dynasties made this one of the richest places in Europe, a magnet to which great talent was naturally attracted. Much of that heritage remains intact and surprisingly well preserved today, and can be seen in the form of magnificent architecture and some really outstanding museums. This is a city for serious travelers; those looking for history, art, and culture rather than natural splendor or foot-stomping merriment.

Because of its proximity to Munich and its location at the junction of major transportation routes, Augsburg makes an excellent alternative base for daytrips throughout Bavaria.

GETTING THERE:

Trains to Augsburg depart Munich's main station very frequently, taking about 30 minutes for the run. Return service operates until after midnight.

By car, Augsburg is 42 miles northwest of Munich. Take the A-8 Autobahn to the Augsburg-Ost exit and park in one of the multi-story car parks near Königsplatz.

PRACTICALITIES:

Avoid going to Augsburg on a Monday, when most of its attractions are closed. The local **Tourist Information Office**, phone (0821) 50-20-70, is at Bahnhofstrasse 7, 2 blocks east of the train station. **Bicycles** may be rented at the train station from April through October. Augsburg is in the Land of **Bayern**, and has a **population** of about 250,000.

FOOD AND DRINK:

There is a fairly wide selection of restaurants and cafés in every price range. Among the best choices are:

Sieben Schwaben Stuben (Bürgermeister-Fischer-Str. 12, 1 block south of St. Anne's Church) Swabian specialties in an Old World atmosphere. $$

Fuggerkeller (Maximilianstr. 38, 1 block north of the Schaezler Palace) An elegant cellar restaurant in a historic mansion. Swabian and International cuisine. X: Sun. $$

Fuggerei Stube (Jakoberstr. 26, by the Fuggerei) A popular grill restaurant. Reservations advised, phone (0821) 308-70. X: Sun. eve., Mon. $$

Ratskeller (Rathausplatz 2, in the Town Hall basement) Swabian and Bavarian specialties under a vaulted brick ceiling. X: Sun. eve., Mon. $

SUGGESTED TOUR:

Augsburg's main **train station** *(Hauptbahnhof)* (1) was built in 1845 and is today the oldest in any large German city. Leave it and follow Bahnhofstrasse past the tourist office to Königsplatz. Continue along Bürgermeister-Fischer-Strasse and turn right onto Maximilianstrasse. This elegant old street was once part of the *Via Claudia Augusta,* an ancient Roman road leading north from Verona. At that time Augsburg, named after the emperor Augustus, was the capital of the province of Rhaetia. Today this broad thoroughfare is part of the famous Romantic Road, a heavily promoted tourist route from Würzburg to Füssen going by way of Rothenburg and Augsburg.

The early 16th-century **Fugger Palais** (2) was the town residence of one of the wealthiest families on Earth. Jakob Fugger the Rich, financier of emperors and a man of incredible power, lived here until his death in 1525. Be sure to see the inner courtyards, particularly the **Damenhof** with its curiously Florentine appearance. It is accessible through the main entrance.

Now follow the map to the **Römisches Museum** (Roman Museum) (3), located in a former Dominican church. Many valuable artifacts from Augsburg's Roman era are displayed in this magnificent setting, including a superb gilded horse's head from the 2nd century A.D. The museum is open on Tuesdays through Sundays, from 10 a.m. to 5 p.m., closing at 4 p.m. from October through April.

Return to Maximilianstrasse and visit the **Schaezler Palais** (4), facing the Hercules Fountain of 1602. The palace itself features a stunning rococo ballroom, once used to entertain Marie Antoinette on her way to marry Louis XVI, and now houses the city's two major art museums. The first of these, nearest the entrance, is the **Deutsche Barockgalerie** (German Baroque Gallery) with its important works from the 17th and 18th centuries. But the real treasures are in the **Staatsgalerie** (State Gallery), reached via a connecting passage through the festival hall. The well-known portrait of **Jakob Fugger the Rich* by Albrecht Dürer is here, along with many great masterpieces of the Renaissance. Both museums are open during the same times as the Roman Museum, above.

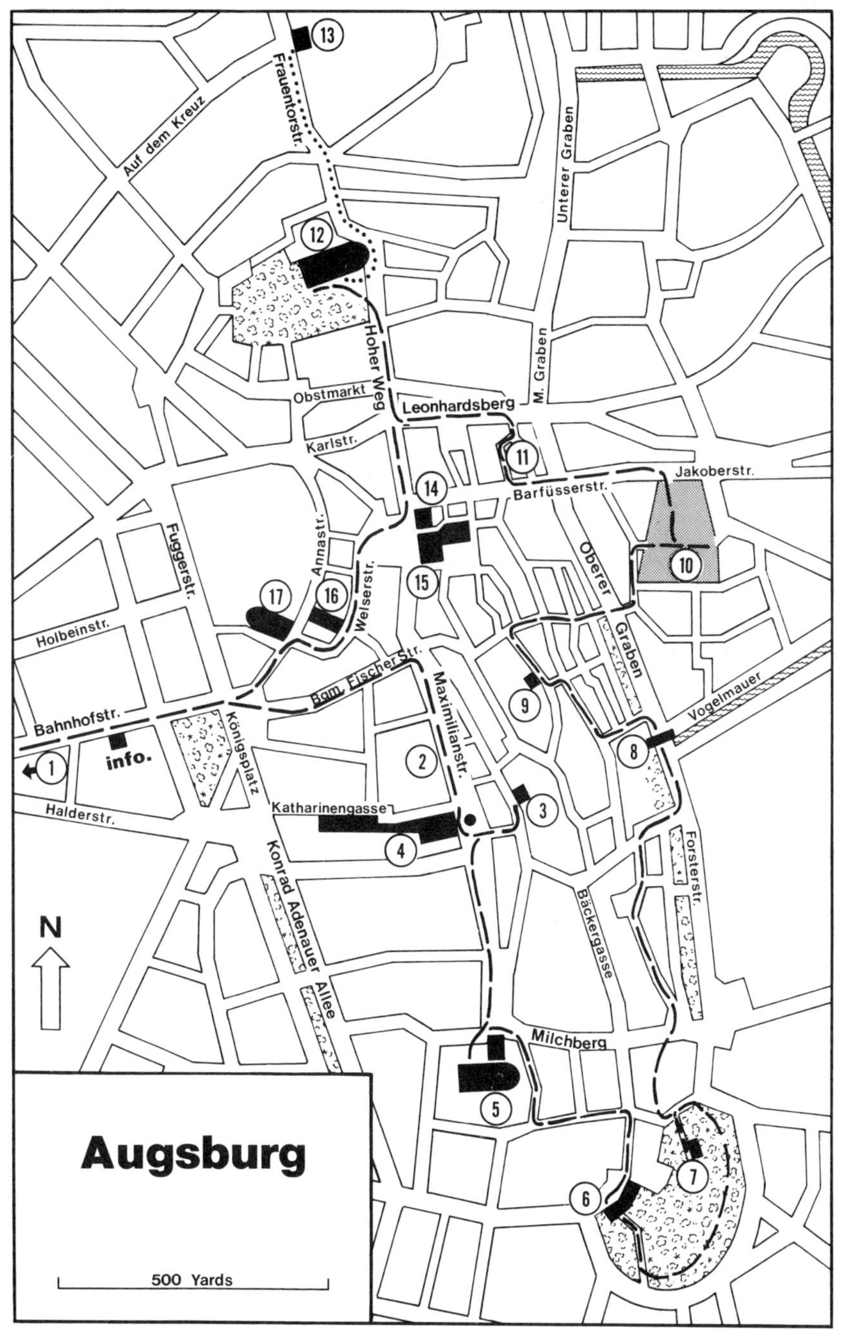
Augsburg
500 Yards
N
Auf dem Kreuz
Frauentorstr.
Unterer Graben
M. Graben
Hoher Weg
Obstmarkt
Leonhardsberg
Karlstr.
Jakoberstr.
Barfüsserstr.
Annastr.
Welserstr.
Oberer Graben
Fuggerstr.
Holbeinstr.
Bgm. Fischer Str.
Maximilianstr.
Vogelmauer
Bahnhofstr.
Königsplatz
info.
Halderstr.
Katharinengasse
Forsterstr.
Konrad Adenauer Allee
Bäckergasse
Milchberg
1
2
3
4
5
6
7
8
9
10
11
12
13
14
15
16
17

At the far end of Maximilianstrasse is the Catholic **Basilica of SS. Ulrich and Afra** (5) and, adjoining it, the smaller Protestant **Church of St. Ulrich**. Together they symbolize the spirit of the Peace of Augsburg, an agreement of 1555 that brought religious freedom to the peers of the realm, although not to their subjects. Both are worth visiting, with the Catholic church being the more interesting. St. Afra, a Swabian who died a martyr in A.D. 304 during the rule of Diocletian, is buried in its crypt along with St. Ulrich, a 10th-century Swabian bishop who saved Augsburg from the Huns.

Continue on to the **Rotes Tor** (Red Gate) (6), a fortified bastion first built in 1546. Go through the entrance on its right and into a park, passing a large open-air theater in which opera performances are given during July and August. Amble around through the park and turn left at the herb garden, then left again through a courtyard of the 17th-century Heilig-Geist-Spital to the **Handwerkermuseum** (Hand Crafts Museum) (7). This free exhibition of local handicrafts is open every day except on Saturdays, from 2–6 p.m.

Now follow the map through a former Dominican convent, exiting through a gate onto Margarentenstrasse. Continue along the Schwibbogengasse and a stream to the 15th-century **Vogel Tor** (Bird Gate) (8), opposite which are impressive sections of the medieval city wall, moats, and a watermill.

Turn left on Neuer Gang and right on Mittlerer Lech, then cross the little stream into the romantic old Lechviertel district. A right on Vorderer Lech brings you to the **Holbein Haus** (9), where the artist Hans Holbein the Elder, born in Augsburg in 1465, lived during the early 16th century. The original house was destroyed in 1944 but later reconstructed. Now a city art gallery for special exhibitions, it has some memorabilia on Holbein and is open on Tuesdays through Sundays, from 10 a.m. to 5 p.m.; closing at 4 p.m. from November through April.

The route leads across the busy Oberer Graben and into what is probably the most significant sight in Augsburg. The **Fuggerei** (10) is hardly where Jakob Fugger the Rich lived. It is, however, where he shrewdly took out insurance on his soul, buying eternal salvation through an act of charity. For the unbelievably low rent of 1.72 Marks a year, poor, elderly, deserving Catholics from Augsburg can live out their days in comfort and dignity in this, the world's first public housing development. The payment, equal to one Rhenish Guilder, has remained unchanged since the Fuggerei was opened in 1519. In addition, the residents must also promise to pray every day for the souls of the Fuggers.

The Fuggerei is actually a rather attractive town-within-a-town, complete with its own walls and gates, which are closed at night for security. Although the houses appear to be quite old, most are post-

The Perlachturm and the Rathaus

war reconstructions with modern facilities. One of the few originals to survive is now a **museum**, furnished as it was during the 17th and 18th centuries. Located at Mittleren Gasse 13, it is open from April through October, daily from 9 a.m. to 5 p.m. The house next door at number 14 is also an original, and was occupied by one Franz Mozart, the composer's great-grandfather, from 1681 to 1693.

Exit onto Jakoberstrasse and follow the map to the **Bertold Brecht Haus** (11) at Auf-dem-Rain 7. Born here in 1898, the famous author of the *Threepenny Opera* later moved to America before settling down after the war in East Berlin, where he died in 1956. His leftist leanings made him a pariah in Augsburg, but now that he's safely dead his house has become a tourist attraction. It's open on Tuesdays through Sundays, from 10 a.m. to 5 p.m.; closing at 4 p.m. from November through April.

A left on Leonhardsberg and a right on Hoher Weg leads to the ***Dom** (Cathedral) (12), a romantically beautiful structure begun in the 9th century and enlarged in the Gothic style during the 14th century. To the left of its main entrance, midway to the west end along the south side and protected by a gate, there is a fascinating ***bronze door** decorated with strange reliefs depicting both mythology and the Old

Testament. This dates from the 11th century. Equally ancient are the **stained-glass windows of the Prophets**, said to be the oldest of their kind in the world. There are several altar paintings by Hans Holbein the Elder, and other excellent works of art.

From here you might want to make a short **side trip** north to visit the **Mozart Haus** (13) at Frauentorstrasse 30. Wolfgang Amadeus was, of course, born in Salzburg, but his father Leopold was raised here, and the house is an interesting museum of Mozart memorabilia. The family's fortunes had certainly improved since the time that Wolfgang's great-grandfather Franz lived in the Fuggerei! The house is open on Mondays, Tuesdays, Thursdays, and Fridays, from 10 a.m. until noon and 2–5 p.m.; closing at 4 p.m. on Fridays.

Continue down Hoher Weg to the **Perlachturm** (14), originally built in the 12th century as a watchtower but extended to its present height of 256 feet during the 17th century. You can climb to the top from April through September, daily from 10 a.m. to 6 p.m., for a bird's-eye ***view** of the town and countryside. The Alps are visible when a yellow flag is flown. Hidden behind the tower is a tiny church that also dates from the 12th century.

Next to the tower is the early 17th-century **Rathaus** (Town Hall) (15), badly damaged during the last war but now so completely restored that it seems to have been built only yesterday. Perhaps after it ages a bit, it will once again be considered as one of the finest Renaissance structures in Germany. Its spectacular **Golden Hall** may be visited on weekdays from 10 a.m. to 6 p.m., provided it's not in use.

The adjacent **Rathausplatz** is a handsome open square, embellished with a 16th-century statue of the emperor Augustus. Around it are a number of inviting **outdoor cafés** and pubs, which you might be in need of by now.

Walk down Philippine-Welser-Strasse past the former residence of the Welser family at number 24. Like the Fuggers, this dynasty was incredibly rich, and at one time actually owned most of Venezuela. Unfortunately, they left little behind and have since fallen into obscurity. Their house is now occupied by the **Maximilian Museum** (16), which displays some outstanding souvenirs of Augsburg's past. It is open on Tuesdays through Sundays, from 10 a.m. to 4 p.m.

St.-Annakirche (St. Anne's Church) (17) is entered through a side door to the left in the Annahof. In 1518 Martin Luther found sanctuary in this former Carmelite monastery, which has been Protestant since the Reformation. Inside, there is a remarkable burial chapel of the Fuggers, and the famous **Portrait of Luther* by Lucas Cranach the Elder. The church is open daily from 10 a.m. to noon and 2:30–6 p.m. From here it is a relatively short walk back to the train station.

A Daytrip from Munich or Frankfurt

*Nürnberg

(Nuremberg)

Often regarded as the most German of German cities, Nürnberg makes a fascinating daytrip destination whose very name recalls a contradiction of images. It is at once the perfect medieval city, the toy capital of the world, the setting for Wagner's incomparable opera *"Die Meistersinger,"* and a charming center of intellect and culture. Yet, Nürnberg was the place chosen by Hitler for the infamous Nazi rallies of the '30s, and the city that lent its proud name to the despicable laws of racial purity. In retribution, it was practically leveled during World War II, and is still best known for the war-crime trials held there after the collapse of the Third Reich. Since then, the old part of town has been largely restored to its former appearance so that it at least *looks* ancient. It is commonly known in English as Nuremberg.

Not really old as medieval cities go, Nürnberg was founded about 1040 as a military stronghold by Emperor Heinrich III. With the downfall of the Imperial House of Hohenstaufen in the 13th century it became a free city, fortunately located at the junction of several important trade routes. During this period the arts flourished with such local talents as Albrecht Dürer and Hans Sachs. Prosperity came to end with the Thirty Years War, when Nürnberg's population and wealth declined greatly. It was not until the Industrial Revolution of the 19th century that the city, by now a part of Bavaria, regained its prominent position in German affairs.

This daytrip can easily be taken from Frankfurt as well as from Munich.

GETTING THERE:

Trains depart **Munich's** main station at least hourly for Nürnberg, about 100 minutes away by IC or EC express. Return service operates until mid-evening.

Trains leave **Frankfurt's** main station hourly for Nürnberg. Most of these are of the IC or EC class and take about two hours and 20 minutes for the journey. Return trains run until mid-evening.

By Car from **Munich**, take the A-9 Autobahn 103 miles north to Nürnberg.

By car from **Frankfurt**, take the A-3 Autobahn 138 miles southeast to Nürnberg.

PRACTICALITIES:

Several of Nürnberg's best attractions are closed on Mondays. The local **Tourist Information Office**, phone (0911) 23-36-32, is in the main train station, with a branch at Hauptmarkt 18. Nürnberg is in the Land of **Bayern** and has a **population** of about 490,000.

FOOD AND DRINK:

The local specialty is Bratwurst, those little sausages that taste better here than anywhere else. Nürnberg is also noted for its Lebkuchen cookies, excellent Franconian wines, and superb beer. Among the choice restaurants are:

Goldenes Posthorn (Glöckleinsgasse 2, across from St. Sebald's Church) Inventive Franconian cuisine, in business since the 15th century. Reservations and proper dress required, phone (0911) 22-51-53. X: Sun. $$$

Nassauer Keller (Karolinenstr. 2, opposite St. Lorenz Church) Traditional cuisine in the cellar of a 13th-century house. Reservations and proper dress required, phone (0911) 22-59-67. X: Sun. $$

Heilig Geist Spital (Spitalgasse 12, on the Pegnitz River) An authentic wine tavern, very popular with tourists. $ and $$

Bratwurst Häusle (Rathausplatz 1, across from the Old Town Hall) A boisterous, fun place for grilled sausages and sauerkraut. X: Sun., holidays. $

Bratwurstglöcklein (In the Handwerkerhof by the Königstor) A rustic place for bratwurst, sauerkraut, potato salad, and beer. X: Sun., holidays, winter. $

SUGGESTED TOUR:

Begin your walk at the **main train station** *(Hauptbahnhof)* (1), where the tourist office is located. From here use the underground passageway to reach the **Königstor** (2), a part of the massive old fortifications. These walls, constructed over a period of centuries, remain intact today and give Nürnberg a medieval appearance that is largely missing from other major German cities. Next to the tower is an entrance to the **Handwerkerhof**, a courtyard of small shops where present-day craftsmen carry on in the medieval tradition. You may want to return here later.

Stroll along Königstrasse to the **St.-Lorenz-Kirche** (St. Lawrence's Church) (3). Built between the 13th and 15th centuries, this is the city's largest house of worship. It contains some remarkable works of art, including the 16th-century **Annunciation* by Veit Stoss that hangs suspended in the choir. Other pieces to look for are the tabernacle by Adam Kraft, to the left of the high altar, and the wonderful stained-glass windows in the choir.

Opposite the front of the church is the tower-like **Nassauer Haus**, parts of which date from the early 13th century. It is reputed to be the oldest dwelling in town, and now houses a delightful restaurant. Continue along Königstrasse, here reserved for pedestrians, to the Museum Bridge. To your right is one of those wonderful scenes so typical of Nürnberg. The **Heilig-Geist-Spital** (4), a 14th-century almshouse spanning the Pegnitz River, still serves its original purpose and also contains a very popular *Weinstube* and restaurant.

You are now only steps from the **Hauptmarkt** (main market place) (5), an open area usually filled with farmers' stalls. The traditional *Christkindlmarkt* is held here each December for the sale of toys and ornaments. Facing the east side of the square is the 14th-century **Frauenkirche** (Church of Our Lady), which provides a free spectacle every day at noon in the form of mechanical figures acting out the story of the Golden Bull of 1356. Step inside to see the famous Tucher altarpiece from 1440.

One of the best-known sights in Nürnberg is the ***Schöner Brunnen** (Beautiful Fountain) in the northwest corner of the square. Dating from the 14th century, it is decorated with 40 sculpted figures arranged in four tiers, and surrounded by a 16th-century wrought-iron grille. Now walk up to the **Altes Rathaus** (Old Town Hall) (6), where you can take a gruesome tour through the 14th-century dungeons and visit the torture chamber. The cells are open from May through September, on Mondays through Fridays from 10 a.m. to 4 p.m.; and on weekends from 10 a.m. to 1 p.m.

St.-Sebaldus-Kirche (St. Sebald's Church) (7) was begun in 1225, making the transition from the Romanesque to the Gothic style. Enter through the west portal and visit the ***Shrine of St. Sebaldus**, a wonderful 16th-century bronze sculpture containing the silver coffin of Nürnberg's patron saint. There are several other exceptional works of art, including a sunburst Madonna on a north aisle pillar, a Crucifixion group by Veit Stoss near the main altar and, in the south aisle, a stone sculpture by Adam Kraft of Christ bearing the Cross.

A climb up Bergstrasse leads to the ***Albrecht Dürer Haus** (8), where the great artist lived from 1509 until his death in 1528. The first three floors are open as a museum, and give a good impression of the surroundings in which he lived and worked. The house is open daily

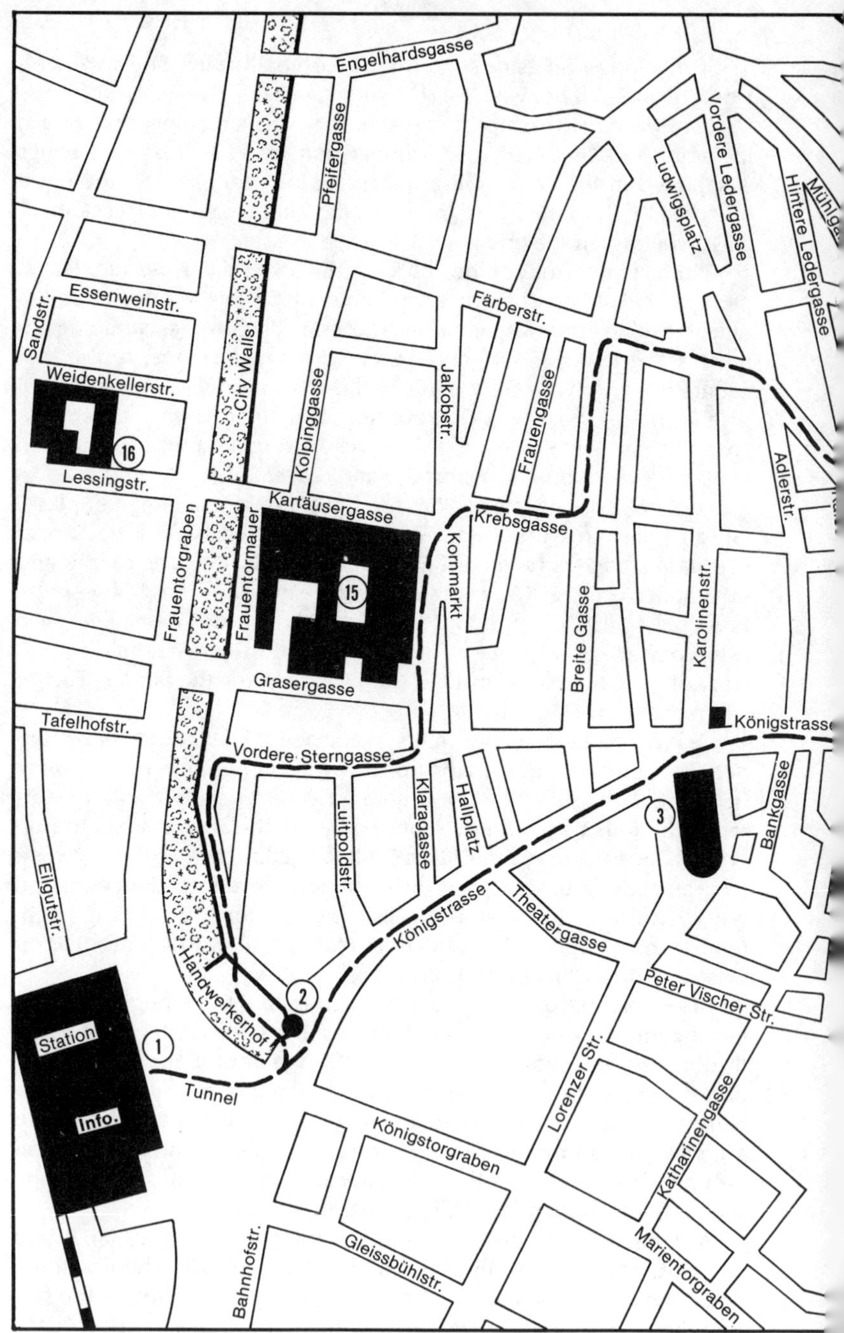
Engelhardsgasse
Pfeifergasse
Ludwigsplatz
Vordere Ledergasse
Hintere Ledergasse
Färberstr.
Essenweinstr.
Sandstr.
Weidenkellerstr.
City Walls
Kolpinggasse
Jakobstr.
Frauengasse
Adlerstr.
16
Lessingstr.
Kartäusergasse
Krebsgasse
Frauentorgraben
Frauentormauer
15
Kornmarkt
Breite Gasse
Karolinenstr.
Grasergasse
Königstrasse
Tafelhofstr.
Vordere Sterngasse
Luitpoldstr.
Klaragasse
Hallplatz
3
Bankgasse
Eilgutstr.
Königstrasse
Theatergasse
Handwerkerhof
2
Peter Vischer Str.
Station
1
Tunnel
Lorenzer Str.
Info.
Königstorgraben
Katharinengasse
Gleissbühlstr.
Bahnhofstr.
Marientorgraben

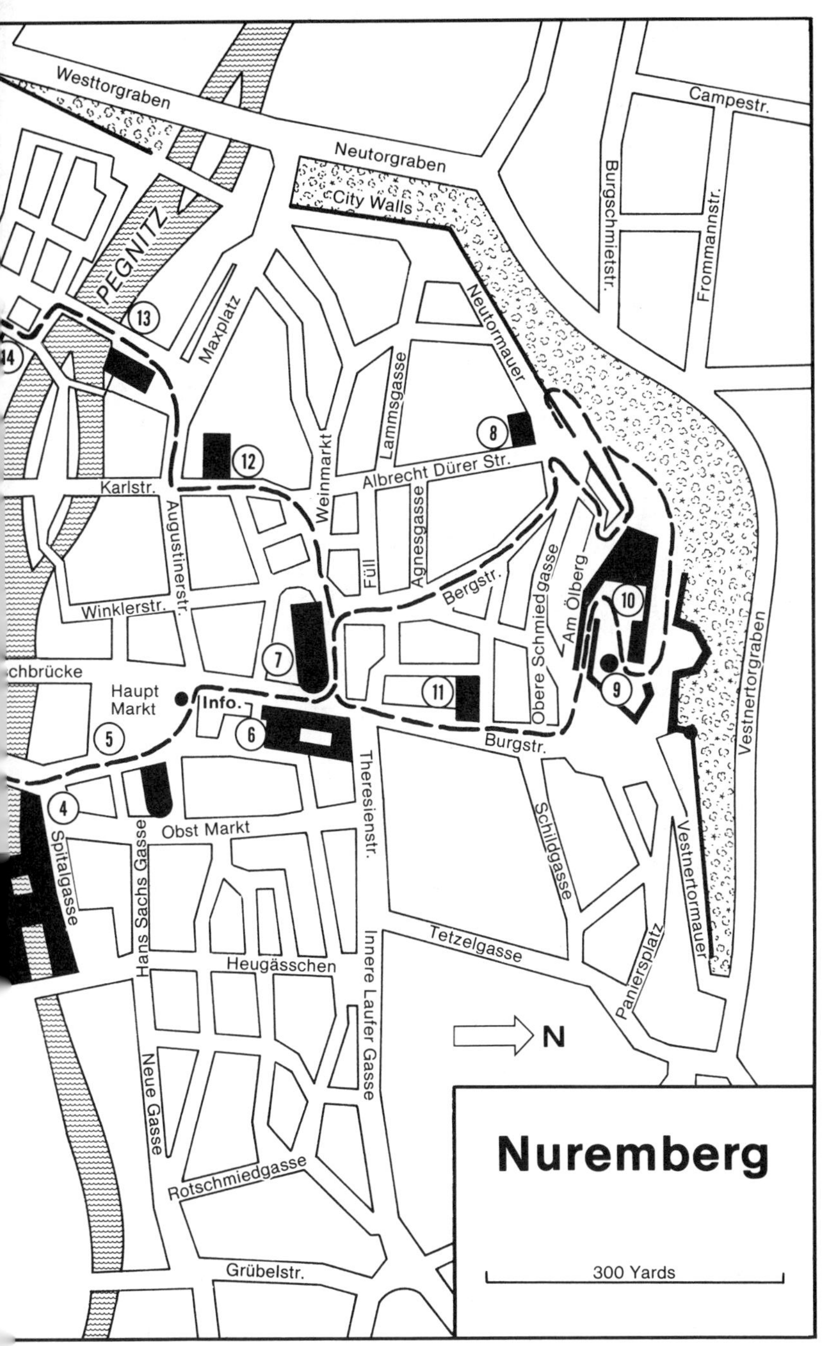
Westtorgraben
Neutorgraben
City Walls
Campestr.
Burgschmietstr.
Frommannstr.
PEGNITZ
Maxplatz
Neutormauer
Lammsgasse
Weinmarkt
Albrecht Dürer Str.
Karlstr.
Augustinerstr.
Agnesgasse
Füll
Bergstr.
Obere Schmiedgasse
Am Ölberg
Winklerstr.
Vestnertorgraben
Haupt Markt
Info.
Burgstr.
Theresienstr.
Schildgasse
Vestnertormauer
Obst Markt
Spitalgasse
Hans Sachs Gasse
Tetzelgasse
Paniersplatz
Heugässchen
Innere Laufer Gasse
N
Neue Gasse
Rotschmiedgasse
Grübelstr.
Nuremberg
300 Yards
4
5
6
7
8
9
10
11
12
13

except on Mondays, from 10 a.m. to 5 p.m. On weekdays during the winter season it opens at 1 p.m., and is open on Wednesday evenings all year round. The picturesque square next to this has some attractive **outdoor cafés**.

Follow the map uphill and through a garden to an opening in the town wall, from which you will have a marvelous ***view** of the square. Return through the garden and stroll past the **Fünfeckiger Turm** (Pentagonal Tower), which dates from 1040 and is regarded as the oldest structure in Nürnberg. Adjoining this are the Imperial Stables, now used as a youth hostel. You are now within the precincts of **Nürnberg Castle**, a residence of all acknowledged German kings and emperors from 1050 to 1571. Continue on to the 13th-century **Sinwellturm** (9), a massive round tower that may be climbed for the best possible panoramic view of the city. Close to this is the **Tiefer Brunnen** (Deep Well), a source of water since the earliest days. It, too, may be visited.

The major part of the castle, the **Kaiserburg** (10), was begun in the 12th century, although most of what you see today dates from the 15th and 16th centuries. There are frequent guided tours through its Gothic interior visiting, among other rooms, the interesting 12th-century **chapel**, a double-deck affair where emperors worshipped above the heads of lesser folk. The castle is open daily from 9 a.m. to noon and 12:45–5 p.m.; closing at 4 p.m. in winter.

Walk down and turn right on Burgstrasse. This leads to the **Fembo Haus** (11), a excellent museum of life in old Nürnberg, located in a well-preserved Renaissance mansion. Be sure to see the large model of the Old City on the fourth floor. The museum is open on Tuesdays through Sundays, from 10 a.m. to 5 p.m.; during winter from 1–5 p.m.

The route again passes St. Sebald's Church, then follows Weinmarkt and Karlstrasse to the ***Spielzeug Museum** (Toy Museum) (12). A wealth of delightful playthings from all over the world is on display, ranging from simple dolls to elaborate model railway setups. Toys have been a major Nürnberg industry for centuries, making a visit here especially appropriate. The museum is open on Tuesdays through Sundays, from 10 a.m. to 5 p.m.; closing at 9 p.m. on Wednesdays.

Continue on to the **Maxbrücke** (13), a bridge with stunning views up and down the Pegnitz River. The large half-timbered structure to your left, the Weinstadel, was built in 1446 as a home for lepers. Later used for wine storage, it is now a residence for university students. Adjacent to this is the Wasserturm, a part of the older 14th-century fortifications. From here the Pegnitz is spanned by a covered wooden footbridge called the **Henkersteg**, or hangman's bridge, to whose solitary dwelling it led. To the right, the view of the medieval walls arched over the river is equally engaging.

Follow the map past the 15th-century **Unschlitthaus** (14), a former

Nürnberg Castle rises above the square by the Dürer House

granary, and through a more modern part of town to the formidable **Germanisches National Museum** (Germanic National Museum) (15). Dedicated to the many aspects of German art and culture from prehistoric times to the 20th century, this vast treasure house requires several hours to see properly. It is open on Tuesdays through Sundays, from 9 a.m. to 5 p.m.; and also on Thursday evenings from 8–9:30 p.m.

Railfans and kids, as well as some otherwise normal people, will really enjoy a visit to the **Verkehrsmuseum** (Transportation Museum) (16) just beyond the walls on Lessingstrasse. Its collection of old trains features the *Adler,* the first locomotive to operate in Germany, and "mad" King Ludwig II's incredible private cars. Three floors of exhibits are almost entirely devoted to railroading, with a special treat being the huge model train layout *(Modellbahn),* which runs hourly on the half-hour. There is an inexpensive cafeteria with local dishes and drinks served in a 19th-century machine shop setting. The museum is open daily from 10 a.m. to 5 p.m., closing an hour earlier on Sundays and in winter.

A Daytrip from Frankfurt or Munich

Würzburg

Although situated on the Main River, Würzburg really belongs to the south of Germany. This "Town of the Madonnas" is renowned for its splendid Residenz and other triumphs of the Baroque style, as well as for its delicious wines. Curiously enough, and despite its central location, Würzburg is all too often overlooked by foreign tourists as they scurry from Heidelberg to Rothenburg and Munich. That's a pity, for this lovely old town at the northern end of the famed "Romantic Road" has a lot to offer the traveler.

Würzburg dates from at least the 7th century, and its history is filled with the comings and goings of saints, kings, and emperors; including the likes of Charlemagne and Frederick Barbarossa. The noted sculptor Tilman Riemenschneider worked here most of his life, was elected mayor, and in 1525 led a peasant revolt for which he was imprisoned.

Würzburg's greatest era, however, was the 18th century. It was then that the ruling prince-bishops moved down from their fortress on the Marienberg and into the magnificent new Residenz, where they set a style of unparalleled opulence. By the early 19th century the grandeur subsided as the town became a part of Bavaria. The vast destruction of World War II led to a near-total restoration, so that the Würzburg you see today looks very much as it did in centuries past.

This trip can be taken from either Frankfurt or Munich, and makes a good stopover between them.

GETTING THERE:

Trains leave **Frankfurt's** main station hourly for the 80-minute ride to Würzburg. Most are of the IC or EC class. There is good return service until mid-evening.

Trains depart **Munich's** main station about hourly for the 2½-hour run to Würzburg. Most are of the IC class. Return service operates until mid-evening.

By car from **Frankfurt**, Würzburg is 73 miles to the southeast via the A-3 Autobahn.

By car from **Munich**, Würzburg lies 173 miles to the northwest. Take the A-9 Autobahn to Nürnberg, then the A-3 to Würzburg.

The Residenz

PRACTICALITIES:

Würzburg may be visited in any season, but avoid coming on a Monday, when the most important sights are closed. There is a local **Tourist Information Office** in front of the train station, phone (0931) 374-36; and at the Marktplatz, phone (0931) 373-98. **Bicycles** may be rented at the station from April through October. Würzburg is in the Land of **Bayern** and has a **population** of about 127,000.

FOOD AND DRINK:

The local Franconian wines, in their characteristic *Bocksbeutel* flask, are superb, as is the local beer. Some good restaurant choices are:

Hotel Rebstock (Neubaustr. 7, 4 blocks south of the Town Hall) A centuries-old palace, now a luxury hotel, with a gourmet restaurant and a wine tavern. X: early Jan. Restaurant X: Sun. eve., Tavern X: Tues. $$$ and $$

Ratskeller (Langgasse 1, in the Town Hall) A vaulted cellar restaurant with local wines and country cooking. X: Early Feb. $$

Zur Stadt Mainz (Semmelstr. 39, 5 blocks north of the Residenz) An old inn famed for its local cuisine. X; Mon., late Dec.-late Jan. $$

Schiffbäuerin (Katzengasse 7, across the river, 2 blocks north of the Old Bridge) A famous fish restaurant. X: Sun. eve., Mon., mid-July-mid-Aug. $$

Juliusspital (Juliuspromenade 19, 6 blocks northwest of the Residenz) An historic tavern with hearty local specialties and superb wine from their own vineyard. X; Wed., Feb. $$

Bürgerspital Weinstuben (Theaterstr. 19, 3 blocks northwest of the Residenz) A characteristic old wine tavern with Franconian cooking. X: Tues., mid-July-mid-Aug. $

SUGGESTED TOUR:

Leave the **train station** (1) and pass the tourist office located just outside. From here follow the map to Würzburg's main attraction, the ***Residenz** (2). Primarily the work of the renowned architect Balthasar Neumann, this magnificent Baroque palace was built between 1720 and 1744 as a residence for the prince-bishops of Würzburg, who had previously lived in the Marienberg fortress.

Inside, the most spectacular sight is of the ***Grand Staircase**. As you approach the first landing you become aware of a dazzling ceiling depicting the four continents known at that time. This fresco, one of the largest on Earth, is regarded as the supreme achievement of the Venetian master, Giambattista Tiepolo. The **Weisser Saal** (White Hall), an elegant monochromatic masterpiece of pure rococo, provides visual relief before continuing on to the **Kaiser Saal** (Imperial Hall). Again, Tiepolo outdid himself on the frescoes and, together with the architect Neumann and the sculptor Antonio Bossi, created one of the most splendid interior spaces in Germany. There are other wonderful rooms to see before leaving the palace, especially the **Garden Room** on the ground floor. The Residenz is open on Tuesdays through Sundays from 9 a.m. to 5 p.m.; and from 10 a.m. to 4 p.m. from October through March. The admission includes a guided tour.

The **Hofkirche** (Court Chapel), another part of the complex, is entered from the outside. This marvelous accomplishment by the same team is in every way equal to what you've seen in the palace proper. A gate next to this leads into the delightful **gardens**, which deserve to be explored thoroughly.

Stroll down Hofstrasse to the **Dom** (Cathedral) (3). Begun in the 11th century on the site of an earlier cathedral, it has been greatly modified in the years since, including some modern works installed as part of a postwar restoration. There are several fine sculptures by Tilman Riemenschneider, particularly the tombs of the prince-bishops Rudolf von Scherenberg and Lorenz von Bibra. Also noteworthy is the outstanding Schönborn Chapel, designed by Balthasar Neumann, in the north transept.

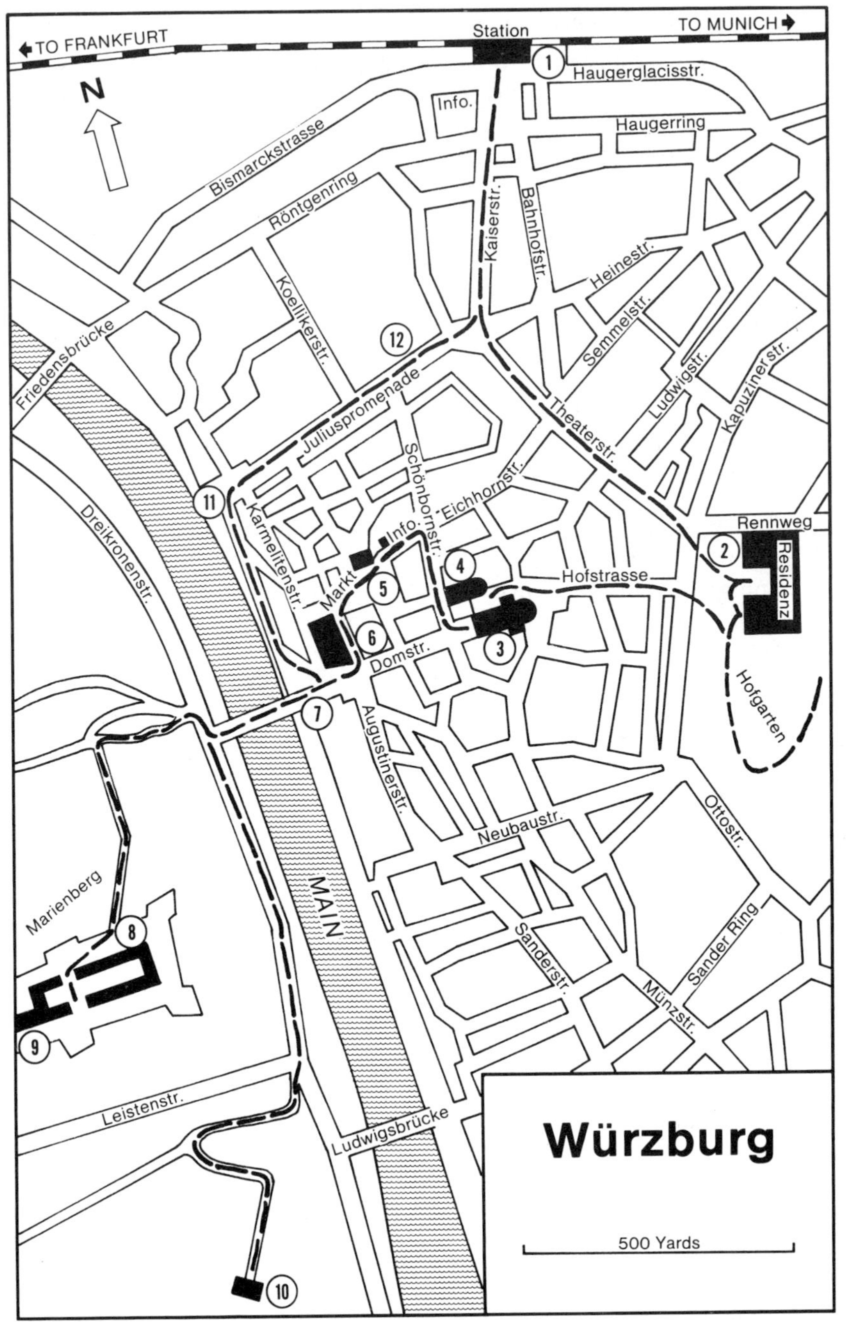

TO FRANKFURT
Station
TO MUNICH
N
Info.
Haugerglacisstr.
Haugerring
Bismarckstrasse
Röntgenring
Kaiserstr.
Bahnhofstr.
Heinestr.
Semmelstr.
Ludwigstr.
Kapuzinerstr.
Koellikerstr.
Friedensbrücke
Juliuspromenade
Theaterstr.
Schönbornstr.
Eichhornstr.
Info.
Karmelitenstr.
Markt
Rennweg
Residenz
Hofstrasse
Domstr.
Dreikronenstr.
Hofgarten
Augustinerstr.
Ottostr.
Neubaustr.
MAIN
Marienberg
Sanderstr.
Sander Ring
Münzstr.
Leistenstr.
Ludwigsbrücke
Würzburg
500 Yards
1
2
3
4
5
6
7
8
9
10
11
12

The **Neumünster** (4), just a few steps away, has a fine Baroque façade at its west end. Much of this church dates from the 11th and 13th centuries and was built on the burial site of the Irish monk St. Kilian, who was murdered here in 689. Again, the rich interior has several excellent sculptures by Riemenschneider. There is a small garden on the north side, called the **Lusamgärtlein**, in which the famous 13th-century minnesinger Walther von der Vogelweide is supposed to be buried.

From here follow the map to the **Marktplatz** (5). There are two remarkable structures on its north side. One of these is the **Haus zum Falken**, a former inn with a fabulous rococo facade, which now houses the main tourist office. The other is the late-Gothic **Marienkapelle** (St. Mary's Chapel). Enter through its north portal and take a look at the tombstone of Konrad von Schaumberg—another great carving by Riemenschneider—and the tomb of Balthasar Neumann, the architect who brought so much splendor to Würzburg.

Walk around to the **Rathaus** (Town Hall) (6), a picturesque complex of buildings from different eras, one of which dates from the 13th century. Step inside and visit the Wenzelsaal, named for King Wenceslas, who dined here in 1397. You can do the same, but only downstairs in the Ratskeller.

As you walk around this area, you may notice that many of the old houses have small statues of the Virgin set into corner niches. This is why Würzburg is called the "Town of the Madonnas."

The **Alte Mainbrücke** (Old Bridge) (7) still carries traffic over the Main River, as it has since the 15th century. This medieval span is beautifully adorned with statues of saints. Stroll across it and climb up to the **Festung Marienberg** (Marienberg Fortress) (8), home to the prince-bishops from the 13th to the 18th centuries. There is, of course, a great view of the town from here. Defensive fortifications of some sort have existed on this hill since about 1000 B.C., but the earliest part now remaining is the **Marienkirche** (St. Mary's Church) in the courtyard, consecrated in 706.

Be sure to see the ***Mainfränkisches Museum** (Franconian Museum) (9), located in the former Zeughaus (Arsenal) of the fortress. A showcase for the arts and artifacts of Würzburg, it contains an entire gallery of sculptures by Tilman Riemenschneider as well as works by Tiepolo and others. The displays of **wine making** are especially interesting as this hill is itself covered with vineyards. The museum is open daily from 10 a.m. to 5 p.m., closing at 4 p.m. from October through March. The new Fürstenbau Museum, concerned with Würzburg's history, is now open in the south wing on Tuesdays through Sundays.

Return to the bridge. Before crossing it, you may want to visit the **Käppele** (10), a Baroque pilgrimage church on a nearby hill. Built by

Festung Marienberg from the Alte Mainbrücke

Balthasar Neumann in the 18th century, it has some wonderful frescoes by Matthias Günther, and a fabulous **view** of both the Marienberg and Würzburg.

Recross the ancient bridge and walk along the bank of the river to the **Old Crane** (11), an 18th-century reminder that Würzburg was also a port town. There is an attractive **outdoor beer garden** overlooking the water's edge adjacent to this; just the place to relax after a hard day's sightseeing. If you'd rather sample the local wine, why not stop instead at the *Weinstuben* of the **Juliusspital** (12), an atmospheric old institution founded in 1576. While there you might ask to see the rococo apothecary and the gardens. From here it is only a short way back to the train station.

A Daytrip from Frankfurt

Triberg

The legendary Black Forest lies tucked away in a remote corner of Germany, often overlooked by foreign tourists. Simple geography keeps them away. One glance at the map shows you how difficult it can be to include this enchanted region—known in German as the *Schwarzwald*—into most practical itineraries. But that doesn't rule out sampling at least a bit of its magic on a lengthy but delightful daytrip from Frankfurt.

Triberg is probably the best spot for a first-time visit to the Black Forest. It has just about everything—waterfalls, mountain trails, a *gemütlich* atmosphere, good restaurants, and a fabulous museum filled with cuckoo clocks. It is easy to reach by rail, and not too difficult to get to by car. You could make the journey more worthwhile by staying overnight in the region and also visiting Freiburg, described in the next few pages.

GETTING THERE:

Trains leave Frankfurt's main station at 2-hour intervals for the direct 3-hour ride to Triberg, offering spectacular scenery during the last half-hour. Return service operates until early evening. Other routings are possible by making a change at Offenburg. Railpass holders will get their money's worth on this trip!

By car, Triberg is 165 miles south of Frankfurt. Take the A-5 Autobahn to the Offenburg exit, then continue on the B-33 road.

PRACTICALITIES:

Triberg should be visited in the warm season, when all the trails around the waterfall are sure to be open. Good weather is important. The local **Tourist Information Office**, phone (07722) 812-30, is in the Kurhaus near the waterfalls entrance. Triberg is in the Land of **Baden-Württemberg** and has a **population** of about 6,000.

In the Schwarzwald Museum

FOOD AND DRINK:

There are many places to eat and drink in this popular mountain resort. Some good choices are:

Parkhotel Wehrle (on the Marktplatz) Elegant, with trout prepared 20 different ways, along with wild game and other dishes. $$$

Hotel Pfaff (Hauptstr. 85, near the waterfalls entrance) Known for its trout dishes. Outdoor tables available. X: Wed. in off-season, Nov. $$

Zur Lilie (at the waterfalls entrance) A rather rustic but enjoyable place with simple food. X: Fri. in winter. $

Hotel Tanne (Wallfahrtsstr. 35, near the church) A simple inn with good food. X: Tues. in off-season, Nov. $

SUGGESTED TOUR:

The **Triberg Train Station** (1) is isolated in a forested valley. From there you can either take a DB bus (railpasses accepted), a taxi, or just walk slightly uphill for three-quarters of a mile to the **Markt Platz** (Market Place) (2). The Gutach stream, a few yards to the right of the main street, pokes its rushing waters between a clutter of inns, restaurants, and shops—none very elegant but all quite appealing. The **Rathaus** (Town Hall) (3) is worth a visit to see the exceptionally rich wood carvings in its council chamber, a true reflection of the local folk art of which the town is so proud. It is open on Mondays through Fridays, from 9 a.m. to noon and 2–4 p.m.

Continue uphill past a multitude of cuckoo-clock shops and enter the woods. In a few yards you will see an attractive café with a small watermill. Just beyond this is a **tollhouse** (4) where you pay a small fee to visit the **waterfalls**. From this point upwards, the Gutach stream tumbles down over seven cascades into a romantic glen for a drop of over 500 feet, making it the highest *Wasserfälle* in Germany.

Climb the path alongside the rushing torrent until you reach the top. Once there, descend a short distance to a bridge with a sign pointing the way to the Wallfahrtskirche. Cross it and pass another tollhouse. You are now on the **Panorama Weg,** a woodland trail with stunning views of the surrounding mountains and forests. Going past an onion-domed church, you will soon come to a **boating pond** (5), where an outdoor café invites you to stop for lunch or a drink.

Now follow the map to the **Wallfahrtskirche** (Church of Our Lady of the Pines) (6), which you saw from the path. Built in 1705, this small pilgrimage church has a marvelously Baroque interior. Its beautifully carved **high altar** is particularly outstanding, and contains the original small image of the Virgin that was attached to a pine tree here in the late 17th century. According to legend, this caused a miraculous healing spring to appear, attracting pilgrims for many years.

Continue down the street to the ***Schwarzwald Museum** (Black Forest Museum) (7), one of Germany's best local history museums. Here you can get a good impression of Black Forest life in the hard times before the region became a tourist center. Woodcarving, clockmaking, and mining were the predominant industries, and all are well represented in the museum. Individual rooms re-create the workshops and homes of long ago, while a hundred-foot-long tunnel offers a small taste of what the mines must have been like. Another section traces the development of a more modern local industry, radio communications, over the years. The most fascinating exhibits, however, are the ***mechanical music machines,** ranging from huge orchestrions to tiny bird-call boxes. Many of these can be operated by inserting a coin, and are an absolute delight to watch and hear. The most famous products of the Black Forest—**cuckoo clocks**—are also displayed in great variety. Triberg is a good place to purchase one of these noisy contraptions, should you feel so inclined. The museum is open daily from mid-may through September, 9 a.m. to 6 p.m.; and daily during the rest of the year from 9 a.m. to noon and 2–5 p.m.

Crossing the Hauptstrasse, walk down Luisenstrasse to the **Kurhaus** (8), a modern structure housing a concert hall, meeting rooms, and the tourist office. Here you can rest in a pleasant garden before returning to the train station.

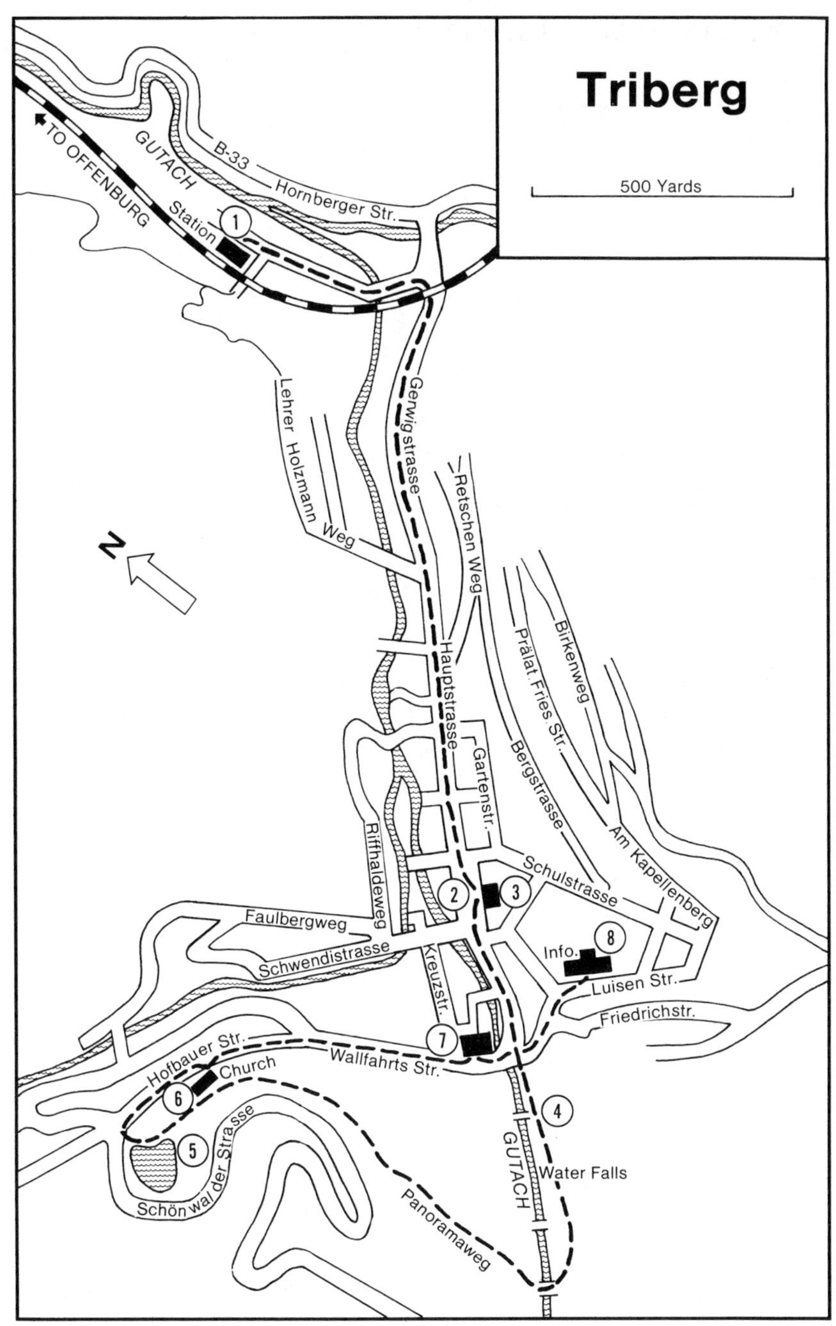

Triberg
500 Yards
TO OFFENBURG
GUTACH
B-33
Hornberger Str.
Station
1
Lehrer Holzmann Weg
Gerwigstrasse
Retschen Weg
N
Birkenweg
Prälat. Fries Str.
Hauptstrasse
Gartenstr.
Bergstrasse
Am Kapellenberg
Riffhaldeweg
Schulstrasse
2
3
Faulbergweg
8
Info.
Schwendistrasse
Kreuzstr.
Luisen Str.
Friedrichstr.
Hofbauer Str.
7
Wallfahrts Str.
Church
6
4
Schönwalder Strasse
5
GUTACH
Water Falls
Panoramaweg

A Daytrip from Frankfurt

Freiburg

One of Germany's most appealing cities remains unspoiled by mass tourism. Located in the extreme southwest corner of the country, Freiburg-im-Breisgau (its official name) lies far enough off the beaten path to discourage most travelers from going there. Those who do go are in for a real discovery. This delightful place on the edge of the Black Forest is not only exceptionally attractive, but also has plenty of character—and eccentricities. Where else do forest streams run down the gutters of the streets? How many other towns have a mountain right in their very center? Freiburg's main attraction, however, lies in the sunny disposition of its people, who manage to be easygoing and cosmopolitan at the same time; a heritage, no doubt, from over four centuries of Austrian rule as well as strong ties to nearby France and Switzerland. The presence, since 1457, of a major university also adds a certain youthful vitality.

Although this is a one-day trip, you might prefer to stay overnight and combine it with nearby Triberg, described previously. There is bus service between them.

GETTING THERE:

Trains of the EC and IC classes depart Frankfurt's main station hourly for the 2½-hour run to Freiburg. A change at Mannheim is sometimes necessary. Good return service operates until early evening, with other trains running all night long.

By car, Freiburg is 168 miles south of Frankfurt via the A-5 Autobahn. Use the Freiburg-Nord exit.

PRACTICALITIES:

Most of Freiburg's museums are closed on Mondays. The town claims to get more sunshine than any other city in Germany, so you'll probably enjoy good weather. The local **Tourist Information Office**, phone (0761) 36-89-00, is at Rotteckring 14, opposite Colombi Park. **Bicycles** may be rented at the train station from April through October. Freiburg is in the Land of **Baden-Württemberg** and has a **population** of about 180,000.

Münsterplatz and the Cathedral

FOOD AND DRINK:

Freiburg abounds in good restaurants, a few of which are:

Ratskeller im Kornhaus (Münsterplatz 11, facing the north side of the cathedral) Traditional local cuisine in a 15th-century cellar. X: Sat. eve., Mon. $$

Schlossberg Dattler (at the top of the cable car) A large, rustic place with a great view and outdoor terraces. X: Tues. $$

Greiffenegg-Schlössle (Schlossbergring 3, near the Schwabentor) Wild game and other dishes, overlooking the town. X: Mon., Feb. $$

Zum Roten Bären (Oberlinden 12, near the Augustiner Museum) Traditional Black Forest specialties in one of Germany's oldest and most atmospheric inns. $$

Grosser Meyerhof (Grünwälderstr. 7, 2 blocks northeast of the Martinstor) A beerhall with good food. X: Mon. eve., Tues. $

A very cheap lunch can be had from one of the many vendors at the farmers' market in Münsterplatz, held daily except on Sundays.

SUGGESTED TOUR:

Leave the **main train station** *(Hauptbahnhof)* (1) and follow Eisenbahnstrasse to the tourist office at the corner of Rotteckring. Continue down the pedestrianized Rathausgasse to **Rathausplatz** (2), a very charming old square bordered on the west by both the new and old town halls. The statue in its center is of a Franciscan friar, Berthold Schwarz, who is supposed to have invented gunpowder here in 1353. Enter the picturesque courtyard of the **Neues Rathaus** (New Town Hall), which was created by linking together two 16th-century houses. A carillon plays folk tunes here each day at 12:03 p.m.

Turn right on Franziskanerstrasse and pass the 13th-century St. Martin's Church, noted for its beautiful Gothic cloisters. Opposite this is the famous **Haus zum Walfisch.** Originally built in 1516 as a home for Emperor Maximilian I, it later served as a refuge for the humanist, Erasmus of Rotterdam, and is now a bank. Note the magnificent oriel window above its doorway.

Continue on to the ***Cathedral** *(Münster)* (3), widely regarded as one of the great masterpieces of Gothic architecture. Its superb 380-foot-high **tower** is among the very few in Germany to have been completed during the Middle Ages. It may be climbed on Tuesdays through Saturdays from 10 a.m. to 5 p.m., and on Sundays from 1–5 p.m. Construction on the cathedral began around 1200 and took over 300 years to complete, resulting in a rather engaging mixture of styles. The interior has several excellent works of art, including an early 16th-century triptych of the *Coronation of the Virgin* by Hans Baldung on the ***high altar**. This and other treasures can be seen better by taking one of the guided tours from the south transept entrance. Another outstanding altarpiece, this by Hans Holbein the Younger, is in the University Chapel to the right. The **stained-glass windows** in the south transept date from the 13th century.

A lively ***farmers' market** is held in the adjacent area every day except Sundays and some holidays, from 7 a.m. to 1 p.m. **Outdoor cafés** line the square in good weather, making this a wonderful place to sit down and enjoy all the activity. Some of the buildings have survived the ages and are still in good condition, especially the blood-red, turreted 16th-century **Kaufhaus** (Merchants' Guild House) on the south side.

Now follow the map to the lower station of the **Schlossberg Seilbahn** (cable car) (4), which carries you to the top of Freiburg's downtown mountain. Purchase an "up" ticket *(Bergfahrt)* only, since you will be walking down. Stroll along the trail overlooking the city and descend to the medieval **Schwabentor** (Swabian Gate) (5), a part of the old fortifications. Take a look at the street leading into town—Oberlinden—which has the characteristic *Bächle,* or little streams

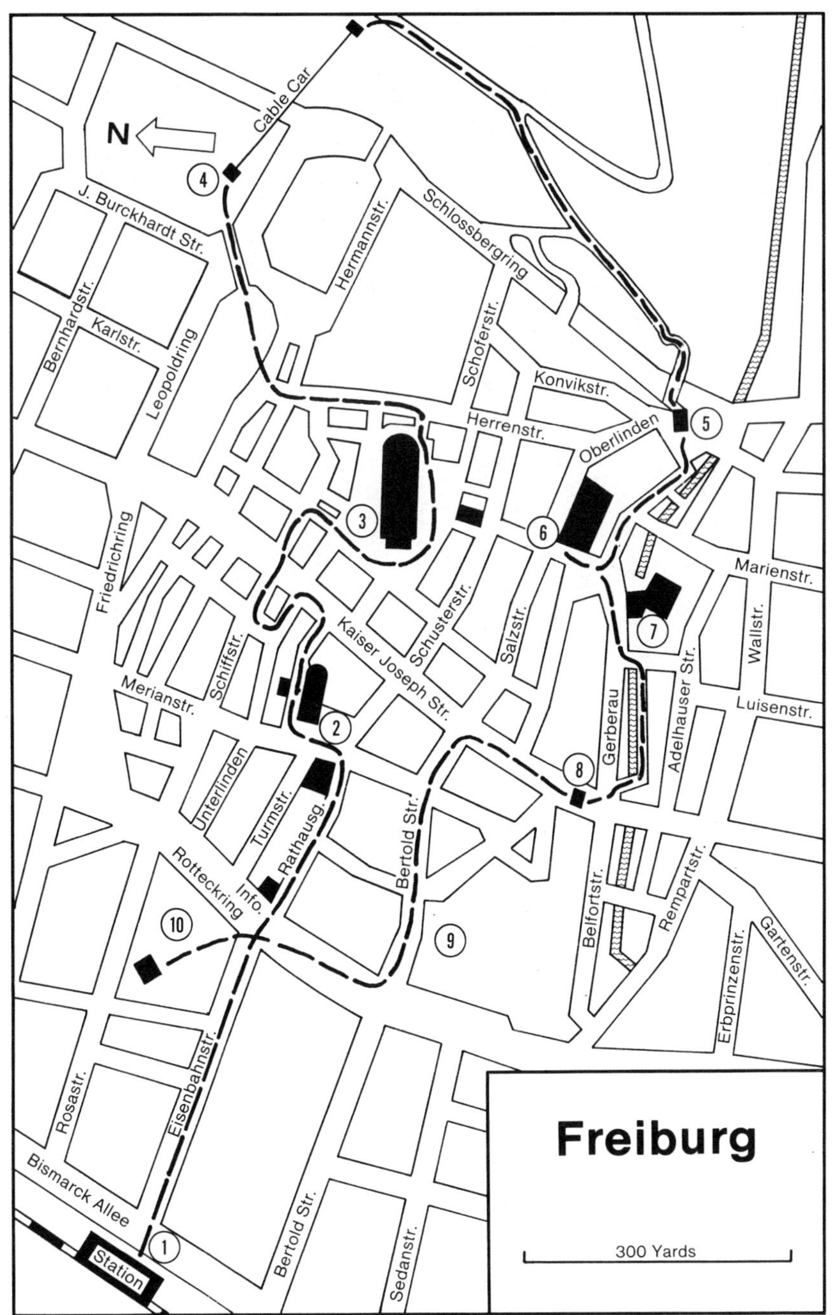
Freiburg
N
Cable Car
J. Burckhardt Str.
Bernhardstr.
Karlstr.
Leopoldring
Hermannstr.
Schlossbergring
Schoferstr.
Konvikstr.
Herrenstr.
Oberlinden
Friedrichring
Schusterstr.
Salzstr.
Marienstr.
Wallstr.
Adelhauser Str.
Luisenstr.
Gerberau
Kaiser Joseph Str.
Schiffstr.
Merianstr.
Unterlinden
Turmstr.
Rathausg.
Bertold Str.
Info.
Rotteckring
Belfortstr.
Rempartstr.
Erbprinzenstr.
Gartenstr.
Eisenbahnstr.
Rosastr.
Bismarck Allee
Station
Sedanstr.
300 Yards
1
2
3
4
5
6
7
8
9
10

The Martinstor town gate

running in the gutters that formed the medieval sewage system. Unwary pedestrians and drivers keep falling into these traps.

From the gate, the route goes through a colorful old district alongside a canal to the ***Augustiner Museum** (6). Housed in a former 13th-century monastery, its magnificent collections span over ten centuries of art. At least an hour will be needed to even sample the treasures on display, including some of the most illustrious names in painting. The museum is open on Tuesdays through Sundays, from 10 a.m. to 5 p.m.; remaining open until 8 p.m. on Wednesdays.

You may be interested in the nearby **Natur und Völkerkundemus Museum** (Natural History and Ethnology Museum) (7), also occupying an old monastery. Continue along the canal to the magnificently medieval **Martinstor** (8), the other surviving town gate.

Turn left on Bertholdstrasse and go by the main buildings of the **University** (9), which was founded as far back as 1457 and is now among the leading centers of higher education in Germany. Wander around them and follow Rotteckring to **Colombi Park** (10), a nice place to rest before returning to the train station.

A Daytrip from Frankfurt

Rüdesheim

Wine lovers will rejoice in a trip to Rüdesheim, Germany's favorite wine village. The vintages have been flowing here for some two thousand years, ever since the Romans settled the area and began growing grapes. You can have a wonderful time sampling the result—some of Germany's (and the world's) best white wines—or in just exploring this delightful town and its surroundings. Whatever you do, you won't be alone. Rüdesheim is *very* popular with tourists from all over the globe, but you'll be seeing a whole lot more than most of them on this do-it-yourself daytrip.

The suggested tour begins in the neighboring village of Assmannshausen and includes a ride across the Rhine to Bingen. If these don't interest you, it is entirely possible to spend the whole day in Rüdesheim and not get bored. Tipsy perhaps, but not bored.

GETTING THERE:

Trains depart Frankfurt's main station for Rüdesheim and Assmannshausen several times each morning, some from the main level and some from the lower S-Bahn level. In addition, there are trains and buses from Wiesbaden, which is easily reached by S-Bahn commuter trains. The direct trip takes about one hour. Return service operates until mid-evening. Be sure to check the schedules carefully, especially to determine whether the train you want also stops in Assmannshausen. If not, it is only a short distance by bus or taxi from Rüdesheim.

By car, leave Frankfurt on the A-66 Autobahn and stay on it past Wiesbaden to Eltville. From there take the B-42 road into Rüdesheim, which is about 45 miles west of Frankfurt.

PRACTICALITIES:

This trip should be taken between April and the end of October, when all of the attractions are open. Good weather is essential. The **Tourist Information Office** for Rüdesheim, phone (06722) 29-62, is at Rheinstrasse 16, near the KD Line pier. In Bingen, they are at Rheinkai 21, phone (06721) 142-69. **Bicycles** may be rented at the Rüdesheim train station from April through October. Rüdesheim is in the Land of **Hessen** and has a **population** of about 10,000.

FOOD AND DRINK:

There is an extremely wide selection of places to eat and drink in the Rüdesheim area. A few are:

In Assmannshausen:

Krone (Rheinuferstr. 10, near the train station) An old inn overlooking the Rhine; classic German cuisine. X: Jan., Feb. $$$+

Altes Haus (Lorcherstr. 5, 1 block northwest of the chair lift lower station) An historic 16th-century inn with good food. X: Wed., Tues. off-season, Jan.–mid-Mar. $$

Lamm (Rheinuferstr. 6, 4 blocks north of the train station) Good meals at low prices. X: mid-Nov.–mid-Mar. $

Near the Niederwald Monument:

Jagdschloss Niederwald (near the top of the chair lift) A ducal hunting lodge featuring traditional wild game and other dishes. X: Jan.–mid-Feb. $$$

In Rüdesheim:

Traube-Aumüller (Rheinstr. 6, near the Brömserburg Castle) A good choice in a touristy location. X: Nov.–Mar. $$

Felsenkeller (Oberstr. 39, near the lower station of the cable car) A pleasant country-style inn. $$

Zum Bären (Schmidtstr. 24, 1 block east of the market place) Local specialties at a fair price. X: Mon. off-season. $$

In addition, there are many attractive wine taverns with food on and around the Drosselgasse.

SUGGESTED TOUR:

Those making the complete tour should begin at the **train station** in **Assmannshausen** (1). Follow the map through this romantic old village, whose existence was first documented in 1108. Oddly enough, it is the home of Germany's best *red* wines. The narrow streets lead past several half-timbered houses and an interesting late-Gothic church to the **chair lift** *(Seilbahn)* (2). Purchase a combination ticket to Rüdesheim and be seated for a comfortable ride to the Niederwald. Along the way you will have superb high-level views across the Rhine Valley.

Getting off at the top, walk around past the **Jagdschloss** (3), a former hunting lodge of the dukes of Nassau. It is now a very attractive hotel and restaurant complete with another panoramic vista. From here take a leisurely stroll of about one-half mile or so along a forest road to the **Niederwald Denkmal** (4), one of the most colossal monuments on Earth. A late-19th-century expression of overblown nationalism, its heroic figure of *Germania* symbolizes the unification of Germany achieved in 1871 and is still deeply revered by the German people—although to foreign eyes it may seem somewhat amusing. The enormous bronze relief depicts military heroes surrounding Kai-

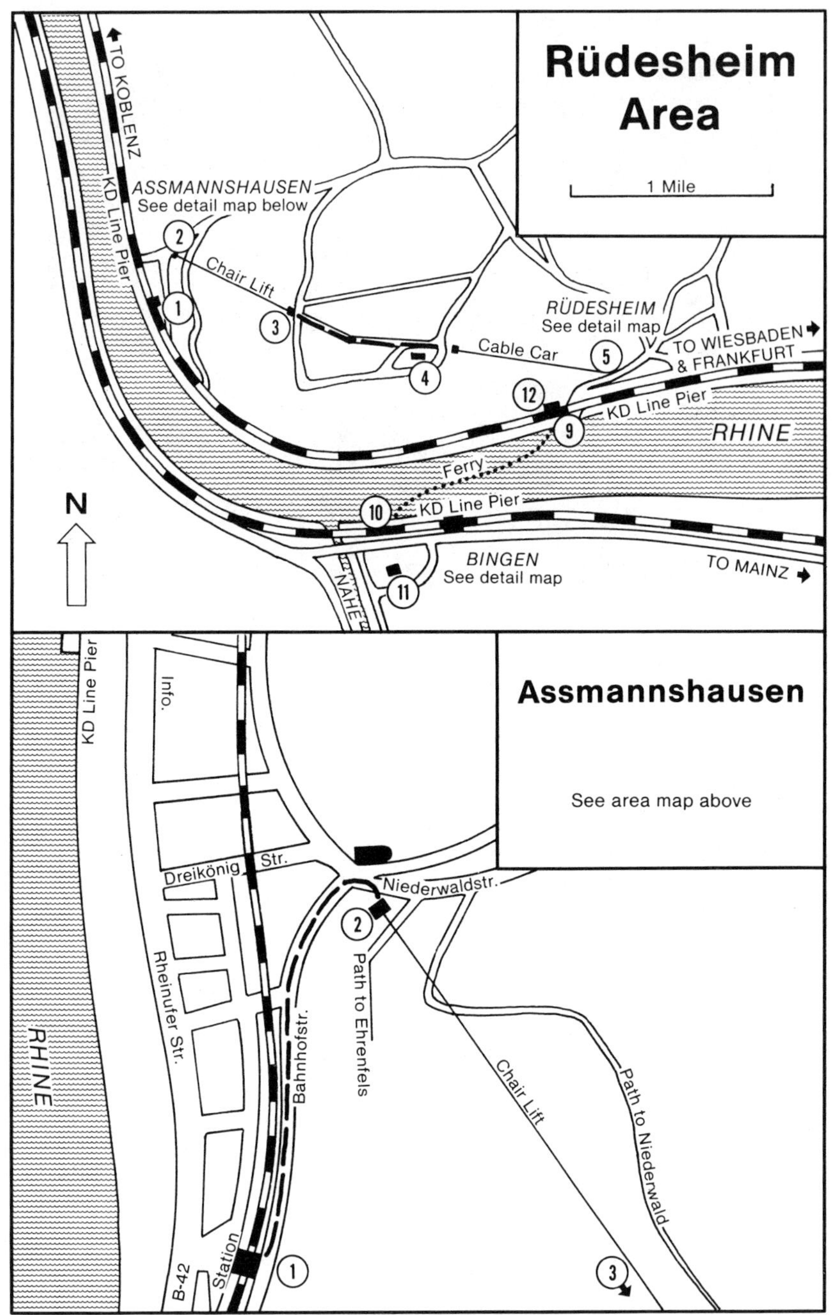

Rüdesheim Area
1 Mile
TO KOBLENZ
KD Line Pier
ASSMANNSHAUSEN
See detail map below
Chair Lift
Cable Car
RÜDESHEIM
See detail map
TO WIESBADEN & FRANKFURT
KD Line Pier
RHINE
Ferry
KD Line Pier
BINGEN
See detail map
TO MAINZ
NAHE
N
1
2
3
4
5
9
10
11
12
Assmannshausen
See area map above
KD Line Pier
Info.
Dreikönig Str.
Niederwaldstr.
Rheinufer Str.
Bahnhofstr.
Path to Ehrenfels
Chair Lift
Path to Niederwald
RHINE
Station
B-42
1
2
3

The Drosselgasse

ser Wilhelm I and Bismarck, and of course there is a fabulous ***view** across the Rhine.

Take the nearby **cable car** *(Seilbahn)* down across the vineyards to its **lower station** (5) in Rüdesheim. Make a right on Oberstrasse to the **Brömserhof** (6), an aristocratic residence dating from 1542. The interior now features a curious exhibition known as **Siegfried's Mechanisches Musikkabinett**, an amazing collection of antique self-playing musical instruments dating from the 18th to the 20th centuries. This is open daily from mid-March through mid-November, from 10 a.m. to 10 p.m.

Rüdesheim is world-famous for the **Drosselgasse** (Thrush Alley), a narrow lane that is usually jam-packed with hundreds of thirsty visitors. You may want to return here later to relax in one of its many colorful wine taverns. Until then, however, there are several other worthwhile sights.

Continue to the bottom and turn left on Rheinstrasse, passing the tourist office. The **Marktplatz** (Market Place) has an interesting 14th-century parish church. At the eastern end of the Rheinstrasse is the **Adlerturm** (Eagle's Tower) (7), built in the 15th century as part of the medieval defense fortifications.

Return along the bank of the Rhine to the ***Brömserburg** (8), an ancient castle built on late-Roman foundations between the 11th and 14th centuries. Formerly a refuge for the archbishops of Mainz, this

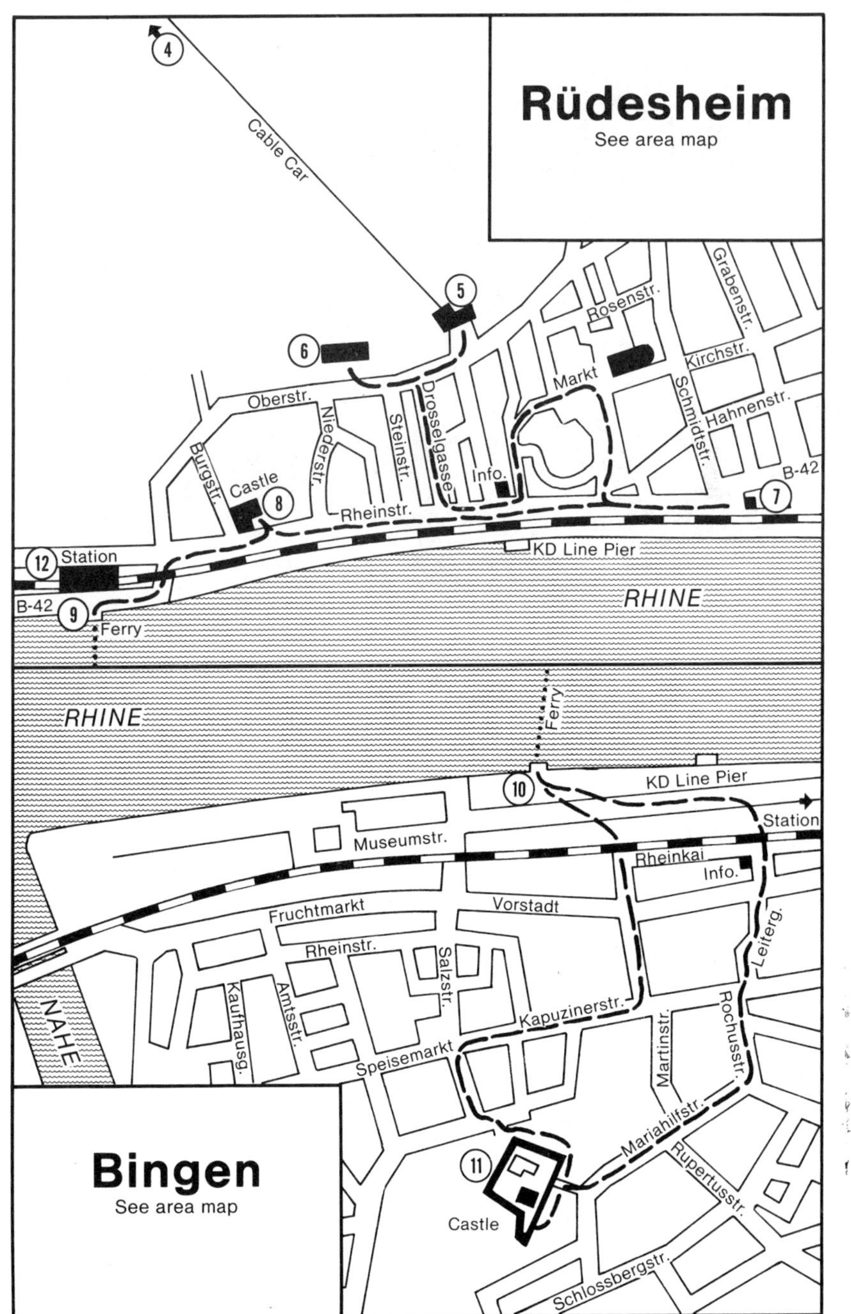
Rüdesheim
See area map
Cable Car
4
5
6
7
8
9
12
Rosenstr.
Grabenstr.
Kirchstr.
Markt
Schmidtstr.
Hahnenstr.
Oberstr.
Niederstr.
Steinstr.
Drosselgasse
Burgstr.
Castle
Info.
B-42
Rheinstr.
Station
KD Line Pier
RHINE
Ferry
RHINE
Ferry
10
KD Line Pier
Station
Museumstr.
Rheinkai
Info.
Fruchtmarkt
Vorstadt
Leiterg.
Rheinstr.
Salzstr.
Kaufhausg.
Amtsstr.
NAHE
Kapuzinerstr.
Martinstr.
Rochusstr.
Speisemarkt
Mariahilfstr.
11
Rupertusstr.
Castle
Schlossbergstr.
Bingen
See area map

The Brömserburg

formidable structure now houses the outstanding ***Rheingau Wine Museum**, a must-see for any visitor to Rüdesheim. Displays here cover the entire scope of wine-making—and drinking—down through the ages. The museum is open from March until November, daily from 9 a.m. to noon and 2–6 p.m.

A short stroll along the river brings you to the **passenger ferry dock** *(Personenfähre)* (9). From here you can take a quick boat ride to Bingen, just across the Rhine.

Leave the **Bingen ferry landing** (10) and follow the map past the tourist office up to **Burg Klopp** (11), a heavily rebuilt castle whose origins probably date from the Roman era. There is an exceptionally good view of the Rhine Valley from here, but the main attraction is the **Binger Heimat Museum** (Bingen Folk Museum). Step inside to see some remarkable exhibits dating from prehistoric times until the Frankish period. Probably the most interesting of these is the collection of 2nd-century Roman doctor's instruments. The museum is open from May through October, on Tuesdays through Sundays, from 9 a.m. to noon and 2–5 p.m.

Return to the ferry dock and Rüdesheim. The **train station** (12) is just across from the dock, but you will most likely want to enjoy a bit of wine sampling along the Drosselgasse before heading back to Frankfurt.

A Daytrip from Frankfurt

*Trier

The greatest collection of Roman remains to be found anywhere north of the Alps is in Trier, which bills itself as Germany's oldest town. According to an ancient legend, this was founded around 2000 B.C. by Trebeta, son of Semiramis, the queen of Assyria. Historians say otherwise, although archaeological digs do reveal some trace of human habitation dating from that era. What is actually documented is that the town, then called *Augusta Treverorum,* was established in 16 B.C. by the Roman emperor Augustus on the site of an earlier Celtic settlement.

Whatever its true age, Trier is certainly a fascinating place. Several of its Roman structures remain in use today, along with well-preserved buildings from just about every era since. For centuries this city was among the most important in Europe; at one time second only to Rome. Those days have long since ended, and Trier is now a relatively minor provincial place. Although it is quite some distance from Frankfurt, its attractions are so compelling that a journey is more than worthwhile.

GETTING THERE:

Trains of the IC class depart Frankfurt's main station at least hourly for Koblenz, where you change to a regular train to Trier. The total journey takes under three hours, and follows an exceptionally beautiful route along the Rhine and Mosel rivers. Return service operates until mid-evening.

By car, leave Frankfurt on the A-66 Autobahn, then take the A-3 north past Limburg and head west on the A-48 to the Trier exit. The total distance is about 150 miles.

PRACTICALITIES:

Trier can be visited in any season, but note that most of the major attractions are closed on Mondays from November through March, and every day during December. Some of its museums close early on Sundays, and all day on major holidays. The local **Tourist Information Office**, phone (0651) 480-71, is next to the Porta Nigra. **Bicycles** may be rented at the train station from April through October. Trier is in the Land of **Rheinland-Pfalz** and has a **population** of about 97,000.

Porta Nigra

FOOD AND DRINK:

Trier is heavily touristed, so it has plenty of restaurants and cafés. Some choices are:

Hotel Porta Nigra (facing the Porta Nigra) A modern hotel with 3 restaurants. $$ and $$$

Brunnenhof (in the Simeonstift next to the Porta Nigra) Typical German food in an 11th-century building. $$

Zum Domstein (Hauptmarkt 5) Popular for its local and Roman specialties, with a superb selection of Mosel, Saar, and Ruwer wines. $$

Ratskeller zur Steipe (Hauptmarkt 14) In a cellar under the Town Banqueting Hall, also has outdoor tables. X: Mon., Jan.–Easter. $

Museum Café (in the Rhineland Museum) A pleasant, modern place for light meals. Opens into the gardens. $

SUGGESTED TOUR:

Leave the **main train station** *(Hauptbahnhof)* (1) and walk down Bahnhofstrasse and Theodor-Heuss-Allee to the ancient ***Porta Nigra** (2), the very symbol of Trier and one of the finest Roman relics anywhere. Built towards the end of the 2nd century A.D. as a massive fortified gate, it was converted into a church about 1040 and later restored to its original appearance by Napoleon after 1804, when Trier was a part of France. No mortar was used in its construction; instead, the stone blocks are joined by iron clamps. The name, meaning black gate, derives from its present color—the result of centuries of pollution. Stroll through the inner courtyard, where unsuspecting enemies could be trapped from all sides. An exploration of its bulky interior can be made any day from 9 a.m. to 6 p.m. in season (9 a.m. to 1 p.m. and 2–5 p.m. in off-season), but not on Mondays from January through March, or at all during December. A joint ticket covering all of the Roman sites is available.

Adjoining this is the **Simeonstift**, a former collegiate building from the 11th century that now houses the tourist office, a restaurant, and the **Städtisches Museum**. The latter is devoted primarily to the history of Trier from prehistoric to modern times.

Walk down Simeonstrasse past the very unusual **Dreikönigenhaus** at number 19, a nobleman's town residence dating from 1230. Note the strange location of its original entrance—at an upper level where it could only be reached by a retractable ladder, a safety feature in those days of unrest.

Continue on to the ***Hauptmarkt** (3). The stone cross in this main square was erected in 958 as a symbol of the town's right to hold a market. Near this stands a lovely 16th-century fountain, while the entire busy scene is dominated by the Gothic **Church of St. Gangolf.** One particularly outstanding building is the **Steipe**, a colorful 15th-century banqueting house that now houses the Ratskeller. It was restored after heavy damage in World War II.

Now turn down the Sternstrasse to the ***Dom** (Cathedral) (4), a powerful fortress-like structure dating in part from Roman times. Over the centuries this was enlarged and rebuilt several times, the most visible changes having occurred during the 12th century. Its interior is an engaging mixture of Romanesque, Gothic, and Baroque styles. Don't miss the **Treasury** *(Domschatzmuseum)* to the right of the high altar, which is open on Mondays through Saturdays from 10 a.m. to noon and 2–5 p.m., and on Sundays and holidays from 2–5 p.m. From November through March it is open daily from 2–4 p.m. only. Among its treasures are the 10th-century Altar of St. Andrew, one of the great masterpieces of the Ottonian period. The precious Holy Robe, supposedly worn by Christ at His trial, is kept permanently in a shrine.

Stroll through the cloisters, then visit the adjacent **Liebfrauenkirche** (Church of Our Lady) (5). One of the earliest Gothic churches in Germany, it was built in the form of a Greek cross during the 13th century, and is noted for its elegant, light-filled interior.

Closeby, on Windstrasse, is the **Bischöfliches Museum** (6). On display here are some fascinating 4th-century paintings from the palace of the Roman emperor Constantine, discovered under the cathedral in 1945. There are also several medieval statues and other places of ancient religious art. The museum is open on Mondays through Saturdays, from 9 a.m. to 1 p.m. and 2–5 p.m.; and on Sundays and holidays from 1–5 p.m.

The enormous **Palastaula** (7), a few steps away, is the only surviving part of Constantine's great imperial palace. Once the throne room of the emperor, this colossal structure from about A.D. 310 now sees service as a Protestant church. Take a look inside, then walk around to the adjoining **Palace of the Electors**, an 18th-century rococo building presently used for government offices.

Paths through the palace gardens lead to the **Rheinisches Landesmuseum** (Rhineland Museum) (8), probably the best collection of Roman antiquities in Germany. Allow plenty of time to take it all in, from gold coins to mosaics to huge monuments. The displays also feature archaeological finds dating from prehistory as well as a rich selection of medieval art. There is an attractive **museum café** facing the gardens, a fine place for a light lunch. The museum is open on Mondays through Fridays, from 10 a.m. to 4 p.m.; on Saturdays from 9:30 a.m. to 1 p.m.; and on Sundays and holidays from 9 a.m. to 1 p.m., but closes on some major holidays.

From here you may want to make a short side trip to the **Amphitheater** (9), the oldest Roman structure in Trier. Over 20,000 spectators once jammed its terraces to watch the gladiators fight, a form of spectacle that continued into the Christian era. Be sure to climb down into the cellars under the arena, and to examine the side chambers that served as cages. Much of the stone work was exploited as a quarry during the Middle Ages, but enough remains to imagine yourself back in the 1st century A.D., when it was built. The Amphitheater is open during the same times as the Porta Nigra (2).

A stroll down Olewiger Strasse brings you to the ***Kaiserthermen** (Imperial Baths) (10). Not much of this extraordinary 4th-century structure remains above ground, but the maze of passageways below is fantastic and well worth exploring. The baths were established by the emperor Constantine and were among the largest in the entire Roman empire. Strangely enough, they were never completed nor used for their intended purpose. The ruins are open during the same times as the Porta Nigra (2).

If you're still bursting with energy you might want to walk down to the Mosel River to see a few more sights, otherwise you can save some steps by following the map back into town via Neustrasse and Brückenstrasse.

The long route takes you first to the 2nd-century **Barbarathermen** (11) on Südallee. These Roman baths were used for several centuries

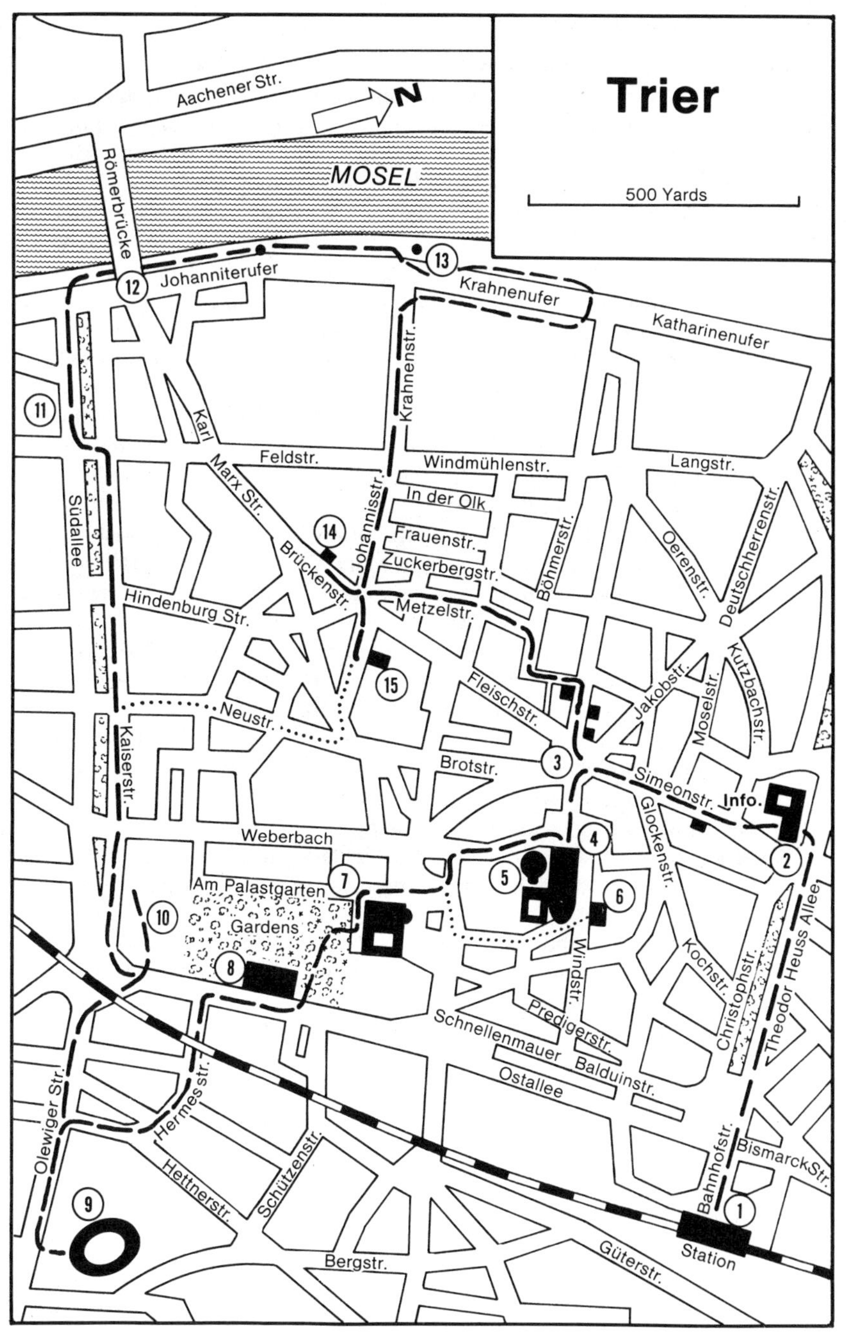
Trier
500 Yards
N
MOSEL
Aachener Str.
Römerbrücke
Johanniterufer
Krahnenufer
Katharinenufer
Krahnenstr.
Karl Marx Str.
Feldstr.
Windmühlenstr.
Langstr.
In der Olk
Frauenstr.
Zuckerbergstr.
Johannisstr.
Brückenstr.
Böhmerstr.
Oerenstr.
Deutschherrenstr.
Südallee
Hindenburg Str.
Metzelstr.
Fleischstr.
Jakobstr.
Moselstr.
Kutzbachstr.
Neustr.
Kaiserstr.
Brotstr.
Simeonstr.
Info.
Glockenstr.
Weberbach
Am Palastgarten
Gardens
Windstr.
Kochstr.
Christophstr.
Theodor Heuss Allee
Predigerstr.
Schnellenmauer
Balduinstr.
Ostallee
Olewiger Str.
Hermesstr.
Hettnerstr.
Schützenstr.
Bahnhofstr.
Bismarck Str.
Station
Güterstr.
Bergstr.
1
2
3
4
5
6
7
8
9
10
11
12
13
14
15

and were once larger than the Kaiserthermen. What little remains of their past glory is in derelict condition and requires a vivid imagination to visualize, although the effect of really *ruined* ruins can be quite romantic. Take a look from the street before deciding to enter. The opening times are nearly the same as for the Porta Nigra (2).

The **Römerbrücke** (Roman Bridge) (12) is just a few steps away. Its stone piers were built in the 2nd century A.D. and still carry the weight of heavy traffic. The upper parts, originally of wood, were replaced with masonry arches during the 14th century, and again in the 18th. Walk down steps to a path along the Mosel River and follow it past the **Zoll Kran** (Customs Crane), dating from 1774, and the **Alte Kran** (Old Crane) (13), which goes all the way back to 1413. Both are in excellent condition, and the latter's treadmill can be seen by peeking in the window. The busy adjacent street, Krahnenufer, is difficult to cross here, so walk north to the traffic light and return to Krahnenstrasse, which you follow into town.

Of all the people born in Trier, the one who had the greatest impact on society was undoubtedly Karl Marx, who lived from 1818 until 1883. His birthplace at Brückenstrasse 10 is open as the **Karl Marx Haus** (14), where both the life of communism's prophet and the worldwide spread of socialism is traced in minute detail. Perhaps you can find a clue, in the memorabilia or in the house itself, as to why Marx was so tragically mistaken in his understanding of how the world works. It's worth a try, and it can be done on Tuesdays through Sundays, from 10 a.m. to 6 p.m.; and on Mondays from 1–6 p.m., with shorter hours from November through March.

End your tour on a brighter note by paying a visit to the joyful **Spielzeugmuseum** (Toy Museum) (15), installed in three upper floors on Nagelstrasse. Although some of the toys are antiques, the majority are of recent enough vintage to evoke childhood memories. Hidden away in a corner of the third floor is a display of toys from the Third Reich, including a miniature tin Hitler riding in an open Mercedes! The museum is open daily from 11 a.m. to 6 p.m.

Return to the train station via the 11th-century **Frankenturm** at Dietrichstrasse 5—one of the oldest surviving dwellings in Germany—and the Hauptmarkt (3).

A Daytrip from Frankfurt

*Cologne

(Köln)

The skyline of Cologne is completely dominated by its magnificent cathedral, Germany's largest and one of the greatest on Earth. This ancient city on the Rhine has long been in the center of things. Having begun life as a Roman camp in 38 B.C., it was raised to city status around A.D. 50 and given the name *Colonia Claudia Ara Agrippinensium*—a mouthful soon shortened to *Colonia.* After the fall of the Roman Empire this was Germanized to *Köln,* its official designation to this day. With nearly a million inhabitants, Cologne is now the fourth-largest metropolis in the nation (after Berlin, Hamburg, and Munich) and a world leader in commerce. Its extraordinary museums alone make this a highly worthwhile daytrip destination, especially on a rainy day.

GETTING THERE:

Trains, mostly of the EC and IC classes, leave Frankfurt's main station at least hourly for Cologne *(Köln)*, a journey of about 2¼ hours. Return trains run until late evening.

By car, leave Frankfurt on the A-66 Autobahn, then turn northwest on the A-3 to Cologne *(Köln)*. The distance is 116 miles.

PRACTICALITIES:

Cologne may be explored in any season, but avoid coming on a Monday, when the museums are closed. Apart from the cathedral, these are the city's major attractions. Mass insanity prevails during the **Carnival** season, especially from the Thursday prior to the seventh Sunday before Easter until the start of Lent. The local **Tourist Information Office**, phone (0221) 221-33-40, faces the front of the cathedral. Cologne is in the Land of **Nordrhein-Westfalen** and has a **population** of about 999,000.

FOOD AND DRINK:

Cologne is renowned for its unique dishes such as *Rievkoche* (potato pancakes and applesauce), *Himmel un Ärd* (apples and potatoes), *Kölsche Kaviar* (not caviar, but blood sausage with onions), and *Halve Hahn* (not half a chicken, but a fancy cheese sandwich). These are all washed down with *Kölsch,* a light but potent beer served in tiny glasses. Some of the most unusual and enjoyable food is served at inexpensive beerhalls by colorful waiters affectionately called *Köbesse.*

Some good restaurant choices are:

Bado-La Poêle d'Or (Kömodienstr. 52, near the Municipal Museum) One of the best in Germany, famous for its nouvelle French cuisine. Reservations are essential, phone (0221) 134-100. X: Sun., Mon. lunch, holidays, late July. $$$+

Weinhaus im Walfisch (Salzgasse 13, 2 blocks south of Gross St. Martin Church) Serving traditional local specialties for four centuries. X: Weekends, holidays. $$

Alt Köln (Trankgasse 7, between the cathedral and the train station) A favorite old tavern with local dishes. $$

Ratskeller (Alter Markt, behind the Old City Hall) Solid German cuisine. $$

Früh (Am Hof 12, 1 block south of the cathedral) Cologne specialties in an Old World setting, makes its own beer. $ and $$

Brauhaus Sion (Unter Taschenmacher 5, 1 block south of the Roman-Germanic Museum) Traditional local specialties in a Kölsch beer hall. $

Museum Cafeteria (in the Wallraf-Richartz-Ludwig Museum) Light, healthy food in a cheerfully modern setting. X: Mon. $

SUGGESTED TOUR:

The **main train station** *(Hauptbahnhof)* (1) is located in the very heart of Cologne, just a few steps from the tourist office. Directly facing this is the ***Dom** (Cathedral) (2), one of the world's most stupendous Gothic structures. Begun in 1248 on the site of an earlier cathedral— and a Roman temple—it was far from complete when construction came to a standstill in the early 16th century. After that, not much happened until a wave of romantic nationalism swept the country in the mid-19th century. In the end it was political rather than religious considerations that led to the final completion in 1880. The Protestant rulers of Prussia felt a need to placate the Catholic Rhineland, and the newly united nation would clearly benefit from a symbol embodying the spirit of medieval Germany in its Gothic design.

Enter the cathedral via its magnificent west portal. The sheer verticality of the nave is awe inspiring, as are the medieval stained-glass windows, but the real treasures lie beyond the crossing. In a glass

The Cultural Center and the rear of the Cathedral

case behind the high altar you will find the most precious object of all. This is the ***Dreikönigenschrein** (Reliquary of the Three Kings), a 12th-century masterpiece of the goldsmiths' art alleged to contain the bones of the Magi, which were brought from Milan in 1164 by Emperor Frederick Barbarossa. It was the veneration of these relics during the Middle Ages that attracted countless pilgrims to Cologne and thus provided the impetus for building the present cathedral.

The medieval **choir** leading up to this has some outstanding stalls and statuary, while in the ambulatory there are two fabulous works of art. The first of these is the ***Gero Cross**, dating from 976, which is regarded as the oldest monumental cross from the Middle Ages and is located in the Cross Chapel to the left of the choir. On the other side, in the Lady Chapel directly across the chancel, is the 15th-century ***Dombild**, a triptych celebrating the Adoration of the Magi and the two patron saints of Cologne—Ursula and Gereon. More riches can be found in the **Treasury**, located just off the north transept and open on Mondays through Saturdays, from 9 a.m. to 5 p.m. (4 p.m. in winter); and on Sundays from 12:30–4 p.m. Before leaving the cathedral, you may want to test your athletic ability by climbing over 500 steps to the top of the **south tower** for a fantastic view. Good luck!

Every time a hole is dug in Cologne there is a very real possibility of striking Roman ruins. An outstanding example of this happened in 1941, when workers were digging a bomb shelter next to the cathedral. What came to light was the wonderfully pagan **Dionysos Mosaic**, a 22-by-34-foot celebration of wine and revelry. In recent years the modern ***Römisch-Germanisches Museum** (3) was built around this to display a vast collection of local archaeological finds. Step inside and enjoy the marvelously inspired presentation of life in ancient Colonia, complete with room settings that look as though the Romans had just gone out for a stroll. Don't miss this museum, which is open on Tuesdays through Sundays from 10 a.m. to 5 p.m.; remaining open until 8 p.m. on Wednesdays and Thursdays.

The small **Diocesan Museum**, just a few steps away on the same open square, may interest you with its exquisite collection of ancient and medieval religious art. Now walk around to the nearby ***Wallraf-Richartz Museum / Museum Ludwig** (4), two institutions combined to form one of the greatest art galleries in all of Europe. It occupies a large segment of a spectacular cultural center wedged between the cathedral and the Rhine, which also houses the **Philharmonie** concert hall and the **Cinemathek** film theater. Allow plenty of time to peruse the many art treasures of this double museum, ranging all the way from the medieval to an exceptionally rich collection of American Pop. On display are paintings by the Cologne masters of the 14th to 16th centuries, Rembrandt, Dürer, Cranach, Rubens, Van Dyck, and many others. The sections devoted to modern art, called the Museum Ludwig, includes works by Picasso, Kandinsky, Dali, Max Ernst, Oldenburg, Rauschenberg, and Warhol—to name a few. Photographers will enjoy the small **Agfa Foto-Historama** with its collection of old cameras and changing print exhibitions next to the excellent cafeteria on the ground floor. The museum complex is open on Tuesdays through Thursdays, 10 a.m. to 8 p.m.; and on Fridays through Sundays from 10 a.m. to 6 p.m.

Return to the front of the cathedral and turn left onto the pedestrians-only Hohe Strasse, the main shopping street. Follow this to Gürzenichstrasse, where you make a left. The **Gürzenich** building, dating from 1441, still fulfills its original purpose as a banqueting hall. Martinstrasse leads to the **Altes Rathaus** (Old City Hall) (5), originally built in the 14th century but considerably altered since. Its Renaissance loggia is particularly attractive. Just in front of this is the open excavation of a 12th-century **Mikwe**, a ritual bath of the Jewish ghetto that was destroyed after the 15th-century expulsion order. You can ask at the City Hall reception desk for a key to see it. Also nearby, at number 1 Kleine Budengasse, is the entrance to the underground **Roman Praetorium** with remains from the 1st through the 4th centuries A.D. It is usually open on Tuesdays through Sundays, from 10 a.m. to 5 p.m.

An alleyway next to the City Hall leads to the Alter Markt and then to the imposing **Gross St. Martin Church** (6). Along with the cathe-

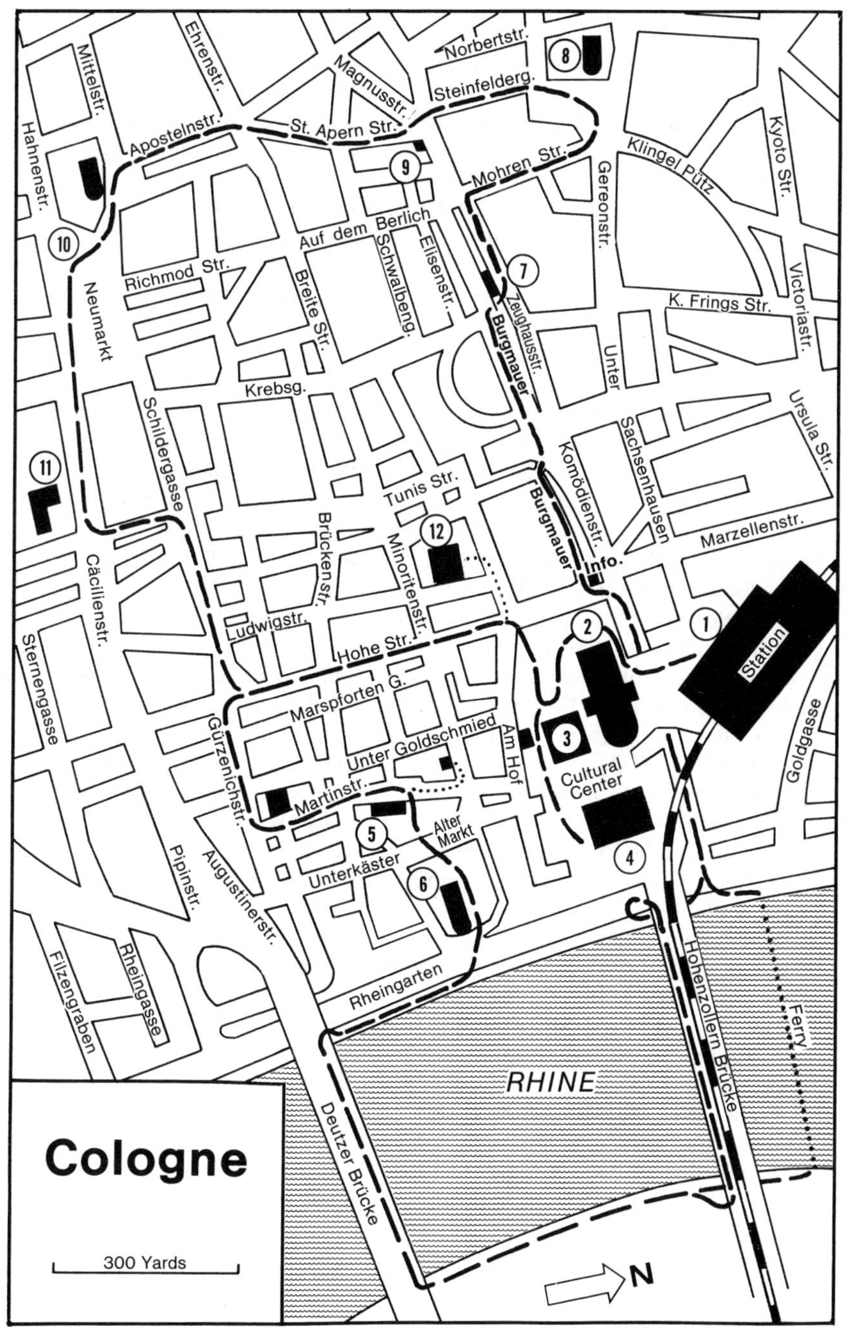
Cologne
300 Yards
N
RHINE
Station
Info.
Cultural Center
Mittelstr.
Hahnenstr.
Ehrenstr.
Magnusstr.
Norbertstr.
Steinfelderg.
Apostelnstr.
St. Apern Str.
Mohren Str.
Klingel Pütz
Kyoto Str.
Gereonstr.
Auf dem Berlich
Schwalbeng.
Elisenstr.
Richmod Str.
Breite Str.
Neumarkt
Zeughausstr.
Burgmauer
K. Frings Str.
Victoriastr.
Unter Sachsenhausen
Krebsg.
Ursula Str.
Schildergasse
Komödienstr.
Tunis Str.
Brückenstr.
Minoritenstr.
Marzellenstr.
Cäcilienstr.
Ludwigstr.
Hohe Str.
Sternengasse
Marspforten G.
Gürzenichstr.
Unter Goldschmied
Am Hof
Martinstr.
Alter Markt
Goldgasse
Unterkäster
Pipinstr.
Augustinerstr.
Rheingarten
Filzengraben
Rheingasse
Deutzer Brücke
Hohenzollern Brücke
Ferry
1
2
3
4
5
6
7
8
9
10
11
12

dral, this fortress-like structure—begun in 960 and completed in the mid-13th century—is a landmark of Cologne. This is the heart of the historic **Old City**, a maze of narrow, winding streets lined with reconstructed medieval houses and numerous restaurants, taverns, and outdoor cafés.

Stroll through the Fisch Markt and along the river's edge, where a flight of steps will take you up to the Deutzer Bridge. Cross the Rhine on this and turn left on the path along its opposite bank. From here you will have a marvelous view of the renowned Cologne skyline. Return to the city either on the ferry shown on the map, or by walking along the footpath on the south side of the Hohenzollern railway bridge.

You have now seen most of the tourist attractions in Cologne. If time allows, a further exploration can be made by following the map to the **Kölnisches Stadtmuseum** (Cologne Municipal Museum) (7), located in a former arsenal, with its entrance on Zeughausstrasse. The displays here, including arms and armor, are concerned with the history of the city and may be seen on Tuesdays through Sundays, from 10 a.m. to 5 p.m.; remaining open on Thursdays until 8 p.m.

Continue on to the **Church of St. Gereon** (8), which dates in part from Roman times. Many changes were made since then, making this a particularly interesting structure to visit.

A short stroll down Steinfeldergasse will bring you to the **Römerturm** (Roman Tower) (9), a part of the original town walls built around A.D. 50. Although small, its mosaic brick patterns are highly intriguing. Now follow St. Apern Strasse, lined with elegant antique shops, and Apostelnstrasse to **Neumarkt** (10). This lively market square is dominated by the massive **Church of the Holy Apostles**, an 11th-century structure in the Rhineland Romanesque style.

Another attraction is the **Schnütgen Museum** (11), housed in the desanctified 12th-century Church of St. Cecilia on Cäcilienstrasse. The superb collection of ancient religious artifacts, many of ivory, gold, or wood, are strikingly displayed in a setting of serene purity. It is open on Tuesdays through Sundays, from 10 a.m. to 5 p.m. From here you can return via Hohe Strasse to the train station.

Along the way you might want to make a little detour on An der Rechtschule to the recently-installed **Museum für Angewandte Kunst** (Museum of the Applied Arts) (12), a century-old institution that has at last found a worthy home. Its collections range from medieval crafts to the post-modern designs of today, and they can all be seen on Tuesdays from 10 a.m. to 8 p.m., and on Wednesdays through Sundays from 10 a.m. to 5 p.m.

Section VII

DAYTRIPS IN

AUSTRIA

- from Vienna
- from Salzburg

Fortunately for visitors to Austria, the country's two most popular attractions are also its best bases for daytrips. This makes it quite easy for you to enjoy the many charms of Vienna and Salzburg, while at the same time probing the rest of the country for experiences that are simply not available in the cities. Just take a break in your urban sightseeing and make a few one-day excursions into the nearby countryside; visiting mountains, lakes, vineyards, country palaces, salt mines, a pilgrimage center, and even another city or two where tourists are rare and the pleasures unspoiled. Along the way you can relish regional cuisine at low prices; ride ancient steam trains, cable cars, and boats; take mountain hikes or explore by bicycle; plunge deep into the earth; or ascend to the top of a snow-capped mountain.

None of these daytrips are difficult. All of them can be taken with or without your own car, and all get you back to your base city in plenty of time for dinner and a good night's sleep. The first four excursions use Vienna as a base, the fifth is halfway between Vienna and Salzburg and is equally accessible from either, while the last two are intended to be taken from Salzburg.

GETTING AROUND:

Trains are probably the best mode of transportation for all but the first of the daytrips. Even on that one exception, it is possible to travel by train over most of the route, using a bus to finish it. In case you haven't ridden them lately, the **Austrian Federal Railways** (ÖBB) operate frequent trains that are completely modern and comfortable, if not the speediest in Europe. Many of their routes pass through spectacular countryside. **Vienna** has two major central stations, the **Westbahnhof** and the **Südbahnhof**. Note which one your train is leaving from. **Salzburg** has only one main station, the **Hauptbahnhof**.

Eurailpasses (see page 18) are accepted throughout the country, but if you're only visiting Austria you'll save money by using the **Rabbit Card** instead. Valid for unlimited hops on any trains all over Austria on any four days during a ten-day period, this economical pass is available in either first-or second-class versions, for adults or for juniors up to the age of 26. It is sold at ticket counters in train stations throughout Austria, and must be used along with your passport. The free brochure describing it has a handy rail map of the entire country. Current **schedules** can be checked by calling (0222) 1717 in Vienna; or (0662) 1717 in Salzburg.

Buses leave from **Vienna's** Wien-Mitte Bus Station on Landstrasser Hauptstrasse, by the Air Terminal and the Hilton Hotel. For schedules call (0222) 7501. In **Salzburg**, they depart from the square in front of the train station. For information phone (0662) 167.

Travel by **car** is excellent throughout Austria, and strongly recommended for the first trip in this chapter. The roads compare well with those of Germany. Although the **road map** given away free by the tourist office is adequate, you may want one with more detail, such as the *Michelin Map Number 426 - Austria,* generally available in bookstores. Ask the National Tourist Office for their free brochure on *Automobile Travel and Car Rental in Austria,* which gives plenty of advice.

ADVANCE PLANNING INFORMATION:

The **Austrian National Tourist Office** has branches throughout the world, including New York, Chicago, Houston, Los Angeles, Montreal, Toronto, Vancouver, London, Sydney, and Tokyo. The address of their New York office is: 500 Fifth Ave., Suite 2009, New York NY 10110, phone (212) 944-6880.

A Daytrip from Vienna

Northern Burgenland

For those traveling by car, a tour through the northern part of Burgenland is just about the easiest and most enjoyable daytrip that can be taken from Vienna. If you're dependent on public transportation, you'll find it more difficult but still completely possible and well worth the effort.

Perhaps you've never heard of Burgenland. This is hardly surprising as Austria's youngest province isn't exactly overrun with overseas tourists. It is, however, a favorite vacation spot for the Viennese, other Austrians, Germans, and visitors from Eastern Europe. All of this means that you'll have a genuine experience as opposed to one created for *Ausländers,* and that it won't be very expensive. Although Burgenland begins a mere 12 miles from Vienna, there are so many unusual things to enjoy that an early start is strongly recommended.

The countryside of northern Burgenland is dominated by Europe's strangest lake, the 124-square-mile *Neusiedler See,* a shallow paradise for birds and water-sports enthusiasts surrounded by miles of tall reeds and the hauntingly beautiful *puszta* plain extending over the horizon into Hungary. There are no mountains at all, but miles and miles of vineyards, beyond which gentle hills lead to the provincial capital of Eisenstadt. Although barely more than a village, this small town is rich in musical memories and has some outstanding attractions as well.

GETTING THERE:

Trains on the S-Bahn suburban service depart Vienna's Südbahnhof (South Station) hourly for the 50-minute ride to **Neusiedl-am-See**, whose station is almost a mile from the town. Bikes can be rented at the station, and there are occasional buses. Trains run at least every 2 hours from the Neusiedl station to **Eisenstadt**, a ride of 40 minutes. There is no direct train service from Eisenstadt back to Vienna, and taking a bus is much faster than doing the whole train trip in reverse. All trains are second-class locals.

Buses leave Vienna's Wien-Mitte Bus Station, near the air terminal and the Hilton Hotel, several times in the morning for **Neusiedl-am-See**. This ride take a bit over an hour and drops you off at the Hauptplatz in Neusiedl. *There is no bus service from Neusiedl to Rust and Mörbisch, so you will have to bike it or skip these two villages.* Buses from Neusiedl's Hauptplatz to the Domplatz in **Eisenstadt** run almost hourly and take 45 minutes. **Return buses** from Eisenstadt to **Vienna** leave at least hourly and take about 80 minutes.

By car, take the B-10 road southeast from Vienna, changing to the B-50 at Parndorf, then the B-51 into **Neusiedl-am-See**. After your visit, follow the map via Rust and Mörbisch to Eisenstadt. From there the B-59 and B-16 roads will return you to Vienna. The total driving distance for the day's outing is a bit under 100 miles.

GETTING AROUND:

If you don't have a car and you want to see Rust and Mörbisch as well as Neusiedl and Eisenstadt, you might consider renting a **bicycle** *(Fahrrad)* at the Neusiedl train station and returning it to the Eisenstadt station. The total pedaling distance is about 38 miles, most of which is flat and much of which is over separate bike trails. This service is available from April through October only. If you travel to Neusiedl by train the rental fee is cut in half, and you might want to make reservations by calling the Neusiedl station at (02167) 2437. Maps of bike trails in Burgenland are available free at local tourist offices.

PRACTICALITIES:

Northern Burgenland is at its best between late spring and early fall. Some of the attractions are closed on Mondays, and good weather is essential. The **Local Tourist Information Offices** for the stops along this tour are at: Hauptplatz 1, **Neusiedl-am-See**, phone (02167) 2229; Rathaus, **Rust**, phone (02685) 502; Hauptstrasse, **Mörbisch**, phone (02685) 8430; and Hauptstrasse 35, **Eisenstadt**, phone (02682) 2710. For the entire region you could contact the **Provincial Tourist Office** at Schloss Esterházy, Eisenstadt, phone (02682) 3384.

FOOD AND DRINK:

Burgenland's "Pannonian" cuisine is strongly influenced by neighboring Hungary. Expect to find spicy paprika dishes such as *Gulyas* (goulash) along with lake fish, duck, goose, and wild game. Some typical deserts are *Palatschinken* (crêpes with jam), and *Mohnstrudel* (poppy seeds and raisins in pastry). The local wines are among Austria's best, especially those from Rust. The area abounds in good restaurants, including:

In Neusiedl-am-See:

Barth-Stuben (Franz-Liszt-Gasse 37, 2 blocks east of the Rathaus) Best in town, attracts diners from Vienna for its inventive dishes. Outdoor garden tables available. Reservations preferred, phone (02167) 2625. X: Mon., late Nov., late Jan. $$$

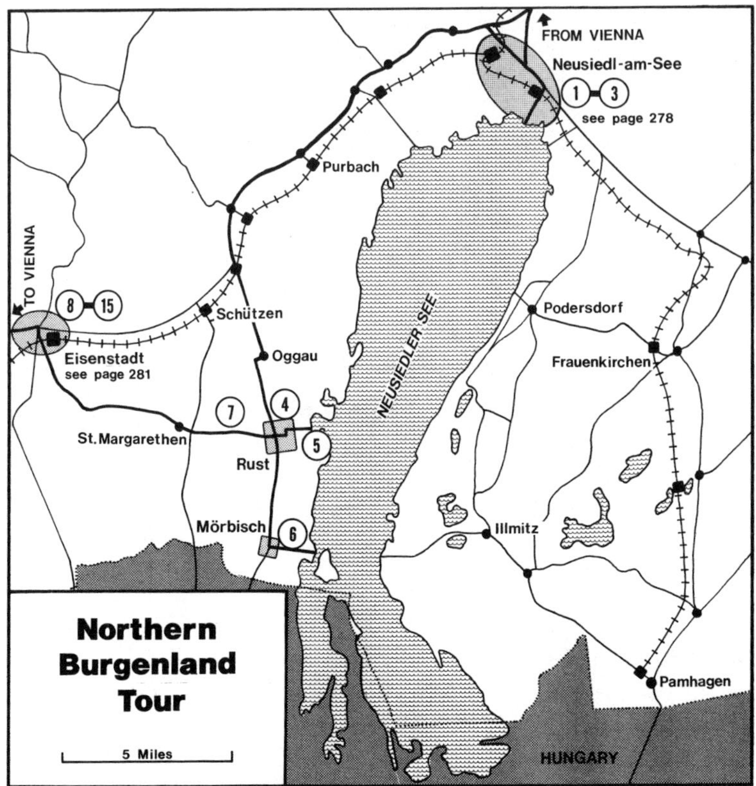

Rathausstüberl (Kirchengasse 2, near the Rathaus) A friendly place with outdoor garden tables. Noted for Pannonian-style grills and fish, as well as salads. X: Wed. $

Around Rust:

Taubenkobel (Hauptstrasse 33 in nearby Schützen, 5 miles northwest of Rust) Renowned for its sophisticated cuisine in a rustic setting. Reservations suggested, phone (02684) 2297. X: Mon. $$ and $$$

Rathauskeller (Rathausplatz 1 in the center of Rust) Simple foods, but a great selection of local wines for tasting. X: Wed. and Dec.–Jan. $

In Eisenstadt:

Schlosstaverne (Esterházyplatz 5, opposite the palace) A tourist place with gypsy music, but still a good choice. Typical Austrian and Hungarian dishes. $$

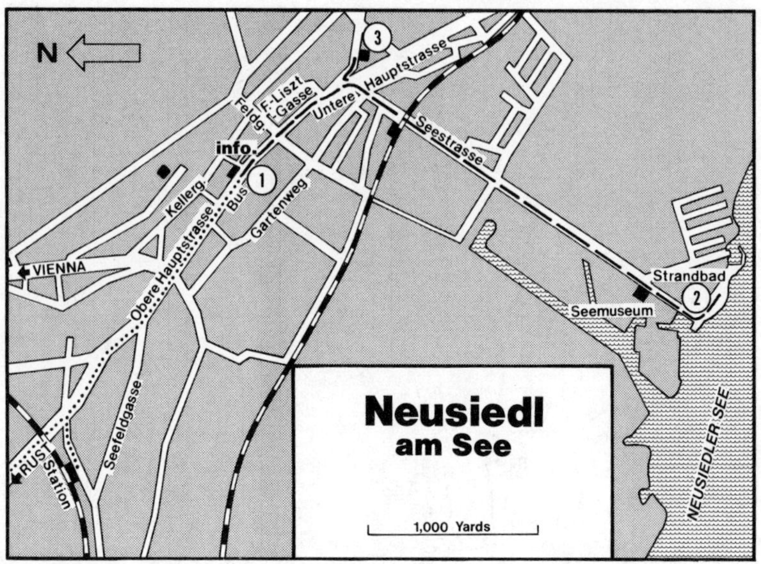

SUGGESTED TOUR:

The most prominent feature of northern Burgenland is its mysterious ***Neusiedler See** (Lake Neusiedl), one of the largest inland bodies of water in Europe and certainly the strangest. What can you say about a lake that sometimes isn't there? Or that has no obvious source, nor any natural outlet? Its warm and slightly salty water comes mostly, of course, from underground springs and is lost by evaporation. The southern end of the lake is in Hungary, and from there its level is artificially regulated by a canal to the Danube River. Most of the time, the lake is less than 7 feet deep at any given spot, and considerably shallower in most places, so it can actually be walked across. Doing this without an expert guide is dangerous, however. Strong winds sometimes blow the water to one shore, creating tricky currents and leaving the other side dry.

The Neusiedler See is almost completely surrounded by a belt of tall reeds growing in marshlands up to a mile wide. Much of it is a nature preserve with over 250 kinds of birds, most notably storks, nesting near its shores. You won't have enough time on a daytrip to study much of the wildlife, but you will be able to rent a boat for an hour or so. Besides being a paradise for nature lovers, the lake serves as a micro-climate regulator for the surrounding vineyards that produce some of Austria's very best wines. Enjoy!

Along the Strandbad at Neusiedl-am-See

Begin your tour at the resort village of **Neusiedl-am-See**, located at the lake's northern end. *Those coming by train will have to travel nearly a mile by bus, bike or on foot to its center.* Neusiedl's **Hauptplatz** (Main Square) (1) is where buses from Vienna and to Eisenstadt stop. Facing this square is the Rathaus (Town Hall), and behind it the 15th-century **Pfarrkirche**, a Gothic parish church with an unusual pulpit. On a low hill behind this are the ruins of **Burg Tabor**, a fortress from the 13th century.

Continue down Untere Hauptstrasse and turn right on Seestrasse. The road soon becomes a causeway, going through a mile of reeds to the **Strandbad** (2), a lively beach area on the water's edge. Here you can rent an electric, sail, pedal, or row boat by the hour and have some fun exploring the lake while dodging the multitude of windsurfers. There is also an outdoor café, and the **Seemuseum** with its collections of local flora and fauna, which can be seen from Easter through October, daily from 9 a.m. to noon and 1–5 p.m.

Return to Untere Hauptstrasse and turn right on Kalvarienbergstrasse to the nearby **Pannonisches Heimatmuseum** (Museum of Local Pannonian Life) (3), where room settings, furnishings, tools, costumes, crafts, and the like bring back memories of bygone times. It is open from May through October; on Tuesdays through Saturdays from 2:30–6:30 p.m.; and on Sundays and holidays from 10 a.m. to noon and 2:30–6:30 p.m.

Leave Neusiedl-am-See and drive (or pedal) along the west side of the lake to the popular village of Rust, a distance of 19 miles. *If you're dependent on public transportation, you'll have to skip this and go directly to Eisenstadt (8) by bus from Neusiedl's Hauptplatz, or by train.*

***Rust** (4) is famous for both its wines and its storks, who nest on its roofs and chimneys from April through August during their annual migrations from Egypt. The old part of the village is exceptionally well preserved, with many Renaissance and Baroque houses gracing the narrow lanes. **Wine cafés**, often called *Buschenschänken* or *Heurigen* and sometimes hidden away in courtyards, offer delicious opportunities to taste the local vintages. In the center of the village is the **Rathausplatz** (Town Hall Square), overlooked by the Gothic **Fischerkirche** (Fishermen's Church). Still surrounded by a defensive wall, this was built between the 12th and 16th centuries, and has some noteworthy 15th-century frescoes as well as an organ from 1705.

As in Neusiedl, you can follow a mile-long causeway through the reeds to the **Seebad** (5), a beach and boat landing where you can again rent a boat by the hour, or have a lakeside alfresco snack or drink at the Seerestaurant Rust.

Leave Rust and continue south for 3½ miles to ***Mörbisch** (6), a delightful lake village right on the Hungarian border. The Magyar influence is very strong here, with low, whitewashed, galleried houses colorfully festooned with flowers and bunches of corn. The **Heimathaus** at Hauptstrasse 53 is a small local museum in a characteristic old wine house, near the church and the tourist office.

Head back toward Rust and turn left. Just before **St. Margarethen** is the peculiar **Römer Steinbruch** (Roman Quarry) (7), whose limestone was used by the ancient Romans for strongholds, and later by Austrians for building much of Vienna. Modern sculptors work the site today, transforming it into a bizarre landscape of ever-changing shapes.

Continue on to ***Eisenstadt**, an exceptionally interesting small town that became the capital of Burgenland province in 1925. Although it dates from at least the 12th century, Eisenstadt didn't amount to much until the Esterházy family, descendants of Attila the Hun, made it their seat in the 17th century. They were largely responsible for establishing Hapsburg rule in Hungary, of which this was then a part.

Schloss Esterházy (8), the old family palace, was built in the Baroque style on medieval foundations between 1663 and 1672. It is now used by the provincial government, but still belongs to the Esterházys. The great composer **Joseph Haydn**, who developed the symphonic form, worked here on and off for some 30 years in the service of the family, producing a rich musical heritage that still lives on. Performances of his works, often with musicians in period costumes, are

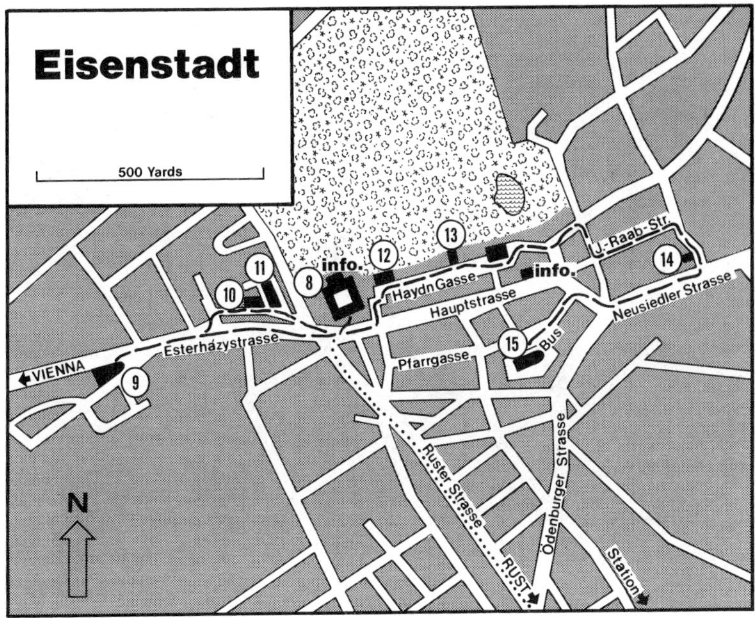

given frequently in the **Haydn Saal**, an elaborate concert hall within the palace. This and other rooms can be seen on guided tours lasting some 30 minutes and given in English on request. Schloss Esterházy is open to tourists daily from Easter through October, and on weekdays only the rest of the year, with tours starting hourly from 9 a.m. to 4 p.m.

Follow the map to the exceedingly Baroque **Bergkirche** (9), a church, mausoleum, and indoor Calvary rolled into one. The remains of Joseph Haydn, who died in 1809, rest there although his head did not rejoin the rest of the body until much later, having been stolen by grave robbers and eventually given to a Vienna museum. Be sure to follow the **Stations of the Cross**, with their life-size wooden figures in niches along an indoor passage that winds its way uphill through the strange **Kalvarienberg** (Calvary Hill) to the belfry, from which there is an excellent view. Visits may be made from April through October, daily from 9 a.m. to noon and 2–5 p.m.

Return on Esterházystrasse and follow around to Unterbergstrasse, a small street in what was once a barred Jewish ghetto. Today, the **Austrian Jewish Museum** (10) celebrates the rich cultural heritage of all Austrian Jews throughout history. Considered to be one of the best museums of its type in Europe, it is open from late May through late October, on Tuesdays through Saturdays, from 10 a.m. to 5 p.m. Just

Atop the Bergkirche

a block to the north is a historic Jewish cemetery that was desecrated in 1938 but reconstructed after the war.

The **Landesmuseum** (Provincial Museum) (11), nearby on Museumgasse, focuses on regional history. Among its displays are some remarkable Celtic and Roman artifacts, items relating to wine making, and local folk crafts. It is open on Tuesdays through Sundays, from 9 a.m. to noon and 1–5 p.m.

Return past Schloss Esterházy, behind which is a nice park, and follow the map to Haydn Gasse. The **Museum of Austrian Culture** (12) has displays on medieval Austrian history along with changing exhibitions, shown from mid-March through October, on Tuesdays through Sundays from 9:30 a.m. to 4:30 p.m.

Joseph Haydn lived in the simple house at number 21 from 1766 to 1778. It is now the **Haydn Museum** (13), where manuscripts and personal belongings are shown in an undisturbed setting. Even if you don't go inside, at least have a look at the lovely courtyard. Visitors are welcome from Easter through October, Tuesdays through Sundays, from 9 a.m. to noon and 1–5 p.m.

Now follow the map past another spot associated with Haydn, the rustic **Gärtenhäuschen** (14) or little garden house. Continue around to **Domplatz** (15), whose 15th-century Gothic church was elevated to cathedral status in 1960. Buses for Vienna leave from this square, and there is a simple outdoor café where you can wait. If you're driving, the best route is via the B-59 and B-16 roads.

A Daytrip from Vienna

The Schneeberg

A trip to the Schneeberg is strictly for fun. It may not be exactly towering by Alpine standards, but Vienna's very own "Snow Mountain" is close at hand and is just the place for a day's escape form the rigors of sightseeing. Rising some 6,811 feet above sea level, it carries a mantle of snow throughout much of the summer, and in winter provides perfectly enjoyable skiing. The views are magnificent, the air is clean, and you can even try a little bit of mountain hiking if you like.

Being the highest peak in the province of Lower Austria is not the Schneeberg's only attraction. Thousands of people go there just to experience the marvelous old *Schmalspurige Dampfbetriebene Zahnradbahn* (narrow-gauge steam-operated cog-wheel railroad) that chugs and clangs its smoky way for 6 miles in a mere 80 minutes, gaining 3,980 feet of altitude in the process. Built in the 1890s, these primitive trains still carry wooden cars with hard seats, and are an absolute delight for both railfans and normal people alike. They take you almost to the top of the mountain, to a point where you can relish the view and perhaps have lunch or a few drinks; or you can continue on foot over good trails to the very summit to say that you've been there.

GETTING THERE:

Trains leave Vienna's Südbahnhof (South Station) several times daily from about 6:30 to 9 a.m. for the 1½-hour ride to Puchberg-am-Schneeberg where you board the steam train. Some of these are direct, some split en route, and others require a change at Wiener Neustadt. Service is best on summer weekends. Return trains run from Puchberg to Vienna until late evening. It is imperative that you check the schedules in advance as they change seasonally and are subject to variations. All of the trains are second-class locals.

By car, take the A-2 Autobahn south from Vienna to the Wiener Nuestadt exit, then the B-26 west to Puchberg-am-Schneeberg. The total distance is 45 miles.

PRATICALITIES:

Avoid making this trip between early November and late April, when the cog-wheel steam train does not operate. Service is best on summer weekends, but it can also be crowded then. Some **warm, layered clothing** should be brought along as it is much cooler atop the mountain. A light jacket or sweater should suffice in summer. **Clear weather** is essential for enjoyment of this trip, and an early start is strongly recommended. The local **Tourist Information Office**, phone (02636) 2201, is on Wiener-Neustadt-Strasse in Puchberg, near the train station. For information about the cog-wheel steam train phone (02636) 2225-0. **Bicycles** may be rented at the station from April through October. The Schneeberg is in the Land of **Niederösterreich.**

FOOD AND DRINK:

There are several adequate tourist restaurants in Puchberg. Two good places for meals or drinks on the mountain are:

Berghaus Hochschneeberg (Atop the mountain, near the terminus) Simple Austrian food in an old stone hotel from 1898. X: Nov. through Mar. $

Damböck Haus (15-minute walk from the upper train terminus, following a trail with green blazes) Rough-and-ready mountain fare in a friendly rustic hikers' hut. $

SUGGESTED TOUR:

Begin at the **Puchberg-am-Schneeberg Train Station** (1), where you purchase a special ticket for the ***cog-wheel steam train** and obtain a seat reservation card *(Platzkarte)*. You won't need a ticket if you're traveling on a Eurailpass or Rabbit Card, but the seat reservation is still required. It may be possible to make this reservation while on the train from Vienna; ask the conductor.

Take a moment to examine the cog-wheel steam locomotives before boarding the train. Built in the 1890s, they look as though their front axles have collapsed, but this peculiar angle relative to the track is to keep the fireboxes level while climbing the mountain. The engine is at the downhill end of the train to prevent any coaches from giving you an excessively thrilling ride in the event of a coupling failure. Depending on your tolerance for the acrid smell of coal smoke, you may want to ride in the car next to the locomotive so that you can watch the engineer at work.

The first 45 minutes is spent climbing through a forest with ever-changing views of the valley, the mountain huts, and the babbling brooks. This is followed by a scheduled 15-minute rest stop at the **Baumgartner Haus** (2), where you can get off for refreshments while the engine takes a drink of water.

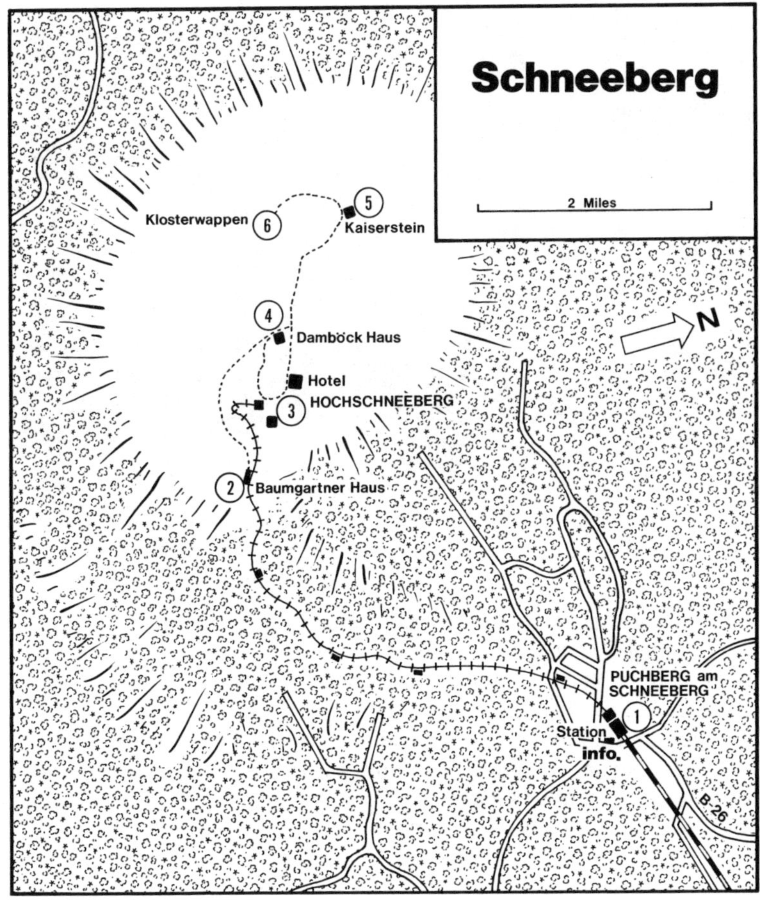

The climb now becomes much steeper, soon passing the timberline and entering a region of Alpine tundra. There are two tunnels in this stretch—close the windows quickly when the train enters them or be overwhelmed by its smoke! The upper station, **Hochschneeberg** (3), is reached 80 minutes after leaving Puchberg. Here you should make reservations for the return journey. Next to the hut are sidings where trains are parked, awaiting their afternoon trips down. Their fires are kept going, making it fascinating to walk among the black, sooty, hissing beasts. On the other side of the tracks is a rather strange chapel, the **Elizabethkirche**, which was visited in 1902 by Kaiser Franz Joseph, who came by train.

Train halt at the Baumgartner Haus

It is only a short stroll to the **Berghaus Hochschneeberg**, a sturdy but primitive small hotel that opened when the tracks first reached these heights. Meals and drinks are available there, as are hiking maps *(Wanderkarten)* of the area.

From the station, you can walk along a wide trail with green blazes, going around the Waxriegel summit (6,193 feet) and in 15 minutes reaching the **Damböck Haus** (4), a hut maintained by the Austrian Touring Club *(ÖTK)* that offers cheap meals, rustic *Gemütlichkeit,* and even simple overnight accommodations. In the Austrian Alps, hikers do not sleep in tents or carry cooking equipment. Instead, they make use of some 700 such huts. This explains the small rucksacks that Austrian hikers carry in contrast the huge backpacks common to Americans. The ecological lessons are clear; Austria is a nation of hikers and climbers, yet the mountains remain pristine.

From here it is an hour's hike to the **Kaiserstein** (5), which has another hut at an altitude of 6,760 feet. A ridge trail with red blazes leads shortly to the main summit, the ***Klosterwappen** (6), for a magnificent view from a height of 6,811 feet of the Pre-Alps as far as Vienna's Wienerwald, and across the Höllental Valley to the Raxalpe and the High Alps.

There are several trail options taking you back to the upper train station, but the easiest, quickest, and safest route is to just retrace your steps.

A Daytrip from Vienna

*Graz

Much of Austria's traditional Old World atmosphere lingers on in Graz, yet paradoxically the nation's second-largest city is regarded as being its most progressive. It is this blending of the past with the future that makes Graz such a worthwhile destination for its relatively few visitors. The hordes of mass tourism haven't exactly flocked there yet, doubtlessly because the city's charms are subtle and well hidden in a maze of alleyways and courtyards, just waiting to be uncovered by inquisitive travelers on foot. There are no three-star "must-see" attractions as such, but several excellent museums highlight one of the most delightful urban walking tours in this part of Europe.

Besides being Austria's "other city," Graz is the capital of its second-largest province, Styria; the seat of two universities with a combined student population of about 30,000; a lively center of avant-garde culture; and a green place of parks and gardens. Its name comes from the Slavic word *gradec,* meaning a small castle, as defensive installations stood atop the downtown Schlossberg hill since the 9th century, guarding the narrow Mur Valley—a strategic approach to Vienna—from the Turks. A town developed by the 12th century, eventually becoming an imperial city of the ruling Hapsburgs. Graz continued to prosper as a provincial capital even after the court moved to Vienna in the 17th century, and flourished especially during the 19th-century rule of the enlightened Archduke Johann.

GETTING THERE:

Trains depart Vienna's Südbahnhof (South Station) at 2-hour intervals for the 2½-hour express run to Graz. Other fast trains require an easy change at Bruck-an-der-Mur. The last express back to Vienna leaves Graz at about 8:30 p.m.

By car, the fast route is to take the A-2 Autobahn all the way to Graz, which lies 124 miles southwest of Vienna. A more scenic, but considerably slower, route goes by way of Semmering and Bruck-an-der-Mur.

PRACTICALITIES:

Graz is at its best on weekdays from April through October. On weekends and holidays its streets are dead, and its museums closed by noon or 1 p.m. Some of the major attractions are closed completely from November through March. The local **Tourist Information Office**, phone (0316) 83-52-41, is at Herrengasse 16, a block south of the Hauptplatz. **Bicycles** can be rented at the station from April through October. Graz is the capital of Land **Steiermark** and has a **population** of about 243,000.

FOOD AND DRINK:

Graz has a fine selection of good-value restaurants serving traditional Styrian cuisine. Some choices are:

Hofkeller (Hofgasse 8, a block west of the Burg) Elegant dining in traditional surroundings, fine Austrian and International specialties. Reservations advised, phone (0316) 70-24-39. X: Sun. $$$

Stainzerbauer (Bürgergasse 4, a block south of the cathedral) A local favorite for hearty Styrian cuisine, always crowded. $$

Krebsenkeller (Sackstrasse 12, just south of the Neue Galerie) A complex of small dining rooms around a hidden 16th-century courtyard. $$

Goldene Pastete (Sporgasse 28, 2 blocks south of the Folklore Museum) Local dishes in a friendly 16th-century inn. X: Sat., Sun., late Aug. $$

Landhauskeller (Schmiedgasse 9, 2 blocks southeast of the Hauptplatz) A traditional rustic *Weinstube* with outdoor tables in summer. X: Sun., holidays. $

Gambrinuskeller (Färbergasse 6, 2 blocks northwest of Glockenspielplatz) Grilled meats, salads, and Balkan specialties, with a summer terrace. X: Sun., holidays. $

SUGGESTED TOUR:

The **main train station** (*Hauptbahnhof*) (1) is about a mile west of the Old Town quarter, where the tour begins. This is easily reached by taking tram number 3 or 6 from the front of the station to the Hauptplatz. Board the front entrance of the tram and pay the driver. If you prefer to walk, just follow Annenstrasse slightly downhill to the river, cross the bridge, and take Murgasse to the Hauptplatz.

Lying at the foot of the Schlossberg hill, in the center of the Old Town, the ***Hauptplatz** (Main Square) (2) is the very heart of old Graz. Its lively use as an open-air farmers' market and general meeting place continues to this day, made all the more pleasant by several outdoor cafés. Triangular in shape, the *platz* was laid out as far back as 1164

In the Hauptplatz

and was historically used as a place of justice. The **fountain** in its center is topped with a statue of Archduke Johann, the 19th-century patron who did much to develop Graz as a cultural and scientific center.

To the north of the statue, on the Schlossberg hill, stands the famous 16th-century **Uhrturm** (Clock Tower), virtually the trademark of Graz. The heavily decorated 17th-century **Luegg House** at the corner of Sporgasse is the most elaborate of the fine old houses lining both sides of the square, several of which, especially those on the west side, are from the Renaissance period. Along the south side rises the 19th-century **Rathaus** (City Hall), whose massive bulk dominates the entire *platz*.

The narrow Franziskanergasse leads through an ancient butchers' quarter to some of the oldest streets and passageways in town, whose original medieval houses were later given Baroque façades. The tiny, well-hidden Kapaunplatz is especially attractive. With its front facing the river, the **Franziskanerkirche** (Franciscan Church) (3) was founded by the Minorites around 1240, along with its adjacent monastery. Later transferred to the Franciscans, the church has a 14th-century choir, a nave from 1520, and a fortified tower from 1636. Take a look at its cloister if the gate facing the Franziskanerplatz is open.

Continue on the twisting Neue-Welt-Gasse to Schmiedgasse, once the street of the blacksmiths, for a wonderful view of the Hauptplatz. Now follow the map past the Grazer Congress (Convention Center) and casino to the renowned **Landesmuseum Joanneum** (4), founded by Archduke Johann in 1811 and the oldest public museum in Austria. Actually, the two buildings here are only the core of an extensive provincial museum complex that is scattered all over town, covering a broad range of subjects. The entrance facing Raubergasse is for the mineralogical and natural history collections, while the applied arts department and the world-famous ***Alte Galerie** of the fine arts from the Middle Ages through the Baroque period is entered from Neutorgasse. One of Graz's major attractions, the latter features works by Pieter Brueghel the Younger and both Cranachs, along with magnificent medieval **stained-glass windows**, an altarpiece depicting the murder of Thomas à Becket, and the exquisite *Admont Madonna* carving from 1400. The Alte Galerie is open on Tuesdays through Fridays, 10 a.m. to 5 p.m.; and on weekends and holidays from 10 a.m. to 1 p.m.

Now take Landhausgasse to Herrengasse, the main street of the Old Town quarter. The 15th-century **Gemaltes Haus** at number 3, once a ducal residence, is beautifully decorated with frescoes from 1742. To the right is the imposing **Landhaus**, the provincial parliament of Styria, built in the 16th century in the Italian Renaissance style. This structure also houses the Tourist Information Office. Its real beauty, as with many buildings in town, does not become apparent until you stroll through its **inner courtyards** . These are elegantly detailed in an almost Mediterranean manner with up to three levels of flower-bedecked arcades, and with a well canopy so finely crafted in bronze that it looks like wrought iron.

The same building complex includes the adjoining ***Landeszeughaus** (Provincial Arsenal) (5), a four-story armory built in the mid-17th century that is today the leading tourist attraction of Graz. Virtually unaltered over the centuries, it is still stocked with the original 16th- and 17th-century weapons intended to be used in defending Austria against the Turks. About 30,000 items can be examined, including some 3,000 suits of armor, nearly 8,000 firearms, cannons, mortars, swords, halberds, and other military weapons of that era. The armory and its contents became obsolescent in the early 18th century when the likelihood of a Turkish invasion disappeared, after which the equipment would have been dispersed had it not been for a petition from the people of Styria to Empress Maria Theresa to keep it intact in honor of their militia's loyal service. Intact and well-preserved it has remained ever since. Visits may be made from April through October only, Mondays through Fridays, 9 a.m. to 5 p.m.; and on weekends and holidays from 9 a.m. to 1 p.m.

Perhaps attracted by all those armaments, Napoleon once spent the night across the street at Herrengasse 13. Just a few steps from this is the **Stadtpfarrkirche** (Town Parish Church) (6). Although built

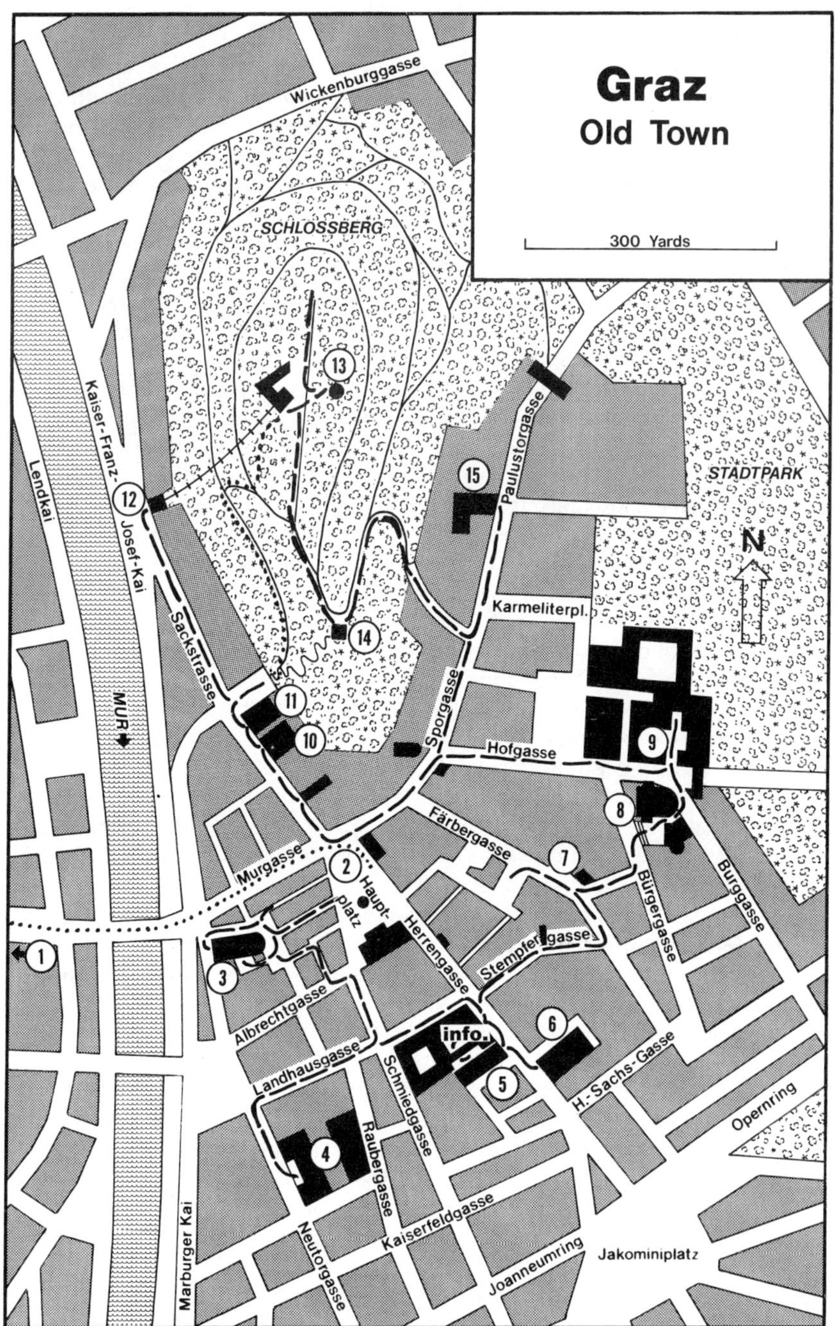
Graz
Old Town
300 Yards
Wickenburggasse
SCHLOSSBERG
STADTPARK
Kaiser-Franz-Josef-Kai
Lendkai
MUR
Sackstrasse
Paulustorgasse
Karmeliterpl.
Sporgasse
Hofgasse
Färbergasse
Murgasse
Hauptplatz
Herrengasse
Bürgergasse
Burggasse
Stempfergasse
Albrechtgasse
Landhausgasse
Schmiedgasse
info.
H.-Sachs-Gasse
Opernring
Raubergasse
Kaiserfeldgasse
Neutorgasse
Marburger Kai
Joanneumring
Jakominiplatz
N
1
2
3
4
5
6
7
8
9
10
11
12
13
14
15

in the early 16th century, it was later given a Baroque façade and acquired a steeple in 1781. Step inside to see a painting by Tintoretto, the *Assumption of the Virgin*, which decorates the altar. Across the street is a small alleyway named in honor of J.B. Fischer von Erlach, the great architect of the Austrian Baroque, who was born there in 1656.

Return on Herrengasse and turn up the winding Stempfergasse, noting the house at number 6. Until recently, this was thought to have been the home of the astronomer Johannes Kepler, who taught in Graz for a while. Its arcaded courtyard is interesting, and is partially occupied by an atmospheric wine tavern.

Turning left on Enge Gasse brings you to a wonderful little square called **Glockenspielplatz** (7). Appropriately, a musical show with animated wooden figures emerging from a wall above a café and dancing to old folk tunes is put on daily at 11 a.m. and 6 p.m., and other times as well. Take a look into the courtyard at house number 5, which has a 17th-century open staircase; and at the arcaded Renaissance courtyard behind house number 7. The nearby **Mehlplatz** has some exceptionally handsome buildings.

Now follow the map to the late-Gothic **Domkirche** (Cathedral) (8), up a flight of open stairs from Bürgergasse. On the south outside wall of the church, near the steps, is the famous *Landplagenbild* fresco from the 15th century. Although quite faded, it still depicts in no uncertain terms the greatest afflictions of those times—the plague, the locusts, and those nasty Turks. Built between 1438 and 1462 by Emperor Friedrich III on the site of an earlier church, the cathedral is noted for its lovely **high altar** made of colored marble in 1730, its choir stalls, its tombs, and its Renaissance reliquaries on either side of the archway leading to the choir.

Immediately south of the cathedral is the splendid mid-17th-century **Mausoleum** of Emperor Ferdinand II, who died in 1637. Part of its emphatically Baroque interior is to an early design by native-son J.B. Fischer von Erlach, and is the only example of his work in Graz. It may be seen on guided tours only, on Mondays through Saturdays from 11 a.m. to noon and 2–3 p.m.

Cross Hofgasse to examine what little remains of the former imperial palace, the **Burg** (9), dating from the 15th century. Most of it was replaced with dull government offices during the 19th and early 20th centuries; but you can still see the **Burgtor**, a palace gate that opens into the Stadtpark (Municipal Park); and the **Gothic Staircase** of 1499 with its noted double spiral construction, hidden away at the far end of the main courtyard.

Hofgasse leads past the early 19th-century **Schauspielhaus**, the city's leading theater, now known mostly for its avant-garde produc-

Along the Sporgasse

tions. At the corner of Sporgasse, at number 22, is the **Deutschritter-ordenshaus** (House of the Teutonic Order), whose early Renaissance courtyard should be seen. Across the street stands the **Stiegenkirche**, an interesting church from the early 17th century that can be reached only by climbing two flights of stairs.

There is no climbing involved on the Sporgasse, however. It's downhill all the way on this atmospheric winding lane, passing outdoor cafés and boutiques as you head back to the Hauptplatz. Make a right on Sackstrasse and take a look at the hidden 16th-century courtyard behind number 12. Close to this, at number 16, is the **Neue Galerie** (New Gallery) (10), a small art museum belonging to the Joanneum, which features modern Austrian works from the 19th century to the present. It is housed in the 17th-century **Herbertstein Palace**, once the city residence of the ruling princes. The museum is open on Mondays through Fridays, 10 a.m. to 6 p.m.; and on weekends and holidays from 10 a.m. to 1 p.m.

There is another palace next door at number 18, where the Archduke Franz Ferdinand, heir to the Austro-Hungarian throne, was born in 1863. In 1914 he was assassinated at Sarajevo in what was to be the opening round of World War I. Today, the Khuenburg Palace houses the **Stadtmuseum** (City Museum) (11), where the history of Graz is on display on Tuesdays through Saturdays from10 a.m. to 6 p.m.; and on Sundays and holidays from 10 a.m. to 1 p.m.

Stroll into the Schlossbergplatz, from the end of which you can climb a steep 395-foot stone staircase to the summit of Graz's midtown hill. Or you could continue down the street to the **Schlossbergbahn Funicular Railway** (12) and ride up in comfort instead.

However you get to its top, the ***Schlossberg** (Castle Hill) offers great views across Graz and central Styria. Defensive fortifications guarding the Mur Valley have crowned this summit since at least the 9th century, but all were demolished in 1809 on orders from a victorious Napoleon. All, that is, except for two towers that were spared upon payment of 3,000 guilders by the citizens of Graz.

One of these is the octagonal **Glockenturm** (Bell Tower) (13) dating from 1588, which contains Styria's largest bell, the four-ton "Liesl." Just north of it is an **Open-Air Theater** where opera and dramatic performances are given in what remains of the old casemates. You might want to stop at the nearby **Schlossberg Café** for a much-deserved alfresco drink or snack, especially if you walked up.

Continue along a downhill road to the other surviving structure and the very symbol of Graz, the 16th-century **Uhrturm** (Clock Tower) (14). Take a very careful look at its 18th-century clock with four faces, and then at your own watch. Notice anything wrong? No, it's not the time, it's the hands. The *big* ones tell the hour; the *small* ones the minute! Why? Perhaps it's easier to read at a distance that way.

Follow the map downhill to Paulustorgasse, which leads to one last attraction before returning to the Old Town quarter. This is the **Steirisches Volkskundemuseum** (Styrian Folklore Museum) (15), where period room settings, local costumes, and historical items are displayed in a former monastery. Another branch of the Joanneum, it is open from April through October, on Mondays through Fridays from 9 a.m. to 4 p.m.; and on weekends and holidays from 9 a.m. to noon. From here you can meander down Sporgasse to the Hauptplatz for a tram ride back to the station.

A Daytrip from Vienna

Mariazell

Austria's foremost place of pilgrimage, the home of its national shrine, is so beautifully situated that a daytrip there from Vienna is worthwhile for the scenic splendor alone. As a bonus, you can visit a magnificent basilica of great religious and historical significance, ride to the top of a mountain for panoramic views, and take a short hike or steam-tram ride to a lovely lake. The town itself is a year-round resort, with many pleasant diversions.

Located in a snug valley between mountains in the northernmost reaches of Styria, Mariazell began its long history as a venerated site on December 21, 1157. According to tradition, that's when five monks set up a lonely priory in the forest, erecting a statue of the Virgin that was soon thought to be performing miracles. A pilgrimage church was built in 1200, and in 1377 the king of Hungary attributed his victory over the Turks to the Virgin of Mariazell, beginning a tide of pilgrimage that has not ceased to this day. For many centuries, it was this cult that enhanced the union of Austria with the Hapsburg dynasty. Today's visitors are drawn not only for devotional reasons, but also for the sheer natural pleasures this small resort offers. Railfans will find this to be a particularly enticing trip.

GETTING THERE:

Trains leave Vienna's Westbahnhof (West Station) frequently for the 45-minute ride to St. Pölten, where you change to the old narrow-gauge *Mariazellerbahn,* built in 1905 and still one of the most scenic mountain rail lines in Austria. Trains on this line depart several times in the morning and early afternoon, taking about 2½ hours to reach Mariazell. Return service operates until late afternoon.

By car, leave Vienna on the A-1 Autobahn and head west to the St. Pölten exit, then take the B-20 south into the mountains. Mariazell is 86 miles southwest of Vienna.

PRACTICALITIES:

Mariazell flourishes all year round, although a few minor sights are closed in winter. The historic steam tram operates on weekends and holidays, from July through September. The local **tourist office**, phone (03882) 2366, is at Hauptplatz 13, to the left of the basilica. **Bicycles** may be rented at the train station from April through October. Mariazell is in the Land of **Steiermark** and has a **population** of about 2,500.

FOOD AND DRINK:

Some especially good choices are:

Jägerwirt (Hauptplatz 2, directly across from the basilica) Traditional Austrian fare with an old-fashioned country atmosphere. X: Mon., Dec. $$

Edelweiss Mountain Hut (Atop the Bürgeralpe, a short walk from the upper cable-car station past the observation tower) A rustic Alpine retreat with indoor and outdoor tables. $

SUGGESTED TOURS:

From the **Mariazell Train Station** (1) it is a pleasant 10-minute walk along a path marked Bahnhofpromenade into the town proper. Follow Leberstrasse past the parking lot and turn left on Grazer Strasse to the Hauptplatz, or main square.

Rising in front of you is the great ***Basilica** (2) that grew out of the pilgrimage church of 1200. The present structure dates from the 14th century, but was greatly enlarged and altered during the late 17th century. Its appearance may seem rather strange, what with two squat, bulbous Baroque towers flanking the original Gothic spire and porch. Inside, however, it is a triumph of the Baroque style, resplendent in its elaborate plaster work and paintings. The main focus of pilgrimage, the ***Gnadenkapelle** or Chapel of Miracles, is in the center of the nave. A silver baldachin designed in 1727 by J.E. Fischer von Erlach the Younger shelters the original 12th-century statue of the Virgin of Mariazell, or *Magna Mater Austriae,* the Austrian national shrine. The silver grille around it was donated in 1756 by Empress Maria Theresa.

Beyond this is the **High Altar** of 1704, a famous creation by Austria's master of the Baroque, J.B. Fischer von Erlach the Elder. The **Treasury** (*Schatzkammer*), up a few steps, has a wonderful collection of votive offerings dating from medieval times to the present, along with valuable items of ecclesiastical art. It is open from May through October, from 10 a.m. to noon and 2–3 p.m.

A path leads uphill from the rear of the church to the **Kalvarienberg** (Mount Calvary) (3), passing Stations of the Cross and a display of mechanical nativity figurines.

Return to the Hauptplatz and follow Wiener Strasse for 2 blocks to

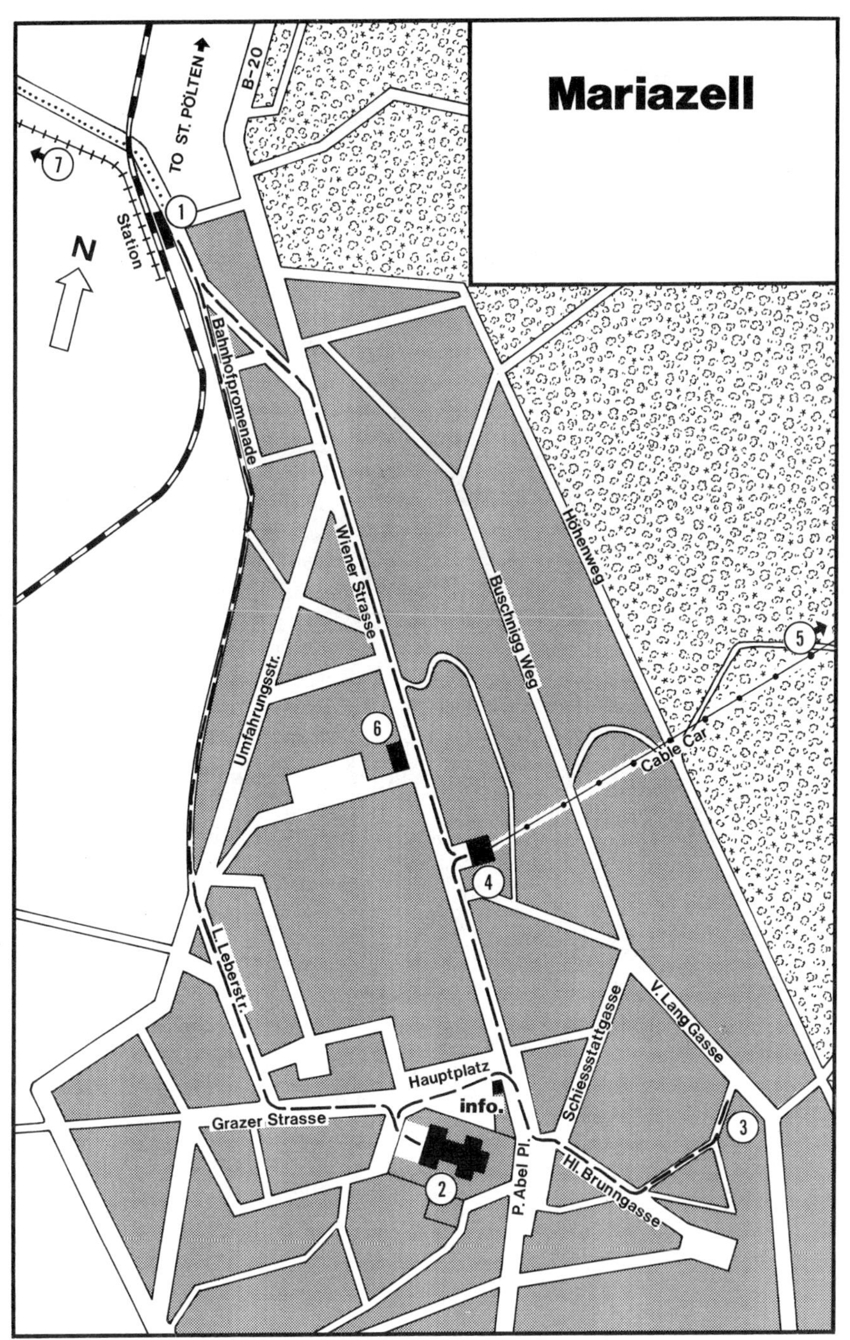
Mariazell
TO ST. PÖLTEN
B-20
Station
N
Bahnhofpromenade
Wiener Strasse
Buschnigg Weg
Höhenweg
Umfahrungsstr.
Cable Car
L. Leberstr.
Hauptplatz
info.
Grazer Strasse
P. Abel Pl.
Schiesstattgasse
V. Lang Gasse
Hl. Brunngasse
1
2
3
4
5
6
7

The Basilica

the lower station of the **Bürgeralpebahn Cable Car** (4), which quickly lifts you up to the 4,150-foot-high ***Bürgeralpe Plateau** (5) for a bird's-eye view of the surrounding mountains and lakes. A sham-medieval observation tower, just up the path, allows you to climb above the tree line for an even better look. Several invigorating forest strolls following marked trails can be taken from here. In winter this becomes a popular ski area, especially favored by family groups.

Back in town, continue down Wiener Strasse to the **Heimatmuseum** (Museum of Local History) (6). Open on Mondays through Saturdays from July through September, it features rustic room settings and folk arts from times gone by.

The route on the map returns you to the train station in about 10 minutes. From there, you might want to make a side trip of about 2 miles to the **Erlaufsee** (7), a lovely lake surrounded by impressive mountains. While this makes an excellent walk, if you happen to come on a weekend or holiday from July through September you could ride there on the delightful ***Museumstramweg** instead. Running with open cars from the train station to the lake, this claims to be the world's oldest remaining steam tram and, along with the train ride from St. Pölten provides a memorable experience. Ask at the tourist office for current schedules.

A Daytrip from Vienna or Salzburg

Linz

Largely devoted to the steel and chemical industries, Linz may at first seem an odd destination for a daytrip. Yet, the nation's third-largest city and the provincial capital of Upper Austria does have its charms, especially in the fact that not many overseas tourists go there. This leaves its well-restored Old Town district on the banks of the Danube and its delightful Pöstlingberg hill uncluttered and unspoiled, ready to be savored without the crush of mass tourism.

Linz began life in the 2nd century A.D. as the Roman camp of *Lentia,* guarding the Danube Valley and the overland salt route to Bohemia. Its strategic position on the river made it a natural center of trade from the Middle Ages on, eventually becoming a major industrial giant that today boasts one of Europe's largest and most advanced steel mills. The early development of railways, starting when Austria's first train ran from Linz to Budweis in Czechoslovakia as early as 1832, brought a further prosperity that is still reflected in the city's handsome buildings and streets.

As well as being a daytrip destination, Linz is a good stopover place for those traveling between Vienna and Salzburg. Doing this could allow enough time for an interesting side trip to the nearby world-famous Abbey of St. Florian.

GETTING THERE:

Trains depart Vienna's Westbahnhof (West Station) at least hourly for Linz, a ride of slightly under 2 hours. Return service operates until late evening.

Trains depart Salzburg at least hourly for the 90-minute ride to Linz, with returns running until late evening.

By car from Vienna, it's the A-1 Autobahn all the way. Linz is 115 miles west of Vienna.

By car from Salzburg, Linz is 82 miles to the northeast via the A-1 Autobahn.

PRACTICALITIES:

The castle and two museums are closed on Mondays, while the modern art gallery is closed on Sundays. Good weather is necessary to enjoy the Pöstlingberg. There is a branch office of the local **Tourist Information Office** in the train station, phone (0732) 540-00. The main office is at Altstadt 17, 1 block west of the Hauptplatz, phone (0732) 27-74-83. With a **population** of about 200,000, Linz is the capital of Land **Oberösterreich.**

FOOD AND DRINK:

Being a prosperous business center, Linz has no shortage of good restaurants and cafés. A local specialty is the *Linzer Torte,* an almond cake with jam. Some choice places to eat along the walking route are:

Allegro (Schillerstrasse 68, 3 blocks northeast of the Volks Garten) The best and most elegant restaurant in town, with imaginative *nouvelle* Austrian cuisine. For reservations phone (0732) 66-98-00. X: Sun., Aug. $$$

Mühlviertlerhof (Graben 24, near the Alter Dom) Traditional Austrian cuisine in a slightly rustic setting. $$

Wachauer Weinstube (Pfarrgasse 29, just east of the Hauptplatz) Mostly known for its wines from the Danube Valley, this tavern has simple but delicious food as well. X: Sun. $$

Klosterhof (Landstrasse 30, south of the Hauptplatz) A sprawling restaurant with many rooms and a beer garden. Hearty traditional Austrian fare. $

Gasthof Aigner (Atop the Pöstlingberg, near the pilgrimage church) A friendly place with good home cooking, indoors and out. $

SUGGESTED TOUR:

Leave the **main train station** (*Hauptbahnhof*) (1) and follow the map through the Volks Garten park and up the main shopping street, Landstrasse, turning right on Bethlehemstrasse. The **Stadtmuseum** (City Museum) (2), also known as the *Nordico* because it was once a school for Scandinavian students, has collections pertaining to local history, including costumes, furniture, paintings, and a model of Linz as it appeared in 1740. It is open on Mondays through Fridays, from 9 a.m. to 6 p.m., and on weekends from 1–5 p.m.

A left turn on Fadingerstrasse brings you to Museumstrasse. On the right is the **Francisco Carolinum Museum** (3), which is mostly devoted to natural history. If you're interested, the doors are open on Tuesdays through Fridays from 9 a.m. to 6 p.m., and on weekends from 10 a.m. to 4 p.m.

The Hauptplatz with its Dreifaltigkeitssäule

Head west on Museumstrasse and Graben, turning right on Domgasse. The **Alter Dom** (4) or *Jesuitenkirche* was built in the 17th century and served as Linz's cathedral from 1785 until 1909. Its aisleless interior is richly decorated in the ornate Jesuit style; the elaborately carved choir stalls, pulpit, and high altar harmonizing with the pink marble columns and intricate plaster work. The great composer Anton Bruckner, born nearby in 1824, was organist here from 1856 until 1868, and the Krismann organ on which he played is still in use.

Follow the narrow Domgasse around to the **Stadtpfarrkirche** (City Parish Church) (5), a Gothic structure built in the 13th century but totally remodeled in the Baroque style in 1648. To the right of its high altar is a tomb containing the heart of Emperor Frederick III, who lived in Linz from 1489 until his death in 1493. The rest of him is in St. Stephen's Cathedral in Vienna. Anton Bruckner was organist here, as well.

A tiny lane called Pfarrgasse leads into the grandiose **Hauptplatz** (6), one of Europe's most impressive main squares. In its center stands, to no one's surprise, the almost ubiquitous **Dreifaltigkeitssäule** (Trinity Column)—a feature common to many an Austrian town. Erected in 1723, it commemorates in white marble the deliverance of Linz from the plague and the Turks. Rising to a height of 85 feet and beautifully carved with angels, this is perhaps the epitome of Baroque Trinity columns.

Turn north and cross the Nibelungen Bridge over the Danube and into the modern suburb of Urfahr. Continue up Hauptstrasse, turning right on Blütenstrasse to the "Lentia 2000" indoor shopping mall, which also houses the **Neue Galerie—Wolfgang Gurlitt Museum** (7). If you're momentarily tired of the Baroque, this will come as a welcome relief. The collections feature works by Austrian and German artists of the 19th and 20th centuries, including such talents as Gustav Klimt, Egon Schiele, Oscar Kokoschka, Franz von Lenbach, and Max Liebermann. There are also frequent temporary exhibitions. The museum is open on Mondays through Saturdays from 10 a.m. to 6 p.m., remaining open until 10 p.m. on Thursdays. From November through April it is also open on Sundays, from 10 a.m. to 1 p.m.

Follow the map past the Linz-Urfahr train station to the adjacent Pöstlingberg Bahnhof (8), a small station where you can board a rather quaint old tram for one of the most enjoyable trolley-car rides anywhere. With departures every 20 minutes, this is the steepest non-cog tram line in the world, and goes right through suburbs and countryside to the top of the 1,765-foot-high ***Pöstlingberg hill** (9), a ride of 20 minutes. The **view** from the summit, sweeping across the Danube Valley and taking in all of Linz, extends in clear weather to the beginning of the Alps. This is a perfect spot to take a short break at one of the cafés or restaurants near the upper station.

At the very top stands a Baroque **Pilgrimage Church** (*Wallfahrtskirche*) of 1738, noted for its 18th-century Pietà of carved wood. Nearby is the **Grottenbahn**, a thoroughly delightful ride on a miniature railway through a fairy-tale grotto (*Märchengrotte*) installed deep inside the old defensive fortifications. Don't miss this special treat, even if you don't happen to have a kid in tow.

Return to town and re-cross the river to the Hauptplatz. A right turn on Hofgasse takes you through the oldest part of town and up to the **Schloss** (10), a 15th-century castle that once guarded the bridge across the Danube. Rebuilt several times and used by the military as late as World War II, it is today a somewhat uninspired structure, but definitely worth a visit to see the splendid ***Schlossmuseum**, or Provincial Museum of Upper Austria. All manner of things are on display here, including Bronze-Age artifacts, Roman remains, armor, medieval sculpture, furniture, costumes, musical instruments, and so on. There is a rich collection of folk art with room settings, toys, tools, and religious objects; and even a section devoted to railways and cider making; as well as special exhibitions from time to time. Visits may be made on Tuesdays through Saturdays from 9 a.m. to 5 p.m., and on Sundays from 10 a.m. to 4 p.m. It is closed on Mondays.

Continue through the castle. On the outside terrace, facing the river, is an outdoor café where you can enjoy a drink or snack before marching on.

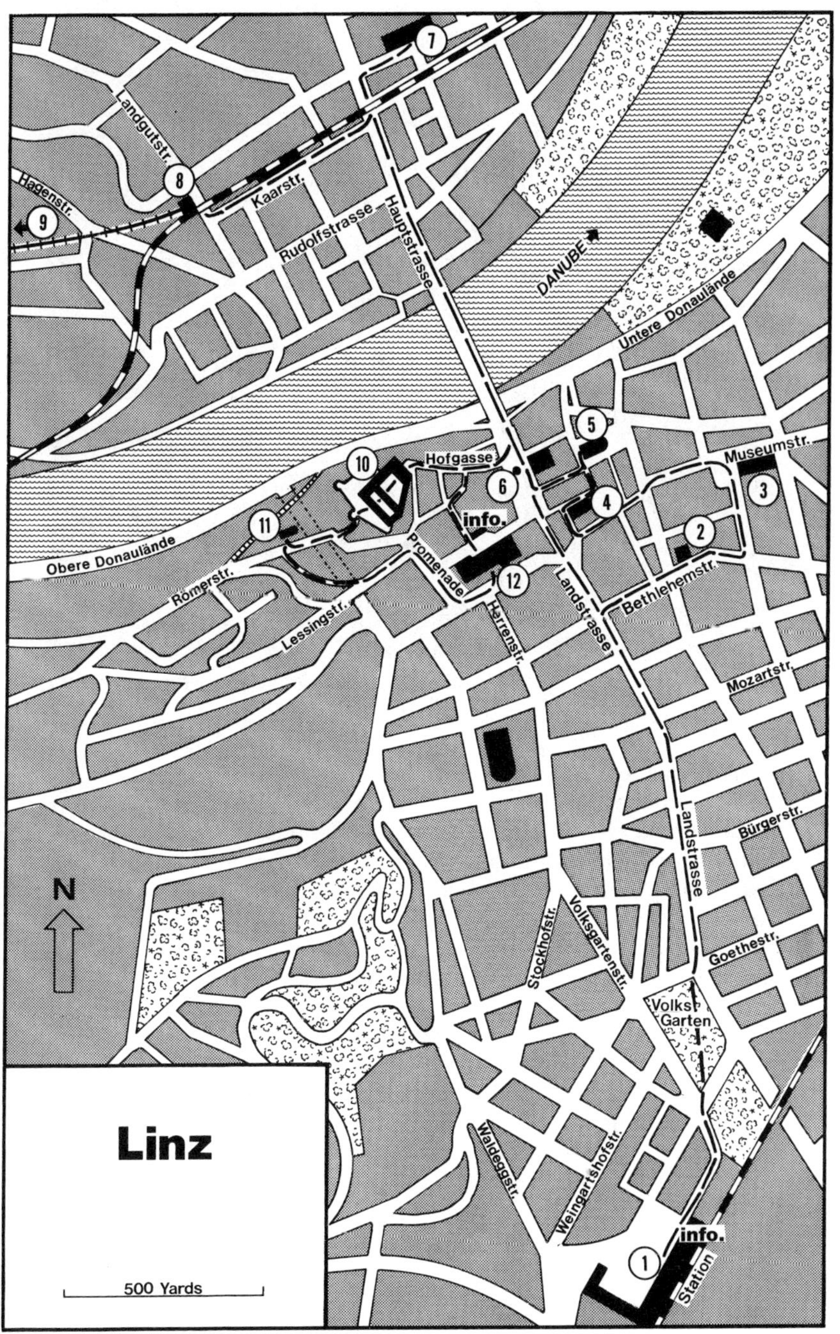

Linz
500 Yards
N
Landgutstr.
Hagenstr.
Kaarstr.
Rudolfstrasse
Hauptstrasse
DANUBE
Untere Donaulände
Museumstr.
Hofgasse
info.
Obere Donaulände
Römerstr.
Lessingstr.
Promenade
Herrenstr.
Landstrasse
Bethlehemstr.
Mozartstr.
Bürgerstr.
Goethestr.
Stockhofstr.
Volksgartenstr.
Volks Garten
Waldeggstr.
Weingartshofstr.
Station

Boarding the Pöstlingberg tram

A passage through the western curtain wall brings you down steps to Römerstrasse and what is possibly the oldest church in Austria, the **Martinskirche** (11). Built on Roman foundations, it might be of pre-Carolingian origin, but in any case was documented as early as 799. Altered somewhat over the years, it still preserves most of its form along with some 15th-century frescoes.

A narrow path called the Flügelhofgasse leads downhill to Lessingstrasse and the 16th-century **Landhaus** (12), the seat of the provincial government. In its inner courtyard is an octagonal fountain representing the planets, which honors the astronomer and mathematician Johannes Kepler, who taught in this building from 1612 to 1626. The same complex also houses the **Minoritenkirche**, a rococo church of the 18th century with an unusually fine interior.

The nicest route back to the Hauptplatz is via Altstadt and Hofgasse. From the main square you can take tram number 1 or 3 back to the main train station (*Hauptbahnhof*).

*Hallstatt

You've probably seen pictures of Hallstatt, that tiny village clinging to a miniscule patch of Earth between a mountain and a lake, whose image graces many a travel poster and guidebook cover. Easily one of the most photogenic spots in all of Europe, Hallstatt is also one of the oldest settlements in this part of the Continent. *Hall* is an ancient Celtic word for salt, for the early Celts were mining the white gold here as far back as 1000 B.C., long before they migrated west to France and Britain. The late Bronze and early Iron ages (900–500 B.C.) are in fact known as the Hallstatt Era after the advanced civilization that once flourished here. Numerous artifacts from that epoch have been unearthed and are displayed in the local Prehistoric Museum, while what may be the world's oldest salt mine is still in operation and may easily be visited.

With all it has to offer, Hallstatt has become a very popular weekend destination among the Austrians themselves. Besides sheer beauty and historical significance, it offers boating possibilities on a lovely lake, short hikes in the surrounding hills, a tour of the salt mine, an interesting Gothic church with a bizarre charnel house, and a full range of tourist amenities.

GETTING THERE:

Trains (marked for Vienna) depart Salzburg almost hourly for Attnang-Puchheim, where you change to another train for Hallstatt, going by way of Bad Ischl. The total journey is about 2½ hours, with returns usually running until mid-evening. The Hallstatt station is across the lake from the village, connected by a ferry that meets each train.

Buses leave from the square in front of Salzburg's train station for Bad Ischl, where you change to another bus for Hallstatt. The total journey takes about 3½ hours and runs several times in the morning, with returns until late afternoon.

By car, leave Salzburg on the B-158, heading southeast to Bad Ischl, then take the B-145 and local roads south to Hallstatt. The total distance is 48 miles. A tunnel under the village connects with the parking lot. Don't even think of driving in town.

PRACTICALITIES:

Avoid making this trip between mid-October and the beginning of May, when nearly everything is closed. Train service is reduced between late September and May. Be sure to bring along a light sweater or jacket if you plan to visit the salt mines. Good weather will greatly enhance your enjoyment of this trip. The **Tourist Information Office**, phone (06134) 208, is in the modern Kongresshaus on Seestrasse, south of the Marktplatz. Hallstatt is in the Land of **Oberösterreich**, and has a **population** of about 1,500.

FOOD AND DRINK:

There are many places to eat, all geared to the tourist trade. Some of the better choices are:

Grüner Baum (Marktplatz 104) Known for its fresh lake fish, this small hotel restaurant has a terrace on the water. X: Nov.–Mar. $$

Seewirt (Zauner) (Marktplatz 51) Traditional Austrian cuisine on the main square. $$

Weisses Lamm (Dr.-Morton-Weg 166, near the Marktplatz) Austrian cooking, the best choice in its category. $

SUGGESTED TOUR:

The **Hallstatt Train Station** (1), really just a rustic halt, lies across the dark, brooding, fjord-like **Hallstätter See** from the village. Wedged between the steep mountains of the souhtern Salzkammergut region, this lovely but somewhat mysterious lake sets just the right mood for the strange sights to come. Get an outside seat on the small ferry that carries you in 10 minutes to the **Boat Landing** (2) at ***Hallstatt-Markt**, the historic center of the ancient village. While at the pier you might ask about sightseeing boat trips (*Rundfahrten*). Rentals of electric, pedal, or row boats are available nearby.

Those coming by car or bus should begin by walking downhill from the parking lot to the Marktplatz.

The attractive **Marktplatz** (Market Square) (3) is lined with flower-bedecked inns, shops, and cafés; a great place to stop for a bit of refreshment. In its center is a fountain along with another one of those ubiquitous Trinity columns. At the bottom of the square, facing the lake, stands the Protestant Church, which dates only from the 19th century but whose organ is from 1790. This region of Austria was once a Protestant stronghold.

Continue down Seestrasse to the **Prehistoric Museum** (4), whose displays taken from local excavation sites will give you a better understanding of the salt mines and how they worked in ancient times. The prosperity created by trading in "white gold" is evident from the rich

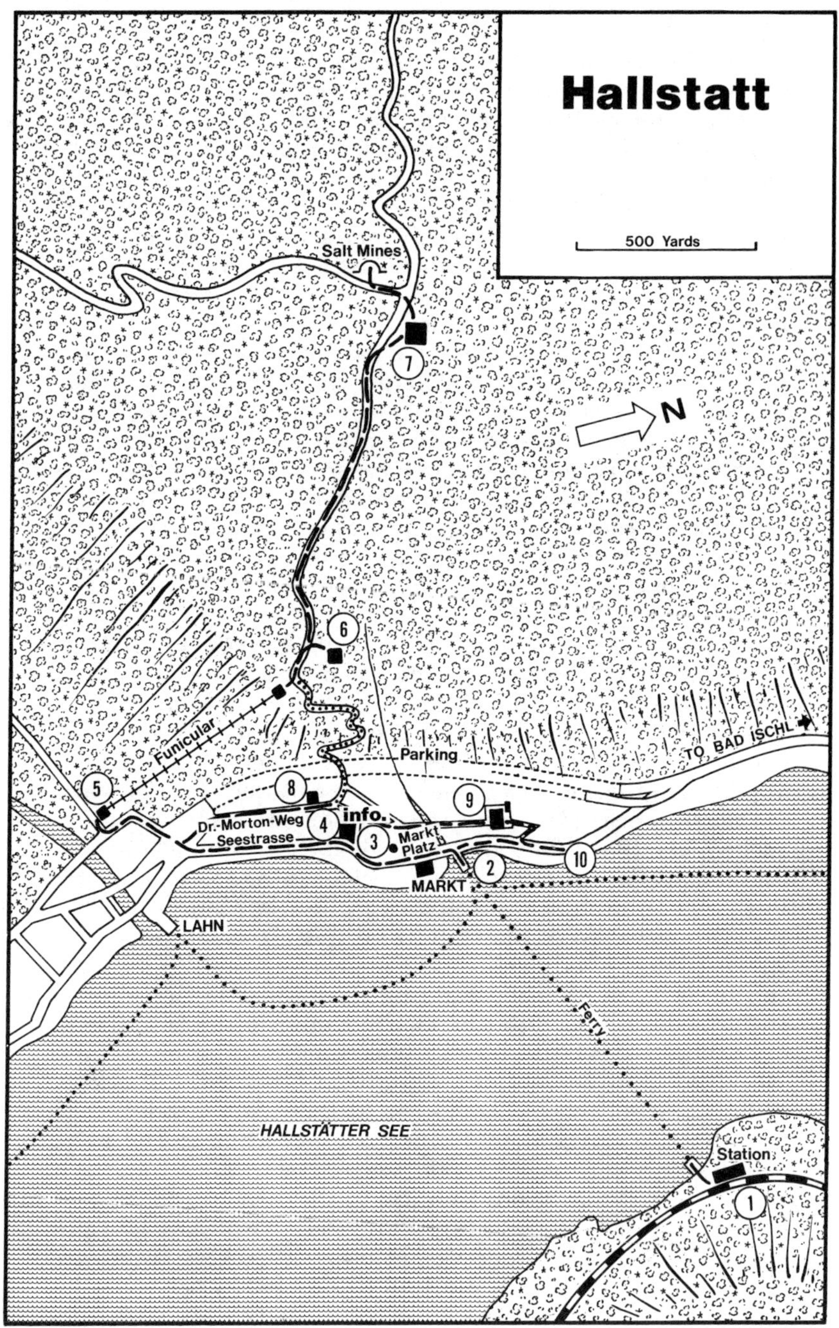
Hallstatt
500 Yards
Salt Mines
N
7
6
Funicular
Parking
TO BAD ISCHL
5
8
9
Dr.-Morton-Weg
4
info.
3
Markt Platz
Seestrasse
MARKT
2
10
LAHN
Ferry
HALLSTÄTTER SEE
Station
1

foreign ornamentations that were apparently common among the miners of 2,500 years ago. The museum is open daily from May through September, from 9:30 a.m. to 6 p.m.; and during April and October daily from 10 a.m. to 4 p.m. Its entrance fee includes a visit to the Folk Museum.

Seestrasse now follows along the edge of the lake, where you can rent small boats by the hour. You will soon come to the settlement of **Lahn** and the lower station of the **funicular** (5) that quickly carries you up the Salzberg mountain. Buy a one-way ticket if you intend to walk down via the scenic Salzbergweg trail.

Close to the upper station is the **Rudolfsturm** (6), a medieval fortification built in 1284 by Duke Albrecht I and named after his father, Rudolf I, who founded the Hapsburg dynasty in 1273. This once defended the salt mines against invasion by the prince-bishops of Salzburg. For many centuries the tower was the residence of the mine managers, and is now a restaurant and outdoor café. With its superb views, this is a good place to stop for refreshments before or after the mine tour. Scattered around the area are the scanty remains of an **Iron-Age burial ground** (*Gräberfeld*), where some 2,000 prehistoric graves have been excavated since 1846.

Follow the path to the main building of the ***Salt Mines** (*Salzbergwerk)* (7), buy a ticket, and join the group for a subterranean tour through the oldest still-operating salt mine in the world. You will be issued protective clothes to put on over your own, including a rather silly cap. A guide leades you along a narrow tunnel to a cavern, from which you descend deep into the earth on a polished wooden slide. The workings of a salt mine are explained around what amounts to an underground lake, where chambers are flooded with water to produce brine. This then flows through pipelines called *Soleleitungen* for about 25 miles to an evaporation plant at Ebensee, a process that has been used since 1607. Prior to that the salt was just hacked out. Climbing to an upper level, you board a little miners' train for a ride back into sunlight. The salt mine tour is offered daily from June through mid-September, from 9:30 a.m. to 4:30 p.m.; and in May and from mid-September until mid-October from 9:30 a.m. to 3 p.m. *It is not suitable for small children, nor for claustrophobic or disabled persons.*

Return to the upper station of the funicular. You can either ride back on this or walk down the Salzbergweg, a delightful trail following a small stream with waterfalls. Whichever way you choose, your next visit should be to the **Heimat Museum** (Folk Museum) (8) on Dr.-Morton-Weg. Housed in the village's oldest secular building, which dates from the 14th century, the displays of folk art and objects of ordinary life in times past trace the history of Hallstatt and its salt mining industry. It is open during the same times as the Prehistoric Museum and uses the same ticket.

The classic view of Hallstatt

Follow the map to the beautifully sited Catholic ***Pfarrkirche** (Parish Church) (9), with its tiny cemetery and charnel house. The church was built in the 15th century and is noted for its ***winged altarpiece** from 1515, its late-Gothic frescoes, and its unusual tower with a pagoda-style roof. The adjacent **cemetery** seems much too small for the village, but overcrowding is avoided by a unique, if somewhat macabre, solution in use since 1600. After being buried for 10 years or so, the bodies are dug up to make room for more. Their skulls are then bleached, and often decorated with pictures and the names of their former owners. Thousands of these are stored in the **Charnel House** (*Beinhaus*) beneath the Chapel of St. Michael next to the graveyard. The door is usually open, so pop in for a look.

A stepped path leads down to the main street. By walking away from the village you will soon come to a spot where the most impressive pictures of Hallstatt are taken. Snap away, then return to the boat landing or parking lot.

A Daytrip from Salzburg

Hallein

It's only a few minutes from Salzburg, but the ancient town of Hallein is a long way removed in the type of experiences it offers. You can ride a cable car up a mountain on the German border, plunge into the bowels of the earth while exploring a salt mine that has been worked since Neolithic times, visit a prehistoric farm before seeing a remarkable museum of Celtic antiquities, and even trace the origin of that most beloved of Christmas carols, "Silent Night."

Hallein owes both its history and its very name to salt, the prefix "hal" being an ancient Celtic word for the mineral. It developed during the Middle Ages as a place where precious salt was extracted from brine coming down from the hillside mines. Some of its medieval past remains intact, while many of the narrow streets are still lined with 17th- and 18th-century houses. Next to the 15th-century parish church is the home and grave of the composer Franz-Xaver Gruber (1787–1863), whose one famous work is still sung by millions the world over.

GETTING THERE:

Trains leave Salzburg several times before 9 a.m. and after 11 a.m. for the short 20-minute ride to Hallein. Some of these are expresses, others second-class locals. Return service operates until late evening.

Buses depart frequently from the square in front of Salzburg's train station for Hallein, a ride of 40 minutes. You can get off at Kornsteinplatz near the tourist office in the center of Hallein, or at the train station. Returns run until mid-evening.

By car, leave Salzburg on the B-160 road past Hellbrunn and continue south on the B-159 to Hallein, a total distance of 11 miles. There is a parking lot by the lower cable car station, or you could drive up to the salt mine instead.

PRACTICALITIES:

Avoid going to Hallein between the beginning of November and the end of April, when virtually everything is closed. Bring along a light sweater or jacket as the salt mine is chilly. The local **Tourist Information Office**, phone (06245) 5394, is in the center of Hallein at Unterer Markt 1. **Bicycles** may be rented at the train station. Hallein is in the Land of **Salzburg,** and has a **population** of about 11,000.

Waiting to enter the Salt Mine

FOOD AND DRINK:

Hohlwegwirt (Salzachtal Bundesstrasse Nord 62, B-160, 3 miles north of Hallein on the west side of the river) Highly regarded for its inventive variations on local cuisine. For reservations phone (06245) 2415. X: Mon. $$$

Gasthof Hager (Salzachtal Bundesstrasse 10, 4 blocks southwest of the train station) Austrian cuisine with a contemporary touch, right in town. X: Wed. $$

SUGGESTED TOUR:

Leave the **train station** (1) and follow the map across the river, passing the tourist office, to the lower station of the **Salzbergbahn Cable Car** (2). You can save some money by purchasing the combination ticket (*Kombitarif.*) that includes the cable car, mine tour, and mining museum; and grants a reduction (*Ermässigung*) at the Celtic Farm and Hallein's Keltenmuseum. The 10-minute ride gently lifts you over a thousand feet above the valley to the attractive resort village of **Bad Dürrnberg**, where the cable car's **upper station** (3) is within a half-mile of the German border. It is also possible to drive there.

Follow the path and street downhill to the ***Salzbergwerk Dürrnberg** (Salt Mine) entrance (4). Here you'll be given a group number. When this is displayed, the group enters a changing room and is issued protective clothing for the subterranean trek. The group then goes to the mine shaft and boards electric wagons, which carry you underground as far as the salt deposits. From there on the tour is by foot, mostly some 3,000 feet beneath Germany as this mine works the same salt deposits as the famous mine in the nearby Bavarian town of Berchtesgaden. There are stops at displays explaining how the salt is extracted, and at dioramas depicting Celtic miners at work in the Dürrnberg mines as early as 700 B.C., along with artifacts of their prehistoric religion. Descending to the lower levels is exciting as you travel rapidly downwards through the mountain on polished wooden slides, visiting an underground salt lake along the way. The visit ends with another electric wagon ride back to daylight. Taking a total of about 1½ hours, the salt mine tour is offered daily from May through September, 9 a.m. to 5 p.m.; and in October from 10 a.m. to 2 p.m. *It is not recommended for small children, nor for disabled or claustrophobic persons.* There is a small **Museum of Salt Mining** (*Bergbaumuseum*) in an old wooden "Solestube" building near the parking lot by the mine entrance.

You might want to take a break at one of the simple **outdoor cafés** near the mine entrance, where you can sit down with a drink or light meal and enjoy the mountain view.

Just above the mine entrance is a reconstructed prehistoric **Celtic Farm Village** (*Kelten-Freilichtschau*) (5) in the style of about 500 B.C., complete with a prince's burial site. A detailed English explanation of everything is available on request. The village is open from May through September, 10 a.m. to 5 p.m.; and in early October from 11 a.m. to 4 p.m.

Continue steeply uphill to the early-17th-century **Pilgrimage Church of Maria Dürrnberg** (6), constructed of the same local pink marble that is still quarried today.

Return to the upper station of the cable car. Adjacent to this is the **Kurgarten** (7), a lovely garden with one of those strange open pavilions called *Gradierwerke* where you march around a covered track breathing salt-air fumes that are supposed to be good for your health. It's free, so try it. There are instructions in English.

Take the cable car back down to Hallein and follow the map through the old part of town to the **Stadtpfarrkirche** (parish church) (8), where Franz-Xaver Gruber, the composer of "Silent Night," was organist for 28 years in the mid-19th century. His organ is still in use, and his house next door still occupied. In front of this is his grave, a national shrine of sorts, and nearby a plaque in English placed there in 1934 by the schoolteachers of Los Angeles, honoring his "Universal Message of Peace and Good Will."

The route on the map takes you through the picturesque *Altstadt* to the ***Keltenmuseum** (9), a superb and quite modern museum of local life among the prehistoric Celts, the salt trade through the ages,

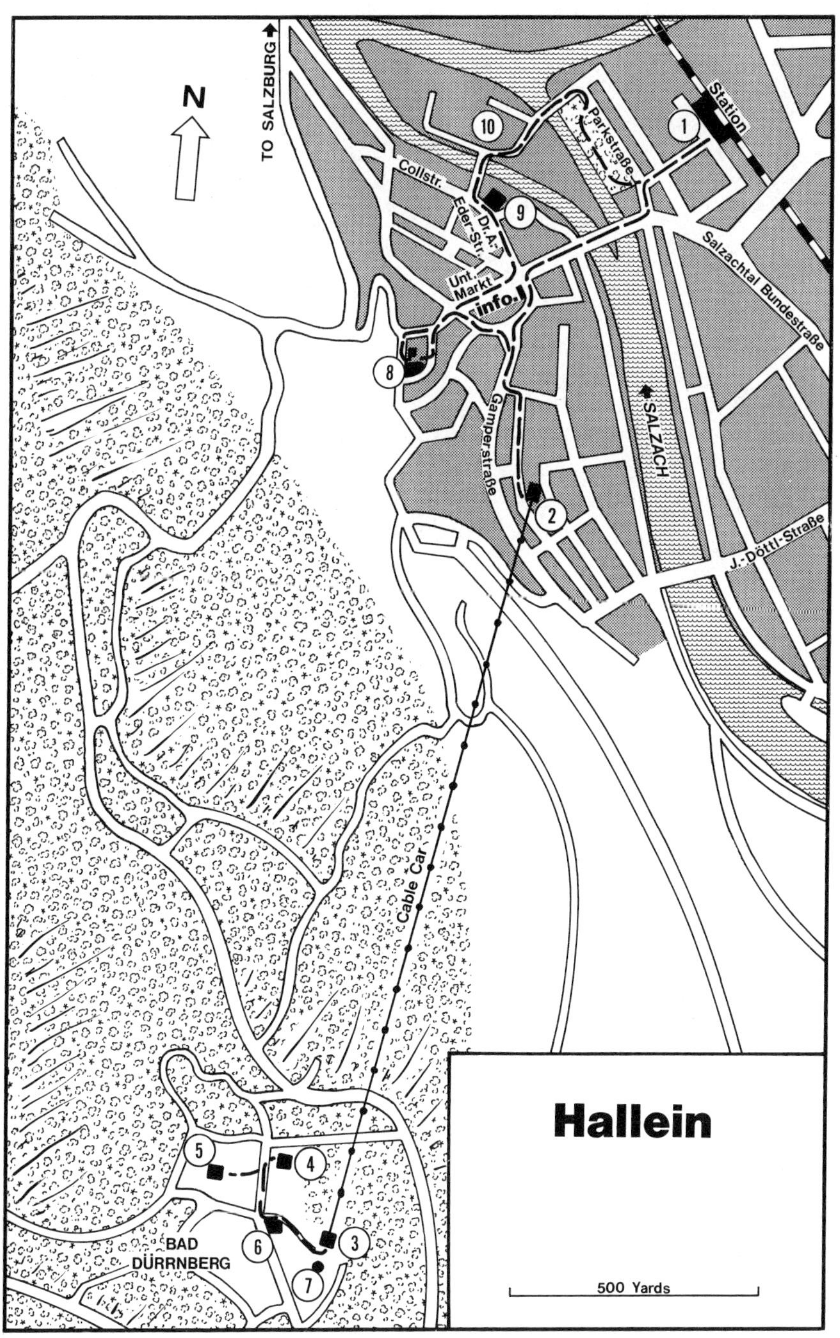
N
TO SALZBURG
Station
Parkstraße
Collstr.
Dr.-A.
Eder-Str.
Unt. Markt
info.
Salzachtal Bundesstraße
SALZACH
Gamperstraße
J.-Döttl-Straße
Cable Car
BAD DÜRRNBERG
1
2
3
4
5
6
7
8
9
10
Hallein
500 Yards

An Iron-Age grave in the Keltenmuseum

regional folklore, and memories of Franz-Xaver Gruber. Among the outstanding exhibits are an Iron-Age grave complete with skeleton, a diorama of prehistoric salt mining techniques, tools, implements, and jewelry; room interiors and costumes from the last century; and personal belongings of F.X. Gruber including the guitar on which "Silent Night" was first played. The Keltenmuseum is open daily from May through September, 9 a.m. to 5 p.m.; and in October from noon until 5 p.m.

The best way back to the station takes you past the **Saline Works** (10), where brine is converted into salt on an island in the Salzach River, and through the Town Park.

Section VIII

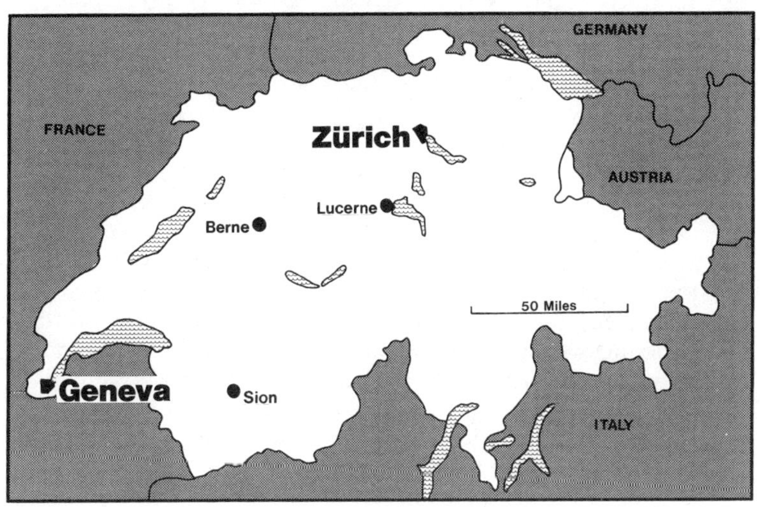

DAYTRIPS IN

SWITZERLAND

• from Zürich • from Geneva

On two-dimensional maps, Switzerland sure looks like a daytripper's paradise. It has all of the right elements—compactness, an immense cultural diversity, great cities, natural splendor, a fascinating history, and a fabulous transportation system supported by national prosperity. It also has the Alps, which both contributes to the pleasures and complicates things a bit. You don't just go through these hills, you must often go far out of your way to get around them.

Still, there are many wonderful daytrips that can be made from the two major cities as well as from other centers. The three trips described here represent just a small sample of what's possible. The first is best taken from Zürich (or Basle), the last from Geneva (or Lausanne), and the middle one from either city or from anywhere else north of the mountains.

GETTING AROUND:

Trains are an easy way to reach the daytrip destinations in this section, which are all served by the **Swiss Federal Railways** (*SBB/CFF/FFS*). In addition, there are numerous private railways, especially in the more mountainous areas. In general, mainline services are fast, clean, comfortable, and operate at hourly intervals. The Swiss have a mania for punctuality, so you can actually set your watch by train arrivals. Most visitors will find the second-class cars to be more than adequate, making first-class travel a waste of money. Except for some luxury international expresses and a very few tourist excursion trains, there is never a need to make reservations. **Bicycles** may be rented at most railway stations, with reductions for ticket holders.

Eurailpasses (see page 18) are accepted for all regular services and some lake steamers. They *do not* cover the most expensive of the private mountain railways. The national passes are more useful as they include rural postal buses and municipal transit systems in addition to trains and boats, but they are not necessarily cheaper. Check the current prices carefully in light of your travel plans. The passes available through travel agents are the **Swiss Pass**, offered for 8 or 15 consecutive days, or for one month; the **Swiss Flexipass** for use on any 3 days within a 15-day period; and the **Swiss Card**, which is not really a pass at all but which entitles you to a round-trip ticket from any Swiss border town or airport to any destination in the country along with a 50% discount on all Swiss railways, buses, and lake steamers for one month. All three plans are available in either first- or second-class versions.

Roads throughout Switzerland are superb, but be sure that your vehicle has the annual road-toll "Vignette" sticker before getting on a superhighway. Cars rented in Switzerland include this; those coming from outside the country can purchase one at the border or at some post offices.

ADVANCE PLANNING INFORMATION:

The **Swiss National Tourist Office** has branches in cities throughout the world, including New York, Chicago, Los Angeles, San Francisco, Toronto, London, Sydney, and Tokyo. The address of the New York office is: 608 Fifth Avenue, New York NY 10020, phone (212) 7575944.

A Daytrip from Zürich

*Lucerne

(Luzern)

Lucerne has been the Swiss tourist town *par excellence* ever since the mid-19th century, when British travelers first discovered the Alps and the Swiss did their best to make them feel at home. Queen Victoria herself came for a month in 1868. Long a favorite retreat for celebrities and the idle rich, Lucerne remains a prime destination for countless visitors from all around the world. Yet, it is no tourist trap. The attractions here are so genuine, the setting so magnificent, that nearly everyone who comes has a great time in spite of the camera-toting hordes.

There was a town here long before tourism was invented, of course. It began around A.D. 750 with the founding of a Benedictine monastery on the site where the Hofkirche now stands. The opening of the St. Gotthard Pass in the 13th century made the village an important trading center on the route between Italy and northern Europe. To free itself of oppressive rule by the Hapsburgs of Austria, Lucerne joined the alliance of the Forest Cantons in 1332, in effect forming the nucleus of the Swiss nation. During the Reformation it remained staunchly Roman Catholic, as it is today.

Lucerne's stunning location, at the foot of the Alps where the Reuss River flows out of Switzerland's most beautiful lake, would alone make it a major attraction. Add to that the well-preserved medieval Old Town by the water's edge, the world-class cultural offerings, and the ease with which lake and mountain excursions can be made, and you have what is surely one of the most desireable destinations in all of Europe. You may very well want to return for a few days to take the classic lake cruise and ascend the Pilatus and Rigi mountains by rack railway or cable car.

GETTING THERE:

Trains depart Zürich's main station hourly for the 50-minute ride to Lucerne (*Luzern*), with return service until late evening.

By car, Lucerne is 35 miles southwest of Zürich via the N-3 and N-14 highways.

PRACTICALITIES:

Lucerne is at its best from April through October, especially when the sun is shining. Most of its sights are open daily, but some small museums close on Mondays in summer as well as a few other days in winter. The **Tourist Information Office**, phone (041) 51-71-71, is at Frankenstrasse 1, just west of the train station. **Bicycles** may be rented at the station, and could be useful for the two side trips described. Lucerne has a **population** of about 63,000 and is in the Canton of **Luzern**. **German** is the predominant language.

FOOD AND DRINK:

Out of a multitude of tourist-oriented restaurants, a few good choices are:

Zum Raben (Kornmarkt 5, behind the Altes Rathaus) Creative, contemporary cuisine in the heart of the Old Town. For reservations phone (041) 51-51-35. $$$

Old Swiss House (Löwenplatz 4, a block south of the Lion Monument) Swiss and Continental cuisine in an Old World setting. $$

Wilden Mann (Bahnhofstrasse 30, a block west of the Jesuit Church) A popular tavern in Lucerne's most charming old inn. $$

Weinhof (Weystrasse 12, a block north of the Hofkirche) A good value for local dishes. X: Sat. $

SUGGESTED TOUR:

Leave the **Bahnhof** (train station) (1) and turn left along the Reuss River, a tributary of the Rhine and the natural outlet for the **Vierwaldstättersee** (Lake of the Four Forest Cantons). Otherwise known as Lake Lucerne, this begins here and meanders on for some 20 miles to the southeast. To your right is the delightful ***Kapellbrücke** (2), one of the oldest covered wooden bridges anywhere. Built in 1333, its walkway is decorated with over a hundred 17th-century paintings depicting local and Swiss history, the town's patron saints, and legendary stories. Attached to the bridge, in mid-stream, is the octagonal stone ***Wasserturm** (Water Tower). The cellar of this former medieval lighthouse was once used as a damp dungeon, and the upper floors as torture chambers. According to an improbable legend, the town's name derives from the *lucerna* (lamp in Latin) that hung from it. Later the town treasury, the tower is now a clubhouse.

Cross the bridge into the Old Town, noting the early-16th-century **Zur Gilgenhaus** with its sharply-pointed round tower on the river's edge to the right. The author Victor Hugo stayed here in 1839. Turn left into **Kapellplatz**, whose 12th-century church is the oldest in Lu-

On the Kapellbrücke

cerne. Continue on to the **Kornmarkt** and the **Altes Rathaus** (Old Town Hall) (3). Completed in 1606, it is in the Italian Renaissance style but with a determinately Swiss roof. The adjacent clock tower dates from around the 14th century. Take a look at the arcades by the river, where a **market** is held on Tuesdays and Saturdays. Just east of the town hall is the **Am Rhyn Haus**, an early-17th-century mansion that now houses an excellent gallery of late works by Picasso. This small museum is open daily from April through October, 10 a.m. to 6 p.m.; and on Fridays through Sundays in winter, from 11 a.m. to noon and 2–5 p.m.

From here it is only a block west to the ***Weinmarkt** (4), the most picturesque square in the Old Town. This was the center of activity in the Middle Ages; a place where trade flourished, pageants were held, and outlaws were hanged. The fountain in its center is a copy of an original from 1481 that represents armed warriors and the patron saint of soldiers. All around the square are beautifully painted old houses, some with their characteristic *erkers,* or oriel windows.

Now follow the map through another lovely square, the **Hirschenplatz**, where the poet Goethe stayed at the Goldener Adler inn during 1779. Continue on through Schwanenplatz to the east side of town and the elegantly-spired ***Hofkirche** (5), the main church of Lucerne. Beginning as the 8th-century monastery from which the town grew, it evolved into a great basilica that was almost totally destroyed by fire on Easter Sunday of 1633. Only the two slim towers survived the conflagration. The late-Renaissance church you see today was completed in the 17th century, and is surrounded on all sides by unusual **arcades** in the Tuscan style containing the tombs of Lucerne's oldest families. Step inside to see the richly-carved choir stalls and pulpit from 1639, as well as the renowned **organ** of 1650 with its 80 stops and 4,950 pipes.

As long as you're in this part of town, you might want to make a **side trip** to what many consider to be Lucerne's stellar attraction. You can either walk about one mile east or take bus number 2 from Haldenstrasse to the fabulous ***Verkehrshaus der Schweiz** (Swiss Transport Museum) (6) on the edge of the lake near the Lido. Now, this may not exactly sound like an exciting prospect; but once you've seen the marvelous old trains, cars, cycles, boats, and various aircraft; the operating model of the St. Gotthard railway across the Alps; and the original NASA space capsules; you'll probably want to spend hours here. In addition, there are sections on telecommunications, navigation, and tourism, as well as the famous **Longines Planetarium** and the **Hans Erni Museum** of contemporary art. The largest institution of its kind in Europe, the Verkehrshaus complex is open daily and has full restaurant and cafeteria facilities.

Back in town, you can turn north on Löwenstrasse to visit three of Lucerne's classic old attractions. The first of these is the **Panorama** (7), an enormous circular painting from 1879 of the sort that was popular in Victorian days. It depicts in stark reality the retreat of the French army into Switzerland during the Franco-Prussian War, and can be viewed daily from mid-March until late October.

A short stroll north of this is the famous **Löwendenkmal** (Lion Monument) (8). This immense sculpture of a dying lion in agony, hewn from the natural rock face in 1821, commemorates the 786 Swiss Guards who perished defending King Louis XVI from the revolutionary mob in the Tuileries of Paris in 1792. In the past, the Swiss had provided mercenaries for the various courts of Europe; today they guard only the Pope in Rome.

The **Gletschergarten** (Glacier Garden) (9), a few steps to the north, is rather interesting. A natural glacial formation dating from the last Ice Age, it features 32 large potholes created by the pressure of melting ice, along with a museum of prehistoric fossils and displays of local history. It is open daily from March through October.

Follow the map to the 14th-century ***Museggmauer** (10), one of the best-preserved fortified town walls in Europe. Nearly 3,000 feet long, it is graced with nine defensive towers and a parapet walk. During the summer season you can climb the **Schirmerturm** near its center for a sweeping **panoramic view** of the town and its lake.

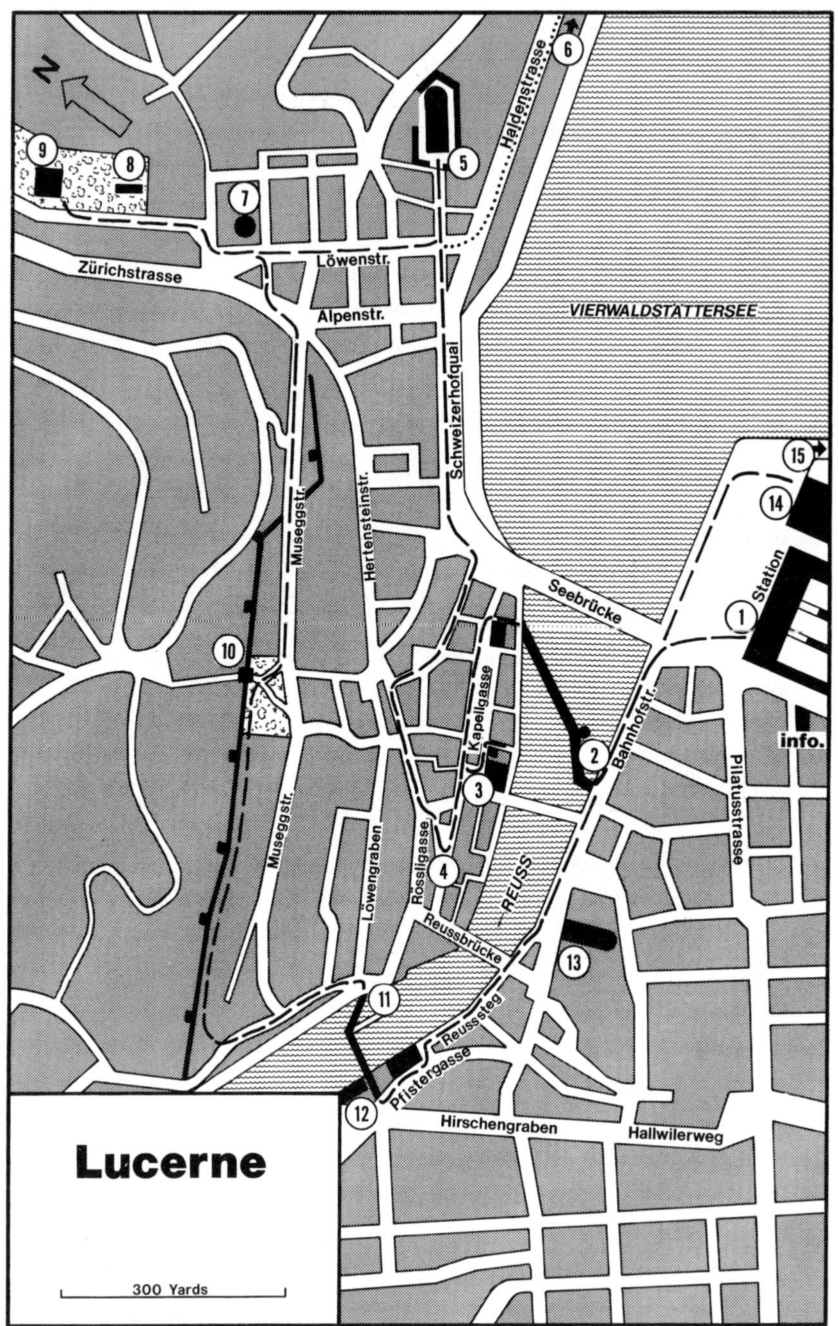
N
Haldenstrasse
Zürichstrasse
Löwenstr.
Alpenstr.
VIERWALDSTÄTTERSEE
Schweizerhofquai
Museggstr.
Hertensteinstr.
Seebrücke
Station
Kapellgasse
Bahnhofstr.
info.
Pilatusstrasse
Museggstr.
Löwengraben
Rössligasse
REUSS
Reussbrücke
Reusssteg
Pfistergasse
Hirschengraben
Hallwilerweg
Lucerne
300 Yards
1
2
3
4
5
6
7
8
9
10
11
12
13
14
15

Continue along the ramparts to their western end, then descend on Brüggligasse to the early-15th-century **Spreuerbrücke** (11), another covered wooden bridge of immense charm. Its walkway is decorated with 44 painted panels depicting the medieval *Totentanz* (Dance of Death) that so obsessed a society often decimated by the bubonic plague. There is a tiny 16th-century chapel in the middle of the bridge, and great views of the Old Town.

Cross the bridge. Immediately to your right is the **Naturmuseum** (12), which features displays on the natural history of central Switzerland, a collection of local archaeological finds, and dioramas on the lives of the early lake people. The museum is open every day except Mondays and major holidays. Turn left into Pfistergasse, passing the new **Historisches Museum** of local history in a 16th-century arsenal at number 24.

Now follow the Reusssteg path along the river to the **Jesuitenkirche** (13), Switzerland's first church in the Jesuit style. Completed in 1677, its simple façade belies the splendid rococo interior of 1750.

Continue along the water's edge past the train station (1) and the boat landing, from which wonderful ***cruises** on the lake are offered, to the **Kunstmuseum** (14). Housed in the imposing Kunst-und Kongresshaus of 1933, this is Lucerne's major art museum and features Swiss paintings from the 15th century to the present, along with works by major European artists. It is open on Tuesdays through Sundays, from 9 a.m. to noon and 2–5 p.m.

If time permits and interest compels, you might want to make a **side trip** to a real music-lover's mecca, the ***Richard Wagner Museum** (15) in the suburb of Tribschen. The great composer lived in the isolated lakeside Victorian house from 1866 until 1872, and it was here that he completed *Die Meistersinger* and *Siegfried,* and worked on the *Götterdämmerung*. On display in a highly evocative setting are some original scores, musical instruments, and personal effects recalling Wagner's life in exile here with Cosima von Bülow, the daughter of Franz Liszt and wife of a famous conductor. Visits may be made from mid-April through mid-October, on Tuesdays through Saturdays from 9 a.m. to noon and 2–6 p.m., and on Sundays from 10:30 a.m. to noon and 2–5 p.m. In winter it is open on Tuesdays, Thursdays, Saturdays, and Sundays. You can reach it by taking bus number 6 or 7 from the train station to the Wartegg stop, followed by a short stroll, or by walking or cycling two miles south along the lakefront.

A Daytrip from Zürich or Geneva

*Berne

(Bern)

Switzerland's capital is also its best-preserved city, and perhaps its most colorful as well. The Middle Ages are still alive in the heart of the Old Town, which is enlivened with numerous gaily-painted Renaissance fountains and some four miles of *Lauben,* those 18th-century stone arcades that make Berne's streets so attractive and yet ever so practical. This is a city to savor for its wealth of distinctive details, and a place to enjoy for its sense of good bourgeois living.

Unlike most old cities, Berne began life quite abruptly—in 1191 to be exact. Duke Berchtold V of Zähringen wanted to build a fortified town in his domain, and the steep promontory rising from a loop in the Aare River seemed the perfect spot from a defensive standpoint. There the city was laid out in a grid pattern with the old castle of Nydegg to protect it. An ancient legend is still told concerning the first animal to be killed by the duke while hunting in the area. It was a bear, hence the name Berne. In truth, a bear emblem was used on the Zähringen coat of arms long before the duke was born, and remains the ubiquitous symbol of the city to this day.

Berne was granted its freedom in 1218 and joined the Swiss Confederation in 1353. In 1405 the city nearly burned to the ground, but was rebuilt in stone. It was not until 1848 that Switzerland finally found it necessary to form a real government, complete with a constitution modeled on the American example. The choice of Berne as the seat of the new Parliament was hardly surprising as it combined a central location with the wealth and staunchly conservative values so long associated with that country.

GETTING THERE:

Trains depart Zürich's main station frequently for the 70-minute ride to Berne, with returns until late evening.

Trains depart Geneva's main station at least hourly for Berne, a ride of about 1¾ hours. Returns run until late evening.

By car from Zürich, Berne is 76 miles to the southwest via the N-1 highway.

By car from Geneva, Berne is 97 miles to the northeast via the N-1, N-9, and N-12 highways.

PRACTICALITIES:

Some of Berne's most important attractions are closed on Mondays or holidays. Colorful outdoor **markets** are held on Tuesdays, Thursdays, and Saturdays around or near the Bärenplatz. The **Tourist Information Office**, phone (031) 22-76-76, is in the train station complex at street level. Berne has a **population** of about 137,000 and is in the Canton of **Berne. German** is the predominant language.

FOOD AND DRINK:

You can fortify yourself for the walking tour by devouring Berne's famous specialty, the *Berner Platte,* which consists of assorted meats and sausages heaped over a mound of potatoes, sauerkraut, or beans. Some restaurant choices are:

Schultheiss Stube (in the Schweizerhof Hotel by the train station) Excellent cuisine in friendly surroundings, regarded as Berne's best. $$$

Grosser Kornhauskeller (Kornhausplatz 18, in the Kornhaus) Enjoy a *Berner Platte* in this big beer cellar under an 18th-century granary. X: Mon. $$

Klötzlikeller (Gerechtigkeitsgasse 62, near the Justice Fountain) Berne's oldest wine tavern has been in this cellar for over three centuries. Light meals are served. X: Sun. $

Zu Webern (Gerechtigkeitsgasse 68, near the Justice Fountain) An inexpensive place for typical Swiss dishes. X: Sun., Mon. $

SUGGESTED TOUR:

Berne's underground **main train station** (1) is part of a vast, modern communications and shopping complex. Rather than riding the first escalator up to street level, follow the passage to the right past ruins of the **Christoffelturm**, a 14th-century town gate now preserved as part of the station. The second escalator from the end takes you up to the **Heiliggeistkirche** (Church of the Holy Ghost) (2), a Protestant Baroque masterpiece completed in 1729.

Berne is famous for its four miles of arcades, called *Lauben,* which have been sensibly sheltering pedestrians from the elements since at least the 18th century. These start here and line most of the streets in the Old Town. Follow Spitalgasse past the Piper Fountain of 1546 to the Käfigturm (3), a prison tower erected in 1641 on the site of a 13th-century town gate. It remained in use as a jail until 1897 and today decorates the adjacent Bärenplatz, a lively square where outdoor markets are held.

Continue on the busy **Marktgasse**, a pedestrian street filled with attractive shops in old arcaded buildings. In its center are two more

The Schützenbrunnen in the Marktgasse

16th-century fountains, the *Anna Seilerbrunnen* and the *Schützenbrunnen,* the latter depicting a marksman in armor standing over an armed bear shooting a gun. At the next square, to the left, is the strangely demented **Kindlifresserbrunnen** (Ogre Fountain), on which a figure of a giant devours little children, a feast he has been enjoying since 1544.

The intersection is dominated by the ***Zytgloggeturm** (Clock Tower) (4), a Berne landmark first built around 1191 and later reconstructed. Its 16th-century clock mechanism springs into action at four minutes before each hour, providing a splendid show of marching bears and other creatures on the side facing Kramgasse. A tour of its inner workings is offered at 4:30 p.m. daily from May through October. Ask at the tourist office for details.

While on the subject of time and motion, you might want to visit the nearby **Albert Einstein Museum** (5), located upstairs at Kramgasse 49. This is where the great physicist lived from 1903 until 1905, and where he developed his Special Theory of Relativity leading to the famous equation $E = mc^2$, the basis of atomic energy. You can put on your thinking cap there from Tuesdays through Fridays, 10 a.m. to 5 p.m.; and on Saturdays from 10 a.m. to 4 p.m.

The street you're on, the ***Kramgasse**, has been wonderfully preserved, with many restored houses dating from the 16th to the 18th centuries. Take a look at the picturesque oriel windows and corner turrets on some of them. There are three old fountains in the center of the street, each worth examining.

Continue straight ahead on the Gerechtigkeitsgasse, an equally attractive pedestrian street. In its center is a fountain called the **Gerechtigkeitsbrunnen**, on which a sword-wielding statue of Justice stands over the severed heads of the Pope, an emperor, a sultan, and for some obscure reason, the mayor of Berne.

Cross the Nydegg Bridge, with its spectacular **views** up and down the Aare River, to the **Bärengraben** (Bear Pits) (6). Live bears, the mascots of Berne, have been kept in captivity since the 15th century, and have occupied this particular spot since 1857. Bear food (*Bärenfutter*) is sold should you care to bribe them into performing cute tricks.

Recross the bridge and turn down Junkerngasse, a street lined with arcades and fine patrician homes. The ***Munster** (7), a magnificent Protestant church of cathedral-like proportions, was begun in 1421 but not completed until 1893. The ***tympanum** over its main doorway depicts the Last Judgement with over 200 figures carved in stone. Relatively few of its interior furnishings survived the Reformation, although some of the stained-glass windows as well as the 16th-century choir stalls did and are quite attractive. You can climb to the top of its **tower** for a wonderful ***panorama** of the Old Town and a glimpse of the Bernese Alps in the distance. Another great view can be had by simply strolling out onto the **terrace** adjacent to the church.

Continue along Münstergasse to Casinoplatz and turn left, crossing the Kirchenfeldbrücke, a bridge with excellent outlooks from both sides. At its far end is the **Schweizerisches Alpines Museum** (Swiss Alpine Museum) (8), a must-see if you have any interest in mountains, whether to climb or just admire them. Not only are there the expected maps, skis, and alpenstocks; but also displays of how the mountain people live. The museum is open on Tuesdays through Sundays from 10 a.m. to 5 p.m., and on Mondays from 2–5 p.m. In winter it closes between noon and 2 p.m.

Just across Helvetiaplatz stands the **Bernisches Historisches Museum** (9), a pseudo-Gothic castle containing artifacts of regional history along with folk art, costumes, tapestries, and room settings. It is open on Tuesdays through Sundays from 10 a.m. to 5 p.m.; except that during the winter it is open daily but closed from noon to 2 p.m..

Retrace your steps across the bridge and turn left through a little park onto the Bundesterrace, an open platform with fine views of the river. A right turn through an archway leads to the Bundesplatz and the front entrance of the massive **Bundeshaus** (10), the home of the **Swiss Parliament**. Free ***guided tours** are given daily except on holidays or when Parliament is in session. These begin at 9, 10, and 11

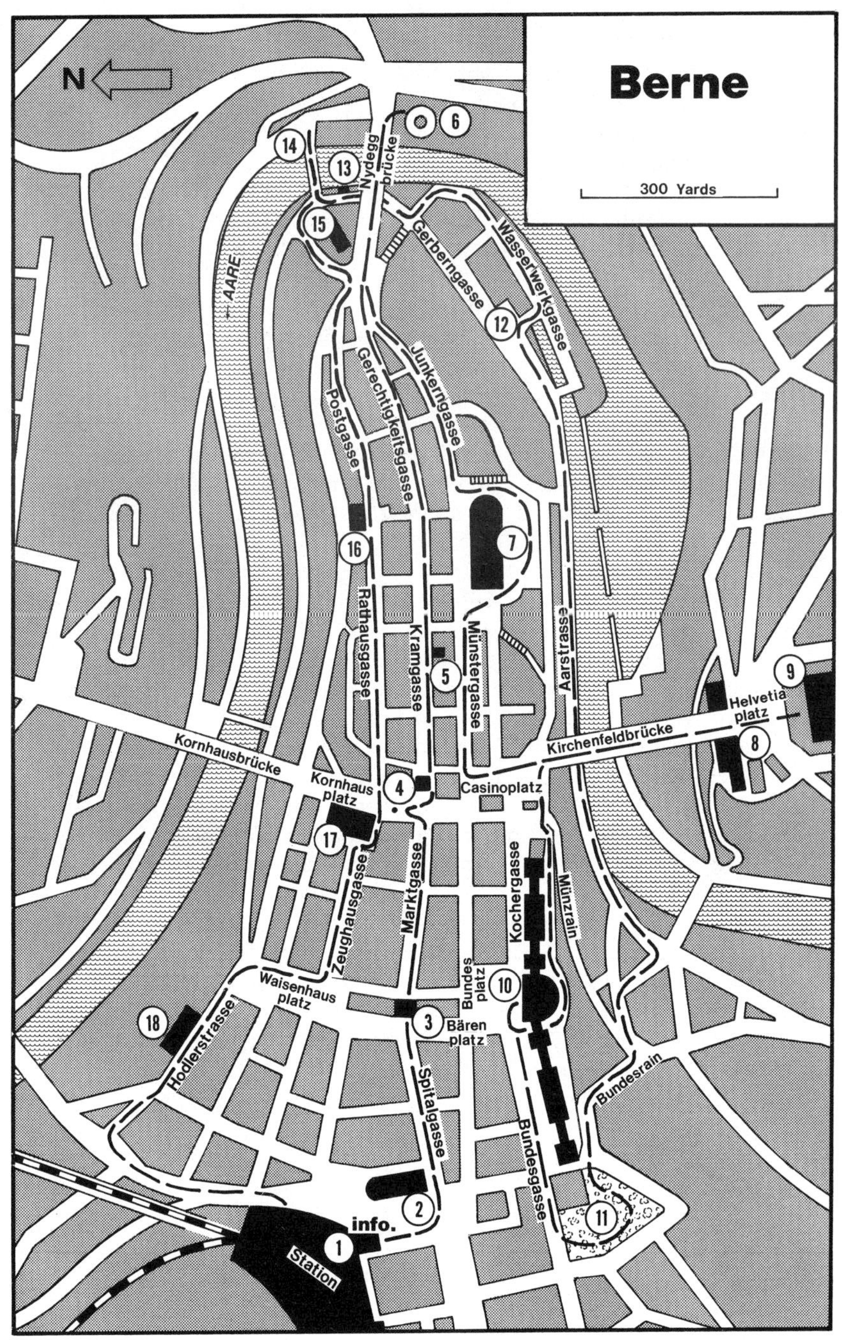

Berne
300 Yards
N
AARE
Nydegg brücke
Gerberngasse
Wasserwerkgasse
Junkerngasse
Gerechtigkeitsgasse
Postgasse
Rathausgasse
Kramgasse
Münstergasse
Aarstrasse
Kornhausbrücke
Kirchenfeldbrücke
Helvetia platz
Kornhaus platz
Casinoplatz
Zeughausgasse
Marktgasse
Kochergasse
Münzrain
Waisenhaus platz
Bundes platz
Bären platz
Hodlerstrasse
Spitalgasse
Bundesgasse
Bundesrain
info.
Station
1
2
3
4
5
6
7
8
9
10
11
12
13
14
15
16
17
18

a.m., and 2, 3, and 4 p.m.; with no 4 p.m. tour on Sundays. The multilingual guide explains the interesting workings of Swiss democracy as you pass through the chambers and sit at delegate's desks during the 45-minute visit.

You have now just about come full circle on the walking tour, but if you have both time and energy left you might want to continue on to some sights overlooked by most tourists. To do this, follow the map to the **Kleine Schanze** (11), a 17th-century bastion that is now a park. The striking monument near its center commemorates the founding of the Universal Postal Union, an international regulatory agency, here in 1875. Take the steps down to the Bundesrain and follow the map along the river, passing a weir that channels some of the water toward a group of old mills. At **Mühlenplatz** (12) make a right turn into the early industrial section, then a left on Wasserwerkgasse. Continue under the Nydegg Bridge. At number 5 Mattenenge you will find steps leading under a house to the **Ländtetor** (13), the remains of a 13th-century landing stage for river barges.

Cross the **Untertorbrücke** (14), a bridge completed in 1489. At its far end is the 13th-century Felsenburg, once a gate and now a residence. Return to Läuferplatz, noting its 16th-century Messenger Fountain. Now climb the Nydeggstalden to the **Nydeggkirche** (15), a 14th-century church built on the foundation wall of the ancient Nydegg fortress that was destroyed around 1270.

Postgasse leads to the **Rathaus** (Town Hall) (16) of 1406, a well-restored building with an unusual exterior staircase. Continue along Rathausgasse to the **Kornhaus** (17), an early-18th-century granary that houses a small museum and, in the basement, a popular restaurant.

Now follow the map to Berne's famous ***Kunstmuseum** (18), easily one of the finest art museums in Switzerland. Its collections cover the span of European painting, especially of the 19th and 20th centuries, with an emphasis on Swiss works. Several rooms are devoted to the talents of native-son Paul Klee (1879–1940). The museum is open on Tuesdays from 10 a.m. to 9 p.m., and on Wednesdays through Sundays from 10 a.m. to 5 p.m. It is closed on Mondays. From here it is only a short walk back to the train station.

A Daytrip from Geneva

Sion

Visitors traveling through Switzerland's lovely Rhône Valley are often astonished by the sudden sight of two fairy-tale castles perched precariously atop twin hills. What these dreamlike bastions have been guarding for centuries is the two-thousand-year-old town of Sion, one of the great medieval treasures of the Alps. Little known to overseas tourists, the capital of the Valais and the first Helvetian town to adopt Christianity is a real gem.

The two peaks that rise so dramatically from the town's center were originally settled by Celtic tribes. When the Romans came they called the place *Sedunum*. Sion, known in German as *Sitten,* was the seat of a bishopric ever since the 4th century. At the beginning of the 11th century the Church was granted secular as well as sacred authority over the valley, an arrangement that lasted, in part, as late as the 19th century. Happily, the bishops were benevolent rulers throughout this period, with the result that the town has remained staunchly loyal to the Roman Catholic Church ever since. Sion today is a prosperous, lively regional center; one that is fun to explore and one in which reminders of the past live on for future generations to enjoy.

GETTING THERE:

Trains, mostly of the EC or IC class, depart Geneva's main station at least hourly for the 2-hour ride to Sion, with return service until late evening.

By car, Sion is 98 miles east of Geneva via the N-1 to Lausanne followed by the N-9.

PRACTICALITIES:

Avoid coming to Sion on a Monday, when several of its attractions are closed. One or two minor sights are closed on weekends and holidays instead. Sion is at its best between late spring and early fall, and requires good weather to enjoy. The walking tour involves a **stiff uphill climb** to the castles, which may be difficult for some. The local **Tourist Information Office**, phone (027) 22-85-86, is at 3 Place de la Planta, corner of Rue de Lausanne. Sion has a **population** of about 25,000 and is in the Canton of **Valais**. **French** is the predominant language.

FOOD AND DRINK:

Sion's most famous dish is *raclette,* a hearty combination of hot cheese melted over boiled potatoes. It goes well with the local white wine, *Fendant.* A few restaurant choices are:

L'Enclos de Valère (Rue des Châteaux by the Valère hill) A garden restaurant with French cuisine. Reservations advised, phone (027) 23-32-30. $$$

La Pergola (116 Rue de Lausanne, near the tourist office) Italian specialities in a small hotel. $

SUGGESTED TOUR:

Leaving the **train station** *(Gare)* (1), use the underground passageway to reach Avenue de la Gare and follow this to Rue de Lausanne. Make a right turn here for one block, then go left onto Rue de la Tour. Stroll through the park on your left and follow the map to the 12th-century **Tour des Sorciers** (Witches' Tower) (2), all that remains of the medieval town walls.

Retrace your steps on Rue de la Tour and continue on to the **Cathedral of Notre-Dame-du-Glarier** (3). Largely rebuilt in the Gothic style during the 15th century, it has a striking 12th-century Romanesque ***tower**. The most noted interior feature is the 16th-century **triptych** of the Tree of Jesse behind the high altar. Opposite the cathedral is the **Eglise de Saint-Théodule**, a church built during the rule of Cardinal Mathieu Schiner, a local *Valaisan* who in the 16th century attempted to overcome French influence and create a powerful state ranging from Swabia to Milan. He failed in this endeavor and was defeated by King Francois I of France at the Battle of Marignano just outside Milan. Schiner's ideas remained alive, however, and ultimately helped lead to the present Swiss Confederation.

Walk a few steps down Rue St.-Théodule and turn left onto Rue de Conthey. Just before Grand Pont there is an arcade opening to the right, leading to an inner courtyard and the **Maison Supersaxo** (4). This glorious mansion was built in 1505 by the wealthy Jörg auf der Flüe who, changing his name to Georgius Supersaxo, became a rival of the powerful Cardinal Schiner. The sumptuous interior with its remarkable ***carved ceiling** may be visited by climbing the staircase on any day except weekends and holidays, from 10 a.m. to noon and 2–5 p.m.

The arcade exits onto Rue de Lausanne. Turn left and, passing Grand Pont, take the narrow Ruelle de la Lombardie passageway until you get to a tiny fountain. Here turn left and climb the steps leading to Rue du Vieux College. You are now in the heart of the colorful old Lombardie district, an area that still echoes the Middle Ages. Follow around to **Place de la Théâtre** (5) and continue down steps to Rue des

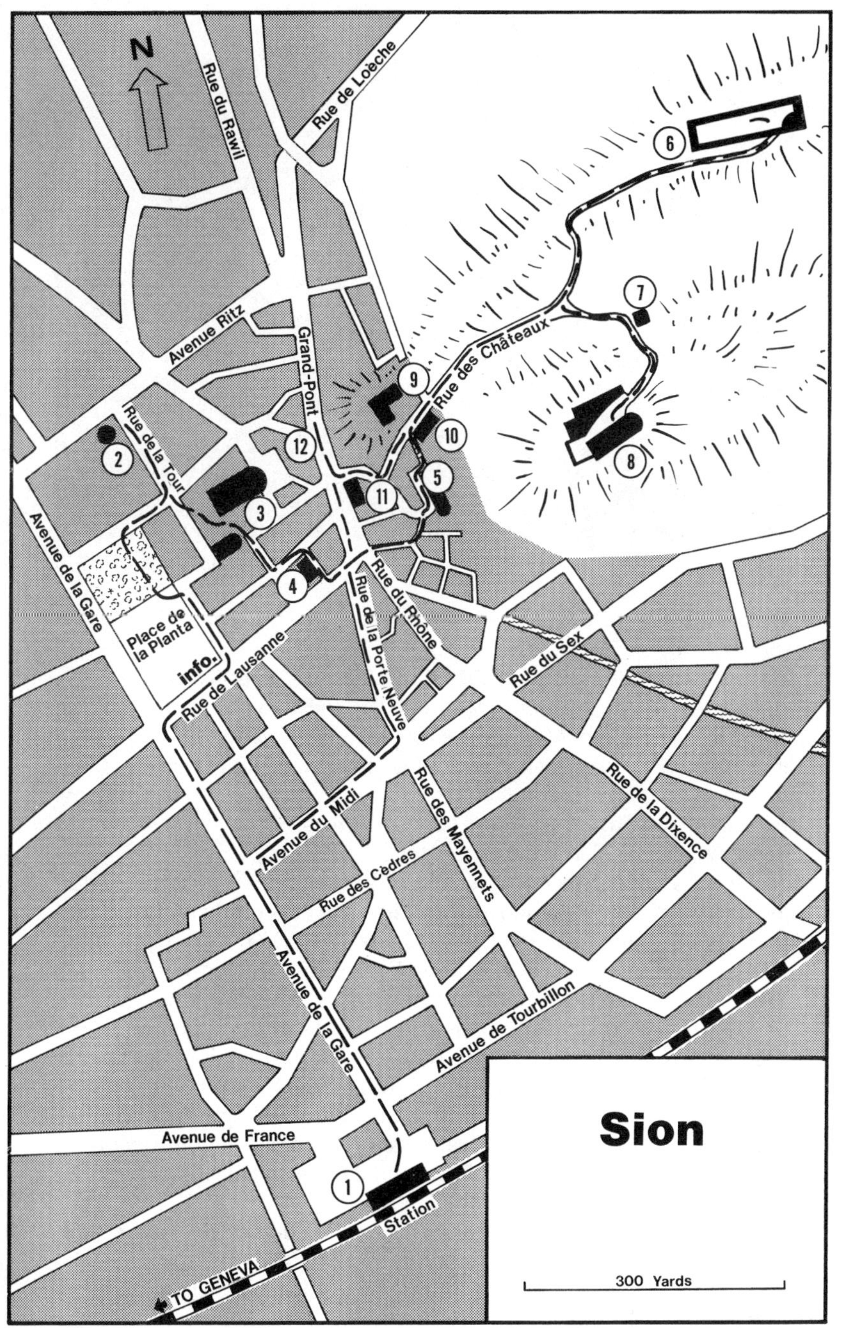
N
Rue du Rawil
Rue de Loèche
Avenue Ritz
Grand-Pont
Rue des Châteaux
Rue de la Tour
Avenue de la Gare
Place de la Planta
info.
Rue de Lausanne
Rue de la Porte Neuve
Rue du Rhône
Rue du Sex
Rue de la Dixence
Avenue du Midi
Rue des Mayennets
Rue des Cèdres
Avenue de Tourbillon
Avenue de la Gare
Avenue de France
Station
TO GENEVA
Sion
300 Yards
1
2
3
4
5
6
7
8
9
10
11
12

Château de Tourbillon

Châteaux. A right turn here will take you uphill to a saddle between the two hills.

The 13th-century **Château de Tourbillon** (6), a castle that is now in ruins, caps the higher peak. Although the climb to it is very steep, the effort is worthwhile. Most of the fortress, formerly the bishop's summer residence, was destroyed by fire in 1788. What remains is fascinating to explore, particularly the tower and the still-extant chapel with its 15th-century frescoes. Needless to say, the ***view** from this height is spectacular.

Sion's stellar attraction, the **Hill of Valère,** rises opposite Tourbillon and is fortunately much lower. Climb the easy gradient, going past the Romanesque **Tous-les-Saints Chapel** of 1325 (7). Above it is the fortress-church of ***Notre-Dame-de-Valère** (8), erected between the 11th and 15th centuries. Once a cathedral, its primitive interior is one of the most unusual in Europe. The famous ***organ** was built in the 1380s and remains in use to this day—the oldest functioning organ in the world. As you wander about you will discover many other strange things about the Valère, such as the 15th-century mill right in the church, next to the nave, as well as an arsenal where ammunition was made. This was, after all, both a cathedral and a defensive bastion; the bishops doubling as the rulers of the land.

Just opposite the church entrance is the ***Musée de Valère** (Museum) in a series of fortress buildings running down the hill. Enter the complex to see the outstanding displays of religious objects, furniture, costumes, and folkloric items relating to local life in past centu-

Notre-Dame-de-Valère

ries. Both the church and the museum are open on Tuesdays through Sundays, from 10 a.m. to noon and 2–5 p.m.

Exit at the bottom of the complex and return to Rue des Châteaux, following it back into town. At the intersection of Rue du Tunnel you will find the **Musée Cantonal des Beaux-Arts** (Cantonal Art Museum) (9), housed in the former **Château de la Majorie**, once a residence for church officials. The collections here are mostly concerned with works by artists associated with the Valais region, most notably those by Raphael Ritz (1829–94). Just across the street is the **Musée d'Archéologie** (10), an outstanding small gallery of local archaeological finds and other artifacts from ancient times. Both museums are open on Tuesdays through Sundays, from 10 a.m. to noon and 2–5 p.m.

Continue down to Grand Pont. On the corner stands the **Hôtel de Ville** (Town Hall) (11), a 17th-century structure with a splendid astronomical clock, elaborately carved doors and, inside the entrance, the oldest Christian inscription in Switzerland, dating from as far back as A.D. 377. You can usually step inside to see this on weekday mornings and afternoons.

A short stroll up Grand Pont takes you past a lovely **fountain** (12) and some interesting façades. The walking tour is now over, but you might want to poke around the many little alleyways that dart off in all directions, particularly those in the Lombardie quarter. On the other hand, there's a lot to be said for merely plopping down at one of the attractive outdoor cafés and relaxing over a glass of the local wine.

Section IX

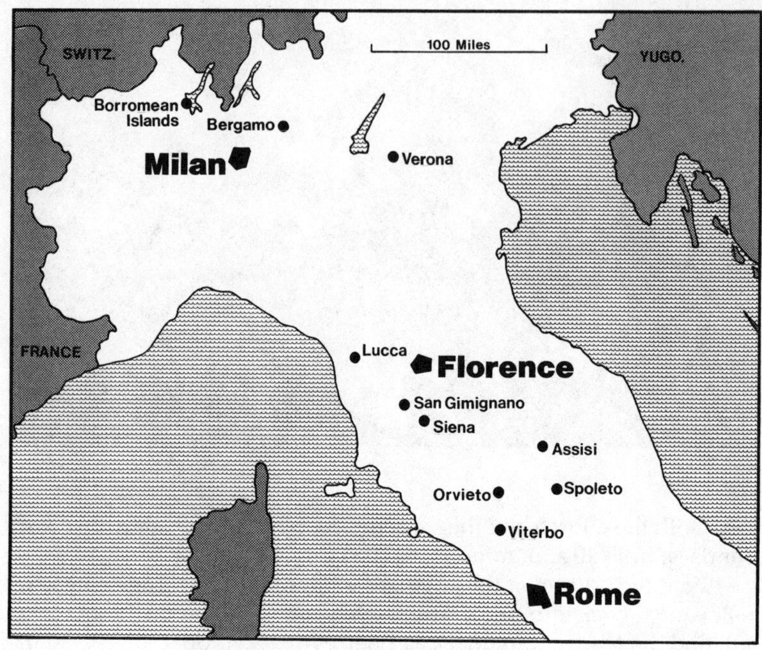

DAYTRIPS IN

ITALY

• from Rome • from Florence • from Milan

At first glance, Italy may not seem to be the most promising place for the daytrip approach to travel. Its long, thin shape and generally mountainous terrain—combined with a somewhat underdeveloped transportation system—makes most trips into the hinterland slower and more problematic than is usually the case north of the Alps. Nevertheless, Italy does offer a few exceptional opportunities for easy one-day excursions from its major cities. This section takes a close look at four such trips that can be made from Rome, three from Florence, and another three from Milan.

The range of attractions covered in these daytrips include such treats as ancient settlements that predate even the Romans, five intriguing hill towns, a few under-discovered gems including Lucca and Bergamo, famous places such as Siena and Verona, one of the world's major centers of pilgrimage, and a gorgeous lake nestled in the snow-capped Alps.

Many additional daytrip destinations are thoroughly described in our companion guidebook, ***Daytrips in Italy***, which follows the same format and features 40 one-day adventures from Rome, Florence, Milan, Venice, and Naples—including walking tours of the base cities themselves.

GETTING AROUND:

Trains are a satisfactory way of reaching all of the daytrip destinations in this section, although in a few cases **buses** are preferable. The **Italian State Railways** *(FS)* network has been noticeably improved in recent years with new equipment, smoother tracks, and better on-time performance. Happily, its fares remain low. The fastest trains are the new first-class-only **ETR 450** *Pendolino* types, for which a supplementary charge is made that includes reservations and a meal. Other luxury trains are those of the **EC** and **IC** classes, both charging premium fares unless you have a railpass. These usually carry second- as well as first-class cars, and sometimes require reservations. Ordinary expresses are designated **EXPR** *(Espresso),* semi-expresses **DIR** *(Diretto),* and slow locals **LOCALE** *(Accelerato).*

Eurailpasses (see page 18) are accepted by the Italian State Railways, but if you're visiting only Italy you should consider these economical alternatives instead: The **BTLC Italian Railpass** is valid for unlimited travel on the Italian State Railways for periods of 8, 15, 21, or 30 consecutive days and is sold in both first- and second-class versions, for either adults or children. The **Italy Flexi Railcard** provides the same benefits at a slightly higher per-day cost on any 4 days in a 9-day period, on any 8 days in a 21-day period, or on any 12 days in a 30-day period. As with most railpasses, they should be purchased before going to Europe. Ask your travel agent.

Roads in Italy are excellent, especially the **Autostrade** superhighways with their high speeds and high tolls. When shared by three or more people, driving might be as inexpensive as train travel, and allows greater flexibility.

ADVANCE PLANNING INFORMATION:

The **Italian Government Tourist Office** has branches throughout the world, including New York, Chicago, San Francisco, Montreal, Tokyo, and London. The address of their New York office is: 630 Fifth Avenue, New York NY 10111, phone (212) 245-4822.

A Daytrip from Rome

Viterbo

Many towns in Italy claim to be the most perfectly preserved holdover from the Middle Ages, but in the area near Rome that honor almost surely belongs to Viterbo. Calling itself the "City of the Popes" because no fewer than five pontiffs lived there during the 13th century, the town has kept its splendid old buildings and highly atmospheric medieval quarter almost totally intact.

Viterbo began as a settlement of the ancient Etruscans, those enigmatic people about whom so little is known, and was later conquered by the Romans. Its great period of development was during the Middle Ages, when it rivaled Rome itself. After the papacy moved to Avignon the town declined, ultimately becoming the minor provincial capital that it remains today.

GETTING THERE:

Trains depart Rome's Termini Station several times in the morning for Orte, where you change to a local for Viterbo's Porta Fiorentina Station. The total trip takes about 2 hours. There is also direct railcar service from Rome's San Pietro Station, just south of the Vatican, which also takes about 2 hours. Return service on both routes operates until mid-evening.

By car, take the Via Cassia (Route S-2) north from Rome to Viterbo, a distance of 50 miles.

PRACTICALITIES:

Some sights in Viterbo are closed on Sundays, Mondays, and major holidays. Good weather will make this trip more enjoyable. The local **Tourist Information Office,** phone (0761) 234-776, is at Piazza Verdi 4; while the provincial office, phone (0761) 234-795, is at Piazza dei Caduti 16, 2 blocks northwest of Piazza del Plebiscito. Viterbo is in the region of **Latium** and has a **population** of about 59,000.

FOOD AND DRINK:

Viterbo has essentially the same cuisine as Rome. The local wine is the famous *Est! Est!! Est!!!,* a slightly sweet white from nearby Montefiascone. Some good restaurant choices are:

In the San Pellegrino district

La Zaffera (Piazza San Carluccio, at the west end of Via San Pellegrino) In the medieval San Pellegrino quarter, with a garden. X: Mon. $$$

Scaletta (Via Marconi 45, 2 blocks southwest of Pza. Verdi) An old favorite in a commercial district. X: Mon. $$

Da Ciro (Via Cardinale La fontaine 74, 2 blocks southwest of the Fontana Grande) A convenient location on the north side of the San Pellegrino quarter. X: Fri. $$

Trattoria Tre Re (Via Macel Gattesco 3, 2 blocks north of Pza. del Plebiscito) Very popular with local businessmen. X: Thurs. $

SUGGESTED TOUR:

Leave the **Porta Fiorentina train station** (1) and follow the map through a gate in the well-preserved medieval walls to **Piazza Verdi** (2), where the local tourist office is located. Continue on through a succession of narrow streets to the ***Museo Civico** (Municipal Museum) (3), which you should see before its afternoon closing. Housed in a former convent around an elegant 13th-century cloister, the museum is noted for its wonderful collection of **Etruscan objects** and sarcophagi from nearby digs. Some of these, dating from as far back as the 7th century B.C., are inscribed in the strange alphabet of the still-undeciphered Etruscan language. There are also early Roman works on display. The art gallery upstairs has among its treasures a magnificent **Pietà* and a *Flagellation,* both by the 16th-century Roman painter Sabastiano del Piombo, as well as the *Incredulity of St. Thomas* by Salvator Rosa, a romantic artist of the 17th century. Visits may be made from 8 a.m. to 1:30 p.m., daily except on holidays. During the summer season it is also open from 3:30 to 6 or 7:30 p.m., except on Sundays and holidays.

While at the museum, be sure to visit the adjacent **Church of Santa Maria della Verità**. First built in the 12th century and later altered, it is beautifully decorated with 15th-century frescoes by Lorenzo da Viterbo, restored after suffering bomb damage during World War II. The church is closed between noon and 3 p.m.

The route now leads through the Porta Romana gate, rebuilt in 1653, to the **Fontana Grande** (4). Easily the most beautiful fountain in Viterbo, it has been merrily bubbling away since the 13th century. A left turn on Via delle Fabbriche brings you into the unspoiled San Pellegrino district, where time has stood still since the Middle Ages.

The utterly delightful ***Piazza San Pellegrino** (5) is one of the most picturesque little squares in Italy. The stark Alesssandri Tower beyond its western end dates from the 13th century, as do many of the unusual structures around it.

Pick your way through the maze and continue on past the shady Piazza della Morte, crossing the historic Ponte del Duomo bridge with its scanty Etruscan remains. Piazza San Lorenzo, another splendid medieval square, was built on the site of the ancient Etruscan acropolis, some of whose stones are incorporated in surrounding houses. At the western end of this is the 12th-century **Duomo** (Cathedral) (6), with a later façade and a 14th-century bell tower. The restored Romanesque interior has some interesting columns, floor mosaics, and remnants of 12th-century frescoes.

Viterbo's most impressive piece of architecture is undoubtedly the ***Palazzo Papale** (Papal Palace) (7), built in the 13th century as a home for the popes who stayed there to avoid troubles in Rome. Its Gothic loggia, outside staircase, massive arches, and battlements make a dramatic sight against the clear Italian sky. A conclave of cardinals, meeting here in 1268 to elect a new pope, was unable to reach a decision for over two years. Tired of the procrastination, the local ruler first locked them in, then removed the roof, and finally cut off the food supply. Hunger did the trick, and soon a new pope, Gregory X, was elected. From this incident came the rules by which popes are elected

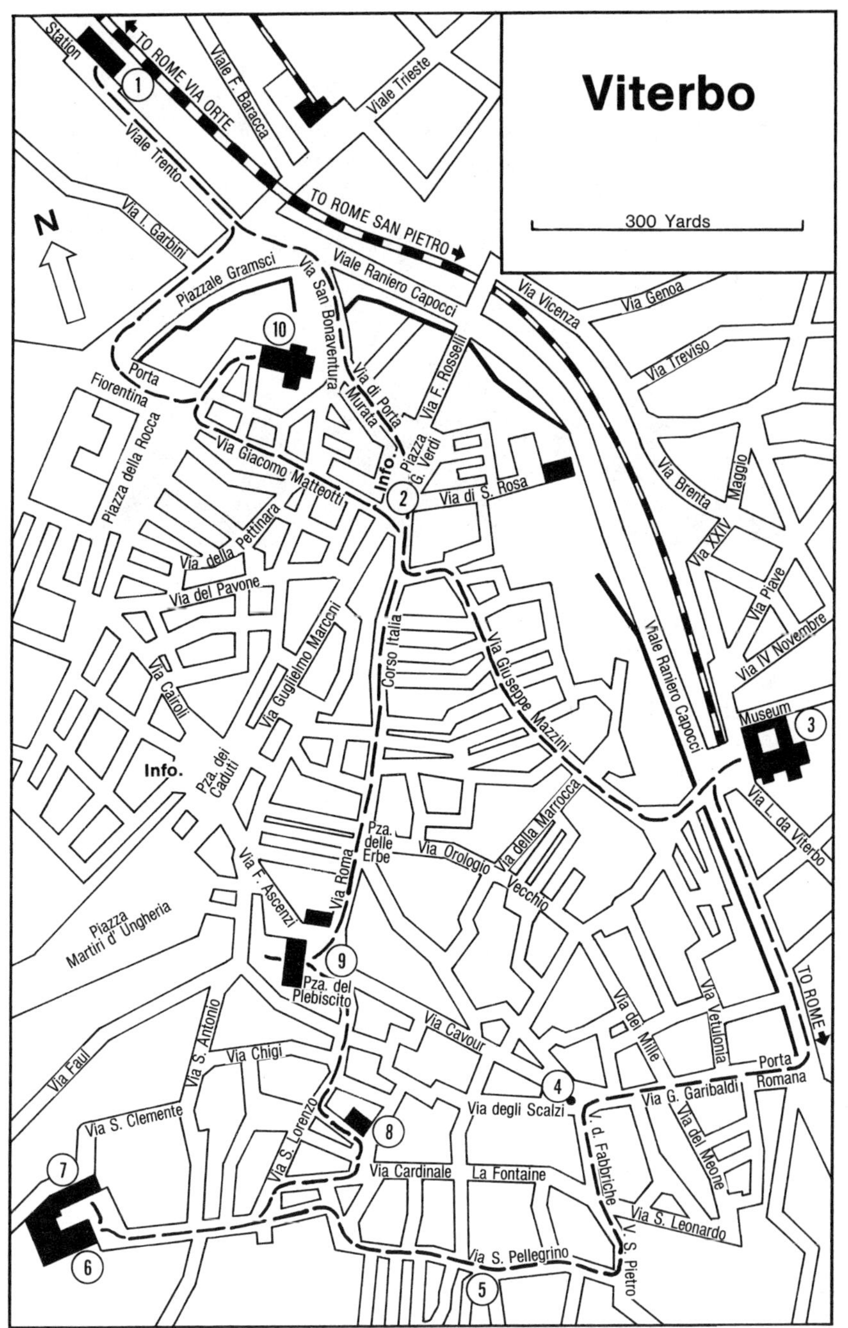
Viterbo
300 Yards
N
Station
TO ROME VIA ORTE
TO ROME SAN PIETRO
TO ROME
Viale F. Baracca
Viale Trieste
Viale Trento
Via I. Garbini
Piazzale Gramsci
Via San Bonaventura
Viale Raniero Capocci
Via Vicenza
Via Genoa
Via Treviso
Porta Fiorentina
Via di Porta Murata
Via F. Rosselli
Piazza della Rocca
Via Giacomo Matteotti
Info.
Piazza G. Verdi
Via di S. Rosa
Via Brenta
Via XXIV Maggio
Via della Pettinara
Via del Pavone
Via Piave
Via IV Novembre
Via Guglielmo Marconi
Corso Italia
Via Giuseppe Mazzini
Viale Raniero Capocci
Via Cairoli
Museum
Info.
Pza. dei Caduti
Via L. da Viterbo
Pza. delle Erbe
Via Orologio
Via della Marrocca
Vecchio
Via F. Ascenzi
Via Roma
Piazza Martiri d' Ungheria
Pza. del Plebiscito
Via Cavour
Via dei Mille
Via Vetulonia
Via S. Antonio
Via Chigi
Via Faul
Porta Romana
Via G. Garibaldi
Via degli Scalzi
Via S. Clemente
Via S. Lorenzo
V. d. Fabbriche
Via del Meone
Via Cardinale La Fontaine
Via S. Leonardo
Via S. Pellegrino
V. S. Pietro
1
2
3
4
5
6
7
8
9
10

The Palazzo Papale

to this day in the Vatican. The palace may usually be visited on Mondays through Saturdays, from 10 a.m. to 12:30 p.m.

Return to Piazza della Morte and stroll over to the **Church of Santa Maria Nuova** (8), a 12th-century church of great charm. The tiny outdoor pulpit on its left façade was once used by St. Thomas Aquinas for preaching. Walk behind this and turn right on Via San Lorenzo, a street lined with interesting buildings.

The **Piazza del Plebiscito** (9) is the busy center of the Old Town. On its west side stands the 15th-century **Palazzo Comunale**, whose exquisite courtyard can be reached through a passage, revealing some very nice views. To the north is the 13th-century Palazzo del Podestà with its beautiful 15th-century clock tower.

The route now leads past the animated Piazza delle Erbe and down the long Corso Italia, a favorite street for strolling. When you reach Piazza Verdi, turn left and follow Via Matteotti uphill to the **Church of San Francesco** (10). Built in the Gothic style in 1237, it has an interesting outdoor pulpit on the façade. Step inside to see the tombs of two popes who died in Viterbo, Hadrian V and Clement IV. From here it is an easy walk through the Porta Fiorentina back to the train station.

A Daytrip from Rome

Orvieto

The first sight of Orvieto never fails to astonish visitors. Perched high atop a rocky mound overlooking the rich Umbrian countryside, this ancient town is famous for both its delicious white wine and its spectacular cathedral. These attractions plus its convenient location midway on the main highway and rail line between Rome and Florence act as a magnet for tourists, who come by the thousands. The pity is that so few of them ever venture beyond the cathedral square to explore the magnificently well-preserved medieval town itself. The walking tour described here probes deeply into this and leads you to some intriguing sights.

Orvieto's history was determined by its easily defended site, a natural fortress if ever there was one. Although it was already inhabited during prehistoric times, it was those mysterious Etruscans who developed the first real settlement here around 800 B.C. This was destroyed by the Romans in the 3rd century B.C., after which the population moved down to the valley. Orvieto again served its defensive role during the Barbarian invasions and the troubled period that followed. In the Middle Ages it became a stronghold of the popes, who often had to flee Rome.

GETTING THERE:

Trains depart Rome's Termini Station several times in the morning for the 90-minute run to Orvieto. Most of these are marked for Milan or Venice. Return service operates until mid-evening.

By car, take the A-1 Autostrada north from Rome to Orvieto, a distance of 75 miles, and park near the cathedral.

PRACTICALITIES:

Orvieto may be visited at any time, but note that the two small museums are closed on Mondays. Clear weather is essential for the magnificent views. The local **Tourist Information Office**, phone (0763) 41-772, is directly opposite the cathedral. Orvieto is in the region of **Umbria** and has a **population** of about 22,500.

FOOD AND DRINK:

Orvieto's white wine, available either dry *(secco)* or slightly sweet *(abboccato),* is world famous. Some good restaurant choices are:

Maurizio (Via del Duomo 78, a block northwest from the cathedral) A longtime favorite in a great location. X: Tues. $$

Dell' Ancora (Via di Piazza del Popolo 7, just off the west end of Pza. del Popolo) Real country cooking. X: Thurs., Jan. $$

Del Cocco (Via Garibaldi 4, just south of Pza. della Repubblica) A favorite with the locals. X: Fri. $

Co-op CRAMST "San Francesco" (Via Maitani 17, 1 block west of the cathedral, hidden in an alleyway) Combination restaurant, cafeteria, and pizzeria. Popular with the young crowd. X: Sun. $

SUGGESTED TOUR:

The **train station** (1) is, naturally, down in the valley. Take one of the frequent buses to the upper town. Tickets are sold in the station's bar and must be canceled on board the bus, which may go to the cathedral, or take you to Piazza XXIX Marzo (2) instead—in which case you can follow the map to the cathedral.

The flamboyant facade of Orvieto's ***Duomo** (Cathedral) (3) is literally covered with dazzling multicolored mosaics and splendid bas-reliefs. Whether you admire the effect or consider it a study in wretched excess, there is no doubt that it is certainly impressive. The structure itself, a perfect example of the Italian Gothic style, was begun in 1290 to house the relics of the Miracle of Bolsena. The amount of money lavished on its construction was surely due to the fact that many of the popes of that time took refuge in Orvieto, safe from the deadly plots of Rome.

Compared to the façade, the simple interior seems uncluttered and almost restrained—although the alternating layers of black and white stone lend a strange spatial effect. In the north transept is the **Corporal Chapel**, where the relics of the Miracle of Bolsena are kept in a sumptuous 14th-century reliquary within a tabernacle. It seems that in 1293 a priest in nearby Bolsena, plagued by doubts, was convinced of the presence of Christ in the host as it dripped blood onto the altar linen. Pope Urban IV, residing in Orvieto at the time, considered this to be a true miracle and ordered the construction of the cathedral to shelter the blood-stained cloth.

The greatest art treasures of the cathedral are in the **Chapel of San Brizio**, occupying the south transept. These are the incomparable ***frescoes** depicting the *Apocalypse,* begun in 1447 by Fra Angelico

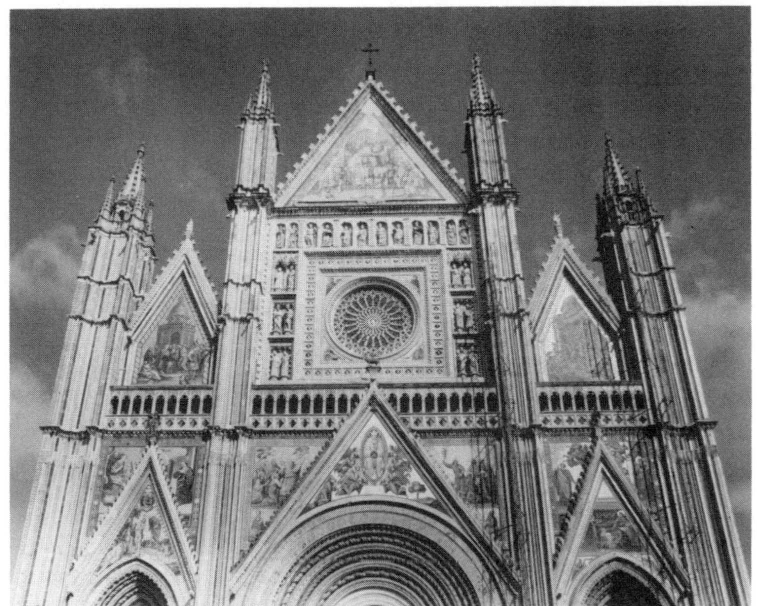

The Cathedral's ornate façade

and completed in 1504 by Luca Signorelli. Among the greatest masterpieces of the Renaissance, they supposedly provided the inspiration for Michelangelo in his painting of the Sistine Chapel ceiling in the Vatican. The cathedral is closed between 1 and 2:30 p.m.

Standing next to the cathedral is the 13th-century **Palazzo dei Papi** (Papal Palace) (4). This stark, monumental Gothic structure, built as a residence for the popes, houses the **Museo dell' Opera del Duomo** (Cathedral Museum). Climb the outside staircase and step inside to see a fascinating, if slightly disorganized, collection of religious art associated with the cathedral. The most impressive piece on display is the *Madonna* polyptych by Simone Martini, a 14th-century painter from Siena. The museum is open daily except Mondays, from 9 a.m. to 1 p.m. and 2–5 p.m.

Across the square from the cathedral is the **Museo Civico Archaeologico** (5), also known as the Claudio Faina Archaeological Museum, which specializes in Etruscan objects from the local area. Its collection is a must if you have an interest in the subject, and may be seen daily except on Mondays, from 9 a.m. to 1 p.m. and 3–7 p.m.

The route now leaves the bus tours behind and follows a complicated path through a colorful old neighborhood, with several places where you can look out across the valley. Follow it to **Piazza della Repubblica** (6), the heart of the Old Town. In the center of this is the 16th-century town hall, while to the east stands the 12th-century **Church of Sant' Andrea** with its strange 12-sided bell tower. It was in this church that Pope Innocent III announced the Fourth Crusade in 1216. Excavations beneath it have revealed the remains of a 6th-century church on top of Etruscan and Roman ruins. These can be seen by asking the caretaker.

Continue down Via Loggia dei Mercanti and enter a world that has hardly changed since the Middle Ages. By carefully following the map you will come to the solitary 11th-century ***Church of San Giovenale** (7), a very primitive structure of immense charm. Enter via the side door to admire the cool simplicity of its frescoed interior, a treat not to be missed even though few people ever pay a visit.

The route leads through more delightful medieval streets back to Piazza della Repubblica (6), then continues on to the lively **Piazza Capitano del Popolo** (8). The **Palazzo del Popolo** (People's Palace), an immense structure from the 12th century, was first built as an ecclesiastical seat and later used as a palace for the Captain of the People. It has long dominated the square, where outdoor markets are held on Saturdays.

Stroll down the main street, Corso Cavour, to Piazzale Cahen and the ruins of an old fortress, now a public park. Just beyond this is the **Pozzo di San Patrizio** (St. Patrick's Well) (9), dug in 1527 on orders from Pope Clement VII as a precaution against the town's water supply being cut off by a siege. It is over 200 feet deep and lined with two remarkably intertwined staircases that never meet except at the bottom. You can have the somewhat eerie experience of going down it, but remember that what goes down must come up. Descents may be made any day from 9 a.m. to 7 p.m. (6 p.m. in winter). Only a few yards to the west of this are the ruins of an Etruscan temple.

Return to the train station by taking one of the frequent buses from the stop in front of the former funicular, a fantastic 19th-century contraption that hasn't run in decades but which hopefully might be restored. Those interested in exploring the ancient **Etruscan Necropolis** (10) can do so by walking downhill along the road to the station, a distance of nearly a mile. Dating from at least the 4th century B.C., this well-preserved area of chamber tombs is utterly fascinating. The strange inscriptions above the burial entrances are probably the names of the deceased, although the language has never been deciphered. The tomb area is open until sunset and there is no charge. You can get on the bus to the station at the stop *(Fermata)* opposite the tombs.

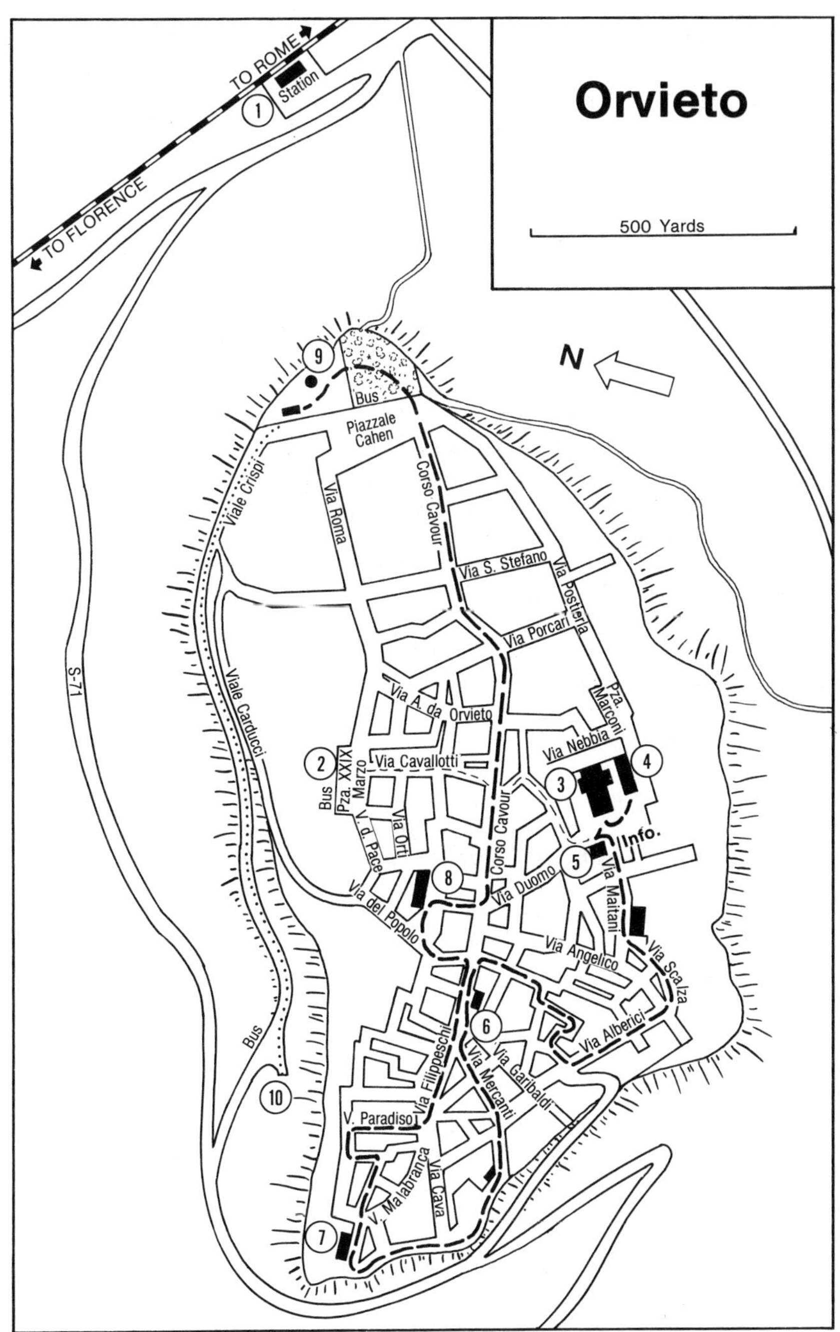
Orvieto
500 Yards
N
TO ROME
Station
TO FLORENCE
S-71
Bus
Piazzale Cahen
Viale Crispi
Via Roma
Corso Cavour
Via S. Stefano
Via Postieria
Via Porcari
Viale Carducci
Via A. da Orvieto
Pza. Marconi
Via Nebbia
Via Cavallotti
Pza. XXIX Marzo
V. d. Pace
Via Orti
Info.
Via Duomo
Via Maitani
Via del Popolo
Via Angelico
Via Scalza
Via Alberici
Via Filippeschi
Via Mercanti
Via Garibaldi
V. Paradiso
V. Malabranca
Via Cava

A Daytrip from Rome

Assisi

Few places are as completely permeated with the memory of a single person as Assisi is with Saint Francis. Miraculously, the steady stream of pilgrims and tourists who come in veneration or out of curiosity have not managed to undo the gentle tranquility of this ancient Umbrian hill town.

Assisi began as an Umbrian settlement strongly influenced by the nearby Etruscans, and later developed into the Roman town of *Asisium.* After the usual destruction by the Barbarians, it became subject to the duchy of Spoleto and eventually, in the 12th century, was a republic in its own right. From the beginning of the 16th century until the unification of Italy in the mid-19th, it was a peaceful part of the Papal States.

Saint Francis was born in Assisi in 1182, the son of a wealthy merchant and his French wife. After a dissolute youth and a year's imprisonment during a war with Perugia, he became disenchanted with the worldly life and embraced absolute poverty. Through his personal example and teachings, a new religious order was founded with the blessings of the Pope, in time becoming known as the Franciscans. According to tradition, he received the stigmata during a vision on September 14, 1224. Two years later he died in a nearby village. His simple faith, kindness, and love of nature has made him one of Christendom's most cherished saints.

GETTING THERE:

Trains marked for Ancona depart Rome's Termini Station several times in the morning. Take one of these as far as **Foligno** and change there to a local train for Assisi. The total trip takes about 2½ hours. Check the schedule carefully as a change at Orte instead of Foligno may be required. Return service operates until early evening.

By car, Assisi is 110 miles northeast of Rome. Take the A-1 Autostrada north to Orte, then the S-3 past Spoleto to Foligno, and finally the S-75.

The Basilica di San Francesco

PRACTICALITIES:

Assisi may be visited at any time, but expect crowds on holy days, especially the Feast of Saint Francis in early October. Some minor sights are closed on Mondays. The local **Tourist Information Office**, phone (075) 81-25-34, is at Piazza del Comune 12. Assisi is in the region of **Umbria** and has a **population** of about 25,000.

FOOD AND DRINK:

Some good restaurant choices are:

Il Frantoio (Via Fontebella 25, 3 blocks southeast of the basilica) Luxurious dining, with an outdoor terrace. X: Mon. in winter. $$$

Buca di San Francesco (Via Brizi, 2 blocks west of Pza. del Comune) In a basement wine cellar, with outdoor tables on a terrace. X: Mon., July $$

Medioevo (Via Arco dei Priori 4, just south of Pza. del Comune) A highly romantic ambiance. X: Wed., Jan. $$

Umbra (Vicolo degli Archi 6, just south of Pza. del Comune) In a small hotel, with a garden terrace. X: Tues. $$

Girarrosto la Fortezza (Vicolo della Fortezza 2, just north of Pza. del Comune) Good food in an atmospheric setting. X: Thurs. $

Pallotta (Via San Rufino 4, just east of Pza. del Comune) A nice place for an inexpensive meal. X: Tues. $

SUGGESTED TOUR:

The Assisi **train station** (1) is located in the village of Santa Maria degli Angeli at the foot of the Subasio mountain. Buses depart about every 30 minutes for the three-mile journey uphill to the walled town of Assisi. Tickets can be purchased in the station, and must be canceled on board the bus. Buy a return ticket at the same time.

Get off the bus at Porta San Pietro (2) and walk uphill to the famed ***Basilica di San Francesco** (Basilica of Saint Francis) (3), the main attraction of Assisi and the goal of countless pilgrimages. It was begun as early as 1228, just two years after the saint's death, and already consecrated by 1253. There are actually two churches, one on top of the other, built over a crypt containing the tomb of Saint Francis.

Begin your visit in the ***Lower Church**, whose dark vaulted interior is lined with magnificent frescoes. Artists came from all over Italy to add their contributions, bringing about a new kind of naturalistic art imbued with the Franciscan spirit. Be sure to bring along plenty of coins for the light switches, otherwise you may miss some of the best treasures. The most famous of these is the **Madonna with St. Francis* by Cimabue, on the wall of the right transept, from which the often-reproduced portrait of the saint is derived. Other noted artists represented are Giotto, Simone Martini, Pietro Lorenzetti, and Andrea da Bologna. In the middle of the nave are steps leading down to the **crypt**, only discovered in 1818, where Saint Francis is buried. Return to the Lower Church and take the steps from the right transept up to the main **cloisters**, from which you can visit the **Treasury** *(Tesoro)* with its famed collection of medieval art, and the bookstore.

Continue climbing to the **Upper Church**, whose well-lit interior is in complete contrast to the lower. The transepts are lined with badly damaged frescoes by Cimabue, although his **Crucifixion* still retains much of its intense power. The walls of the nave are decorated with a famous cycle of 28 ***frescoes**, mostly by Giotto, depicting the *Life of Saint Francis*. Begin at the right transept to see them in chronological order. Above these are another two cycles of frescoes, those on the north wall showing scenes from the Old Testament, and on the south wall the New Testament.

The Basilica is open to tourists from 8 a.m. to 7 p.m. (6 p.m. in winter), but not on Sunday mornings or some holy days. From November through March it closes for lunch between noon and 2 p.m. Decent dress is required, as in most Italian churches.

Now follow the colorful Via San Francesco, perhaps stopping at the **Oratorio dei Pellegrini** (Pilgrim's Oratorio) (4), a tiny chapel em-

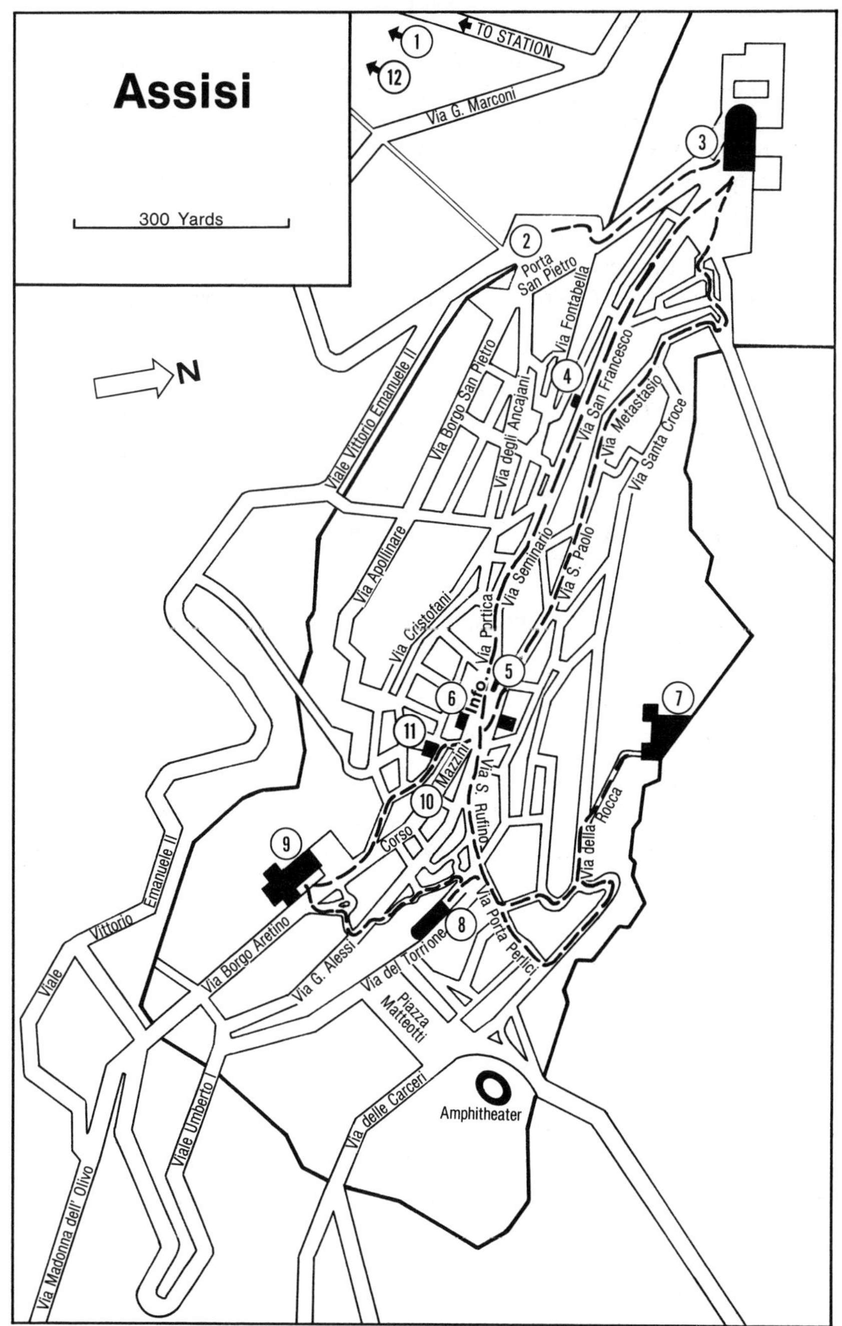
Assisi
300 Yards
N
TO STATION
Via G. Marconi
Porta San Pietro
Via Fontabella
Viale Vittorio Emanuele II
Via Borgo San Pietro
Via degli Ancajani
Via San Francesco
Via Metastasio
Via Santa Croce
Via Apollinare
Via Seminario
Via S. Paolo
Via Cristofani
Via Portica
Info.
Mazzini
Via S. Rufino
Corso
Via della Rocca
Via Borgo Aretino
Via G. Alessi
Via del Torrione
Via Porta Perlici
Piazza Matteotti
Amphitheater
Via delle Carceri
Viale Umberto
Via Madonna dell' Olivo
Viale Vittorio Emanuele II
1
2
3
4
5
6
7
8
9
10
11
12

bellished with delightful 15th-century Umbrian frescoes. Continue on to remnants of the former Church of San Nicolo, whose crypt now houses the small **Museo Romano Comunale** (5) with its displays of Etruscan and Roman antiquities. A tunnel from here gives access to the old Roman Forum beneath the present day piazza. The museum is open daily from 9:30 a.m. to 8 p.m. in summer; and from 10:30 a.m. to 1 p.m. and 3–6:30 p.m. in winter.

The **Piazza del Comune**, just steps away, is the main square of Assisi. On its north side stands the remarkable **Temple of Minerva**, dating from the reign of Augustus and now serving as a church. Next to it is the tall 13th-century Torre Comunale tower and, to the left, the Palazzo del Capitano del Popolo, a palace from the same century. Along the south side you will find the **tourist office** and the **Palazzo dei Priori** (Town Hall) (6), which houses the **Pinacoteca** (Municipal Art Gallery) on its ground floor. This small museum has a good collection of Umbrian frescoes and other art works. It is open daily from 9:30 a.m. to noon and 3–7 p.m. in summer; and in winter from 10:30 a.m. to 1 p.m. and 3–6:30 p.m.

Leave the square on Via San Rufino and follow the complicated route uphill through picturesque streets to the **Rocca Maggiore** (Castle) (7). First built in the 12th century, it was reconstructed in the 14th and is still in fine condition. The ***views** from its summit are spectacular; while the interior may be explored from 9 a.m. to 8 p.m. in summer, and 10 a.m. to 4 p.m. in winter. On the way down you might want to go a little out of the way to see the scanty remains of a **Roman amphitheater.**

The **Duomo San Rufino** (Cathedral) (8) was begun in 1140 and has some interesting carvings around its doors and windows. Its façade is considered to be a masterpiece of Umbrian Romanesque architecture. Step inside to see the font, at the beginning of the right aisle, where Saint Francis, Saint Clare, and the emperor Frederick II Hohenstaufen were baptized. The small museum, crypt, and a Roman well may be seen on request.

Continue downhill to the **Chiesa di Santa Chiara** (9), a church erected in the 13th century to house the remains of Saint Clare, who founded the Order of the Poor Clares and was the companion of Saint Francis. Its plain facade, embellished with a lovely rose window, is supported by monumental buttresses. Inside, be sure to visit the **Chapel of San Giorgio** on the south side. This contains the famous Byzantine crucifix that is said to have spoken to Saint Francis, revealing to him his mission in life.

On the way back to Piazza del Comune you will pass the **Oratorio di San Francesco Piccolino** (10), a simple stone structure believed to have been the birthplace of Saint Francis. Nearby is the **Chiesa Nuova**

The Rocca Maggiore

(New Church), built in the 17th century on the supposed site of Saint Francis's parents' house.

Head back to the Basilica of Saint Francis (3) via the interesting route on the map, then continue down to the bus stop at Porta San Pietro (2). Take a look at the adjacent **Chiesa di San Pietro** a 13th-century abbey church with an unusual facade, before boarding a bus back to the train station. If you have a wait there, you may want to visit the **Basilica di Santa Maria degli Angeli** (12, off the map), just a few blocks south of the station. Within its nave is the **Capella della Porziuncola,** a small 4th-century chapel used by Saint Francis, and the Capella del Transito, where he died in 1226.

A Daytrip from Rome

Spoleto

Spoleto is best known today for its annual Festival of Two Worlds, founded in 1958 by the Italian-American composer Gian-Carlo Menotti. The same qualities that first attracted the festival should bring you here, too. A small Umbrian hill town of great antiquity and unspoiled character, Spoleto has the additional merit of being easy to reach. Although it possesses no great sights as such, its exceptionally well-preserved core does contain a large number of remarkable Roman and medieval structures of more than passing interest. As a bonus, the town is blessed with a truly cosmopolitan ambiance—a blend of rural Italy with a touch of international sophistication. In short, Spoleto is a delightful destination for a relaxed and thoroughly enjoyable daytrip.

An ancient Umbrian center of unknown origin, *Spoletium* became a Roman colony in 242 B.C. Twenty-five years later it successfully repelled an attack by Hannibal, giving Rome the needed time to reorganize its defenses and save the republic. During the Middle Ages it was the seat of a fairly large duchy, and in the 14th century became part of the Papal States, yielding to the new Kingdom of Italy in 1860.

GETTING THERE:

Trains, usually marked for Ancona, depart Rome's Termini Station several times in the morning for the under-2-hour ride to Spoleto. One of these requires a change at Orte. Return service operates until mid-evening.

By car, take the A-1 Autostrada north almost to Orte, then the S-3 past Terni and into Spoleto. Park as close to Piazza della Libertà as possible. Spoleto is 81 miles northeast of Rome.

PRACTICALITIES:

Spoleto is crowded during the Festival of Two Worlds, held annually between mid-June and mid-July. Good weather is essential as almost all of this trip is out of doors. The local **Tourist Information Office**, phone (0743) 28-111, is at Piazza della Libertà. Spoleto is in the region of **Umbria** and has a **population** of about 38,000.

The Duomo

FOOD AND DRINK:

The major gastronomic experience of Spoleto is the black truffle *(Tartufo),* found on local hillsides. Other specialties are a pasta called *Stringozzi,* and a variety of game dishes. The local wine is *Trebbiano Spoleto,* a rather strong white.

Some choice restaurants are:

Il Tartufo (Pza. Garibaldi 24, between the train station and the upper town) Considered to be the best restaurant in Spoleto. X: Wed., late July. $$$

Sabatini (Corso Mazzini 52, 2 blocks north of Pza. della Libertà) A traditional restaurant with Umbrian specialties. X: Mon., Jan. $$

La Barcaccia (Pza. Fratelli Bandiera 3, just west of the town hall) A good choice in the heart of the Old Town. X: Tues., Jan. $

Il Panciolle (Largo Muzio Clemente 4, 3 blocks west of the cathedral) A charming local restaurant on a quiet, shady little square. X: Wed. $

SUGGESTED TOUR:

Spoleto's international flavor becomes apparent the moment you step outside the **train station** (1, off the map) and confront the overpowering 1962 sculpture by Alexander Calder. From there it is a pleasant one-mile walk to Piazza della Libertà, fairly level most of the way until you get to the steep Via Porta Fuga. Just go straight ahead and follow the route on the map. There is also a frequent bus service from the station if you'd rather ride.

The **Piazza della Libertà** (2) is the real start of this walk. On its east side is the tourist office, while the west opens onto the ancient **Roman Theater**, built in the 1st century A.D. Unearthed in recent years, it has been restored and is once again used for performances.

Via Brignone leads east towards the Roman Arch, a relic from the 3rd century B.C. that still spans the road. Just before this turn left onto Via Arco de Druso. The small **Arch of Drusus** (3), dating from A.D. 23, commemorates the victories of General Drusus—the adopted son of Augustus—over the Germanic tribes. To the right of it is the interesting small **Church of Sant' Ansano**, built around the walls of a 1st-century Roman temple. In its crypt is the Chapel of Sant' Isacco, a primitive Christian church within the old temple.

Continue on through the **Piazza del Mercato**, where a lively open-air market is held on Mondays through Saturdays on the site of the Ancient Roman forum. The route now leads through some quaint old streets to the Bishop's Palace, in whose courtyard is the lovely 12th-century **Church of Sant' Eufemia** (4). Step inside to see the unusual women's galleries above the aisles and the 15th-century triptych behind the altar.

Via di Visiale leads past the **Casa Romano**, a Roman house from the 1st century A.D. supposedly owned by the mother of the emperor Vespasian. Its restored interior may usually be seen by inquiring at the adjacent **Palazzo Comunale** (Town Hall) (5) on Piazza del Municipo. The town hall also houses the **Pinacoteca**, a small art museum displaying mostly Umbrian works. It is open on Wednesdays through Mondays, from 10 a.m. to 1 p.m. and 3–7 p.m.

Now walk uphill to the massive 14th-century **Rocca** (Fortress) (6), built as a stronghold for the pope's representatives. In the late 15th century it was home to none other than the notorious Lucrezia Borgia. After the unification of Italy it became a prison and remained so until 1982. It is now open to the public and may be visited on Mondays through Saturdays, from 10 a.m. to 7:30 p.m.

Around the rear of the castle, spanning a narrow valley, is the remarkable ***Ponte delle Torri** (Bridge of Towers) (7). Erected in the 14th century over Roman foundations, this 755-foot-long bridge and aqueduct is supported by pillars up to 262 feet in height, the center two

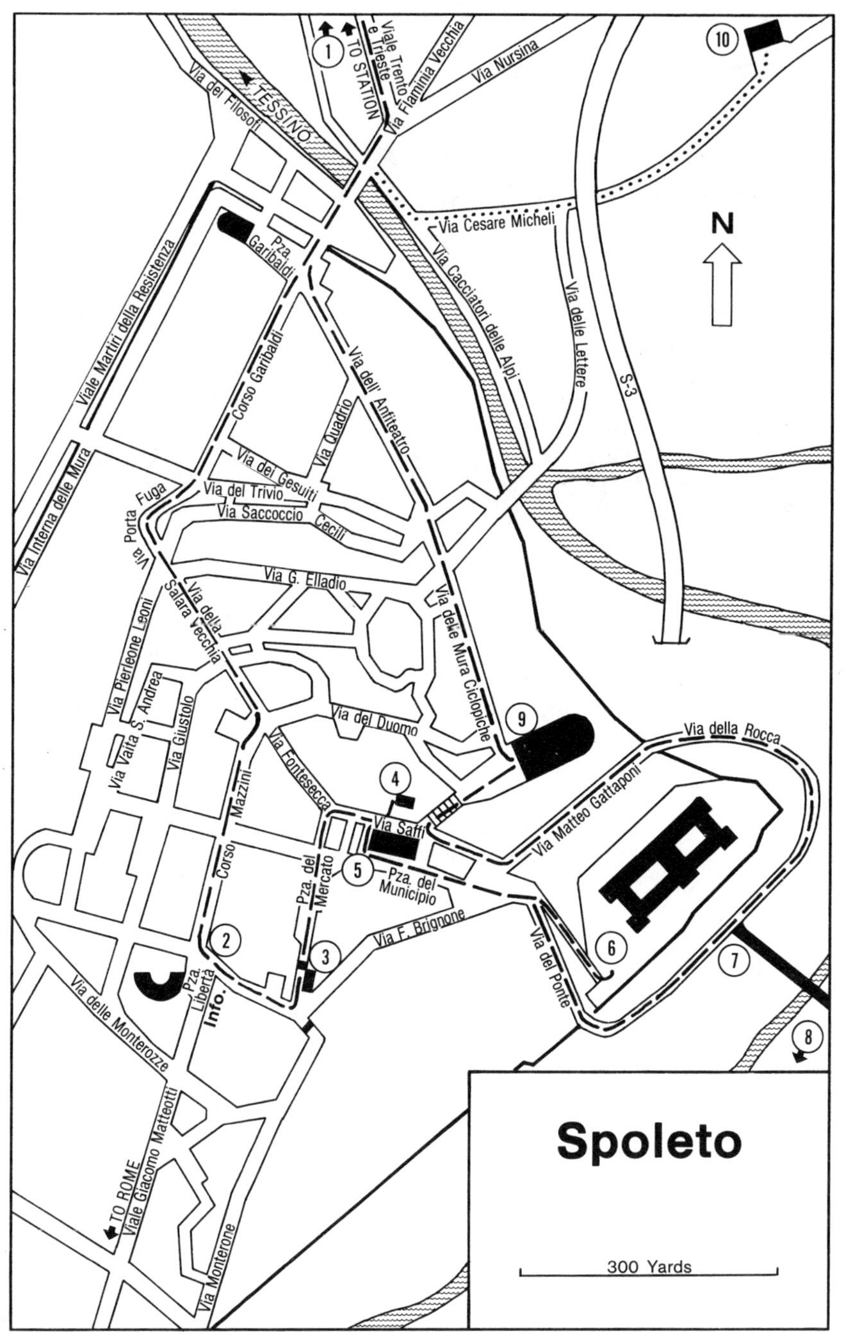

Spoleto
300 Yards
N
TO STATION
TO ROME
TESSINO
Viale Trento e Trieste
Via Flaminia Vecchia
Via Nursina
Via dei Filosofi
Via Cesare Micheli
Via Cacciatori delle Alpi
Via delle Lettere
S-3
Pza Garibaldi
Viale Martiri della Resistenza
Via Interna delle Mura
Corso Garibaldi
Via dell' Anfiteatro
Via Quadrio
Via dei Gesuiti
Via del Trivio
Via Saccoccio
Cecili
Via Porta Fuga
Via G. Elladio
Via della Salara Vecchia
Via delle Mura Ciclopiche
Via Pierleone Leoni
Via S. Andrea
Via Vaita
Via Giustolo
Via del Duomo
Via Fontesecca
Corso Mazzini
Via della Rocca
Via Matteo Gattaponi
Via Saffi
Pza. del Mercato
Pza. del Municipio
Via F. Brignone
Via del Ponte
Pza. Libertà
Info.
Via delle Monterozze
Viale Giacomo Matteotti
Via Monterone
1
2
3
4
5
6
7
8
9
10

The Ponte delle Torri

of which are hollow for use as defensive towers. A stroll across it offers breathtaking views and the opportunity for a short country walk to the nearby **Church of San Pietro** (8, off the map). Begun in the 5th century, it later acquired a lavish 12th-century facade depicting strange narrative folk fables.

Return around the other side of the fortress. Along the way are little signs reserving the harvest rights for truffles on the hillside. Back in town, you will soon come to the top of the spectacular stairway that leads down to the ***Duomo** (Cathedral) (9), a very beautiful and unusual sight. Consecrated in 1198 and altered over the years, it has a marvelous Renaissance porch, eight rose windows, and a majestic tower. Inside, there are some wonderful ***frescoes** in the apse including the noted *Coronation of the Virgin,* which were the last works by Fra Filippo Lippi who died here in 1469 and whose tomb is in the chapel to the right. The first chapel on the south aisle, nearest the entrance, contains a splendid *Madonna Enthroned* by the 15th-century Umbrian painter Pinturicchio, while the interior west façade is decorated with a bust of Pope Urban VIII by Bernini. The cathedral is closed from 1–3 p.m.

The shortest route back to the train station is shown on the map. From the bridge you might want to make an easy side trip to the nearby **Church of San Salvatore** (10), one of the oldest Christian churches in Europe. It was begun as early as the 4th century and altered in the 9th. The interior is extremely atmospheric and contains several excellent Roman columns.

A Daytrip from Florence

*San Gimignano

Perched high atop a hill and completely surrounded by its ancient walls, the small town of San Gimignano is an incredibly well-preserved holdover from the Middle Ages. It is famous throughout the world for the 13 surviving medieval towers that give its skyline the startling appearance of a miniature Manhattan. There were once more than 70 of these structures, built during the 12th and 13th centuries both as status symbols and for family defense during those violent times.

The Etruscans probably had a settlement on this site, but there are no actual references to San Gimignano prior to the Middle Ages. Its location, overlooking fertile farmland and near the old road linking Rome with the north, brought a measure of prosperity until, unable to defend itself, it fell under the rule of Florence in 1353. A backwater ever since, it has remained practically unchanged to this day.

Located seven miles from the nearest rail station or highway, San Gimignano is not quite as easy to reach as most of the other daytrip destinations, but its allure is so extraordinary that a little extra effort is well worthwhile. Its name, by the way, is pronounced *Sahn Gee-meen-YAHN-oh*.

GETTING THERE:

Trains, bound for Siena, depart Florence's main station several times in the morning, sometimes requiring a change at Empoli. Get off the train at Poggibonsi, about 70 minutes from Florence, and continue by TRA-IN bus to San Gimignano's Porta San Giovanni stop, a 20-minute ride. Bus tickets are sold at the newsstand in the Poggibonsi station, and cancelled on board. Return service usually operates until mid-evening, but check locally.

Buses depart several times in the morning from the SITA terminal near the west side of Florence's main train station. Some of these go direct to San Gimignano while others require a change at Poggibonsi. Purchase two tickets (one for return) before boarding and cancel one of them on board. The average run is just over one hour, much faster than the train/bus combination above. Again, check the return schedules.

By car, San Gimignano is 34 miles southwest of Florence. Take the *Superstrada del Palio* highway in the direction of Siena and exit at Poggibonsi, after which it is seven miles on local roads to San Gimignano.

PRACTICALITIES:

Most of the sights are closed on Mondays from October through March; otherwise San Gimignano may be visited on any day. Clear weather is essential for the glorious views. An **outdoor market** is held on Thursday and Saturday mornings. The local **Tourist Information Office** *(Pro Loco)*, phone (0577) 94-00-08, is on Piazza del Duomo. They provide a wide variety of useful services and sell bus tickets. San Gimignano is in the region of **Toscana** and has a **population** of about 7,000.

FOOD AND DRINK:

Being a major tourist attraction, the town has many restaurants and cafés. Some good choices are:

Le Terrazze (Pza. della Cisterna 23, in the La Cisterna Hotel) Offers both a country-inn atmosphere and a view. X: Tues., Wed. lunch, Winter. $$$

Bel Soggiorno (Via San Giovanni 41, near Porta San Giovanni) A medieval ambiance with a view of the town. X: Mon. $$

La Griglia (Via San Matteo 34, near Pza. del Duomo) Grilled foods in pleasant surroundings. X: Thurs., Jan., Feb. $$

La Stella (Via San Matteo 75, on the way to Porta San Matteo) Home-grown foods. X: Wed. $

Taverna Paradiso (Via San Giovanni 6, just off Pza. della Cisterna) Pizza and a range of other foods. X: Mon. $

A favorite dessert in these parts is *Panforte,* a sinful concoction of nuts, candied fruits, and honey. The local red wine is *Chianti,* of which the *Classico* variety is best. An interesting white wine is *Vernaccia di San Gimignano.*

SUGGESTED TOUR:

Begin your walk at the **Porta San Giovanni** (1), a magnificent town gate erected in 1262. It is right next to the bus stop and the parking lot. Before entering, take a look at the impressive guard room perched above the gate.

Via San Giovanni is a colorful old street lined with medieval buildings, a taste of things to come. Follow it past the **Arco dei Becci** gate, an opening in the original 11th-century inner walls that leads to the ***Piazza della Cisterna** (2). Named for the beautiful 13th-century **fountain** in its center, this delightful square is paved with bricks in a her-

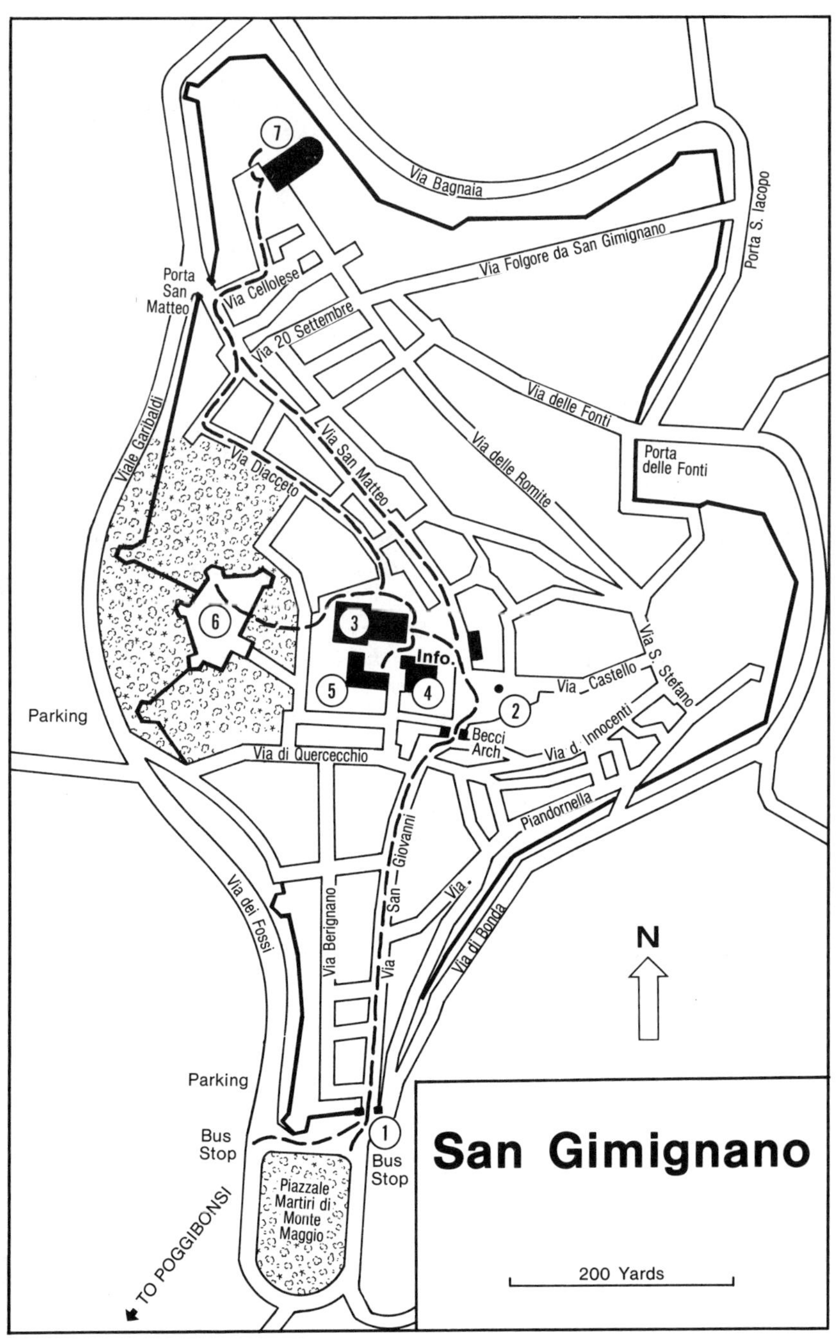
San Gimignano
Via Bagnaia
Porta S. Iacopo
Via Folgore da San Gimignano
Porta San Matteo
Via Cellolese
Via 20 Settembre
Via delle Fonti
Porta delle Fonti
Viale Garibaldi
Via Diacceto
Via San Matteo
Via delle Romite
Via S. Stefano
Via Castello
Info.
Parking
Becci Arch
Via d. Innocenti
Via di Quercecchio
Piandornella
Via San Giovanni
Via Berignano
Via dei Fossi
Via
Via di Bonda
N
Parking
Bus Stop
Bus Stop
Piazzale Martiri di Monte Maggio
TO POGGIBONSI
200 Yards

ringbone pattern. It is said that if you walk around the fountain you will surely return to San Gimignano. The famous **towers** rise all around you, a legacy of times when height meant safety. Many Italian towns were once graced with these fascinating structures, but most of them were torn down as the cities developed, a progress that happily bypassed sleepy old San Gimignano. Take a look at the Palazzo Tortoli at number 7, an elegant 14th-century house in the style of Siena.

Now stroll into the adjacent Piazza del Duomo, whose name is somewhat of a misnomer. The **Collegiata** (Collegiate Church) (3), dominating the west side, is often referred to as the *Duomo* (Cathedral) although it never was one. Begun in the 13th century, the church has been enlarged and greatly modified over the years. The Romanesque interior is noted for its outstanding frescoes, especially the *Martyrdom of Saint Sebastian* by Benozzo Gozzoli, a mid-15th-century work on the inside of the entrance wall flanked by two wooden statues of the *Annunciation*. Above this there is a fine *Last Judgment* by Taddeo di Bartola. Covering the length of the right aisle are ***frescoes** depicting scenes from the New Testament, while the left aisle tells stories from the Old Testament.

Be sure to visit the ***Capella di Santa Fina** chapel at the end of the right aisle. Dedicated to San Gimignano's patron saint, a young girl who died in 1253 at the age of 15 after years of suffering, it is widely regarded as a high point of Renaissance art. An admission is charged for this, which is also valid for the Torre Grossa and the town's museums. The church is closed from 12:30–3 p.m.

To the left of the chruch stands the **Palazzo de Popolo** (People's Palace) (4), which has been the Town Hall since the 13th century. Its tower, the ***Torre Grossa** (Fat Tower), is the highest in town and may be climbed for a marvelous panorama. On the way up stop at the **Sala del Consiglio** (Council Chamber), where Dante argued the case for a Tuscan alliance in 1300. In the same room there is a vast fresco of the *Maestà* by Lippo Memmi, painted in 1317. Continue up to the **Museo Civico** (Municipal Museum) on the second floor, where you will see a fine collection of Sienese and Florentine paintings from the 13th to the 15th centuries.

Now the climb really begins, all 177 feet of it. A medieval ordinance forbade any other structures from reaching this height, and as this is the only tower open to the public, you can put all of your energy into it. The ***view** from the top is really worth it.

Returning to Earth, stroll over to the **Museo d'Arte Sacra / Museo Etrusco** (5) in the lovely Piazza Pecori. Religious art from the Middle Ages is featured along with a small but interesting display of Etruscan and Roman artifacts found in the vicinity. All of the museums, including the Palazzo del Popolo and the Torre Grossa, are open daily from

View from the Rocca di Montestaffoli

April through September (except on May 1), from 9:30 a.m. to 12:30 p.m. and 3–6 p.m. From October through March they are open every day except on Mondays and major holidays, from 9:30 a.m. to 12:30 p.m. and 2:30–5:30 p.m.

Now follow the map to the ruined **Rocca di Montestaffoli** (6), a fortress built by the Florentines in 1353 but later demolished. It is now a public park, the perfect spot for a picnic, and offers the most unforgettable ***view** of San Gimignano's skyline.

Via Diacceto leads, down steps, from the north side of the church to the Porta San Matteo, another main gateway into the town erected in 1262. Just beyond this is the **Chiesa di Sant' Agostino** (Church of Saint Augustine) (7), a rather plain 13th-century structure containing some remarkable art. Among the most noted works here are the frescoes in the choir depicting the *Life of Saint Augustine,* a lively cycle of 15th-century masterpieces by Benozzo Gozzoli. While there, don't miss the lovely **cloisters** to the left of the church, which closes between noon and 3 p.m.

Return on Via San Matteo to the Piazza della Cisterna, where you can sit down at an outdoor café for some well-earned refreshment before heading back to Florence.

A Daytrip from Florence

*Siena

While Florence is the embodiment of the Renaissance, its ancient rival is resolutely rooted in the Middle Ages. One of the great sights of Italy, Siena is built atop the convergence of three clay hills whose soil yields the pigment *Burnt Sienna.* A complete circuit of medieval walls still encloses the perfectly preserved buildings and narrow, twisting streets that thread their way to the magnificent Piazza del Campo, one of the very finest public squares in the world.

Siena's origins go back to the time of the Etruscans, later being established as a Roman military colony, *Saena Julia,* under the emperor Augustus. It was not until the 12th century that the town became a free republic and assumed a position of importance rivaling that of Florence. The period preceding the mid-14th century saw great prosperity and an unprecedented building boom. Then, in 1348, the plague struck and devastated the city. Siena was decimated once again in 1555 by the Spaniards and became a part of Tuscany, an arrangement that lasted until the unification of Italy in the 19th century.

Unlike the other great tourist centers of Italy, Siena has largely insulated itself from a changing world, remaining inward-looking, reserved, and just a little bit aloof. Its speech is the purest, most musical Italian spoken anywhere; its art and architecture a superlative example of unspoiled Gothic.

Siena is divided into 17 wards, or *Contrade,* to which individual citizens devote an almost fanatical allegiance. Twice every year, on July 2nd and August 16th, these districts compete in a spectacular medieval horse race called the *Palio,* an event that draws huge crowds from all over the globe. No mere tourist attraction, this is the real thing—as it has been for many centuries.

GETTING THERE:

Trains depart Florence's main station several times in the morning for the 1½-hour ride to Siena. Some of these require a change at Empoli, others are direct. Return service operates until mid-morning.

Buses are considerably faster than trains on this route. Departures, almost hourly, are from Florence's SITA Terminal near the west side of the main train station. The *Rapida* buses take about one hour, the locals longer. Purchase tickets before boarding and cancel them on board. Return buses run until mid-evening.

By car, Siena is 42 miles south of Florence on the *Superstrada del Palio* highway. Park near Piazza Gramsci (2) as driving is forbidden in the historical center.

PRACTICALITIES:

Siena's main sights are open daily, except that the Palazzo Pubblico closes on Sunday afternoons and a few holidays. The art museum is also closed on Mondays. Mass insanity rules during the *Palio* races, held every year on July 2nd and August 16th. The local **Tourist Information Office**, phone (0577) 28-05-51, is at Piazza del Campo 56. Siena is in the region of **Toscana** and has a **population** of about 60,000.

FOOD AND DRINK:

Chianti Classico is the best local wine, while oenophiles will enjoy sampling other great Italian wines at the Enoteca Italica. Siena is famous for its *Panforte,* a rich loaf of nuts, candied fruits, and honey. Some good restaurants along the walking route are:

Guido (Vicolo Pettinaio 7, between Pza. Tolomei and Pza. del Campo) Dining in a medieval setting. X: Wed. $$

Al Mangia (Pza. del Campo 42) Overlooking the main square, with outdoor tables. X: Mon. $$

Il Campo (Pza. del Campo 50) Opens onto the main square, outdoor seating available. X: Tues. $$

Nello-La Taverna (Via del Porrione 28, just off the northeast corner of Pza. del Campo) A traditional old tavern. X: Sun. eve., Mon. $$

Da Mugolone (Via dei Pellegrini 8, between Pza. del Campo and the rear of the cathedral) A popular restaurant in the Old Town. X: Thurs., Sun. eve. $$

Al Marsili (Via del Castoro 3, between the Palazzo Chigi-Saracini and the cathedral) Famous for pasta and steak. X: Mon. $$

Severino (Via del Capitano 6, between the Pinacoteca and the cathedral) Exceptionally good value with a friendly atmosphere. X: Sun. $$

Grotta Santa Caterina (Via della Galluzza 26, near the house of St. Catherine) A rustic place, locally popular. X: Mon. $$

SUGGESTED TOUR:

The **train station** (1) is down in the valley and off the map. Buy a bus ticket in the station and board the bus to town, disembarking at **Piazza Gramsci** (2). Those coming by bus from Florence will get off at Piazza San Domenico (11).

Follow the map past Piazza Matteotti to Piazza Salimbeni, where the flavor of the city begins in earnest. The building at the center of the piazza, the Gothic-styled **Palazzo Salimbeni**, dates from the 14th century and is flanked by two equally impressive palaces from the 15th and 16th centuries. All three are occupied by a bank that has been here since 1624. Via Banchi di Sopra, the main street of Siena, leads to Piazza Tolomei and its marvelous **Palazzo Tolomei**. Built in 1205, this elegant Gothic structure is the oldest private mansion in town. Continue straight ahead to the intersection of Siena's three most important streets and the **Loggia della Mercanzia**, a 15th-century open arcade that once sheltered a commercial tribunal.

You are now just steps from one of Europe's most compelling sights, the ***Piazza del Campo** (3). Popularly known as *Il Campo,* this magnificent public square in the shape of a sloping shell is the very hub of Siena. It is here that the twice-yearly *Palio* race is held, and here that citizens have gathered since medieval times. At its highest point the **Fonte Gaia** (Fountain of Joy) splashes merrily while locals and tourists alike refresh themselves at the many outdoor cafés. The open area, bordered by exquisite buildings, is divided by paving stones into nine segments representing the Council of Nine, merchants who governed Siena in the 13th and 14th centuries.

Dominating the scene is the 334-foot-high ***Torre del Mangia**, built in the 14th century, and the adjoining **Palazzo Pubblico** (Town Hall) (4), begun in 1297. At the base of the tower are the Renaissance arches of the **Capella di Piazza,** a chapel commemorating the end of the plague. From the inner courtyard to its right you can get a wonderfully framed view of the tower, and a look at the statue of Mangia, the gluttonous medieval bell-ringer for whom it was named.

Enter the Palazzo Pubblico from a doorway to the right and climb up to the first floor. The **Sala del Mappamondo** (Globe Room) has among its treasures a **Maestà* fresco of the Virgin surrounded by saints, an early masterpiece by native-son Simone Martini. The next room is famous for its 14th-century allegorical frescoes of the **Effects of Good and Bad Government*. Designed to inspire the civic leaders, this is one of the most important secular paintings from the Middle Ages and is especially fascinating for its rendering of street scenes in Siena, many of which are surprisingly recognizable. Continue on through the other rooms, all filled with superb, mostly Sienese, art. Upstairs, there is a loggia where pieces of the original 15th-century Fountain of Joy are displayed. The one in the piazza is a 19th-century copy. Wandering around, you will come to a doorway leading to the tower. If you can possibly negotiate the 332 steps, do so—the ***view** from the top presents a dramatic panorama of the medieval city. The Palazzo complex is open daily from mid-March through mid-November, 9:30 a.m. to 7:45 p.m., closing on Sundays at 1:45 p.m. During the rest of the year

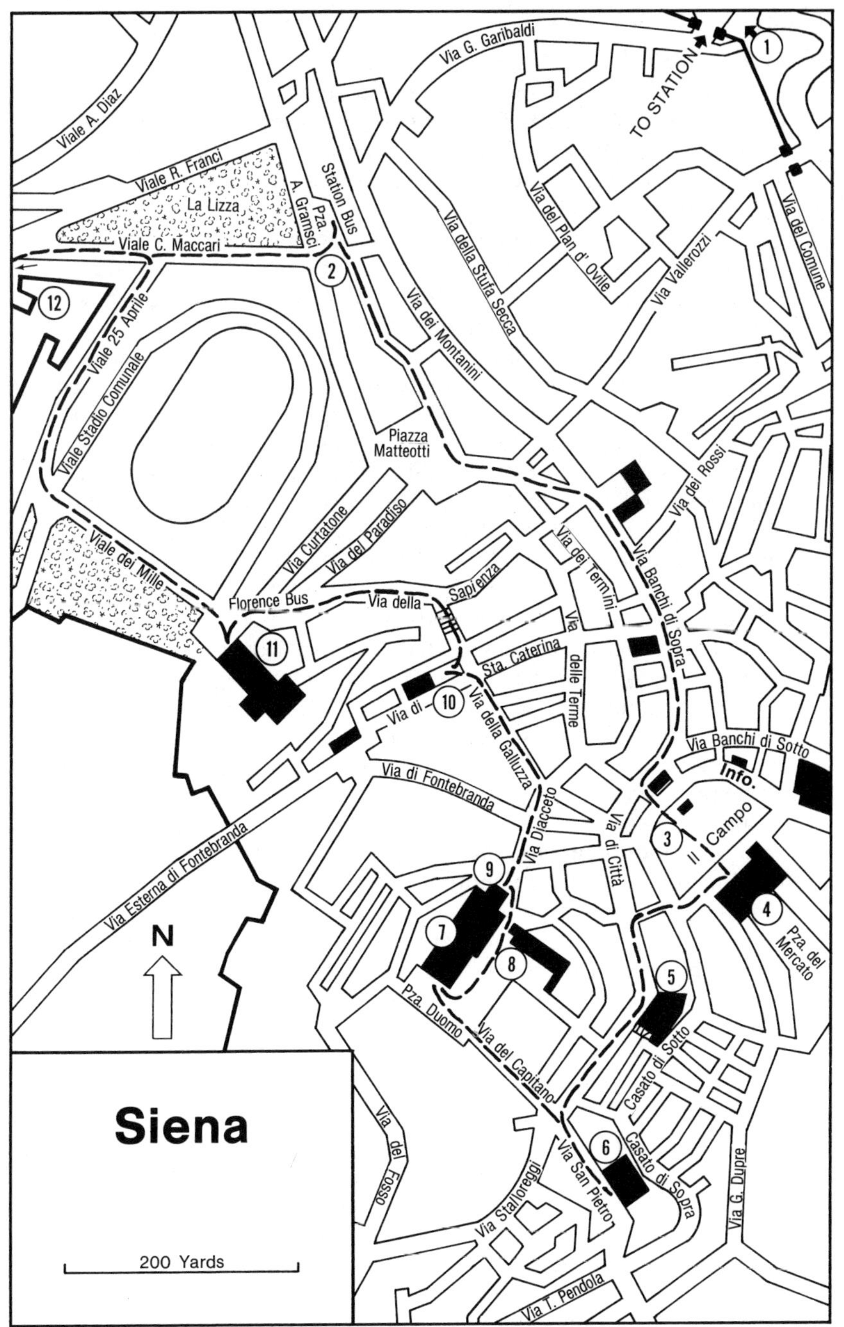

Siena
200 Yards
N
TO STATION
Via G. Garibaldi
Viale A. Diaz
Viale R. Franci
La Lizza
Viale C. Maccari
Pza. A. Gramsci
Station Bus
Via della Stufa Secca
Via del Plan d' Ovile
Via Vallerozzi
Via del Comune
Via dei Montanini
Viale 25 Aprile
Viale Stadio Comunale
Piazza Matteotti
Via Curtatone
Via del Paradiso
Viale dei Mille
Florence Bus
Via della
Sapienza
Via dei Termini
Via Banchi di Sopra
Via dei Rossi
Via delle Terme
Sta. Caterina
Via di
Via della Galluzza
Via Banchi di Sotto
Info.
Via di Fontebranda
Via Diacceto
Via di Città
Il Campo
Pza. del Mercato
Via Esterna di Fontebranda
Pza. Duomo
Via del Capitano
Casato di Sotto
Casato di Sopra
Via San Pietro
Via Stalloreggi
Via del Fosso
Via G. Dupre
Via T. Pendola
1
2
3
4
5
6
7
8
9
10
11
12

it is open daily from 9:30 a.m. to 1:45 p.m.

Leave the square by the tiny Vicolo del Bargello alleyway and turn left onto Via di Città. The **Palazzo Chigi-Saracini** (5) at number 89 is an outstanding 14th-century palace now housing a world-famous musical academy. Step inside its courtyard, where free impromptu concerts are frequently held.

Follow the map to the **Pinacoteca Nazionale** (6), an art museum specializing in Sienese painting from the 12th to the 16th centuries. It is housed in the splendid early-15th-century Palazzo Buonsignori. Virtually every artist who worked in Siena is represented in the vast collection, all arranged in chronological order so you can better understand the stylistic evolution. The museum is open on Tuesdays through Saturdays from 8:30 a.m. to 7 p.m. (closing at 2 p.m. in mid-winter), and on Sundays from 8:30 a.m. to 1 p.m.; but not on some holidays.

Continue up Via San Pietro and Via del Capitano to the highest point in town, Piazza del Duomo. The extremely ornate—and somewhat fussy—façade of the ***Duomo** (Cathedral) (7) overwhelms this square with its intricate designs. Although begun in the Romanesque style in 1196, it evolved into Tuscan Gothic during the two centuries of its construction, and remains perhaps the best example of that genre.

When a larger cathedral was started in rival Florence the Sienese, not to be outdone, decided to use the present building as the transept of a truly enormous church. The plague of 1348, however, soon put an end to that scheme and the work was never resumed. You can see the remains of the huge, unbuilt nave in the small piazza on the right by the bell tower.

Inside, the cathedral is every bit as interesting as its exterior promises. The ***floor** is unique, illustrating Biblical and other scenes with inlaid marble executed by more than 40 leading artists between the mid-14th and mid-16th centuries. Some of the better sections are usually covered for protection, but are generally on view in late summer. The magnificently carved octagonal marble ***pulpit**, borne on nine columns, was created in the late 13th century by Nicola Pisano and his pupils.

Be sure to visit the ***Libreria Piccolomini**, just off the left aisle. One of the most beautifully decorated rooms in Italy, it is renowned for its ten early-16th-century frescoes depicting the life of Pope Pius II. The famous statue of the *Three Graces,* in the center of the room, is a 3rd-century Roman copy of a Greek original.

Stroll over to the ***Museo dell' Opera del Duomo** (Cathedral Museum) (8), housed in what remains of the 14th-century attempt to add a gigantic nave to the cathedral. Nearly all of the works on display here come from the cathedral and represent an enormous treasury of religious art. Don't miss the original carvings from the cathedral fa-

Looking into the Piazza del Campo

çade (most of the present ones are copies), done in the late 13th century by Giovanni Pisano—easily among the best Gothic statuary in Italy. On the upper floors are the noted early-14th-century **Maestà* by Duccio, which marked a new era in Sienese painting, and the *Blessed Agostino with Four of his Miracles* by Simone Martini. You can climb out on the roof for excellent views. The museum is open daily from 9 a.m. to 7:30 p.m., closing in winter at 1:30 p.m.

The steps behind the cathedral lead to the **Battistero** (Baptistry) (9), noted for its remarkable 15th-century baptismal font designed by Jacopo della Quercia. Another work to look for is Donatello's dramatic *Feast of Herod,* one of the earliest uses of perspective. The baptistry is dark, so make sure you have coins for the light switches. It is open daily from 9 a.m. to 1 p.m. and 3–6 p.m.

Continue along Via di Diacceto and turn left into **Via della Galluzza**, one of the most picturesque streets in Siena. Here the Middle Ages come alive in a dark, narrow, and mysterious setting, with many arches connecting the ancient buildings. This leads to the **Sanctuario di Santa Caterina** (10), a place of pilgrimage since 1464. St. Catherine of Siena, a patron saint of Italy, was born here in 1347 and took the veil at the age of eight. Her life and works are celebrated in this small complex of buildings, open daily from 9 a.m. to 12:30 p.m. and 3–6 p.m.

Follow the map to the **Basilica di San Domenico** (11), a rather austere brick church begun in the 13th century. This is where Saint Catherine worshipped, and several of the works inside are devoted to her. Don't miss the **Capella di Santa Caterina**, a chapel on the right side of the nave with two masterpieces by Sodoma and a reliquary containing the preserved head of the saint. There is a nice view from the terrace beyond the apse.

A delightful way to end your day in Siena is to visit the **Enoteca Italica,** a national wine-tasting cellar in the 16th-century **Medici Fortress of Santa Barbara** (12). You can sample the best of Italian vintages by the glass here, either on an outdoor terrace or in the atmospheric old dungeons. The wines flow every day from 3 p.m. until midnight.

A short walk along Viale Cesare Maccari brings you to Piazza Gramsci, where you can get a local bus to the train station. Those going all the way to Florence by bus should return to Piazza San Domenico (11).

A Daytrip from Florence

Lucca

Often overlooked in favor of the more famous towns of Tuscany, Lucca is a refreshing escape from the tourist hordes and yet remains every bit as fascinating as the rest. It is completely encircled by massive 16th-century ramparts that offer delightful opportunities for strolls with a view. The streets within the well-preserved medieval center are both level and uncrowded, making this one of the most eminently walkable of cities. Although it has no major tourist sights, Lucca is filled with a charm that never fails to impress discriminating visitors.

Originally settled by the Ligurians and later the Etruscans, Lucca became a Roman colony in 180 B.C. Despite incessant wars with Pisa and Florence during the Middle Ages, the town has always been prosperous, a happy situation reflected by its splendid buildings. In 1805 Napoleon gave it to his sister as a principality, and in 1847 it was incorporated into the Grand Duchy of Tuscany, soon to become part of the Kingdom of Italy.

GETTING THERE:

Trains, mostly bound for Viareggio, depart Florence's main station several times in the morning. The average time to Lucca is about 90 minutes; a change at Pistoia might be required. Return service operates until late evening.

Buses leave from the LAZZI terminal just opposite the east side of the main train station in Florence. Buy your ticket before boarding for the 70-minute ride. The bus station in Lucca is at Piazzale Verdi at the west end of the ramparts.

By car, Lucca is 46 miles west of Florence via the A-11 Autostrada. The most convenient parking inside the walls is at Piazza Napoleone.

PRACTICALITIES:

Lucca may be enjoyed at any time, but remember that its major museum is closed on Mondays and some holidays. The local **Tourist Information Office**, phone (0583) 49-36-39, is at Via Veneto 40, just south of Piazza Napoleone. There is also a local tourist office at Piazzale Donato, by the western end of the ramparts, where **bicycles** may be rented. Lucca is in the region of **Toscana** and has a **population** of about 89,000.

FOOD AND DRINK:

The restaurants of Lucca offer unusually good dining for your money. Some good choices are:

Buca di Sant' Antonio (Via della Cervia, near Pza. San Michele) The most famous restaurant in town, specializes in game dishes. Reservations needed, phone (0583) 55-881. X: Sun. eve., Mon., July $$$

Giglio (Pza. del Giglio, near Pza. Napoleone) A traditional restaurant in an old building. X: Tues. eve., Wed. $$

Sergio (Pza. dei Bernardini 7, between the cathedral and the Guinigi Tower) A contemporary ambiance above a square. X: Mon. eve., Tues. $$

Da Giulio (Via San Tommaso 29, near the northwest corner of the ramparts) Very popular with the local crowd, an exceptional value. X: Sun., Mon., Aug. $

There are two good local wines, the red *Colline Lucchesi* and the white *Montecarlo*. Lucca is famous for its olive oil.

SUGGESTED TOUR:

Leaving the **train station** (1), follow the map through the Porta San Pietro gate and into the Old Town. Via Vittorio Veneto leads to the main square, **Piazza Napoleone**, dominated on the west by the handsome 16th-century Palazzo della Provincia. Turn right and continue on to the ***Duomo** (Cathedral) (2), an 11th- to 13th-century Romanesque structure that appears to be leaning against its bell tower. Its richly decorated façade with three tiers of arches is in the style of nearby Pisa, although it looks unfinished for lack of a top pediment.

The interior, rebuilt in the Gothic style during the 14th century, has a fine inlaid marble floor. The cathedral's greatest treasure, from a religious point of view, is the ***Volto Santo** (Holy Face), a wooden effigy of Christ on the Cross housed in its own little temple in the middle of the north aisle. There is an utterly fantastic story associated with this; one that drew pilgrims to Lucca for many years. According to this legend, the figure was carved by Nicodemus shortly after the Crucifixion, and remained hidden for centuries. Through a vision, an Italian bishop found it in Lebanon and cast it adrift on an unmanned boat. Miraculously, it appeared off the Italian shore near La Spezia. Naturally, there was a dispute as to which town got it. To solve this, the Crucifix was placed on a cart drawn by two untamed oxen who would go wherever God willed them. They went to Lucca. The flaw in the tale is that the figure seems to be of 11th-century origin. In any case, the people of Lucca love their statue and take it for a ride around town every September 13th. The temple housing it was built in 1484 by Lucca's own Matteo Civitali.

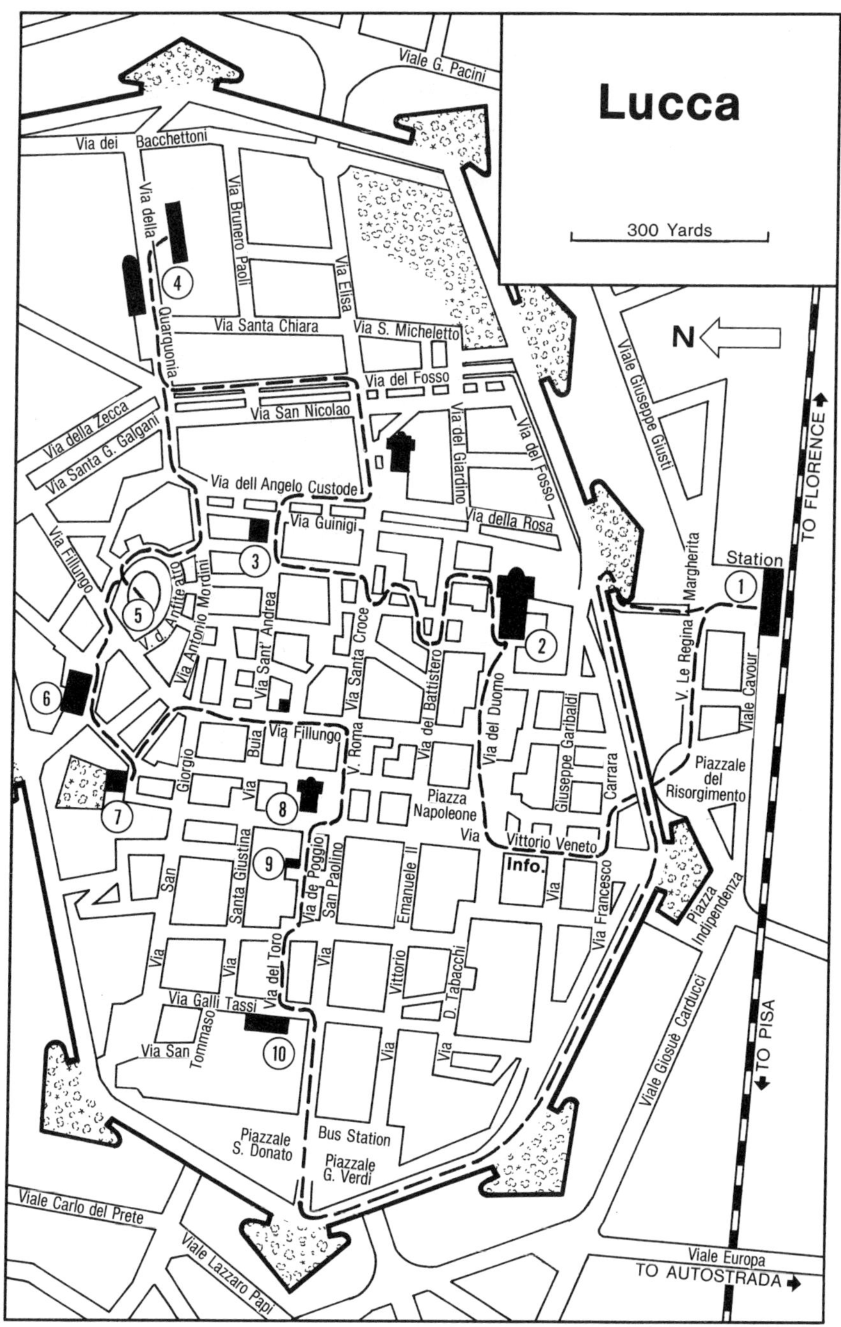
Lucca
300 Yards
N
Viale G. Pacini
Via dei Bacchettoni
Via della Quarquonia
Via Brunero Paoli
Via Elisa
Via Santa Chiara
Via S. Micheletto
Via del Fosso
Via San Nicolao
Via della Zecca
Via Santa G. Galgani
Via dell Angelo Custode
Via del Giardino
Via del Fosso
Via Guinigi
Via della Rosa
Via Fillungo
V. d. Anfiteatro
Via Antonio Mordini
Via Sant' Andrea
Via Santa Croce
Via del Battistero
Via del Duomo
Via Fillungo
Via Buia
Via San Giorgio
V. Roma
Piazza Napoleone
Via Vittorio Veneto
Info.
Via Giuseppe Garibaldi
Via Carrara
Via de Poggio
Via San Paolino
Via Santa Giustina
Via Vittorio Emanuele II
Via Francesco Carrara
Via del Toro
Via D. Tabacchi
Via Galli Tassi
Via San Tommaso
Piazzale S. Donato
Bus Station
Piazzale G. Verdi
Viale Carlo del Prete
Viale Lazzaro Papi
Viale Europa
TO AUTOSTRADA
Viale Giosuè Carducci
TO PISA
Piazza Indipendenza
Piazzale del Risorgimento
Viale Cavour
V. Le Regina Margherita
Station
Viale Giuseppe Giusti
TO FLORENCE
1
2
3
4
5
6
7
8
9
10

The cathedral has several other works of art, foremost of which is the celebrated ***Tomb of Ilaria del Carretto**, an early-15th-century masterpiece by Jacopo della Quercia in the north transept. To the right of this, in a chapel, is a famous painting of the *Madonna with St. Stephen and St. John the Baptist*. Returning towards the west end, the third chapel in the south aisle has a marvelous *Last Supper* by Tintoretto. Just before exiting, note the sculpture near the center door of *St. Martin and the Beggar*. The cathedral is open daily from 7:30 a.m. to noon and 3–7 p.m.

Now wind your way through the ancient streets to a most peculiar sight, the 14th-century **Torre Guinigi** (3). There is nothing unusual about medieval Italian town palaces with towers, but this one is topped by full-grown trees and, what's more, you can climb up and sit in the shade under them. The ***view** is absolutely marvelous and well worth the effort. Ascents may be made daily, April through September, from 9 a.m. to 7 p.m.; and from 10 a.m. to 4 p.m. the rest of the year.

Continue on, following the map, past the 13th-century **Chiesa di Santa Maria Forisportam**, a church so named because it was then outside the gate of the original Roman walls. **Via del Fosso**, divided by a small canal, is all that remains of a medieval defensive moat. Stroll along it to the statue of the Madonna atop a column, then turn right on Via della Quarquonia.

The **Museo Nazionale** (National Museum), housed in the impressive 15th-century **Villa Guinigi** (4) just outside the Old Town, contains a rich collection of art and artifacts. The ground floor rooms are filled with Roman, Etruscan, and even Ligurian items found locally, along with Lucchese sculpture from the 8th through the 14th centuries. The painting galleries, upstairs, include among their treasures two large major works by Fra Bartolommeo. There is also some interesting furniture, textiles, and inlay work. The museum is open on Tuesdays through Sundays from 9 a.m. to 2 p.m., with shorter hours from October through March. It is closed on Mondays and major holidays.

Retrace your steps and continue on Via dell' Anfiteatro, which follows the walls of the **Anfiteatro Romano** (5), or what's left of it. Built in the 2nd century A.D. to house ten thousand spectators, the Roman arena became a quarry after the fall of the empire; many of its stones being used in church construction. Some remained, however, and medieval dwellings were built incorporating the original walls with newer masonry. As you walk down the street you will be able to clearly pick out the Roman stones and arches from the later fabric. Enter the first archway into Piazza del Mercato, an **outdoor market place** in the center of the arena. The atmosphere here is charged with ancient memories, especially after the last vegetable sellers have gone home.

The **Chiesa di San Frediano** (6), a nearby church, was built in the

Atop the Torre Guinigi

12th century on the site of a 6th-century basilica. Its rather austere façade is topped with a wonderful **mosaic** depicting Christ and the Twelve Apostles. Inside, there is a magnificent 12th-century ***font** in the right aisle, carved with the story of Moses, the Good Shepherd, and the Apostles. The **Trenta Chapel**, on the left, has some fine reliefs by Jacopo della Quercia. Also on the left aisle is the Chapel of St. Augustine with a fresco illustrating the transport of the Volto Santo to Lucca, a legend you already came across in the cathedral and may be curious about.

Just a few steps away stands the elegant 17th-century **Palazzo Pfanner** (7). Enter the simple doorway and wander around the delightful 18th-century statuary gardens, built up against the town's ramparts. The splendid galleried staircase leads to a small exhibit of local costumes.

Follow the map down Via Fillungo, a narrow pedestrian street steeped in the atmosphere of the Middle Ages. The **Torre delle Ore**, a 13th-century clock tower on the left, is one of the few medieval towers that survive in a town once full of them. A right turn on Via Roma brings you to the Piazza San Michele, a large open square on the site of the Roman forum. Note the open Renaissance loggia of the Palazzo Pretorio at the southwest corner.

The Chiesa di San Michele in Foro

The **Chiesa di San Michele in Foro** (8) is a church with a marvelously oversized ***façade**, easily the most impressive in town. Crowned with an enormous statue of the Archangel Michael, it was built in the 13th century for a planned enlargement of the 12th-century church that never took place. Step inside to see, on the first altar in the south aisle, the terracotta *Madonna and Child* by Andrea della Robbia and, in the north transept, a panel painting of *Four Saints* by Filippo Lippi.

It is now only a few steps to the **Casa di Giacomo Puccini** (9) on Via di Poggio. Born in this house in 1858, the renowned composer studied music in Lucca before moving on to Milan. Opera lovers will want to go upstairs to see the small museum devoted to his life. It is open on Tuesdays through Sundays from 10 a.m. to 6 p.m., closing at 4 p.m. from October through March, and closed on some holidays.

Continue straight ahead to the **Pinacoteca Nazionale** (National Gallery) (10) in the 17th-century Palazzo Mansi. Its sumptuous interior houses a good collection of paintings, primarily from the Renaissance through the 19th century, but the real attraction here is the rich decor. It is open on Tuesdays through Sundays, from 9 a.m. to 7 p.m., closing at 4 p.m. on holidays.

Now wander past the bus terminal at Piazzale Verdi and the nearby local tourist office (which also rents bicycles) onto the 16th-century ***fortifications** that completely encircle the Old Town. These tree-shaded ramparts offer wonderful views as well as a delightful route back to the train station, and are a favorite place among the locals for pleasant strolls or bike rides.

A Daytrip from Milan

Bergamo

Another one of those marvelously well-preserved medieval hill towns that often get overlooked by tourists, Bergamo makes an easy and highly satisfying daytrip from nearby Milan. Perhaps would-be visitors are put off by its spacious, pleasantly modern but unexciting Lower Town. Those who ascend to the ancient walled Upper Town, however, are in for a visual treat, an unspoiled holdover from the Middle Ages that never fails to work its special magic.

Originally a Gallic settlement, Bergamo fell to the Romans in 197 B.C. and was named *Bergomum*. It remained an unimportant place until the 12th century when it joined the Lombard League and soon came under the control of Milan. After years of internal fighting between the noble families, it finally threw in its lot with Venice, to whom it belonged from 1498 till 1797. Conquered by Napoleon and later under Austrian domination, it played a pivotal role in the *Risorgimento* that led to Italian unity in the mid-19th century.

GETTING THERE:

Trains leave Milan's Centrale Station shortly before 9 a.m., and at other times from Milan's Garibaldi or Lambrate stations, for the 50-minute ride to Bergamo. Return service operates until mid-evening, with a few trains terminating at Garibaldi or Lambrate stations in Milan, both easily reached by subway.

By car, Bergamo is 30 miles northeast of Milan via the A-4 Autostrada. Avoid driving in the Upper Town.

PRACTICALITIES:

Bergamo may be visited at any time, but note that the Art Museum is closed on Mondays and some holidays. Fine weather is necessary to enjoy the views. The local **Tourist Information Office**, phone (035) 232–730, is at Piazza Vecchia 9, in the Upper Town. Bergamo is in the region of **Lombardia** and has a **population** of about 120,000.

FOOD AND DRINK:

There is an unusually good selection of restaurants—some of which serve the local specialty, *Polenta e Ucelli di Bergamo,* a dish of small roasted birds in cornmeal mush. A few choices in the Upper Town are:

Taverna del Colleoni (Pza. Vecchia 7, on the main square) Dining in a 16th-century setting, with outdoor tables in summer. X: Mon., Aug. $$$

Agnello d'Oro (Via Gombito 22, between the Rocca and Pza. Vecchia) An old inn with a cozy ambiance. X: Mon., Jan. $$

Trattoria Barnabò (Via Colleoni 31, west of Pza. Vecchia) A great value in regional cooking. X: Thurs. $

SUGGESTED TOUR:

From the **train station** (1) in the **Lower Town** *(Città Bassa)*, you can either take a bus to the funicular (3) (one ticket covers both), or walk the pleasant distance of nearly one mile. On foot, follow Viale Papa Giovanni XXIII to **Piazza Matteotti** (2), a monumental open square beyond the 19th-century Porta Nuova gate that marks the 15th-century town boundaries. To the right is the Teatro Donizetti, an opera house named for the composer Gaetano Donizetti, born in Bergamo in 1797. All of the broad streets and elegant squares around you are the result of an urban plan developed around 1900, when the Lower Town still had relatively few buildings.

Continue straight ahead to the lower station of the **funicular** (3) that quickly lifts you to the ancient **Upper Town** *(Città Alta)*, perched high above the plain. Follow the map uphill from the picturesque Piazza del Mercato delle Scarpe to the **Rocca Fortress** (4), built in 1331 and enlarged by both the Viscontis of Milan and the Venetians. In 1848 it was used by the Austrians as a platform from which to bomb the Lower Town. Just beyond this lies the lovely **Park of Remembrance** with its closeup views of the Upper Town as well as a sweeping **panorama** of the surrounding countryside.

Return to the square and amble up the narrow Via Gombito, passing on the left the **Torre Gombito**, erected in 1100 to an impressive height of 210 feet but later lowered to 170 feet for fear of instability.

A hundred yards or so beyond this the street opens into what has to be one of the most beautiful squares in Italy, the ***Piazza Vecchia**, historically the center of Bergamo. The atmosphere of times long gone by is so intense here that you may feel transported into another era. At the far end, crowned with the winged lion of Venice, is the **Palazzo della Ragione**, built in 1198, destroyed by fire in 1513, and rebuilt in 1554. On its right, a 14th-century covered staircase leads to the main floor of the palace, which was used as a town hall during the times of the Venetian Republic.

An elegant little 18th-century **fountain** splashes away in the center of the square, while to the right, beyond the staircase, the **Torre Civ-**

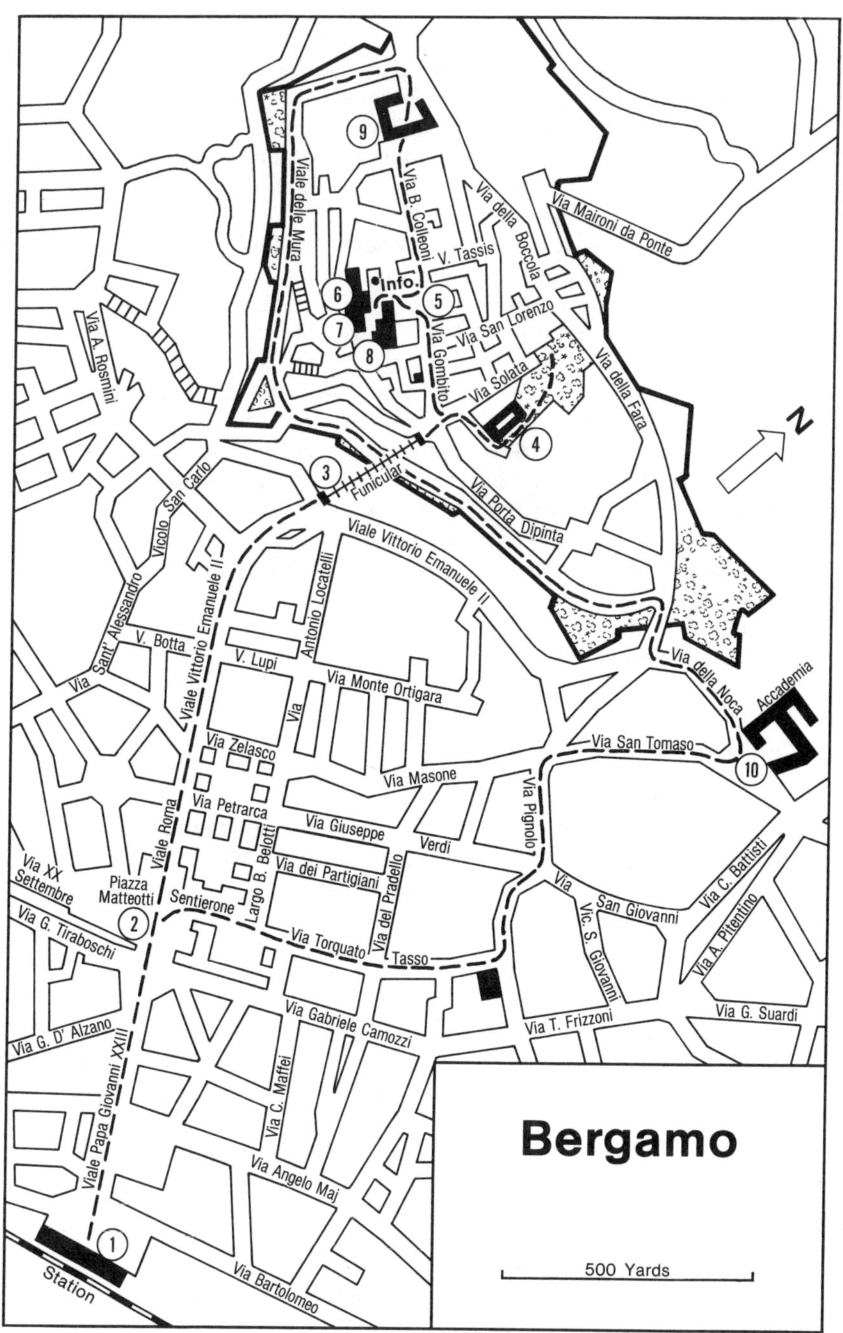
Bergamo
500 Yards
N
Info.
Viale delle Mura
Via B. Colleoni
V. Tassis
Via della Boccola
Via Maironi da Ponte
Via San Lorenzo
Via Gombito
Via Solata
Via della Fara
Funicular
Via Porta Dipinta
Viale Vittorio Emanuele II
Via A. Rosmini
Vicolo San Carlo
Via Sant' Alessandro
V. Botta
V. Lupi
Via Antonio Locatelli
Via Monte Ortigara
Via della Noca
Accademia
Via San Tomaso
Via Zelasco
Via Masone
Via Pignolo
Via Petrarca
Viale Roma
Via Giuseppe Verdi
Largo B. Belotti
Via dei Partigiani
Via del Pradello
Via XX Settembre
Piazza Matteotti
Sentierone
Via G. Tiraboschi
Via Torquato Tasso
Via San Giovanni
Vic. S. Giovanni
Via C. Battisti
Via A. Pitentino
Via G. Suardi
Via T. Frizzoni
Via Gabriele Camozzi
Via G. D' Alzano
Via C. Maffei
Viale Papa Giovanni XXIII
Via Angelo Maj
Via Bartolomeo
Station

ica rises to a height of 175 feet. This 12th-century tower was built by a Ghibelline family to lord it over their Guelph neighbors and later, in the 15th century, acquired a clock and a bell that still sounds the curfew every evening at 10 o'clock. In more recent times an elevator was installed, making it easy for you to reach the platform for an intimate **view** across the rooftops.

Pass under an archway to the ***Capella Colleoni** (6). Exceedingly flamboyant in its multicolored marble, this chapel rises above the question of taste and becomes, instead, a gem of Lombardian Renaissance architecture. Built in 1476 to receive the remains of that great *condottiere,* the soldier-of-fortune Bartolomeo Colleoni who at various times served both Venice and Milan, it houses the exquisite tomb of his daughter as well as, perhaps, himself, although this is not known for certain. Step inside to see the **frescoes** by Tiepolo, the delicate **sarcophagus** by Amadeo of Pavia, and the leader's **equestrian statue** executed in gilt wood by the German master, Sisto Siry of Nürnberg. The chapel is open daily from 9 a.m. to noon and 3–6 p.m.

Adjacent to this is the ***Basilica di Santa Maria Maggiore** (7), a Romanesque structure begun in 1137 on the site of an 8th-century church. Its marvelous north porch gives a hint of the splendors to be found within its wildly Baroque interior, lavishly redecorated during the late 16th century. Be sure to examine the elaborately carved 18th-century ***confessional**, the Florentine and Flemish ***tapestries**, the inlaid wooden **choir stalls** from the 16th century, and the 14th-century **frescoes** in the north transept. The basilica is closed between 12:30 and 3 p.m.

At the far end of the square is the **Duomo** (Cathedral) (8), a 15th-century building with an 18th-century interior and a 19th-century dome and façade. Although richly decorated with some fine paintings by Tiepolo and others, it is of less interest than the two previous churches.

Stroll past the small **Baptistry**, a charming 14th-century octagonal structure adorned with statues, and return to Piazza Vecchia (5). From here follow Via Colleoni to Piazza Mascheroni. A small gateway opens into **Piazza Cittadella** (9), bordered by buildings that were once a residence of the ruling Viscontis, and later a seat of the Austrian overlords. They now house the modest Archaeological and Natural History museums.

Continue on to Largo Colle Aperto and turn left on Viale delle Mura, built atop the imposing fortified walls erected by the Venetian Republic in the 16th century. Along here you will have glorious **views** of the pre-Alps, the Lower Town, the plains of Lombardy and, if the weather is really clear, the spires of Milan's cathedral. At Porta San Giacomo bear left and follow the map to the Porta Sant' Agostino at the foot of the Upper Town.

Piazza Vecchia and the Torre Civica

Just beyond this, turn left on Via della Noca, really a pedestrian way, and walk down to the ***Accademia Carrara** (10), an outstanding art museum famous for the exceptionally high quality of its collections. The gallery is not large enough to intimidate or exhaust you, but can certainly provide at least an hour's enjoyment of superb paintings. It mostly deals with the northern Italian schools but includes some foreign works as well. This special treat is open on Wednesdays through Mondays, from 9:30 a.m. to 12:30 p.m. and 2:30–5:30 p.m.

Now bear right and stroll up Via San Tomaso, making a left onto Via Pignolo—two picturesque streets lined with fine old buildings. A right turn at the interesting **Chiesa di San Spirito** brings you onto Via Torquato Tasso, ending at the Sentierone, an elegant promenade with outdoor cafés on one side and the Donizetti Opera House on the other. This is a fine place to rest before heading back to the station.

A Daytrip from Milan

The Borromean Islands

The Italian Lake District in the foothills of the Alps north of Milan has been a favorite vacation paradise for many generations of Europeans. These long, thin bodies of sparkling water combine mountain grandeur with the luxurious vegetation of a Mediterranean land, providing welcome relief from the summer heat of the cities. For tourists, they also offer a brief chance to escape those steady cultural treks through museums, churches, and palaces.

Which of the lakes is best for an enjoyable daytrip is a matter of taste. Each has its virtues, but only Lake Maggiore has the Borromean Islands—easily among the most memorable sights in Italy. Three of these can be visited, including the strange fantasy world of Isola Bella, the impossibly picturesque Isola dei Pescatori, and the lush gardens of Isola Madre. To finish the day, you may want to ride a cable car to the summit of Monte Mottarone for a glorious view of the lake and the nearby Swiss Alps.

The Borromean Islands are easily reached by boats from Stresa, a fashionable lake resort on a major rail line. Lake Maggiore, barely three miles across at its widest point, is some 40 miles long, extending from the plains of Lombardy north to Locarno in Switzerland.

GETTING THERE:

Trains leave Milan's Centrale Station several times in the morning for Stresa, a ride of about one hour. There are also slower local trains from Milan's Garibaldi Station, taking about 90 minutes. Return service operates until mid-evening.

By car, Stresa is 50 miles northwest of Milan via the A-8 Autostrada and the S-33 road. Park near the pier.

PRACTICALITIES:

The Borromean Islands may be visited any day from about late March through October. Good weather is essential for this trip. The local **Tourist Information Office** in Stresa, phone (0323) 30-150, is in the Palace of Congesses at Piazzale Europa 1, midway between the train station and the pier. Stresa and the islands are in the **Piemonte** region.

In the Gardens on Isola Bella

FOOD AND DRINK:

Lake Maggiore is an international resort, with a wide selection of restaurants and cafés. Some choices are:

In Stresa:

Hôtel des Iles Borromées (Corso Umberto I, between the pier and the cable car) A grand resort hotel in the 19th-century tradition, with a renowned luxury restaurant. $$$

Emiliano (Corso Italia 48, near the pier) Considered to be the best restaurant in the area. Reservations needed, phone (0323) 31-396. X: Tues., Dec. $$$

Ariston (Corso Italia 60, near the pier) Dining at a small hotel with a view of the lake. X: Dec.–Feb. $$

Luina (Via Garibaldi 21, 1 block inland from the pier) Excellent food in a convenient location. X: Nov.–Mar. $$

Pappagallo (Via Principessa Margherita 46, just off Corso Umberto I) Pizza and popular Italian dishes. X: Wed. $

On Isola Bella:

Elvezia (across from the pier) A small inn with a restaurant. X: Nov.–Mar. $$

On Isola dei Pescatori:

Verbano (behind the church) Outdoor dining with a view. X: Wed., Nov.–Mar. $$

SUGGESTED TOUR:

Leaving the **train station** (1) in Stresa, turn right and then left onto Via Duchessa di Genova. A right on Via De Martini will take you past the **tourist office** (2). Continue down Via Roma and Via Tomaso to the large boat terminal on the **pier** (3). There are other small boats operating from the lakefront around here, but these are more expensive than the regular scheduled boats from the pier. Buy a ticket good for stops at Isola Bella, Isola Superiore (a.k.a. *dei Pescatori*), Isola Madre, and return. If you intend to extend your trip to include Villa Taranto (7) you should get the more expensive ticket that goes at least that far. Posted signs in English explain all of the options, but ask for a free schedule brochure *(Orario)* so you can plot your moves as the day progresses.

Board the boat to Isola Bella, a hop of about five minutes. Always ask to make sure that you are on the right boat so you don't wind up somewhere else on this very large lake.

***Isola Bella** (4) is almost completely a creation of man. Originally just a rock inhabited by few people, it was transformed in the 17th century by Count Borromeo into its present dream-like fantasy of stepped gardens, incredible statuary, and a lavish palace. There is no other place on Earth quite like this; and while all of it is grossly overdecorated, the island never fails to enchant—or at least amuse—its many visitors. The whole ensemble is still owned, along with Isola Madre, by the Borromeo family.

Buy a ticket and enter the **Palace**. You can either join a guided tour or just stroll through on your own. Some of the opulent chambers are of historic interest—Napoleon slept in one and Mussolini held a 1936 conference of European leaders in another. A descent to the **grottoes** takes you into a different world. Returning to the palace above, walk out into the spectacular ***gardens**, where white peacocks stroll amid exotic vegetation and bizarre sculptures. Try to allow an hour for both the palace and gardens, which are open daily in season from 9 a.m. to noon and 1:30–5:30 p.m.

Return to the pier and take the next boat to **Isola Superiore** (5), more popularly known as **Isola dei Pescatori** for the fishermen who live there. Wander around the back alleyways of the tiny village and go down to the water on the side opposite the pier, where local children play along the rocky beach. Be sure to visit the simple but inspiring **church** and the tiny graveyard behind it. From here, the narrow Via Ugo Ara squeezes its way between venerable houses to a little **park** at the island's northwestern end. Some people complain that Isola dei Pescatori has been ruined by mass tourism, but they've probably never been beyond the commercialized pier area, to which you should now return for a boat ride to the next island.

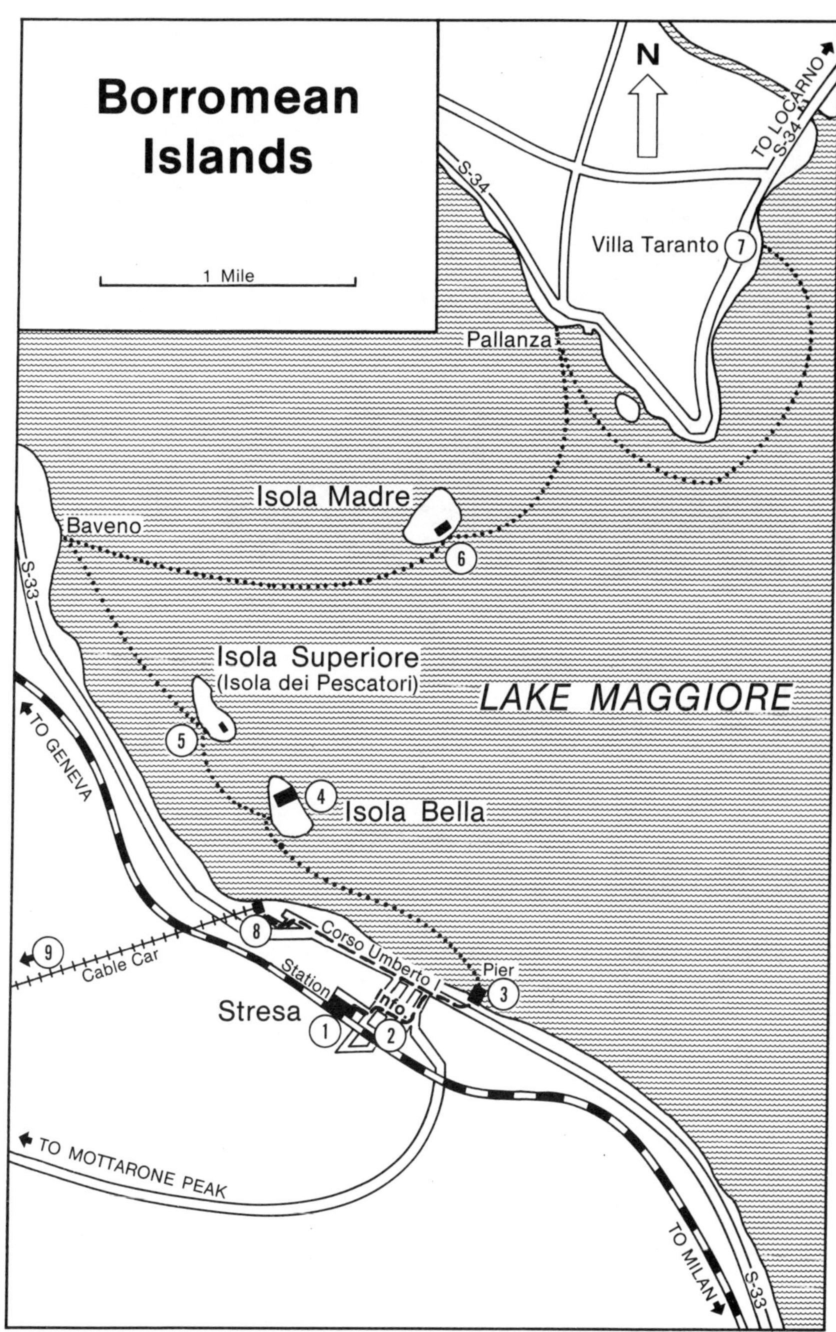

Borromean Islands
1 Mile
N
TO LOCARNO
S-34
S-34
Villa Taranto
7
Pallanza
Isola Madre
Baveno
6
S-33
Isola Superiore
(Isola dei Pescatori)
LAKE MAGGIORE
TO GENEVA
5
4
Isola Bella
8
Corso Umberto I
9
Cable Car
Station
Pier
3
Info
Stresa
1
2
TO MOTTARONE PEAK
TO MILAN
S-33

The pier at Isola Superiore

***Isola Madre** (6) is the largest, the least-visited, and in some ways the most delightful of the Borromean Islands. It too has a villa, but compared to the outrageous palace on Isola Bella this is a pretty simple affair, with interesting portraits and mementos of the Borromeo family's history on display. The main attraction, though, is the setting itself—a semi-tropical world of luxuriant ***gardens** and natural splendor with the Alps for a backdrop. Visits may be made on any day in season, from 9 a.m. to 5:30 p.m.

At this point you will probably want to return to Stresa. Those with an interest in gardens might prefer to continue on to the ***Villa Taranto** (7), a botanical paradise reached by boat after first making a stop at Pallanza. An enormous variety of flora from all over the world is cultivated in a magnificent setting. The gardens are open daily from April through October, from 8:30 a.m. to 6:30 p.m.

Back in Stresa, you can get an overall view of the lake and the surrounding mountains by taking the cable car (or driving by the route on the map) to the top of **Monte Mottarone**. The lower station (8) is a bit less than one mile from the pier. Follow Corso Umberto I along the water's edge to the point where it turns inland, then take Via Borromeo and Via Torino to Lido and board the cable car for the ride up. The **summit** (9), at 4,900 feet, offers a marvelous alpine panorama extending as far south as Milan.

A Daytrip from Milan

*Verona

The ancient, romantic city of Verona is best known as the setting for a story that never happened. Or did it? Fantasy mixes with reality here, and you can easily imagine Romeo and Juliet strolling through these timeless streets.

The very origins of Verona are as cloudy as the Shakespearean tragedy it gave life to. Two thousand years ago it was already an important city, and an old one even then, having been occupied since prehistoric times. For the Romans it was a vital strategic center, situated on the plains just south of a point where the Alps could be crossed. Verona's greatest era was under the Scaligers, from 1260 to 1387, followed by a dark period at the hands of the Viscontis. From 1405 to 1796 it flourished under Venetian rule. Then came the French, succeeded by the Austrians in 1814. In 1866 Verona finally became part of a unified Italy.

Few cities in Europe have preserved their past quite as well. Several Roman structures remain in use today, including the third-largest Roman amphitheater in the world. A lingering medieval atmosphere still fills the streets, and there are many splendid Renaissance buildings to enliven the scene. On top of this, Verona is a lively, likeable place that is easily enjoyed on foot.

GETTING THERE:

Trains depart Milan's Centrale Station for Verona's Porta Nuova Station fairly frequently until about 9 a.m., the trip taking a bit less than 90 minutes. Return service operates until late evening.

By car, take the A-4 Autostrada east from Milan to the Verona-Sud exit, a distance of 98 miles.

PRACTICALITIES:

Verona may be visited in any season, but avoid coming on a Monday or major holiday, when nearly everything is closed. The local **Tourist Information Office**, phone (045) 59-28-28, is at Via Dietro Anfiteatro 6, behind the Arena. Verona is in the region of **Veneto** and has a **population** of about 260,000.

FOOD AND DRINK:

The local cuisine of Verona is similar to that of its long-time ruler, Venice. One local specialty is *Pandoro,* a delicate light cake. The best regional wines are the dry white *Soave,* the fragrant red *Valpolicella,* and the light red *Bardolino*. Some good restaurant choices are:

12 Apostoli (Corticella San Marco 3, a block southwest of Pza. delle Erbe) Very old and world famous. For reservations call (045) 59-69-99. X: Sun. eve., Mon., mid-June. $$$

Nuovo Marconi (Via Fogge 4, a block northwest of Pza. dei Signori) Great food in elegant surroundings. Phone (045) 59-19-10 to reserve. X: Tues. eve., Sun. $$$

Accademia (Via Scala 10) Conveniently located just east of Via Mazzini. X: Sun. eve., Wed. $$ and $$$

Ciopeta (Vicolo Teatro Filarmonico 2, a block west of Pza. Brà) A small inn with good-value meals. X: Fri. eve., Sat. $$

Corte Farina (Corte Farina 4, 3 blocks north of the Arena, a block west of Via Mazzini) A great pizzeria with budget prices. X: Mon. $

SUGGESTED TOUR:

From the **Porta Nuova train station** (1) you can either take a bus or walk the dull three-quarter-mile distance to Piazza Brà. Along the way you will pass through the Porta Nuova gate, a part of the massive 16th-century town walls. **Piazza Brà** is entered through the Portoni della Brà, erected in 1389 by the Viscontis as part of their defences. To the right is the bulky 17th-century Palazza della Gran Guardia and, just beyond, the neoclassical Palazzo Barbieri, now the city hall. On the opposite side of the park is the Liston, a fashionable promenade lined with lively cafés and restaurants.

The main attraction in the Piazza Brà is the ***Arena** (2), the third-largest amphitheater of the Roman world. It was built in the 1st century A.D. and is still in excellent condition. Only four arches of the outermost wall survived the earthquake of 1183, but the inner section is virtually complete. You can climb all over the interior, which seats some 20,000 spectators who in the past may have enjoyed gladiatorial contests during the Roman era, executions in the Middle Ages, tournaments during the Renaissance, and plays in the 19th century. It is now used for operas during July and August, of which the most spectacular is that perennial favorite by Verdi, Aïda. The Arena is open every day except Mondays and a few holidays, from 8 a.m. to 6:45 p.m., closing earlier in winter and at 1:30 on performance days.

Now follow Via Mazzini, a pedestrians-only street lined with quality shops, to the **Casa di Giullietta** (House of Juliet) (3) at Via Cappello 23. Step into the courtyard to see the famous **balcony** from which

Juliet's Balcony

Shakespeare's characters exchanged their declarations of love. The building dates from the 13th century, but no evidence of any real Romeo and Juliet exists. It's a nice illusion, however, and you can go out on the balcony to complete it. The house is open on Tuesdays through Sundays, from 8 a.m. to 6:45 p.m.

Stroll over to the ***Piazza delle Erbe** (4), a market place on the site of the Roman forum. Amid the colorful bustle of the market stands the Madonna of Verona fountain, erected in 1368 and now the symbol of the city. All around you are various houses, palaces, and towers, some dating as far back as the 12th century.

Pass under the Arco della Costa, which has a whalebone hanging from it, and into **Piazza dei Signori** (5), a surprisingly quiet and dignified square in the midst of so much commotion. An opening on the right leads into the courtyard of the Mercato Vecchio from which you may ascend all 270 feet of the 12th-century **Torre dei Lamberti** by elevator for a marvelous **view**, any day except Mondays. Stroll back into Piazza dei Signori, where a statue of Dante recalls the poet's stay here after being exiled from his native Florence. Behind him is the Loggia del Consiglio, the finest Renaissance structure in Verona.

Among the more unusual sights in town are the **Arche Scaligeri** (Tombs of the Scaligers) (6), reached through an archway at the far end of the Piazza dei Signori. These outdoor canopied Gothic structures are the most elaborate medieval tombs in Italy, a fitting memo-

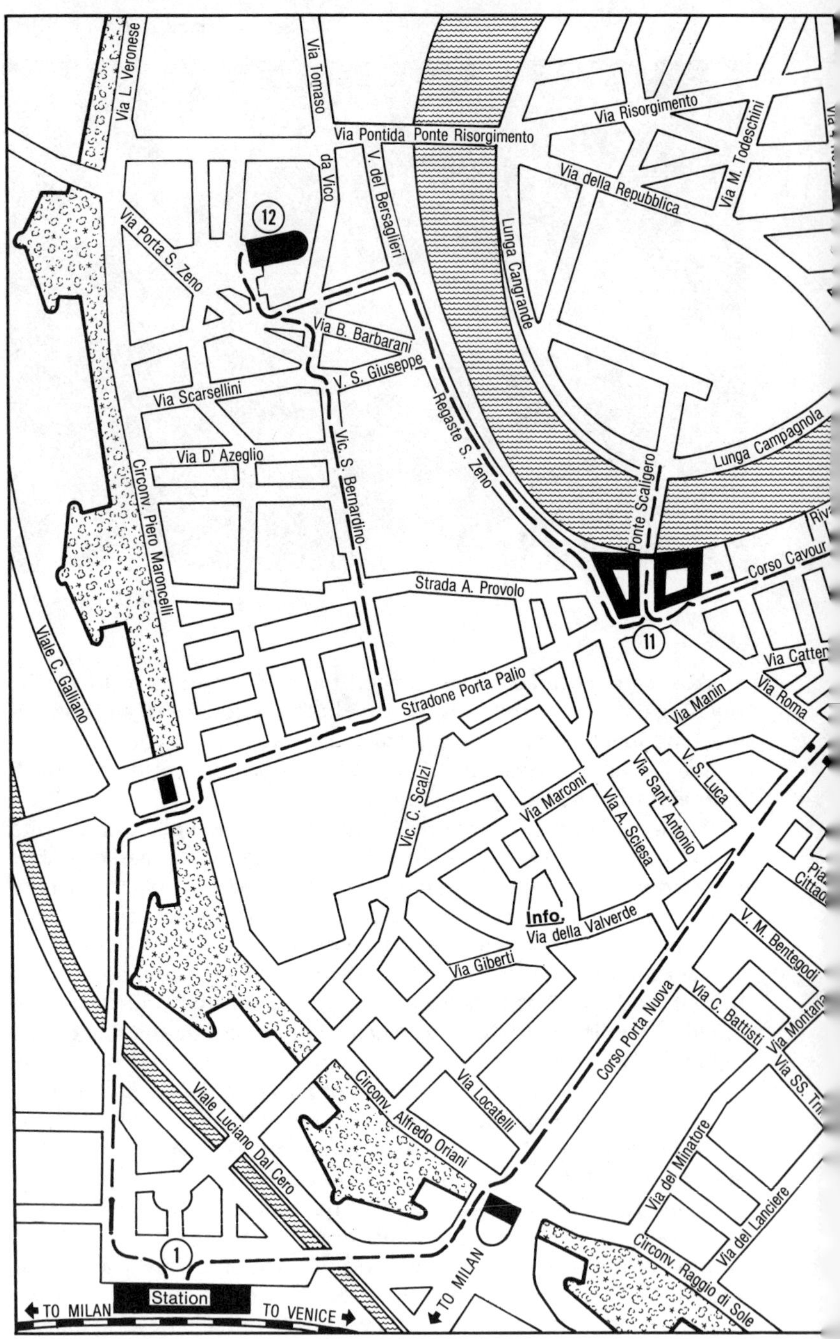

Via L. Veronese
Via Tomaso da Vico
Via Pontida
Ponte Risorgimento
Via Risorgimento
Via M. Todeschini
Via della Repubblica
V. del Bersaglieri
12
Via Porta S. Zeno
Lunga Cangrande
Via B. Barbarani
V. S. Giuseppe
Via Scarsellini
Regaste S. Zeno
Lunga Campagnola
Via D' Azeglio
Circonv. Piero Maroncelli
Vic. S. Bernardino
Ponte Scaligero
Corso Cavour
Strada A. Provolo
11
Viale C. Galliano
Stradone Porta Palio
Via Manin
Via Roma
V. S. Luca
Via Sant' Antonio
Via Marconi
Via A. Sciesa
Vic. C. Scalzi
Info.
Via della Valverde
Via Giberti
V. M. Bentegodi
Corso Porta Nuova
Via C. Battisti
Via Locatelli
Circonv. Alfredo Oriani
Viale Luciano Dal Cero
Via del Minatore
Via del Lanciere
Circonv. Raggio di Sole
1
Station
TO MILAN
TO VENICE
TO MILAN

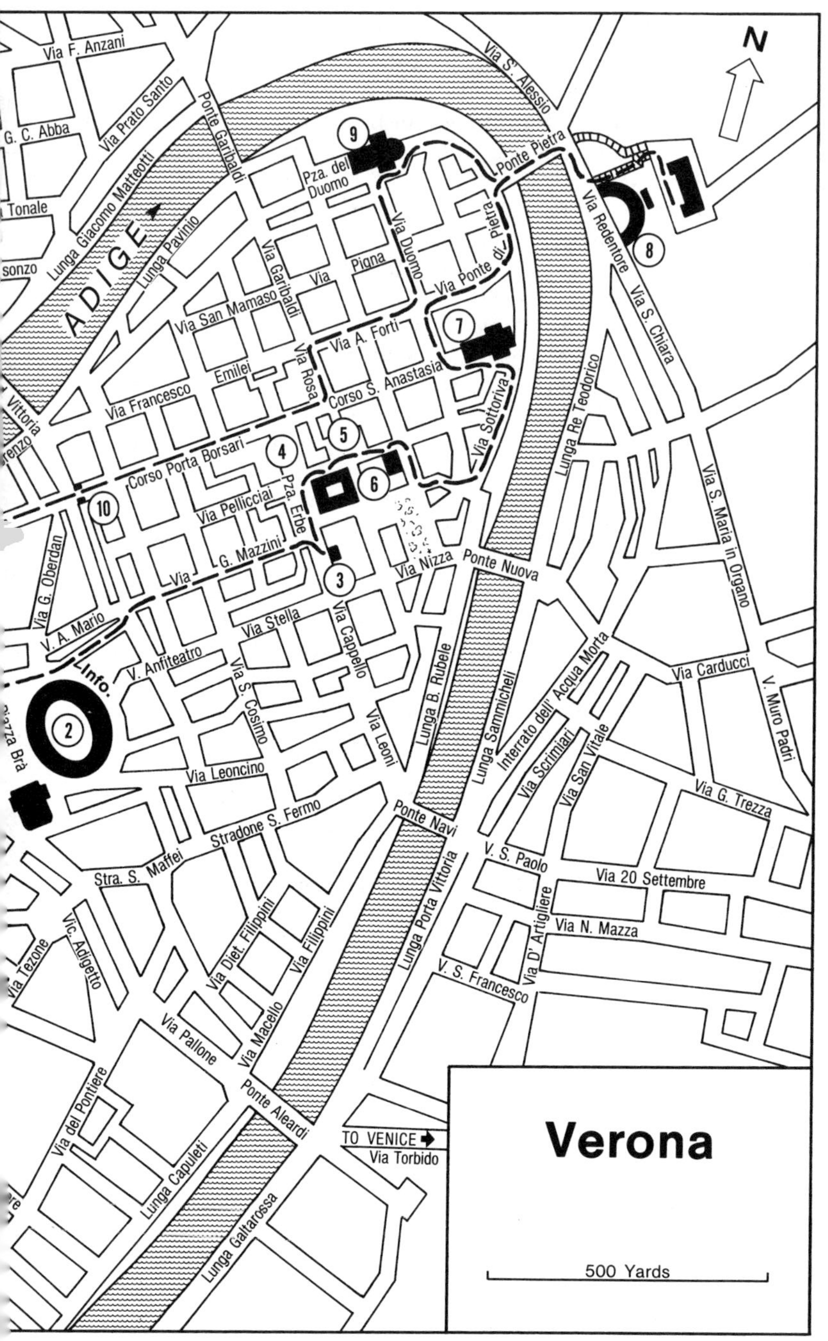

N
ADIGE
Via F. Anzani
G. C. Abba
Via Prato Santo
Tonale
Lunga Giacomo Matteotti
Ponte Garibaldi
Lunga Pavinio
Via S. Alessio
Ponte Pietra
Pza. del Duomo
Via Duomo
Via Ponte di Pietra
Via Redentore
Via S. Chiara
Via Garibaldi
Via Pigna
Via San Mamaso
Via A. Forti
Via Rosa
Emilei
Via Francesco
Corso S. Anastasia
Via Sottoriva
Lunga Re Teodorico
Vittoria
Corso Porta Borsari
Via Pellicciai
Pza. Erbe
Via G. Oberdan
Via G. Mazzini
Via Nizza
Ponte Nuova
Via S. Maria in Organo
V. A. Mario
Via Stella
Via Cappello
Lunga B. Rubele
Lunga Sammicheli
Interrato dell' Acqua Morta
Via Carducci
V. Muro Padri
Info.
V. Anfiteatro
Via S. Cosimo
Via Leoni
Via Scrimiari
Via San Vitale
Via Leoncino
Via G. Trezza
Stradone S. Fermo
Ponte Navi
V. S. Paolo
Via 20 Settembre
Stra. S. Maffei
Lunga Porta Vittoria
Via D' Artigliere
Via N. Mazza
Vic. Adigetto
Via Tezone
Via Diet. Filippini
Via Filippini
V. S. Francesco
Via Macello
Via Pallone
Via del Pontiere
Ponte Aleardi
TO VENICE
Via Torbido
Lunga Capuleti
Lunga Galtarossa
Verona
500 Yards

rial for the Scaliger dynasty. Note in particular the one over the doorway of the adjacent **Chiesa di Santa Maria Antica** church, surmounted by an equestrian figure. The tombs can be seen from the street, or visited close up on any day except Mondays or holidays, from 9 a.m. to noon and 2:30–6 p.m.

Make a right turn onto Via Arche Scaligeri past the so-called Romeo's House at number 4, a medieval building in poor condition. Continue down Via Ponte Nuova and turn left into Via Sottoriva, a picturesque street with porticoed houses in the Venetian Gothic style.

The **Chiesa di Sant' Anastasia** (7), although a huge church, doesn't look like much from the outside. Its interior, however, is quite another story. Begun in 1290 by the Dominicans, it was completed in the 15th century. Step inside to see the famous holy-water **stoups** supported by hunchback human figures. The fresco of **St. George and the Princess,* in the Giusti Chapel at the end of the left transept, is a major 15th-century work by Pisanello. Note also the terracotta reliefs by Michele da Firenze depicting the life of Christ, in the Pellegrini Chapel to the right of the chancel.

The route now leads across the Adige River to the **Teatro Romano** (Roman Theater) (8), an outdoor structure dating from the 1st century B.C. Performances of Shakespeare's plays are given here in July and August. From the theater you can take an elevator to the **Museo Archaeologico** (Archaeological Museum) in the former convent above, which also offers a fine view. The theater complex is open daily except on Mondays and some holidays, from 8 a.m. to 6:45 p.m., closing at 1:30 p.m. in winter and on performance days. It is not actually necessary to go in, however, as you can see a great deal from the steps to the left of its entrance. Continue climbing those same steps all the way to the **Castel San Pietro** at the top of the hill for a sweeping panoramic **view** of Verona, a worthwhile effort.

Return to the river and follow the map to the ***Duomo** (Cathedral) (9), begun in the 12th century on the site of an earlier church. It was altered in later years, acquiring a splendid campanile designed by Verona's great Mannerist architect, Michel Sanmicheli, in the 16th century. Inside, the major art works include a fabulous 16th-century **Assumption* by Titian, over the first altar on the left. Another interesting work, this by Liberale da Verona, is the *Epiphany* above the second altar on the right. The polished marble enclosure around the chancel, dating from 1534, is by Sanmicheli.

Continue on, following the route on the map, through the **Porta Borsari** (10), a well-preserved Roman gateway from the 1st century A.D. Beyond this is the Corso Cavour, a remarkable street lined with Gothic, Renaissance, and Baroque structures, foremost of which is Sanmichele's **Palazzo Bevilacqua** at number 19. In a little park next to the castle stands the **Arco dei Gavi**, a reconstructed 1st-century Roman triumphal arch.

The ***Castelvecchio** (11) is a massive medieval stronghold built in the 14th century by the ruling Cangrande II Scaliger as a refuge from his unruly subjects. It was later put to various uses by the Venetians, the French, and the Austrians, finally becoming a museum in 1925. There are two distinct parts, the fortress and the palace, linked by a keep that also forms the head of the Ponte Scaligero, a bridge across the river. Badly damaged during World War II, the complex has been thoroughly restored and is once again used as an ***art museum**. Enter through the courtyard to see the superb collection of medieval sculptures as well as the many fine paintings from the 16th through the 18th centuries, including works by Veronese, Tintoretto, Bellini, Tiepolo, Guardi, and others. As you cross into the last section of the museum you can get a good look at the famous equestrian statue of Cangrande I, magnificently displayed on a plinth over the courtyard. The Castelvecchio is open on Tuesdays through Sundays, from 8 a.m. to 6:45 p.m.

Be sure to stroll across the heavily fortified and utterly delightful ***Ponte Scaligero** (Scaliger Bridge) to the far side of the river for a wonderful view. At this point you could easily return by way of Via Roma to Piazza Brà, where there are many cafés and where you can get a bus to the train station. To do this, however, is to miss one of the major sights of Verona, reached by following the route on the map.

The 12th-century ***Chiesa di San Zeno Maggiore** (12) is among the best Romanesque churches in Italy. Its celebrated primitive **bronze doors** depict scenes from the Old and New Testaments as well as events in the life of Saint Zeno. Enter through the cloister to the left. The spacious interior is quite unusual and contains, above the high altar, one of the most important early Renaissance paintings in Italy, the noted **San Zeno Triptych* by Mantegna. The balustrade near this is decorated with fine statues of Christ and the Apostles. Below, in the crypt, is the tomb of Saint Zeno himself. The church is usually open daily, from 7 a.m. to 12:30 p.m. and 3:30–6 p.m. Leaving it, the best route back to the train station is shown on the map, or you could take a bus.

Section X

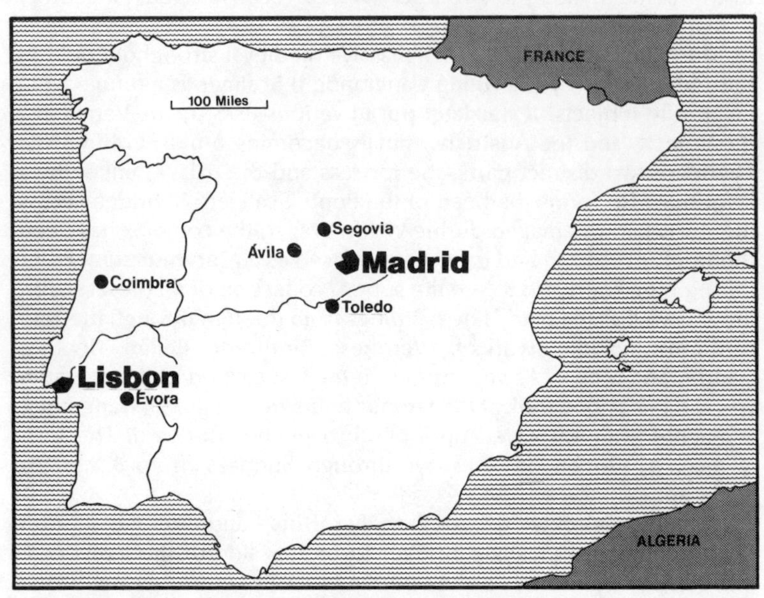

DAYTRIPS IN
SPAIN and PORTUGAL

- **from Madrid**
- **from Lisbon**

Daytrips are becoming a more attractive way to explore the Iberian peninsula as the rail and highway systems there keep getting better. Both Spain and Portugal offer a heady combination of cultures and sights that simply cannot be matched anywhere else in the world. Not only is there a rich Roman past with monuments to rival even Italy's, but—unique in Europe—a strong North African Moorish culture that has left the landscape dotted with exquisite Islamic-influenced architecture. Both of these forces combined with trends from northern Europe to create an intriguing Spanish style along with a very different but equally engrossing Portuguese way of life.

The five daytrips described in this section can only hint at what these two countries have to offer, but all are exceptionally interesting and easy enough to make. The first three are to destinations close to Madrid, while the remaining two use Lisbon as a base.

GETTING AROUND:

Spain's national railway, known locally as **RENFE**, has improved significantly in recent years. Madrid is the hub of its 8,000-mile network, making most towns in Spain relatively easy to reach from the centrally-located capital. Note that Madrid has three mainline stations—*Atocha,* near the center of the city; *Chamartin,* at the northern edge of town; and *Norte* (or *Principie Pío*), in a valley behind the Royal Palace. **Reservations** are required for most express trains, such as the *Talgos* and *Rapidos,* but not for the locals that you'll be using on these daytrips. The already-low **fares** can be cut substantially by traveling round-trip on one of the frequent *Dias Azules* (Blue Days), of which there are about 300 a year.

Portugal, whose national railway is known as **CP**, offers very good service on the main north-south route, with less frequent trains on its other lines. Lisbon has four mainline stations—*Santa Apolónia,* just east of the Alfama district; *Barreiro,* on the south side of the harbor, reached by ferry from the downtown *Terreiro do Paço; Rossio,* in the city center; and *Cais do Sodré,* on the harbor just west of the center. **Reservations** are required for *Rapido* trains.

Eurailpasses (see page 18) are accepted in both Spain and Portugal, but the low fares there make them hardly worthwhile unless you are also traveling in other European countries such as France. Spain offers the cheaper **Spanish Railpass**, available for unlimited travel in Spain only on any 4 days during a 15-day period, or on any 8 or 15 consecutive days, in either first or second class. Portugal has its own **Tourist Ticket** for 7, 14, or 21 consecutive days of unlimited train travel in either class within that country.

Buses are often faster and more frequent than trains in both countries, especially for out-of-the-way destinations, and are recommended for several of the daytrips in this section.

Driving is good in both countries as long as you stick to the main roads. An International Driving Permit, available in America from the AAA, is required in Spain and strongly recommended for Portugal.

ADVANCE PLANNING INFORMATION:

The **National Tourist Office of Spain** has branches in cities around the world, including New York, Miami, Chicago, Los Angeles, Toronto, and London. Their New York address is: 665 Fifth Avenue, New York NY 10022, phone (212) 759-8822. The **Portuguese National Tourist Office** has a branch in New York at 590 Fifth Avenue, New York NY 10036, phone (212) 354-4403; as well as others in Montreal, Toronto, and London.

A Daytrip from Madrid

* Segovia

For over two millennia, Segovia has guarded the northern slopes of the Sierra de Guadarrama chain north of Madrid. The ancient walled town and its fairy-tale castle ride like a ship atop an isolated rock overlooking the confluence of two mountain streams. Compact, rich in historic attractions, and filled with genuine charm, it later became a romantic retreat for Spanish artists and poets, and eventually a major sight for foreign visitors. This is surely one of the best daytrips that can be made from Madrid.

Originally an Iberian settlement, Segovia was captured by the Romans around 80 B.C. and until the fall of the empire served as an important military outpost at the junction of two major roads. It became the seat of a bishop under the succeeding Visigoths, but in the 8th century A.D. was conquered by Islamic Moors from North Africa, who ruled until about 1085. Segovia then reverted to Christianity, becoming a royal residence in 1284. Isabella the Catholic was proclaimed Queen of Castile here in 1474, opening the door to Spanish unification. The town's leading role in the popular (but unsuccessful) *Comunero* uprising of 1520 led eventually to a decline that continued until its well-preserved delights were rediscovered at the dawn of the 20th century.

GETTING THERE:

Trains depart the underground *(Apeadero)* level of Madrid's Atocha Station several times in the morning for the scenic 2-hour run to Segovia. They can also be boarded at Madrid's Recoletos, Nuevos Ministerios, and Chamartin stations a few minutes later. All trains are second-class only and do not require reservations. Return service operates until mid-evening.

Buses are a slightly faster way to reach Segovia. They depart from Madrid's La Sepulvedana terminal at Paseo de la Florida 11, near the Norté train station. Buses operate hourly and take about 90 minutes for the run.

By car, Segovia is about 55 miles northwest of Madrid. Take the A-6 *Autopista* highway to the Collado-Villalba exit, then the N-601 north to Segovia.

The Alcázar at Segovia

PRACTICALITIES:

Try to avoid visiting Segovia on summer weekends, when it's overrun with tourists. The major attractions are open daily all year round, but a few minor sights are closed on Mondays. The local **Tourist Information Office**, phone (911) 43-03-28, is at Plaza Mayor 10. Segovia has a **population** of about 40,000 and is in the region of **Castile-León**.

FOOD AND DRINK:

Segovia is famous for its excellent restaurants, which attract diners from Madrid in all seasons. *The* great local dish is *Cochinillo Asado* (roast suckling pig), while other specialties include *Cordero Lechal* (roast suckling lamb), *Cochifrito* (lamb stew), and *Sopa Castellana* (soup of ham, paprika, and poached egg). Out of an embarrassment of riches, a few choice restaurants are:

Mesón de Cándido (Plaza de Azoguejo 5, by the Aqueduct) A national institution, one of Spain's oldest and best restaurants. Specializes in local cuisine, especially *cochinillo*. Reservations suggested on weekends, phone (911) 42-81-03. $$$

Mesón Duque (Calle Cervantes 12, 2 blocks west of the Aqueduct) This friendly old place with colorful decor specializes in *cochinillo* and other local meat dishes. Reservations suggested on weekends, phone (911) 43-05-37. $$

La Oficina (Calle Cronista Lecea 10, a block east of Plaza Mayor) Another atmospheric old restaurant with local cooking, offers good-value set-price meals. $$

Mesón del Campesino (Calle de Infanta Isabel 12, a block southeast of Plaza Mayor) Local specialties at low prices makes this a favorite of the younger crowd. X: Thurs. $

Try to finish your sightseeing before sitting down to a copious, leisurely, and rather late Segovia lunch.

SUGGESTED TOUR:

Leave the **train station** *(Estación de Ferrocarril)* (1) or the **bus terminal** *(Estación de Autobuses)* (2) and take town bus number 3 or a taxi to **Plaza Mayor** (3) in the heart of the old walled town, passing the spectacular Roman aqueduct en route. You *could* get there on foot, but it's a long, dull, uphill walk. Still known to diehards by its former name, Plaza del General Franco, the main square of Segovia is lined with arcaded buildings, cafés, the tourist office, and the 17th-century Town Hall *(Ayuntamiento)*.

At the western end of the square stands the ***Cathedral** (4), the last great Gothic structure erected in Spain. The Renaissance was already in full bloom when the conservative Spaniards started this project in 1525 to replace a former cathedral that was destroyed in the *Comunero* insurrection of 1520. Built of honey-colored stone, it carries the Gothic ideal to extremes with its many delicate pinnacles and buttresses. The domes above the crossing and atop the tower, however, are a concession to the newer classical style of the Renaissance.

Step inside to admire the 16th-century Flemish stained glass in some of the windows, the Flamboyant choir stalls, and the lovely ***Cloister** *(Claustro)* that was part of the old cathedral. Leading off from this is a small **Museum** *(Museo)* with a 17th-century gilt carriage used in the Corpus Christi procession, and the **Sala Capitular** with its remarkable Flemish tapestries. During summer the cathedral is open daily from 9 a.m. to 7 p.m.; from October through May it is open on Mondays through Fridays from 9:30 a.m. to 1 p.m. and 3–6 p.m., and on weekends and holidays from 9:30 a.m. to 6 p.m.

Now follow the map to Segovia's foremost attraction, its ***Alcázar** (5). This fairy-tale castle, bristling with crenellations, turrets, and conical towers, was probably built in the 13th century on Moorish or even Roman foundations and remodeled several times since, most notably in the 14th and 15th centuries. Originally a royal residence, it was

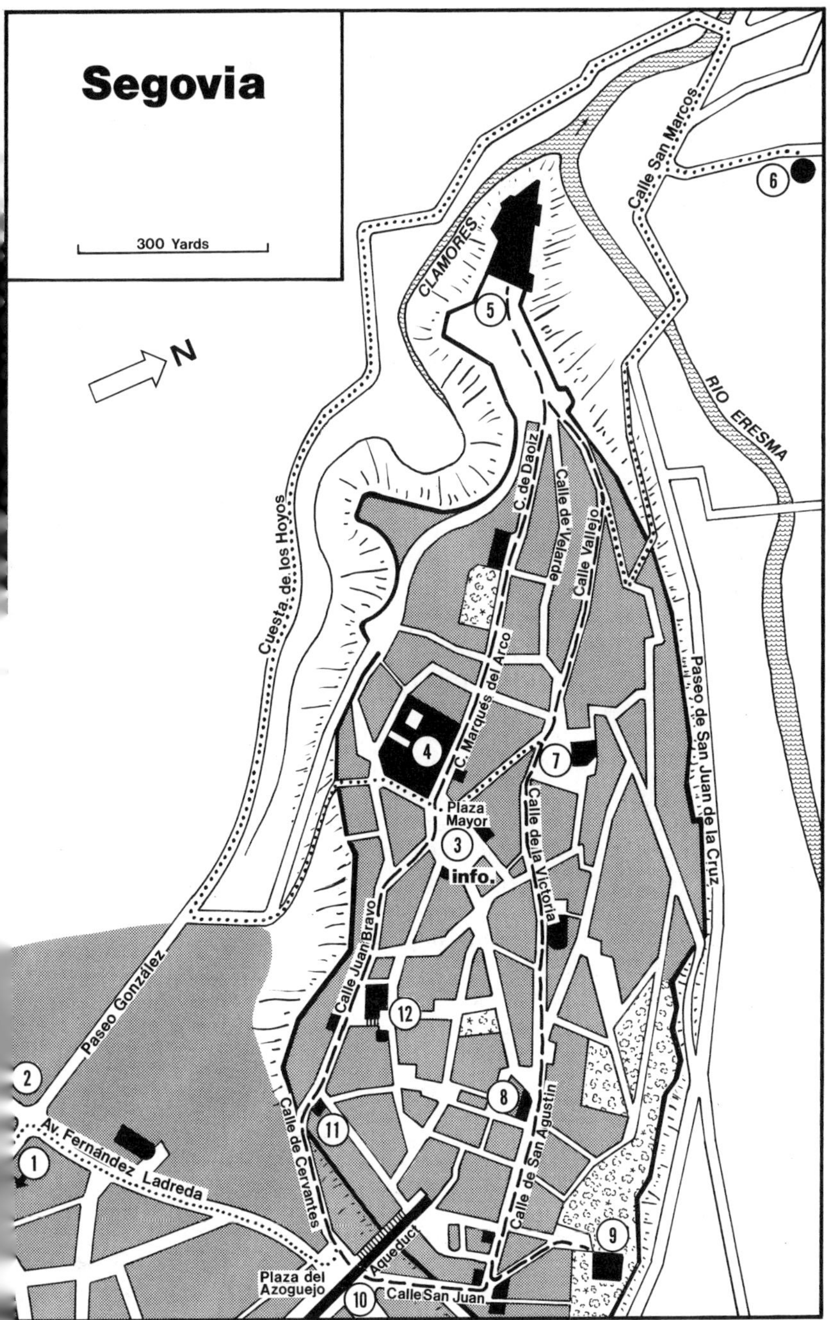
Segovia
300 Yards
N
CLAMORES
Calle San Marcos
RIO ERESMA
Cuesta de los Hoyos
C. de Daoiz
Calle de Velarde
Calle Vallejo
C. Marqués del Arco
Paseo de San Juan de la Cruz
Plaza Mayor
info.
Calle de la Victoria
Calle Juan Bravo
Paseo González
Av. Fernández Ladreda
Calle de Cervantes
Calle de San Agustín
Aqueduct
Plaza del Azoguejo
Calle San Juan
1
2
3
4
5
6
7
8
9
10
11
12

converted into an artillery academy in the 18th century. A disastrous fire in 1862, allegedly set by cadets who wanted to move the school to Madrid, led to an almost total reconstruction in the highly romantic style of the late 19th century. Only the massive keep by the entrance survives intact from the original structure. For a terrific view of the Alcázar, be sure to make the side trip to the valley floor, described below.

Enter the castle via the drawbridge and explore the various rooms, mostly filled with armor, weapons, tapestries, and period furnishings. The decorations, especially the *Mudéjar* ceilings and *esgrafiado* plasterwork, are exquisite. Be sure to climb to the top of the medieval keep, the **Torre de Juan II**, for a panoramic ***view** of Segovia and the surrounding countryside. The Alcázar is open daily from 10 a.m. to 7 p.m., closing at 6 p.m. in winter.

If you feel up to it, a very scenic ***side trip** can be made by following the route on the map through the Puerta de Santiago gate and down a path to the valley. Cross the Eresma stream and bear left. A road to your right leads to the **Iglesia de la Vera Cruz** (6), a highly unusual church built in 1208 by the Knights Templars on a site once occupied by a Roman temple and later by a mosque. Clearly inspired by the Holy Sepulchre in Jerusalem, it has a circular plan with 12 sides and a two-story church within the church, in which knights of the order once stood guard over an alleged piece of the True Cross, since removed. There is an excellent **view** from its tower. La Vera Cruz is open on Tuesdays through Sundays, from 10:30 a.m. to 1:30 p.m. and 3:30–7 p.m., closing at 6 p.m. in winter.

Continue along Calle San Marcos for the most fabulous vistas of the Alcázar; it is from a point near the next bridge that the ***classic views** of Segovia's castle are taken. Cross the span and bear left along the Clamores stream on the Cuesta de los Hoyos road. Turn left at the first intersection and climb the steps through the town walls, returning to Plaza Mayor (3).

Whether you made the side trip or not, your next destination should be the **Iglesia de San Esteban** (7). This 13th-century Romanesque church is noted for its fine exterior gallery, and especially for its high tower with a pyramidal roof. Just west of this, at Calle de los Desamparados 5, is the **pension** where the great poet Antonio Machado lived from 1919 until 1932. You can visit his simple lodgings from Tuesdays through Sundays, from 4–6 p.m.

Stroll east on the Calle de la Victoria, passing a fortified mansion from about 1200 known as the **Casa de Hércules** after a Roman figure on its tower. Beyond this is the 12th-century church of **La Trinidad**. Continue on Calle de San Agustin to the **Museo Provincial de Bellas Artes** (8), a small museum of mostly local art located at number 12.

Accommodated in a restored 16th-century house with *Mudéjar* decorations, the collection includes some interesting old views of the town. It is open on Tuesdays through Saturdays, from 10 a.m. to 2 p.m. and 4–6 p.m.; and on Sundays from 10–2 p.m.

Straight ahead is the **Plaza del Conde de Cheste**, a small triangular space lined with a remarkable group of medieval mansions, some dating from the 14th century. Just north of it stands the deconsecrated **Iglesia de San Juan de los Caballeros** (9), an 11th-century church that was once the favored burial spot for Segovia's leading families. It now houses the **Museo de la Familia Zuloaga**, an art gallery devoted to the works of the potter Daniel Zuloaga (1852–1921) and the famous painter Ignacio Zuloaga (1870–1945). The museum is presently closed for renovation.

Follow the map downhill on Calle San Juan to Plaza del Azoguejo and the magnificent ***Roman Aqueduct** (10). Widely regarded as one of the finest surviving Roman structures anywhere, and certainly one of the largest, it was probably built in the late 1st century A.D. during the reign of the emperor Trajan. Nearly a half-mile long, its two tiers of arches soar some 92 feet above the lowest street level. The huge granite blocks are held together without mortar or clamps, yet the only damage it ever sustained was at the hands of the Moors in 1071, when 35 arches were destroyed. These were replaced in the 15th century on orders from Queen Isabella.

There are several excellent restaurants nearby, where you could enjoy a late, leisurely lunch. If you've seen enough, you can also take bus number 3 from here back to the train station, or continue on to Plaza Mayor and leave from there.

Calle de Cervantes leads uphill, returning you to the Old Town. Just inside the walls stands the **Casa de los Picos** (11), a 15th-century fortified mansion distinguished by the unusual pyramidal stones covering its facade. It is now used as an art school and sometimes has exhibitions of student work. Continuing on, you soon come to Plaza de San Martin, an intriguing multi-level open square dominated by the **Iglesia de San Martin** (12). This 12th-century Romanesque church has an interesting exterior gallery in the regional style. In the upper part of the square is the 15th-century **Torreón de Lozoya** tower, part of an old fortified town mansion; while on the main street is the **Casa del Siglo XV**, a house of the 15th century thought by some to be the birthplace of Juan Bravo, who led the failed commoners' insurrection of 1520. Even though he tried to overthrow the government, Juan Bravo is still regarded as a hero and his statue is just across the street, which is also named for him. Continue on this back to Plaza Mayor (3), where the walk began.

A Daytrip from Madrid

Ávila

Ávila's claim to being closer to Heaven than any other town in Spain can be taken both physically and spiritually. At an altitude of 3,700 feet, it is the highest provincial capital in the land and at the same time the most representative home of Spanish mysticism. *La ciudad de cantos y santos,* the "city of stones and saints," is a deeply evocative place of brooding, melancholy beauty whose fame lies in its association with that most robust of medieval mystics, Saint Teresa of Jesus. From a distance the town appears as one vast fortress, its massive 11th-century walls still standing guard against an infidel who never returned. Few places have so awesome a power to inflict their personality on the visitor as does Ávila.

There was a settlement here in prehistoric times, which later became the Roman town of *Avela.* A decline set in during the Moorish occupation that followed. When the Moors were at last driven from Toledo in 1085, the new king, Alfonso VI of Castile, charged his son-in-law, Raimondo de Borgoña, with the repopulation of Ávila. To this end the massive fortifications that remain virtually unchanged today were quickly built. Now secure against any invader, Ávila prospered until the expulsion of its most talented citizens, the Moriscos, in 1609. After that it fell into a long sleep from which it has only recently awakened.

Saint Teresa of Jesus was born in Ávila in 1515. She was one of the most remarkable women in history, a great mystic whose works have influenced the Catholic Church to this day. You will find traces of her life all along the walking route, along with those of her contemporary, Saint John of the Cross.

GETTING THERE:

Trains depart the underground *(Apeadero)* level of Madrid's Atocha Station several times in the morning for Ávila, a run of about 2 hours. They can also be boarded at Madrid's Recoletos, Nuevos Ministerios, and Chamartin stations a few minutes later. In addition, there are a few fast express trains out of Madrid's Chamartin or Norte *(Príncipe Pío)* stations, which require reservations. Return service runs until mid-evening.

The monumental Puerta de Alcázar

Buses operated by several companies depart from different terminals in Madrid for the 2-hour ride to Ávila. Ask locally for current information.

By car, Ávila is about 70 miles northwest of Madrid. The fastest route is via the N-VI and A-6 *Autopista* highways northwest to Villacastín, then the N-110 west to Ávila.

PRACTICALITIES:

Nearly all of the sights of Ávila are open daily. Winters here tend to be severe, but the summers are quite pleasant. A colorful ***fiesta*** honoring Saint Teresa is held from the 7th through the 15th of October, while the exuberant **Summer Celebration** is in late July. The local **Tourist Information Office**, phone (918) 21-13-87, faces the front of the cathedral. Ávila has a **population** of about 43,000 and is in the region of **Castile-León**.

FOOD AND DRINK:

The cooking of Ávila tends to be simple but of high quality, as mostly local ingredients are used. The one specialty is *Yemas de Santa Teresa,* an egg-yolk-and-sugar confection once distributed to the poor by the saint. Some good restaurants are:

El Fogón de Santa Teresa (in the Valderrabanos Hotel facing the cathedral) Castilian cuisine in luxurious surroundings. $$$

El Molino de la Losa (on the Adaja River just north of the bridge) Dine on local specialties in a restored ancient water mill. Also a great place for drinks. X: Mon. in off-season. $$

Mesón del Rastro (Plaza Rastro 1, 2 blocks east of La Santa) A colorful old place with traditional Castilian cuisine, long popular with visitors. $$

Palomar (Calle Tomás L. de Victoria, a block east of Plaza Victoria) Local Castilian dishes at modest prices. $

SUGGESTED TOUR:

From the **train station** (1) it's a three-quarter-mile walk to the old walled town, or you could take a taxi or local bus there. On foot, follow Avenida de José-Antonio west to a large monastery, then Calle del Duque de Alba to Plaza de Santa Teresa. Facing this busy square is the monumental **Puerta de Alcázar** (2), one of the nine gateways that pierce the forbidding 11th-century ***ramparts**. The entire circuit of these, over a mile and a half in length, and up to 40 feet high and 10 feet thick, is completely intact and seems to have been built just yesterday. Indeed, aside from some minor modifications made in the 14th century, these are the same walls that have successfully defended Ávila for over 900 years. You can walk atop a section of them later in the trip.

Stroll through the gate and turn right to Ávila's austere **Cathedral** (3), nearly as military a structure as the walls themselves. Begun in 1135 in the Romanesque manner, its lingering construction soon evolved into the Gothic, with Renaissance elements added later. Enter via the west front, whose door is flanked with stone carvings of two "wild men" of obscure meaning.

The **interior** is unusually bright for a Spanish church, as most of its dark stained-glass windows were destroyed by the Lisbon earthquake of 1755. These were replaced with much lighter glass, enhancing the effect of the strangely mottled yellow-and-red stone in the older sec-

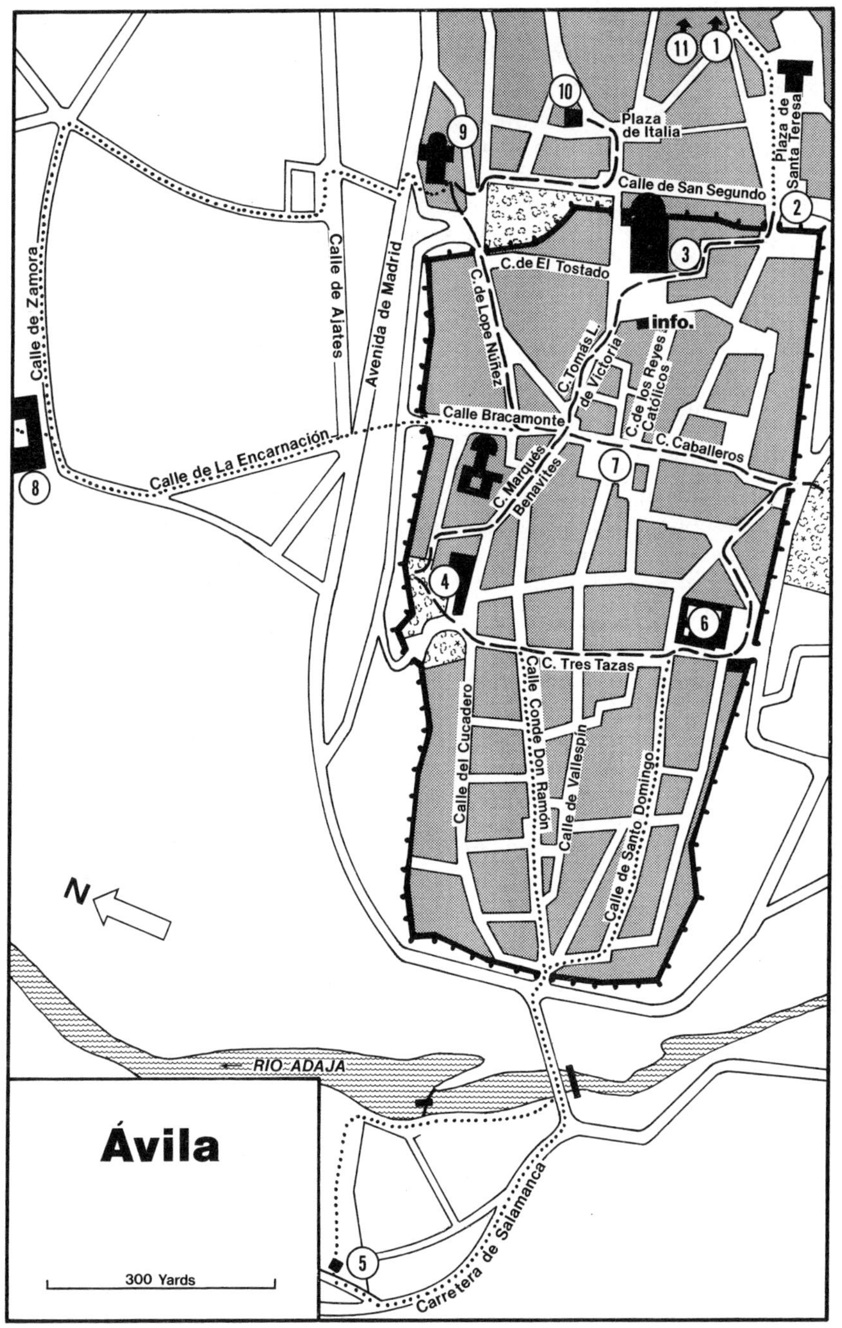
Ávila
300 Yards
N
Plaza de Italia
Plaza de Santa Teresa
Calle de San Segundo
C. de El Tostado
C. de Lope Núñez
info.
C. Tomás L. de Victoria
C. de los Reyes Católicos
Calle de Zamora
Calle de Ajates
Avenida de Madrid
Calle Bracamonte
C. Caballeros
Calle de La Encarnación
C. Marqués Benavites
C. Tres Tazas
Calle del Cucadero
Calle Conde Don Ramón
Calle de Vallespín
Calle de Santo Domingo
RÍO ADAJA
Carretera de Salamanca
1
2
3
4
5
6
7
8
9
10
11

tion toward the east. Take a look at the remarkable **choir stalls** in the Renaissance style, carved in the mid-16th century by a Dutch artisan. Above the high altar in the *Capilla Mayor* (chancel) is a gorgeously painted **altarpiece** from about 1500.

Walk around the double ambulatory in the apse, the oldest part of the cathedral. This is actually embedded into the town walls and forms a part of the defensive structure. In the center, behind the high altar, is the huge alabaster **tomb** of Alonso de Madrigal, a 15th-century bishop of Ávila, who was popularly known as "El Tostado" due to his dark complexion. Nearby is the small **cathedral museum**, which displays relics, a huge 16th-century monstrance, and a minor portrait by El Greco among its many treasures. The cathedral is open daily from 8 a.m. to 1 p.m. and 3–7 p.m.; from October through April it closes at 5 p.m.

Follow the map through ancient streets to the **Parador Raimundo de Borgoña** (4), a government-operated tourist inn occupying a rebuilt 15th-century palace. From its gardens you have easy access to the sentry path atop the ***town walls**. A short walk along this will reward you with a magnificent ***view** of Ávila and an appreciation of just why these are often considered to be the finest medieval fortifications in Europe.

From here, an interesting **side trip** of a little more than a mile can be made through an older, more desolate neighborhood, then across the river for the most spectacular view possible of the old walled town. Follow the route on the map, exiting the ramparts and crossing the Adaja River. To your left is an attractive old bridge, the **Puente Viejo**, which is no longer in use. Bear right to **Los Cuatro Postes** (5), a strange open structure of four stone columns enclosing a cross. The ***view of Ávila** from this point is unsurpassed, a vision right out of the Middle Ages. An alternative route back to town is to amble right down to the river, turn right, and follow its banks past an old mill that is now a restaurant and café.

Back in town, your next stop should be at **"La Santa,"** the **Convento de Santa Teresa** (6). Built on the very spot where Saint Teresa of Jesus was born in 1515, this 17th-century Baroque church houses an ornate chapel dedicated to the saint, and a tiny garden in which she played as a child. A small museum of relics, displaying one of her fingers, is adjacent. The convent church is open daily from 9 a.m. to 1 p.m. and 3:30–7 p.m.

Just outside the church, next to a gate in the walls, is the **Palacio de Núñez Vela**, a late-16th-century Renaissance mansion with an unusual façade and a classic inner patio. It now serves as a courthouse. Turn left into Plaza del General Mola, a small square dominated by the **Casa de Oñate**, also known as the Guzmán Palace. Another outstanding mansion, it is surmounted by a powerfully battlemented tower from the early 16th century. Continue on to Plaza del Rastro, where a gateway leads beyond the walls into a **park** overlooking the valley.

Calle de los Caballeros heads north to **Plaza de la Victoria** (7), Ávila's arcaded main square. A local folk market is held here on Fridays from 9 a.m. to 2 p.m.

You can make a worthwhile **side trip** from here by following the map to the **Monasterio de la Encarnación** (8), less than a half-mile to the north. Saint Teresa of Jesus lived in this convent for some 29 years beginning in 1533, eventually serving as prioress. Inside, there is a small **museum** of her life, in which you can see her cell, furnishings, and personal effects. Some of the rooms in which she experienced her visions may be visited. Entered from a courtyard, the museum is open daily from 10 a.m. to 1 p.m. and 4–7 p.m. The map shows an alternative route back to town that brings you directly to the next attraction.

Of the multitude of religious structures in Ávila, one of the most interesting is the ***Basilica de San Vincente** (9). Begun in the 12 century in the Romanesque manner, it took over 300 years to complete and makes the transition into the Gothic style. According to tradition, the church is built on the spot where the young Saint Vincent and his two sisters, saints Sabina and Cristeta, were brutally executed by the Romans around A.D. 303 for having stomped on an altar of Jupiter. Their tomb, the **Sepulcro de los Niños Mártires**, lies under a strange, almost Oriental, 15th-century baldachin, and depicts their martyrdom in gruesome detail. It was long believed that whoever made a false oath while touching this would suffer grievous harm. Down in the **crypt** there is a venerated figure of the Virgin once alleged to have been carved by Nicodemus and brought here by Saint Peter. The rock on which Saint Vincent and his sisters perished is also there. Visits to the basilica may be made daily, from 10 a.m. to 1 p.m. and 4–6 p.m.

Stroll south along the walls to the protruding apse of the cathedral and turn left into Plaza de Italia. Just north of this is the **Casa de los Deanes** (10), a 16th-century Renaissance deanery that now houses the **Provincial Museum**. Inside, there is a fine 15th-century *triptych attributed to Hans Memling, antique Spanish furniture, folkloric items, and local archaeological finds. It is open on Tuesdays through Saturdays from 10 a.m. to 2 p.m. and 5–8 p.m.; and on Sundays from 10 a.m. to 2 p.m.

Returning to the station, you might want to stop at the **Convento de San José** (11). Also known as the Convento de los Madres, this was the first of a series of convents founded by Saint Teresa. It now houses a small museum of her life, which is open daily from 10 a.m. to 1 p.m. and 3:30–6 p.m.

A Daytrip from Madrid

*Toledo

At first sight, Toledo looks uncannily like the 16th-century painting of it by El Greco. Upon closer examination, the town becomes even more of a vision right out of the Middle Ages. Trapped atop a rocky mound, almost surrounded by a deep gorge of the rushing Tagus River, Toledo is a gem in an otherwise harsh, desolate landscape. Once the capital of Spain, still the seat of its Primate, this ancient place is a living monument to the past.

Originally the chief city of the Carpentani, an early Iberian tribe, Toledo was captured by the Romans in 192 B.C. and given the name *Toletum*. Between the 6th and 8th centuries A.D. most of Spain was ruled by the Germanic Visigoths, who made the town their capital. During the period of Moorish occupation, from 712 to 1085, Toledo became a great center of trade whose tolerant population embraced Muslims, Jews, and Mozarabic Christians alike. With the help of El Cid, the town was liberated in the 11th century and became the residence of the Christian kings of Castile.

The Middle Ages were the greatest period of Toledo's long history. Then an ecclesiastical and intellectual center, it saw the beginning of the Spanish Inquisition in 1480 and the expulsion of its Jewish residents in 1492. After Philip II moved his court to Madrid in 1561, however, the town lost importance. Nothing of great significance happened there again until the Civil War of 1936–39, when the long siege of its Alcázar again helped change the course of Spanish history.

Toledo is perhaps best known as the home of El Greco. Born on the island of Crete in 1541, Domenikos Theotokopoulos moved to Spain in 1577 and established himself as a successful artist. Known locally as "The Greek" *(El Greco)* by Spaniards who had trouble pronouncing his name, he spent the rest of his life in Toledo, dying there in 1614. Many of his most important works can still be seen in the town.

Toledo's proximity to Madrid makes it a very popular destination for tourists, who tend to crowd into the three most famous sights and then leave. The tour described here covers much more than that, exploring places overlooked by the mobs.

In the Plaza de Zocodover

GETTING THERE:

Trains depart Madrid's Atocha Station several times in the morning for the 80-minute run to Toledo, with return service operating until mid-evening.

Buses leave Madrid's Estación del Sur de Autobuses station frequently for Toledo, a ride of about one hour.

By car, Toledo is 44 miles southwest of Madrid via the N-401 road. Avoid driving in the center of town.

PRACTICALITIES:

Several of Toledo's best sights are closed on Mondays, and have reduced hours on Sundays. If you can, go in the off-season, or linger late in the day as the town is often overrun with packaged group tours. Beware of avaricious "guides" and tourist-trap restaurants. Among several annual **festivals**, the celebration of Corpus Christi is the most spectacular. It climaxes on the Thursday of the ninth week after Holy Week. The *Fiesta de la Virgen del Sagrario* in mid-August is another important event. The local **Tourist Information Office**, phone (925) 22-08-43, is just north of the Puerta de Bisagra. Toledo has a **population** of about 53,000 and is in the region of **Castile-La Mancha**.

FOOD AND DRINK:

The great delicacy of Toledo is *Perdiz Estofada* (stewed partridge), with other game dishes common. Among meats, lamb is usually the best. Prices tend to be high, so check the *menús del dia* and *platos combinados* for daily specials. Some choice restaurants are:

Asadar Adolfo (Calle Hombre de Palo 7, just north of the cathedral) Toledo's best restaurant features lighter, innovative versions of local cuisine in a 14th-century house. Reservations recommended, phone (925) 22-73-21. X: Sun. eve. $$$

Méson Aurelio (Calle Sinagoga 1, just north of the cathedral) Castillian cuisine and local game specialties in a casual setting. X: Mon. $$

Hierbabuena (Calle Cristo de la Luz 9, near the mosque) Excellent local dishes in attractive surroundings) X: Sun. eve., Mon. $$

Sinaí (Cuesta de los Reyes Católicos, near the Sinagoga de Santa Maria la Blanca) Moroccan and Kosher cuisine in the old Jewish quarter. X: Tues. and all evenings. $$ and $

El Nido (Plaza de la Magdalena 5, 2 blocks south of Zocodover) Popular with students for its fixed-price menus. X: Mon. $

SUGGESTED TOUR:

From the **train station** (1) it's a stiff but interesting uphill trek into the Old Town. You can avoid this by taking bus number 3 or 6 (or a taxi) directly to Plaza de Zocodover. If you decide to hoof the three-quarter-mile distance, just follow the map across the 13th-century **Puente de Alcántara** bridge, under the town walls, up long steps, and through the Moorish **Arco de la Sangre** archway.

However you get there, **Plaza de Zocodover** (2) is the animated center of daily life in Toledo. Its name derives from the Arabic *souk* (market place), as it was a venue for horse trading during Moorish times. Today it is lined with busy cafés, many with outdoor tables. You'll be coming back this way later in the tour, when you might want to stop for a drink.

Calle del Comercio, a bustling narrow shopping thoroughfare, leads directly to the ***Cathedral** (3). Still the seat of the Catholic Primate of Spain, this is the most important single attraction in Toledo. There was a Visigothic church on the site ever since the 6th century, which was used as a mosque during the Moorish occupation and demolished in 1227 to make way for the present structure. The cathedral you see today was mostly completed by the late 15th century. It is essentially in the Gothic style, but with a distinctly Spanish character later embellished with Baroque trimmings.

Inside, the cathedral contains a wealth of artistic treasures includ-

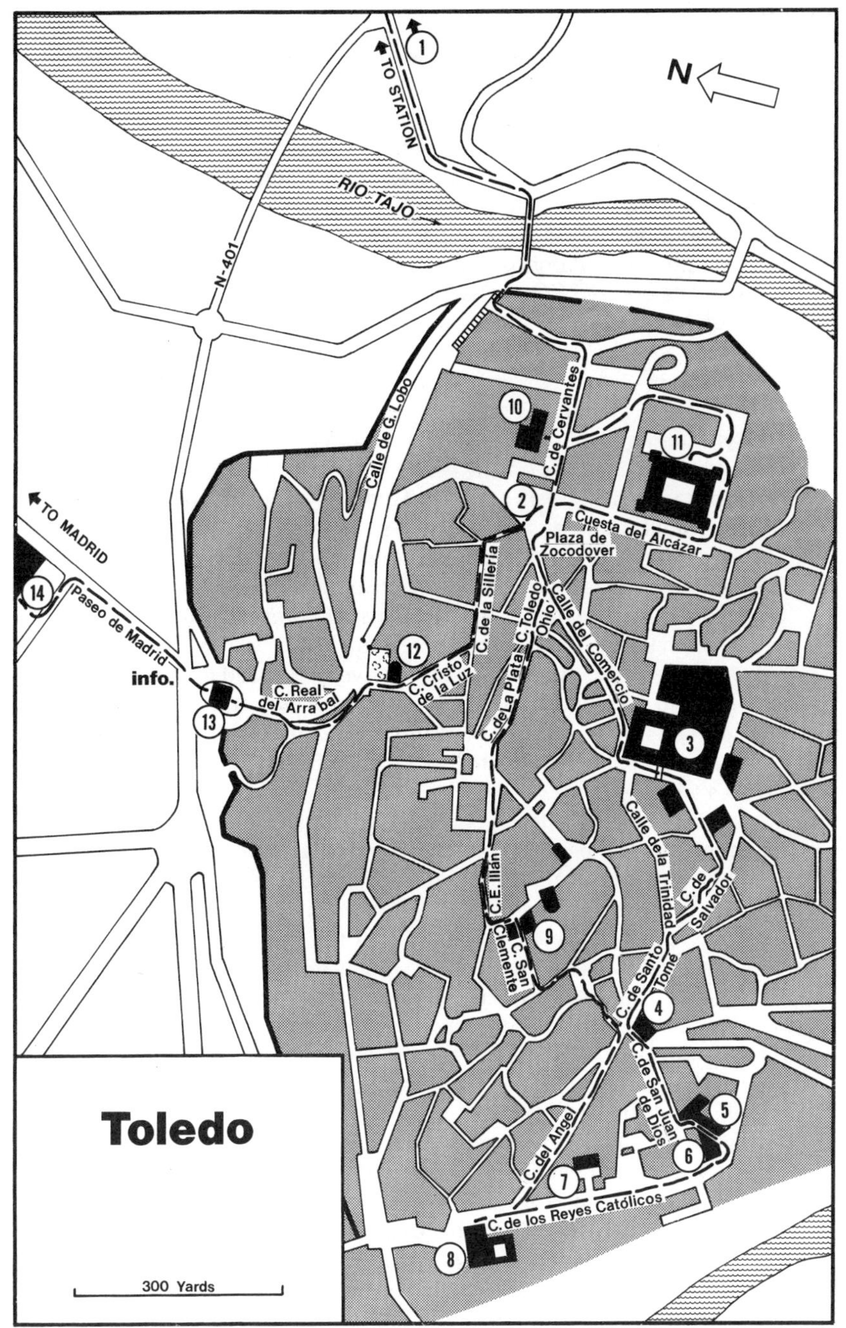
Toledo
N
TO STATION
RIO TAJO
N-401
TO MADRID
Paseo de Madrid
info.
C. Real del Arrabal
Calle de G. Lobo
C. de Cervantes
Cuesta del Alcázar
Plaza de Zocodover
C. de la Sillería
C. Cristo de la Luz
C. Toledo Ohio
Calle del Comercio
C. de La Plata
Calle de la Trinidad
C. de Salvador
C. E. Illán
C. San Clemente
C. de Santo Tomé
C. de San Juan de Dios
C. del Angel
C. de los Reyes Católicos
300 Yards

ing the famed ***Transparente**, a gigantic 18th-century marble altar done up in a theatrical rococo manner. Equally stunning is the centrally-located ***Coro** (choir) with its magnificently carved stalls depicting the conquest of Granada in 1492. A splendid collection of 27 paintings by El Greco along with some by Velázquez, Goya, and others is displayed in the ***Sacristy**, while the ***Tesoro** (treasury) exhibits an incredible 400-pound monstrance made in part from the first gold brought back from America by Columbus. Mass according to the ancient Visigothic rite is still celebrated in the **Capilla Mozárabe** under the south tower. The **cloister**, visited on the way out, provides a beautiful transition back into the town. The cathedral is open daily from 10:30 a.m. to 1 p.m. and 3:30–7 p.m., closing at 6 p.m. from October through April.

The square in front of the cathedral is bounded on the south by the **Ayuntamiento** (Town Hall), rebuilt in the early 17th century by El Greco's son, and on the northwest by the Archbishop's Palace. Follow the map west to the **Iglesia de Santo Tomé** (4), an unpretentious church with one fabulous attraction. El Greco's masterpiece, the monumental ****Burial of the Count of Orgaz***, is still where the artist put it in 1586. This painting depicts a miracle in which two saints descend from Heaven to bury the count, while at the top his soul is received into Heaven. Even though the count, who had given large sums to this church, died in the 14th century, the artist shows everyone dressed in 16th-century costume and included both his son and himself in the composition. The church is open on Tuesdays through Saturdays from 10 a.m. to 1:45 p.m. and 3:30–6 p.m., and on Sundays from 10 a.m. to 1:45 p.m. It closes a bit earlier in winter.

Continue down Calle de San Juan de Dios to the **Casa y Museo del Greco** (5). The painter El Greco may or may not have lived in precisely this old house, but he did reside in the neighborhood and this property is known to have been owned by his landlord. Be that as it may, the house has been splendidly restored to its 16th-century condition and is as interesting for the insight it sheds on bourgeois life in Renaissance Toledo as it is for the El Greco paintings. Be sure to visit the charming garden and the adjoining museum, which has a collection of minor works by the master and his contemporaries. The most outstanding pieces are his *View of Toledo* and the individual portraits of Christ and the Apostles. The Casa del Greco is open on Tuesdays through Saturdays from 10 a.m. to 2 p.m. and 4–7 p.m. (6 p.m. in winter), and on Sundays from 10 a.m. to 2 p.m.

Step across the narrow side street to the ***Sinagoga del Tránsito** (6), one of the two surviving synagogues in the old *Judería,* or Jewish Quarter. It was founded in 1366 by the king's treasurer, Samuel Ha-Levi, who was later executed by his boss, Pedro the Cruel. After the expulsion of the Jews from Toledo in 1492 it became a Christian church dedicated to *Nuestra Señora del Tránsito,* but it is now used as the **Sephardic Museum** of Jewish life in Spain. Incredibly enough, the original Hebraic inscriptions and tombs have survived through the centuries, making this a fascinating place to visit. It is open on Tuesdays through Saturdays from 10 a.m. to 2 p.m. and 4–7 p.m. (6 p.m. in winter), and on Sundays from 10 a.m. to 2 p.m.

Head down Calle de los Reyes Católicos to the other remaining synagogue, the **Sinagoga de Santa María la Blanca** (7). If the name seems odd, the interior is stranger still. Built in the style of a mosque about 1180 as the principal place of worship for Toledo's 12,000 Jews, the building was seized by a Christian mob led by Saint Vincent Ferrer in 1405 and used as a church. It later became a military barracks but has since been restored to its original condition. With its luminous white interior and rows of graceful horseshoe arches, this is one of the loveliest little sights in town. It is open daily from 10 a.m. to 2 p.m. and 3:30–7 p.m., closing at 6 p.m. in winter.

A bit farther down the street is the **Monasterio de San Juan de los Reyes** (8), erected in the late 15th century as a burial place for the Catholic monarchs, Ferdinand and Isabel. As it turned out, they were actually interred at Granada following the final victory over the Moors, but their church in Toledo remains a perfect example of the Isabelline style, a highly ornamental form of Flamboyant Gothic mixed with Spanish motifs. The double-decked **Claustro** (cloister) with its Mudéjar vaulting is particularly attractive. Be on the lookout for chains hung from the exterior of the apse; these were once worn by Christian prisoners of the Muslims who were set free after the reconquest. The monastery is open daily from 10 a.m. to 1:45 p.m. and 3:30–7 p.m., closing at 6 p.m. in winter.

Stroll up Calle del Angel almost back to the Santo Tomé church, then turn north following the map. From here on, any remaining tourist hordes will vanish as you enter a quiet, unspoiled part of town. The **Iglesia de San Román** (9) is an outstanding 13th-century Mudéjar church that now houses a modest **museum** of Visigothic cultural artifacts from the pre-Moorish period. There's not an awful lot to see here, but the church itself has some marvelous late-Romanesque frescoes that make a visit worthwhile. It is open on Tuesdays through Saturdays from 10 a.m. to 2 p.m. and 4–6:30 p.m., and on Sundays from 10 a.m. to 2 p.m. The ticket is also valid for the Santa Cruz art museum, coming up next.

Return to Plaza de Zocodover (2) via a series of colorful back streets, the last of which commemorates the links between this Toledo and the other one on Ohio. By now, you're probably yearning for a rest stop; luckily, the main square is lined with attractive cafés with outdoor tables.

The one attraction of Toledo that doesn't usually close for a lunch break is the ***Museo de la Santa Cruz** (10), a first-rate art museum installed in a beautiful 16th-century hospital and orphanage. It's just a few steps from the Plaza de Zocodover, so saunter on over and enjoy the ***22 paintings by El Greco**, the Flemish tapestries from the Renaissance, the 15th-century ***Zodiac Tapestry** originally made for the cathedral, the fine Toledo swords, and the many other treasures of the fine and applied arts. There is also an archaeological section with prehistoric and Roman artifacts. The museum is open on Tuesdays through Saturdays from 10 a.m. to 6:30 p.m., on Sundays from 10 a.m. to 2 p.m., and on Mondays from 10 a.m. to 2 p.m. and 4:30–6:30 p.m.

Looming over everything else in Toledo is its mighty **Alcázar** (11), a massive citadel two blocks to the south. The Romans had a fortress on this site, as did the Visigoths and later the Moors. This one began in the 13th century and was converted into a royal palace for Charles V, the Holy Roman Emperor, in the early 16th century. Many times it was demolished, and many times it was rebuilt. In 1882 it became a military academy, only to be totally ruined during the Civil War in 1936. What you see today is a reconstruction largely glorifying Franco's Fascist rule. Still, it is interesting, and the bullet-riddled office of the commandant, Colonel Moscardó, adds a brilliant touch of propaganda. The Alcázar is open on Tuesdays through Sundays, from 9:30 a.m. to 1:30 p.m. and 4–6:30 p.m.

Return to the Plaza de Zocodover via the Cuesta del Alcázar. Strength permitting, there are a few more sights that might interest you. Begin by following the map to the **Mezquita del Cristo de la Luz** (Mosque of Christ of the Light) (12). If the name makes about as much sense as the Synagogue of Santa María, the explanation is the same. Built around 987 on even earlier Visigothic foundations, the tiny mosque was converted to Christian use in the 12th century. The "Light" refers to the legend that El Cid, after liberating Toledo, discovered a hidden Visigothic lamp there that had been miraculously burning since before the Moorish occupation. For entry, ask the gardener, who can also show you the 14th-century **Puerta del Sol** gate, accessible from the adjacent garden.

Continue down to the **Puerta Nueva de Bisagra** (13), a monumental 16th-century gateway in the town walls. The tourist office is directly across from this. In just a short stroll down the Paseo de Madrid you will reach the **Hospital de Tavera** (14), a 16th-century structure that contains a private museum. The treasures inside include El Greco's last work, the ***Baptism of Christ***; others by the master; a *Portrait of Charles V* by Titian; the *Bearded Woman* by Ribera; work by Tintoretto, and rooms of period furnishings. It is open daily from 10 a.m. to 1:30 p.m. and 3:30–6 p.m. From here you can easily find your way back to the station.

A Daytrip from Lisbon

Coimbra

Portugal's ancient university town was also its first capital, and remains a colorfully romantic place with its steep, twisted, and narrow streets echoing to youthful exuberance. As in centuries past, Coimbra basks in a poetic atmosphere that is hard to define but easy to enjoy.

Originally a settlement of the Iron Age, it was known to the Romans as *Aeminium* and became the seat of a bishop when the nearby Roman city of *Conimbriga* was destroyed during the 6th century A.D. A little more than a century later the Iberian peninsula fell to the Moors from North Africa. Under their rule, Coimbra flourished as a commercial center and meeting place of Islamic and Christian cultures. Recaptured by the Christians in 1064, the town continued to prosper.

Portugal's first monarch, Afonso III, made Coimbra his capital in 1139, a status it held until the royal court moved to Lisbon in 1255. The national university founded in Lisbon in 1290 was first transferred to Coimbra in 1308, moving there permanently in 1537 under the patronage of King João III. It soon became one of the most prominent humanist centers of the Renaissance, and today still dominates the town.

GETTING THERE:

Trains depart Lisbon's Santa Apolónia station several times in the morning for Coimbra-B station, a trip of 2 or 3 hours. The faster *Rapido* trains require reservations, plus a supplement for the fastest *ALFA* train. The outlying Coimbra-B station is about a mile from Coimbra-A station in the heart of town where the tour begins; there are frequent connecting trains or you can take a taxi.

By car, Coimbra is 124 miles northeast of Lisbon via the A-1 (E-3) Auto Estrada highway. There is a large parking lot just north of the Coimbra-A station.

PRACTICALITIES:

The major museum and a few of the minor sights are closed on Mondays and holidays. Student life is at its liveliest during the *Queima das Fitas* **festival** at the end of term in early May. Coimbra's **Tourist Information Office** *(Turismo),* phone (039) 238-86, is on the Largo da Portagem square opposite the bridge. The town has a **population** of about 80,000 and is in the **Costa da Prata** region.

FOOD AND DRINK:

Nearly all of the restaurants are in the Lower Town or just across the river, so plan on having lunch between noon and 2 p.m., before making the climb to the Upper Town. Some choice restaurants are:

Dom Pedro (Avenida Emídio Navarro 58, near the Largo da Portagem) Regional and International specialties in a classically Portuguese dining room. Reservations recommended, phone (039) 291-08. $$$

O Alfredo (Avenida João das Regras 32, just across the river) A bustling place for typical Portuguese food. Reservations suggested, phone (039) 81-46-69. $$$

Café Santa Cruz (Praça 8 de Maio, next to the Mosteiro de Santa Cruz) An old-fashioned place long popular with students, locals, and visitors alike for meals or just drinks. $

Democrática (Travessa do Rua Nova 7, just west of the Mosteiro de Santa Cruz) Huge meals at very low prices. X: Sun. $

SUGGESTED TOUR:

Leave the **Estação Coimbra-A** (downtown train station) (1) and walk straight ahead for two blocks to **Largo da Portagem** (2), a large open square next to the bridge. The tourist office is near its southeast corner. Coimbra is divided into three segments, all accessible from this point. The **Baixa** (Lower Town) is the commercial heart by the river, the **Alta** (Upper Town) is the historic center and home of the university, while the **Santa Clara** district across the river has some unusual attractions. This walking tour visits all three.

Follow the map through back streets to **Praça do Comércio**, an old market square dating from medieval times. Public executions, *autos-da-fé,* festivals, and other entertainments were once held here. The 13th-century church in the north corner, **Igreja de São Tiago**, has interesting doorways and nicely carved columns. Continue down the narrow Rua Coelho and Rua da Louca to **Praça 8 de Maio**, the very heart of Coimbra.

Directly across the square is the ornate ***Mosteiro de Santa Cruz** (Monastery of the Holy Cross) (3), founded in 1131 and heavily altered in the Manueline style during the 16th century. To its left is the town hall, and to the right a marvelously old-fashioned café. Step inside the church to admire its splendid interior. Afonso Henriques, who as Afonso I was Portugal's first king, lies buried in a gracefully carved tomb to the left of the high altar. On the other side is the tomb of his son, Sancho I, the country's second king. The walls of the nave are covered with blue *azulejo* tiles representing the Holy Cross and the life of Saint Augustine, while the ***pulpit** is one of the most remarkable works of the Renaissance in Portugal. Be sure to visit the ***Claustro do Silêncio**

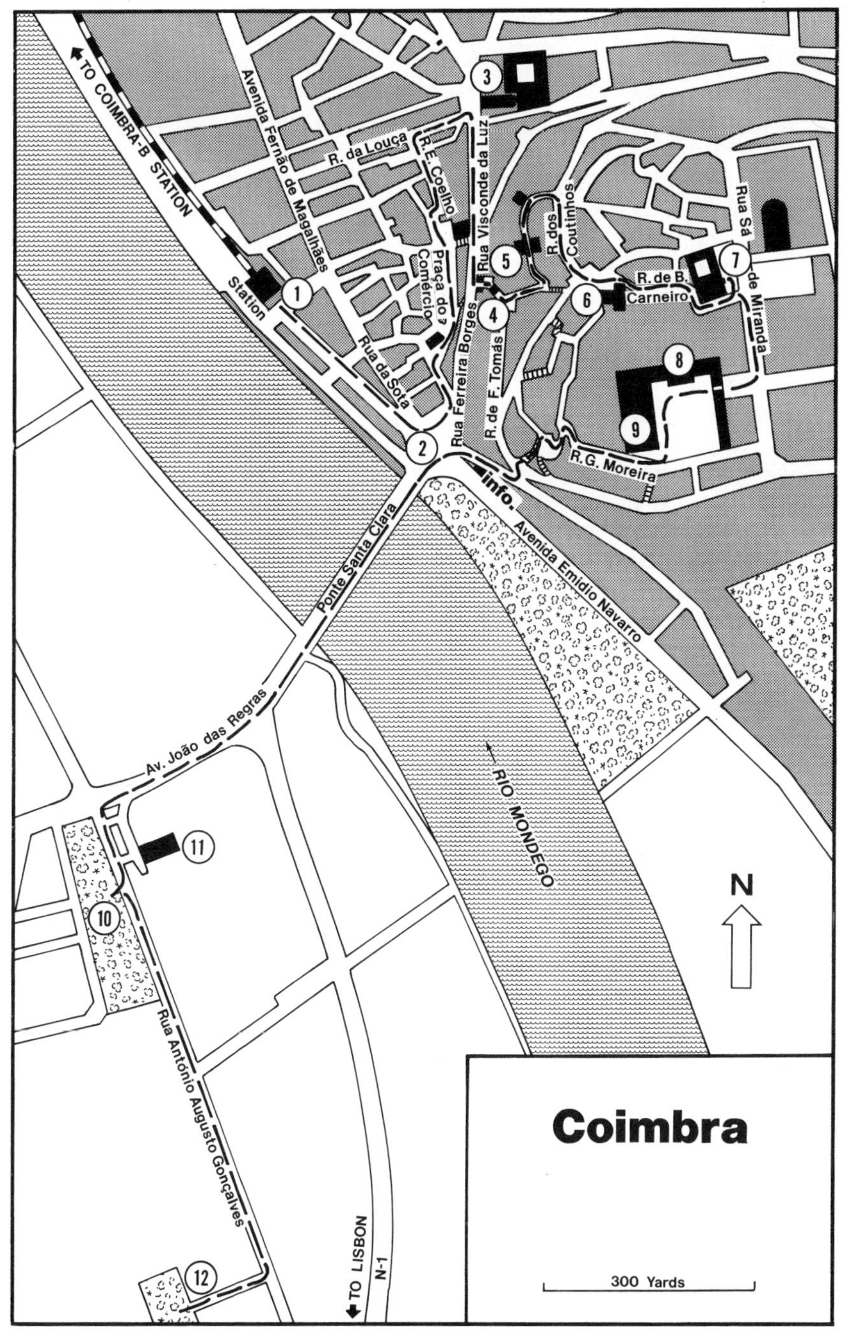

TO COIMBRA-B STATION
Station
Avenida Fernão de Magalhães
R. da Louça
R. E. Coelho
Rua Visconde da Luz
Praça do Comércio
Rua da Sota
Rua Ferreira Borges
R. de F. Tomás
R. dos Coutinhos
R. de B. Carneiro
Rua Sá de Miranda
R. G. Moreira
Info.
Avenida Emídio Navarro
Ponte Santa Clara
Av. João das Regras
RIO MONDEGO
Rua António Augusto Gonçalves
TO LISBON
N-1
N
1
2
3
4
5
6
7
8
9
10
11
12
Coimbra
300 Yards

(Silent Cloister), reached through a doorway in the north transept. From here a stairway leads to the *coro alto* gallery with its carved stalls depicting the voyages of Vasco da Gama. The monastery is open daily from 9 a.m. to noon and 2–6 p.m.

Following Rua Visconde da Luz will bring you to the two surviving gateways of the ancient city. From here the route makes a steep climb into the Upper Town, where there are few restaurants. If you haven't had lunch yet, it would be a good idea to do so now. Turn left and go up a few steps through the first gate, the **Porta da Barbacã**. Just beyond this a right turn leads through the **Arco de Almedina** (4), parts of which date from the 9th century. Its name derives from *medina,* the Arabic word for city. The tower rising above was Coimbra's first town hall, rebuilt in the 16th century.

You are now in the **Alta** district, a tangle of narrow alleyways leading to the University at the top of the hill. Make the first possible left and climb the steps. To your right is a steep passageway called **Escadas de Quebra-Costas**, literally meaning the steps of broken backs. Rather than risk getting stuck in there after an ample Portuguese lunch, turn instead to the left and follow Rua de Sobre-Ripas to the **Palácio de Sub-Ripas** (5). Completed in 1547, this unusual residence occupies both sides of the alleyway and incorporates parts of earlier buildings as well as the town wall. Just beyond it is the **Torre do Anto**, a 9th-century defensive tower that now houses a non-profit shop for local handicrafts.

Turn right and right again onto Rua dos Coutinhos, leasing past the Science Museum to the **Sé Velha** (Old Cathedral) (6), a Romanesque gem from 1170 that resembles a fortress more than a church. The doorway on the north side, added in 1530, provides a touch of the Renaissance to an otherwise austere structure. Step inside to see the splendid Flamboyant Gothic ***altarpiece** and the beautiful 13th-century ***cloisters**, reached through a door in the south aisle. The church is open daily from 9 a.m. to 12:30 p.m. and 2–5 p.m.

A stroll up Rua de Borges Carneiro brings you to the ***Museu Nacional Machado de Castro** (7), one of the most magnificent museums in Portugal. The building itself, formerly the Bishop's Palace, was erected over a Roman cryptoportico that once supported their forum and now serves as a basement. Inside, you will find a rich colleciton of ***sculpture**, particularly of the Renaissance, as well as paintings and other works of art. The spooky ***underground section**, in the galleries once used as a granary, displays *in-situ* artifacts dating from Roman and even prehistoric times. Visits may be made on Tuesdays through Sundays from 10 a.m. to 12:30 p.m. and 2–4:30 p.m. The 16th-century **Sé Nova** ("New" Cathedral) is adjacent.

Follow Rua Sá de Miranda past the modern university buildings

The Sé Velha

and turn right into the **Universidade Velha** (Old University). Formerly the palace of King João III, these buildings were donated to the school in 1537 and are still in use. Passing through the **Porta Férrea** (Iron Gate) of 1634, you enter a large courtyard dominated by an 18th-century bell tower. A staircase to the right leads to the **Via Latina** (8), a covered gallery where once only Latin was spoken. From there you can visit the **Sala dos Capelos** (Ceremonial Hall), hung with portraits of the kings of Portugal, and other rooms.

Cross the courtyard and enter the **Capela de São Miguel**, an elaborate chapel in the Manueline style, dedicated to Saint Michael. Its 17th-century *azulejo* tiles, highly decorated ceiling, and Baroque ***organ loft** of 1733 are a testament to the size of the school's endowment. A small **museum** of sacred art is adjacent.

To the left of the chapel is the university's renowned library, the ***Biblioteca Joannina** (9). Ring the bell for entrance into a world of Baroque splendor. The *trompe l'oeil* ceilings are breathtaking, while the walls of gilded opulence rival anything else in Portugal. Most of the attractions of the Old University are open daily from 9:30 a.m. to 12:30 p.m. and 2–5 p.m.

From the edge of the courtyard you can get a magnificent ***view** of the town and countryside. Descend the steps opposite the library and follow the map past a clutter of colorful houses known as the *Palacios Confusos* to the river.

Cross the bridge over the Mondego River and walk along Avenida João das Regras to the entrance of **Portugal dos Pequenitos** (10), a fantasy garden intended for children but equally enchanting to grown-ups. Built to the scale of a five-year-old, the park contains diminutive reproductions of houses and public buildings typical of the various regions of Portugal and its former colonies, including Africa, Goa, Macao, and Brazil. Most of the structures can be entered and contain appropriate exhibits. The garden is open daily from 9 a.m. to 7 p.m., closing at 5:30 p.m. in winter.

Stroll over to the nearby **Convento de Santa Clara-a-Velha** (11), a 14th-century convent that was vacated in the 17th century due to frequent flooding. Now reduced to ruins, it is an evocative spot charged with memories of Queen Isabel and the tragic Inês de Castro. Although rarely visited by tourists, there is a caretaker who will let you in. The "new" convent that replaced it in 1649 is on a hill a few blocks away.

Continue down Rua Gonçalves to the **Quinta das Lágrimas** (Villa of Tears) (12) where, according to a legend immortalized by the great 16th-century poet Camões, Inês de Castro, mistress of Prince Pedro and mother of his illegitimate children, was murdered on the orders of King Afonso IV in 1355. In the terrible story that followed, Pedro, now king, had the body exhumed and crowned queen. The garden and the Fountain of Love are open to visitors. From here it is an easy walk back to the station.

A Daytrip from Lisbon

Évora

Évora may indeed be the "museum city" of Portugal, but in many ways it is even more inviting as an unpretentious, rather sleepy, rural town that hasn't changed an awful lot in centuries. There are precious few of the trappings of a vanished empire here; no grandiose palaces or world-famous sights to lure the tourist hordes. What you will find instead is a charming, comfortable country place that just happens to be crammed with fascinating little bits and pieces of the nation's past.

Set atop a low hill overlooking the surrounding plains, Évora has occupied a strategic site since prehistoric times. The Romans captured it in the 2nd century B.C. and later named it *Liberalitas Julia,* only to lose out to the Germanic Visigoths in the 5th century A.D. Like most of the Iberian peninsula, Évora was overrun by the Moors from Africa during the 8th century and prospered under their enlightened rule until 1165. That's when Fearless Gerald struck. Geraldo Sem Pavor was a swashbuckling rogue who won the new king's pardon by liberating Évora from the Muslims. Under cover of darkness—so that improbable story goes—Geraldo singlehandedly scaled the town walls using lances as a ladder, hurled the guards to their deaths below, then leaped to the ground and, fighting off the Moors with one hand, used the other hand to open the gates for the Christian army.

After that, Évora became an important place, a major center of learning, and a sometimes residence for the kings of Portugal. All of this ended when Spain defeated Portugal in 1580. The town never recovered from that disaster, and suffered further when its university was closed in 1759, not to reopen until 1975. Today, the artifacts of its rich history, from the Romans to the Moors to the Renaissance, remain intact to delight those travelers willing to go a little out of the way to experience them.

GETTING THERE:

Trains to Évora leave once or twice in the morning from Lisbon's Barreiro Station, on the south side of the harbor. There are connecting ferry boats from the Praça do Comércio (Terreiro do Paço) terminal in downtown Lisbon, where you also buy the train ticket. Be sure to leave by 7:30 a.m. for the 3-hour journey. A return service runs in the early evening.

Buses are a bit faster and more frequent than trains on this route. Operated by Rodoviária Nacional, they leave from Avenida Casal Ribeiro 18 in Lisbon and take about 2½ hours to reach Évora.

By car, Évora is 90 miles southeast of Lisbon. Cross the suspension bridge and take the A-2/E-4 highway south, then the N-10, N-4, and N-114 roads east.

PRACTICALITIES:

The major museum of Évora is closed on Mondays and major holidays. A great country fair and folk festival, the **Feira de São João**, is held annually around the last two weeks of June. The **Tourist Information Office** *(Turismo)*, phone (066) 226-71, is on the main square at Praça do Giraldo 73. Évora has a **population** of about 50,000 and is in the region of **Alto Alentejo**.

FOOD AND DRINK:

Meals in Évora tend to be basic and quite substantial, with little pretense at refinement. A few local specialties are: *Porco à Alentejana* (pork with clams), *Feijoada Alentejana* (pork with beans), *Borrego* (lamb), and *Cabrito* (kid). Some restaurant choices are:

Cozinha de Santo Humberto (Rua da Moeda 39, just west of Praça do Giraldo) An atmospheric place for local cuisine, especially game. Reservations preferred, phone (066) 242-51. X: Thurs. $$$

Pousada dos Lóios (by the Roman Temple) Regional and international dishes in a 15th-century monastery, now a government-run tourist inn. Outdoor tables available in the cloister. Reservations preferred, phone (066) 240-51. $$$

Guião (Rua da República 81, near the Senhora da Graça church) A large, old-fashioned restaurant serving local specialties. X: Mon. $$

Martinho (Largo Luis de Camões 24, 4 blocks northwest of Praça do Giraldo) A local favorite for local cooking. $

Faisca (Rua do Raimundo 33, just west of the tourist office) Inexpensive regional foods. X: Sun. $

SUGGESTED TOUR:

From the **Estação** (train station) (1) you can either take a cab or walk the three-quarter-mile distance to Évora's lovely main square, the **Praça do Giraldo** (2). Named for the town's liberator, this was once the Roman forum. Many ancient buildings from that era survived intact until the late 16th-century when—alas—they were torn down by the local ruler as unwelcome reminders of a heathen past. Toward the north end of the plaza is a marble Renaissance **fountain** that was given

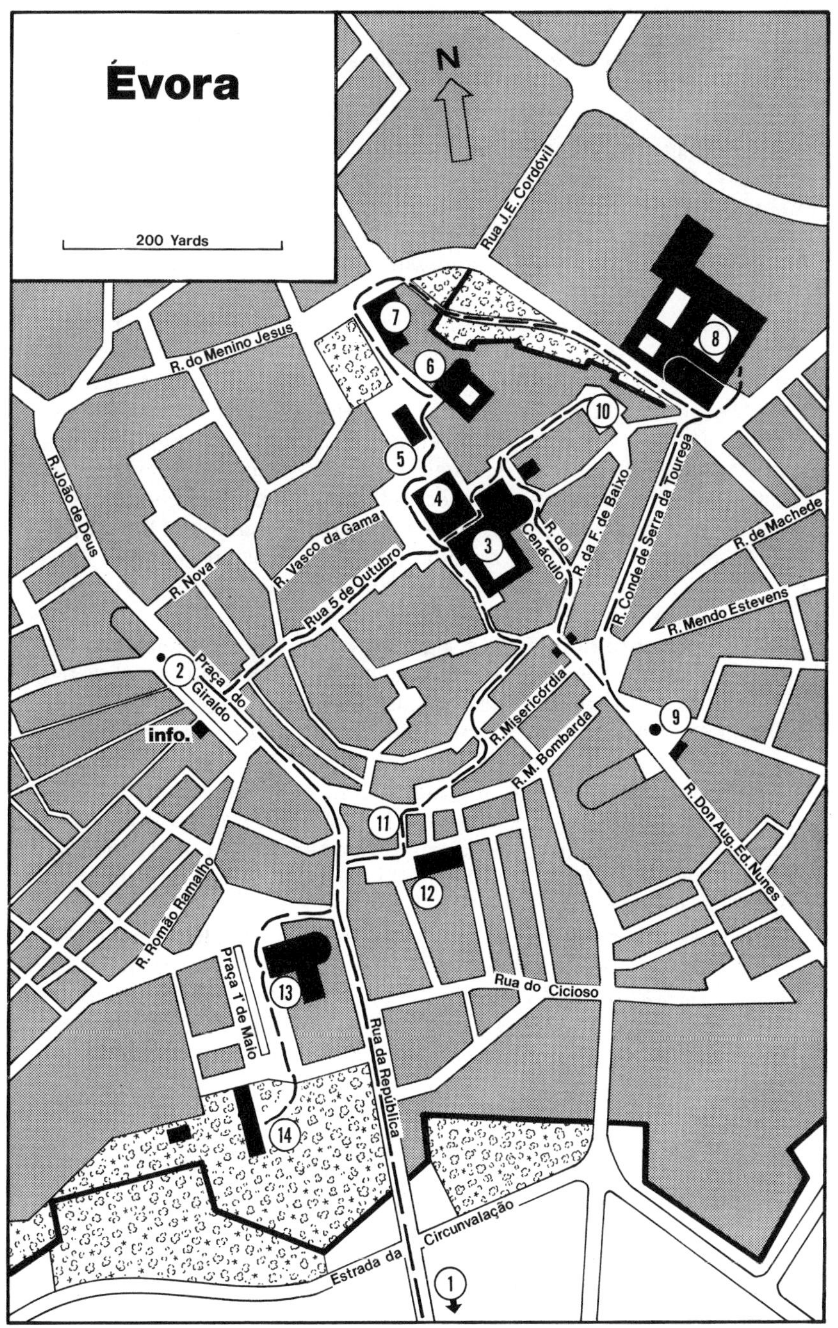
Évora
200 Yards
N
Rua J.E. Cordóvil
R. do Menino Jesus
R. João de Deus
R. Vasco da Gama
R. Nova
Rua 5 de Outubro
R. do Cenáculo
R. da F. de Baixo
R. Conde de Serra da Tourega
R. de Machede
R. Mendo Estevens
Praça do Giraldo
info.
R. Misericórdia
R. M. Bombarda
R. Don Aug. Ed. Nunes
R. Romão Ramalho
Praça 1° de Maio
Rua do Cicioso
Rua da República
Estrada da Circunvalação
1
2
3
4
5
6
7
8
9
10
11
12
13
14

a metal crown by King Philip II of Spain after deciding in 1580 that he was also the king of Portugal.

Rua 5 de Outubro leads directly to the ***Sé** (Cathedral) (3), a massive and austere granite structure surmounted by intriguing conical towers. In many ways it resembles a fortress as much as it does a church. Begun in 1186, the cathedral makes the leap between the Romanesque and Gothic styles, albeit in a ponderous way. Its main doorway is, however, decorated with outstanding 14th-century **statues of the Apostles**.

Inside, there is a magnificent ***dome** above the crossing, a pair of Gothic rose windows, a multicolored 15th-century statue of the pregnant Virgin set in a Baroque chapel to the left, an elevated ***choir** over the west end with wonderfully carved Renaissance stalls, and a neoclassical chancel from the 18th century. Be sure to visit the 14th-century ***Claustro** (cloisters), reached via a door near the entrance. The cathedral's treasures are exhibited in the **Museu de Arte Sacra** in the south tower, including a rare 13th-century ivory ***carving of the Virgin and Child** that unfolds to become a triptych depicting her life. The cathedral is open daily from 9 a.m. to noon and 2–5 p.m.; the museum and cloisters, however, are closed on Mondays.

The former Bishop's Palace, right next door, houses the **Museu de Évora** (Regional Museum) (4). This is where most of the surviving artifacts of Évora's splendid Roman past are kept, along with medieval and Renaissance sculpture, and both Flemish and Portuguese paintings. Don't miss the 3rd-century marble relief of a possessed woman, the 16th-century triptych of the Crucifixion in Limoges enamel, or the 13 paintings depicting the life of the Virgin that were once above the high altar of the cathedral. Also on display are *azulejo* tiles, antique furnishings, and other items. The museum is open on Tuesdays through Sundays, 9 a.m. to noon and 2–5 p.m.

Évora's only remaining Roman structure is its **Templo Romano** (5), a temple from the 2nd or 3rd century A.D. that survived partly intact because it was bricked up during the Middle Ages and continued to be used for various purposes until 1870. Located at the highest point in town, it is thought by some to have been dedicated to the goddess Diana, but there is no proof of this.

Most of the adjacent 15th-century **Convento dos Lóios** is now a *pousada* (government-run tourist inn) where you can have an elegant meal or stay overnight in comfort, but its church, the **Igreja de São João Evangelista** (6), is still privately owned and may be visited. Step through its Flamboyant Gothic portal to see the nave lined with exquisite *azulejo* tiles, a painting whose eyes and feet seem to move, and a medieval cistern filled with human bones. These and other curiosities can be seen daily from 9 a.m. to noon and 2–5 p.m.

The Templo Romano

Just north of this is a palace owned by the same family that owns the church. Forming part of the medieval town walls, the **Paço dos Duques de Cadaval** (7) was begun in the 14th century and served as an occasional residence for several Portuguese kings. Later remodeled, it became a center of humanist learning and home to the dukes of Cadaval. A small art gallery in it is open to the public, and you'll get a good **view** of the lower town from the gardens to the left.

Bear right and stroll downhill past remains of the Roman and Visigothic walls, going through a park to **Universidade de Évora** (8).

Founded in the 16th century by the Jesuits, it was closed in 1759 after that order was suppressed throughout Portugal. It was not until 1975 that the university reopened; until then the buildings were used as a high school. The old structure, in the Italian Renaissance style with Baroque overtones, has an exceptionally nice **cloister** that you can wander in to see.

Follow the map to the **Largo das Portas de Moura** (9), a small square of immense charm that quietly evokes several different epochs of Évora's past. The simple spherical marble **fountain** in its center dates from the Renaissance, while the 16th-century **Casa Cordovil** on the south side has touches of a Moorish fantasy.

Return toward the cathedral and pick your way through the narrow alleyways behind it to the **Solar dos Condes de Basto** (10), an ancient royal residence that was mostly rebuilt in later centuries, but which still incorporates parts of the Roman and Visigothic walls. There are some excellent closeup views of the cathedral's strange towers from here.

Continue via a passageway to the front of the church and turn left, following the route on the map through a picturesque arched alley called the **Travessa da Caraça** (11) to the **Igreja Nossa Senhora de Graça** (12). Dedicated to Our Lady of Grace, this 16th-century Renaissance church has an incredible **façade** decorated with four colossal figures of Atlas dangling over the roof ridge while supporting huge terrestrial globes. Whatever its artistic merit, it certainly is different.

Just two blocks to the west is one of Portugal's strangest sights. Hidden away in the **Igreja de São Francisco** (13) church is its macabre ***Capela dos Ossos**, a chapel tastefully lined with the skulls and bones of some 5,000 humans. Two shriveled corpses—one a small child—hang from a wall. As if to accentuate the sense of inescapable mortality, a sign over the door proclaims (in Latin) "Our bones are waiting for yours." You can view these grisly remains on any day, from 9 a.m. to 12:30 p.m. and 2:30–6 p.m.

On the same square as the church is the **Museu de Artesanato**, a free exhibition of local handicrafts, where you can also purchase unusual gifts or souvenirs. It is open on Tuesdays through Sundays, from 10 a.m. to noon and 2–5:30 p.m. Continue a few steps south to the **Jardim Público** (14), a public garden partially surrounded by the medieval town wall. Near its entrance is the remaining section of the late-15th-century **Palácio de Don Manuel**, an occasional home of several Portuguese kings. It as here that Manuel I commissioned Vasco da Gama in 1497 to find a sea route to India. The restored Ladies Gallery of the palace is now used for art exhibitions. From here you can return to Praça do Giraldo (2) or walk back to the station.

Index

Cathedrals and Museums are listed individually under those category headings.

More

DAYTRIPS

TRAVEL GUIDES BY EARL STEINBICKER

DAYTRIPS LONDON

Explores the inner and outer boroughs of the great metropolis on 7 one-day walking tours, then describes 23 daytrips to destinations throughout nearby southeastern England. 39 large maps, 58 photos, 240 pages.

DAYTRIPS IN BRITAIN

Most of Britain's best attractions lie within daytrip range of London, Edinburgh, or Glasgow. This popular guidebook takes a close look at 60 of the most exciting destinations and shows you how to enjoy them. 65 maps, 107 photos, 353 pages.

DAYTRIPS IN FRANCE

Describes 45 great one-day excursions—including 5 walking tours of Paris, 23 daytrips from the city, 5 in Provence, and 12 along the Riviera. Glossaries, 55 maps, 89 photos. 2nd edition, 336 pages.

DAYTRIPS IN HOLLAND, BELGIUM AND LUXEMBOURG

Many unusual places are covered on the 40 daytrips in this guidebook, along with all of the favorites plus the 3 major cities. Glossaries, 45 maps, 69 photos, 288 pages.

DAYTRIPS IN GERMANY

55 of Germany's most enticing destinations can be savored on daytrips from Munich, Frankfurt, Hamburg, and Berlin. Walking tours of the big cities are included. Glossaries, 62 maps, and 94 photos. 3rd edition, 336 pages.

DAYTRIPS IN ITALY

Features 40 one-day adventures in and around Rome, Florence, Milan, Venice, and Naples; including walking tours of the major cities as well as lesser-known places. Glossaries, 45 maps, 69 photos, 288 pages.